USA's Best

TRIPS

99 THEMED ITINERARIES ACROSS AMERICA

Sara Benson,
Amy Balfour, Alison Bing, Becca Blond, Jennifer Denniston,
Lisa Dunford, Alex Leviton, David Ozanich, Danny Palmerlee,
Brandon Presser, Karla Zimmerman

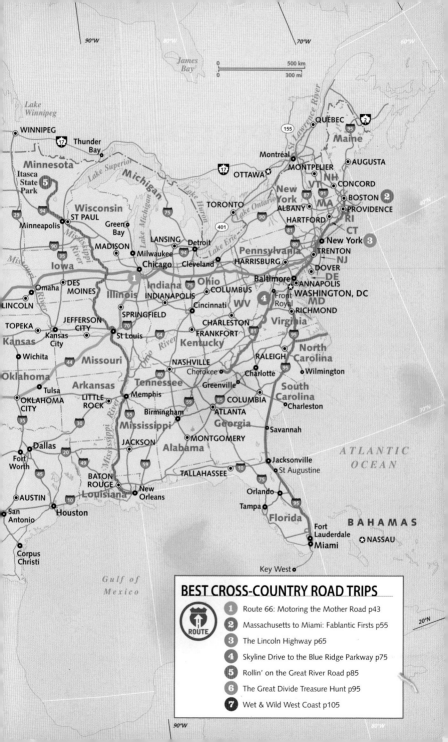

90°W 80°W 70°W 60°W

James
Bay

0   500 km
0   300 mi

Lake
Winnipeg

● WINNIPEG
🛡17 Thunder
Bay

Minnesota
Itasca
State
Park 🛡5

🛡94
🛡29
● Minneapolis
🛡90
● ST PAUL
🛡35

Wisconsin
Green ●
Bay
● Milwaukee
🛡94
● MADISON

Lake Superior

Michigan

Lake Michigan

Lake Huron

🛡17 OTTAWA ✪
155
● QUÉBEC
🛡2

Maine

Montréal ●
MONTPELIER ●
● AUGUSTA
NH
VT 🛡91 CONCORD ●
87 🛡 BOSTON ●🛡2
New ● ALBANY
York 🛡90 MA PROVIDENCE ●
HARTFORD ● RI
CT

TORONTO ●
Lake Ontario

401

St Lawrence River

40°N

Minneapolis
Iowa

Mississippi River

● DES
MOINES
● Omaha
🛡35

Illinois
LANSING ●
● Detroit
Chicago 🛡75
● Cleveland ●
HARRISBURG ●

Indiana Ohio
INDIANAPOLIS ● COLUMBUS ●

🛡1

Pennsylvania
90 🛡
🛡80
● New York 🛡3
TRENTON ●
NJ
DOVER ●
DE

● LINCOLN
TOPEKA ●
Kansas
Kansas ●
City

🛡70
JEFFERSON ●
CITY
SPRINGFIELD ●
● St Louis
🛡64

Cincinnati ● WV
CHARLESTON ●
FRANKFORT ●
🛡81
Kentucky

Baltimore ●
ANNAPOLIS ●
🛡4 WASHINGTON, DC
Front MD
Royal ● RICHMOND

Virginia 🛡95

Missouri
🛡44
● Wichita

Ohio River
NASHVILLE ●
Cherokee ●
🛡40

RALEIGH ●
● Charlotte 🛡95

North
Carolina
● Wilmington

Oklahoma
● Tulsa
OKLAHOMA
CITY
🛡35

Arkansas
LITTLE ● Memphis
ROCK
🛡55

Tennessee
Greenville ●

🛡85 COLUMBIA ●

South
Carolina
● Charleston

● Dallas
Fort
Worth
🛡20
🛡45

🛡59
Birmingham ●
🛡40
JACKSON ●
Mississippi

Alabama
🛡59

ATLANTA ●
Georgia
● Savannah

Mississippi River

● MONTGOMERY

AUSTIN ●
🛡10
San
Antonio ●

BATON
ROUGE ●
Louisiana
● New
Orleans

TALLAHASSEE ●
🛡10
● Jacksonville
🛡75 ● St Augustine

ATLANTIC
OCEAN

30°N

● Corpus
Christi

Gulf of
Mexico

Orlando ●

Tampa ●
🛡95
Florida
Fort
Lauderdale ●
● Miami

BAHAMAS

✪ NASSAU

20°N

Key West ●

BEST CROSS-COUNTRY ROAD TRIPS

🛡
ROUTE

90°W 80°W

USA'S BEST TRIPS

Everyone knows road-tripping is the ultimate way to experience the USA. You can drive up, down, across, around or straight through every state on the continental map. We're here to help you narrow down the options. Whether you're on a quest for that perfect Pacific Northwest microbrewery pint, fresh lobster right off the boat in Maine or the coolest classic all-night diners in New Jersey, we've got you covered. Our authors drove, paddled, walked, cycled, rode the rails and hopped buses all across the country to bring you their 99 favorite trips.

Maybe you've climbed the Statue of Liberty, toured the National Mall in Washington DC, peeked over the edge of the Grand Canyon or crossed the Golden Gate Bridge a dozen times before. But have you slept in a wigwam motel on Route 66, ridden the solar-powered Ferris wheel on Santa Monica Pier or stood at the headwaters of the mighty Mississippi River? From epic to eclectic, urban to outdoorsy, tear-jerkingly historical to downright wacky, our trips will take you places you've never been – or even imagined existed – before.

Statue of Liberty, New York

"Our authors drove, paddled, walked, cycled, rode the rails and hopped buses all across the country…"

"Ever since Henry Ford invented the Tin Lizzie, Americans have gone nuts for road-tripping."

Cross-Country Road Trips

Ever since Henry Ford invented the Tin Lizzie, Americans have gone nuts for road-tripping. Before learning to get their kicks on Route 66 (p43), they cruised west on the Lincoln Highway (p65). History's a nice bonus, but classic road trips are all about the scenery, right? Judge for yourself on the Mississippi's Great River Road (p85), up and down the Continental Divide (p95) or on the naturally wet and wild West Coast (p105).

An endless highway in eastern California

ROUTE 66: MOTORING THE MOTHER ROAD

MASSACHUSETTS TO MIAMI: FABLANTIC FIRSTS

⊕ St Augustine's old quarter, Florida p61

⊖ The High Line, Manhattan, New York p58

⊘ Bodie Island lighthouse, North Carolina's Outer Banks p59

HIGHWAYS VS BYWAYS

The USA has four million miles of public roads. But don't worry: interstate highways only account for 1%. That still leaves plenty of off-the-beaten-path scenic byways (http://byways .org) for curious travelers.

THE LINCOLN HIGHWAY

⊕ Flaming Gorge National Recreation Area, Utah p71

⊖ Downtown Pittsburgh, Pennsylvania p67

SKYLINE DRIVE TO THE BLUE RIDGE PARKWAY

"road trips are all about the scenery, right? Judge for yourself on the Mississippi's Great River Road..."

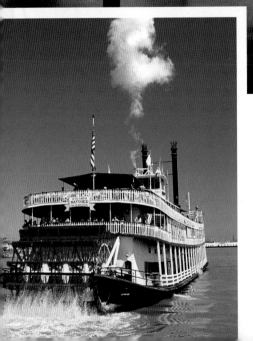

ROLLIN' ON THE GREAT RIVER ROAD

Mississippi River in New Orleans, Louisiana p92

Steamboat *Natchez,* New Orleans, Louisiana p92

THE GREAT DIVIDE
TREASURE HUNT

⬖ Yellowstone National Park,
Wyoming p98

⬖ Elk in Rocky Mountain
National Park, Colorado p99

WET & WILD
WEST COAST

> "go road-tripping all around the USA, a country big enough to embrace souls full of wanderlust..."

◉ **Routes**

Somewhere between Key West (p297) and the Southwest's deserts (p543), you decided on a five-year plan: invest in a killer car stereo and go road-tripping all around the USA, a country big enough to embrace souls full of wanderlust like yours. When spring is in the air, go cruisin' Florida's East Coast (p285) or do a Gulf Coast (p449) jaunt through Texas. In summer, trace the music heritage of the Crooked Road (p155) and afterwards don't miss that famous fall foliage along the Natchez Trace Parkway (p245). No wheels? No problem. Tour the Southwest by train (p535), climb aboard Amtrak (p627) in California or take a ferry through Alaska's Inside Passage (p677).

LOCATION SCOUT

The Worldwide Guide to Movie Locations (www.movie-loca tions.com/places/usa/usa.html) points out famous silver-screen filming spots in all 50 states, from Oregon's *Twilight* and Idaho's *Napoleon Dynamite* to Florida's *The Truman Show*.

Food & Drink

When you've been driving for hours, nothing's more important than what's on your plate next. (We've driven across three states just for that perfect slice of lemon meringue pie.) Start feasting in the Golden State by taking chef Alice Waters' (p611) culinary tour and dallying in California's lesser known wine countries (p621). Answer New Mexico's official state question – "red or green?" – on a green chile adventure (p561) then become a barbecue expert (p537) in Texas' Hill Country. Cowgirls and boys will tell you where the beef is (p383) in the Great Plains, and you'll need to loosen your belt for down-on-the-farm feasts (p331) in the Midwest. On the East Coast, it's all about crustaceans on our Maine lobster tour (p205) and crab quest (p149) through Maryland.

A GREEN CHILE ADVENTURE p561
Red or green in New Mexico? We vote green.

KEEP ON TRUCKIN'

Next-generation food trucks are delivering haute gourmet and wildly multicultural meals on wheels to the hungry denizens of NY, LA, San Francisco, Seattle and more. Track 'em down on Twitter.

A MOVEABLE FEAST p331
Local artisanal cheese at Fromagination, in Madison, Wisconsin

CAJUN COUNTRY ROAD TRIP p231
Boiled crawfish, a Cajun country staple

ALICE WATERS' CULINARY TOUR p611
Zuni Café, San Francisco, California

"from Florida's white-sand beaches and islands, to prairie grasslands rolling across the Great Plains..."

Outdoors

Nature is alive and kicking in the USA, from Florida's white-sand beaches and islands, to prairie grasslands rolling across the Great Plains, to the Rocky Mountains raising their jagged teeth along the Continental Divide, and onward to the tallest trees on earth, standing sentinel over Pacific shores. Go dippin' down the Cascades (p653), tripping through Grand Teton and Yellowstone (p491) and leaf-peeping in New England (p191), or find out where the buffalo (p411) roam out West. Stand on the edge of the Grand Canyon (p529), then experience it from the bottom up while rafting the Colorado (p573). Explore the untamed wilderness of Big Bend (p459) and the Everglades (p303) or stay civilized by skiing Colorado (p479).

WEEK IN THE GRAND CANYON p529
South Kaibab Trail, Grand Canyon National Park, Arizona

GO WILD IN THE EVERGLADES p303
Everglades National Park, Florida

DIPPIN' DOWN THE CASCADES p653
Umpqua Hot Springs, Oregon

History & Culture

Forget those stuffy history lessons you learned as a child. Traveling the USA means experiencing the living, breathing stories of millions of immigrants and their tapestry of varied traditions. Dig up San Antonio's Spanish and Mexican roots (p431), or ramble through Amish Country (p343). Even dusty centuries past come alive when you take a Civil War tour (p141) or follow Oklahoma's tribal trails (p389) into the Old West (p399). Culture vultures, get rockin' in the Midwest (p353), tap your toes from Music City to Dixieland (p223), amble through Santa Fe's art scene (p539) and uncover literary New England (p179). Got a short attention span? Maine's 60 lighthouses in 60 hours (p209) trip is designed just for you.

SAN ANTONIO MARIACHIS & MACHACADO p431
San Antonio Fiesta, San Antonio, Texas

DO MORE DIGGING

History hounds will find even more travel itineraries that take in an astonishing number of nationally registered historic sites, from Florida shipwrecks to stops on the Underground Railroad, at www.nps.gov /history/nr/travel.

WILD WEST WYOMING p485
Cheyenne Frontier Days rodeo, Cheyenne, Wyoming

60 LIGHTHOUSES IN 60 HOURS p209
West Quoddy Light, in Quoddy Head State Park, Maine

② Offbeat

Home of UFO fanatics, funky outsider art, towering monuments of eccentricity and haunted houses galore, the USA has enough weird stuff to fill a lifetime of vacations. Our offbeat adventures will take you to the wildest, most way-out-there destinations. Pop-culture addicts can drive from **The Simpsons to The Shining** (p671) in Washington or zoom from **Hell to the moon** (p515) in Idaho. Afterward, speculate about aliens and **visionary outsider art** (p455) in Texas, hang out with iconoclasts in **weird Vermont** (p199) or commune with the dead in **freaky Florida** (p313). Monster roadside oddities abound across the country: witness Sue, the World's Largest Holstein Cow, and a host of Wall Drug billboards, in the **offbeat Dakotas** (p417), or the World's Largest Ball of Twine in the Midwest, a **treasure chest of kitsch** (p365).

ODDBALL ART & ALIENS p455
Cadillac Ranch, Amarillo, Texas

THE WACKY WEB

Looking for a tattoo emporium, a gallery of candy-bar wrappers, a prized collection of B-movie posters or the 8-track archive? Find these and more at the Museum of Online Museums (www.coudal.com/moom).

WEIRD VERMONT p199
Ben & Jerry's, Waterbury, Vermont

OFFBEAT DAKOTAS p417
Novelty rides outside Wall Drug, South Dakota

Cities

We picked a dozen of the USA's biggest, brawniest and just plain boldest cities, then gave ourselves 48 hours to pack everything in, from famous urban sights and sounds, to underground culture and high-falutin' foodie haunts, to indie rock bars for grabbing a drink after midnight. So just pick a city, any city, and start exploring. It's as easy as A, B, C (as in, Austin – p425, Boston – p167, Chicago – p325). Are sexy San Francisco (p603), Miami (p279), Los Angeles (p581) or Las Vegas (p523) more your scene? We've got those urban magnets covered, too. Need some mood elevation? Traipse from the skyscrapers of Manhattan (p117) to the "Mile High City" of Denver (p467) and Seattle's (p633) space needle. Last but not least, don't forget New Orleans (p217), aka the Big Easy, fueled by jazz, chicory coffee and love.

⊕ **48 HOURS IN NEW ORLEANS** p217
New Orleans' French Quarter, Louisiana

⊖ **48 HOURS IN MIAMI** p279
Ocean Dr, South Beach, Miami, Florida

Contents

SOUTHWEST TRIPS 521

CALIFORNIA TRIPS 579

PACIFIC NORTHWEST TRIPS 631

BEHIND THE SCENES 683

Trips by Theme

ROUTES

TRIP

FOOD & DRINK

TRIP

OUTDOORS

TRIP

HISTORY & CULTURE

TRIP

OFFBEAT

TRIP

CITIES

TRIP

Trips by Season

Expert-Recommended Trips

Trip Builder

TRIPS	THEME	CHAPTER	PAGE	DISTANCE	DURATION
60 Lighthouses in 60 Hours	(HISTORY & CULTURE)	New England	p209	375 miles	3 days
Maine Lobster Tour	(FOOD & DRINK)	New England	p205	200 miles	3 days
Skyline Drive to the Blue Ridge Parkway	(ROUTE)	Best Cross-Country Road Trips	p75	520 miles	6 days
The Great Smokies	(OUTDOORS)	The South	p265	180 miles	5 days
A Civil War Tour	(HISTORY & CULTURE)	New York, Washington DC & the Mid-Atlantic	p141	320 miles	2 days
The Crooked Road: Heritage Music Trail	(ROUTE)	New York, Washington DC & the Mid-Atlantic	p155	145 miles	3 days
Cruisin' Florida's East Coast	(ROUTE)	Florida	p285	475 miles	6 days
Overseas Highway to Key West	(ROUTE)	Florida	p297	150 miles	3 days
Rockin' the Midwest	(HISTORY & CULTURE)	Great Lakes	p353	450 miles	4 days
48 Hours in Chicago	(CITY)	Great Lakes	p325		2 days
San Antonio Mariachis & Machacado	(HISTORY & CULTURE)	Texas	p431	10 miles	3 days
Best of Hill Country BBQ	(FOOD & DRINK)	Texas	p437	110 miles	4 days
Wild West Legends	(HISTORY & CULTURE)	Great Plains	p399	935 miles	6 days
Oklahoma's Tribal Trails	(HISTORY & CULTURE)	Great Plains	p389	390 miles	4 days
Once-in-a-Lifetime Glacier	(OUTDOORS)	Rocky Mountains	p503	60 miles	4 days
The Great Divide Treasure Hunt	(ROUTE)	Best Cross-Country Road Trips	p95	2100 miles	10 days
Retro-Modern Palm Springs	(HISTORY & CULTURE)	California	p589	16 miles	2 days
Life in Death Valley	(HISTORY & CULTURE)	California	p597	350 miles	3 days
Pacific Northwest Grand Tour	(OUTDOORS)	Pacific Northwest	p639	1675 miles	3 weeks
The Simpsons to the Shining	(OFFBEAT)	Pacific Northwest	p671	700 miles	6 days
Week in the Grand Canyon	(OUTDOORS)	Southwest	p529	500 miles	7 days
Written in Stone: Utah's National Parks	(OUTDOORS)	Southwest	p553	400 miles	8 days

MEGA TRIP	DISTANCE	DURATION	DESCRIPTION	BEST TIME TO GO
The Maine Attractions	400 miles	5 days	Take a week to wind your way along the craggy coast of Maine in search of fresh lobster and the flickering glow of lighthouses that harken back to a bygone era.	Jun-Aug
Taking the South's High Roads	750 miles	12 days	Treat yourself to a two-week taste of bluegrass country, stretching from pastoral Shenandoah's Skyline Drive along the southern spine of the Appalachians to the Great Smoky Mountains.	Sep-Oct
Capital Culture Corridor	575 miles	6 days	Experience America's heart-rending history at famous battlefields, then get your feet tappin' at time-worn music halls and feast on country cookin' deep in Appalachia.	Aug-Oct
Florida's Sun-Soaked Beaches & Islands	685 miles	10 days	For bikini-clad sun seekers, surfers and other party people, this lazy coastal road trip takes its sweet time beach hopping south to sultry Miami and across the Keys' lotusland.	Dec-Apr
Sights & Sounds of the Midwest	450 miles	6 days	Get your groove back at killer indie rock, rap, jazz and blues venues, then let yourself be blown away by the Windy City, the prairie's undisputed cultural capital.	May-Sep
A True Taste of Texas	190 miles	1 week	The Lone Star state's Spanish and Mexican heritage spices up riverside San Antonio, just a short jaunt from the Hill Country, where back-roads barbecue is king.	Mar-May
Real Cowboys & Indians	1445 miles	10 days	Everything you've dreamed about in the Wild West can be found on this 10-day trip across the plains, including an eye-opening cultural journey through contemporary Native American lands.	May-Sep
Ultimate Rocky Mountain Highs	1135 miles	2 weeks	From top (Glacier's Going-to-the-Sun Rd) to bottom (Silver City, New Mexico), this incredible Rockies ramble will prove irresistible to four-seasons outdoor fanatics and lovers of postcard scenery.	Jul-Sep
Definitive SoCal Desert Escape	550 miles	6 days	From midcentury modern architecture in Palm Springs to extreme living in Death Valley, this is the ultimate one-week tour of some of Southern California's most beautiful desert landscapes.	Feb-Apr
Wild & Weird Pacific Northwest	2535 miles	4 weeks	Skyscraping volcanic ranges, idyllic islands and virgin rain forest mix it up with offbeat cities, microbreweries and pop-culture movie and TV locations on this laidback month-long escape.	Jun-Sep
Epic Southwestern Tribal Lands	1010 miles	2 weeks	The Southwest's signature red-rock landscapes and canyon oases carved by wind and water are on tap for this adventure around the Four Corners, a stronghold for Native American traditions.	May-Jun & Sep-Oct

The Authors

SARA BENSON
An author of 30 travel and nonfiction books, Sara has contributed to dozens of Lonely Planet travel guides. Midwestern by birth and a coastal Californian by choice, Sara has traveled extensively to every state except Alaska – follow her adventures online at www.indietraveler.net. Her favorite trip was Go Wild in the Everglades (p303).

AMY BALFOUR
Amy fell for the Great Plains after a 1990s road trip. Since then she's hiked the Badlands, pigtailed over the Black Hills, raced trains in Nebraska, pushed through Kansas tallgrass and savored Oklahoma's best chicken-fried steak. She's researched six US Lonely Planet guides. Her favorite trip was Where the Buffalo Roam (p411).

ALISON BING
Over 15 years in San Francisco, Alison has done everything you're supposed to do there and many you're not, including falling in love on the Haight bus and gorging on Mission burritos before Berlioz symphonies. Alison holds degrees in art history and international diplomacy – respectable credentials she regularly undermines with outspoken culture commentary for foodie magazines, radio, TV and books, including Lonely Planet's *San Francisco, California* and *Coastal California* guides. Her favorite trip was Alice Waters' Culinary Tour (p611).

BECCA BLOND

Becca Blond lives in Boulder, Colorado, which she covered, along with the rest of the Rocky Mountain states, for Lonely Planet's *USA* guide. She was the coordinating author of *Arizona, New Mexico & Grand Canyon Trips* and has contributed to more than 30 Lonely Planet travel guides. Her favorite trip was The Great Divide Treasure Hunt (p95).

JENNIFER DENNISTON

Jennifer, who lived in Albuquerque for five years and now lives in Iowa, spends months every year road-tripping across the USA. After years of returning to northern New Mexico, falling in love with its landscape and distinct culture, the region remains one of her favorite spots in the country. Her favorite Trip was A Green Chile Adventure (p561).

LISA DUNFORD

In the 15 years Lisa has lived in Texas she has driven the length and breadth of her large adopted state several times. She worked as a restaurant reviewer and features department editor at the *Corpus Christi Caller-Times* newspaper before becoming a freelance writer. She's always on the look-out for good brisket or an old dance hall; her favorite trip was Best of Hill Country BBQ (p437).

ALEX LEVITON
Californian by birth and Southern by home-ownership, Alex lived in a tobacco warehouse in Durham for five years and, although now back in San Francisco, has a fondness for the fireflies, front porches and pace of life in North Carolina. Her favorite trip was Eclectic Americana in the Triangle (p257).

DAVID OZANICH
When not writing about the East Coast for Lonely Planet or sipping cocktails in swanky hotel bars, David writes plays and young-adult novels. Most recently he coauthored the Likely Story series for Knopf. He lives in Greenwich Village and his favorite trip was The Crooked Road: Heritage Music Trail (p155).

DANNY PALMERLEE
Danny is a freelance writer and photographer based in Portland, Oregon. He has written numerous Lonely Planet guidebooks and his work has appeared in publications around the globe. He loves the North Umpqua River in southern Oregon, hates the black flies of the North Cascades and wishes he could hike the Oregon Coast with Elbridge Trask. His favorite trip was Dippin' Down the Cascades (p653).

BRANDON PRESSER

After spending his childhood summers collecting starfish along the Maine coast, Brandon perfected his "pahk the cah" Bostonian drawl while attending Harvard University. These days Brandon is a full-time freelance travel writer and has authored well over a dozen Lonely Planet guides. His favorite trip was Ivy League Secrets & Superstitions (p173).

LONELY PLANET AUTHORS

Why is our travel information the best in the world? It's simple: our authors are independent, dedicated travelers. They don't research using just the internet or phone and they don't take freebies, so you can rely on their advice being well researched and impartial. They travel widely, to all the popular spots and off the beaten track. They personally visit thousands of hotels, restaurants, cafés, bars, galleries, palaces, museums and more – and they take pride in getting all the details right and telling it how it is. Think you can do it? Find out how at lonelyplanet.com.

KARLA ZIMMERMAN

As a life-long Midwesterner, Karla is well-versed in the region's beaches, ballparks, breweries and pie shops. When she's not home in Chicago watching the Cubs – er, writing for websites, books and magazines, she's out exploring. Karla has written several Lonely Planet guidebooks covering the USA, Canada, Caribbean and Europe. Her favorite trip was A Moveable Feast (p331).

CONTRIBUTING EXPERTS

Josh Chicoine is lead singer and guitarist for the M's and co-director of the Chicago International Movies and Music Festival (www.cimmfest.org). He offers recommendations for places to hear live music on p353.

Robert Lee Hodge has been engaging in Civil War reenactments for three decades as a self-proclaimed "hardcore" reenactor, and was a subject of Tony Horwitz's *Confederates in the Attic*. Robert lends us his expertise on p251.

Lee Klein is an award-winning food critic for the *Miami New Times* alternative weekly newspaper. He shares his secrets for finding Miami's most intriguing Latin American hole-in-the-walls, star chefs' tables and more on p279.

Cindy Lovell, PhD, is the Executive Director of the Mark Twain Boyhood Home & Museum in Hannibal, Missouri. She shares Twain lore and Hannibal hotspots in a book-lovers' tour of Twain's hometown on p377.

Chris and Sylvia Mackey, both UT graduates, are long-time residents of Austin. They own the Star of Texas Inn and run Austin Folk House B&B. Chris & Sylvia contributed to our Austin trip on p425.

Tony Merchell is a well-known architectural historian of Southern California's desert regions. He talks about his love of midcentury modern design in Palm Springs on p589.

Shipherd Reed hauls a copper-plated trailer around Arizona and New Mexico to record the stories of underground miners – a vanishing breed – for the University of Arizona's Miners Story Project (www.minersstory.org). He shared his insights on p567.

Steven Thompson is Senior Program Manager for the National Parks Conservation Association in Whitefish, Montana, and is the editor of www.crownofthecontinent.net. He has been hiking Glacier's trails for 20 years and gives us the park lowdown on p503.

Alice Waters, chef and author, revolutionized modern eating by championing local, organic, sustainable foods, which she does for us on p611. Her groundbreaking restaurant, Chez Panisse, is in Berkeley.

BEST CROSS-COUNTRY ROAD TRIPS

When does a place become so famous, or exert such an irresistible pull on the imagination, that it truly becomes an American icon? We'll tell you: when it's part of a classic American road trip.

Get your kicks on Route 66, snaking across the USA's heartland from the prairie capital Chicago to the palm trees of Los Angeles. Discover the often forgotten Lincoln Hwy, America's first transcontinental route, which really stretches from sea to shining sea. Roll alongside the mighty Mississippi, searching out the best blues music, barbecue and small-town life. Ride the spine of the West's rugged Continental Divide, or cascade down the tamer Appalachians on Shenandoah's Skyline Drive and the Blue Ridge Highway.

PLAYLIST ♫♪

Sneer all you want, indie rockers. We know what classic tunes will get all the party people in the back seat singing along (or maybe playing air guitar):

- "King of the Road," Roger Miller
- "This Land Is Your Land," Sharon Jones & the Dap-Kings
- "I've Been Everywhere," Johnny Cash
- "Truckin'," Grateful Dead
- "Crosstown Traffic," Jimi Hendrix
- "Runnin' Down a Dream," Tom Petty
- "Life Is a Highway," Rascal Flatts
- "Born to Be Wild," Steppenwolf

Can't leave the ocean behind? Cruise the Atlantic Coast from Massachusetts to Miami, peeking at the quirky side of US history. Or go west and soak up the spectacular beauty of the Pacific coast via jaw-dropping highways that stretch all the way from Mexico to Canada.

Some of the USA's most iconic road trips might be in your own backyard. Turn the page and find out.

TRIP TRACKER

- [ ] **1** Route 66: Motoring the Mother Road
- [ ] **2** Massachusetts to Miami: Fablantic Firsts
- [ ] **3** The Lincoln Highway
- [ ] **4** Skyline Drive to the Blue Ridge Parkway
- [ ] **5** Rollin' on the Great River Road
- [ ] **6** The Great Divide Treasure Hunt
- [ ] **7** Wet & Wild West Coast
- [ ] **8** 48 Hours in Manhattan
- [ ] **9** East Coast Ivory Towers
- [ ] **10** New Jersey Diners: Open 24 Hours
- [ ] **11** New York's Adirondack State Park
- [ ] **12** A Civil War Tour
- [ ] **13** Maryland Crab Quest
- [ ] **14** The Crooked Road: Heritage Music Trail
- [ ] **15** Dollhouse Delaware
- [ ] **16** 48 Hours in Boston
- [ ] **17** Ivy League Secrets & Superstitions
- [ ] **18** Literary New England
- [ ] **19** The Great Rhode Island Bicycle Tour
- [ ] **20** Leaf Peeps & Harvest Eats
- [ ] **21** Weird Vermont
- [ ] **22** Maine Lobster Tour
- [ ] **23** 60 Lighthouses in 60 Hours
- [ ] **24** 48 Hours in New Orleans
- [ ] **25** Music City to Dixieland: A Musical Roots Run
- [ ] **26** Cajun Country Road Trip
- [ ] **27** Antebellum South
- [ ] **28** Driving the Natchez Trace Parkway
- [ ] **29** Historic Battles of the Civil War
- [ ] **30** Eclectic Americana in the Triangle
- [ ] **31** The Great Smokies
- [ ] **32** Kentucky Bluegrass & Horse Country
- [ ] **33** 48 Hours in Miami
- [ ] **34** Cruisin' Florida's East Coast
- [ ] **35** Doing Disney & More
- [ ] **36** Overseas Highway to Key West
- [ ] **37** Go Wild in the Everglades
- [ ] **38** High Life Down on the Gulf Coast
- [ ] **39** Freaky Florida
- [ ] **40** North Florida Backwaters & Byways
- [ ] **41** 48 Hours in Chicago
- [ ] **42** A Moveable Feast
- [ ] **43** Michigan's Gold Coast
- [ ] **44** An Amish Country Ramble
- [ ] **45** Lake Lovers' Trail
- [ ] **46** Rockin' the Midwest
- [ ] **47** Dylan, Moose & More on Highway 61
- [ ] **48** Rich in Kitsch
- [ ] **49** 48 Hours in St Louis
- [ ] **50** Twain Tour
- [ ] **51** Here's the Beef
- [ ] **52** Oklahoma's Tribal Trails
- [ ] **53** Plains, Cranes & Automobiles
- [ ] **54** Wild West Legends
- [ ] **55** On the Pioneer Trail
- [ ] **56** Where the Buffalo Roam
- [ ] **57** Offbeat Dakotas
- [ ] **58** 48 Hours in Austin
- [ ] **59** San Antonio Mariachis & Machacado
- [ ] **60** Best of Hill Country BBQ
- [ ] **61** Cattle Country Drive
- [ ] **62** Gulf Coast Jaunt
- [ ] **63** Oddball Art & Aliens
- [ ] **64** Big Fun in Big Bend
- [ ] **65** 48 Hours in Greater Denver
- [ ] **66** Summit Colorado: the 14er Club
- [ ] **67** Colorado Ski Country
- [ ] **68** Wild West Wyoming
- [ ] **69** Tripping Through Grand Teton & Yellowstone
- [ ] **70** Going Boho in Bozeman's Big Sky Country
- [ ] **71** Once-in-a-Lifetime Glacier
- [ ] **72** Champagne & Powder in Sun Valley
- [ ] **73** Hot Potatoes & Hot Lava: Offbeat Idaho
- [ ] **74** 48 Hours in Las Vegas
- [ ] **75** Week in the Grand Canyon
- [ ] **76** Southwest by Train
- [ ] **77** Santa Fe Arts Amble
- [ ] **78** Four Corners Cruise
- [ ] **79** Written in Stone: Utah's National Parks
- [ ] **80** A Green Chile Adventure
- [ ] **81** Gunfighters & Gold Miners
- [ ] **82** Rafting the Colorado
- [ ] **83** 48 Hours in Los Angeles
- [ ] **84** Retro-Modern Palm Springs
- [ ] **85** A Wild Ride in the Parks
- [ ] **86** Life in Death Valley
- [ ] **87** 48 Hours in San Francisco
- [ ] **88** Alice Waters' Culinary Tour
- [ ] **89** Tree Time in Sequoia & Kings Canyon
- [ ] **90** California's Other Wine Countries
- [ ] **91** All Aboard Amtrak
- [ ] **92** 48 Hours in Seattle
- [ ] **93** Pacific Northwest Grand Tour
- [ ] **94** International Selkirk Loop
- [ ] **95** Dippin' Down the Cascades
- [ ] **96** Journey Through Time Scenic Byway
- [ ] **97** Whistle-Stop Brewery Tour
- [ ] **98** The Simpsons to the Shining
- [ ] **99** Up the Inside Passage

Route 66: Motoring the Mother Road

WHY GO Snaking across the nation's belly, this fragile ribbon of concrete was the USA's original road trip, connecting Chicago with Los Angeles in 1926. Neon signs, motor courts, pie-filled diners and drive-in theaters sprouted along the way. Many remain, and tracing Route 66 today is a time-warped journey through small-town America.

Nostalgia and kitsch are your constant companions on the old thoroughfare. Nicknamed the "Mother Road" and "Main Street USA," Route 66 became popular during the Depression, when Dust Bowl migrants drove west in beat-up jalopies. After WWII, middle-class motorists hit the road for fun in their Chevys. Eventually bypassed by interstates, Route 66 was decommissioned in 1985. Driving it nowadays means seeking out blue-line highways and gravel frontage roads.

The route kicks off in downtown Chicago on Adams St just west of Michigan Ave. Before embarking fuel up at ❶ **Lou Mitchell's**. As if double-yolked eggs and thick-cut French toast aren't enough, Lou's serves free doughnut holes while you wait for your table, a free dish of ice cream after your meal and free Milk Duds (women only) to take on the road.

The insulin surge will propel your twisty, trafficky ride out of the city. Stay on Adams St for 1.5 miles until you come to Ogden Ave. Go left, and continue through the suburbs of Cicero and Berwyn. Brown "Historic Route 66" signs, while few and far between, do pop up at crucial junctions to mark the way. At Harlem Ave, turn left (south) and stay on it briefly until you jump onto Joliet Rd. After 6 miles,

TIME
14 days

DISTANCE
2400 miles

BEST TIME TO GO
May – Sep

START
Chicago, IL

END
Santa Monica, CA

43

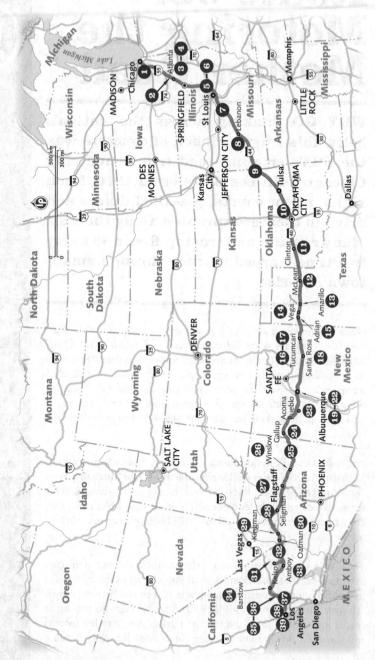

Joliet Rd joins southbound I-55 (at exit 277), and you'll be funneled onto the interstate.

Luckily, it's a short stint on the big bad freeway. At exit 269 rejoin Joliet Rd heading south, which merges with Hwy 53. Soon the good stuff starts rising from the cornfields: a giant fiberglass spaceman in Wilmington, chili cheese fries at Braidwood's diner, a vintage gas station in Odell, and more.

2 Funks Grove, a 19th-century maple-sirup farm south of Shirley (exit 154 off I-55), is one of a kind. Yes, that's "sirup" (with an "i"), which means the product is naturally sweet, versus artificially enhanced. Try it at the farm-house shop, or explore the trail-laced nature center and brooding graveyard nearby.

Get back on Old Route 66 (a frontage road that parallels the interstate here), and in 10 miles you'll reach the throwback hamlet of **3 Atlanta**. Pull up a chair at the **4 Palms Grill Cafe**, where thick slabs of gooseberry, peach, sour-cream raisin and other retro pies tempt from a glass case. Tall Paul, a giant statue of Paul Bunyan clutching a hot dog, and the old-timey murals splashed across Atlanta's buildings provide the route's top photo op in Illinois.

Keep following the brown "66" signs, leaving corn dogs, Abe Lincoln shrines, farms and grain silos in your wake. Before driving into Missouri, detour off I-270 at exit 3. Follow Hwy 203 south, turn right at the first stoplight and drive west to the 1929 **5 Old Chain of Rocks Bridge**. Open only to pedestrians and cyclists these days, the mile-long span over the Mississippi River has a 22-degree angled bend (cause of many a crash, hence the ban on cars).

Adventure doesn't just whisper in your ear as you swoop over the Mississippi River (back on I-270) toward Missouri. It grabs the wheel, presses the accelerator and powers you into St Louis, a can-do city that's launched westbound travelers for centuries.

To ogle the city's most iconic attraction, exit onto Riverview Dr and point your car south toward the 630ft-tall Gateway Arch, a graceful reminder of the city's role in westward expansion. For up-close views of the stainless-steel span and the Jefferson National Expansion Memorial surrounding it, turn left onto Washington Ave from Tucker Blvd (12th St). The memorial honors Thomas Jefferson, the westward-thinking president behind the Louisiana Purchase and the Lewis and Clark Expedition.

Jefferson was also an early fan of ice cream, so if you don't have time for monuments, honor his culinary vision with a creamy treat from ❻ **Ted Drewes Frozen Custard.** Follow Tucker Blvd south to Gravois Ave, turn right onto Chippewa St then scan for the icicle-trimmed shack surrounded by custard-craving masses. But no worries, lines move fast and half the fun is deciding which of 27 toppings to swirl into your "concrete" – so thick they hand it to you upside down.

NAVIGATING THE NITTY GRITTY

Because Route 66 is no longer an official road, it doesn't appear on most maps. We've provided high-level directions, but you'll fare best using one of these additional resources: free turn-by-turn directions at www.historic66.com; the illustrated "Here It Is!" map series (Ghost Town Press); or the EZ66 Guide for Travelers (National Historic Route 66 Federation).

   We've pointed out the don't-miss motels for when you need to rest your head, but there are plenty of others to choose from along the road. Part of the fun is rolling up in a random small town and plopping down at the local motor court.

From here, I-44 closely tracks – and sometimes covers – chunks of original Mother Road (yup, they repaved paradise, put up a four-lane interstate). One bright spot? Kitschy billboards touting ❼ **Meramec Caverns.** This family-mobbed attraction and campground ($18 to $25) has lured roadtrippers with offbeat ads since 1933.

From gold panning to riverboat rides, you'll find a day's worth of distractions, but don't miss the historically and geologically engaging cave tour. Note to kitsch seekers: the restaurant and gift store are actually inside the mouth of the cave. Check it out.

The nostalgic, 1940s-era ❽ **Munger Moss Motel** keeps the Route 66 spirit alive in Lebanon with a bright neon sign and Route 66–themed rooms. In the morning take Hwy 96 to Civil War–era Carthage and its 66 Drive-in Theatre.

ABE MANIA

Illinois is the Land of Lincoln, according to local license plates, and the best place to get an Honest Abe fix is Springfield, on Route 66 about 200 miles downstate from Chicago. Abe fans get weak-kneed at the holy trio of sights: **Lincoln's Tomb** (in Oak Ridge Cemetery), the **Lincoln Presidential Museum & Library** (www.alplm. org) and the **Lincoln Home** (www.nps.gov/liho), all in or near downtown.

From Joplin, follow Hwy 66 to Old Route 66 then hold tight: Kansas is on the horizon. The tornado-prone state holds a mere 13 miles of Mother Road (less than 1% of the total) but there's still a lot to see.

After passing through mine-scarred Galena, stop at the red-brick ❾ **Eisler Brothers Old Riverton Store** and stock up on batteries, seasonal flowers, turkey sandwiches and Route 66 memorabilia. The 1925 property looks much like it did when built – note the pressed-tin ceiling and the outhouse – and it's on the National Register of Historic Places. From there, cross Hwy 400 and continue to the 1923 Marsh

Rainbow Arch Bridge, from where it's 3 miles south to Civil War–minded Baxter Springs.

The "Mother Road" moniker first appeared in John Steinbeck's novel *The Grapes of Wrath*. In this Depression-era classic, the Joad family trekked west across Oklahoma on Route 66, an exodus route for hundreds of thousands of real-life migrants escaping the drought-stricken region during the Dust Bowl years. For turn-by-turn directions through Oklahoma's 426 miles of drivable Mother Road, download the Oklahoma Route 66 Trip Guide (www.oklahomaroute66.com).

From Afton to Tulsa, Route 66 parallels I-44 (now a toll road), crossing it twice before entering Vinita, a mere side dish to Clanton's Café and its lip-smacking chicken-fried steak. Continuing west, ponder the world's largest concrete totem pole near Foyil, pay homage to Renaissance wrangler Will Rogers in Claremore, swoop over the Verdigris River then snap a photo of the 80ft-long Blue Whale, the happiest creature to ever get beached in the town of Catoosa.

THAT BURGER MAKES ME CRY

The first onion-fried burger was served in 1926 in El Reno, Oklahoma. Today, this kickin' delicacy (ground beef combined with raw onions then caramelized on the grill) wows diners at burger joints statewide. El Reno serves a 750-pounder during May's **Fried Onion Burger Festival**. The rest of the year, visit **Roberts** (300 S Bickford Ave), **Jobe's** (1220 Sunset Dr) or **Johnnie's Grill** (310 S Rock Island) – all in El Reno.

Art-deco Tulsa is Oklahoma's second-largest city. It's also the hometown of Mother Road route-maker Cyrus Avery, "The Father of Route 66." From 193rd St, gritty 11th St slices west across the city's northern flank, a light industrial area packed tight with used-car dealerships and budget motels.

In Arcadia, 90 miles southwest, the cavernous, red-painted Round Barn dukes it out with a 66ft bottle of pop for your attention. The latter is the eye-catching calling card for ❿ POPS, a glass-walled gas station built in 2007. The station's spare, space-age contours are kept grounded by the retro charms inside – 530 varieties of soda pop ($1.99 each), a burger-and-shake-serving diner and clerks who don't mind answering your inevitable soda-pop questions. And yes, they do sell Avery's Kitty Piddle.

It's boots and chaps and cowboy hats in Oklahoma City, home of the fantastic National Cowboy & Western Heritage Museum. Most other cowboy attractions are corralled south of downtown in Stockyards City where you can watch a cattle auction, buy a custom-made cowboy hat or carve into a savory sirloin. The Field of Empty Chairs at the Oklahoma City National Memorial

& Museum is a moving reminder of the 168 men, women and children killed by a terrorist explosion here on April 19, 1995.

Route 66 rolls west from town on NW 39th St. Tip your hat to Garth Brooks in Yukon, the country crooner's former hometown. The Mother Road joins Business I-40 for 20 miles then parallels I-40, linking several diner-loving small towns. West of Hydro, look for the distinctive out-thrust, live-over porch at Lucille's Service Station, built in 1929.

RIGHT NEAR ROUTE 66

Late millionaire Stanley Marsh said he planted the 10 vintage 1949 to 1963 cars at the freely accessible **Cadillac Ranch** art installation in salute to Route 66. It's not actually on "the road," but it's right near – west of Amarillo on the southern I-40 feeder between exits 60 and 62.

Flags from all eight Mother Road states fly high beside the memorabilia-filled ⑪ **Oklahoma Route 66 Museum**, in Clinton. This fun-loving treasure trove, run by the Oklahoma Historical Society, isn't your typical mishmash of photos, clippings and knick-knacks (though there is an artifact-filled Cabinet of Curios). Instead, it uses music and videos to dramatize six decades of Route 66 history. Last exhibit? A faux-but-fun drive-in theater.

Continue west to Erick, hometown of "King of the Road" composer Roger Miller. With the song's breezy first line floating from your speakers ("Trailers for sale or rent…"), it's an easy cruise through Texola into the Lone Star State.

Vestiges of the Mother Road are few on the Texas panhandle plains and New Mexico desert – mostly it's I-40 frontage. The old route does detour into towns like miniscule McLean, where the ⑫ **Devil's Rope Museum** contains two Route 66 memorabilia-filled rooms. West, at First and Main Sts, a little old Philips station is another photo op. Subsequent towns offer little but you can't miss the 190ft-tall cross in Groom or the old VW Beetles planted nose-in-dirt as art at Conway.

Getting into Amarillo, the ⑬ **Big Texan Steak Ranch & Motel** – with its giant cowboy sign, flashing lights, longhorn limousine and shooting arcade – is as kitsch as they come. Between Georgia and Western on W 6th Ave, antiques, boutiques and bars fill the old buildings.

The route wanders into ⑭ **Vega**, where you'll find a nicely restored Magnolia gas station and Dot's Mini-Museum, a collector's packed shack that's freely open when the owner is around. The 1950s diner-style ⑮ **Midpoint Cafe** in Adrian marks the halfway point between LA and Chicago, and serves some darn good "ugly crust" pie.

From here, it's 63 miles past the chiles on the New Mexico welcome sign and through the vast desert flatness of the Llano Estacado, named after the seas of stalklike yucca, to **16** **Tucumcari**. With plenty of roadside kitsch and old-school neon, this tiny ranching town is a favorite of Route 66 aficionados looking for a remnant of the old Southwest, a Southwest before the damming of the rivers, the arrival of Snowbirds and the ubiquitous Comfort Suites. Hunker down at the 1936 **17** **Blue Swallow Motel**, a roadside classic with pull-in garages beside some rooms, vintage decor, and blue neon boasting its "100% refrigerated bar."

The interstate stretches endlessly from Tucumcari to the horizon, dry and windy, mile after mile, with the emptiness of the plains falling to the east and flat-topped mesas dotted with piñon popping out of the nothingness as you head west. For a taste of the trek without cruise control, air conditioning and a loaded iPod, loop along old Route 66 through **18** **Santa Rosa** and stop at the Route 66 Automobile Museum, on Will Rogers Ave, before returning to the 21st century on I-40.

After 1936 Route 66 was re-aligned from its original path north through Santa Fe to a direct line west through Tijeras Canyon, sandwiched between the 10,000ft limestone-capped granite Sandia and Manzano Mountains, and into **19** **Albuquerque**. Today, the city's **20** **Central Ave**, an eclectic treasure trove of Route 66 landmarks peppered with boho coffeehouses and funky restaurants, tattoo parlors and New Age shops, follows the post-1937 route.

Exit I-40 at Carlisle St, head south and turn right onto Central Ave for the best stretch of the old road, a 7-mile cruise through trendy Nob Hill and downtown Albuquerque, past the low-flung adobes and quirky museums (think rattlesnakes, atomic bombs and turquoise) of Old Town and over the Rio Grande River. Indulge in some local, organic fare and a tequila flight at breezy **21** **Artichoke Café**, just west of I-25, and don't miss the spectacular tile-and-wood artistry of the **22** **Kimo Theater**, across from the old Indian trading post downtown. This 1927 icon of pueblo deco architecture blends Native American culture with art deco design; the prominent swastika, for example, is a Navajo symbol for life, freedom and happiness, and a Hopi symbol of their nomadic tradition.

West from Albuquerque, vestiges of old Route 66 continue to cluster in the cities, so it's back to the interstate for the 60-mile drive to **23** **Acoma Pueblo**. Known as "sky city," this Native American community perched on a 370ft sandstone mesa vies with the Hopi village of Old Oraibi and Taos Pueblo for the title of longest continuously inhabited settlement in the United States. Tribal members have lived in the pueblo since AD 1150 and many of the dwellings remain much as they have for centuries, with no sewer, water or electricity.

Allow a few hours for a walking tour to the mesa, and then zip along the interstate 90 miles to ㉔ **Gallup**, where Route 66 dips off I-40 to act as the main drag past beautifully renovated buildings. Continuing on the interstate, it's another 70 miles over the Arizona border to the surreal ㉕ **Petrified Forest National Park**. The "trees" here are fragmented, fossilized 225-million-year-old logs; in essence, wood that has turned to stone, scattered over a vast area of semidesert grassland. Many are huge – up to 6ft in diameter – and several trails spur off the park's 28-mile paved scenic drive.

Catch the sunset over the Painted Desert from the park's Kachina Point before driving a final hour to the lonesome little town of Winslow (made famous by the Eagle's "Take It Easy"), for forty winks at ㉖ **La Posada**. Designed by Mary Colter for Fred Harvey, the early-20th-century entrepreneur who codified Southwestern style in his hotels and restaurants along the Santa Fe Railroad, this 1929 hotel features elaborate tile work, glass-and-tin chandeliers and Navajo rugs. Colter created some of the most famous buildings in the Southwest, including several that blend magnificently into the limestone of Grand Canyon National Park, but many consider this rambling hacienda to be her masterpiece. Small, period-styled rooms are named for former guests, including Albert Einstein and Gary Cooper, and there's a decent restaurant.

Hit the road before breakfast, as you'll find better options 60 miles west in historic ㉗ **Flagstaff**. With a low-key vibe and an inordinate number of outdoor shops catering to both the fleece-clad local crowd and Grand Canyon visitors, this high-country college town makes a pleasant morning stroll. Route 66 follows the railroad tracks to the pedestrian-friendly downtown, where you can grab a vegan scone or tofu scramble with your coffee at Macy's on S Beaver St, and let the kids shake the morning out of their bodies at Thorpe Park, before rejoining the interstate for the 75 miles to tiny ㉘ **Seligman**. The Snow-Cap Drive-In here, a Route 66 favorite, has been in the Delgadillo family since it opened in 1953.

The Mother Road arcs northwest from Seligman away from I-40 through blink-and-miss-them towns for 90 miles back around to I-40 and quiet ㉙ **Kingman**, home to a couple of fun museums, before corkscrewing west as County Hwy 10 into the rugged Black Mountains. Twist and turn 30 miles up through Sitgreaves Pass and down past the tumbleweeds and saguaro to the old mining town of ㉚ **Oatman**. When the gold was mined out in 1942 and Route 66 was rerouted south in 1952, closing six of the town's seven gas stations, this little settlement reinvented itself as a movie set and unapologetic

Wild West tourist trap. Feed carrots to the wild burros, catch a gunfight and grab an icy something in the musky old saloon of the 1902 Oatman Hotel, where Clark Gable and Carole Lombard spent their wedding night in 1939, before returning to the glare of the Arizona sun for the final 25-mile stretch to the California border.

LA-bound drivers rarely detour off I-40 – but travelers who follow faded Route 66 stencils north from Needles though the ③ **Mojave Desert** discover tumbleweed landscapes bypassed by freeways. West along Goffs Rd, you'll spot ③ **Goffs Schoolhouse and Railway Depot**, once abandoned but recently restored as repositories of Mojave Desert history.

For dessert in the desert, veer off Route 66 at Fenner onto I-40, and head 28 miles to Kelbaker Rd, where you'll turn north 22 miles to **Kelso Depot** (www.nps.gov/moja/index.htm). The Mojave National Preserve's main visitor center is located in this renovated railway station, where the 1924 lunch counter has recently reopened to reward intrepid travelers with $5 pie à la mode.

Crossing I-40 south at Fenner on Route 66, you'll pass ghost towns signposted by lonesome railroad markers and boarded-up gas stations: ③ **Amboy** (purchased in 2005 by nostalgic fast-food magnate Albert Okura, who re-opened the 1950s gas station), Bagdad (long-gone namesake location of 1987 German cult classic *Bagdad Café*), Siberia (now vanished) and Ludlow (largely ruined).

Signs of life return as you reach Barstow, ominously immortalized in Hunter S Thompson's *Fear and Loathing in Las Vegas:* "We were somewhere around Barstow, on the edge of the desert, when the drugs began to take hold…" Barstow is also home to the ③ **Route 66 Mother Road Museum**, featuring classic cars, vintage photos and priceless auto-repair signage ("Some things we fix good").

In nearby Victorville, Uma Thurman hit the Mother Road with a vengeance in Quentin Tarantino's 2004 *Kill Bill Vol 2* after a pitstop at ③ **Emma Jean's Holland Burger Café**. Try their killer Brian Burger, with grilled green chiles, melted Swiss and a half-pound patty on thick sourdough bread. Afterwards, waddle into the ③ **California Route 66 Museum** to glimpse the life's work of trash-maestro Miles Mahan: a scavenged 9ft tin hula dancer amid a "Cactus Garden" of wine bottles stuck to fence posts.

Take I-15 out of Victorville, then rejoin Route 66 heading south towards the San Bernardino suburbs to reach the cartoonish ③ **Wigwam Motel**, which movie buffs may recognize as the Cozy Cone Motel in Pixar's 2006 animation *Cars* (originally titled *Route 66*). Each recently renovated 1949 concrete tepee has its own diminutive bathroom and guestroom, complete with wagon-wheel bedstead. In the morning, follow Foothill Blvd/Route 66 West through retro-suburban ㊳ **Pasadena**, where you'll spot midcentury homes, motels and diners along palm-lined streets.

For a Hollywood ending to your trip with a minimum of LA traffic, plan to take Arroyo Seco Parkway in the early afternoon to Los Angeles, where Sunset Blvd connects you to Santa Monica Blvd (aka Hwy 2, formerly Route 66). When you reach the Pacific, park and ride off into the sunset on the solar-powered, 130ft Ferris wheel at the western terminus of Route 66: ㊴ **Santa Monica Pier**.

Amy Balfour, Alison Bing, Jennifer Denniston, Lisa Dunford & Karla Zimmerman

TRIP INFORMATION

GETTING THERE
I-90/94 barrels through downtown Chicago. Exit at Congress Pkwy, and in rapid succession: turn left at State St, right at Jackson Blvd, left at Michigan Ave, and left onto Adams St.

DO
Acoma Pueblo
Native American mesa-top village, 16 miles south of I-40. Price includes photography permit, museum entrance and ¾-mile walking tour. ☎ 800-747-0180; www.cabq. gov; I-40 exit 102, NM; adult/child $20/10; ◷ 9am-4pm; ♿

California Route 66 Museum
Road-tripping artifacts and a recreated folk-art landmark: Miles Mahan's Hula-ville, made entirely of roadside trash. ☎ 760-951-0436; www.califrt66museum.org; 16825 South D Street, Victorville, CA; admission free; ◷ 10am-4pm Thu-Mon, 11am-3pm Sun; ♿

Devil's Rope Museum
Part of this ranching museum is dedicated to a recreated diner and locals' Route 66 remembrances. ☎ 806-779-2225; www. barbwiremuseum.com; 100 Kingsley St, McLean, TX; admission $2; ◷ 10am-4pm Tue-Sat

Eisler Brothers Old Riverton Store
Their soft-drink fountain runs heavy on syrup so if you like it sweet fill 'er up. ☎ 620-848-3330; www.eislerbros.com; 7109 SE Hwy 66, Riverton, KS; ◷ 7:30am-8pm Mon-Sat, noon-7pm Sun

Funks Grove
The Funk family cooks up mighty fine maple sirup at their tree-studded farm. ☎ 309-874-3360; www.funksmaplesirup.com; 5257 Old Route 66, Shirley, IL; admission free; ◷ 9am-5pm Mon-Sat, 1-5pm Sun, with variations; ♿

Kimo Theater
Pueblo deco theater with performances ranging from Nutcracker to Second City, puppet shows to film festivals. ☎ 505-768-3544; www.cabq.gov; 423 Central Ave NW, Albuquerque, NM; admission varies; ♿

Meramec Caverns
Hiding place of 1870s outlaw Jesse James. ☎ 573-468-3166; www.americascave.com; Stanton, MO; adult/child $19/9.50; ◷ 9am-7pm May & Jun, 8:30am-7:30pm Jul & Aug, shorter hours rest of the year; ♿

Oklahoma Route 66 Museum
Outside, visit the tiny Valentine Diner. ☎ 580-323-7866; www.route66.org; 2229 W Gary Blvd, Clinton, OK; adult/child $4/1; ◷ 9am-5pm Mon-Sat, 1-5pm Sun, with variations, closed Sun & Mon Dec & Jan; ♿

Old Chain of Rocks Bridge
Walk or cycle across the Big Muddy from Illinois to Missouri; there's free parking by the bridge entrance. Old Chain of Rocks Rd, Madison, IL; ◷ 9am-dusk

Petrified Forest National Park
Silica dissolved from volcanic ash hardened into quartz, thus "petrifying" the wood of fallen logs. ☎ 928-524-6228; www.nps. gov/pefo; I-40 exit 311, AZ; 7-day entry per vehicle/bicycle & motorcycle $10/5; ◷ 8am-5pm, with seasonal variations; ♿

Route 66 Mother Road Museum
Roadside attractions galore inside rambling 1911 "Casa del Desierto" Harvey House, plus photo exhibits, books and gifts. ☎ 760-255-1890; www.route66museum.org; 681 N First Ave, Barstow, CA; admission free; ◷ 10am-4pm Fri-Sun; ♿

EAT
Artichoke Café
After crossing the country, fueled by nostalgia and kitsch, it's time for ginger crab-cakes and pumpkin ravioli. ☎ 505-243-0200; 424 Central SE, Albuquerque, NM; mains $14-25; ◷ 11am-2pm Mon-Fri, 5:30-10pm Tue-Sat, 5:30-9pm Sun & Mon

Big Texan Steak Ranch & Motel

Originally built on the old route (Amarillo Blvd) in 1959, the owner relocated when I-40 was constructed. The first Big Tex sign still towers over the Old West–style motel rooms and Texas-shaped cement pond. ☎ 800-657-7177; www.bigtexan.com; 7700 I-40 E, Amarillo, TX; mains $18-40; ☺ 7:30am-10:30pm

Emma Jean's Holland Burger Café

Dinky diner with grilled burgers, well-lubricated fries and mountainous blackberry cobbler, made from scratch. Cash only. ☎ 760-243-9938; www.hollandburger.com /home.html; 17143 North D St, Victorville, CA; mains $5-8; ☺ 5am-2:45pm Mon-Fri, 6:30am-12:30pm Sat

Lou Mitchell's

Lou's old-school waiters deliver fluffy pancakes and omelets, with a side of Milk Duds, by Route 66's starting point. ☎ 312-939-3111; 565 W Jackson Blvd, Chicago, IL; mains $5-10; ☺ 5:30am-3pm Mon-Sat, 7am-3pm Sun

Midpoint Cafe

Vibrant vinyl chairs and 1950s-esque knick-knacks form the backdrop for this burger joint and gift shop. ☎ 806-538-6379; cnr Business 40 & CR 22, Adrian, TX; mains $3-7; ☺ 8am-4pm Mar-Dec

Palms Grill Cafe

Fork into the blue plate special (sure to be gravy-smothered) or slabs of pie. ☎ 217-648-2233; 110 SW Arch St, Atlanta, IL; mains $4-9; ☺ 8am-5pm Sun-Thu, 8am-8pm Fri & Sat

POPS

Schedule dinner for sunset, when POPS illuminates its Paul Bunyan–sized soda bottle. ☎ 405-928-7677; www.pops66.com; 660 W Hwy 66, Arcadia, OK; mains $5-15; ☺ 10:30am-9pm daily, breakfast 6-10:30am Sat & Sun; ♿

Ted Drewes Frozen Custard

Swirl in one of 27 toppings – raspberry to caramel to M&M's – to make a concrete. ☎ 314-481-2652; www.teddrewes.com; 6726 Chippewa St, St Louis, MO; mains under $5; ☺ 11am-11pm Feb-Dec; ♿

SLEEP

Blue Swallow Motel

A must for anyone looking for that quint-essential Mother Road vibe. Seven hundred miles west of Lebanon, Missouri. ☎ 575-461-9849; www.blueswallowmotel.com; 815 E Tucumcari Blvd, Tucumcari, NM; r $66; ♿ 🐾

La Posada

Harvey Hotel reminiscent of days when travel meant crystal on the rails, not plastic in the car. Circa 1929. ☎ 928-289-4366; www.laposada.org; 303 E 2nd St Winslow, AZ; r $120-160; ♿ 🐾

Munger Moss Motel

Munger and Moss? Surnames of the original owner's first two husbands. ☎ 417-532-3111; www.mungermoss.com; 1336 E Route 66, Lebanon, MO; r from $40

Wigwam Motel

Get your kitsch on Route 66: stay snug in a concrete tepee, with kidney-shaped pool out the back. ☎ 909-875-3005; www.wigwammotel.com; 2728 West Foothill Blvd, San Bernardino, CA; r $63.50-75; ♿

USEFUL WEBSITES

www.historic66.com
www.nps.gov/history/nr/travel/route66

LINK YOUR TRIP

www.lonelyplanet.com/trip-planner

Massachusetts to Miami: Fablantic Firsts

WHY GO Follow the quirky, often has-to-be-seen-to-believed course of US history all the way down the Atlantic seaboard, from the Ivy League's hallowed halls to Miami Beach's oldest dive bar. This coastal road trip is stuffed full of offbeat US originals.

Famous figures have long been coining nicknames for the USA: "the melting pot," "land of the free," "home of the brave," but it was David Bowie that got it right when he said "Ch-ch-changes!" True, he wasn't exactly talking about the 50 states in that song, but change is the hallmark of the American spirit. After all, it was the willingness to change that turned a motley crew of overtaxed colonies into the world's capital of capitalism. So, in honor of the country's pioneering panache, we've charted a special trip down the Atlantic Coast. It's a tribute to the savvy trendsetters who have helped shape this great nation over the last 400 years. You're gonna love our menagerie of fabulous firsts – in fact, we're pretty sure you'll be back for seconds.

Our first first is tucked deep within the hallowed halls of the nation's first college, Harvard. The ① **Hasty Pudding Theatricals**, the USA's first acting troupe, takes the stage every February to dispel the myth that this old-school Ivy Leaguer is a stronghold of pseudo-intellectual guffawing and library-bound geeks. What started centuries ago as a fraternity's reenactment of famous historical events has gradually turned into an elaborate drag burlesque musical. Everything's over the top – from the cartoonlike costumes to the clanging oompah-pah of the house band it's rude and crude, and each act overflows with slapstick humor and ridiculous wordplay. Past show titles include "Some Like it Yacht" and "Acropolis Now." "Vowel Movement" is perhaps the crudest tune in the history of modern musical theatre. Even the characters have painfully punderful names: there was that trollop who spoiled the spelling bee, Connie Lynn Guist, and who could forget the pious

TIME
10 days

DISTANCE
2000 miles

BEST TIME TO GO
Mar – Aug

START
Boston, MA

END
Miami, FL

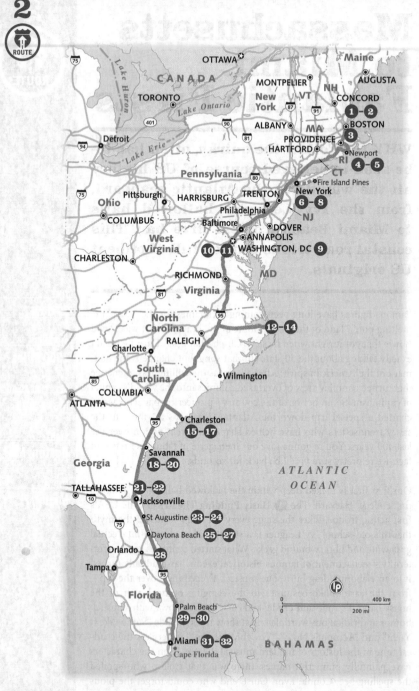

and naive Stella Virgin? Despite the bombast and frenzied ado, each annual show still honors the all-male Shakespearian performance model; however, today's no-holds-bard renditions surely have the poor playwright spinning in his grave. As the plumage-crowned cancan dancers close the satin curtains, make your way back to downtown Boston for a restful night's sleep at the **②** **Omni Parker House**, the nation's first "grand hotel" (also the longest continuously operating hotel in America – it opened in 1855). Although most of the traditional trimmings have been replaced with swish modern design, lavish common spaces still hint at the building's illustrious past.

In the morning, it's time to pay tribute to one of the USA's best-known creations, the franchise. We're not sending you to McDonalds, there's no need to grimace. We've got something else in mind – a traditional, cop-fattening repast at the first **③** **Dunkin' Donuts**. Gorge on glazed, double chocolate, and jelly-filled treats à la Homer Simpson while taking in the doughnut-hole-in-the-wall's facsimiled decor. Caffeinate with a round of Dunkaccinos (or any of the other trademarked buzzwords) while reading the perfect capitalist fairytale. Once upon a time in 1948, Bill Rosenberg opened a humble doughnut shop (the one you're sitting in). It was originally called "Open Kettle" but the name quickly changed. Soon after, a licensing agreement was reached, contracts were signed, and by 1963 there were more than 100 branches throughout the USA. Things went global in 1970 when Japan said *konichiwa* to the burgeoning conglomerate, and today there are over 5000 links in this ever-expanding chain.

If factory-line fare leaves you less than beaming, then hop back on your wheels and continue south along I-95 for a meal at the opposite end of the dining spectrum. America's first members-only resort, **④** **Bailey's Beach Club**, is a veritable WASP nest occupying a private slice of chalky gray sand in Newport, Rhode Island. If your surname isn't Vanderbilt and you don't have a roman numeral attached, then chances are slim – make that impossible – that you'll get to nibble their foie gras and crack open the bubbly. In fact, the members list is so tightly guarded even Donald Trump got the proverbial talk-to-the-hand! Don't despair though; locals joke that Bailey's Beach is the most hideous strip of sand around and, besides, New-

FIRST CLASS
The advent of American industry spawned the nation's first aristocrats, and the idyllic Rhode Island town of Newport was the *it* spot to erect a sumptuous summer mansion. Year after year wealthy families would try to keep up with the Joneses – Italianate palazzos were mimicked, French chateaux reproduced inch by inch, and English manors cloned from steeple to cellar. Check out www.newportmansions.org for details on touring these wondrous allegories of capitalism.

port has plenty of other opportunities for us plebeians to nab a fancy nosh. Our favorite is the **⑤** **White Horse Tavern** on Marlborough St. Founded by a pirate in 1687, this gambrel-roofed tavern is one of the oldest establishments in the United States. In 1708 the restaurant secured its place in the annals of American history when local council members charged their meal to the public treasury, thus creating the country's first "business lunch." Although eye patches and talking parrots have been gradually replaced with popped collars and navy-blue blazers (a "business casual" dress code is strictly enforced), the lovely dining room is still very much a step back in time. Just watch your footing – the floorboards are very uneven!

Check into the first entirely sustainable LEED-approved (Leadership in Energy and Environmental Design) hotel in New York City, the ❻ **Crosby Street Hotel**. Being green has never been so easy in this stunning hotel located in SoHo (on…wait for it…Crosby St). Each room is individually decorated in delightful style by the hotel's owner, with dress-forms and rich textiles highlighting the marvelous rooms and their great views of downtown Manhattan. Stay in the city's first ever "Meadow Suite," with your own private terrace garden. Or head down to the Crosby Bar for afternoon champagne tea while surrounded by appealing and whimsical contemporary art. Sunday nights offer a movie club with cocktails and classic cinema in a chic screening room.

COCKTAIL HOUR

Cocktail connoisseurs will want to hit the birthplace of the Bloody Mary, here called the "Red Snapper." The **King Cole Bar** in the **St Regis Hotel** (just off 5th Avenue on East 55th Street; www.starwoodhotels.com/stregis) is elegant and refined. Sip your drink while admiring the Maxfield Parrish mural that gives the bar its name.

Across town, the Meatpacking District, once a bastion of seedy leather bars, cow carcasses and prostitutes, has been aggressively gentrified over the past decade. It is now home to chic eateries, even chicer boutiques, and perhaps the most popular new attraction in the city: ❼ **The High Line**. Inspired by the Promenade Plantee in Paris, this is the first elevated park in New York. A wonder of urban reinvention, the High Line was an abandoned railway that ran from the meatpacking plants to the Westside rail yard. Locals banded to turn the tracks into much-needed public space in this section of Manhattan. It runs north from Gansevoort St to West 20th and is marvelous in every way. You'll get great and unexpected views of the city as you wind through the quarter-mile stretch that's stuffed with lovely gardens of meadow plants and birch trees. Bring a cup of coffee and a croissant and sit on the myriad benches or chaise lounges for some of the best people-watching you'll ever get. Jaded New Yorkers get excited about very little but this park has had people buzzing ever since it opened in early 2009. Not to be missed!

For a trip into old-timey New York, catch a ride with Famous Fat Dave in his authentic vintage checkered cab for his ❽ **Five Borough Eating Tour**. If it isn't the oldest cab in operation, it's certainly the first and only that chauffeurs you around the city in old-world glamour. Dave, a real cabbie, will pick you and your friends up in his "Wheels of Steel" and take you to the forgotten corners of the city in search of delicacies such as the famed hot dog at the very first Nathan's, in Coney Island (local legend has it this was the home of the first ever hot dog), the first pizza available "by the slice" (now a New York gastronomic stalwart), at Patsy's in Harlem, or even more esoteric firsts such as the "first American fried chicken with Spanish flavor," in Washington Heights. Whatever that means, it was great chicken! Along the way, Dave shares bits of New York history as you travel from seafood joints on City Island to the Bronx's own "Murder Burger" with a nightcap at the Italian bakeries of

DETOUR About an hour and a half from NYC by car or train is one of the first gay resorts, the **Fire Island Pines** (www.fipines.com). Accessible only by ferry, this is where the boys go to summer. Relax on the beach then hit low tea and high tea (for cocktails, not English breakfast) at the dockside bars. Don't forget your Speedos!

Greenwich Village. This unique experience is one of the best times we've ever had in New York City, and trust us when we tell you we've had some pretty good times there.

Continuing down the coast, it's a quick few hours to Washington DC, where we're going to see the first ladies collection at the ❾ **National Museum of American History**, part of the Smithsonian Institute. Several gowns are on display (including glamourpuss Jackie Kennedy's) along with White House china and various other items belonging to West Wing doyennes from Martha Washington to Michelle Obama. While you're there, check out the kitchen of the first lady of cooking, Julia Child.

Across the Potomac River is ❿ **Old Town Alexandria**, first settled in 1695 in what was then the British Colony of Virginia. After an afternoon spent in the company of first ladies and historical Virginia, let's celebrate with a nod to the first woman herself at the impeccable ⓫ **Restaurant Eve**. Catering to beltway boys and government gals on dates, Eve is hidden down a cloistered entryway. Its menu packs a sophisticated French-American punch that's delicious but not overly precious. This is nationally recognized Irish chef Cathal Armstrong's first restaurant on New World shores. Try the mojito.

Keep going and you'll run into North Carolina, in the endearing Dirty South, where y'all might-could learn a thing or two about minding your manners and slowin' wayyyy down. Your first stop is the ⓬ **Outer Banks**, amply blessed by the geography gods (with a side of kitsch). Two hundred miles of pristine sandy white beaches and stately lighthouses share a sub-mile-wide strip of land with drive-through convenience stores and beachwear shacks with ubiquitous shark-jawed entrances. North Carolina throws down the first-in-flight gauntlet (take that, birthplace-of-aviation Ohio!) at Kitty Hawk, home to the ⓭ **Wright Brothers Memorial**. Orville and Wilbur might have drawn up their glider plans in Dayton, but it was the Outer Banks' gentle winds and soft landings that were the catalyst for the Red Baron, NASA and frequent-flyer-mile clubs. The complex encompasses several museums, a hilltop memorial and historic outbuildings and flight markers.

Most restaurants in the Outer Banks serve crab with a side order of anthropomorphic mascots, so head to the first green-certified restaurant in North Carolina, **14 Basnight's Lone Cedar Café**. Come early to wander the fresh herb garden and pier, and then feast, with a sunset backdrop, on delectable seafood and vegetables. You can actually taste the commitment to sustainable farming and fishing. Bring your own freshly caught fish, and the chefs will prepare it any way you like.

Head into the deepest of the Deep South by traveling down a state to South Carolina, where the area around **15 Charleston** was host to many firsts in the United States: the first temporary European settlement (Spanish, 1526), the first decisive American victory in the Revolutionary War (Sullivan's Island; June 28, 1776), the first public library (1698) and, that all-important first, the first submarine to be used in combat, the **16 HL Hunley**. In 1861, two Confederate steam-gauge manufacturers teamed up with Horace L Hunley, a Louisiana businessperson, to create an underwater secret weapon. The hand-cranked craft was the only underwater vessel to sink an enemy ship until WWI. The museum is a working archaeological site, and visitors get to peer into the 90,000-gallon tank at the *Hunley,* where eight very tightly cramped men sunk the USS *Housitonic* in six minutes.

THE FIRST HYPHENATED AMERICAN

In 1587, Virginia Dare became the first English child born on American soil, on Roanoke Island in the Outer Banks. The colony's governor left soon thereafter for supplies, returning from England three years later to find a deserted colony. To this day, no one knows what happened; however, several Englishmen later reported seeing a young English maid captured by a Native American tribe. Was this Virginia Dare? DNA tests are under way to find out.

Sleep with the echo of our first president at the **17 John Rutledge House Inn**, the private home to one of the signers of the Constitution. George Washington mentioned the fab breakfast here in his diary, and the restored rooms and elegant common space evoke colonial times.

The most fablantic town in Georgia is, of course, **18 Savannah**. The literate city filled with antebellum mansions and haute cuisine was made even more famous by what's known as "the book" – *Midnight in the Garden of Good and Evil*, a Southern Gothic true crime novel based on a local hustler's murder by a well-known antiques dealer. To see the original home to the transvestite star Lady Chablis from the book, shimmy into **19 Club One**, the first multistory entertainment complex in Savannah. For the oldest mansion in Savannah, head thee to the ⑳ **Olde Pink House**. Sure, it's touristed and, yes, the surly staff's attitude is de rigueur, but it dates from 1771, serves up some of the finest biscuits and she-crab soup around, and, well, it's *pink*. (The original red bricks have bled through the white stucco, creating the effect.)

From steamy Savannah, slide south down the coast into the Sunshine State. Just outside Jacksonville, ㉑ **American Beach** is an adorably sleepy stretch of gorgeous white sand that played an important part during the USA's pre–Civil Rights era. In 1935, AL Lewis, Florida's first African American millionaire, built the first beach resort for African Americans along Florida's then-segregated shores. In America Beach's heyday, busloads of vacationers thronged to motels, restaurants and nightclubs where superstars like Louis Armstrong, Duke Ellington and Ray Charles played. Check out the independent film *Sunshine State,* which brings American Beach's tangled racial and class history to life.

Linger longer on Amelia Island in the seaport town of Fernandina Beach, with its fetching Victorian mansions. At Florida's oldest still-standing hotel (those hurricanes are ferocious, folks!), ㉒ **Florida House Inn**, the rollicking good-time atmosphere of the Frisky Mermaid Bar & Grille's bluegrass jams and shag-dancing nights is contagious. US presidents, moneyed Rockefellers and Old Hollywood film stars have all slept in the historic rooms upstairs.

Further south, ㉓ **St Augustine** lays claim to the title of being the oldest continuously occupied European settlement in North America. (To be fair, the Spanish first tried to settle Pensacola on Florida's Panhandle in 1559, only to be wiped out by a hurricane.) Today this 16th-century city suffers from too many ticky-tacky tourist trappings (hello, Fountain of Youth!). But walk the narrow cobblestone streets of its old quarter and you'll uncover beautifully preserved historic buildings, including the one-time residence of Napoleon's nephew. Yes, *that* Napoleon. Flickering candles illuminate stone-walled ㉔ **Taberna de Gallo**, which mimics a mid-18th-century pub, where colonial re-enactors sing sea shanties that get progressively rowdier – sing along and bang on the tables with your beer stein.

But enough of Ye Olde Past for a while. Florida coastin' spells F-U-N, nowhere more so than at partyin' ㉕ **Daytona Beach**. Think of it all as good family fun with a side of sleaze, just to keep things interesting. Although Fort Lauderdale's halcyon spring-break days were raunchier and rowdier, Daytona is where MTV shot its first spring-break special in 1986, sparking an anything-goes revolution. Traipse along the carnivalesque boardwalk, past beach bums' bars where draft beer sloshes around in plastic cups year-round. One look at Daytona Beach's perfectly planar miles of hard-packed sand, and you'll know why Nascar's first auto-racing dragway took place here in 1948. Just over a decade later, the modern ㉖ **Daytona Speedway**, known for its steep-banked turns angled at a death-defying 31 degrees, opened as the fastest course for stock cars ever built. You can (virtually) sit in the driver's seat or work on the pit crew at the heart-pounding **㉗ Daytona 500 Experience**.

Halfway from Jacksonville to Miami, Titusville is the launching pad for touring Florida's Space Coast, a land of many firsts. The "space race" was won when the US landed the first humans on the moon, and north of Cape Canaveral is the **㉘ Kennedy Space Center**. It's hard not to feel your heart and mind electrify as you tour NASA's working facilities, walking underneath a real Saturn V rocket and touching a piece of lunar rock, then strapping yourself into a bone-shaking shuttle-launch simulator.

> **DETOUR** Still got some gas left in the car? From Miami Beach it's only a 30-minute drive south and across two causeways out to Key Biscayne and **Cape Florida** (www.floridastateparks.org/capeflorida), harboring the oldest operating light station on the Florida coast, first built in 1826. Climb 109 steps to the tippy-top for panoramic views of the bay and the surrounding state park's top-ranked white-sand beach. The lighthouse is open for exploring and twice-daily guided tours Wednesday to Sunday.

Zoom south on I-95 to posh **㉙ Palm Beach**, the playground of rich-and-famous billionaires on Florida's Gold Coast. Gated compounds with palatial mansions line the Intra-Costal Waterway, but unless you've got VIP celebrity connections, there's no way to get a peek inside. Unless, of course, you visit the beaux arts–styled White-hall, now the **㉚ Flagler Museum**. Finished in 1902, Whitehall was arguably the first private residence in the USA to have both central heating and air-conditioning. The mansion also features pink aluminum-leaf wallpaper (at the time, more expensive than gold). Its Grand Hall was the largest single room of any Gilded Age mansion, outfitted with Gatsby-esque billiards tables. (Gruesome tip: railroad tycoon Henry Flagler died after tumbling down a staircase here, so watch your step!) Incidentally, Palm Beach County is home to another infamous first: its voter ballot recount in 2000 helped lead to the first-ever US Supreme Court intervention in a presidential election.

Keep truckin' south to your final destination, Miami. South Beach (SoBe) grabs the most beautiful beaches by day and the hottest clubs at night. But don't overlook its quieter art-deco historic district, where lofty hotels with tropical lobbies just scream "Miami!". Get into the retro swing of things at the **㉛ Art Deco Gift Shop**, offering architectural walking tours of glamorous art-deco addresses from yesteryear and today. Afterward dive into Miami's noir side at shady **㉜ Mac's Club Deuce**, bohemian Miami Beach's oldest neighborhood bar. You should expect to see everyone from transgendered ladies to hardcore bikers to Hollywood A-list celebs doing a little slumming at the Deuce. *¡Viva la revolución social!*

Sara Benson, Alex Leviton, David Ozanich & Brandon Presser

TRIP INFORMATION

GETTING THERE
From Boston, cross over the Charles River to Cambridge and make your way down I-95.

DO

Art Deco Gift Shop
Browse Bakelite jewelry and reproduction posters, then pick up an iPod walking tour and map. ☎ 305-531-3484; www.mdpl.org; 1001 Ocean Dr, Miami, FL; admission free, tour prices vary; ⏲ 9:30am-7pm

Daytona 500 Experience
A shrine to all things Nascar; make reservations for race-car ride-alongs. ☎ 386-681-6800; www.daytona500experience.com; 1801 W International Speedway Blvd, Daytona, FL; adult/child from $25/20; ⏲ 10am-6pm, with seasonal variations; ♿

Five Borough Eating Tour
Get a personal tour of New York's hidden culinary wonders with Dave the cabbie in his vintage checkered cab. www.famousfatdave.com; New York, NY; tours from $200

Flagler Museum
Tour this elaborate 55-room Jazz Age mansion ("more wonderful than any palace in Europe," one newspaper opined), completed in just 18 months as a gift from Henry Flagler for his bride. ☎ 561-655-2833; www.flaglermuseum.us; 1 Whitehall Way, Palm Beach, FL; adult/youth $18/10; ⏲ 10am-5pm Tue-Sat, noon-5pm Sun

Hasty Pudding Theatricals
A drag-tastic musical hidden deep within Harvard's hallowed halls. ☎ 617-495-5205; www.hastypudding.org; 12 Holyoke St, Cambridge, MA; ⏲ Feb & Mar

High Line
New York's first elevated park winds its way through Manhattan's West Side. www.thehighline.org; entrances at Gansevoort St, West 20th St, New York, NY; admission free; ⏲ 7am-8pm winter, 7am-10pm summer

HL Hunley
A working underwater archaeological site of a Civil War submarine with a museum and gift shop. ☎ 877-448-6539; www.hunley.org; 1250 Supply St, N Charleston, SC; admission $12; ⏲ 10am-5pm Sat, noon-5pm Sun; ♿

Kennedy Space Center
An all-in-one science museum, theme park and astronaut tribute. Buy advance tickets for lunch with a NASA astronaut. ☎ 321-449-4444; www.kennedyspacecenter.com; Orsino, FL; adult/child from $38/28; ⏲ 9am-6pm; ♿

National Museum of American History
Get to know your first ladies at this highlight of the Smithsonian. ☎ 202-633-1000; www.americanhistory.si.edu; National Mall, 14th St & Constitution Ave NW, Washington DC; admission free; ⏲ 10am-5:30pm

Olde Pink House
Dine with locals, tourists and ghosts at the 1771 mansion. ☎ 912-232-4286; 23 Abercorn St, Savannah, GA; mains $14-31; ⏲ 5-10.30pm Sun-Thu, 5-11pm Fri & Sat

Wright Brothers Memorial
Sprawling museum with gift shop, flight demonstrations and historical buildings. ☎ 252-441-7430; www.nps.gov/wrbr; Hwy 158 Bypass Milepost 8, Kill Devil Hills, NC; adult/child $4/free; ⏲ 9am-6pm Memorial Day-Labor Day, 9am-5pm off-season; ♿

EAT & DRINK

Bailey's Beach Club
Newport's members-only WASP nest on a private beachfront property. Sprouting Rock Beach Association; ☎ 401-847-1900; 34 Ocean Dr, Newport, RI

Basnight's Lone Cedar Café
Fresh seafood, vegetables and an on-site herb garden. ☎ 252-441-5405; www.lonecedarcafe.com; Nags Head-Manteo Causeway, Nags Head, NC; mains $8-36; ⏲ 11:30am-3pm Thu-Sun, 5pm-close daily, closed Jan & early Feb; ♿

Club One
Savannah bar and social institution featuring drag shows, karaoke, an often-pulsating dance floor and the tasty Bay Café. ☎ **912-232-0200; www.clubone-online.com; 1 Jefferson St, Savannah, GA; mains $7-12, entry fees vary; 5pm-3am**

Dunkin' Donuts
Responsible for thousands of pot bellies, Dunkin' Donuts' first link in the worldwide chain opened on a street named Artery. Coincidence? ☎ **617-472-9502; www.dunkindonuts.com; 543 Southern Artery, Quincy, MA; doughnuts $0.85; 24hr;**

Mac's Club Deuce
Knockin 'em back since 1926, this neighborhood fixture is deliciously seedy – if you're a dive-bar aficionado, that is. ☎ **305-673-9537; 222 14th St, Miami, FL; 8am-5am**

Restaurant Eve
A fine meal is guaranteed at this highlight of emerging epicurean Alexandria. ☎ **703-706-0450; www.restauranteve.com; 110 S Pitt St, Alexandria, VA; mains $15-35; 11:30am-2:30pm Mon-Fri & 5:30-10pm Mon-Sat, lounge open to 11:30pm**

Taberna de Gallo
Pitchers of sangria and imported Spanish wines overflow inside a living-history bar. ☎ **904-825-6830; www.staugustinegovernment.com/visitors; 53 St George St, St Augustine, FL; noon-5:15pm Wed & Thu, noon-9pm Fri & Sat, 1-5:15pm Sun**

White Horse Tavern
Home to the first "business lunch," this upscale dining all-star was founded by a pirate in 1687. ☎ **401-849-3600; www.whitehorsetavern.com; 26 Marlborough St, Newport, RI; from 11:30am**

SLEEP

Crosby Street Hotel
This spectacular sustainable SoHo hotel has so much going for it you might never leave its cozy and chic confines. Bar and restaurant too. ☎ **212-226-6400; www.firmdale.com; 79 Crosby St, New York, NY; r from $495**

Florida House Inn
Lodgings at this historic hostelry look long in the tooth, but all have air-con and private baths (some have fireplaces). ☎ **904-261-3300; www.floridahouseinn.com; 20-22 S 3rd St, Fernandina Beach, FL; r $109-279**

John Rutledge House Inn
In a house old enough to have hosted George Washington for breakfast, there are 19 historic rooms in an elegant setting. ☎ **800-476-9741; www.johnrutledgehouseinn.com; 116 Broad St, Charleston, SC; r from $175**

Omni Parker House
The nation's longest continuously operating hotel anchors the heart of historical downtown Boston. ☎ **617-227-8600; www.omnihotels.com; 60 School St, Boston, MA; r $199-599;**

USEFUL WEBSITES
www.discovernewengland.org
www.visitflorida.com

LINK YOUR TRIP
TRIP
8 48 Hours in Manhattan p117
16 48 Hours in Boston p167
33 48 Hours in Miami p279

www.lonelyplanet.com/trip-planner

The Lincoln Highway

WHY GO America's first transcontinental highway coincided with the dawn of its love affair with cars. Fall in love with the road all over again as you navigate some of the most unusual sites while traveling from New York's legendary 42nd St to San Francisco's Lincoln Park.

Like the rumored "real America," the Lincoln Hwy exists somewhere in the ether between myth, memory and capitalism. Begun in 1913 and completed by 1925, it allowed cross-country road-trippers (as opposed to wagon trainers) to make the epic trip from sea to shining sea. Today the original route has been merged with a smorgasbord of others, making a strict adherence to the 1920s version nearly impossible. But this northern auto trail (even when you fake it a bit) still manages to trace a unique path through the heart of the USA. (Route purists should consult one of the many local Lincoln Hwy organizations or investigate the resources at http://lincolnhighway.jameslin.name.)

It seems only appropriate for such an iconic highway to begin at the Crossroads of the World: ❶ **Times Square** at 42nd St and 7th Ave. Grab a bagel and some coffee and head west out of town towards the Holland Tunnel, the original route out of New York and into New Jersey. If you woke up this morning and got yourself a gun, then you'll want to light a cigar as you trace the winding labyrinth of highways to the New Jersey Turnpike, made famous in the opening credits of *The Sopranos*.

The Lincoln Hwy heads south through Newark, Elizabeth and into ❷ **Princeton**, home of nattily dressed professors, and with a picture-perfect town center that is ideal for strolling. The big iron gates of Princeton University, one of the eight Ivy League universities that dot the Mid-Atlantic and New England, abut the highway. The campus is a delight to behold and is easy to explore. Make sure to check out the art museum.

TIME
10 – 12 days

DISTANCE
2905 miles

BEST TIME TO GO
Apr – Oct

START
New York, NY

END
San Francisco, CA

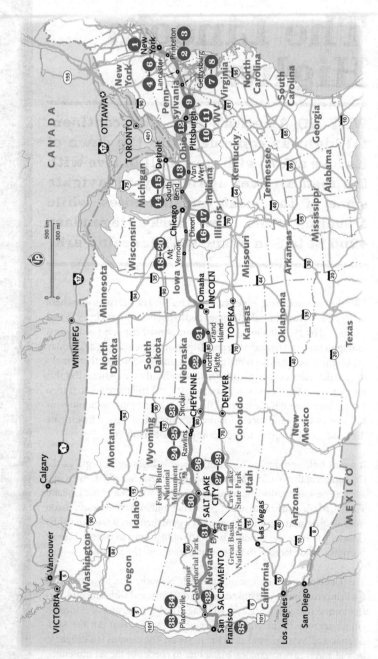

For lunch, pop into ❸ **Lahiere's**, where you'll find a thoughtful yet whimsical continental menu to go with your dry white wine and dog-eared copy of Proust. A recent visit offered up pork belly BLT sliders as part of an affordable prix fixe lunch menu. This place has been serving the local cognoscenti since 1919.

At this point, route purists will want to head southwest through Trenton and into Philadelphia, following the original highway. But we're going to keep on trucking past Philly to find the Pennsylvania Dutch in ❹ **Lancaster**. Yes, it's Amish country. Get your inner Kelly McGillis and Lukas Haas on when you play witness in the land of Mennonites. If you like quilts and old-timey farming equipment you are going to be in hog heaven. If not, you will still find a burgeoning arts community and some great dining.

Rest your weary head at the ❺ **Lancaster Arts Hotel**, a boutique inn that's in a renovated tobacco warehouse and filled with works by local artists. Added bonus: it has a bar and restaurant in the lobby! Or head to downtown Lancaster to the chic ❻ **Belvedere Inn** for an equally top-notch dinner in this dimly lit romantic restaurant in a garland-decorated townhouse with a roaring fireplace. Pumpkin ravioli, grilled shrimp, steamed mussels and more provided one of the finer meals we came upon along the highway.

Shove off west again towards York and ❼ **Gettysburg**, both along the original Lincoln Hwy, which in this part of the country is more or less interchangeable with Rte 30. Just west of the Civil War supersite you'll find the perplexing, captivating ❽ **Mr Ed's Elephant Museum**, which boats thousands of elephant-shaped curios large and small – one of them even talks to you. This textbook distillation of the roadside attraction also has an entire room devoted to Pez – grade-A strange, so obviously a must.

All along this section of Rte 30 you will notice several murals and "Roadside Giant" sculptures decorating the 200-mile ❾ **Lincoln Highway Heritage Corridor Roadside Museum**. Markers designate the historic route and lead you past intriguing sites such as the Shoe House (outside York, Pennsylvania, along Rte 30) and the creepiest mountainside girlie bar we've ever encountered.

Eventually you'll pull into ❿ **Pittsburgh**, where we invite you traveling maniacs to feel "like a steel town girl on a Saturday night." Allow us to point you in the direction of the ⓫ **Andy Warhol Museum**, celebrating the hometown hero. Lovingly archived "time capsules" packaged by Andy during his storied career are highlights and add fascinating context to the iconic works of art that cover five floors in this industrial space.

The Lincoln (aka Hwy 30) rolls into Ohio after brushing a wee section of West Virginia, then crosses the Ohio River to East Liverpool – once the nation's pottery capital thanks to its rich clay deposits. If that isn't enough to warrant a stop, the death mask of Pretty Boy Floyd is. The FBI caught up with "public enemy number one" near East Liverpool in 1934 and Floyd lost the ensuing shootout. The local mortician embalmed him at ⑫ **Sturgis House** – now an antique-stuffed B&B where you can see spooky gangster artifacts in the basement.

THE SUMMER WHITE HOUSE

Bedford Springs (www.omnibedfordsprings.com), home of rejuvenating spa treatments for 200 years, is a majestically restored historic hotel replete with columns and porticos, just a mile south of historic Bedford. President James Buchanan conducted the country's business here during long-ago summers. Achingly beautiful and sophisticated, enjoy the Springs Eternal Spa and historic golf course. The Tap Room even serves draught root beer! Heaven.

From downtown, take scenic Hwy 267/Lisbon St northwest, which reconnects to Hwy 30 as it climbs steeply toward Lisbon. On the road beyond, football-crazed Canton, cute collegey Wooster, haunted Mansfield and cornfields flash by. Then, just before the border, a neon sign beckons in Van Wert: "Young Fried Chicken Day and Night." The Davis family has been cooking bird here at ⑬ **Balyeat's Coffee Shop** for almost 50 years. You'll hurt their feelings if you don't stop and indulge, at least for a slice of butterscotch pie.

In Indiana the highway zips by Ft Wayne, the state's second-largest city, after which road-trippers must choose: follow the newer Lincoln alignment by staying on Hwy 30, or take the older one via Hwy 33. We suggest the latter: you'll chug by Churubusco and its legendary turtle; Amish-tinged Goshen; and Elkhart, maker of RVs and brass instruments.

ASK A LOCAL "My personal favorite [along the Lincoln Hwy] has to be the restored 1927 Coffee Pot. Ironically, coffee is neither brewed nor served there; but the 2½-story pot is a funky photo op just west of Bedford. Its 'cousin,' the World's Largest Tea Pot, is located on the Lincoln Hwy 147 miles west in Chester, WV."

Olga Herbert, executive director, Lincoln Highway Heritage Corridor, Ligonier, PA

The road becomes Lincoln Way as it heads into ⑭ **South Bend**, the University of Notre Dame's home. You know how people in certain towns say, "football is a religion here"? They mean it at Notre Dame, where *Touchdown Jesus* lords over the 80,000-capacity stadium (it's a mural of the resurrected Christ with arms raised, though the pose bears a striking resemblance to a referee signaling a touchdown). Less visited but worth a stop is the ⑮ **Studebaker National Museum** near downtown. The vintage carmaker was the pride of South Bend for its stylish vehicles – icons in the early days of road-tripping – but it couldn't keep pace with Detroit and folded in the 1960s.

Rejoin Hwy 30 in Valparaiso, and motor into Illinois. The road runs through Chicago's southern suburbs, then turns northwest. In Aurora take Hwy 31 north to Geneva, and exit west on Hwy 38. Flat cornfields dominate the view right up to ⑯ **Dixon**. Now Illinois may be the Land of Lincoln, but Dixon is all about another presidential son: Ronald Reagan. Dutch spent his childhood here, and there's no greater homage than the portrait that hangs in the ⑰ **Dixon Historic Center** – made from 14,000 red, white and blue jellybeans.

Take Hwy 2 to Sterling, and rejoin Hwy 30, which crosses the mighty Mississippi into Iowa and lands in the city of Clinton. From here, an original alignment shoots northwest, but we'll stick to Hwy 30. It tracks the original route through most of Iowa, rolling west on a farm-flanked path to the Missouri River. Iowa's scenery is so bucolic (white farmhouses, red barns, towering silos), it's easy to think you've got the state figured out before you've driven 30 miles. But don't forget, Iowa picked Barack Obama during its first-in-line presidential caucus in 2008, and the state was one of the first to allow same-sex marriage.

Small-town assumptions are also proved wrong – politely – in walkable ⑱ **Mt Vernon**. This happenin' hamlet comes with a nationally acclaimed chef, an indie movie theatre, sassy boutiques and charming antique stores. There's even a Justin boot–selling java joint known for its oatmeal chocolate chip cookies (it's called Fuel, on 1st St E). The lauded chef is Matt Steigerwald, owner of the bustling ⑲ **Lincoln Cafe**. The eatery's red-brick walls and artsy decor set a cozy but convivial mood. Seasonal mains and sides (think wild king salmon, duck-fat potatoes and red-chile grilled rapini) change biweekly. Cornell College's historic 1877 ⑳ **Brackett House** is a guest lodge for the college and a welcoming inn for road-weary travelers. Four homey bedrooms – patterned wallpaper, carpet, a few antiques – work well for families and small groups.

Hwy 30 continues through the heartland, threading past a quiltlike display of farms, tractors and checkerboard fields. Near Denison, hometown of TV mom Donna Reed, Hwy 30 bends south, picking up steam for a swooping ride through Missouri Valley and a 9-mile push to the Missouri River.

In Nebraska, Hwy 30's soothing pattern of passing trains, whistlestop silos and regimental cornfields quickly induces "byway hypnosis." To shake off the pastoral fugue, imagine tens of thousands of covered wagons bumping west here in the mid-1800s. The California and Mormon trails entered the state near Omaha; the Oregon Trail joined them west of Grand Island. All three tracked the Platte River. Check out the pioneer lifestyle at Grand Island's sprawling ㉑ **Stuhr Museum of the Prairie Pioneer**. May through August, blacksmiths, dressmakers and other period re-enactors go about their daily routines in the 1899 Railroad Town. Kids can ask questions and sometimes join the action.

From here, Hwy 30 parallels I-80, the Platte River and Union Pacific railroad tracks. Around 600,000 sandhill cranes refuel in this area in late winter and early spring, drawing birdwatchers to Platte-hugging observatories. Original alignments, including the Gothenburg stair steps, split from Hwy 30 west of Kearney. Visit www.lincolnhighwaynebraskabyway.com for a general location map. In Cozad, Hwy 30 swings under a bright 100th-meridian sign.

All those trains that've passed you? They're approaching or leaving Union Pacific's Bailey Yard in North Platte, the world's largest railroad changing station. Daily, 10,000 cars chug through; of those, 3000 are sorted to different tracks. Watch this intricate ballet from the upper floors of the ㉒ **Golden Spike Tower & Visitor Center**. Docents share train expertise – and a few bad jokes – as you peer down at the 315-mile network of tracks.

THE MIDDLE OF SOMEWHERE

In 1914, a marker 2 miles east of Cozad, Nebraska, noted the Lincoln Hwy's midpoint. Nowadays, because the route has changed so many times, it may be impossible to determine the halfway point. Those hankering for a midtrip toast should celebrate 3 miles west of Kearney, Nebraska. In the 1920s and early 1930s this was the site of the 1733 Ranch, a gigantic barn proclaiming itself the midpoint between Boston and San Francisco. It was 1733 miles to both.

Near Ogallala, pioneer trails curve north to Scottsbluff while the Lincoln Hwy crosses into the mountain time zone as Hwy 30. It links Sidney and Kimball before rolling into the "Equality State" of Wyoming, where "the Rail Splitter's" highway runs parallel to modern I-80 as it zips past the state's cowboy-capital-on-the-prairie, Cheyenne. The highway then climbs into the Medicine Bow mountain range and zooms past a 12.5ft-tall bust of the highway's namesake. Even when you're going 75mph, it's impossible to miss Abe Lincoln's trademark sideburns, beard and glasses chiseled into a massive stone monument over I-80 at exit 323. The monument sits atop the 8640ft Sherman Pass summit, marking the highway's highest point.

It's a long haul across Wyoming's windswept prairie to tiny Sinclair, and ㉓ **Su Casa**. The popular restaurant serves some of the best Mexican dishes around and is worth the drive. Constructed in 1923, Sinclair is an oil refinery town with a story behind its name – ask the locals if you're curious. Wandering its historic downtown is itself a trip – it's filled with Spanish-style hacienda architecture that feels more like old Mexico than the Wyoming prairie.

Six miles west of Sinclair is ㉔ **Rawlins**, a Wild West railway town, and your home for the night. All the usual chain motel suspects, and sadly not much else, cram both ends of town; grab a room at your preferred brand then pay a visit to the ㉕ **Wyoming Frontier Prison Museum** after dark. A real former penitentiary, constructed in 1872 and in operation until 1981, it once housed such notorious outlaws as Butch Cassidy. Today the Romanesque turret-crowned building looks fit for a horror-movie set – and did in fact serve as the location for the low-budget 1988 horror flick *Prison* – and gives a ghoulishly good night tour (on weekends June through August).

Hit the road after breakfast for the 123 miles to Green River, where John Wesley Powell began his epic 1869 Colorado River descent – look for the original put-in at what's now called Expedition Island Park – and swing south to explore **26 Flaming Gorge National Recreation Area**. A dam has submerged and tamed part of the wild river Powell once mapped, but the fiery red rock formations he named its gorge for remain a striking sight.

From Green River, it's 170 miles over the state line on I-80 to **27 Salt Lake City**. Founded in 1849 by Church of Latter Day Saints leader Brigham Young and 148 followers, Salt Lake was home to more than 70,000 Mormon pioneers by 1869 and today wears its Mormon heritage on its sleeve. Ten-acre Temple Sq, with a museum, visitor center and the spectacular Tabernacle Choir (performances Sunday 9:15am and Thursday 8pm), serves as the lifeblood of this 170-year-old faith, one of the most culturally and politically conservative in the country. Sites showcasing church history and culture blend seamlessly with the city's eclectic restaurants and brewpubs. Poke through new, used and rare treasures at **28 Sam Weller's Bookstore** before nestling into one of the most comfortable beds on the Lincoln Hwy at the red-brick **29 Peery Hotel**.

 DETOUR Detouring north just past Little America 60 miles on Hwy 30, flat grasslands give way to a weird rock desert of flat-top sandstone boulders, sandy dunes, sage-dusted desert and a desolate river valley of the very impressive **Fossil Butte National Monument**. The monument is home to some of the world's most well-preserved fossils – more than 80 fish, reptiles, mammals and plants are displayed in the on-site visitor center.

Just west of Salt Lake City on I-80, following the route of the Lincoln Hwy, you can't miss the oddly turreted marina rising like a temple from the salt flats of the **30 Great Salt Lake**. Fifteen thousand years ago, Lake Bonneville, three times as deep and 80% of the area of Lake Michigan, submerged this valley, and its remains are the largest salt-water lake in the western hemisphere. Walk barefoot through the surreal crunch of the shore, splash the therapeutic brine on your face, and pick up some beef, elk and buffalo jerky for the road; Dave sells the excellent "Deb's Best Jerky" from his truck in the marina parking lot, weather permitting.

DETOUR Stop at **Cave Lake State Park** and splash in the wonderfully hidden **Steptoe Creek** on your way 60 miles to **Great Basin National Park**. Famous for **Lehman Caves** and its bristlecone pines, arguably the oldest organism on earth and fundamental to climate research, this jewel features a scenic drive to a blessedly cool 10,000ft, delightful aspen-lined creeks and hiking.

The endless white of the Great Salt Lake Desert stretches for miles in every direction. It looks like the earth's skin itself, exposed and cracked. The 1916 guide to the Lincoln warned travelers to buy gas any time they could, and while it's not as imperative today, you'll want to stock up on water and keep a close eye on the fuel gauge. Zip past Bonneville Salt Flats, the site of the 600mph world record in land speed, and head 123 miles to West Wendover before cutting south on Alt 93 into Nevada's desolate, dry and rocky gold- and copper-mining country.

DETOUR

Approaching the Sierra Nevada, swing north toward Truckee and Lincoln Hwy's alternate route through the Donner Pass. In 1846, the Donner party of homesteaders was stranded here for months in 22ft of snow. Rescuers found only half the pioneers alive, surviving on boiled ox hides and their companions' corpses. Off Hwy I-80, **Donner Memorial Park** (www.parks.ca.gov) offers lakeside campsites ideal for gruesome ghost stories.

It's two hours to the tiny mining town of Ely, tonight's destination. Follow the main drag to **31 Hotel Nevada**. Built in 1929 as the tallest building in the state, this musty old-school gambling hall with antler chandeliers and taxidermy on the walls gives a taste of Nevada before the grandeur of Steve Wynn and the flash of Cirque de Soleil.

Hwy 50 follows the Lincoln Hwy west from Ely through Nevada's mesmerizing Basin and Range country 345 miles to California. North-to-south running mountains cut the landscape into long, flat strips of sagebrush-covered basin; you drive like a bat out of hell through the wide stretches of desert flatlands and wind slowly up into rounded mountain passes. *Life* magazine called this the Loneliest Road in America; pick up a "passport" at the hotel and allow a day to explore old mining towns and historic markers along the journey.

Heading south along Hwy 50, staggering slopes frame teal-blue **32 Lake Tahoe**. Skiers brake here for giddy runs down Tahoe's highest summit – but intrepid travelers press onward to **33 Placerville**, where gold prospectors once blew fortunes on saloon benders and the Hangtown Fry, an oyster-bacon omelette that cost the equivalent today of $153. Placerville's **34 Cozmic Café** offers an updated take on the Wild West: organic brunches downstairs, honky-tonk and yoga upstairs, plus microbrews in an old mine shaft.

"you can see the point of the Lincoln Hwy: golden sunsets and bold new directions."

Another hour west is Sacramento, where the original Lincoln Hwy route veers south on Hwy 99 through Stockton and west on 580 to Oakland. Historical sticklers hop the ferry, but the Bay Bridge gets you to San Francisco faster.

On the northwestern edge of San Francisco, Lincoln Hwy reaches the sparkling Pacific at Lincoln Park. The road ends at the **35 Legion of Honor**, but the imagination takes flight with museum collections ranging from Impressionist masterpieces to censored R Crumb comics. From here, you can see the point of the Lincoln Highway: golden sunsets and bold new directions.

Amy Balfour, Alison Bing, Becca Blond, Jennifer Denniston, David Ozanich & Karla Zimmerman

TRIP INFORMATION

GETTING THERE

From New York's West 42nd St, head south on 7th Ave. Follow signs for the Holland Tunnel, which will whisk you under the Hudson River towards the New Jersey Turnpike.

DO

Andy Warhol Museum

A superb museum dedicated to the maestro of pop; a must for any serious art fan. ☎ 412-237-8300; www.warhol.org; 117 Sandusky St, Pittsburgh, PA; adult/child $15/8; ◔ 10am-5pm Tue-Thu, Sat & Sun, 10am-10pm Fri, closed Mon & major holidays

Dixon Historic Center

Ronald Reagan's old high school has been converted into a shrine, complete with jellybean likeness. ☎ 815-288-5508; www.dixonhistoriccenter.org; 205 W Fifth St, Dixon, IL; suggested donation $3; ◔ 9am-4pm Mon-Fri, 10am-4pm Sat

Flaming Gorge National Recreation Area

Straddling the Utah and Wyoming state line, it comprises 201,000 acres of protected scenery surrounding Flaming Gorge Reservoir; most facilities, including the visitors center, are in Utah. ☎ 435-789-1181; www.fs.fed.us/r4/ashley/recreation/flaming_gorge/index.shtm; admission $5; ◔ main visitor center 9am-5pm Jun-Aug

Golden Spike Tower & Visitor Center

Docents await on the 8th-floor observation deck. ☎ 308-532-9920; www.goldenspiketower.com; 1249 N Homestead Rd, North Platte, NE; adult/child $6/4; ◔ 9am-7pm Mon-Sat, 1-7pm Sun May-Sep, with variations; ♿

Legion of Honor

More than 4000 years of art overflow in this faux-French palace: mummies, mega-Impressionists, experimental drawings John Cage made with eyes closed. ☎ 415-750-3600; www.famsf.org/legion/index.asp; Lincoln Park, San Francisco, CA; adult/senior/student/under 12yr $10/7/6/free; ◔ 9:30am-5:15pm Tue-Sun; ♿

Mr Ed's Elephant Museum

A roadside oddity in classic style, see thousands of elephant curios of every shape and size – including one that talks! ☎ 717-352-3792; www.mistereds.com; 6019 Chambersburg Road, Ortanna, PA; admission free; ◔ 10am-5pm

Sam Weller's Bookstore

This independent biblio-heaven with a progressive slant has been a Salt Lake City institution since 1929. ☎ 801-328-7586; www.samwellers.com; 254 S Main St, Salt Lake City, UT; ◔ 10am-7pm Mon-Sat; ♿

Studebaker National Museum

Gaze at the shiny fleet of classic beauties from the Lincoln Hwy's heyday. ☎ 574-235-9714; www.studebakermuseum.org; 201 S Chapin St, South Bend, IN; adult/6-18 yr $8/5; ◔ 10am-5pm Mon-Sat, noon-5pm Sun

Stuhr Museum of the Prairie Pioneer

Beyond Railroad Town, visit a Pawnee lodge and a log-cabin settlement. ☎ 308-385-5316; www.stuhrmuseum.org; 3133 W US Hwy 34, Grand Island, NE; adult/child May-Sep $8/6, Oct-Apr $6/4; ◔ 9am-5pm Mon-Sat, noon-5pm Sun; ♿

Wyoming Frontier Prison Museum

The guided tours are well worth the small admission fee, especially the creepy after-dark one offered on summer weekends. ☎ 307-342-4422; www.wyomingfrontierprison.org; 500 W Walnut St, Rawlins, WY; admission free, tours adult/child $7/6; ◔ 8am-7pm May-Sep

EAT

Balyeat's Coffee Shop

Fried chicken, roast pork, Salisbury steak, meatloaf – did we mention there's meat at this little diner? Pie, too. ☎ 419-238-1580; 133 Main St, Van Wert, OH; mains $6-12; ◔ 6am-9pm Tue-Sat, 6am-7:30pm Sun

Belvedere Inn

Extremely well-prepared cuisine in a chicly appointed townhouse. Romantic, delightful and unexpectedly refined. ☎ 717-394-2422; www.belvedereinn.biz; 402 N Queen St, Lancaster, PA; mains $10-30; ☷ 11am-2pm Mon-Fri, 5-11pm Sun-Thu, 5pm-midnight Fri & Sat, bar open until 2am daily

Cozmic Café

Buckwheat waffles, "Nachos Nirvana," yoga classes and rap battles in an 1859 landmark. ☎ 530-642-8481; www.thecozmiccafe.com; 594 Main St, Placerville, CA; mains $6-9; ☷ 8am-8pm Mon-Sat, 8am-5:30pm Sun, pub open until midnight Fri-Sun; Ⓥ

Lahiere's

Charming contemporary French-American restaurant that's been serving the people of Princeton since 1919. ☎ 609-921-2798; www.lahieres.com; 5-11 Witherspoon St, Princeton, NJ; mains $10-30; ☷ 11:30am-2:30pm, 5:30-9:30pm Mon-Fri, 11:30am-2pm & 5:30-10pm Sat, closed Sun

Lincoln Cafe

Bring a bottle from the Lincoln Wine Bar. ☎ 319-895-4041; www.foodisimportant.com; 117 1st St W, Mt Vernon, IA; mains under $15; ☷ 11am-2pm Tue-Sat, 10am-2pm Sun, 5-9pm Tue-Thu, 5-9:30pm Fri-Sat; ♿

Su Casa

A taste of old Mexico in the high desert, this restaurant has been serving "south of the border" classics to crowds for decades now. ☎ 307-328-1745; 705 Lincoln Ave, Sinclair, WY; mains $5-10; ☷ 11am-7pm

SLEEP

Brackett House

Three bedrooms have sun porches ideal for cozying up with a book. ☎ 319-895-4425; www.cornellcollege.edu/brackett-house; 418 2nd St SW, Mt Vernon, IA; r $68-102

Hotel Nevada

A 1929 gambling hall locked in a time warp. Look for the three-story neon miner and ask for a luxury room. ☎ 775-289-6665; www.hotelnevada.com; 501 Aultman, Ely, NV; r $45-110; ☖

Lancaster Arts Hotel

Excellent boutique hotel filled with original art, which offers an appealing alternative to standard issue road motels. Worth the price. ☎ 717-299-3000; www.lancasterartshotel.com; 300 Harrisburg Ave, Lancaster, PA; r $129-359

Peery Hotel

Spring for a room with two queen beds at this gracious 1910 jewel in downtown Salt Lake City. ☎ 801-521-4300; www.peeryhotel.com; 110 W Broadway, Salt Lake City, UT; r $79-120; ♿ ☖

Sturgis House

Flowery wallpaper, heavy drapes and a gangster past fill this six-room B&B in a Victorian mansion. ☎ 330-382-0194; www.sturgishouse.com; 122 W 5th St, East Liverpool, OH; s/d incl breakfast $65/80

USEFUL WEBSITES

www.lincolnhighwayassoc.org
www.lincolnhighwaynews.com

LINK YOUR TRIP

TRIP

www.lonelyplanet.com/trip-planner

Skyline Drive to the Blue Ridge Parkway

WHY GO Running through Virginia and North Carolina, this National Scenic Byway is the most visited area of national parkland in the USA, with almost 20 million road-trippers a year. The 469-mile road meanders through both quintessentially bucolic pasturelands and imposing Appalachian vistas...time to break out your convertible '37 coupé.

TIME
6 days

DISTANCE
520 miles

BEST TIME TO GO
Aug – Oct

START
Front Royal, VA

END
Cherokee, NC

You can thank the Great Depression for both the Virginian Skyline Drive and the North Carolinian Blue Ridge Parkway. Although the idea of a scenic byway between the Shenandoah National Park and the Great Smokies had been around for a generation, Americans hadn't yet invented road-tripping as a pastime. Work on the Blue Ridge Parkway began in earnest in 1933, when the government harnessed the strength of thousands of out-of-work mountaineers in the Civilian Conservation Corps. In Virginia, the centerpiece of the ribbon-thin Shenandoah National Park, which crowns the northern end of the parkway, is the jaw-dropping beauty of Skyline Drive, which runs for just over 100 miles high atop the Blue Ridge Mountains. Unlike the massive acreage of western parks like Yellowstone or Yosemite, Shenandoah is at times only a mile wide.

Straddling the northern entrance to the park is the tiny city of ❶ Front Royal. Although it's not among Virginia's fanciest ports of call, this lush riverside town offers all the urban amenities one might need before a camping or hiking trip up in the mountains.

But before you head into the national park, drive a few miles north of Front Royal (towards Winchester) to ❷ Dinosaur Land. This spectacularly lowbrow shrine to concrete sculpture is not to be missed. Although it's an "educational prehistoric forest," with over 50 life-

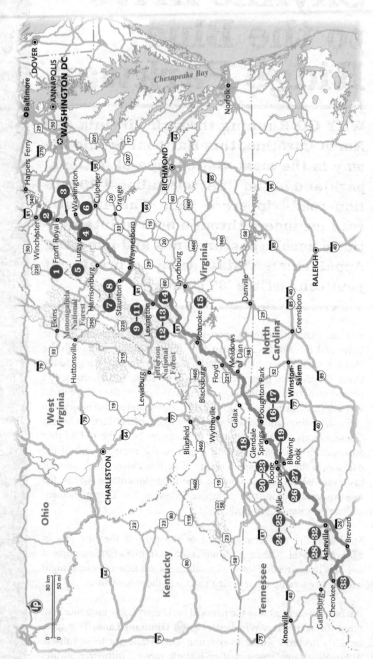

size(ish) dinosaurs (and a King Kong for good measure), you'd probably learn more about the tenants by fast-forwarding through *Jurassic Park 2*. But that's not why you've stopped here, so grab your camera and sidle up to the triceratops for memories that will last a millennium.

❸ Skyline Drive is the scenic drive to end all drives. The more than 75 overlooks, with views into Virginia's Shenandoah Valley and the Piedmont, are all breathtaking, even after you've seen the first 70. In spring and summer, endless variations on the color green are sure to enchant, just as the vibrant reds and yellows will amaze in autumn. This might be your chance to finally hike a section of the Appalachian Trail, which crosses Skyline Drive at 32 places. (Be sure to keep your eyes peeled for governors of South Carolina!) An ideal location to stay the night on the Skyline Drive is ❹ Skyland, which sits on the highest peak of the Shenandoah National Park. Skyland was founded as an upscale resort in 1888, but the current form was built in the 1920s and it still retains some of those design elements, if showing a little wear and tear. An important request to make is for a "room with a view" of the Shenandoah Valley below, so you can sit on your balcony and gaze at the lights of the little towns and farms in the distance. All things considered, Skyland can't be beat for easy access to the Appalachian Trail, which zigzags right through the property. Have a meal in the great big sleek dining room with spectacular views. Drinkers will be happy to know they have a taproom featuring nightly (local!) entertainment. Try the Prohibition Punch, which is sweet and fruity and sure to refresh your tired soul.

From Skyland you can also venture to a couple of sites down the mountain that are well worth checking out. Back up at Thornton Gap (about Mile 32) head west, where you'll find the wonderful ❺ Luray Caverns. Here you can take a one-hour, roughly 1-mile guided tour of these caves, opened to the public over a hundred years ago. Among the largest and most famous caverns in the

GARDEN MAZE ALERT

Next to the Luray Caverns is an excellent opportunity to play Shelley Duvall and Scatman Crothers. Go screaming *Shining*-style through the **Hedge Maze**, but beware! This maze is harder than it looks and some could spend longer inside it than they anticipated. Paranormal and psychic abilities are permitted, but frowned upon, when solving the maze. Redrum! Redrum!

east, Luray boasts what is surely a one-of-a-kind – the Stalacpipe Organ – in the pit of its rocky belly. This crazy contraption has been banging out melodies on the rock formations for decades. As the guide says, the caves are 400 million years old, "*if* you believe in geological dating." No matter what you believe, you'll be impressed by these fantastic underground expanses.

Feeling hungry after all that spelunking? Then head east towards Washington (the town, not the capital) and settle in for some five-star dining at the

❻ Inn at Little Washington, a sacred destination on the epicurean trail. Founded more than 30 years ago by Patrick O'Connell and his partner, it has been named one of the "10 Best Restaurants in the World" by the *International Herald Tribune*. But the inn's pleasures come at a price so beware – the dinner prix fixe started at $148 on a recent visit and goes higher on weekends. It is worth every penny. First of all, the service is, unsurprisingly, impeccable, and the food hits all the grace notes. For the first course you might try the beet fantasia or the eggs in an egg (once prepared for the Queen of England on her visit to American shores). Next, you could try the pecan-crusted soft-shell crab tempura with Italian mustard fruit.

> **DETOUR**
>
> If you're still not ready to go sightseeing in Shenandoah, drive 30 miles further north on Rte 340 to Harpers Ferry, West Virginia, for the **John Brown Wax Museum** (www.johnbrownwaxmuseum.com). Located on the town's main drag, it tells the dramatic story of this famed (if not quite successful) abolitionist in several waxy dioramas. Yes, it's a wax museum about slavery, riots, treason and, ultimately, the gallows. Bizarre and generally unsettling, this place is a must-see for aficionados of the wax arts.

The "pepper crusted tuna pretending to be a filet mignon capped with seared duck fois gras on charred onions with a burgundy butter sauce" is a popular main course. Others prefer the "medallions of rabbit loin wrapped in house cured pancetta surrounding a Lilliputian rabbit rib roast resting on a pillow of English pea puree." So, yeah, any questions? Go. Toss your credit score to the wind and just go. To really make the evening count, reserve one of the achingly perfect rooms at the adjacent inn from which the restaurant gets its name.

At the southern terminus of Skyline Drive is the wonderfully revitalized town of **❼ Staunton**. Their Trinity Church has 12 Tiffany Studios stained-glass windows but the town's real showstopper is **❽ Blackfriars Playhouse**. The theater is a painstakingly authentic re-creation of the original London Blackfriars Playhouse. Shows are presented as they were in Shakespeare's day, with the lights from chandeliers kept on, and traditional seating on benches, Lord's chairs, or gallants' stools directly onstage. The specialty here is Elizabethan and Jacobean drama, naturally. This is not to be missed by any theater lover.

About half an hour south of Staunton is the wonderfully sexy town of **❾ Lexington**, home of the achingly beautiful colonnades of Washington and Lee University and the imposing Virginia Military Institute. Don't miss the li'l charmer of a town. Just a few miles north on Rte 11 is **❿ Hull's Drive-In Movie Theater**. This totally hardcore artifact of the golden age of automobiles is a living museum to the road trips your parents remember. It plays only new releases (sadly no *American Graffiti* or *Pee-Wee's Big Adventure*) on weekends, so you are left at the mercy of Hollywood's latest trifle. But even the latest installment of *Star Trek* should look good on a warm, starry Virginia night.

You can pick up some fresh movie snacks from the best joint in Lexington, the ⑪ **Patisserie Café**. Situated in what looks like a French farmhouse at the head of the loop through town, this superb bakery has dozens of homemade choices that come prepackaged for easy takeout. You can eat on site, too.

Before we send you back to the Blue Ridge Parkway, head south on Hwy 81 to the gorgeous ⑫ **Natural Bridge** and its fantabulous potpourri of amusements. Natural Bridge is a legitimate natural wonder – and is even claimed to be one of the "Seven Natural Wonders of the World," though just who put that list together remains unclear. Soaring 200ft in the air, this centuries-old rock formation is wondrous in its beauty and provides a true respite from the trials and tribulations of the road. Those who aren't afraid of a little religion should hang around for the "Drama of Creation" light show that plays nightly underneath and around the bridge.

Around Natural Bridge are several other attractions of varying kitsch value. Best to keep moving to the truly unnatural part of the complex: the outrageously out-of-place and therefore ingenious ⑬ **Foamhenge**. What's that, you say? You mean a life-size replica of England's most famous mystery site built entirely out of foam? Yes, and this crown jewel of the Blue Ridge foothills is one of the most ridiculous and incredible sights in the state of Virginia. The utter ludicrousness of Foamhenge is its sole reward, and will change your life like a trip to Fatima. Bring your druid/pagan claptrap and see if anything happens at sundown on the solstice.

MULE SKINNER BLUES?

The **Blue Ridge Music Center** (www.blueridge musiccenter.net) is a large, grassy outdoor amphitheater right off the BRP (milepost 213). It offers programming that focuses on local musicians carrying on traditions of Appalachian music. Bring a lawn chair and sit yourself down for some old-timey tunes. At night you can watch fireflies glimmer in the darkness.

Head back to the Blue Ridge Parkway and drive south towards Roanoke. This portion of the BRP has gentle, rolling hills and not too many overly sharp curves. A good place to stop is ⑭ **Blackhorse Gap**, where the Appalachian Trail crosses the parkway. Oak and hickory trees rise in Jefferson National Forest to create green walls of foliage on either side of the road.

Check into the Tudor-style ⑮ **Hotel Roanoke** after a long day's drive. This grand dame has presided over this city at the base of the Blue Ridge Mountains for the better part of a century and provides a welcome respite. Downstairs is the Pine Room for those requiring a stiff drink, and a formal restaurant, the Regency Room.

If you've got a couple of hours still in you, head 'cross state lines to rest your head in North Carolina at ⑯ **Bluff's Lodge**. As one of the only noncamping accommodations on the parkway, the lodge's rooms are lovely enough, but it's the deck with an outdoor fireplace that draws us to this location, as it practically forces one to roast s'mores while singing campfire songs or watching meteor showers. However, the choice of whether to stay at Hotel Roanoke or Bluff's Lodge is moot. The most important question is whether you want to arrive at **⑰ Bluff's Lodge Coffee Shop** by breakfast or lunch. The "cafeteria" with easy-wipe vinyl menus and a knick-knack gift store (candles! local pottery! grits!) looks like any roadside pit stop on the outside, but step inside for the best biscuits in North Carolina, nay, on Earth. Come at breakfast for a side of eggs with your biscuits. Come at lunch for a side of fatback. Call ahead for the fried chicken, cooked to order for 30 to 40 minutes in a well-seasoned cast-iron skillet, or order the barbecue, western NC–style (heavy on the tomato), served between corncakes sealed with a layer of – why not? – melted cheese.

For a bit of Italia in Appalachia, head off the parkway at Milepost 258/259 until you get to Glendale Springs and the **⑱ Holy Trinity Episcopal Church**. The fresco artist Benjamin F Long, now famed for work such as the TransAmerica dome in Charlotte, started in the High Country in the late 1970s after returning from eight years apprenticing for Italian masters. Visit his Last Supper fresco in Glendale Springs; his models for the work were local residents (the model for Thomas was Long himself).

A rite of passage for every North Carolinian child is the Appalachian- and Old West–themed amusement park, the **⑲ Tweetsie Railroad**. A 1917 coal-fired steam locomotive starts your journey through a gloriously campy 1950s-style Wild West show, past marauding Indians and heroic cowboys. Midway rides, Western shops selling toy guns, fudge and no-holds-barred Olde Tyme souvenirs, and family-friendly shows complete a full day's worth of innocent Americana that would make even Garrison Keillor blush.

You can debate the park's lack of political correctness with students from nearby Appalachian State over dinner in **⑳ Boone**, a chilled-out university town that brings a heaping dose of culture to the otherwise outdoorsy area. To check out the college-town vibe and do some shopping or eating, head to **㉑ King St**, the Blue Ridge version of the classic college-town main drag. Or, to stick with the mountaineer vibe and eat one-seventh your weight in one sitting, stop in at the **㉒ Dan'l Boone Inn**, which has been serving up family-style meals since the 1960s – the three-meat-and-five-veg menu hasn't changed much since then.

The classic Southern/country staples are all here – green beans, country ham biscuits, stewed apples and fried chicken – and in massive quantities.

Spend a day off the parkway after Boone. First, get your fingernails dirty at **23 Foggy Mountain Gem Mine**. While there are a half-dozen spots near or on the parkway to go gem mining, many have cartoon mascots and tour-bus parking that cater to large crowds (we trust you can find the billboards pointing out the way, if you'd rather). The smaller Foggy Mountain was founded and is operated by graduate gemologists. Kids (and anyone who has ever made a mud pie) will love buying a bucket of rocks and digging through for guaranteed semiprecious gems from all over the world, North Carolina included. After sifting through your rocks in a miner's flume line, ask on-site gemologists to cut and mount your hand-picked gems in any number of settings.

Continue on Hwy 105 for 1.5 miles and take a right on Broadstone Rd, reaching the **24 Mast Farm Inn and Simplicity Restaurant**, a 200-year-old farmhouse inn and restaurant. You will get a personalized menu with items like "Slow chicken Nascar style but mighty low on points and Ashe County cheese trucked over by Junior Johnson" or "Hot potato and leek vichyssoise buddies from West Jefferson singin' Elvis tunes while cruisin' 421 by Wilkesboro." You're probably getting the drift 'round now that y'all might-could stay a while at this homage to Southern hospitality. Sumptuous linens and claw-footed tubs in the main house might tempt you, but the front-porch rockers, wood-burning stoves and a log cabin will draw many visitors to the cottages.

The next day, head into Historic Valle Crucis, to the **25 Original Mast General Store**. The first of a band of general stores in the Blue Ridge Mountains, it still sells some of the same products it did when it opened in 1883. Still the gathering spot for locals, and now visitors, it sells a dozen types of bacon, traditional handmade hard candy, games of pick-up sticks and paddle ball, signs that read "Hippies Use Side Door," and a complete selection of women's bonnets.

JAM, LOCAL STYLE

There's no better area in North Carolina to see traditional music than the hills of the High Country. Check locally for details, but this lot will get you started.

Mrs Hyatt's Oprahouse, in Asheville (Thursday evening); **Old Fort Mountain Music Jam**, Rocket Building, Old Fort (Friday evening); **Historic Orchard at Altapass**, Milepost 328, Little Switzerland (weekend afternoons); **Mountain Home Music Concert Series**, at Blowing Rock Auditorium in Boone (Saturday evening, or turn to WECR 102.3 at 8pm); **Jim and Jennie's High Country Music Barn**, at Crossnore (Saturday evening).

Head down Hwy 184 to Hwy 105 to reach **26 Grandfather Mountain**, a Unesco biosphere reserve worthy of a day trip. The grounds hold a wildlife habitat with black bear, river otters and bald eagles, plus a nature preserve with miles of hiking trails, but most people come here to walk the famous mile-high swinging bridge. The 228ft bridge stretches over a precipitous chasm that exposes visitors (safely) to the full force of mountain winds and a panoramic mountain vista. On a particularly gusty day, listen to the bridge's steel girders sing. Follow the parkway south to reach ㉗ **Linville Falls**. These river gorges and waterfalls are accessed by a criss-cross network of trails in one of the more quiet corners of the Grandfather Mountain area. During the week and in the off-season months, you can find secluded spots worthy of meditating on the sheer awesomeness of a multifaceted waterfall. Plan on spending at least an hour or two here, and bring comfortable shoes.

"not only can you camp nearby, you can do it in an honest-to-Mongolian-goodness yurt…"

Continue south to ㉘ **Asheville**, the hippified mountain town that defies a singular categorization. A mixture of Blue Ridge folk traditions, New Age healing centers and a burgeoning Slow Food outpost, Asheville rightfully tops countless "best places to live/visit/see-art-deco-architecture" lists. The town is about two hours south of Linville Falls, so you'll be plenty ready for bed. Not a lot of cities offer the chance to sleep in the woods a nine-minute drive from downtown. But this is Asheville, so not only can you camp nearby, you can do it in an honest-to-Mongolian-goodness yurt at ㉙ **Campfire Lodgings**. It blends the best of country camping (fire pits, mountain views) and the city (free wi-fi, clean bathrooms). From downtown, take I-26 towards Weaverville.

Spend some time perusing the ㉚ **Grove Arcade**, the pinnacle of Asheville's art-deco architecture (and the center of fab downtown shopping). The surrounding blocks offer the best of Asheville sightseeing, and city diner crossed with organic farm restaurant ㉛ **Early Girl Eatery**. Early Girl has quickly become an institution for serving delightfully new "health" food such as biscuits with vegetarian herbed gravy alongside farmstead cheeseburgers slathered with basil mayo.

Finally, end your scenic byway journey at the largest private home in the US: the ㉜ **Biltmore Estate**. The French chateau–style super-mega-mansion (175,000 sq ft; over four *acres* of living space), built by the railroad and shipping baron Vanderbilt family in the 1890s, helped turn Asheville into a progressive artist colony. Hundreds of artisans and craftspeople arrived to help create the intricate woodwork, linens, stained glass and gardens that grace the estate's grounds.

Continue about 60 miles through the Pisgah and Nantahala National Forests to the southern end of the Blue Ridge Parkway: Cherokee, the capital of the Cherokee Indian Reservation. Bypass the casino and plastic headdress shops for the ㉝ **Museum of the Cherokee Indian**. Many generations of deerskins, pots and woven skirts share space with life-size dioramas and a computer-animated lesson, covering 12,000 years of Cherokee history.

Alex Leviton & David Ozanich

TRIP INFORMATION

GETTING THERE

Front Royal is 69 miles west of Washington DC, via I-66.

DO

Biltmore Estate

An entire day's worth of architecture, history, scenery and a little 250-room summer house. ☎ 800-411-3812; www.biltmore.com; 1 Approach Rd, Asheville, NC; adult/teen/child $60/30/free; ⏱ house 9am-5.30pm, restaurant & shop hrs vary; ♿

Blackfriars Playhouse

Don't miss this stunning reproduction of a 17th-century English theater, with performances of Shakespeare and the like. ☎ 504-851-1733; www.americanshakespearecenter.com; 10 S Market St, Staunton, VA; tickets $20-40; ⏱ show times vary

Dinosaur Land

Virginia's own Jurassic Park with 40 or so "life-size" dino "sculptures." ☎ 540-869-2222; www.dinosaurland.com; 3848 Stonewall Jackson Hwy, White Post, VA; adult/child $5/4; ⏱ 9:30am-5:30pm, closed Jan & Feb

Foggy Mountain Gem Mine

Semiprecious stones guaranteed in each bucket; a gemologist on site. ☎ 828-963-4367; www.foggymountaingems.com; 4416 Hwy 105 S, Boone, NC; buckets $15-110; ⏱ 10am-6pm; ♿

Grandfather Mountain

A Unesco biosphere reserve with hiking trails and a swinging bridge. ☎ 800-468-7325; www.grandfather.com; 2050 Blowing Rock Hwy at Hwy 221 (Milepost 305), Linville, NC; adult/child $15/7; ⏱ 8am-1hr before sunset, 9am-5pm winter; ♿

Grove Arcade

Locally made jewelry, clothes and furniture, plus restaurants, art deco architecture and a deli. ☎ 828-252-7799; www.grovearcade.com; 1 Page Ave, Asheville, NC; ⏱ 10am-6pm Mon-Sat, noon-5pm Sun, hours vary by store

Holy Trinity Episcopal Church

Take an unexpected detour to see Italian-inspired frescoes. ☎ 336-982-3076; www.churchofthefrescoes.com, www.benlongfrescotrail.com; 120 Glendale School Rd, Glendale Springs, NC; admission free; ⏱ 9am-5pm

Hull's Drive-In Movie Theater

Step back in time to the 1950s. Utterly fab. ☎ 540-463-2621; www.hullsdrivein.com; 2361 N Lee Hwy, Lexington, VA; admission $5; ⏱ double feature starts 9:15pm

Linville Falls

Hike down to a series of multilevel waterfalls. www.ncwaterfalls.com/lin1.htm; Milepost 316.3, Linville Falls, NC; admission free; ⏱ dawn-dusk; ♿

Luray Caverns

The coolest caverns in Virginia – with the unique Stalacpipe Organ and a garden maze. ☎ 540-743-6551; www.luraycaverns.com; 970 US Hwy 211 West, Luray, VA; adult/child $21/10; ⏱ 9am-7pm summer, 9am-4pm or 5pm winter

Museum of the Cherokee Indian

Artifacts and exhibits trace the history of the Cherokees. ☎ 828-497-3481; www.cherokeemuseum.org; 589 Tsali Blvd, Cherokee, NC; adult/child $9/6; ⏱ 9am-5pm daily year-round, 9am-7pm Mon-Sat summer; ♿

Natural Bridge & Foamhenge

A truly marvelous natural formation at the base of the Blue Ridge Mountains and a replica of Stonehenge made entirely of foam. ☎ 540-291-2121; www.naturalbridgeva.com; Rte 11 just north of Rte 130, Natural Bridge, VA; adult/child $15/10; ⏱ 8am-dark

Original Mast General Store

Over 130 years of selling everything from cradles to caskets. ☎ 828-963-6511; www.mastgeneralstore.com; Hwy 194, Valle Crucis, NC; ⏱ 7am-6.30pm Mon-Sat, noon-6pm Sun; ♿

Tweetsie Railroad
A theme park based around a historic steam train. ☎ 828-264-9061; www.tweetsie.com; 300 Tweetsie Railroad Ln, Blowing Rock, NC; adult/child $31/22; 🕑 9am-6pm Fri-Sun May-Sep & holidays, daily Jun-Aug; ♿

EAT

Bluff's Lodge Coffee Shop
Biscuits and fried chicken worthy of a road trip by themselves. ☎ 336-372-4499; Milepost 241, Doughton Park, NC; mains $2.50-18; 🕑 8am-8pm; ♿

Dan'l Boone Inn
Family-style dining for the very, very hungry, since the 1960s. ☎ 828-264-8657; www. danlbooneinn.com; 130 Hardin St, Boone, NC; mains adult $9-16, children $4-9; 🕑 11.30am-9pm Mon-Fri, 8am-9pm Sat-Sun, dinner only Mon-Fri in winter; ♿

Early Girl Eatery
Classic Southern diner fare with a farm-grown twist; especially good for breakfast. ☎ 828-259-9292; www.earlygirleatery.com; 8 Wall St, Asheville, NC; mains $3-14; 🕑 7.30am-3pm Mon-Fri, 9am-3pm Sat & Sun, 5-9pm Tue-Thu, 5-10pm Fri & Sat; ♿ 🐾

Inn at Little Washington
One of the best restaurants ever — you should sell a kidney and make a reservation. ☎ 540-675-3800; www.theinnatlittlewashington.com; cnr Middle & Main Sts, Washington, VA; dinner prix fixe $148-165; 🕑 5:30-11pm

Patisserie Café
Fantastic, yummy bakery in a French farmhouse, with food to go or stay. ☎ 540-462-6000; www.patisseriecafe.net; 107 N Main St, Lexington, VA; mains $5-10; 🕑 11am-7:30pm Mon-Fri, 9am-3pm Sat, closed Sun

SLEEP

Bluff's Lodge
Be sure to ask for a room with a view. ☎ 336-372-4499; www.blueridgeresort. com; Milepost 241.1, Doughton Park, NC; r $85-105; 🕑 late Apr-Nov; ♿

Campfire Lodgings
Quiet, scenic campsite with yurts 10 minutes from downtown. ☎ 828-658-8012; www. campfirelodgings.com; 116 Appalachian Village Rd, Asheville, NC; campsites $30-50, yurts & cabins $105-150; ♿

Hotel Roanoke
Large, full-service Tudor-style hotel in the heart of Roanoke. ☎ 540-985-5900; www. hotelroanoke.com; 110 Shenandoah Ave, Roanoke, VA; r $150-300

Mast Farm Inn and Simplicity Restaurant
Inn, cabins and restaurant in buildings dating back to the late 1700s. ☎ 828-963-5857; www.mastfarminn.com; 2543 Broadstone Rd, Banner Elk, NC; r $99-269, cabins $149-459; restaurant prix fixe $37.50; 🕑 restaurant 6-8.30pm Thu-Sat plus holidays

Skyland
Resort located high atop the Shenandoah National Park off Skyline Drive. ☎ 800-999-4714; www.visitshenandoah.com; Mile 41 Skyline Drive, VA; r $89-200

USEFUL WEBSITES
www.nps.gov/blri
www.blueridgeparkway.org

LINK YOUR TRIP
www.lonelyplanet.com/trip-planner

Rollin' on the Great River Road

WHY GO This epic roadway traces the meanderings of the Mississippi River, past eagles' nests and juke joints, pine forests and plantations. Covering more than 2000 bluesy miles, it unfurls through major cities like Minneapolis, Memphis and New Orleans, though its heart beats as Main Street in retro small towns.

TIME
10 days

DISTANCE
2000 miles

BEST TIME TO GO
May – Jul

START
Lake Itasca, MN

END
New Orleans, LA

Despite the name, the Great River Road is not a single highway, but a series of linked federal, state and county roads running along both sides of Old Man River. The eastern route pokes through Wisconsin, Illinois, Kentucky, Tennessee and Mississippi. The western route curves through Minnesota, Iowa, Missouri, Arkansas and Louisiana. The one constant, wherever you are: the green paddle-wheel sign that marks the way.

Begin where the river begins, in Minnesota's ❶ Itasca State Park. A carved pole denotes the headwaters of "the Mighty Mississippi" – a good thing, because it's puny enough to mistake for a creek. Wade in the knee-deep flow and hop over a couple of stepping stones, then boast you walked across the Father of Waters. The park also offers canoeing, hiking, biking and camping, plus a lodge and hostel, all operated according to the principles of "Minnesota nice" (the state's proverbial hospitality).

From here, the River Road whips through piney northwoods and towns known for lakes, lumberjacks and fishing. A classic example is ❷ Bemidji, 30 miles northeast of Itasca, which delivers mustachioed, broad-shouldered Paul Bunyan. Standing 18ft and weighing 2.5 tons, he raises his concrete head by the visitors center, flanked by Babe, his faithful blue ox. Together they make a mighty photo op. Did we mention they created the Mississippi? As legend has it, Babe was hauling the tank wagon that paved the winter logging roads with ice. One day it sprang a leak, which trickled down to New Orleans and formed the Big Muddy.

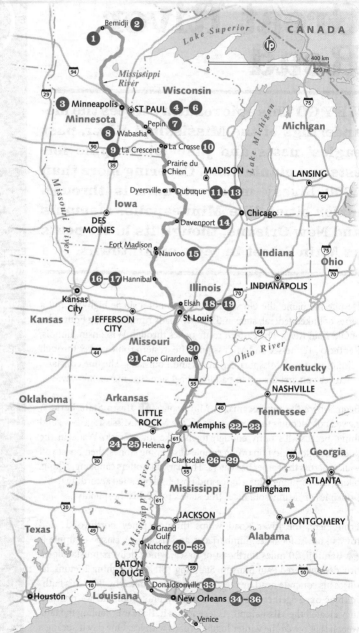

The road drifts west then south for 350 miles, taking strides on remote Forest Service lanes, gravel roads and county highways that skirt wee communities like Cuyuna, home to wood-tick races each June (we're talking small bloodsucking insects running on a wooden board). It eventually drops into glassy, high-rise ❸ Minneapolis. The Riverfront District at downtown's northern edge makes a fine pause for its parks, museums, theaters, bars and polka clubs. A stone's throw downstream, 50,000 students hit the books (and live music venues) at the University of Minnesota. If you want to rock, Minneapolis is your stopover.

If you want a night on a tugboat and *Great Gatsby* ambiance, twin city ❹ St Paul is your place, 10 miles east. The four-room ❺ Covington Inn floats in a tug moored smack in the Mississippi; watch the river traffic glide by while sipping your morning coffee. Later, stroll over to ❻ WA Frost & Company. The tree-shaded, ivy-covered patio is straight out of a novel by native son F Scott Fitzgerald, perfect for a glass of wine, beer or gin. Soak it up with locally sourced dishes like the artisanal cheese plate and pan-roasted whitefish.

Twenty-five miles beyond St Paul, near Hastings, the River Road splits into eastern and western sections as the Mississippi becomes the border between states. It's the Minnesota–Wisconsin line at this juncture, and our trip starts flip-flopping between the two to cover the best sights.

Stay on the Minnesota side (Hwy 61) to shoe and pottery purveyor Red Wing, then cross to Wisconsin (Hwy 35) where some of the Mississippi Valley's prettiest landscapes begin. A great stretch of road edges the bluffs beside Maiden Rock, Stockholm and Pepin. While it's tempting to keep on truckin', brake in the latter for the Slow Food stalwart ❼ Harbor View Cafe. Staff write the changing menu on a chalkboard twice daily – once for lunch, once for dinner – a ritual they've kept for more than 25 years. Cross your fingers the list shows the four-cheese stuffed mushrooms, caper-sauced halibut and lemon cake with ginger. There are no reservations, and queues are typical, but there's a full bar inside and deck chairs line the sidewalk outside, each with a water view.

Continue 8 miles southeast to Nelson (where you can nibble at the local cheese factory) and cross back over the river to Wabasha, Minnesota. Large populations of bald eagles flock here each winter, where they indulge in waterside trees for nesting and fat silvery fish for chowing as they migrate. Learn all about it at the ❽ National Eagle Center and also get acquainted with Donald, Harriet and the other rehabilitated birds who live on site. These creatures are more than majestic – they also write blogs (http://nationaleaglecenter.net/meet-our-eagles).

Stay on Hwy 61 as it opens into a gorgeous drive for nearly 60 miles past sandbars, marshes and untamed green hills en route to La Crescent, Minnesota – aka "the Apple Capital." Orchards sprout from the land and roadside stands sell the tart wares, particularly bountiful from August through October. Strawberries, sweet corn and pumpkins fill baskets during other seasons. Hardy **9 Bauer's Market** is open year-round and offers the added bonus of lawn ornaments – say, a fish-toting gnome or giant mushroom – many painted by a local artist.

ROADIE RESOURCES

Turn-by-turn directions for the Great River Road are complex, spanning an incredible number of highways and byways. We've provided some road information here, but for nitty-gritty instructions you'll need additional resources. A few states maintain their own River Road website – **Minnesota** (www.mnmississippiriver.com), **Wisconsin** (www.wigreatriverroad.org), **Illinois** (www.greatriverroad-illinois.org) and **Iowa** (www.iowagreatriverroad.com) among them. Or check the **National Scenic Byways** (www.byways.org/explore/byways/2279/directions.html) for designated sections.

Cross the Mississippi again via Hwy 61 to La Crescent's twin city La Crosse, Wisconsin. The road (which becomes 3rd St S) swings by the **10 World's Largest Six-Pack**. The "cans" are actually storage tanks for City Brewery, formerly G Heileman Brewing, maker of Old Style lager. As the sign in front says: they hold enough to fill 7.3 million cans, or enough to provide one lucky person with a six-pack a day for 3351 years. Yowza.

Hwy 35 clasps the river for another 60 miles to the old fur trading post of Prairie du Chien. This is also where the final battle of the bloody Black Hawk War was fought in 1832, between the Sauk natives and white settlers.

Motor over the bridge to Marquette, Iowa. Just north, Effigy Mounds National Monument protects Native American ceremonial grounds. In Pikes Peak State Park to the south, shutterbugs can snap photos from the highest bluff (500ft) on the Mississippi.

From Pikes Peak, country roads link with state and US highways for a 60-mile spin to hill-flanked **11 Dubuque**, named for French-Canadian fur trapper Julien Dubuque. At the hands-on **12 National Mississippi River Museum & Aquarium**, at the Port of Dubuque, enjoy a big-screen soar over the river, pilot a simulated barge, or touch river-dwelling creatures in a wet lab. An American alligator lurks in the Mississippi Bayou aquarium, one of six creature-filled habitats.

The historic **13 Hotel Julien** reopened in 2009 after an 18-month $30 million renovation. Top-of-the-line decor and amenities enhance its Victorian roots (the hotel, which dates to 1839, was rebuilt after a 1913 fire). According to lore, Al Capone lodged here when things got "uncomfortable" in Chicago. The Capone Suite comes with a bank vault where the gangster allegedly hid.

In the morning, take Hwy 52 south toward Sabula then follow Hwy 67 to Davenport, Bettendorf, Moline and Rock Island, collectively known as the Quad Cities. The glass-walled **14 Figge Art Museum** sparkles above the River

Road in Davenport. The museum's Midwest Regionalist Collection includes the only self-portrait by *American Gothic* painter Grant Wood; you can also stroll through the world-class Haitian and Mexican Colonial collections.

A leisurely network of roads continues south, with Hwy 61 rolling into Fort Madison. Cross the Mississippi on the Fort Madison Toll Bridge ($1), a double-decker swing span accommodating trains and cars on separate levels.

Take Hwy 96 into striking ⑮ **Nauvoo**, a pilgrimage site for Mormons. Joseph Smith, the religion's founder, brought his flock here in 1839 after they were kicked out of Missouri. Nauvoo (Hebrew for "beautiful place") grew quickly. Almost 12,000 Mormons took up residence, rivaling Chicago's population. By 1846 they were gone. Tension rose, Smith was killed, and Brigham Young led the group west to Utah. Today the tiny town is a historic district loaded with impressive structures, such as the homes of Smith and Young. The centerpiece is the gleaming white temple, built in 2002 on the site of the Mormons' burned-down original sanctuary.

> **DETOUR**
>
> Is this heaven? It's Iowa. Iowa? I could have sworn it was heaven… Road-trippers might see a little heaven themselves at the free **Field of Dreams Movie Site** (www.fodmoviesite.com; open 9am to 6pm April to November), in Dyersville, 30 miles west of Dubuque. While not exactly river related, the movie's farmhouse, baseball diamond and cornfield are certainly inspirational. Bat a few balls, sit on the bleachers or read some film history.

Follow Hwy 96 south to I-72, taking it west across the Mississippi to ⑯ **Hannibal**, Missouri, hometown of writer Mark Twain. From the Mark Twain Boyhood Home & Museum to the Mark Twain Dinette, Hannibal is a big group hug for the humorist. Enjoy Mississippi surf 'n' turf – fried catfish and barbecued ribs – at ⑰ **Lula Belle's Restaurant & B&B**, a former brothel that embraces its racy past with a harmless wink.

Back in Illinois, take Hwy 96 to Hwy 100. Hwy 100 between Grafton and Alton is perhaps the most scenic 15 miles of the entire River Road. As you slip under wind-hewn bluffs, keep an eye out for the turnoff to itty-bitty ⑱ **Elsah**, a hidden hamlet of 19th-century stone cottages, wood buggy shops and farmhouses. Most of the town, including the ⑲ **Maple Leaf Cottage Inn**, sits on two parallel streets. The inn is a flowery, old-school B&B where you can't help but slow down (note: bluffs aren't kind to cell phone reception). Around the bend lies Principia College, a small liberal arts school and one of the few for Christian Scientists.

Just before the town of Alton the Piasa Bird spreads its wings over an old quarry wall. The replica pictograph derives from Native American myths about a massive bird that devours people. A bit further downriver is where Lewis and Clark shoved off for their epic Pacific expedition.

Next up? River City itself, St Louis. The graceful 630ft Gateway Arch swoops over the Jefferson National Expansion Memorial, a tribute to early explorers. The River Road loses a bit of charm as it hurtles south from St Louis on I-55 and Hwy 61. Swing back to the river south of Fruitland, following Hwys 61 and 177 to **20** **Trail of Tears State Park**. Cherokees camped here during their forced march west in the winter of 1838–39. A small museum recounts their tragic journey.

Hwy 177 passes Cape Rock Park where some Lewis and Clark expedition members camped in 1803. In **21** **Cape Girardeau** stroll alongside the 1100ft-long Mississippi River Tales Mural, in which vivid paintings highlight river-related events. Then jump onto I-55 south to **22** **Memphis**, one of the river's most soulful cities. You might have heard of a young chap named Elvis who once lived here. In addition to the homage to the king of rock'n'roll, there's also blues and barbecue almost everywhere you turn. To stay with our theme, hightail to the **23** **Mississippi River Museum**, the place to learn more about the cultural and natural history of the Big Muddy. The museum itself will tell you everything you want to know about the river's relationship with the Civil War, the blues and, of course, transportation. Stick around for a while on Mud Island to engage in riverfront activities like kayaking, river tours, a bankside campsite and a mini-Mississippi replica, which offers the chance to walk 1000 miles of the lower Mississippi in 15 minutes, give or take.

MUSICAL FLOW

Along with cotton and timber, the Mississippi River has long carried music to new ports. Blues, jazz, rock and country genres all met and mixed in the South before traveling upriver, where they got shook up some more. Think Elvis in Memphis; Louis Armstrong in New Orleans; BB King in the Mississippi Delta; Ike and Tina Turner in St Louis; Bix Beiderbecke in Davenport; and the beat goes on.

Pick up the Blues Highway (Hwy 61) in Memphis and drive through the Mississippi Delta, where the blues were born. Robert Johnson, the original blues star, was born in Tunica, Mississippi, a small riverside town that has morphed into a maze of casinos. Then roll through **24** **Helena**, Arkansas, a depressed mill town, and home to the late Sonny Boy Williamson. Sonny Boy was a regular on King Biscuit Time, the first blues radio show in the country. BB King listened religiously as a child, and considers Sonny Boy a major influence. The show, which begins weekdays at 12:15pm, is still running (on KFFA 1360AM, and via King Biscuit Time podcast) and has been hosted by Sunshine Sonny Payne for 60 years or so. It broadcasts out of the **25** **Delta Cultural Center**, which showcases the influence of the river and the Arkansas Delta as much as it boasts about the area's best blues, historical and current. During weekdays, you can watch Sonny Boy's show, recorded at the Cultural Center.

Cross east over the river towards the Mississippi town of **26** **Clarksdale**, the hub of Delta blues country. This is where you'll find the Crossroads, at the intersection of Hwy 61 and Hwy 49, where Robert Johnson made his mythical deal with the devil and became America's first guitar hero. And it's here where live music and blues history are most accessible. Stay at the ㉗ **Shack Up Inn**, an old plantation where a cotton gin and sharecroppers' cabins have been converted into guestrooms stuffed with kitsch antiques. The owners are warm and fun, and are tuned in to the local live-music scene.

The ㉘ **Delta Blues Museum**, in downtown Clarksdale, has the best collection of blues memorabilia in the Delta, including Muddy Waters' reconstructed Mississippi cabin. Creative multimedia exhibits also honor BB King, John Lee Hooker, Big Mama Thornton and WC Handy, whose original 1912 compositions popularized the 12-bar blues. Swing back towards the Crossroads for dinner. That smoky sweetness in the air is coming from ㉙ **Abe's**, a local barbecue joint that's been in business since 1924. The ribs melt off the bone, and its barbecue beef, pork and ham sandwiches are popular too. Apparently when Robert Johnson was mingling with Satan, old Abe was getting a barbecue sauce recipe from Jesus. At least that's what the menu reports.

Historic antebellum mansions will greet you in ㉚ **Natchez**, Mississippi. In the 1840s there were more millionaires per capita here than anywhere in the world. When Union soldiers marched through with orders to torch the place during the Civil War, there weren't any men in town. They were all off fighting. Legend has it that the women greeted the soldiers at their doors and said something like, "Now boys, leave your guns outside and come sit a spell. You must be exhausted." Yes, Southern hospitality saved the city. And the mansions are still open to visitors during the twice-annual pilgrimage seasons, held in the spring and fall.

"when Robert Johnson was mingling with Satan, old Abe was getting a barbecue sauce recipe from Jesus."

Care to taste mansion life? Dine at ㉛ **The Castle**, a restaurant set at the Dunleith, gorgeous and ringed with Corinthian columns. The night scene, when the house is illuminated, is unforgettable, and it's widely considered to be the best kitchen in town. But Natchez gets down and dirty too. When Mark Twain passed through during his riverboat captain days, he crashed in a room above the local saloon. ㉜ **Under the Hill Saloon** remains the best bar in town, with terrific (and free) live music on weekends. The name works, because the saloon is built into a hillside and overlooks the wide, languid Mississippi. And you can still crash upstairs at what is now called the Mark Twain Guesthouse. Reserve your bed at the bar.

Cross the Louisiana state line and Hwy 61 bleeds into I-110 south, which merges with I-10 in Baton Rouge. Head, via Hwys 44 south, 70 west and 18, to Donaldsville, just off Louisiana's River Road (actually a series of highways that skirt both sides of the Mississippi all the way to the Gulf of Mexico). While there are some beautiful antebellum mansions in the area, Donaldsonville's claim to fame is the ㉝ **River Road African American Museum**. Step inside to learn about the region's seldom-told African American history. You'll learn the truth about slave ships, the vicious toils of slavery, slave revolts, the Underground Railroad, reconstruction and Jim Crow, from antiques, artifacts, photographs and video interviews. When slaves escaped the Donaldsonville plantations, they ran or floated south to New Orleans (where they could blend in with free blacks), rather than hike north, where they would have to cross Mississippi, Tennessee and Missouri to find freedom.

THE PHATWATER CHALLENGE

If you're into aquatic self-propulsion (ie you dig kayaking) then you'll enjoy the **Phatwater Challenge** (www.kayakmississippi.com), a marathon kayak race (the future Olympic sport you've never heard of) that runs 45 miles downriver from the Port of Grand Gulf to Natchez, Mississippi. For one day, barge traffic is halted as paddlers own the Mississippi. Join the party, stopping for breaks on beaches and sand bars; you may even see a gator. The race wraps with a bluegrass jam at the **Under the Hill Saloon**.

From Donaldsonville, make your way to Hwy 90 west toward ㉞ **New Orleans**. At Lake Pontchartrain you'll cross a 24-mile-long causeway, the world's largest bridge. When you get into the city limits you'll traverse the gorgeous Crescent City Connection, a four-lane cantilever bridge that crosses the Mississippi and leads into downtown. The history of New Orleans is inextricably linked to its position near the mouth of the Mississippi River. What's known as the USA's most interesting city got that way because of its port-city status through the 18th and 19th centuries. Two-thirds of slaves coming into the country did so through New Orleans, as did a majority of cargo and trade. It quickly became known as an island of culture and remains unique in the USA today.

DETOUR The River Road continues along Hwy 23's west bank to the mouth of Old Man River, 70 miles south of New Orleans. Here you'll find the sport-fishing marina of **Venice**, Louisiana and the **Delta National Wildlife Refuge**, a protected vast estuary. A treasure trove of migrating water fowl, shorebirds and fish (many deliciously edible) abound in these Gulf waters. Boat charters will bring you out to defunct offshore oil platforms to cast off.

Here's your opportunity to finally head down the river aboard the ㉟ **Steamboat Natchez** at Canal St. It offers historic dinner and day cruises – great for families. To spend a bit of outdoor quality time with the Mighty Miss before your journey ends, head to ㊱ **Crabby Jacks** and order a smoked duck po'boy and salad to go, then take it to one of dozens of riverside benches to picnic. Go on, feel free to hum Johnny Cash's "Big River" while you contemplate your now intimate relationship with the 2320 muddy miles that shaped American history.

Amy Balfour, Alex Leviton & Karla Zimmerman

TRIP INFORMATION

GETTING THERE

From Minneapolis, take I-94 west and then Hwy 71 north; it's 220 miles to Itasca State Park.

DO

Bauer's Market

This roadside shop stocks local apples, cider, birdhouses and concrete lawn ornaments. ☎ 507-895-4583; www.bauersmarketplace. com; 221 N 2nd St, La Crescent, MN; ⌚ 8am-6pm Mon-Sat, 10am-5pm Sun

Bemidji Visitors Center

Giant statues of Paul Bunyan and Babe the Blue Ox rise beside the building. ☎ 218-759-0164; www.visitbemidji.com; 300 Bemidji Ave, Bemidji, MN; ⌚ 8am-5pm Mon-Fri, 9am-5pm Sat, noon-4pm Sun Jun-Aug, reduced hrs Sep-May

Delta Blues Museum

Peruse memorabilia, video installations and an entire Muddy Waters wing. ☎ 662-627-6820; www.deltabluesmuseum.org; 1 Blues Alley, Clarksdale, TN; adult/child $7/5; ⌚ 9am-5pm Mon-Sat Mar-Oct, 10am-5pm Nov-Feb; ♿

Delta Cultural Center

Dedicated to the Arkansas Delta's musical and cultural heritage, with a live radio blues show weekdays. ☎ 870-338-4350; www.del taculturalcenter.com; 141 Cherry St, Helena, AR; admission free; ⌚ 9am-5pm Tue-Sat & Mon national holidays; ♿

Figge Art Museum

Studio 1 and the Family Activity Center introduce kids to creativity. ☎ 563-326-7804; www.figgeart.org; 225 W 2nd St, Davenport, IA; adult/child $7/4; ⌚ 10am-5pm Tue, Wed, Fri & Sat, 10am-9pm Thu, noon-5pm Sun; ♿

Itasca State Park

Wade across the Mississippi River at its birthplace (near the Mary Gibbs Center).

☎ 218-266-2100; www.dnr.state.mn.us /state_parks/itasca/index.html; 36750 Main Park Dr, Park Rapids, MN; per vehicle $5; ⌚ 8:30am-4pm; ♿ 🐾

Mississippi River Museum

Enjoy a natural-history lesson on Mud Island. ☎ 901-576-7241; www.mudisland.com; 125 N Front St, Memphis, TN; adult/child $8/5; ⌚ 10am-5pm Apr, May, Sep & Oct, 10am-6pm Jun-Aug, closed Mon; ♿

National Eagle Center

Visit rehabilitated eagles indoors and wild eagles outdoors; November to April is prime time but call ahead to confirm. ☎ 651-565-4989; www.nationaleaglecenter.org; 50 Pembroke Ave, Wabasha, MN; adult/child $6/4; ⌚ 10am-5pm Sun-Thu, 9am-6pm Fri & Sat; ♿

National Mississippi River Museum & Aquarium

An interactive flood table highlights effects of past Mississippi floods. ☎ 563-557-9545; www.mississippirivermuseum.com; 350 E 3rd St, Dubuque, IA; adult/child $10.50/8; ⌚ 10am-5pm, with variations; ♿

River Road African American Museum

Details the harsh reality, heroes and triumphs of Louisiana's African American history. ☎ 225-474-5553; www.africanamerican museum.org; 406 Charles St, Donaldsonville, LA; admission $4; ⌚ 10am-5pm Wed-Sat, 1-5pm Sun; ♿

Steamboat Natchez

Float the Mississippi on a steamboat, but skip the buffet. ☎ 504-586-8777; www.steam boatnatchez.com; Toulouse St, New Orleans, LA; adult/child $25/12.50; ⌚ cruises 11am-1.30pm, 2-4.30pm, 6-9pm; ♿

Trail of Tears State Park

Hike, camp and fish on 3415 woodsy acres. Check the website for visitor center hours. ☎ 573-290-5268; www.mostateparks. com/trailoftears.htm; 429 Moccasin Springs, Jackson, MO; admission free; ⌚ park 7am-10pm, visitor center hours vary; ♿ 🐾

EAT

Abe's
Don't miss the slow-burning tamales and melt-off-the-bone ribs. ☎ 662-624-9947; 616 State St, Clarksdale, MS; mains $3-12; 🕑 10am-9pm Mon-Thu, 10am-10pm Fri & Sat, 11am-2pm Sun; 🖢

The Castle
Upscale continental cuisine is served on the grounds of the sensationally illuminated Dunleith Plantation. ☎ 601-446-8500; www.dunleith.com; 84 Homochitto St, Natchez, MS; mains $18-34; 🕑 7:30-10am daily, 11am-2pm & 6-9pm Mon-Thu, 6-10pm Fri & Sat

Crabby Jacks
New Orleans' best po'boys are served here. ☎ 504-833-2722; 428 Jefferson Hwy, New Orleans, LA; mains $6-12; 🕑 10am-5pm Mon-Fri, 11am-4pm Sat; 🖢

Harbor View Cafe
The book-stuffed, blue-frame Harbor View is a long-standing foodie destination; cash only. ☎ 715-442-3893; 314 First St, Pepin, WI; mains $18-24; 🕑 lunch & dinner Thu-Mon, closed mid-Nov–mid-Mar, with variations

Lula Belle's Restaurant & B&B
Bordello Bomb: Oreos, ice cream and chocolate wedge. ☎ 573-221-6662; www.lula belles.com; 111 Bird St, Hannibal, MO; mains $7-25; 🕑 11am-2pm & 4-8:30pm Mon-Thu, 4-9:30pm Fri & Sat

Under the Hill Saloon
A tremendously fun and historic bar that was once a favorite haunt of Samuel Clemens, riverboat pilot. ☎ 601-446-8023; www.under

thehillsaloon.com; 25 Silver St, Natchez, MS; 🕑 9am-late

WA Frost & Company
Frost serves fine food and drink via its turn-of-the-century interior and Gatsby-esque patio. ☎ 651-224-5715; 374 Selby Ave, St Paul, MN; mains $16-32; 🕑 11am-10pm Sun-Thu, 11am-11pm Fri & Sat

SLEEP

Covington Inn
Pull up the covers in this four-room B&B aboard a Mississippi River tugboat. ☎ 651-292-1411; www.covingtoninn.com; 100 Harriet Island Rd, St Paul, MN; r incl breakfast $150-235

Hotel Julien
Pluses include pillow-top mattresses, granite counters and free wi-fi. ☎ 563-556-4200; www.hoteljuliendubuque.com; 200 Main St, Dubuque, IA; r $119-129, ste $159-179

Maple Leaf Cottage Inn
Iron-rail beds, claw-foot tubs and other antique accoutrements throw the Maple Leaf back in time. ☎ 618-374-1684; www.mapleleafcottages.com; 12 Selma St, Elsah, IL; r incl breakfast $90-110

Shack Up Inn
The Ritz it ain't (this place proclaims proudly), but a must for any self-respecting blues traveler. Two-night minimum on weekends. ☎ 662-624-8329; www.shackupinn.com; 001 Commissary Circle, off Hwy 49, Clarksdale; r from $75; 🐾

USEFUL WEBSITES
www.experiencemississippiriver.com

LINK YOUR TRIP
TRIP

www.lonelyplanet.com/trip-planner

24 48 Hours in New Orleans p217
25 Music City to Dixieland: A Musical Roots Run p223
50 Twain Tour p377

The Great Divide Treasure Hunt

WHY GO Ready to add a wild-adventure-meets-pub-quiz challenge to your great American road trip memory collection? Then drive – as close to parallel as possible – the Continental Divide from Canada to Mexico, and make the odyssey more entertaining by playing this scavenger hunt along the way.

TIME
10 days

DISTANCE
2100 miles

BEST TIME TO GO
Jul – Sep

START
Glacier National Park, MT

END
Animas Peak, NM

Walking the USA top to bottom along the 3100-mile Continental Divide (the great east–west watershed dividing line: all rain falling to its west ends up in the Pacific Ocean; to the east, the Gulf of Mexico) is a hardcore hiker's dream. The Continental Divide Trail (CDT) follows the spine of the Rockies between northern Montana and southern New Mexico and is, along with the Appalachian Trail and the Pacific Coast Trails, part of the triple crown of long-distance hiking. Remote and not entirely finished, it is considered by many to be the most difficult of the top three trails, taking adventurers about six months to complete.

If you're short on time and endurance but still want to see what the hype's about, follow us. This itinerary provides a motorized version of the iconic walk through the mountains, following the north–south highways and byways that run roughly parallel to the USA's famous dividing line – although our driving route comes out almost exactly 1000 miles shorter than the hiking trail. To keep you on your toes, challenge yourself to a metaphorical scavenger hunt while driving. We've identified a list of objects and memories – from summiting a 14er to ghost hunting, soaking in a wilderness hot spring to scouting for turquoise – for you to collect and experience along this iconic 2100-mile road trip.

Grab the trip's first treasure near the start of the hiking trail that inspired it. The CDT begins (or ends, depending which way it's hiked) in Montana's gorgeous ❶ **Glacier National Park**. The park's rugged and

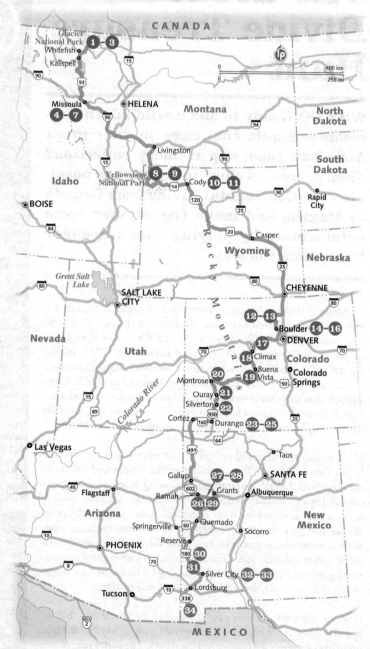

desolate 1600-sq-mile alpine wilderness is home to 200 clear crystal lakes, 50 (sadly shrinking) glaciers and too many rushing waterfalls to count. Spotting animals is common: cougars, grizzlies, black bears and elk all roam freely. Try to see at least two different creatures to add to your treasure hunt checklist.

Enter Glacier through the east entrance and take Going-to-the-Sun Rd west. The CDT crosses the park's 50-mile paved main drag at ❷ **Siyeh Bend**, halfway between St Mary and Logan Pass. Walk at least a few hundred feet down the signature trail: that's task number two on this scavenger hunt. There are numerous hiking trails branching off the CDT around here, and we encourage further exploration because getting off the road is what Glacier's really all about. The road crosses the Continental Divide again atop Logan Pass, where there's a visitor center and a 1.5-mile boardwalk trail to Hidden Lake Overlook. Descending the pass, the road runs parallel to the Continental Divide – it's the 9000ft spine of granite running north, called the Garden Wall.

This is the trip of a lifetime, so spend your first night on the road 7 miles into Glacier's heart. The ❸ **Sperry Chalet** can only be accessed on foot (although mules can be hired to carry gear) via a trail from the parking lot at Lake McDonald Lodge. Leading through wildflower-strewn meadows past jagged peaks and babbling brooks, the hike itself is beautiful. But when you see the 17-room Swiss-style chalet, in a heavenly location on a ridgeline high above Lake McDonald's turquoise shimmer, you'll know the true meaning of high-country nirvana.

Exit Glacier through the western gate in the morning and follow the signs to Hwy 93 south (you'll be quite a bit west of the actual divide, but it passes mostly through wilderness in Montana, making it hard to access by car). For motorists, lively ❹ **Missoula** is a fun pit stop at the end of the 160-mile drive from Glacier. Montana's most culturally diverse town is the type of place where one can hike through a wilderness area, fly fish a blue-ribbon stream and attend the symphony in the same day. Sitting at the convergence of five valleys on the banks of the Clark River, there are seven different wilderness areas within 100 miles – including the amazing Bob Marshall Wilderness Complex between Missoula and Glacier (the Continental Divide splits its rugged, nearly no-roads interior).

Seven miles west of downtown, the ❺ **Smokejumper Visitor Center** is the active base for the heroic men and women who parachute into forests to combat raging wildfires. Its visitor center has thought-provoking audio and visual displays that do a great job illustrating the life of the Western firefighter. When you've finished snooping, check into ❻ **Goldsmith's Bed & Breakfast**, just a stone's toss from the river, back in town. The outdoor deck overlooking the water is the perfect place to kick back with a good novel. For dinner order a handcrafted burger and beer on the patio at ❼ **Iron Horse Brewpub**. Don't miss the saltwater aquarium inside the swank upstairs bar.

Bid "Big Sky Country" goodbye and say hello to "Cowboy State" Wyoming in ⑧ **Yellowstone National Park**, about 300 miles southeast of Missoula. From the north entrance gate, take Grand Loop Rd in a counter-clockwise direction around America's first national park. Established in 1872, Yellowstone is home to half the world's geysers, including perennial crowd pleaser Old Faithful. Snap a picture at the Continental Divide sign crossing east of Old Faithful to add to this hunt's treasure collection; it's on the way to tonight's slumber spot, ⑨ **Lake Yellowstone Hotel & Cabins**. Glowing golden on the lake's northern tip, this historic hotel oozes grand 1920s Western ambience and has the park's most divine lounge. Made for daydreaming, it features big picture windows with lake views, lots of natural light and a live string quartet for background serenading.

Leave Yellowstone via the east entrance and follow Hwy 14 east to Wild West-or-bust ⑩ **Cody**. Keep your eyes peeled in the rearview mirror driving from the park – this 52-mile stretch is considered Yellowstone's most dramatic approach; President Teddy Roosevelt went as far as to dub it "the most scenic 50 miles in the world." Buffalo Bill's old stomping ground is a raucous, well-preserved town that takes its heritage seriously – it was named for orchestrator of Wild West shows William Frederick "Buffalo Bill" Cody. It's now home to the excellent ⑪ **Buffalo Bill Historical Center**, and to the country's longest-running night rodeo – the Cody Nite Rodeo held each evening from June through August. As it's nearly 500 miles of hard driving across the rest of Wyoming to the next destination, stick around town for the raucous broncs and bulls show. A ticket stub from either the rodeo or museum is an acceptable token when tallying this treasure hunt's final points.

FLY FISHING IN MISSOULA

Fans of Brad Pitt and Robert Redford will remember Missoula's moniker from fly-fishing classic *A River Runs Through It*. The movie was set here (although it was actually filmed outside Bozeman, Montana). Still, Missoula is home to some of the state's best angling. Try Rock Creek, 21 miles east. It's a designated blue-ribbon trout stream and favorite local year-round fishing spot. There are a number of shops downtown selling fishing supplies and licenses that also offer guided tours and lessons – extra credit scavenger hunt points here, folks!

HIDDEN TREASURE

For extra credit hike to the **Thorofare Patrol Cabin**, located further from a road than any other occupied building in the contiguous USA. We're not giving away the cabin's location, but here are some clues.

- The cabin is inside Yellowstone Park boundaries, but the 45-mile one-way hike finishes in Grand Teton National Park.

- You will cross the Continental Divide and Yellowstone River.

- From Yellowstone Lake take the Thorofare Trail south; link with the Pacific Coast Trail.

To make up for the punishing wind whiplash of flying at 80mph across the central Wyoming plains (it takes fewer than eight hours, we promise), we've booked you into Colorado's ⑫ **Stanley Hotel**. Perched on a hill overlooking Estes Park, the magnificent old resort, which dates back to 1909, inspired Stephen King to pen his horror classic *The Shining*. Interior shots of the movie version, starring Jack Nicholson, were filmed here. Ghosts supposedly haunt the Stanley, so all the better if you arrive after dark. Grab a tumbler of whiskey at the gorgeous scarred wood bar for strength and join a nightly hotel ghost tour. Then we dare you to book into room 401; staff consider it the most haunted.

Going from one great park to another in only 24 hours is quite an achievement. But ⑬ **Rocky Mountain National Park** waits just west of the Stanley's oversized front doors. The spectacular through-park Trail Ridge Rd (Hwy 34) gives a grand starter glimpse of Colorado's most revered natural treasure. It crosses the Continental Divide at Milner Pass (10,759ft). Get out of the car for a bit – Rocky Mountain's most majestic sights are off-road. Get another notch on the scavenger hunt belt by hiking the 2000ft lung-busting 4-mile ascent to the top of Mt Ida. A picture of the Rocky Mountain high view from the summit will be proof of this task's completion. Explore the park all day; tonight's destination is only 40 miles away.

"the People's Republic of Boulder became the first US city to tax itself specifically to preserve open space."

A model example of a functioning utopian society, the People's Republic of ⑭ **Boulder** (as the locals say) is a liberal university town with a yuppie attitude and a mad crush on the outdoors – in 1967 it became the first US city to tax itself specifically to preserve open space. Check out the signature Flatirons (named for their resemblance to granite irons) to the southwest of downtown – they're famous for rock climbing. Do try to arrive in time for happy hour at the ⑮ **Boulder Café** – in a city known for cheap early bird feasts it stands out and is always packed. That's because it puts its entire seafood raw bar and appetizer menu (which includes eclectic choices like Swiss fondue) at 50% discount for three hours each afternoon. Pair this with half-price drinks and you're in for a bargain-basement gourmet meal. Try to score a seat at the outdoor patio overlooking the city's famous pedestrian-only Pearl St Mall. Bursting with shops, sidewalk cafés and street performers, it's lively, clean and perfect for walking off the king crab legs, oysters and pot of cheese you just consumed.

The charming ⑯ **Hotel Boulderado**, right at the edge of the Pearl St Mall, celebrated a century of service in 2009. Full of Victorian elegance and wonderful public spaces, each antique-filled room is uniquely decorated and boasts luxurious amenities. The basement club is one of the city's most popular cheap-drink and pick-up joints.

You'll have to climb a mountain in the morning to record this adventure's next memory: 14,270ft ⑰ **Grays Peak**. Summiting the 14er (what locals call

14,000ft-plus mountains), off I-70 about 50 miles southwest of Boulder, not only gives you major bragging rights but the hike also takes you to the highest point on the entire Continental Divide. The trail is just 3.5 miles long but ascends 3054ft, which means the climb is pretty damn steep. But the hike is swift, the views from the top sweet and losing your 14er summit virginity a worthy treasure.

Backtrack to I-70 after coming down, continuing west to Copper Mountain and the exit for Hwy 91 south. Sitting at 11,300ft, right on the Continental Divide, ⓲ **Climax** is a full-on ghost town. Although it's now uninhabited, the one-time booming mine town holds the record for having the nation's highest post office and railway station. It's 60 winding miles south from Climax to ⓳ **Cottonwood Hot Springs**, near Buena Vista off Hwy 24. The five soaking pools are rustic, with fantastic views (the stars can be amazing). Reward yourself by staying in a cabin with a private soaking pool.

Cut west on Hwy 50 towards the San Juan Mountains and experience the next piece of treasure on this great hunt – ⓴ **Black Canyon of the Gunnison National Park** – come morn. Here a dark narrow gash above the Gunnison River leads down a 2000ft-deep chasm that's as eerie as it is spectacular. No other canyon in the USA combines the narrow openings, sheer walls and dizzying depths of the Black Canyon, and a peek over the edge evokes a sense of awe (and vertigo) for most. The park's 6-mile South Rim Rd passes 11 overlooks at the edge of the canyon, some reached via short trails.

Sandwiched between imposing peaks, the tiny town of ㉑ **Ouray**, south of the park on Hwy 550, just might be that little bit of paradise John Denver waxed lyrical about in "Rocky Mountain High." Here the mountains don't just tower over you, they actually embrace you – barely quarter of a mile of valley floor is left for the town. Ouray is filled with the usual quaint shops and cafés, and is known for its healing natural hot-springs swimming pool. Between Ouray and ㉒ **Silverton** – a boom-bust-boom silver town with serious charm and outdoor activities potential – Hwy 550 is called the Million Dollar Hwy because its roadbed contains valuable ore. The moniker fits in more ways than one – it's also considered one of the most scenically spectacular drives in the USA.

㉓ **Durango**, another 50 miles south of Silverton on Hwy 550, is the region's hub. With the San Juan mountains dominating the periphery this good-looking old mining town filled with graceful Victorian architecture is now known for its fat single-track bike trails and awesome microbreweries. If you're a beer geek, you'll love ㉔ **Ska Brewing Company**. Once mainly a production facility for making and canning their brews, now sold in liquor stores statewide, today the brewery's small tasting room has grown into a popular après-work local watering hole. Stop by the bar for a beer and, if you're lucky, some barbecue and live music. Make sure to pick up a six-pack or a few bombers to take away; they are imperative to completing this trip's final mission. Spend the night at the museum-worthy ㉕ **Strater Hotel** – find the Stradivarius violin or gold-plated commemorative Winchester rifle to collect another check mark. Couples hint: the hot tub can be reserved for two by the hour, a major romantic plus.

Hwy 160 goes west from Durango to Cortez, where the road drops south to the New Mexico border and becomes Hwy 491 through the remote Navajo Nation to Gallup, the mother town on New Mexico's Mother Road, Route 66. If the scenery between Cortez and Gallup evokes a sense of déjà vu you might be a movie buff: this highway used to be called Route 666 and was featured in the cult classic *Natural Born Killers*. It was renamed Hwy 491 not too many years after the movie was released and the devil's highway connotation didn't seem quite so funny.

> **DETOUR** ▶ Animal lovers will want to detour from Hwy 53, 20 miles southeast of Ramah, and pay the **Wild Spirit Wolf Sanctuary** (www.wildspiritwolf sanctuary.org) on Candy Kitchen Rd a visit. It's home to rescued and captive-born wolves and wolf-dog mixes. The sanctuary offers six interactive walking tours per day, where you walk with the wolves that roam the sanctuary's large natural habitat enclosures. On the quarter-mile walk you'll learn more about conservation efforts, the sanctuary's mission and, of course, all about wolves.

A scenic alternative to Route 66, Hwy 53, accessed from Hwy 602 south of Gallup, features a trippy line-up of weird distractions set against a surreal landscape of crimson arches, crumbling pueblos and volcanic craters. First up is ㉖ **El Morro National Monument**. It's said that throughout history travelers have liked to leave their mark on El Morro's 200ft sandstone mastiff. It's covered with thousands of carvings, from pueblo petroglyphs (c 1250) to inscriptions by Spanish conquistadors and Anglo pioneers. Figure out the English name for this graffiti-covered outcrop for bonus points.

Stay green tonight at ㉗ **Cimarron Rose**, an ecofriendly two-room B&B in the Zuni Mountains just west of the Continental Divide on Hwy 53. Two goats and a horse organically fertilize Cimarron's perennial gardens, which provide food and shelter for more than 80 species of birds.

After devouring a big and delicious breakfast the next morning, continue east a few miles to ㉘ **Bandara Ice Cave & Volcano**, where fire and ice collide on the Continental Divide. The privately owned concession features a subterranean ice cave, known to the Pueblo Indians as Winter Lake, with an ice floor that is 20ft thick and never melts – temps stay below 31°F year-round. It's reached via an easy trail from the visitor center. Another trail climbs to a viewpoint looking into Bandara Crater, one of the country's most accessible volcanoes. Snapping a photo of the region's largest cinder cone is the next tick on this treasure hunt's dwindling "to do" list.

Hwy 53 ends 28 miles west in Grants, another Route 66 relic town (this one fading fast), so you should pick up Hwy 117 south, which runs along the western edge of ㉙ **El Malpais National Monument** to the west. The monument, referred to as "rivers of fire" by local Indian tribes (leading anthropologists and geologists believe they witnessed the volcano's last eruption) consists of almost 200 sq miles of 3000-year-old volcanic badlands accessed via a number of hiking trails off Hwy 117 – one leads to a 17-mile-long lava tube system. Keep an eye out for the impressive La Ventura Natural Arch. It's visible from Hwy 117, and photographing it is on today's checklist.

South of crossroads town Quemado, Hwy 117 turns into Hwy 32 (which also is called Hwy 12 and Hwy 180 at different points throughout the journey) as you wind southwest towards the rugged, ultra-remote ㉚ **Gila Wilderness Area**, the largest roadless area outside Alaska and the country's one and only national wilderness. Made up of various national forest and wilderness areas, and split by the Continental Divide, the Gila offers DIY adventures in spades. Our pick is soaking in a series of natural hot mineral springs just a short hike up the Middle Fork River from the main ranger station a half-mile south of the tiny community of Glenwood, on the Gila's western perimeter. South of Glenwood on Hwy 180, just outside Cliff, spend the night at the stunningly situated ㉛ **Casitas de Gila Guesthouse**. Set on 90 acres of wilderness, each adobe-style unit has a fully stocked kitchen and at least one bedroom. There are telescopes and an outdoor hot tub to keep you entertained after dark.

It's less than 30 minutes' drive south from the guesthouse to breakfast at ㉜ **Diane's Restaurant & Bakery** in Silver City. Order the hatch benedict eggs – the house take on the original is doused with New Mexico's beloved green chile pepper stew. ㉝ **Silver City** is the granddaddy of New Mexico's boom-bust-boom-town success stories, with streets dressed in a lovely mishmash of old brick and cast-iron Victorians alongside thick-walled red adobe buildings now housing gourmet coffee shops and galleries. Billy the Kid spent some of his childhood here and the town still retains a Wild West air with a few raucous saloons. After breakfast grab a disposable cooler and ice from a gas station and chill that six-pack of Ska beer you grabbed in Durango. From Silver City it's just under 100 miles to the place where the pavement and this trip's mileage counter end, at the edge of Hwy 9 and Hwy 338 south. Pop the top of your now-cold beer and celebrate 1075 miles in the middle of nowhere, staring at the 8532ft mass of ㉞ **Animas Peak**, the highest point on the Continental Divide in New Mexico. Beyond it, to the south, lies Mexico.

Becca Blond

TRIP INFORMATION

GETTING THERE
Glacier National Park's east entrance is accessed via Hwy 89; 930 miles northwest of Denver, CO, and 360 miles east of Spokane, WA.

DO
Bandera Ice Cave & Volcano
Hike around the side of one of the country's most accessible volcanoes, and down into an ice cave with a 20ft thick floor; located 28 miles west of Grants. ☎ 888-423-2283; www.icecaves.com; Hwy 53, NM; admission $9; ☼ 8am-1hr before sunset; ☝

Black Canyon of the Gunnison National Park
The visitor center is 2 miles inside the park from the entrance. ☎ 970-249-1914; www. nps.gov/blca; S Rim Dr, CO; admission per vehicle $15; ☼ 8am-6pm Jun-Aug, 8am-4pm Sep-May

Buffalo Bill Historical Center
A sprawling complex of five museums, the main showcase is devoted to Buffalo Bill and his world-famous Wild West shows. ☎ 307-587-4771; www.bbhc.org; 720 Sheridan Ave, Cody, WY; adult/child $15/6; ☼ 7am-8pm Jun-Aug, 10am-3pm Tue-Sun Sep-May

El Malpais National Monument
Almost 200 sq miles of lava flows abutting adjacent sandstone, accessed via Hwy 117. The administrative office is in Grants. ☎ 505-285-4641; www.nps.gov/elma; 123 E Roosevelt Ave, Grants, NM; ☼ 8am-4:30pm Mon-Fri

El Morro National Monument
Ancient graffiti 52 miles southeast of Gallup; there's a good onsite restaurant serving New Mexican fare. ☎ 505-783-4226; www.nps. gov/elmo; admission $3; ☼ 9am-7pm Jun-Aug, 9am-5pm Sep-May

Gila Wilderness Area
The main ranger station is 44 miles north of Silver City. ☎ 575-539-2481; Hwy 180, NM; ☼ 8am-4:30pm

Rocky Mountain National Park
Beaver Meadows Visitor Center serves as the park headquarters. It's on Hwy 36 just east of the entrance. ☎ 970-586-1206; www.nps. gov/romo; Hwy 36, CO; per vehicle $25

Smokejumper Visitor Center
The active base's visitor center has thought-provoking audio and visual displays. ☎ 406-329-4900; W Broadway, Missoula, MT; admission free; ☼ 10am-4pm Jun-Aug

Yellowstone National Park
The Albright Visitors Center near the north entrance serves as Yellowstone headquarters. ☎ 307-344-2263; www.nps.gov/yell; Mammoth, WY; hiker/vehicle $12/25; ☼ 8am-7pm Jun-Aug, 9am-5pm Sep-May

EAT & DRINK
Boulder Café
From 3pm to 6pm all appetizers (including the raw bar) and drinks are half price. We think it's the best deal in town. ☎ 303-444-4884; 1247 Pearl St, Boulder, CO; mains $8-25; ☼ 11.30am-10.30pm

Diane's Restaurant & Bakery
Order something doused in green chile at this popular eatery. ☎ 575-538-8722; 510 N Bullard St, Silver City, NM; mains $10-30; ☼ 11am-2:30pm & 5-8:30pm Tue-Fri, 9am-2pm Sat & Sun

Iron Horse Brewpub
It's undergone a multimillion-dollar expansion and now includes a swank, smoke-free upstairs bar known as 501; pub food is served inside and out. ☎ 406-728-8866; 501 N Higgins St, Missoula, MT; ☼ 11:30am-late

Ska Brewing Company
This microbrewery tasting-room bar does weekly barbecues with live music and free food – call for dates, they are never fixed. ☎ 970-247-5792; www.skabrewing.com; 545 Turner Dr, Durango, CO; ☼ 9am-8pm

SLEEP
Casitas de Gila Guesthouse
Adobe-style casitas on 90 acres at the edge of the Gila; rates drop with length of stay.

☎ 877-923-4827; www.casitasdegila.com; off Hwy 180 near Cliff, NM; r $150-200

Cimarron Rose

Cimarron Rose offers two Southwestern-style suites, with tiles, pine walls and hardwood floors (one has a kitchen). The innkeepers take pride in running an ecofriendly hotel. ☎ 505-783-4770, 800-856-5776; www.cimarronrose.com; 689 Oso Ridge Rd, NM; ste $110-185

Cottonwood Hot Springs

Choose from dorms, rooms and cabins; rates include use of the five rustic soaking pools. ☎ 719-395-6434; www.cottonwood-hot-springs.com; 18999 County Rd 306, Buena Vista, CO; dm $35, r/cabin from $100/165; 🌊

Goldsmith's Bed & Breakfast

This delightful B&B, with comfy rooms, is a pebble's toss from the river. ☎ 406-728-1585; www.goldsmithsinn.com; 809 E Front St, Missoula, MT; r from $130

Hotel Boulderado

This 100-year-old National Register of Historic Places landmark has wonderfully romantic Victorian charm. ☎ 303-442-4344, 800-433-4344; www.boulderado.com; 2115 13th St, Boulder, CO; r from $150

Lake Yellowstone Hotel and Cabins

Like all park lodges, this 1920s charmer is nonsmoking and there is no air-con, TV or internet. ☎ 307-344-7311; www.travelyellowstone.com; Lake Country, WY; cabins $135, r $155-230; 🕐 Jun-Oct

Sperry Chalet

This hike-in-only Swiss-style chalet offers phenomenal views. ☎ 888-345-2649; www.sperrychalet.com, www.mule-shoe.com; Glacier National Park, MT; r incl meals $170-300, mule hire $130; 🕐 Jul-Sep

Stanley Hotel

Stephen King was inspired to write *The Shining* after staying at this historic resort. Rooms are posh modern with 42in flatscreen TVs, neutral colors and plush duvets. ☎ 970-586-4964; www.stanleyhotel.com; 333 Wonderview Ave, Estes Park, CO; r from $159, ghost tours $13

Strater Hotel

The world's largest collection of antique Victorian walnut furniture is displayed at this landmark hotel. ☎ 970-247-4431; www.strater.com; 699 Main St, Durango, CO; r $200

USEFUL WEBSITES

www.cdtsociety.org
www.cdtrail.org

LINK YOUR TRIP

www.lonelyplanet.com/trip-planner

TRIP

66 Summit Colorado: The 14er Club p473

69 Tripping Through Grand Teton & Yellowstone p491

78 Four Corners Cruise p543

Wet & Wild West Coast

WHY GO Whether freak-spotting at Venice Beach or whale-watching on the Oregon coast, maximizing time outside is key to this three-state, 1470-mile, nearly border-to-border journey up the US Pacific Coast. En route, you'll hit the wild and quirky places that make the left coast unique, including small towns, big capes and vertigo-inducing coastal parks.

Start in ❶ San Diego with a splash from Shamu the killer whale at Sea World or stay dry and cruise up Hwy 5 to La Jolla. North of the trim whitewashed downtown, immerse yourself in the teeming tide pools and sea caves of ❷ La Jolla Underwater Park Ecological Reserve, where snorkelers spot flashy orange garibaldi, protected state marine fish. Follow your rumbling stomach an hour's drive north on Hwy 5 to ❸ Orange County, the natural habitat of reality TV stars (tanned to match the state fish) and ❹ Taco Loco. This Laguna Beach beach-shack taco stand looks like your typical mellow surfer hangout, but even hardcore Hwy 1 Harley riders go Loco for blackened shrimp tacos and calamari nachos.

Wet meets wild further up coastal Hwy 1 on ❺ Venice Beach Ocean Front Walk, where morning brings a motley crowd of cross-training starlets jogging backwards and aimless stumblers still smarting after last night's impromptu tattoo. From here, follow Hwy 1 past Malibu mansions until the road merges with Hwy 101, where you can take a slight detour to stretch your legs on the palm-lined streets of seaside Santa Barbara. The Pacific seems placid in secluded Santa Barbara, but it goes wild in ❻ Big Sur, a 225-mile drive north that takes four to five hours. Follow Hwy 101 to San Luis Obispo, where you should gas up for the journey west along coastal Hwy 1. From here, the route is slow going (40mph tops) and adrenaline-inducing, with switchbacks scaling steep hillsides while surf crashes against jade-streaked cliffs below.

TIME
12 – 14 days

DISTANCE
1470 miles

BEST TIME TO GO
Jun – Sep

START
San Diego, CA

END
Port Townsend, WA

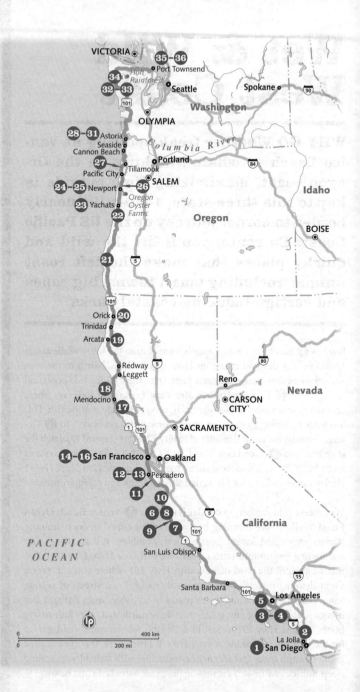

As you approach Big Sur, thrilling stretches of Hwy 1 careen around blind curves and into an alternate reality c 1974, complete with clothing-optional hot tubs. About 25 miles south of the main Big Sur parks, ❼ **Treebones** offers a uniquely Californian choice of accommodations: oceanview campsite; turbine-powered, canvas-clad yurt; or "human nest," a twig tunnel fit for a persnickety hermit, with a futon and ladder access. Flashlights are provided for late-night bathroom treks from yurts, where cozy nights are spent listening to crashing surf by the fireplace. Dinner is available onsite, but incurable romantics and fearless sensualists will head 30 miles north to ❽ **Nepenthe**, where *Tropic of Cancer* author Henry Miller ignored obscenity allegations and wrote with wild abandon. Toast ocean sunsets from the ridge-top terrace with California wine and cheese, or reserve seats inside the redwood-and-adobe lodge for homemade soups and "Green Goddess" salads.

After Treebones' self-serve waffle-and-granola breakfast follow Hwy 1 to ❾ **Julia Pfeiffer Burns State Park**. By the parking lot you'll find the trailhead to the short McWay Falls Overlook Trail, which leads through a tunnel under the highway to spectacular cliffside vistas. Rainbows rise where McWay Falls drop 80ft to the beach, and the bench at trail's end is a prime whale-watching perch in March and April. North along Hwy 1, it's roughly a 30-mile, one-hour drive to the West Coast's masterpiece of architectural aquaculture, the ❿ **Monterey Bay Aquarium**. Picture windows peek right into the bay, rescued sea lions sunbathe on rocky perches and prima ballerina pink jellyfish flit across blue water walls. If schools of silver sardines swimming overhead make your stomach rumble, you're in luck: the onsite restaurant specializes in sustainable seafood.

If Monterey Bay Aquarium is the playground of West Coast sea life, ⓫ **Año Nuevo State Reserve**, 47 miles north on Hwy 1, is more like after-school detention. After an unsuccessful December to March mating season, teenage elephant seals bellyache to anyone within earshot of the refuge for rejects known as Loser's Beach. A 3-mile, 2½-hour round-trip coastal hike heads to observation points overlooking Loser's Beach – any closer could get dangerous when bulls practice their fighting moves. Many seals return to the dunes for molting season April through August, but most haul out to sea from September to October for a major feed before mating season.

THE ULTIMATE CALIFORNIA HOT TUB

To see Big Sur in all its glory, wait until 1am, strap on your hiking shoes and prepare to strip at **Esalen Hot Springs** (www.esalen.org/place /hot_springs.shtml). Since the 1960s, Esalen Institute has hosted daytime workshops with self-help gurus and welcomed visitors who make the quarter-mile cliffside walk to its natural hot springs from 1am to 3am (by prior reservation, at ☎ 831-667-3047, and for $20). Soak away your cares in moonlit tubs built into a cliff, hovering 50ft above crashing breakwaters – but mind those elbows on busy summer nights.

ROUTE

Your own dinner awaits at ⑫ **Duarte's Tavern**, 7 miles up Hwy 1 and about a mile east at the signed turnoff for Pescadero. Start with tangy Pescadero artichoke soup, then take your pick of today's catch pan-fried – fingers crossed for sand dabs, a California delicacy as light and flaky as Dover sole. Nothing could top Grandma Duarte's ollalieberry pie made with berries grown next door – except maybe a hot tub under the stars, perched on a cliff overlooking the Pacific. Nighttime soaks in the cliffside tub are key perks of stays at historic ⑬ **Pigeon Point Lighthouse**, about 3 miles south of the Pescadero turnoff along Hwy 1. Built in 1872, the lighthouse has a still-active 115ft beacon; the light-keeper's house has been thoughtfully restored as a Certified Bay Area Green hostel.

HIGH ADVENTURE, LOW EMISSIONS

To see the West Coast's wild side, go green all the way. Get on the biodiesel-fueled bus with Green Tortoise (www.greentortoise.com) for adventures along the California Coast; on-board berths, parks admission and meals are included (San Francisco to LA: $249). Amtrak offers routes from Seattle to LA, but the most spectacular stretch of track hugs the coastline from San Luis Obispo to Santa Barbara – and you can bring your bike. Otherwise, you can help keep the west wild by considering your carpool options at www.craigslist.org.

After morning hikes along lighthouse coastal trails past thousand-year-old redwoods, ⑭ **San Francisco** awaits just over an hour's drive north along Hwy 1. Past vertigo-inducing vistas and the coastal suburb of Pacifica, Hwy 1 merges briefly with I-280 before veering west and turning into San Francisco's 19th Ave. Hang a left off 19th onto Judah St, then head west until you hit 45th Ave – just four blocks before the street dead ends into La Playa, which skirts blustery Ocean Beach. On the corner of 45th and Judah you'll spot ⑮ **Outerlands**, where beachcombers and ecohipsters converge for heirloom tomato soup with grilled cheese and organic mimosas chased with locally roasted espresso.

Better make that coffee a double: you've got about a 3½-hour drive ahead. Follow the scenic route from La Playa onto Great Hwy, past Ocean Beach and veering east onto Point Lobos Ave, which merges into Geary Blvd. Take Geary east to Park Presidio Blvd and turn left to head north onto Hwy 1 and across a modern marvel: ⑯ **Golden Gate Bridge**. On foggy San Francisco summer days, the bridge's distinctive deco towers disappear into the clouds, only to magically reappear on the sunny north end of the span.

Follow signs for Hwy 101, which will take you north for 87 miles to the exit for State Rd 128 west. Follow this road for 52 miles, initially winding through the woods, then speeding up as it heads straight through ⑰ **Anderson Valley**. This is Mendocino's wine country, with tasting rooms lining State Rd 128 offering a gauntlet of temptations that range from spicy zinfandels to sparkling whites.

The road bumps into Hwy 1 at the coast, where you'll head north 9 miles to Mendocino, a seaside hamlet of whitewashed 19th-century cottages that's been designated a National Historic Preservation District, with a permanent mellow aided by abundant local medical marijuana crops (prescription required). The historic **18** **Joshua Grindle Inn**, perched atop a knoll, is an easy 10-minute stroll from the beach and downtown restaurants. Built by the town's banker in 1879, this B&B maximizes Mendocino's period charm, with wood-beam ceilings, pot-bellied iron stoves, and afternoon tea in the parlor. Awake to home-baked breakfasts on the gingerbread-trimmed porch, overlooking gardens dotted with orange California poppies. Fuel up for the 3½-hour drive to your next pit stop – maybe longer, if you break for beaches, roadside blackberry-picking (August to October) and California gray whale-watching (November through April).

Follow Hwy 1 northeast to Leggett, where you'll veer north onto redwood-lined Hwy 101. North of Redway, follow signs for Avenue of the Giants, a sun-dappled alternate route north through 32 miles of staggeringly tall trees. Merge back onto 101 north, take Exit 713 into downtown Arcata on Hwy 255, then hang a right onto G St to reach **19** **Renata's Crêpèrie**. Arcata is quaint yet progressive, and so are its organic crepes of choice: loaded with sweet seasonal berries or packed with tangy local goat cheese and artichokes. Follow your bliss with heartwarming doses of Americano or hot chocolate, served in hand-warming bowls.

Warming up is wise before you head north along the windswept coast past Trinidad; the temperature suddenly drops north of Orick under the high forest canopy of **20** **Redwood National and State Parks**. These 70 miles of ancient redwoods were spared from clear-cutting in the 1960s by pioneering environmentalists, and today they're duly honored as a World Heritage site and International Biosphere Reserve. To hike through 325 million years of natural history, turn off Hwy 101 2 miles north of Orick onto Davis Rd and take the Trillium Falls Trail to Fern Canyon, where prehistoric ferns drip from 30ft rock walls.

Four miles further north of Orick off Hwy 101, the 10-mile Newton B Drury Scenic Parkway is a detour into another dimension, where visitors instinctively lower their voices so as not to disturb the contemplative silence of these stately redwoods. Pause for an educational pit stop at Prairie Creek Visitors Center and an easy 100yd walk to the Big Tree – at 304ft high and 21ft across, its name is a massive understatement. Drive cautiously; Roosevelt elk roam the area.

After camping at Redwood National and State Parks pack the car and continue north along Hwy 101. About 60 miles north of the parks you'll cross the border into Oregon, where the coastal scenery just gets wilder. The highway hugs the shoreline, snaking through stands of towering Sitka spruce and coastal parks that protect natural rock bridges, tide pools brimming with sea critters, and forest trails.

About 75 miles north of the state line, you'll hit ㉑ **Cape Blanco State Park**, the second most westerly point in the contiguous US (for trivia buffs, Cape Alava, Washington, is the continental US's westernmost point, and both are further west than California's Cape Mendocino, even though Cape Mendocino *appears* more westerly on most maps). Camp out at Cabo Blanco and allow at least a day to explore the wave-pounded beaches and shady trails in and around the park.

"trails take you through moss-laden old-growth forests to rocky beaches, tide pools and blasting marine geysers."

From Cabo Blanco, head 125 miles north to ㉒ **Cape Perpetua Scenic Area**, where trails take you through moss-laden old-growth forests to rocky beaches, tide pools and blasting marine geysers. The cape itself punches like a rocky fist into a tempestuous sea, and its highest point (reached by road or trail) offers one of the finest views on the entire Oregon coast. Cape Perpetua has a beautiful little campground, but for a comfortable treat drive 3 miles north to the town of Yachats and shack up at the ㉓ **Shamrock Lodgettes**, on the mouth of the Yachats River. The nine petite, rustic cabins are tiny but cozy enough to weather the worst winter storms; and on those rare sunny days they offer stunning views through the trees to the ocean.

Twenty-five miles up Hwy 101 you'll hit the town of Newport, where you'll find the outstanding ㉔ **Oregon Coast Aquarium**. Like wandering through a living kaleidoscope, a stroll through this place is an otherworldly experience. The seals and sea otters are cute as can be and the jellyfish room is a near-psychedelic experience. But what really knocks this place off the charts is the deep-sea exhibit through which you walk, surrounded by a Plexiglas tunnel full of sharks, rays and other fish.

ASK A LOCAL

"Go check out the **Historic 804 Trail**. It starts in Yachats and heads north up the beach at Smelt Sands (State Recreation Site). It's part of the old 804 Hwy (a former foot and wagon path), which ran along the beach to Alsea Bay. People traveled south on the beach until they hit Yachats, where the sand ends and they had the forest to deal with."

Dave Rieseck, Yachats, OR

There's nothing like wandering around an aquarium to whet your appetite for seafood. Head down to the docks and into ㉕ **Local Ocean**, a modern but modest seafood restaurant and market serving the best local seafood in town. From Dungeness crab and razor clams to wild salmon and albacore tuna, everything is caught locally and sustainably. In other words, eat as much as you can.

Come check-in time, shun the staid plaster walls of a hotel room and spend the night in a yurt instead. ㉖ **Beverly Beach State Park**, only 6.5 miles up the coast, has tent and RV sites, but the 21 heated yurts offer the truly quintessential Oregon overnight experience. The beach itself lies a short walk away and is wide, long and fabulous for walks and kite flying.

The following morning, head north along Hwy 101 and, 6.2 miles north of Neskowin (or 38 miles north of Beverly Beach), turn left on Brooten Rd. In Pacific City, swing left on Pacific Ave and right on Cape Kiwanda Dr. This puts you on the spectacular Three Capes Scenic Drive, which hugs the coast and passes three rocky and wildly spectacular capes on its way north. The first cape you'll pass is Cape Kiwanda, complete with state park. About 7 miles north of Cape Kiwanda, swing left on Cape Lookout Rd and in another 4 miles you'll arrive at ㉗ **Cape Lookout State Park,**

DETOUR ▶ No trip along the coast is complete without oysters on the half shell, and you can devour them at the source by visiting nearby **Oregon Oyster Farms** (www.oregonoyster.com). The historic farm lies 8 miles inland from Newport, and the drive along Yaquina Bay Rd to get there is half the fun. To reach the farm from Newport, head east on Hwy 20, turn right on SE John Nye Rd and left on Yaquina Bay Rd.

where you can spend the night in a tent, cabin or yurt. The sandy beach at Cape Lookout is vast, pounded by wind-driven breakers and backed by rocks and coastal forest, giving you the sense that you've truly landed in the middle of nowhere. (The northernmost cape, Cape Meares, is not part of this trip.)

From Cape Lookout, head north along Whiskey Creek Rd and take Hwy 131 to Tillamook, where you'll regain Hwy 101. From Tillamook, it's only about 65 miles to Astoria, but you could spend the entire day doing it, stopping for lunch and a quiet wander at Cannon Beach, or for video arcades, candied popcorn and good, old fashioned, tourist-trap cheesiness at Seaside. Both are favorite getaways for Portlanders on the run from the inland summer heat.

Finally, you'll reach ㉘ **Astoria**, whose historic architecture and incredible location make it one of Oregon's finest coastal towns. Astoria lies at the mouth of the Columbia River on Youngs Bay, itself fed by three rivers, the Lewis and Clark, the Youngs and the Walluski. While you're here be sure to drive up to the Astoria Column (elevation 600ft), which offers magnificent views on a clear day. For eats, head to the ㉙ **Ship Inn**, where you can watch tankers ply the mighty Columbia River while devouring an equally mighty basket of halibut fish and chips. For a good night's sleep (which you'll need for tomorrow's drive), shack up at the elegant ㉚ **Rosebriar Inn B&B**, a converted Georgian mansion from the early 1900s.

The following day, get an early start for the three-hour drive north. This stretch of the journey starts with a big scenic bang as Hwy 101 crosses the Columbia River into Washington over the 4-mile ㉛ **Astoria-Megler Bridge**, the longest continuous truss bridge in North America. Completed in 1966, the bridge marked the final link in Hwy 101 which, from then on, ran unbroken from Mexico to Canada. Once you cross the bridge, however, the scenery alternates between snooze-inducing and moderately pretty until you reach the borders of the trip's penultimate and arguably finest reward: **32 Olympic National Park.**

Occupying 990 sq miles of the Olympic Peninsula, the park is one of the rainiest places on earth and shelters some of North America's greatest expanses of old growth temperate rain forest. The park is so big that you can't feasibly see it without basing yourself at various places. This time, keep it simple by heading to Lake Quinault and checking into the splendid **33 Lochaerie Resort,** on the northern shore. A marvelous alternative to the far more famous Lake Quinault Lodge, Lochaerie Resort is a quiet little place with wonderfully cozy cabins warmed by fireplaces and the lingering happiness of past guests. You could easily while away three days here, hiking, canoeing, bird-watching, fishing, clamming or simply wandering the shores of beautiful Lake Quinault. **34 Ruby Beach,** which lies 40 miles northwest of Lake Quinault, makes a great day trip from the resort and is one of the most spectacular beaches along this forbiddingly rocky stretch of the coast.

> **DETOUR**
>
> To really appreciate just how rainy this place is and to experience how wildly that rain can make stuff grow, head to the Tolkeinesque depths of the **Hoh Rainforest**. The dense, moss-covered rain forest is reached via Upper Hoh Rd, which leaves Hwy 101 about 14 miles northeast of Ruby Beach. From Lochaerie Resort, it's about a two-hour trip to the **Hoh River Visitor Center**, where you'll find trailheads into the forest.

From Lake Quinault, follow Hwy 101 as it encircles the peninsula, passing through mystical forest scenery and turnoffs that lead through the grayness to remote Native American outposts and windswept beaches. Finally, 170 miles (about 4½ hours) from Lake Quinault you'll reach **35 Port Townsend,** the final stop on the trip. Set on the northwestern extreme of the Olympic Peninsula, Port Townsend sits at the convergence of Puget Sound and the Strait of Juan de Fuca, directly across from Victoria, British Columbia. It's a marvelous place to close the trip, with splendid Victorian architecture, excellent restaurants and some of the region's very best sea kayaking. Although you'll find plenty of hotels in town, opt instead for a room in one of the former officer housing units of **36 Fort Worden State Park.** (Sharp-eyed film buffs will recognize the setting as the backdrop for the movie *An Officer and a Gentleman.*) The former US Army fortification was built in the late 1890s to protect the strategically important Puget Sound area from outside attack, but is now a lovely state park with beaches, short trails and a thick dose of military history. The perfect place to close the trip is at the park's North Beach, where you might spot a bald eagle swooping down from a treetop snatching a meal from the sea otters just offshore.

Alison Bing & Danny Palmerlee

TRIP INFORMATION

GETTING THERE
Start in San Diego, which hugs the California coast just north of the US–Mexico border.

DO

Año Nuevo State Reserve
Dune hikes reach overlooks above Loser's Beach, where elephant seals bellyflop between dates. ☎ 650-879-2025; www.parks.ca.gov; Hwy 1, CA; parking $10, guided walk $7; 🕒 8:30am-3:30pm Apr-Aug, 8:30am-3pm Sep-Nov, guided walk only Dec-Mar

Cape Blanco State Park
Beach access and great views, plus showers and flush toilets; 4 miles north of Brookings. ☎ 541-332-6774, 800-452-5687; www.oregonstateparks.org; Hwy 101, OR; day use per vehicle $5, tents & RV sites/cabins $16/35; 🚻 ♿

Cape Lookout State Park
Isolated park with vast beach and excellent campgrounds. ☎ 503-842-4981; www.oregonstateparks.org; 13000 Whiskey Creek Rd, Tillamook, OR; day-use $5, campsites $5-20; 🚻 ♿

Cape Perpetua Scenic Area
Rich tide-pool life, rock formations, trails, old-growth forest, views and more. Hwy 101, Yachats, OR; day-use sites $5; 🕒 year-round, campground summer only; 🚻

Fort Worden State Park
Busy state park with hiking and biking trails, excellent beaches, kayak and bike rentals, yoga studio, bleak campground and comfy lodging. ☎ 360-344-4431; www.parks.wa.gov; Port Townsend, WA; admission free; 🕒 year-round; 🚻 ♿

Julia Pfeiffer Burns State Park
Rainbows, waterfalls and whales: nature shows off shamelessly along 0.7-mile McWay Falls Overlook Trail. ☎ 831-667-2315; www.parks.ca.gov; 47225 Hwy 1, Big Sur, CA; day use $10; 🕒 ½hr before sunrise-½hr before sunset; 🚻

Monterey Bay Aquarium
The most impressive sea life you'll see without getting soaked. ☎ 831-648-4800; www.montereybayaquarium.org; 886 Cannery Row, Monterey, CA; adult/student & senior/3-12yr/under 3yr $29.95/$27.95/17.95/free; 🕒 10am-6pm, extended summer hrs; 🚻

Olympic National Park
Home to numerous campgrounds and lodges, beaches, rain forest and high mountain hiking. ☎ 360-565-3130, toll-free 800-833-6388; Olympic Peninsula, WA; admission per vehicle $15; 🕒 year-round; 🚻 ♿

Oregon Coast Aquarium
Exceptional aquarium with seals, sea otters, deep-sea exhibit and jellyfish room. ☎ 541-867-3474; www.aquarium.org; 2820 SE Ferry Slip Rd, Newport, OR; adult/3-12yr/13-17yr/senior $15/9.50/12/13; 🕒 9am-6pm; 🚻

Redwood National and State Parks
Sunlight turns green in this forest primeval, with 2000-year old redwoods and fern-lined canyons. ☎ 707-465-7354 Prairie Creek Visitors Center; www.nps.gov/redw; Newton B Drury Scenic Pkwy, CA; admission free; 🕒 9am-5pm

EAT

Duarte's Tavern
Fresh-caught fish, housemade soups and flaky pies served in a Wild West saloon since 1894. ☎ 650-879-0464; www.duartestavern.com; 202 Stage Rd, Pescadero, CA; mains $12-30; 🕒 7am-9pm

Local Ocean
Seafood restaurant and market with locally caught fish served in sandwiches, tacos and delicious main courses. ☎ 541-574-7959; www.localocean.net; 213 SE Bay Blvd, Newport, OR; sandwiches $7-14, mains $11-25; 🕒 11am-8pm; 🚻

Nepenthe
Sublime sunsets and serviceable sandwiches at Henry Miller's favorite cliffside getaway. ☎ 831-667-2345; www.nepenthebigsur.com; Hwy 1, Big Sur, CA; mains $12.50-36.50; 🕒 9am-10pm

Outerlands

Coastal chills vanish with organic comfort food served on a driftwood-paneled lunch counter. ☎ 415-661-6140; http://outerlandssf.blogspot.com; 4001 Judah St, San Francisco, CA; small plates $6-10; ⏰ 11am-3pm & 6-10pm Tue-Sat, 10am-2:30pm Sun

Renata's Crèpérie

Abundant salads, serious espresso and the Righteous Babe: berries and Nutella atop organic crepes. ☎ 707-825-8783; 1030 G St, Arcata, CA; crepes $6-9; ⏰ 8am-3pm & 5-9pm Fri & Sat, 8am-3pm Wed, Thu & Sun

Ship Inn

Modest but comfy riverside restaurant famous for its fish and chips and tremendous views of the Columbia River. ☎ 503-325-0033; 1 2nd St, Astoria, OR; mains $9-25; ⏰ 11:30am-9:30pm; ♿

Taco Loco

So SoCal: chi-chi seafood quesadillas with blue corn–flour tortillas, 15oz starlet smoothies, and surfer-favorite hemp brownies. ☎ 949-497-1635; www.tacoloco.net; 640 S Coast Hwy, Laguna Beach, CA; dishes $3-11; ⏰ 11am-midnight Sun-Thu, 11am-2am Fri & Sat

SLEEP

Beverly Beach State Park

Large state campground with tents and heated yurts. ☎ 877-444-6777; www.oregonstateparks.org; Hwy 101, OR; tents $13-21, RVs $18-26, yurt $36-41; ⏰ year-round; ♿ 🐾

Joshua Grindle Inn

Unwind 1879-style by the main house fireplaces, or retreat to hideaways in the water tower and saltbox cottage. ☎ 707-937-4143; www.joshgrin.com; 44800 Little Lake Rd, Mendocino, CA; incl breakfast s $119-219, d $165-285

Lochaerie Resort

The six shingled cabins above Lake Quinault are warmed by wood-burning stoves. ☎ 360-288-2215; www.lochaerie.com; 638 North Shore Rd, Olympic National Park, WA; cabins $120-150; ♿

Pigeon Point Lighthouse

Reserve ahead at this certified green lighthouse-keepers' post, with wi-fi and a hot tub. ☎ 650-879-0633; www.norcalhostels.org/pigeon; 210 Pigeon Point Road, Pescadero, CA; dm $25, private rooms $55-100; ⏰ 7:30am-10:30pm

Rosebriar Inn B&B

Elegant 12-room inn with small but comfy rooms, a spacious "carriage house" and a "captain's suite" with kitchenette and awesome views. ☎ 800-487-0224; www.rosebriar.net; 636 14th St, Astoria, OR; r $90-192

Shamrock Lodgettes

Modest but supremely cozy log cabins, "spa" cabins and hotel-style rooms with ocean views. ☎ 541-547-3312; www.shamrocklodgettes.com; 105 Hwy 101, Yachats, OR; r $69-129, cabin $99-189; ♿

Treebones

Spoon inside yurts, camp cliffside or burrow into a "human nest." Rates include self-serve breakfasts. ☎ 877-424-4787; http://treebonesresort.com; 71895 Hwy 1, Big Sur, CA; d incl breakfast $155-245, quad incl breakfast $255, d campsite $65-95

USEFUL WEBSITES

www.hikinginbigsur.com
www.visittheoregoncoast.com

LINK YOUR TRIP

www.lonelyplanet.com/trip-planner

TRIP
83 48 Hours in Los Angeles p581
87 48 Hours in San Francisco p603
92 48 Hours in Seattle p633

NEW YORK, WASHINGTON DC & THE MID-ATLANTIC TRIPS

Along the East Coast, sandwiched between the picturesque hamlets of New England and the gracious plantations of the South, you'll find the Northeast Corridor, which stretches from Washington DC to Boston and includes America's one-and-only truly world-class city: New York. But there is so much more to be discovered in this remarkably beautiful and fascinating area that even locals will be surprised.

After you've spent 48 unforgettable hours in Manhattan, you might want to head upstate to explore the Adirondacks or south to discover the fresh crabs of Maryland and the Du-Pont elegance of dollhouse Delaware. Further south there's the marvelous old-time country music scene that's sprung up in and around the Appalachians along western Virginia's "Crooked Road."

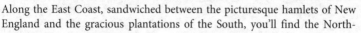 **PLAYLIST** The iconic East Coast has had more than a few songs written in celebration of its incomparable style. Here's a handful to get you started as you cruise the countryside.

- "Take the A Train," Ella Fitzgerald and the Duke Ellington Orchestra
- "Autumn in New York," Frank Sinatra
- "Summer In the City," The Lovin' Spoonful
- "My Old School," Steely Dan
- "Atlantic City," Bruce Springsteen
- "Allentown," Billy Joel
- "Take Me Home, Country Roads," John Denver
- "Good Morning, Baltimore," Original Broadway Cast of *Hairspray*

History buffs will be awed by Civil War battlefields while for city folk and "coastal elites" there's great fun to be had touring the renowned institutions of higher learning, from the Ivy League to William & Mary – or eating your way across New Jersey at its all-night diners. No matter where you find yourself it's guaranteed you will find something unexpected and delightful.

NEW YORK, WASHINGTON DC & THE MID-ATLANTIC

48 Hours in Manhattan

WHY GO Bold and brash New York is a city in flux, moving from one extreme to another in a few short blocks. In 48 hours get a feel for the unique pockets of the city, and do it like a local: on the run, riding the subways, immersed in Manhattan's electric diversity and energy.

TIME
2 days

BEST TIME TO GO
Mar – Dec

START
Lower
Manhattan

END
Little Korea

Start your morning with a jolt in ❶ Lower Manhattan, where thousands of hard-charging finance types come streaming into Wall St every day, determined to make their millions. Dozens of major subway and bus lines converge here, along with the Staten Island and New Jersey ferries. Harried businesspeople with swinging briefcases will bump you along as the moribund streets come alive. Take in the morning rush over a foamy cappuccino at ❷ Financier Patisserie, a Parisian-style bakery hidden inside the historic triangle at Pearl and Mill Lane, near Hanover Sq.

This is the heart of Old New York, where George Washington once slept, ate and worshiped – and was sworn in as the nation's first president. The tiny byways below Wall St are crooked and cobbled, small pathways through a dizzying maze of soaring skyscrapers that eventually lead you to the main thoroughfare of Broadway.

North on Broadway you'll pass two more remnants of pre-Revolutionary New York, ❸ Trinity Church and ❹ St Paul's Chapel, where Washington had his family pew; ahead is the teeming chaos of Chinatown.

Merchants line busy ❺ Canal St, pushing their fake Rolex watches and Louis Vuitton on jostling passersby. Follow the foot traffic east as Canal turns slightly uphill, turning north onto Elizabeth St. The din and excitement of Chinatown will gradually fade as you move into artsy ❻ Nolita, a tiny quadrant of streets north of Little Italy. Martin

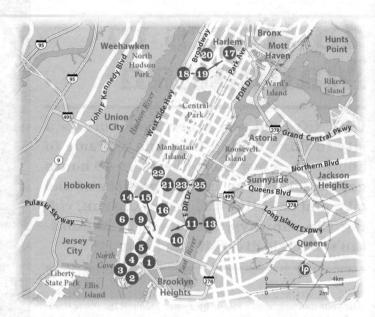

Scorsese grew up on these not-so-mean streets, serving as an altar boy at the ornate marble church on the corner of Prince and Mott Sts. Long before the massive Catholic church was built in midtown, this Irish-Italian structure – the original **7** **St Patrick's Cathedral** – was the seat of the Catholic diocese.

> "It used to be the flophouse for bums and prostitutes but now it's home to the avant-garde..."

Following Prince St to the east brings you to the Bowery, one of New York's most infamous streets. It used to be the flophouse for bums and prostitutes – you'll see the signs of wear and tear in pockmarked graffitied buildings next to brand-new condos – but now it's home to the avant-garde **8** **New Museum of Contemporary Art**. Constructed out of seven white boxes stacked unevenly atop each other, the light-filled museum constantly rotates exhibits, bringing emerging artists and established names and mixing them together for a cutting-edge effect.

The main byway of Nolita, leafy, residential Elizabeth St, is a polyglot of languages and cultures, and has one ancient Italian butcher shop Robert De Niro fans will recognize right away. You'll get a taste of the diversity if you stop for lunch at **9** **Café Colonial**, a French-Brazilian fusion joint with a big, tropical mural on the outside wall and the classic Parisian tin ceiling inside.

Across Houston St and heading east, you are walking the border between the funky Lower East Side on your right and the iconic East Village on your left. When you come across Ave C, head north, into what used to be called ❿ Alphabet City. Comprising Aves A, B, C and D, these four streets entered pop culture lore as the backdrop to the Broadway smash, *Rent*, the story of young creative types struggling to make art (and the rent) in pre-gentrification New York. This was formerly a drug ghetto full of tenement squats but there are new signs of life along these prettied-up avenues, like the bluesy bar ⓫ Louis 649, on the 1st floor of a restored townhouse, with hardwood floors, a resident pit bull and a louche, speakeasy feel. The ⓬ 6th & B community garden is a green space that the city let founder in the 1990s, but which was reclaimed by local residents who turned it into the glowing, fragrant urban oasis it is now. It's fronted by a wrought-iron gate with a half-dozen handprints in it – signifying the "hands on" attitude of the garden keepers – and inside has fruit trees, flowering shrubs, small vegetable plots and a towering, 37ft sculpture of recycled "street treasures" found around the city.

Ave B also leads into ⓭ Tompkins Square Park, the center of '60s rebellion where Jimi Hendrix once gave an outdoor concert and birth-control advocate Margaret Sanger roiled crowds with fiery feminist rhetoric in the 1900s. Now the park's known more for its graceful weeping willows, park benches where neighborhood elders sit, and strong community vibe.

St Marks Pl W passes tattoo parlors and the few remaining punk-rock record stores to 4th St. South along Second Ave, to 2nd St, and one block east, take note of the name – you're on Joey Ramone Pl, named after the legendary rocker from The Ramones.

At the intersection of Bowery and Bleecker, you can stop for the night at the ⓮ Bowery Hotel, where red-tasseled gold keys unlock doors leading to Moroccan-inspired rooms with king-size beds, ornate gold fixtures, swirling ceiling fans and floor-to-ceiling windows. For a bite, slip into the rustic ⓯ Gemma, an Italian trattoria with rough-edged wooden tables and wicker baskets hanging from wide brown beams in the ceiling.

Wake up to a brisk walk uptown to ⓰ Union Square, a buzzing public meeting place marked by a statue of Gandhi on the southeast corner, and an open-air greenmarket most mornings. Then it's onto the subway and up to the historic neighborhood of Harlem for some shopping along 125th St. If you exit the subway at Lexington Ave and 125th St you can work your way west along the busy commercial street, flanked by big-name chain stores and street vendors selling incense, shea butter and perfumes imported from Africa.

South down Lenox Ave you'll pass the famous ⑰ **Lenox Lounge** on your left – James Baldwin, Malcolm X and Fidel Castro are just a few of the celebrated patrons who've tossed back a few while listening to jazz in the back room. Lenox Ave is a wide, breezy boulevard flanked by glorious brownstones and several churches, most of which have fallen on hard times. At the intersection of 116th, at the ⑱ **Malcolm Shabazz Market**, African merchants sell dashikis and wooden carvings. Across Lenox to the west is ⑲ **Amy Ruth's**, the reigning queen of soul food, and a top spot for lunch. Amy Ruth's most famous culinary contribution is fried chicken on waffles (with syrup); it goes perfectly with the small restaurant's Southern charm and checkerboard floors and tablecloths.

You can continue exploring Harlem by heading west to Amsterdam Ave, then south into Morningside Heights, a quiet neighborhood full of Spanish families and Columbia students. The tall Byzantine arches of the ⑳ **Cathedral of St John the Divine** rise above the squat apartment buildings, inviting you to step inside the Romanesque-style granite and limestone structure. It's a century old, but still not complete – blame those pesky spires, almost impossible to get up. Inside you'll find several rose-colored stained-glass windows and the little-visited Poets Corner, a section of wall dedicated to American writers including Robert Frost, Walt Whitman and Edna St Vincent Millay.

MOBY'S NYC

He's a musician, DJ, producer, activist, vegan – and New Yorker. Moby takes us on tour of his favorite hometown haunts.

Tompkins Square Park is a tiny, sun-drenched park that is a microcosm of New York's diversity. "You'll see punk rockers sleeping off their hangovers, hippies playing guitar, Russian immigrants playing chess, Puerto Rican guys on percussion, corporate lawyers pushing $800 strollers," says Moby of his favorite spot to hang out and listen to his iPod. Monday nights, **Arlene's Grocery**, a dive bar near Moby's Lower East Side home, showcases rock 'n' roll karaoke. "I'm a very provincial person," says Moby, who was drafted to play guitar in the karaoke band. "The appeal of a place is largely determined by its distance from my apartment." As such, Moby's rock side project The Little Deaths made its debut at Arlene's. When working on music at 3am, Moby often heads to the oldest part of **Chinatown** (Mott St, south of Canal St) and literally loses himself in his city. "Most of the city is built on a grid system, so this is one of the only places you can do that. All the signs are in Cantonese or Mandarin and the streets are narrow and winding…I'll listen to my headphones, walk around and just get totally lost."

Unpredictability is the secret weapon of the **Slipper Room**, a delectably gaudy East Village cabaret. "You never know what you're going to get there, it might be some terrible band or a bizarre, fantastic burlesque show," says Moby, who is routinely dragged on stage to perform. "Get a couple of drinks in me and I'm shameless."

Simona Rabinovitch

At 96th St you can hop back on the subway and skip down to **㉑ Little Korea**, conveniently next to **㉒ Macy's** department store, in case you had a hankering to ride its old, wooden escalators. Little Korea is centered on 32nd St between Fifth Ave and Broadway, and its noisy, frantic activity goes 24-7. While you walk the street, watching fast-moving chefs preparing the day's meals in open windows, stop at **㉓ Hun Gallery**, a light-filled 2nd-floor space that fills its 2000 sq ft with delicate water paintings, eclectic installations and all manner of modern art. Nearby is the small **㉔ Lee Young Hee Korea Museum**, displaying a collection of Korean clothing, with special emphasis on the brightly colored silks of the ceremonial *hanbok*.

There's no leaving Little Korea without indulging in the preferred local pastime: it's time to loosen up the pipes at **㉕ Grammy Karaoke**. On the floor above Wonjo, itself a crowded and popular 24-hour Korean BBQ spot, Grammy has private rooms for the vocally challenged and liquor readily available to get the party started. If you don't want to sing but like to watch, sit in the main room where the action is – in Korean, of course.

An all-night songfest is a fitting end to a whirlwind visit to the city that never sleeps – an old cliché that's certainly true in K-town.
Ginger Adams Otis

TRIP INFORMATION

GETTING THERE
Regional train, bus and ferry lines all feed into Manhattan, as does the subway.

DO

Cathedral of St John the Divine
Highlights: the Great Rose Window and Great Organ. ☎ 212-316-7540; www.stjohndivine.org; Amsterdam Ave at 112th St; admission free; ⏱ 7am-6pm Mon-Sat, 7am-7pm Sun

Hun Gallery
More than 2000 sq ft of light-filled space showcasing modern art and more. ☎ 212-594-1312; www.hungallery.org; 12 W 32nd St; admission free; ⏱ 11am-6pm Tue-Sat

Lee Young Hee Korea Museum
Brightly colored ceremonial silk *hanboks* and other traditional garb are on display. ☎ 212-560-0722; www.lyhkm.org; 2 W 32nd St; admission free; ⏱ 11am-6pm Mon-Sat

Macy's
An old-fashioned department store stocked with modern designs. ☎ 212-695-4400; www.macys.com; 151 W 34th St; ⏱ 10am-9:30pm Mon-Sat, 11am-8:30pm Sun

New Museum of Contemporary Art
The city's sole museum for contemporary art. ☎ 212-219-1222; www.newmuseum.org; 235 Bowery St; admission $12; ⏱ noon-6pm Wed, Sat & Sun, to 9pm Thu & Fri

St Paul's Chapel
George Washington worshiped here, as did hundreds after 9/11. ☎ 212-233-4164; www.saintpaulschapel.org; 209 Broadway at Fulton St; ⏱ 10am-6pm

EAT

Amy Ruth's
Classic soul food. ☎ 212-280-8779; www.amyruthsharlem.com; 113 W 116th St; mains $12-18; ⏱ open daily, hours vary

Café Colonial
Green palms painted on the wall and big wooden tables make this café fresh and fun. ☎ 212-274-0044; www.cafecolonialny.com; 73 W Houston St; mains $10-28; ⏱ 11am-10pm; ♿

Financier Patisserie
A bit of the West Bank on Wall St. ☎ 212-344-5600; www.financierpastries.com; 62 Stone St; mains $4-12; ⏱ 7am-8pm Mon-Fri, 8:30am-6pm Sat; ♿

Gemma
A lovely trattoria with late-night hours, serving seafood, pasta and antipasto. ☎ 212-505-9100; www.theboweryhotel.com; 335 Bowery; mains $15-39; ⏱ 11am-midnight

DRINK

Grammy Karaoke
Take the tiny elevator up to this Korean karaoke hideaway that never closes. ☎ 212-629-7171; 23 W 32nd St; ⏱ 2pm-6am

Lenox Lounge
The red facade with silver lettering is an iconic image in Harlem, and the back-room jazz worth the $15 cover. ☎ 212-427-0253; www.lenoxlounge.com; 288 Lenox Ave; ⏱ noon-3:30am

Louis 649
No cover to see the jazz, but the musicians expect tips at this couch-filled, cream-walled hangout. ☎ 212-673-1190; www.louis649.com; 649 E 9th St; ⏱ 6pm-4am

SLEEP

Bowery Hotel
Done up like a sultan's modern palace, the Bowery attracts celebrity crowds. ☎ 212-505-9100; www.theboweryhotel.com; 335 Bowery; r $550

USEFUL WEBSITES
www.nyc.gov
www.nycvisit.com
www.lonelyplanet.com/trip-planner

LINK YOUR TRIP

East Coast Ivory Towers

WHY GO The hallowed halls of higher ed are among America's most famous institutions. Journey from Williamsburg to New York to peer behind the ivy-covered walls at some of the East Coast's big guns, and imagine life as a student or professor. You might just enroll all over again.

TIME
4 – 5 days

DISTANCE
380 miles

BEST TIME TO GO
Year-round

START
Williamsburg, VA

END
New York, NY

The history of colleges in this country goes back a long way, since well before the colonies became the United States. Let's start as close to the very beginning as possible at the **1** College of William & Mary, in Williamsburg. Only Harvard has seniority over this classic Virginia college which was founded in 1693 with a grant from King William III and his wife, Queen Mary II.

Visitors will be primarily interested in the **2** William & Mary Historic Campus. The Sir Christopher Wren Building is the oldest school building in continuous use in the USA. It was completed in 1699 and was restored, along with the other historic buildings on campus, by John D Rockefeller, Jr when he was also busy buying up and preserving Colonial Williamsburg. The Wren Building's graceful design, with large brick archways, will fascinate. Originally, the entire college was contained within this building. Thomas Jefferson was in residence when he matriculated through William & Mary in 1760. Sit down on the lawn and imagine yourself as a young scholar in a tricorner hat drinking ale. Afterwards, head to the romantic **3** Crim Dell and its ornate wooden bridge spanning this pond on the heavily forested campus.

Williamsburg has a variety of eating and sleeping options, many of which are located in and around Merchants Sq. Here you can shop for little trinkets, visit the large Barnes & Noble, or pick up some seersucker shorts. If you're planning to spend the night in Williamsburg, you should make reservations at the **4** Fife and Drum Inn, a B&B

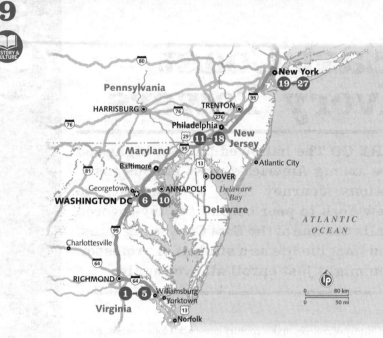

right in the square. From there you'll be able to hear real fifes and drums as the regiments march through nearby historic Williamsburg. You might choose the William and Mary room, which looks out onto the college's Sorority Court. This sunny room has a four-poster bed, a hand-painted floor, and is decorated with a picture of the Wren Building.

DETOUR Want to mix it up with the kids? Head to nearby Yorktown and stop in at the **Yorktown Pub** (☎ 757-886-9964) on Water St. It's popular with students and locals for its inexpensive, tasty food and the relaxed, friendly atmosphere. Hop onto a stool by the front windows and enjoy the view of Yorktown Beach (site of a decisive victory against the British in 1781 that led to the end of the Revolutionary War). Try the St George Golden Ale on tap.

To dine, just step out into the square and you'll find many remarkably good options. The ❺ **Blue Talon Bistro** is an appealing choice. Inside the quaint brick building you'll find a menu with hearty French fare like chicken and mushroom crepes, or salad nicoise. Order the butcher's tasting-board to start, with the chef's selection of cured meats, sausages and pâtés. Sip a nice Bordeaux while, through the large paned windows, you watch kids in rented period costumes trailing behind their parents and fiddling with wooden guns or paper fans.

Continuing up the coast, it's time to get all Northeast corridor about things and head to Washington DC. Specifically, head to ❻ **Georgetown University**. For all intents and purposes, Georgetown is part of DC, but it maintains a unique identity. Besides the university, the area is known for its high-end shops and cafés, as well as for being chronically difficult to park in. Georgetown is an urban campus in many ways, and is divided into three main sections. Hulking **7** **Healy Hall**, a Flemish Romanesque building, is an imposing but beautiful National Historic Landmark. Inside you can visit the cast-iron Riggs Library or the grand Gaston Hall auditorium. The Healy clock tower stands grimly over the area like a disapproving headmaster.

One of the snazziest places to sit down for a meal is the **8** **Café Milano**. This beautiful restaurant has an impressive roster of guests, as even Pope Benedict XVI has been in to sample the homemade pasta. Don't be surprised to see politicos chomping ravioli and gulping wine while they work out some trade deal with lobbyists. The ceilings are covered in murals and the restaurant's mood is fairly casual considering its spectacular food. As a bonus, the restaurant is just down the street from the famous **9** **"Exorcist" Steps**, where Father Karras tumbles to his death after being tossed out the window by the possessed Regan. The character of Father Karras is a priest at Georgetown University.

DETOUR Don't miss a trip to Annapolis for a look at the **United States Naval Academy** (www.navyonline.com). The highlight of any trip to "the Yard" is watching the plebes march in lockstep around Bancroft Hall. Security is tight though so you'll need a photo ID to get on campus. Book a tour through the Armel-Leftwich Visitor Center (☎ 410-293-8687).

Unfortunately, Georgetown doesn't have a ton of great options for spending the night; best to head to the Northwest (NW) section of DC proper and check into the **10** **Hotel Palomar**. This boutique hotel has a trendy restaurant, big spacious rooms with gorgeous bathrooms, and decor with a sort of urban jungle flair – lots of zebra-skin throws and snakeskin-esque carpeting. It's also within walking distance of DuPont Circle and lots of bars.

Moving on north up the corridor, you'll pass through Maryland, Delaware and New Jersey on the way to our next stop. The **11** **University of Pennsylvania**, or UPenn, was founded by Benjamin Franklin. Ever a student himself, in 1749 he decided young men needed an academy of higher learning and, in 1755, Franklin's school became the College of Philadelphia, the first secular university in British North America. Then in 1779, after the American Revolution, the school was renamed and reborn as the University of the State of Pennsylvania.

The campus is as Ivy League gorgeous its genesis suggests. The expansive **12** **Perelman Quad** is studded with modern art (like the classic 1960s "Love" logo) and anchored by several architectural jewels. The monumental **13** **College Hall**, made of green stone and with a gray-slate roof, became forever famous when cartoonist Charles Addams used it as the model for the Addams Family mansion. In turn, the college honored Addams (who studied at UPenn) by naming the ⑭ **Fine Arts Building** after him and placing a silhouette of Addams' kooky, creepy family out front. By all means, enter the Fine Arts Building, with its stunning interior lead-glass aphorisms and ornate balconies.

UPenn's ⑮ **Museum of Archaeology and Anthropology** deserves several hours; the rambling 115-year-old structure is as dramatic as the antiquities it contains. In particular, the ancient China and Egyptian collections – including enormous grinning dragons and numerous dehydrated mummies in various stages of undress – are memorably awesome. Off campus, jump to the other end of the human timeline with a visit to the dazzling ⑯ **Institute of Contemporary Art**, which has an urbanely, artfully futuristic vision.

ASK A LOCAL

"Penn really is beautiful; I especially love walking along Locust Walk. I never get the feeling there are significant town/gown tensions. It has everything you would expect of a major research university – excellent library (the rare-books collection is outstanding), great speakers, performing arts venues. And then there are gems like the Shakespeare Garden outside the Fine Arts Library. For travelers, it's a must-see!"

Jen Dickman, Morristown, NJ

Sansom St is the prime restaurant corridor, and it's hard to go wrong with any of the eateries here. For more futurama, visit ⑰ **Pod**, which is a Steven Starr "theme" restaurant that conjures a neo-Tokyo *Blade Runner* vibe, with cellophane-red booths, molded white plastic chairs and tables, concrete floor and servers in gun-metal gray. Oh, and the sushi and Japanese meals are excellent, too. If you're staying the night in Philadelphia, try the adjacent, perfectly situated ⑱ **Inn at Penn**, where the stylish wood furnishings evoke a Craftsman feel.

"the ancient collections – including enormous grinning dragons and dehydrated mummies in various stages of undress – are memorably awesome."

A couple of hour's drive north, there's a place called New York and it has enough universities to rival Boston for the college-town crown. But the roost is ruled by two dueling divas, one from uptown and the other downtown: ⑲ **Columbia University** and ⑳ **New York University**. Only one of them is Ivy League (Columbia, if you didn't know) and that forever rains on NYU's parades. To its constant chagrin, no matter how many Olsen twins enroll, NYU will never have the same golden luster as fancy-schmancy Columbia. But both are pretty cool schools, all things considered.

Columbia is another of the colonial colleges (founded in 1754 as King's College) and counts both presidents Roosevelt among its alumni. The central campus, in Morningside Heights (Upper Manhattan, near Harlem), can be viewed by strolling ㉑ **Campus Walk**, a public path that cuts between Broadway and Amsterdam through the quad. From here you can admire the ornate beaux arts–style surrounds, designed by the legendary architecture firm McKim, Mead and White in the late 19th century. **22** **Low Memorial Library**, with domed roof and span of columns, is the centerpiece.

Downtown in Greenwich Village, you can find the urban campus of New York University. It has no defined quad, but is centered on **23** **Washington Square Park**, with its famous arch that you've seen in every rerun of *Friends*. Founded later than the other universities, in 1831, NYU is known for its art, business and law schools. NYU (masquerading as UNY) is also where Keri Russell as "Felicity" matriculated. Walk down West 4th St and admire the brick **24** **NYU School of Law** where JFK Jr got his degree. Further east on 4th St is **25** **Bobst Library**, a severe orangey-red brutalist cube of a building, designed by Phillip Johnson, which houses one of New York's largest libraries.

If you're near NYU, unpack your bag at the basic but comfortable **26** **Washington Square Hotel**. From here you'll easily be able to go carousing up and down Bleecker St with the NYUers into the wee hours. And if the next morning's hangover isn't enough to convince you to hightail it home, then drop by the **27** **NYU Office of Admissions** right down the street – surely they'd be happy to hand you an application. Got your transcripts ready?

David Ozanich

> **ASK A LOCAL**
>
> "Unlike a lot of places, **Souen** (☎ 212-627-7150; 28 East 13th St) is more than a crowded co-ed hangout. The food is macrobiotic, so it's all unrefined, unprocessed, and seasonal, but I swear it tastes great. The decor is subdued, the music quiet enough to carry on a conversation. Come for the kuzu stew and stay for the New York tofu cheesecake and homemade soy ice cream!"
>
> *Liz Ureneck, NYU, New York*

TRIP INFORMATION

GETTING THERE
Williamsburg is 50 miles east of Richmond via the I-64.

DO

College of William & Mary
Tours leave from the Office of Undergraduate Admissions. ☎ 757-221-4423; www.wm.edu; 116 Jamestown Rd, Williamsburg, VA; ⊗ tours 10am & 2:30pm daily

Columbia University
The visitors center is in Room 213 of Low Library. ☎ 212-854-4900; www.columbia.edu; 116th St & Broadway, New York, NY; ⊗ tour 1pm daily

Georgetown University
Book an official campus tour through the office of admissions. ☎ 202-687-3600; www.georgetown.edu; 37th St at O St, NW, Washington DC; ⊗ tour hours vary

Institute of Contemporary Art
ICA honors icons like Ant Farm and R Crumb and introduces artists of tomorrow. ☎ 215-898-7108; www.icaphila.org; 118 S 36th St, Philadelphia, PA; admission free; ⊗ noon-8pm Wed-Fri, 11am-5pm Sat & Sun; ♿

Museum of Archaeology and Anthropology
Exhibits include the Americas, Southwest Native Americans, and Native Alaskans. ☎ 215-898-4001; www.museum.upenn.edu; 3260 South St, Philadelphia, PA; adult/child $8/5; ⊗ 10am-4:30pm Tue-Sat, 1-5pm Sun; ♿

New York University
The ultimate urban campus. ☎ 212-998-7200; www.nyu.edu; 50 W 4th St, New York, NY; ⊗ tour hours vary

University of Pennsylvania
No reservations necessary for the one-hour student-led campus tours. ☎ 215-898-7507; www.upenn.edu; Walnut St btwn 34th & 38th Sts, Philadelphia, PA; ⊗ tours 2pm weekdays & noon on fall weekends; ♿

EAT

Blue Talon Bistro
Quaint French restaurant in Merchants Sq, near William & Mary. ☎ 757-476-2583; www.bluetalonbistro.com; 420 Prince George St, Williamsburg, VA; mains $17-28; ⊗ 8am-9pm

Café Milano
Super-chic Italian restaurant where even the pope has dined. Holy Roller! ☎ 202-333-6183; 3251 Prospect St, Georgetown, Washington DC; mains $17-26; ⊗ 11:30am-11pm

Pod
All we'll say is make sure to visit the restroom, and if you want a "pod," make reservations. ☎ 215-387-1803; www.podrestaurant.com; 3636 Sansom St, Philadephia, PA; mains $10-16; ⊗ 11:30am-11pm Mon-Thu, 11:30am-midnight Fri, 5pm-midnight Sat, 5-10pm Sun; ♿

SLEEP

Fife and Drum Inn
Charming B&B in Merchants Sq. ☎ 888-838-1783; www.fifeanddruminn.com; 441 Prince George St, Williamsburg, VA; r $119-325

Hotel Palomar
Boutique hotel near fancy Embassy Row. ☎ 202-448-1800; www.hotelpalomar-dc.com; 2121 P St NW, Washington DC; r $125-500

Inn at Penn
Families should ask about "Bounce Back" packages, which include breakfast. ☎ 215-222-0200; www.theinnatpenn.com; 3600 Sansom St, Philadelphia, PA; r $209-450; ♿

Washington Square Hotel
Cute little hotel near Washington Sq. ☎ 212-777-9515; www.wshotel.com; 103 Waverly Pl, New York, NY; r $200-450

LINK YOUR TRIP
www.lonelyplanet.com/trip-planner

New Jersey Diners: Open 24 Hours

WHY GO What makes a diner? Is it the hours, the neon, the counter, the menu? Is it the jukebox, the clientele? New Jersey and its diners are inextricably linked; to know one is to know the other. On this trip, then, we seek the existential truth of this 3am-coffee-and-cheesecake conundrum.

New Jersey has over 600 diners, more than any other state, so we'll start by restricting ourselves to the boomerang of urbanized northeast Jersey. Locals, save your howls of indignation: we know this leaves out all the great diners elsewhere, but whatta ya gonna do? You really want them all?

Let's begin with a burger. Specifically, a White Mana. Diner scholarship generally acknowledges that the oldest diner in New Jersey is Max's Grill, a 1927 shingle-roofed, maroon O'Mahoney on Harrison Ave (at Manor St) in Harrison. Sadly, Max's Grill is closed, perhaps forever; though the cream-colored lettering announces "Ladies Invited," the grill is quiet.

The Jersey City ❶ White Mana likes to claim it pioneered the fast-food hamburger, which some still call a "slider." First or not, it's a classic of the genre. The tiny chrome-and-white building with the red roof was featured at the 1939 New York World's Fair, and sitting at the circular linoleum counter is a true time warp – as well as a rite of passage for diner aficionados and Jersey City kids.

To get there: from Manhattan's Holland Tunnel, take Hwy 1-9 and follow it north onto frenetic, truck-packed Tonnele Ave. White Mana comes up fast, at Manhattan Ave, but everyone risks the turnoff: from gray-haired matrons to truckers to businesspeople to the quintessential lost souls who frequent Edward Hopper paintings.

TIME
2 – 3 days

DISTANCE
150 miles

BEST TIME TO GO
Year-round

START
Jersey City, NJ

END
Wall, NJ

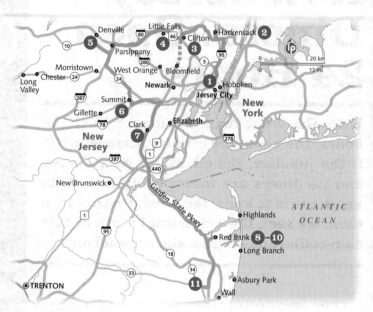

The menu is simplicity itself: burgers, hot dogs, eggs, fries. The equipment? Two small grills, a deep fryer, a toaster oven, and a blender for shakes. The burgers are fresh; no frozen, preformed patties, oh no. The chef grabs a hunk of raw meat with his hand, flattens it with a spatula, tops it with grilled onions and pickle, lays it on a soft bun, and there you go. For $1.12. Cheese is another 10 cents. A "Big Web" – the equivalent of a quarter pounder – is $3.36. Atmosphere is on the house.

For purity, for history, for architecture, this chrome wonder is the quintessential truck-stop diner, and they are a vanishing breed. Another prime example, which in fact argues that *it* was first, is the Hackensack ② **White Manna** (two ns, no explanation, also c 1939); it's got a glass-brick front, more red trim, and smaller potato buns. Are the burgers better? Some make that case, but it's the same experience – order three at a time, and skip lettuce and tomato. They just get in the way.

To get from White Mana to White Manna, continue north on Hwy 1-9 to Rte 46 west, and exit onto River St north (Rte 503/Bergen Turnpike). Then, from White Manna, take Rte 503 back south to I-80 west, take the Garden State Parkway south to exit 153, and take Rte 3 to the ③ **Tick Tock Diner**. "The Tick" is a legend, and it epitomizes another aspect of diner-osity: the restaurant-diner with the mile-long menu. How is it that places offering only a handful of things and others offering everything are both equally and essentially diners? Discuss.

The original Tick was a 1949 Silk City, but the current building was made by Kullman in 1994: the original clock and the neon motto "Eat Heavy" were kept. Though it applies to much, the Tick's motto certainly covers the ever-popular "Disco Fries," which arrive smothered in cheese and gravy. The Tick has the retro chrome and neon, the wry waitstaff, the overwhelming dessert case, the 24-hour breakfasts. It's a home-away-from-home for high schoolers and families and a cure-all for postclub, predawn hangovers. All it lacks are tabletop jukeboxes.

In the same vein is the ❹ **Park West Diner**; to get here, go west on Rte 3, which becomes Rte 46. The Park West has an even classier retro vibe, with a fun planet-and-stars Googie carpet, two-tone booths, a dramatic two-story glass-brick entry, and the scalloped ceiling and inset lights of a Pullman railcar. It's a spruced-up vision of the doo-wop, streamline moderne, art deco '40s and '50s. But the Park West really shines with its food, highlighting, of all things, salads: they arrive like crafted events, towering with mango, straw-berries, perfectly grilled tuna, black-ened shrimp, and feta. Each meal starts with fresh bread and a tasty chickpea salad, and the waitstaff are *nice*.

> **DETOUR** It's not a diner, but it's des-tination dining, Jersey-style: **Holsten's** (www.holstens.com) was the setting for the final scene in the final episode of *The Sopranos*, but it's long been a gourmand's delight. Cheap, fresh hamburgers, homemade ice cream (the shakes are out of this world), and a glass-front confectionery. You'll find Holsten's at 1063 Broad St in Bloomfield; from Rte 3, take exit 153/Broad St.

Yet, with its cutesy mural of Elvis and a pink Cadillac, the Park West tips danger-ously close to pandering nostalgia. Which begs the question: at what point does refurbishing and re-creating an authentic building and time period fall into irredeemable kitsch, becoming yet another *American Graffiti*–style Mel's Diner rip-off? The Park West is not, making the case that authenticity is less about the right look than fresh food, which creates regulars like the actor who played Furio in *The Sopranos*, a native of Paterson, who would no doubt club our kneecaps if we broke bad about the Park West. Which we wouldn't, ever. Sir.

Furthering this particular looks-don't-matter argument is the ❺ **Alexis Diner** in Denville (take Rte 46 west to I-80 and then west to I-287 south to Rte 10 west). There are lots of ugly New Jersey diners; many are flagstone-sided monstrosities with mediocre food served by indifferent staff. As your stomach will tell you, that Jersey boasts 600 diners is not always a good thing.

From the outside, the nondescript Alexis could be mistaken for one of these, though, inside, its pink neon and plum-and-gray decor have a tacky appeal. The Alexis isn't even 24 hours. But it doesn't matter. What matters – the reason the Alexis is voted Morris County's best diner year after year – is the food. Like at the Park West, dishes are fresh and display evidence of thought. The Italian BLT just might be the best sandwich ever made: fresh mozzarella, smoky bacon, green-leaf lettuce and deep-fried tomato on a seasoned focaccia.

GARDENS OF THE GARDEN STATE

New Jersey is called the Garden State, not the Diner State, for a reason: it's packed with farms. Imagine that? And Jersey corn, tomatoes, peaches, apples, and blueberries inspire their own pilgrimages. Here are four farms convenient to north Jersey. All are open daily year-round, but pick-your-own fun only happens in fall. Ya' know, harvest season.

- Alstede Farm, Chester (www.alstedefarms.com)
- Hillview Farms, Gillette (www.hillviewfarmsnj.com)
- Ort Farms, Long Valley (www.ortsfarm.com)
- Wightman's Farm, Morristown (www.wightmansfarms.com)

The Alexis is the ideal place to go Greek: its gyros and Greek salads are delicious and its "taverna specials" are hearty meals that exemplify the best of this particular strain of restaurant-style Jersey diner cuisine. Like '50s nostalgia, what you get at many diners is bland fakery, but not here.

Now we come to another major category of diner: the gleaming, silver roadside railcar, the diner of fantasy – the one photorealist painter John Baeder has made a living capturing and the kind architectural buffs drool over. Like the White Mana, these are prefabricated buildings (though the first were real train cars), and New Jersey has had at least nine manufacturers: such as Silk City, Jerry O'Mahoney, DeRaffele, Kullman and Paramount. Only the last two remain in business.

But are any of them places you'd actually want to eat in?

From the Alexis, take Rte 10 east to I-287 south to Rte 24 east; at exit 8, follow Summit Ave to downtown Summit and the ❻ **Summit Diner**, a 1938 chrome-sided O'Mahoney facing the train station. It's a little worn, inside and out; waitresses display a level of impatience some might call surly. The menu is long, but limited to the grill and the fryer; no shakes. When a despairing customer asked, "How about spinach? You got any green vegetables?" the waitress casually shrugged him off, "Nah, we got green peppers. That's it." The cook uses so much butter, cheese and bacon, the doorway should be posted with instructions: sit, eat, wait for irregular heart rhythm.

"so much butter, the doorway should be posted with instructions: sit, eat, wait for irregular heart rhythm."

And yet, this is the real deal: the Summit is often packed with contractors, pensioners and high school kids. It's an inexpensive working-class place in a town (and a state) that is less working class by the day. It's not *too* worn, and jokes aside, the food is good. So, here we are: diners are not just about the menu and pert greens. They are clientele, history, some attitude.

From Summit, take I-78 east to the Garden State Parkway south; take exit 135 to Central Ave and stop at the ❼ **Clark White Diamond**. This is another, teeny-tiny chrome haven for top-quality burgers, though here the burgers are bigger and the bun has substance (and poppy seeds).

Keep going south on the Parkway to exit 109 and Red Bank. Here, the ❽ **Broadway Diner** is another classic railcar that glows in bubblegum pink, from the tables to the booths to the ceiling. It's got the rotating dessert case, fluffy pancakes, and, at last, tabletop jukeboxes. Yet they don't work. They almost never do. Clearly, the once-essential connection between diners and popular music is gone, so let's mourn and move on: diners are no longer about music.

❾ **Red Bank** is a great town to explore (and window-shop those burgers off), but if you just can't continue, roll yourself into the ❿ **Molly Pitcher Inn** for a well-earned rest.

Finally, there's one more stop, perhaps the most famous of all: the ⓫ **Road-side Diner**. The Roadside is a movie star: it was in 1983's *Baby It's You*, it made a Bon Jovi album cover (*Cross Road*), and in 2008, the Boss himself featured it in the music video "Girls in Their Summer Clothes." Tour buses stop at the Roadside, a burden it somehow overcomes.

This 1950 Silk City railcar has a cool sliding-door entry, 18 counter stools and six booths. It's clean and neat, with original red-and-white tile and wood-work, and exudes a low-key nostalgia (tin advertising signs, a photo of Babe Ruth, golden oldies music). Like Park West, it evokes its era without overdo-ing it. Best of all, the standard, everything-under-the-sun menu is made to order. Burgers are great, and of the chef's egg and tuna salads, a customer nodded reassuringly: "He mixes everything fresh. It doesn't sit."

The Roadside pulls it all together at a nowhere location near the intersection of Rtes 33 and 34. It doesn't epitomize *all* a diner can be – nothing could. In the end, the best diner is always the one where we feel comfortable, the one we call home, the one where we're known and where we'll forgive the occasional bad meal because, like our home, that diner is us.

Jeff Campbell

TRIP 10

TRIP INFORMATION

GETTING THERE
From New York City, take the Holland Tunnel to Hwy 1-9 north/Tonnele Ave to White Mana.

EAT

Alexis Diner
The friendly Alexis gives you fresh baked cookies; if the Italian BLT isn't on the menu, ask for it. ☎ 973-361-8000; http://alexis dinernj.com; 3130 Rte 10 W, Denville; mains $5-20; ⏲ 7am-midnight Sun-Thu, to 1am Fri & Sat; ♿

Broadway Diner
Gotta love the undersea mural and the bad pop music: get down, boogie oogie oogie! ☎ 732-224-1234; 45 Monmouth St, Red Bank; mains $6-18; ⏲ 24hr; ♿

Clark White Diamond
The burger is bigger than the paper plate; the staff are very friendly and they have an Elvis gold record! Cash only. ☎ 732-574-8053; 1207 Raritan Rd at Central Ave, Clark; mains $2-5; ⏲ 24hr; ♿

Park West Diner
Park West gets props for challah bread French toast and buffalo burgers. ☎ 973-256-2767; www.parkwestdiner.com; 1400 US Hwy 46, Little Falls; mains $7-23; ⏲ 24hr; ♿

Roadside Diner
Big, fresh burgers, and don't overlook the dinner specials here. Cash only. ☎ 732-919-1199; 5016 State Rte 33, Wall; mains $4-13; ⏲ 5:30am-8pm Tue-Sat, 5:30am-4pm Sun & Mon; ♿

Summit Diner
Great for breakfast and cheesesteaks, but the grilled cheese is a killer. Cash only. ☎ 908-277-3256; 1 Union Pl at Summit Ave, Summit; mains $4-11; ⏲ 5:30am-8:30pm Mon-Sat, 6:30am-1pm Sun; ♿

Tick Tock Diner
If it's not on the menu, it hasn't been invented yet. Ask for sweet-potato fries instead of regular. ☎ 973-777-0511; www.tictock diner.com; 281 Allwood Rd, Clifton; mains $7-19; ⏲ 24hr; ♿

White Mana
Celebrity clients here include Mike Tyson and Sty Stallone. Cash only. ☎ 201-963-1441; 470 Tonnele Ave, Jersey City; mains $1-4; ⏲ 24hr; ♿

White Manna
You could get milk in a Styrofoam cup and a hot dog, but why? Just decide: cheese or no cheese. Cash only. ☎ 201-342-0914; 358 River St, Hackensack; mains $1-3; ⏲ 24hr; ♿

SLEEP

Molly Pitcher Inn
It's fancy for this trip, but you'll appreciate going upmarket to sleep. Plus, you know where to go for breakfast. ☎ 800-221-1372; www.mollypitcher-oysterpoint.com/molly pitcher; 88 Riverside Ave, Red Bank; r $160-200; ♿

USEFUL WEBSITES
www.dinercity.com
www.njdiners.com

LINK YOUR TRIP

www.lonelyplanet.com/trip-planner

New York's Adirondack State Park

WHY GO New York's wide, northern territory is dominated by an untamed wilderness of craggy peaks with bushy tufts of spruce trees that loom over a series of idyllic, mirrorlike lakes. Strict land control has kept this park almost pristine; it's a treat to spend time in its rough-hewn, rustic confines.

TIME
3 days

DISTANCE
180 miles

BEST TIME TO GO
Apr – Nov

START
Lake George, NY

END
Lake Placid, NY

Enter the Adirondack State Park through the attractive, tourist-friendly enclave of ❶ **Lake George**. This little village is centered on the southern end of the aptly named Lake George, a 32-mile mini-ocean that froths with white-caps on windy days and shines like the placid blue sky on sunny ones. Known as the "Queen of America's Lakes," Lake George has long been the haunt of city-weary artists, history buffs and summer fun seekers.

Not far from the water in downtown Lake George is the ❷ **Fort William Henry Museum**; the fort was built by the British during the French and Indian War (1754–63). It was used as a staging ground for attacks against the garrison that would later become Fort Ticonderoga, and its fall would become the focus of James Fenimore Cooper's epic novel, *The Last of the Mohicans*. Although it's a reconstruction of the 1755 original, the minimalist barracks and dank dungeons certainly seem authentic. Guides dressed in Revolutionary garb muster visitors along, with stops for battle reenactments that include firing period muskets and cannons.

If shivery dungeons aren't frightening enough for you, head along Canada St to the ❸ **House of Frankenstein Wax Museum**, a kitschy little delight that seems oddly out of place in serene Lake George. There are all sorts of monsters and madness in this haunted house (little kids might find it too intense) and if you didn't believe in the Wolfman before, you might after a stop here.

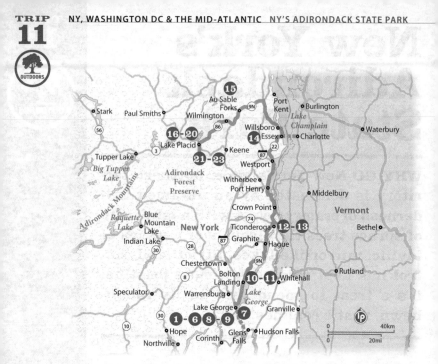

Clear your head with a quick trip around the lake to check out the teeming, wild shoreline and deep blue waters. ❹ **Lake George Steamboat Co's** boats departs from Steel Pier on downtown Beach Rd. Three boats – including the *Minnie Ha-ha,* a paddle wheeler – go out in summer months on one-hour jaunts and half- or full-day trips.

If you'd rather hit the beach, there's a perfect strip for lolling on the waterfront drive appropriately called Beach Rd – but don't expect that crystal-clear, spring-fed lake water to be as warm as the rough sand. Heat up with a volleyball game, or hang out in the picnic area in the sun. Directly behind the beach is the ❺ **Lake George Battlefield** area, a larger, grassier picnic spot. You'll spy the decaying remains of the original Fort William Henry on the green knolls, and a few monuments to long-gone soldiers.

Just south of the battlefield is the entrance to ❻ **Prospect Mountain**. Follow its 5-mile corkscrew drive upward and you'll find dramatic views of the lake and surrounding mountain ranges – the verdant tips of Vermont's Green Mountain range and even some of New Hampshire's granite peaks are visible. ❼ **Davidson Brothers Restaurant and Brewery** can serve you up an English pub dinner, but be prepared to eat buffalo burgers instead of shepherd's pie – that's the house specialty. You can spend the night at the ❽ **Georgian**, a luxury resort, or within the sprawling grounds and sumptuous suites of the ❾ **Fort William Henry Hotel**.

An early start the next morning will see you at ⑩ **Bolton Landing**, north of Lake George, in time for breakfast. Bolton Landing is full of stately, stone megamansions that stretch along Lake George's western shore (Lake Shore Dr). These Tudor and Italianate summer houses were once owned by wealthy New Yorkers, who wryly referred to their piles as "cottages." Check out the Sagamore resort, Melody Manor, Sun Castle and Green Harbor Mansion for four of the best examples of what was once known as ⑪ **"Millionaires Row."**

Move from old money to old military as you leave Bolton Landing and follow the rough Adirondack road to ⑫ **Fort Ticonderoga**, 30 miles northeast. The small town of Ticonderoga is known essentially for two things: the No 2 pencil factory that's long since shut down, and its iconic fort. Since it was taken from the British in 1775 by the "Green Mountain Boys" (a group of independence-loving hotheads from Vermont led by Ethan Allen and Benedict Arnold), Fort Ticonderoga has been synonymous with the American Revolution. Nowadays its buckling stone walls and rickety wooden outposts, affording stellar views of the surrounding lakes, can barely sustain their own weight, let alone that of a 300lb cannon. But every summer the carefully preserved fort opens its doors for tours and reenactments of famous war moments.

DETOUR Take an afternoon visit to **Glens Falls**, about 10 miles south of Lake George along Rte 9. Its chief attraction is the Hyde Collection, a remarkable gathering of art amassed by local newspaper heiress Charlotte Pryun Hyde. In her rambling Florentine Renaissance mansion you'll stumble across Rembrandts, Rubens, Matisses and Eakins, as well as tapestries, sculptures and turn-of-the-century furnishings.

It's a good idea to fuel up on gas and food before leaving Ticonderoga. Grab a bite at the ⑬ **Hot Biscuit Diner**, and then hit the Lakes to Locks Passage – the famously curving, scenic Rte 22 that twists along Lake Champlain toward the historic village of Essex. Each turn brings a new view of Lake Champlain's sculpted shores, pushed up against the foothills of the Green Mountains. On the other side, it's all wavy gold meadows and carefully sculpted fields. A good place to stop for the night is ⑭ **Essex Inn**, built in 1810 when this village was a port stop for boats hauling goods north. The soft-yellow boarding house has all the creaky charm you'd expect from a 200-year-old landmark.

A drive north to Keesville kicks off your morning, as you head toward one of New York's most exciting natural wonders. For those who thrill to nature – or like their nature to be thrilling – there's no beating ⑮ **Au Sable Chasm**, formed by a gushing river that over thousands of years carved its way through deep layers of sandstone, creating 200ft cliffs, waterfalls and rapids.

Au Sable's hiking trails (aided in some places by swinging connecting bridges and a sleek cable car) wind up and down the canyon's nearly 2-mile length. Unique rock formations are marked on hiking maps – look for the Elephant's Head, Devil's Oven, Mystic Canyon, Rainbow Falls and more. When the call of the sun-dappled waters gets too hard to resist, lazily slide downriver in a rented kayak or inner-tube, gazing at the birds and butterflies that fill the light-filled gorge. If adrenaline is your drug, opt for the rafting tours – shooting between ancient rocks at white-water speeds really gets the heart pumping.

> **DETOUR**
>
> Neighboring Vermont is within your reach at Essex – just jump on the stately ferry that crisscrosses Lake Champlain and in 20 minutes you'll be in Charlotte, VT, a quaint hamlet established in 1792 and dedicated to farming and rustic pursuits like making maple syrup and maple syrup candy. The ferry runs all day and can have you back on the New York side of the lake before nightfall.

By day's end, make tracks about 30 miles southwest to Lake Placid, where you can tuck into either the **16 Mirror Lake Inn** or **17 Paradox Lodge** for the night; they're both quaint local-run retreats. Before you begin your Olympic odyssey next morning, stop in at **18 Blues Berry Bakery** or **19 Saranac Sourdough**, two of the best breakfast options.

Take a stroll around downtown Lake Placid and keep an eye out for the 30ft-tall Lake Placid Toboggan Chute (near the post office), one of many Olympic mementoes left in the area. The official **20 Olympic Center**, on Main St, is a large white building where the inside temperatures are kept bone-chillingly cold, thanks to the four large skating rinks where athletes come to train. Hockey fans will recognize this complex as the location of the 1980 "Miracle on Ice," when the upstart US hockey team managed to defeat the seemingly unstoppable Soviets and win Olympic gold. You can relive that and other sports glory days with a visit to the Lake Placid Winter Olympics Museum, inside the center.

Not far from town on Rte 73 is the **21 Mackenzie-Intervale Ski Jumping Complex**, an all-weather training facility for ski jump teams. A 7-mile scenic drive south of the Kodak facility brings you to **22 Mt Van Hoevenberg**, home to Olympic bobsledding.

As you head back to Lake Placid on Rte 73, stop off at the **23 John Brown Farm State Historic Park**, former homestead and final resting place of the famous abolitionist who tried to spark a slave revolt at Harpers Ferry, West Virginia in 1859. Brown and his followers were executed and later interred on his 24-acre farm. You can take a quiet stroll around the fragrant grounds – full of buzzing bees and flowers in summer and icy cross-country ski trails in winter – and study the graves.

Ginger Adams Otis

TRIP INFORMATION

GETTING THERE
Follow Rte 87 north from Saratoga Springs into Adirondack State Park and to the village of Lake George.

DO

Au Sable Chasm
Hike, walk or inner-tube your way around this deep gorge, formed by gushing river waters. ☎ 518-834-7454; www.ausable chasm.com; 2144 Rte 9; adult/child/under 5yr $16/9/free; ⊙ year-round; 🚻 ♿

Fort Ticonderoga
An eerie, rickety and vivid reminder of Revolutionary soldiers' frigid hardships. ☎ 518-585-2821; www.fort-ticonderoga .org; Sandy Redoubt Rd, Ticonderoga; adult/senior/child $15/13.50/7; ⊙ 9:30am-5pm May-Oct; 🚻 ♿

Fort William Henry Museum
Impeccably dressed guides lead informative tours and conduct battle reenactments at this old British fort. ☎ 518-668-5471; www .fwhmuseum.com; Canada St at Rte 9, Lake George; adult/senior/child $14.95/12.95/8; ⊙ 9am-6pm May-Oct; 🚻 ♿

House of Frankenstein Wax Museum
An oddball attraction that's part haunted house, part museum; little kids might not like it. ☎ 518-668-3377; www.frankenstein waxmuseum.com; 213 Canada St, Lake George; adult/child $9/4.50; ⊙ 9am-11pm Jun-Sep, noon-6pm Oct-May

John Brown Farm State Historic Park
Visit the famous abolitionist's former family farm, where he and his sons are buried. ☎ 518-523-3900; John Brown Rd, Lake Placid; admission $2; ⊙ 10am-5pm Wed-Sat, 1-5pm Sun May-Oct; 🚻 ♿

Mackenzie-Intervale Ski Jumping Complex
Suit up and test your ability to withstand heights at this training/competition center. ☎ 518-523-2202, 800-462-6236; www.orda .org; 8 John Brown Rd, Rte 73, Lake Placid; adult/child $10/8; ⊙ hours vary seasonally

Mt Van Hoevenberg
Trolley tour your way along the bobsled and luge training tracks. ☎ 518-523-4436; 8 John Brown Rd, Rte 73, Lake Placid; adult/child $10/8; bobsled rides $30; ⊙ hours vary seasonally; ♿

Olympic Center
Details on 1980 Olympic sites, plus a glimpse at the training rigors undergone by world-class athletes. ☎ 518-523-1655; www.orda .org; 2634 Main St, Lake Placid; adult/child $5/3; ⊙ 10am-5pm; 🚻 ♿

EAT

Blues Berry Bakery
A cheery bakery with fresh-from-the-oven cakes, croissants, brioches, cookies, tarts, éclairs and more. ☎ 518-523-4539; 26 Main St, Lake Placid; mains $2-22; ⊙ 7am-6pm Mon-Sat, 8am-4pm Sun; 🚻

Davidson Brothers Restaurant and Brewery
An old-fashioned pub, with stouts, ales and hearty lagers as well as heaping fish and meat platters. ☎ 518-743-9026; www.david sonbrothers.com; 184 Glen St, Glens Falls; mains $8-22; ⊙ lunch & dinner; 🚻

Hot Biscuit Diner
Heaping plates of fresh eggs, farm bacon, organic burgers, and biscuits from the wood stove oven. ☎ 518-585-3483; http://hot biscuitdiner.com; 14 Montcalm St, Ticonderoga; mains $5-15; ⊙ 8am-7pm; 🚻

Saranac Sourdough
A great deli with fantastic morning coffee and thick, meaty sandwiches that can be packed up to go. ☎ 518-523-4897; 2126 Saranac Ave, Lake Placid; mains $4-12; ⊙ 7am-4pm; 🚻

SLEEP

Essex Inn
A 200-year-old charmer, with seven rooms all decorated with period furnishings, and a wide veranda and back garden. ☎ 518-963-8821; www.theessexinn.com; 2297 Main St, Essex; r with shared bathroom $95, with private bathroom $125-160

Fort William Henry Hotel
A gorgeous megaresort with sweeping mountain and lake views and modern, comfy rooms an arm's length from the water. ☎ 800-234-0267, 518-668-3081; www.fortwilliamhenry.com; 48 Canada St, Lake George; r $159-269

Georgian
A beautiful, sprawling lakeside resort with a marina and pools. The spacious rooms are marred slightly by outdated decor and furnishings. ☎ 518-668-5401; www.georgianresort.com; 384 Canada St, Lake George; r $189-289, ste $389

Mirror Lake Inn
This high-end resort has large rooms with balconies overlooking the water. ☎ 518-523-2544; www.mirrorlakeinn.com; 77 Mirror Lake Dr, Lake Placid; r from $300

Paradox Lodge
Reminiscent of a well-appointed hunting lodge, with cozy fireplaces and Native American print rugs. ☎ 518-523-9078; www.paradoxlodge.com; 76 Saranac Ave, Lake Placid; r $135-245

USEFUL WEBSITES
www.adirondacks.com
www.visitadirondacks.com

LINK YOUR TRIP
www.lonelyplanet.com/trip-planner

A Civil War Tour

WHY GO Millions of Americans have blood ties to the Civil War. The intensity of the Civil Rights movement was fed by proximity to the physical spaces of the nation's other great civil conflict. Physically retracing this phase of American history gives unparalleled insight into other chapters of that narrative.

The Civil War defines the USA. No other conflict of such scale and significance has been fought in, literally, American backyards. Walk or drive by its associated geography, through suburban interchanges and picture-book towns and rolling hills, farmland, forest, swamps and grassy fields, and you are on graves, graves, graves. There are 100,000 American combat dead in a 10-sq-mile area near Fredericksburg, Virginia; that's a grim math that evokes spirits of Western Europe and Central Africa, yet within easy access to the mid-Atlantic urban corridor.

The impact of visiting these spaces in the right mindset can't be overstated. With the right light and the right soundtrack – a low, soft-creeping sunset and the purple chorus of thousands of crickets against an old split-rail fence – a one-two punch of history and physical landscape induces a sort of "stoned by history" afterglow. The effect is followed by a jarring juxtaposition of bloody legacy and bucolic scenery, the latter a happy aftereffect of the decision to keep battlefields untouched and pristine.

These sites are scattered over huge swathes of the American South, but Virginia, in many ways the epicenter of the war, packages some of the conflict's seminal events in a space that includes areas of the prettiest countryside on the Eastern seaboard. So head off, from Georgetown, Washington DC, to time travel as best you can into the war that Oliver Wendell Holmes Jr said "touched with fire" the hearts of those who passed through it.

TIME
2 days

DISTANCE
320 miles

BEST TIME TO GO
Aug – Dec

START
Georgetown, Washington DC

END
Appomattox, VA

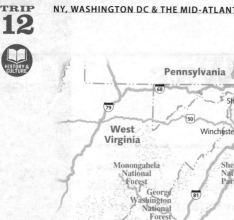
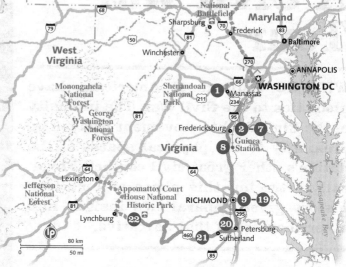

It takes about an hour driving through the tangled knots of suburban sprawl that scar Northern Virginia to reach your first destination: Manassas. Overdeveloped in the mid-1990s, today it is still glutted with gas stations, but the forces of conservation have occasionally prevailed. In the early 1990s the Walt Disney Company proposed an American history–themed park in Haymarket but, to the satisfaction of preservationists, Disney's America did not take over the site of the Battle – actually, battles – of Bull Run. What did assault this area were 35,000 men of the Union Army, in 1861, and what they saw then approximates the view of ❶ **Manassas National Battlefield Park**, today a stretch of gorgeous countryside that has miraculously survived the predations of the army of Northern Virginia real-estate developers.

"Some 32,500 Confederate soldiers were thrust into this backdrop of pastoral North America."

This is as close as any of us will come to 19th-century rural America. From the visitors center, you look out onto green, redefined; in waving hills, dark, brooding tree-lines, the low curve of fields and the soft hump of overgrown trench works.

Some 32,500 Confederate soldiers, as untested and fresh as their enemies, were thrust into this quintessential backdrop of pastoral North America. After a series of charges and countercharges, the Southern line was held by troops under Thomas J "Stonewall" Jackson, an evangelist Virginian who sucked on lemons and rode into battle with one arm above his head to balance his bodily "humors."

Both sides realized a long, hard war was at hand and called up thousands of troops. Europe watched nervously; in a matter of weeks, the largest army in the world was the Union Army of the Potomac. The second biggest was the Confederate States of America Army. A year later, at the Battle of Shiloh, 24,000 people were listed as casualties – more than all the accumulated casualties of every previous American war combined.

Your next stop south on I-95 is ❷ Fredericksburg; if battlefields preserve rural, agricultural America, Fredericksburg is an excellent example of what the nation's main streets once looked like: orderly grids, touches of green and friendly storefronts.

Assuming you're hungry, you're a bit spoiled for choice here. ❸ Bistro Bethem is an excellent main-street corner spot and bustling restaurant in which to perch over period dishes, like quail with cornbread cherry stuffing, on a perfect sunny day. If you need lighter "faire," ❹ Olde Town Wine & Cheese Deli serves up delicious sandwiches and enough gourmet meats and cheeses to keep the average picnic-goer in lunch-basket heaven; mark your entrance to the South by washing your meal down with some sweet iced tea.

> **DETOUR** The Battle of Antietam, fought in Sharpsburg, MD, on September 17, 1862, has the dubious distinction of marking the bloodiest day in American history. The battlesite is preserved at **Antietam National Battlefield** (www.nps.org/anti) in the corn-and-hill country of north-central Maryland. Even geographic nomenclature became violent; the Sunken Road turned into "Bloody Lane" after bodies were stacked there. In the park's cemetery, many of the Union gravestones bear the names of immigrants who died in a country they had only recently adopted.

You don't have to sleep here if you want to power through the tour, but Fredericksburg is defintely worth a linger, and the ❺ Richard Johnston Inn, with its colonially cozy ambience and old-stone air, is an excellent place to rest thy head. Should you just need a caffeine jolt and a bit of soft-folk-music-accented culture, ❻ Griffin Bookshop and Coffee Bar awaits with some mocha-latte infused rocket fuel.

Still, all of this yuppie joy can't hide what put this town on the map: one of the worst blunders in American military history. In 1862, when the Northern Army attempted a massed charge across open terrain at local entrenched Confederate position, a Southern artilleryman looked at the field and uphill slope the Union forces had to cross and told a commanding officer, "A chicken could not live on that field when we open on it." Sixteen charges resulted in an estimated 6000 to 8000 Union casualties.

❼ Fredericksburg & Spotsylvania National Military Park is not as immediately compelling as Manassas because of the thick forest that still covers these battlefields, but the woods themselves are a sylvan wonder. Again, the pretty nature of…well, nature, grows over graves; the nearby Battle of the Wilderness was named for these thick woods, which caught fire and killed hundreds of wounded soldiers after the shooting was finished.

In nearby Chancellorsville, Robert E Lee pulled off his greatest victory when, outnumbered two to one, he *split* his forces and attacked both flanks of the Union army. The audacity of the move caused the Northern force to crumble and flee across the Potomac yet again, but the victory was a costly one; in the course of the fighting, Stonewall Jackson had his arm shot off by a nervous Confederate sentry (the arm, by the way, is buried near the Fredericksburg National Park visitor center; ask a ranger for directions).

The wound was patched, but Jackson went on to contract a fatal dose of pneumonia. He was taken to what is now the next stop on this tour: the **❽ Stonewall Jackson Shrine** in nearby Guinea Station. Here Stonewall lay surrounded by his family, in a small white cabin set against attractive Virginia horse-country, overrun with hanging sprays of purple flowers, daisy fields and trees tied up in the thick strands of gypsy moth nests. After a series of prolonged ramblings, Jackson fell silent, then looked up with a smile, whispered, "Let us cross over the river and rest in the shade of the trees," and died.

DETOUR The Battle of Gettysburg, fought in Gettysburg, PA, in July of 1863, marked the turning point of the war. **Gettysburg National Battlefield** (www.nps.gov/gett) does an excellent job of explaining the course of the combat. Look for Little Round Top, where a Union unit checked a Southern flanking maneuver, and the field of Pickett's Charge, where the Confederacy suffered its most crushing defeat up to July 1863. Abraham Lincoln gave his Gettysburg Address here to mark the victory and the "new birth of the nation" on said country's birthday: July 4.

From here it's not too far along I-95 to **❾ Richmond**, former capital of the Confederacy and modern multicultural tail end of the Northeast urban corridor. The South truly begins here, and the **❿ Virginia Historical Society**, an excellent repository of archival records and creative exhibits, explains just how this invisible line is drawn.

Richmond is a rainbow city, but reports continue of serious income disparities and a divided public memory, both with direct antecedents from the war. **⓫ Monument Ave**, south of W Broad St, which runs through the city's most aristocratic neighborhood, mixes shaggy-bearded Confederate statuary with a sculpture of African American tennis star Arthur Ashe, a nod to diversity in a state that wanted to combine celebrations for Martin Luther King Jr Day with a commemoration of Confederate generals. **⓬ Hollywood Cemetery**, just west of Belvidere St, isn't as controversial as much as elegiac, a mood brought on by the graves of, among others, some 18,000 Southern soldiers.

There are two Civil War museums in Richmond, and they make for an interesting study in contrasts. The ⓭ **Museum of the Confederacy (MOC)** was once a shrine to the Southern "Lost Cause," and still attracts a fair degree of neo-Confederates and their ilk. But the MOC has also graduated into a respected educational institution, and its collection of Confederate artifacts is probably the best in the country. The optional tour of the ⓮ **Confederate White House** is highly recommended for its quirky insights into one of the most fascinating chapters of American history (did you know the second-most powerful man in the Confederacy may have been a gay Jew?).

WHAT'S IN A NAME, PART 1?
Although the Civil War is the widely accepted label for the conflict covered in this trip, you'll still hear die-hard Southern boosters refer to the period as the "War Between the States." What's the difference? Well, a Civil War implies an armed insurrection against a ruling power that never lost its privilege to govern, whereas the name "War Between the States" suggests said states always had (and still have) a right to secession from the Republic.

On the other hand, the ⓯ **American Civil War Center**, located in the old Tredegar ironworks (the main armament producer for the Confederacy), makes an admirable, ultimately successful, effort to present the war from three perspectives: Northern, Southern and African American. The exhibits are lovely and the effect is clearly powerful, reflected in the wall of sticky notes the museum leaves for visitors to jot impressions on.

Richmond has one of the most vibrant African American communities in America, and in a nod to that legacy, we dine in Jackson Ward on a "fish boat" at ⓰ **Croaker's Spot**, soul food's answer to fish and chips: a plate of fried whiting fillets smothered in hot sauce, onions and peppers, with cheese grits and cornbread on the side. For a more refined take on the theme, ⓱ **Julep's** is widely recognized as the cutting edge of Richmond's slew of refined takes on New Southern cuisine.

WHAT'S IN A NAME, PART 2?
One of the more annoying naming conventions of the war goes thus: while the North preferred to name battles for defining geographic terms (Bull Run, Antietam), Southern officers named them for nearby towns (Manassas, Sharpsburg). Although most Americans refer to battles by their Northern names, in some areas folks simply know Manassas as the Battle Of, not as the strip town with a good Waffle House.

Out of many contenders, there are two excellent sleeping options in Virginia's capital: the ⓲ **Massad House Hotel**, a cozy, centrally located study in Tudor-style budget bliss; and one of the poshest palaces of Dixie patricians, the ⓳ **Jefferson Hotel**, a modern execution of the moonlight-and-magnolia cliché.

Petersburg, just south of Richmond, is the blue-collar sibling city to the Virginia capital, its center gutted by white flight following desegregation. ❷⓿ **Petersburg National Battlefield Park** marks the spot where Northern and Southern soldiers spent almost a quarter of the war in a protracted, trench-induced stand-off. The Battle of the Crater, made well known in Charles Frazier's *Cold Mountain*, was an attempt by Union soldiers to break this stalemate by tunneling under the Confederate lines and blowing up their fortifications; the end result was Union soldiers caught in the hole wrought by their own sabotage, killed like fish in a barrel.

Drive south of Petersburg, then west through a skein of back roads to follow Lee's last retreat. It's best to do this drive near sunset, when the trees that line the road burn in brilliant flaming reds and purples; crickets call between the cool spaces in the grass; insects hop against the parachute seedlings of dead dandelions; and the flora and fauna bursts into white clouds, hovering just over the fields that stretch to the indigo-dark crests of the Shenandoah Mountains. This is classic rural America, and for a taste of its weirdness, plus a visit to one of the most hospitable eccentrics you're likely to meet, say hello to Jimmy Olgers and ❷❶ **Olger's Store**, a sort of museum/temple/attic of all things eccentric in Dinwiddie, VA.

> **DETOUR**

Located in one of the prettiest valleys of the Virginia Shenandoahs, **Lexington** deserves your time, especially if you're coming from Appomattox Court House. The town's two major universities both have ties to the war. The Virginia Military Institute sent an entire graduating class into combat for the Confederacy and houses the carcass of Stonewall Jackson's horse, Little Sorrel. Washington and Lee has the body of Robert E Lee and his horse, Traveler (who got the dignity of a burial).

About 85 miles west of here is ❷❷ **Appomattox Court House National Park**, where the Confederacy (and Olgers' own forebear) finally surrendered. The park itself is wide and lovely, and the ranger staff are extremely helpful, but you may want to head back to Richmond for the night; the town of Appomattox is pretty plain.

There are several marker stones dedicated to the surrendering Confederates, and the most touching one marks the spot where Robert E Lee rode back from Appomattox after surrendering to Grant. His soldiers stood on either side of the field waiting for the return of their commander. When Lee rode into sight he doffed his hat; the troops surged towards him, some saying goodbye while others, too overcome with emotion to speak, passed their hands over the white flanks of Lee's horse, Traveler. It's a spot that's dedicated to defeat, and humility, and reconciliation, and the imperfect realization of all those qualities is the character of the America you've been driving through.

Adam Karlin

TRIP INFORMATION

GETTING THERE
From Georgetown in Washington DC, take the Key Bridge across the Potomac to Rte 66 west to get to Manassas, VA.

DO
American Civil War Center
The triple-viewpoint perspective at this institution makes it one of the country's best Civil War museums. ☎ 804-780-1865; www.tredegar.org; 500 Tredegar St, Richmond, VA; adult/student/7-12yr $8/6/2; ⏲ 9am-5pm; ♿

Appomattox Court House National Park
The site of the beginning of America's long, painful process of national reconciliation is gorgeously preserved in southside Virginia. ☎ 434-352-8987; www.nps.gov/apco; 5 Main St, off Hwy 24, Appomattox Court House, VA; admission $4; ⏲ 8:30am-5pm Tue-Sun

Confederate White House
We highly recommend taking a guided tour of Jefferson Davis' old digs at the Museum of the Confederacy; there are quirky tales aplenty hidden in these walls. ☎ 804-649-1861; www.moc.org; 1201 E Clay St, Richmond, VA; admission $3 plus MOC admission; ⏲ 10am-5pm Mon-Sat, from noon Sun

Fredericksburg & Spotsylvania National Military Park
This thickly wooded area is perfect for shady walks. The rangers are incredibly helpful and knowledgeable. ☎ 540-373-6122; www.nps.gov/frsp; 120 Chatham Lane, Fredericksburg, VA; ⏲ 8.30am-6.30pm

Hollywood Cemetery
No matter what your feelings are on the many Confederate soldiers that are buried here, Hollywood Cemetery is supremely elegant and sad. ☎ 804-648-8501; www.hollywoodcemetery.org; 412 S Cherry St, Richmond, VA; ⏲ 8am-5pm

Manassas National Battlefield Park
Perhaps the prettiest battlefield covered on this tour; simply one of the best-preserved spaces on the East Coast. ☎ 706-361-1339; www.nps.gov/mana; 6511 Sudley Rd, Manassas, VA; admission $3; ⏲ 8:30am-5pm

Museum of the Confederacy (MOC)
One of the best museums in the country for viewing actual uniforms, weapons and associated accoutrements from the war. ☎ 804-649-1861; www.moc.org; 1201 E Clay St, Richmond, VA; adult/child $12/7; ⏲ 10am-5pm Mon-Sat, from noon Sun

Olger's Store
This old general store has been converted into an excellent museum of wacky local paraphernalia by true Southern gentleman and host, Jimmy Olgers. www.craterroad.com/olgersstore.html; Hwy 460, Dinwiddie, VA; ⏲ whenever Jimmy says

Petersburg National Battlefield Park
Local rangers provide good insight into the ennui and horror of the first incident of trench warfare in military history. ☎ 804-732-3531, ext200; www.nps.gov/pete; 1001 Pecan Ave, Hopewell, VA; ⏲ 9am-5pm

Stonewall Jackson Shrine
This small cabin is set against one of Virginia's prettiest natural backdrops, and catches the light beautifully at sunset. ☎ 804-633-6076; www.nps.gov/frsp/js.htm; 12019 Stonewall Jackson Rd, Woodford, VA; ⏲ 9am-5pm

Virginia Historical Society
An excellent museum explains why Virginia lies at the center of everything. ☎ 804-358-4901; www.vahistorical.org; 428 North Blvd, Richmond, VA; admission free; ⏲ 10am-5pm Mon-Sat, 1-5pm Sun; ♿

EAT
Bistro Bethem
The New American menu, seasonal ingredients and down-to-earth but dedicated foodie vibe here all equal gastronomic bliss. ☎ 540-371-9999; www.bistrobethem.com; 309 William St, Fredericksburg, VA; mains $15-34; ⏲ lunch & dinner, closed Mon

Croaker's Spot
Richmond's most famous rendition of refined soul food is comforting, delicious and sits in your stomach like a brick pile.

☎ 804-421-0560; www.croakersspot.com; 119 E Leigh St, Richmond, VA; mains $9-19; ⏲ lunch & dinner

Julep's

Where classy, old-school Southern aristocrats like to meet and eat, balanced out by the fresh experimentation of an innovative kitchen. ☎ 804-377-3968; www.juleps.net; 1719 E Franklin St, Richmond, VA; mains $15-30; ⏲ dinner Mon-Sat

Olde Town Wine & Cheese Deli

Damn us as yuppies, but this shop's turkey Reubens are delicious. Oops, our Blackberries are beeping. ☎ 540-373-7877; 707 Caroline St, Fredericksburg, VA; mains $4-7; ⏲ lunch Mon-Sat

DRINK

Griffin Bookshop and Coffee Bar

Not technically a café but great for sipping lattes in recumbent intellectual bliss. ☎ 540-899-8041; www.thegriffinbookshopcoffee bar.com; 723 Caroline St, Fredericksburg, VA; ⏲ daily, hours vary

SLEEP

Jefferson Hotel

They've maintained the almost imperial sense of tradition at this most famed of Richmond hotels. ☎ 804-788-8000; www .jeffersonhotel.com; 101 W Franklin St, Richmond, VA; r $300-800

Massad House Hotel

Massad's great by any standard, but excellent rates and supreme location give it a special place in our hearts. ☎ 804-648-2893; www .massadhousehotel.com; 11 North 4th St, Richmond, VA; r $75-110

Richard Johnston Inn

Well thank goodness: someone made a B&B that's pretty much as cute, friendly and historically evocative as surrounding Fredericksburg itself. ☎ 540-899-7606; www .therichardjohnstoninn.com; 711 Caroline St, Fredericksburg, VA; r $98-210

USEFUL WEBSITES

www.civilwartrails.org
www.pbs.org/civilwar

LINK YOUR TRIP   www.lonelyplanet.com/trip-planner
TRIP

Maryland Crab Quest

WHY GO Come, ye foodies, for the food that best defines Maryland: Callinectes sapidus. The "beautiful swimmer" is better known as the blue crab, served steamed in large shell-flecked social gatherings. Attending a crab feast in a true crab house is the gastronomic distillation of all things Maryland.

TIME
4 days

DISTANCE
320 miles

BEST TIME TO GO
Jun – Sep

START
Baltimore, MD

END
Whitehaven, MD

In some states, when you want to get your smooth on with a girl, you take her out for a nice French meal, or to a cozy Italian joint, or book a table at some cutting-edge fusion culinary chicness.

In Maryland, nothing says "I love you" like spreading newspapers on a table, sticking your thumb up the ass of a bottom-feeding spider, ripping the body of said arthropod cleanly in two and then dismantling the rest of the creature with a mallet and knife. A few beers only add to the romance.

Yes, they know affection in the Old Line State. Although to be honest, a crab feast, Maryland's state meal (thanks to an abundance of the crustaceans in the Chesapeake Bay) is usually not a pairs event. While any self-respecting Maryland girl would go gaga over a good plate of blue crabs, the event tends to be a group affair, an occasion for friends and family to come together and celebrate good food and casualness in that most hallowed of state social halls: the crab house.

These institutions are quintessentially Maryland, and a distinct identifier for a state that lies in an amorphous cultural penumbra between the North, the South and the shadow of the nation's capital. Let's be honest, Maryland is often insecure of its identity. Crabs are the one thing they do best, even better than New Orleans. (Boiled crabs? Pah! Steaming releases the juices.) How much does Maryland care about

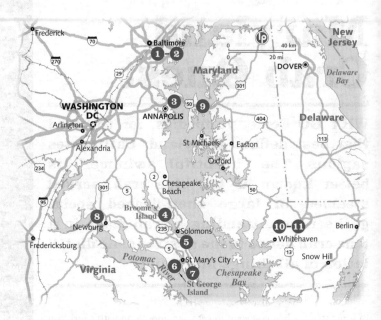

its crabs? Well, they put them on their driver's licenses (no, really). And the physical act of eating together in messy camaraderie, working hard for a little meat that is oh-so-sweet, complemented by sweet white corn, Budweiser and hush puppies, is a ballet most Marylanders are trained in from early childhood, a dance they all know the steps to.

Herein we have described a quest for the best of Maryland's crab houses, yet we've got to admit: the statewide appeal of the venue is partially attributable to its essential sameness across the board. Crabs are comforting, and so are the restaurants they're served in. Inevitably, the crab house decor is uniform: maritime memorabilia, wooden tables, jars of Old Bay, apple vinegar and melted butter, and the smell of fish, frying grease, beer and sawdust.

> *"Done right, the result is sweet, juicy white crabmeat cut by the sharp edge of cayenne, onion and salt."*

Crabs are cooked the same way across the state: steamed in water and beer and Old Bay seasoning; if Old Bay is added afterwards, beware. Done right, the result is sweet, juicy white crabmeat cut by the sharp edge of cayenne, onion and salt.

We'll start in Baltimore, which calls itself the "Crab Cake" to New York's Big Apple. In urban Maryland, this is as good as crabs get, although we are firmly of the opinion that you need to go to the marshy boonies for the best crabs in the state.

1 **Waverly Crabs & Seafood**, on Greenmount Ave, is a slightly tatty joint in a slightly tatty neighborhood, but the prices tend to be cheaper than the competition and the jumbos (the largest class of crab) are really jumbo. The clientele is local, which is another positive sign, as is the mixed Salvadoran, Filipino, black and white staff of pickers, steamers and spicers cooking the crabs behind the counter.

This is a takeout, so you'll be eating your crustaceans at home. For the record, these crab take-aways are more common than actual crab houses, and, often-times, crabs sold out of the back of a waterperson's pickup are of the best qual-ity (and guaranteed to be local; sadly, due to depletion of the Chesapeake Bay and run-off pollution, many "local" crabs are shipped in from southern states, and prepicked crabmeat sold in grocery stores is often from Southeast Asia).

The best sit-down crab joint in Baltimore is **2** **LP Steamers**, which is a quick drive from Fort McHenry. The "LP" stands for Locust Point, one of Charm City's classic blue-collar southside 'hoods; lots of residents here have been employed on the Baltimore docks or are a family member removed from working the waterfront. Steamers stands in the middle of a thin block of Baltimore row houses, and bustles with business from dedicated tour-ists and working-class neighbors. Everything on the menu is good, and everyone working the line is local.

MALES ONLY

Crabs are priced seasonally, so you can expect to pay anywhere from $30 to $80 for a dozen. When buying crabs, be sure to always ask for large or jumbo males. Females shouldn't be har-vested, since they're the mothers of the next generation of dining goodness.

Munching on a fried oyster sandwich doused in hot sauce, we couldn't help smiling when our server asked her friend, in a true Bawlmer accent, about the weather "deeyown the ayshun" (down the Ocean – ie in Ocean City).

It may be the state's capital, but Annapolis isn't the best city in Maryland for crabs – better options are closer in Southern Maryland and the Eastern Shore (by close we mean an hour or so away; Marylanders will drive long distances, even making day trips, for specific crab houses). Still, state politicos do have an excellent option for the vaunted government practice of committee-ing a bill over blue crabs at **3** **Cantler's**, just outside of the city.

Like many crab houses, Cantler's can be approached by road (Forest Beach Rd by Rte 50 east) or boat (a waterfront location is crab-eating industry stand-ard). The soft crabs here are particularly well-respected, probably due to the large on-site peeling sheds, where crabs are allowed to molt.

Some of the tastiest crabs in Maryland are served in the rural trifecta of coun-ties that makes up Southern Maryland. In thin Calvert County, about 45 miles south of Annapolis, the crab cakes at **4** **Stoney's** on Broome's Island are regarded as the best in the state: large, pleasantly lumpy and served amid excellent waterfront ambience. Calvert is good for post-crab drinks, too; on Rte 4 at the tip of Solomons Island is one of the most inexplicably popular bars in the state: the **5** **Tiki Bar**. It's not much more than an outdoor bar with a sand-and-Polynesian-idol-strewn courtyard, but hundreds of party people and boaters from across the Chesapeake create a mini–Bourbon St vibe here on weekends.

BEST. SEASONING. EVER.

You see it everywhere down here: Old Bay seasoning, the deep red, pleasantly hot but unmistakably estuarine spice of Maryland. Made from celery salt, mustard, black and red pepper and other secrets, we put it on our corn, our french fries, our potato chips and, of course, our crabs. A large container of the stuff is the perfect Maryland souvenir, but beware of wiping your face after partaking of the spice: Old Bay in the eyes is incredibly painful.

The crab houses seem to stack thicker the closer you come to the tip of the state's Western Shore, in St Mary's County. Only 60 miles long, yet surrounded by hundreds of miles of water due to its heavily indented coastline, the pineclad beaches of Maryland's oldest county conceal excellent crab shacks, particularly along the Patuxent River. The seafood joints we recommend are known for their steamed crabs and just a bit more. **6** **Evans**, down Piney Point Rd off Rte 5, does good crabs, but is also worth a stop for its quintessentially tidewater location: St George's Island, a speckle of perfectly packaged nature hemmed in by tall, whispering trees, softly lapping tides and loblolly-needle trails.

The further south, the more spread out houses become, as if they are trailing into the Chesapeake Bay and its surrounding forests. Another pretty view and more excellent seafood awaits at the river-encircled end of Wynne Rd, also located off Rte 5. **7** **Courtney's** is run by perennially gruff waterman Tom Courtney and his perennially chatty Filipino wife, Julie. This isn't technically a crab house, but it's one of the most authentic seafood restaurants in Maryland, where anything you're served (well, any seafood) was caught by Tom earlier that day.

Heading north on Rte 5, with a side trip on Rte 234 and a turn onto Hwy 301, leads you to Pope's Creek Rd. The road twists and turns through copses of trees overgrown with ivy and gold-flecked fields, which once hid John Wilkes Booth; Abraham Lincoln's assassin fled into this hinterland after his infamous performance in Ford's Theater.

Today, Pope's Creek (about 4 miles from Newburg) conceals one of the top seafood restaurants in Maryland, a crab-shack-cum-sit-down spot that overlooks the marsh-accented, slow meandering creek itself. **8** **Captain Billy's** is as famous (if not more so) for its oysters as its crabs. Billy's combines the essential elements of Maryland seafood dining: talented frying, casual ambience and beautiful location.

The Eastern Shore is the part of Maryland most connected to water, but it's not as packed with crab houses as one might think; many locals buy their crustaceans directly from watermen or catch them themselves. **9 Harris Crab House** off Rte 50 in the Kent Narrows, just after crossing the Bay Bridge, is highly regarded for its food and enormous wooden waterfront deck, even if it's a bit of a tourist trap.

Finding the best food on the Shore requires a bit of effort and driving. Well, we're loathe to call it Maryland's "best" crab house, as such proclamations have been known to start bar brawls, but it's as sure a contender as any. To reach the grail of this Crab Quest, you need to take Rte

CRUSTACEAN VARIATION

Steamed crabs are never the only item available at crab houses; Maryland menus mix up their shellfish. Try these favorites: crab cakes (crabmeat mixed with bread crumbs and secret spice combinations, fried); crab balls (as above, but smaller); soft crabs (crabs that have molted their shells and are fried, looking like giant breaded spiders – they're delicious); red crab and cream of crab soup; and fish stuffed with crab imperial (crab sautéed in butter, mayonnaise and mustard, occasionally topped with cheese).

50 all the way to tiny MD 347, turn right onto tinier MD 349, and left at even tinier MD 352, before hanging a right onto the thin track that is Clara Rd. There's a gorgeous, friendly B&B down this way, the **10 Whitehaven Hotel** (in Whitehaven; population roughly 30) that overlooks one of the oldest, still-operating ferry crossings in the state.

Also here, nestled in a heart-melting river-and-stream-scape, is the low-slung, laughter-packed **11 Red Roost**. It's a former chicken coop where the lamp shades are crafted from watermen's crab buckets and the waitresses are local teenagers. A bow-tied piano player pounds the keys and croons corny ballads (causing a family sitting next to us to mutter, "we best get out of here"), but that's the only potential drawback. Otherwise, the all-you-can-eat corn (served unshucked!), hush puppies, clam strips, fried chicken and steamed crab feasts are...well, it's a meal fit for a Roman emperor, were Roman emperors from Wicomico county.

Adam Karlin

TRIP INFORMATION

GETTING THERE
Start in Baltimore, on the north side of Greenmount Ave, before moving through the rest of the state.

EAT

Cantler's
The by-consensus best crab house in Annapolis is outside the city, but well worth the drive. ☎ 410-757-1311; www.cantlers.com; 458 Forest Beach Rd, Annapolis; mains from $20; ⏰ 11am-11pm, 11am-midnight Fri & Sat

Captain Billy's
Driving through countryside to get here is half the fun. The other half: delicious food. ☎ 301-932-4323; www.captbillys.com; 11495 Pope's Creek Rd, Pope's Creek; mains $10-30; ⏰ 11am-9pm Tue-Sun, closed winter

Courtney's
This is a small, barebones and thoroughly excellent seafood shack perched over a quiet bend of a picture-perfect river. ☎ 301-872-4403; 48290 Wynne Rd, Ridge; mains $7-25; ⏰ lunch & dinner

Evans
A lovely seafood house on woodsy St George's Island. ☎ 410-994-9944; www.evansseafoodrestaurant.com; 16810 Piney Point Rd, Piney Point; mains $10-32; ⏰ 4-9pm Fri, noon-9pm Sat, noon-8pm Sun

Harris Crab House
Although it gets a bit flooded with tourists, Harris' reputation is well deserved. ☎ 410-827-9500; www.harriscrabhouse.com; 425 Kent Narrow Way, Graysonville; mains $11-30; ⏰ lunch & dinner

LP Steamers
The best in Baltimore's seafood stakes: working class, teasing smiles and the freshest crabs on the southside. ☎ 410-576-9294; www.lpsteamers.com; 1100 E Fort Ave, Baltimore; mains $8-28; ⏰ lunch & dinner

Red Roost
The original legend: tell someone from the Eastern Shore you cracked crabs here and your street (well, Bay) cred rises immediately. ☎ 410-546-5443; www.theredroost.com; 2670 Clara Rd, Whitehaven; mains $15-40; ⏰ daily, hours vary

Stoney's
Another Maryland epic: that of the perfect crab cake, just lumpy, crispy, melty and fat enough for a Chesapeake king. ☎ 410-586-1888; 3956 Oyster House Rd, Broome's Island; mains $12-34; ⏰ lunch & dinner Thu-Sun

Waverly Crabs & Seafood
There's no better spot for takeaway crabs in Baltimore. ☎ 410-243-1181; 3400 Greenmount Ave, Baltimore; crabs priced seasonally; ⏰ to 10pm

DRINK

Tiki Bar
Imagine Bourbon St with all the trashiness and none of the history, plus sand and tidewater breezes. ☎ 410-326-4075; www.tikibarsolomons.com; 85 Charles St, Solomons Island; ⏰ daily, afternoon to late

SLEEP

Whitehaven Hotel
Excellent rooms, views and hosts and nestled on a postcard-corner of the Eastern Shore. ☎ 410-873-2000; http://whitehaven.tripod.com; 2685 Whitehaven Rd, Whitehaven; r $110-150

USEFUL WEBSITES
www.bluecrab.info
http://skipjack.net/le_shore/crab/picking_index.htm

LINK YOUR TRIP

www.lonelyplanet.com/trip-planner

The Crooked Road: Heritage Music Trail

WHY GO Got the Mule Skinner Blues? Then grab your fiddle and hightail it to western Virginia for a toe-tappin', knee-slappin' good time at the historic country, bluegrass and "old time" music venues that speckle the landscape between the Blue Ridge and Appalachian mountain ranges.

Down in Appalachia, where Kentucky meets Tennessee meets Virginia, you'll discover a veritable hotbed of country music history. It's here that such legends as the Carter Family began their musical careers. Virginia has done half the work for you, designating a route called the Crooked Road that carves a winding path through the Blue Ridge Mountains and into the Appalachians.

There are a lot of options for where to begin your journey. A good choice is the teeny, tiny town of ❶ Floyd. This town is a rather surprising blend of rural conservatives mixed with slightly New Age artisans and coffee lovers. Grab a double espresso from an artsy coffeehouse and then head round the corner to peruse the farm tools on sale in the hardware store.

The musical highlight of this curious town is the jamboree at the ❷ Floyd Country Store. Every Friday night, this little store in a clapboard building clears out most of its inventory and lines up rows of chairs around a dance floor. Around 6:30pm the first musicians on the bill start playin' their hearts out on the stage. Pretty soon the room's filled up with locals and visitors hootin' and hollerin' along with the fiddles and banjos. While you listen, you can browse through their extensive selection of music, some of which have endearingly wacky cover portraits. Make your way through the crowd to the deli side of the room and order some ice cream or maybe a root-beer float to go with that bag of penny candy from the barrels up front.

TIME
2 – 3 days

DISTANCE
145 miles

BEST TIME TO GO
May – Oct

START
Floyd, VA

END
Hiltons, VA

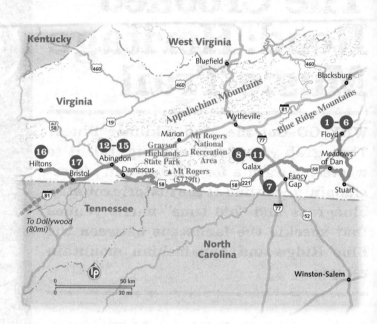

Half the fun of the Friday nights in Floyd is that the music spills out onto the streets. Several jam bands (for want of a better word) twiddle their fiddles in little groups up and down the main road. The listeners cluster round their favorite bands, parking themselves in lawn chairs right on the sidewalk or along the curb. Motorists passing through usually stare at the scene in bewilderment. There's really nothing else like it.

PLAYLIST 🎵

To get in the old-time music mood, try these on for size:

- "In the Jailhouse Now," Jimmie Rodgers
- "East Virginia Blues," Ralph Stanley & The Clinch Mountain Boys
- "Turkey in the Straw," Dock Boggs
- "Mule Skinner Blues," Dolly Parton
- "Hey, Good Lookin'," Tennessee Ernie Ford
- "Keep on the Sunny Side," Carter Family
- "My Clinch Mountain Home," Carter Family
- "Blue Eyes Crying in the Rain," Willie Nelson

There's also nothing like the hottest fried chicken joint in all of Virginia, which is just a few miles down the highway from the central intersection of Floyd. One taste of the buttermilk biscuits slathered with butter and strawberry jam at the all-you-can-eat ❸ **Pine Tavern Restaurant** and your mouth won't stop salivating for the fried chicken and country ham to come. Of course, they also pile on the dumplings, pinto beans, green beans, and mashed potatoes. It's capped by either a fresh fruit or chocolate cobbler. The price for all this? Less than a 12-pack of Bud Light. The restaurant, tucked away between towering pine trees, has been in business since 1927 but new owners have brought their own grandmother's delicious recipes to better serve the traditional Blue Ridge Mountain cuisine. Not to be missed, but prepare to be rolled out at the end.

Floyd has a couple of good options for overnighters. The ❹ **Oak Haven Lodge** is in a fairly new building with big decks and comfortable beds. Some rooms even have a Jacuzzi. Another choice is the aptly named ❺ **Hotel Floyd**, which is also brand new and advertises an "eco-friendly" ethos. Flat-screeen TVs with satellite hookups make it easy being green.

In the morning, stop into the old two-story cedar building that houses ❻ **noteBooks and Black Water Loft**. This combination book, art, and music store has a Haight Ashbury–style coffeehouse on the 2nd floor. Browse books by local artists or relax with a vanilla latte on one of the fraying couches as sun streams through the windows.

DOWN TO EARTH EATS

Those who prefer their food organic or their clothes tie-dyed will be pleased with the earthy offerings at **Oddfella's Cantina** (www.oddfellascantina.com; 110 N Locust St, Floyd). Here you'll find a contemporary menu that's more coastal and organic in its influences. Sip wine while you listen to a local musician strumming away on the small stage under twinkling white lights.

Once you're on the road again, you'll want to head south toward Hwy 58, which makes up a large portion of the Crooked Road. These roads take you past real working farms, some of which have quite the hardscrabble aesthetic – very different from the estate farms and stables of northern Virginia and much of the Shenandoah Valley. When you get to the Blue Ridge Parkway, head south to the ❼ **Blue Ridge Music Center**. This large, grassy outdoor amphitheater offers programming that focuses on local musicians carrying on the traditions of Appalachian music. Performances are mostly on weekends and occasionally during the week. Bring a lawn chair and sit yourself down for an afternoon or evening performance. At night you can watch the fireflies glimmer in the darkness.

Further west is the town of ❽ **Galax**, which is one of the biggest towns and main attractions along the route. In the historic downtown, look for the bright neon marquee of the ❾ **Rex Theater**. This is a big old place, recently restored, with a Friday night show called Blue Ridge Backroads. Even if you can't make it to the theater at 8pm, you can listen to the two-hour show that broadcasts live to the surrounding counties on 89.1 FM.

Galax hosts the Smoke on the Mountain Barbecue Championship (www.smokeonthemountainva.com) on the second weekend in July. Teams from all over crowd the streets of downtown with their tricked-out mobile barbecue units. Judges walk around with signs that read "Silence please. Judging in progress." Booths and games line the streets and live music entertains the crowd. If you aren't lucky enough to be in town for the festival, you can still stop by one of its hosts, the ❿ **Galax Smokehouse**. This popular restaurant has loads of fans and was even called "Best of the Best" by the NBBQN. What's that, you ask? Well, it's the *National Barbecue News*. Did you let your subscription run out? The interior is classic diner/family restaurant and the staff is chipper. No one's puttin' on airs here.

If you think you've got what it takes to play with the boys in the Rex, poke your head into ⓫ **Barr's Fiddle Shop**. This little music shop has got a big selection of homemade and vintage fiddles and banjos along with mandolins, autoharps and harmonicas. You can get a lesson if you have time to hang around, or just admire the fine instruments which hang all over the walls.

If you ease on down the Crooked Road a little further, you'll come to the gorgeous town of ⓬ **Abingdon**. There, like a watery mirage in the desert, is the best hotel for hundreds of miles in any direction. The ⓭ **Martha Washington Inn** is in a regal, gigantic brick mansion built for General Francis Preston in 1832. Pulling up to this country palace after a long day's drive is like arriving at heaven's gates. You can almost hear the angels sing as you climb the stairs to the huge porch with views framed by columns. The rooms are fabulously appointed and have the most comfortable, impossible-to-leave beds in Virginia.

FIDDLE-DEE-DEE

Every second weekend in August for the last 70-some years, Galax has hosted the **Old Fiddler's Convention** (www.oldfiddlersconvention.com), which now lasts for six days. Hosted by the local Loyal Order of the Moose Lodge, musicians come from all over to compete as well as to play. There's also clog dancing!

The Martha Washington is a full-service resort. Have afternoon tea. Book a massage and a facial in the spa. Relax gardenside in a Jacuzzi the size of a pool. Have a Scotch in the President's Club. Read a back issue of the *New Yorker* in the tony library adorned with a wood-inlay globe and an Algonquin Round Table painting above the mantle. And when you're hungry, slip downstairs to the Dining Room for a sumptuous dinner.

If you can possibly pull yourself away from the Martha, Abingdon has several worthwhile activities. The ⓮ **Barter Theatre**, across the street, is the big man on Main St in its historic red-brick building. This regional theater company puts on its own productions of brand-name plays that run in repertory, and include choices such as *Evita* or *The Who's Tommy*.

Just outside of town is a relic from a more recent age, the ⓯ **MoonLite Drive-In**. Bring some beers or grab a Coke from the concession stand and settle in for a double feature picture show. Smoke cigarettes with the cool kids in their pickup.

Another star attraction on the Crooked Road is about 30 miles from Abingdon in the microscopic town of Hiltons. Here at Clinch Mountain is where you'll find the ⑯ **Carter Family Fold**, which has music every Saturday night.

It is overseen by Janette Carter, the youngest daughter of AP and Sara Carter, who, along with sister-in-law Maybelle, formed the core Carter group. (June Carter Cash was Maybelle's daughter.) The music starts at 7:30pm in the big wooden music hall. In the summer there is outdoor seating, too. The hall has replaced the original locale, AP's store, which now houses a museum dedicated to Carter Family history. Also: amateur clog dancing. Be afraid. Be very afraid.

DETOUR Across the Tennessee border, about two hours southwest of Bristol, is the legendary Dolly Parton's personal theme park **Dollywood** (www .dollywood.com). The Smoky Mountains come alive with lots of music and coasters. Fans will enjoy the daily Kinfolk Show starring Dolly's relatives or touring the two-story museum which houses her wigs, costumes, and awards. You can buy your own coat of many colors in Dolly's Closet.

When you wake up at the Martha, you'll want to take advantage of the very dapper breakfast (included in the price) of waffles, pancakes and omelets made to order in the dining room. Bonus points if you dare to wear your cuddly robe downstairs. In nearby Bristol you can attend the ⑰ **Bristol Motor Speedway**, which runs lots of Nascar events. If they're not racing, you can still tour the "world's fastest half-mile" and check out the "The Bristol Experience" in the adjacent museum. Oooh.

Ready to head back home? Pop in one of the CDs you picked up along the way and thrill to old-time music one last time as you ease back to modern life, keeping the wistful memories of banjos and bluegrass tucked safely inside your heart so nobody don't break it again.

David Ozanich

TRIP INFORMATION

GETTING THERE
From Richmond, take the I-64 west to the I-81 and head south to the exit for Floyd.

DO

Barr's Fiddle Shop
Real-as-it-gets country music instrument store. ☎ 276-236-2411; www.barrsfiddle shop.com; 105 S Main St, Galax, VA; ⏱ 9am-5pm

Barter Theatre
Impressive regional theater in Abingdon. ☎ 276-628-3991; www.bartertheatre.com; 127 W Main St, Abingdon, VA; ⏱ showtimes vary, mostly evenings

Blue Ridge Music Center
Outdoor amphitheater on the BR Parkway. ☎ 276-236-5310; www.blueridgemusic center.net; Milepost 213 Blue Ridge Pkwy, Galax, VA; ⏱ weekend shows

Bristol Motor Speedway
Nascar racetrack on the Virginia–Tennessee border. ☎ 423-989-6933; www.bristol motorspeedway.com; 151 Speedway Blvd, Bristol, VA; ⏱ showtimes vary

Carter Family Fold
Old-time music at the old Carter Family digs. ☎ 276-386-6054; www.carterfamilyfold .org; 3 miles NE of 709/614 junction on 614, Hiltons, VA; admission $5; ⏱ 7:30-11pm Sat, museum from 6pm

Floyd Country Store
Home of the Friday Night Jamboree. ☎ 540-745-6649; www.floydcountrystore.com; 206 N Locust St, Floyd, VA; admission $3; ⏱ store 10:30am-5:30pm Tue-Sun, jamboree 7:30pm Fri

Moonlite Drive-In
This fabulous vintage drive-in theater shows new releases. ☎ 276-628-7881; 17555 Lee Hwy, Abingdon, VA; ⏱ double feature from 9pm

noteBooks and Black Water Loft
Artsy bookstore with coffeehouse upstairs. ☎ 540-745-3060; www.notebooksandthe loft.com; 117 N Locust St, Floyd, VA; ⏱ 8am-6pm, to 8pm Fri & Sat

Rex Theater
Broadcasts the Friday night live bluegrass radio show in historic theater. ☎ 276-236-5309; www.rextheatergalax.com; 113 E Grayson St, Galax, VA; ⏱ 8-10pm Fri

EAT

Galax Smokehouse
Great barbecue restaurant in the heart of downtown Galax. ☎ 276-236-1000; www .thegalaxsmokehouse.com; 101 W Main St, Galax, VA; mains $6-15; ⏱ 11am-9pm Mon-Sat, 11am-3pm Sun

Pine Tavern Restaurant
Awesomely good fried chicken and traditional mountain cuisine. Go! ☎ 540-745-4482; www.thepinetavern.com; 611 Floyd Hwy N, Floyd, VA; mains $7-12; ⏱ 4:30-9:30pm Thu-Sat, 11am-8pm Sun

SLEEP

Hotel Floyd
Green motel in downtown Floyd. ☎ 540-745-6080; www.hotelfloyd.com; 120 Wilson St, Floyd, VA; r $75-159

Martha Washington Inn
Superglamorous hotel in a huge 1832 mansion estate. ☎ 276-628-8885; www .marthawashingtoninn.com; 150 W Main St, Abingdon, VA; r $150-500

Oak Haven Lodge
Comfortable lodge just a few minutes outside downtown Floyd. ☎ 540-745-5716; www .oakhavenlodge.com; 323 Webb's Mill Rd, Floyd, VA; r $65-90

LINK YOUR TRIP
www.lonelyplanet.com/trip-planner

Dollhouse Delaware

WHY GO Besides being one of the most obscure states in the union, Delaware weathers a polar split between rampant overdevelopment on her highways and some of the prettiest small towns and well-tended green spaces on the East Coast. On this trip we focus, firmly, on showing off the latter.

You can go on a quest, a journey, if you will, anywhere – even in Delaware. The goal: to find St Andrew's School, where *Dead Poets Society* was filmed. Many American public high schools are architectural monstrosities, but St Andrew's clearly represents something else: nicely manicured greenness, boarding school sensibility and an almost English sense of place.

A love of this particular aesthetic is lost and found in Delaware, a state that blends lush woodland and romantic small roads with long stretches of dreary highway development.

Drive east from Washington DC through Maryland onto Rte 8, which cuts across an overpowering sense of green kept in check by frequent villages, poultry farms and antique shacks, and eventually row after monotonous row of gas stations and vinyl townhouse blocks – the outskirts of ❶ **Dover**.

Past this peripheral ring, Dover unfolds into an attractive grid of red-brick and walkable serenity. This character is exemplified in quaint hotels like the ❷ **State Street Inn**, which splices a refined sense of Old South charm with typically exuberant Northeast hospitality (kind of like Delaware itself).

Around the way are two of Delaware's better free museums: the inordinately packed ❸ **Biggs Museum of American Art**, stuffed with

TIME
1 – 2 days

DISTANCE
60 miles

BEST TIME TO GO
May – Jul

START
Dover, DE

END
Wilmington, DE

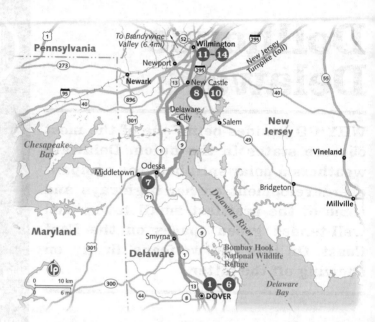

darling examples of Delaware silverware and a nice smattering of American landscapes, and the ❹ **Delaware Public Archives**, where an original signed copy of the Bill of Rights can be viewed for the first six months of the year. The rest of the time it's on display in the National Archives in Washington DC, according to a security guard who clearly resented this state of affairs.

There's a hint of rowdiness afoot in Dover; the town meshes military personnel from nearby Dover Air Force Base (first stop for all returning American war-dead) and the work-hard, play-hard staff of the Delaware state legislature. Seriously – Delaware can party! On a typical Dover Friday night, legislative aides on the town drink tequila and order buffalo wings in ❺ **WT Smithers**, while Annapolis rockers Jimmy's Chicken Shack tear the roof off at the nearby ❻ **Loockerman Exchange (LEX)**, a surprisingly kick-ass gig venue.

Hwy 13 north of Dover is a stretch of commercial ugliness dominated by the casino horse-racing complex of Dover Downs – a preservationist's most lurid nightmare. Leave this behind and veer onto Rte 71 and Noxontown Rd, the turnoff for ❼ **St Andrew's School**. Technically, unless you're a prospective student you can't visit these grounds; call ahead and try to arrange a tour. Friends tell us the school is far more liberal than the strict academy portrayed in *Dead Poets* (it's a co-ed boarding school – do we need to spell it out for you?).

St Andrew's, with its red-brick pavilions, dark wood corridors and lush, roll-ing lawns, embodies the balance of historic and organic charm that is still Delaware's most attractive feature. But it's not the only example of the style.

Heading up Rte 9 takes you to lovely **8** **New Castle**. Unlike many other communities of its size, which tend to give in to quick development cash in the form of fast-food outlets and gas stations, New Castle has realized it can trade in on something better: its aesthetic appeal. The cobblestoned town square, a fringe of lovely park that fronts the Delaware River and well-plotted, dignified middle-class row houses make one weep to think of the McMansions that mar so much of the American suburban landscape.

The right way to sleep and eat in New Castle is old-school style, with colonial banquets heavy on the butter, cream and ye olde hearte attackes, all available at **9** **Jessop's Tavern**. Round out the whole powder-wigged theme with a sleep in the alluringly stone-shod coziness of the **10** **Terry House B&B**, and ask the owner to accompany your breakfast with his excellent ivory-mashing skills on the piano.

ROUTE 9 ON OUR MINDS

It's not rife with dollhouses, but Rte 9 between Odessa and New Castle is one of the prettiest roads in the state, cutting through a picture-perfect wetland-scape of countless swamps draining into the mirror-flat Delaware River. Well, practically perfect; the looming smoke-stacks of Salem Nuclear Power Plant in New Jersey, visible from across the river, aren't the most flattering touch.

It's a scant few miles north of here to **11** **Wilmington**, which epitomizes Delaware class in different angles: from her art deco Design and Art Col-lege to blocks of handsome townhouses that conceal a surpassingly deli-cious local dining scene. **12** **Moro** surprises with a decadently excellent Pacific-rim-cum-steakhouse fusion menu (you don't expect Kobe Pork Milanese in this somewhat bypassed corner of the mid-Atlantic corridor). For more blue-collar countertop fare, **13** **Leo and Jimmy's** has been doing up excellent eats of a meat-between-bread nature for years.

DETOUR One of the reasons Dela-ware has so many doll-houses is because it was basically built by the uberwealthy Dupont family, who turned the Brandywine Valley (6 miles northwest of Wilmington on Rte 52) into their personal Camelot. Today the valley is stuffed with dozens of estates, but the grandest of them all is the old Dupont mansion, **Winterthur** (www.winterthur .org), which stands today as a 175-room country mansion and museum of decorative arts.

As for sleeps, it is universally acknow-ledged that the grandiose **14** **Hotel du Pont** is the best in the state. The palatial grounds and elegantly over-the-top rooms provide a nice offsetting touch to the accumulated cuteness of Delaware's dollhouses.

Adam Karlin

HISTORY & CULTURE

TRIP INFORMATION

GETTING THERE
Drive east from Washington DC onto Rte 50 and then Rte 8 in Maryland to get to Dover.

DO

Biggs Museum of American Art
Who isn't into Delaware's contributions to fine arts and expert silverware? ☎ 302-674-2111; www.biggsmuseum.org; 406 Federal St, Dover; admission free; ☽ 9am-4:30pm, from 1:30pm Sun

Delaware Public Archives
The archives' museum gives good insight into the quirks of America's first state. ☎ 302-744-5000; www.archives.delaware.gov; 121 Duke of York St, Dover; ☽ 8am-4:30pm Mon, Tue, Thu & Fri, 8am-8pm Wed, 9am-5pm Sat

St Andrew's School
Dead Poets Society was filmed on one of the country's prettiest boarding-school grounds. ☎ 302-378-9511; www.standrews-de.org; 350 Noxontown Rd, Middletown

EAT

Jessop's Tavern
Colonial decadence is the name of the culinary game here, as is a general sense of firelit hospitality. ☎ 302-322-6111; www.jessops tavern.com; 114 Delaware St, New Castle; mains $13-22; ☽ 11:30am-9pm Mon-Thu, 11:30am-11pm Fri & Sat, 11:30am-8pm Sun

Leo and Jimmy's
One of Wilmington's oldest and greatest delis is an urban institution, well deserving of both your gnosh and patronage. ☎ 302-656-7151; 728 N Market St, Wilmington; mains $4-12; ☽ 5:30am-4pm; ☷

Moro
Wilmington shocks with fusion wonders. Call ahead and the chef will prepare a personalized menu. ☎ 302-777-1800; www.mororestaurant.net; 1307 N Scott St, Wilmington; mains $24-42; ☽ dinner Tue-Sat

DRINK

Loockerman Exchange (LEX)
LEX attracts some consistently excellent talent throughout the year. Don't miss a show while you're here. ☎ 302-724-6255; www.loockerman.com; 1 W Loockerman St, Dover; ☽ to 1am

WT Smithers
This excellent bar is usually packed, and is a great spot for wings, beers and general bad behavior of the all-American kind. ☎ 302-674-8875; www.wtsmithers.us; 140 South State St, Dover; ☽ 11am-1am

SLEEP

Hotel du Pont
The storied du Pont is the grandest of grande-dame hotels, and the service is nicely laid-back for such a beautiful beast. ☎ 302-594-3100; www.hoteldupont.com; cnr Market & 11th Sts, Wilmington; r $260-430

State Street Inn
The Victorian rooms and vibe at this B&B are well complemented by an exuberantly friendly management team and central location. ☎ 302-734-2294; www.state streetinn.com; 228 N State St, Dover; r $110-135

Terry House B&B
It's corny and comforting, but that's what you're looking for in New Castle, and Terry House doesn't disappoint. ☎ 302-322-2505; www.terryhouse.com; 130 Delaware St, New Castle; r $90-110

USEFUL WEBSITES
www.preservationde.org
www.visitdelaware.com

LINK YOUR TRIP
TRIP

www.lonelyplanet.com/trip-planner

NEW ENGLAND TRIPS

Concocted by a gang of homesick (and uninspired) Brits, the name "New England" has long departed from its literal meaning. Today, the words are synonymous with a memorable medley of sights, smells and sounds. Craggy coastlines dotted with lonely lighthouses. Lobsters, fresh from the sea, served on weathered picnic tables with a heaping portion of corn. The shimmering colors of the autumnal flag flanking a quiet country road. Old, ivy-clad colleges, whose hallowed halls are filled with hot-blooded scholars. New England is indeed all these things, but it's also greater than the sum of its parts. It's an intangible feeling that has moved legions of creative souls – from Hawthorne to Homer – to honor the legendary landscape through myriad oeuvres.

PLAYLIST ♪♪ Push "play" and press your foot to the pedal – New England's yours to explore with this batch of classics.

- "Here It Goes Again," OK Go
- "Just What I Needed," The Cars
- "More Than a Feelin'," Boston
- "Moonlight in Vermont," Willie Nelson
- "The Wives Are in Connecticut," Carly Simon
- "The Impression That I Get," Mighty Mighty Bosstones
- "Land's End," String Cheese Incident
- "Psycho Killer," Talking Heads

The following chapter is a collection of trips that encompasses the best of New England's best. They create a family of unique vignettes that swirls through the region revealing scores of inspiring superlatives. Perhaps you'll be moved to pick up a paintbrush, dust off your typewriters, maybe even get a PhD. Somehow, the country's northeast nook has that effect on folks.

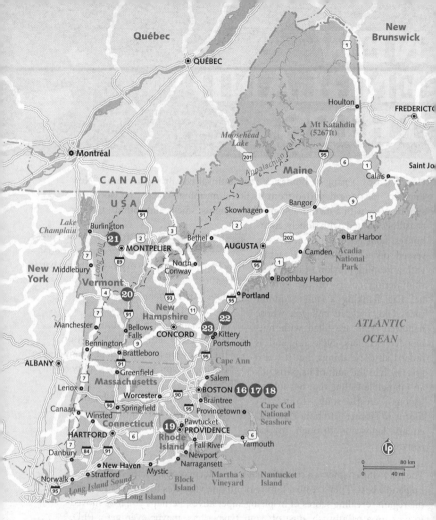

NEW ENGLAND TRIPS

48 Hours in Boston

WHY GO From world-class cuisine and cobbled colonial lanes to vintage shopping and crazed sports fanatics, Boston brews a colorful recipe for chaos. It'll take more than two days to crack Beantown's shell, but this sampler of sights and sounds is a wicked good way to get acquainted (or reacquainted) with the city.

TIME
2 days

BEST TIME TO GO
Year-round

START
Charles St

END
Beacon St

While calculating how to best spend your 48 hours in Boston, start your day with a hearty breakfast and an uncanny mathematical phenomenon at ❶ Paramount, on Charles St. One of the most popular brunch spots for many years and counting, this bustling little joint features delicious fruit spreads and gut-busting sandwiches, but is perhaps best known for its bizarrely convenient seating rotations. Despite the crowded atmosphere, tables always seem to clear out by the time your eyes start searching for a place to rest your bottom. They call it a science. We're pretty sure it's good karma.

Bolster your early jolt of caffeine with a wobbly ride on the ❷ MBTA subway, known to locals simply as "the T." You'll hear the most perfect Bostonian accents as conductors announce upcoming train stations ("next stop *Pahk* Street!"). Boston's T is the country's oldest subway and has been in operation since 1897. Charlie Cards (plastic swipe cards available from any uniformed employee) are rechargeable tickets that save passengers $0.30 per ride. The cards were named after poor old Charlie, a local legend made famous by the Kingston Trio; back in the old days you used to have to pay to get *off* the T and dear Charlie was stuck onboard forever because he couldn't pay the fare.

Exit the T at either Haymarket or State St Station for a leisurely stroll around the cheery marketplace of ❸ Faneuil Hall. Constructed in 1742 as a market and public meeting place, this brick colonial building

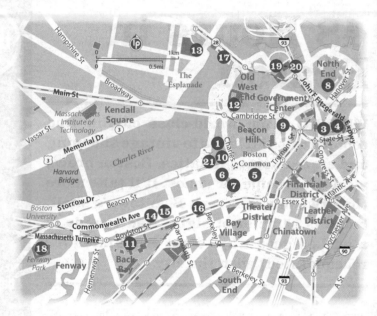

is topped by its signature grasshopper weather vane. Although the hall was supposed to be exclusively for local issues, the Sons of Liberty called many meetings here, informing public opinion about their objections to British taxation without representation. Three additional buildings in the back make up the bulk of the marketplace. Known as **4 Quincy Market**, these granite colonial structures were redeveloped in the 1970s into today's touristy, festive shopping and eating center with over 20 restaurants and 40 food stalls. Try out your Boston drawl as you order a hot bowl of clam *chowda* for lunch, or sample some of the other Boston staples such as baked beans or live lobster.

"Try out your Boston drawl as you order a hot bowl of clam chowda for lunch..."

After spending a disproportionate amount of money at one of the market's homemade-fudge stands, walk off your meal with a stroll through **5 Boston Common** and on to the **6 Public Garden**, a 24-acre botanical oasis of Victorian flowerbeds and weeping willows drooping over a lazy lagoon. Take a good look at the natural splendor while noting that in the 19th century this stunning garden was a tidal salt marsh (like the rest of Back Bay). For the quintessential Boston experience take a ride on the **7 Swan Boats**, a local tradition since 1877.

Ask anyone around town and they'll tell you that the ultimate Boston experience would be incomplete without venturing to the North End and eating at an Italian restaurant tucked away along one of the area's cobbled, medieval-esque streets. The problem is that there are so many great little family-owned joints to choose from and, to make matters worse, Boston's other neighborhoods are speedily stocking up on their fair share of amazing eating establishments. To appease even the harshest of critics, save your trip to Little Italy for dessert at **8** **Mike's**, home of the world's most perfect cannoli. Try your best to ignore the bakery's gaudy decorative mix of mural-sized mirrors framed like Renaissance paintings and buzzing neon lights casting blinding rays upon sweet-toothed customers. If you can't resist the call of the cannoli until after dinner then pick one up on the go as you ponder the infinite dinner options around town. We suggest heading back to Beacon Hill to dine in the smooth, brick wine cellar at **9** **Grotto**, or at celebrity chef Todd English's yuppie pizza paradise **10** **Figs**, but why not stumble upon your own eatery that the guidebooks don't know about. After dinner head to the towering Prudential Center and take a ride all the way to the top for some cocktail clinking at the swank **11** **Top of the Hub**. Drink in the views of the twinkling city lights below while smooth jazz melts over the ivory piano keys in the corner.

FREEDOM TRAIL

The best introduction to revolutionary Boston is the Freedom Trail. The red-brick path winds its way past 16 sites that earned this town its status as the cradle of liberty. The 2.5-mile trail follows the course of the conflict, from the Old State House, where Redcoats killed five men marking the Boston Massacre, to the Old North Church, where the sexton hung two lanterns to warn that British troops would come by sea. Visit the Boston Common information kiosk to pick up a free map or to hook up with a 90-minute guided tour led by the **Freedom Trail Foundation** (www.thefreedomtrail.org).

As the evening winds down, make your way back to Charles St for some beauty sleep before another busy day tomorrow. For 140 years, those staying at 225 Charles St had to be dragged in kicking and screaming in order to spend the night. Today, the wretched Charles St Jail has been transformed into the luxurious **12** **Liberty Hotel**. The hotel's decor playfully references the building's prison past. The restaurant, Clink (chuckle chuckle), preserves some old observation cells and the exquisite lobby soars to a 90ft ceiling (it used to be an indoor exercise space). For views of Boston from across the river, try spending the night at **13** **Hotel Marlowe**. Although the abundance of sassy leopard prints is vaguely reminiscent of a '70s porno, the spicy decor will undoubtedly appeal to the retro swinger in all of us.

Start the morning with a designer breakfast at one of the chichi brunch spots along Boston's effortlessly quirky Newbury St. Afterwards, strut your stuff along the concrete catwalk while doing some serious window shopping, then skip the overpriced boutiques and try your luck at one of the colorful vintage shops. For browsers with an eye for fashion but without a pocketbook to match, **14** **Closet, Inc** (and it does feel like some fashionista's overstuffed closet) is secondhand heaven. You'll never know what you're going to find at **15** **Second Time Around**, but you can be sure that it will have a designer label. Take a detour to Copley Sq and hit up **16** **Filene's Basement**, Boston's ultimate bargain bin. According to legend, the store's original owner, Mr Katz, planned to open a clothing store and decided that "Feline's" would be an appropriately clever name for the shop. He hired an artist to create the store's front sign, but when the artist finished Mr Katz realized that he'd mixed up the "i" and the first "e," writing "Filene's" instead. The name stuck and nowadays it's synonymous with great finds at great prices. The best part about Filene's is its unspoken longevity rule – items are automatically marked down the longer they remain in the store – so dig deep to find the real gems!

RED SOX NATION

First-time visitors to the Red Sox heartland always come away with some piece of memorabilia. If you're really smitten consider becoming an official member of the Red Sox fan club: check out www.redsox.com for more information. Famous fans include Matt Damon, Ben Affleck, Conan O'Brien, Steven Tyler, Rachael Ray and Steve Carell.

Try the immensely popular **17** **Duck Tours** for an abridged version of Boston's sights and history. Crafted from modified amphibious vehicles from WWII, the tour bus/boat splashes around the Charles River then takes to the city streets for a truly unique 90-minute tour.

Finish the day with an honest-to-goodness ballpark wiener at Fenway, home to the beloved **18** **Boston Red Sox**. Watching the rabid fans howl at their favorite players is way more fun than the actual game, but be warned: any back talk about the Sox or praise for the New York Yankees will be met with swift and severe punishment from vigilant devotees. If it isn't baseball season check out Boston's brood of die-hard fans cheering on the other local teams, like the **19** **Boston Bruins** or the **20** **Boston Celtics** (that's S-eltics, not K-eltics), who both play at Banknorth Garden.

After the game there's something that everyone's gotta do, no matter how touristy it may seem: have a drink where everybody knows your name. The Bull & Finch was an authentic English pub (dismantled in England, shipped to Boston and reassembled in a Beacon Hill townhouse). But that's not why hundreds of people descend on the place daily: the pub inspired the TV sitcom *Cheers* and has been thus renamed. Most visitors are disappointed that the interior of **21** **Cheers** bears no resemblance to the TV set. More importantly, tourists are the main clientele, so nobody knows your name (or anybody else's), although after five minutes you're almost guaranteed to hear a patron drunkenly humming the theme song under their breath, and that's reason enough to visit.

Brandon Presser

TRIP INFORMATION

GETTING THERE
Start the trip in the heart of downtown Boston along Charles St near the Park St subway station.

DO
Boston Bruins
The Bruins, under the former star power of Bobby Orr and Ray Bourque, play ice hockey at Banknorth Garden. ☎ 617-624-1900; www.bostonbruins.com; Banknorth Garden, 150 Causeway St; tickets from $32.50; ⊗ mid-Oct–mid-Apr; ♿

Boston Celtics
The Celtics, who've won more basketball championships than any other NBA team, play at Banknorth Garden above North Station. ☎ 617-523-3030; www.celtics.com; Banknorth Garden, 150 Causeway St; tickets from $22; ⊗ mid-Oct–Apr; ♿

Boston Red Sox
The Sox play in Fenway Park, the nation's oldest and most storied ballpark, built in 1912. ☎ 617-267-1700, tours 617-226-6666; www.redsox.com; 4 Yawkey Way; tickets from $28; ⊗ early Apr-early Oct; ♿

Closet, Inc
For shoppers with an eye for fashion but without the income to match. The Closet is a secondhand clothing store that carries high-quality items by acclaimed designers. ☎ 617-536-1919; 175 Newbury St; ⊗ 10am-6pm Tue-Sat, noon-5pm Sun

Duck Tours
Ninety-minute narrated land and water tours of the Charles River and Boston using modified amphibious vehicles from WWII depart from the Prudential Center and the Museum of Science. ☎ 617-267-DUCK; www.boston ducktours.com; Prudential Center; adult /child $32.55/22.05; ⊗ 8.30am-dusk late Mar-Dec; ♿

Faneuil Hall
A brick colonial building topped with the beloved grasshopper weather vane. The hall has earned the nickname 'Cradle of Liberty' due to the heated political movements nurtured here during the American Revolution. ☎ 617-242-5642; www.faneuilhall.com; Congress & North Sts; admission free; ⊗ 9am-5pm, ground fl shops 10am-8pm; ♿

Filene's Basement
The granddaddy of bargain stores, Filene's Basement carries overstocked and irregular items at everyday low prices. ☎ 617-424-5520; 497 Boylston St; ⊗ 9am-9pm Mon-Sat, 11am-7pm Sun

MBTA
The MBTA operates the oldest subway in America, dating back to 1897. It is known locally as "the T." ☎ 617-222-3200; www.mbta .com; one ride $2; ⊗ 5:30am-12:30am; ♿

Second Time Around
Come early and come often, because you never know what you're going to find, but you can be sure it will have a designer label. ☎ 617-247-3504, 617-266-1113; 176 & 219 Newbury St; ⊗ 11am-7pm Mon-Fri, 10am-7pm Sat, 10am-6pm Sun

Swan Boats
A Boston tradition since 1877, the Swan Boats swim around the lazy lagoon in Boston's Public Gardens. ☎ 617-522-1966; www. swanboats.com; Public Garden; adult/under 15yr $2.75/1.50; ⊗ 10am-4pm Apr–mid-Jun, 10am-5pm mid-Jun–Labor Day, noon-4pm Mon-Fri & 10am-4pm Sat & Sun Labor Day-late Sep; ♿

EAT & DRINK
Cheers
However touristy it may seem, have a drink where everybody knows your name. ☎ 617-227-9605; 84 Beacon St; draught beer $5.50; ⊗ 11am-12:30am

Figs
Figs is the brainchild of celebrity chef Todd English. Enjoy whisper-thin crusts topped

with interesting exotic toppings. Case in point: the namesake fig and prosciutto with Gorgonzola. ☎ 617-742-3447; 42 Charles St; pizzas $12-18.25; 🕑 11:30am-10pm Mon-Thu, to 11pm Fri & Sat, noon-10pm Sun

Grotto
As romantic as it is charming, this cramped, brick wine cellar magically transforms into a dim, candlelit hideout for foodies. ☎ 617-227-3434; www.grottorestaurant.com; 37 Bowdoin St; meals $25-45; 🕑 11:30am-3pm Mon-Fri, 5-10pm Sat & Sun

Mike's
A giant gaudy bakery in the heart of the Italian North End neighborhood. The cannoli are a must. ☎ 617-742-3050; www.mikespastry.com; 300 Hanover St; cannoli $2.50; 🕑 8am-10pm Sun-Thu, 8am-11pm Fri & Sat

Paramount
The nexus of the universe's mathematical harmony, Paramount features excellent breakfast fare and a bizarre seating style. ☎ 617-720-1152; 44 Charles St; mains $5.50-22; 🕑 7am-10pm Mon-Thu, 7am-11pm Fri, 8am-11pm Sat, 8am-10pm Sun; 🚻

Quincy Market
This food hall is packed with restaurants and food stalls. Choose from chowder, bagels, Indian, Greek, baked goods and ice cream.

☎ 617-338-2323; cnr Congress & State Sts; meals $5-15; 🕑 10am-9pm Mon-Sat, stalls & restaurants until late; 🚻

Top of the Hub
A brilliant place for bubbly overlooking the city. ☎ 617-536-1775; www.topofthehub.net; Prudential Center, 800 Boylston St; fixed menu $55; 🕑 11:30am-1am Mon-Sat, 11am-1am Sun

SLEEP

Hotel Marlowe
The spicy decor, including sassy leopard prints, will undoubtedly appeal to the retro swinger in all of us. ☎ 617-868-8000; www.hotelmarlowe.com; 25 Edwin H Land Blvd, Cambridge; r from $199; 🚻 🐾

Liberty Hotel
Once a dingy prison for common criminals, this hotel has been decorated playfully with its prison past in mind. Clink, the on-site restaurant, preserves some old observation cells and the lobby has a 90ft ceiling. ☎ 617-224-4000; www.libertyhotel.com; 225 Charles St; r from $314

USEFUL WEBSITES
www.boston.com
www.redsox.mlb.com

LINK YOUR TRIP
www.lonelyplanet.com/trip-planner

TRIP

2 Massachusetts to Miami: Fablantic Firsts p55
8 48 Hours in Manhattan p117
17 Ivy League Secrets & Superstitions p173

Ivy League Secrets & Superstitions

HISTORY & CULTURE

WHY GO Traditionally known for their "old boys club" attitude and ridiculously large endowments (we're talkin' money here), these redbrick bastions of higher learning are steeped in centuries of mystery and intrigue. Get the skinny on what these institutions are really about: parties, public nudity and pizza.

TIME
2 – 3 days

DISTANCE
200 miles

BEST TIME TO GO
Sep – Nov

START
Cambridge, MA

END
New Haven, CT

There's no better place to begin than America's first institution of higher learning: Harvard – the "big H," the "H-bomb," *Hahhhhvahh-hhd*. No matter how you spell it or say it, this saucy institution finds its way into the spotlight more than Paris Hilton. Some of the world's most interesting characters have passed through Harvard's gates: over a dozen American presidents, scores of Nobel prize winners, and a bevy of notable screen actors. Fictional characters too: there was that girl from *Legally Blonde*, the nerd in *With Honors*, the protagonist of the *Da Vinci Code* taught at Harvard, and who could forget *Love Story*'s ill-fated Jennifer Cavalleri.

Give the admissions tour a miss if you aren't into watching prospective students sweat bullets as they sheepishly ask about the SATs. Instead, head to the Holyoke Center for the ❶ **Harvard University Campus Tours**, which are geared to tourists. The one-hour tour ambles between ivy-clad buildings while animated guides chat about the college's humble beginnings. Apparently the sordid history of higher learning in America reads like a twisted Dickens novel (although maybe a little less wordy). You'll learn about Harvard's "house system," which is similar to the dormitories in the Harry Potter series. Students are separated into different houses (*sans* sorting hat, of course) each named for an early president of the university (except Harvard's fourth president, Leonard Hoar – apparently no one wanted a Hoar House on campus…). The tour ends at the infamous ❷ **John Harvard Statue**.

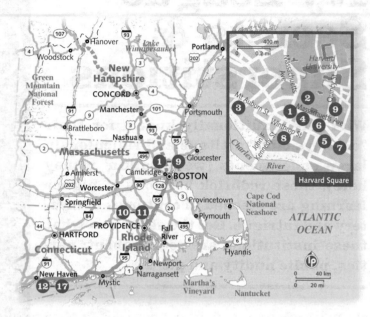

Harvard Square

This sculpture, by Daniel Chester French, is inscribed with "John Harvard, Founder Of Harvard College, 1638" and is commonly known as the statue of three lies: John Harvard was *not* the college's founder, Harvard was actually founded in 1636, and the man depicted isn't even Mr Harvard. This ubiquitous symbol hardly lives up to the university's motto, *Veritas* (truth). Most tourists rub John Harvard's shiny foot for good luck; little do they know that campus pranksters regularly use the foot the way dogs use a fire hydrant.

"The sordid history of higher learning in America reads like a twisted Dickens novel (although maybe a little less wordy)."

After an hour of touring it's time to get off the beaten track and check out the college from a student's perspective. If you've worked up an appetite, try ❸ **Darwin's Ltd** on Mt Auburn St, just west of Harvard Sq. This relaxed deli-cum-café is the choice spot for intellectual types and confirms the theory of "Survival of the Fittest." Grab a leather chair (if you can find a free one), snuggle up with your iMac and enjoy highly evolved sandwiches fusing regional produce and savory meats.

After lunch, head back to Massachusetts Ave to find ❹ **Leavitt & Peirce**. This awesome remnant of old-school Harvard sells an endless selection of tailor-made tobacco, sending Cantabrigians to an early grave for centuries. Give your lungs a break and sneak upstairs to play parlor games in the lofted salon under the watchful eyes of taxidermic elk. Let your new pipe purchase dangle languidly from your puckered lips as you meander among the colonial gridiron between the Harvard's Old Yard and Charles River. Here you will find Harvard's collection of not-so-secret societies, known on campus as Final Clubs. These single-sex clubs are sprinkled all over the place. Have a stroll past the impressive colonial exteriors of the Fox (44 JFK St), Spee (76 Mt Auburn St), Phoenix (72 Mt Auburn St), and the Porcellian (1324 Massachusetts Ave), to name just a few. The most spectacular facade belongs to the **5** **Lampoon Castle** on Mt Auburn St. Although not technically a Final Club, the *Lampoon* is Harvard's humor magazine, and their hang-out just so happens to be a Flemish-style castle chock full of oddities like czarist silverware, props from obscure B-list movies, and even a secret bookcase that opens to reveal a hidden study.

> **DETOUR**
>
> If you aren't sick of popped collars and crimson brick then head up to Hanover, New Hampshire, to check out **Dartmouth College**. Surprise! Free guided walking tours are also available on campus, departing from the 2nd floor of McNutt Hall. Be sure to swing past the **Sphinx Tomb** on East Wheelock St, which belongs to the secretive Sphinx Senior Society.

When it's time to refuel, pack an artery at **6** **Bartley's Burger Cottage** on Massachusetts Ave. Wonderfully kitsch paraphernalia smothers the walls at this carnivore paradise. Tacky debris aside, the juicy burgers are unbeatable and are even named after contemporary celebs. Drool over "Brad Pitt" or one of the other hunks of meat, or try "Dick Cheney," lavished with heart-attack-inducing greasy fixings. Salads are available for the faint of heart, but coming to Bartley's for a hummus platter is like going to the Louvre and not seeing the Mona Lisa. After dinner, walk off the meat sweats and check out **7** **Daedalus**, the choice nightspot for undergrads with a valid ID (or a really good phony). This sleek bar with a tantalizing roof deck bounces virtually every night of the week with gaggles of Final Club folks. When the bars start to close their doors (lest we forget that Massachusetts was founded under Puritanical jurisdiction) head west along Mt Auburn St and make a left on JFK St to find **8** **Pinocchio's**. Soak up that Long Island iced tea with an oh-so-tasty slice of square Sicilian pizza (tomato basil is the student fave) served by surly bakers. During the day this tiny pizza parlor flies under the radar, but in the late evenings it transforms into a stronghold for procrastinating Harvardites.

As the students retreat in the wee hours of the night to tackle their books, hang your hat at the gorgeous **9** **Harvard Faculty Club** on Quincy St, just east of the Old Yard. Despite the name, this stunning colonial mansion is open to all members and friends of the Harvard community (so you better bust out the Rolodex to track down an invitation!). The upstairs bedrooms are swathed in floral prints and covered in a blizzard of doilies. Each room also comes with Cambridge's most precious commodity: a parking space.

In the morning get an early start and take I-95 south out of the Boston city limits to quieter Providence. Here you will find beautiful Brown, the rambunctious younger child of an uptight New England household. Big brothers Harvard and Yale carefully manicure their public image, while the little black sheep of the family prides itself on staunch liberalism and occasional bouts of indecent exposure. A campus tour is a good way to get your bearings and to learn about the artsy-fartsy student body, so stop by the Brown admissions office for a **⑩ Brown University Campus Tour**, led by ubermanic students who have clearly taken lessons in walking backwards without getting plowed by oncoming traffic. If you're in need of more luck after touching John Harvard's foot, head to the **⑪ John Hay Library** and rub the nose of the John Hay statue (although who knows what those cheeky Brown students do to that man's poor honker). Make sure you *don't* visit the four other libraries on campus, as it is commonly believed that those who venture into each structure will be cursed forever and will never marry. If you happen to be bopping around the libraries at the beginning of exam period you might find yourself amid scores of students passing out doughnuts in the buff to their fellow classmates who are busy burning the midnight oil.

PLAYLIST ♫

Nothing's more "quintessential college" than the doo-wop of unaccompanied voices. Download mp3 samples from the websites of these groups and shoo-bee-doo your way across New England.

- "McDonald's Girl," Harvard Din & Tonics
- "We Didn't go to Harvard," Cayuga Waiters
- "Whiffenpoof Song," Yale Whiffenpoofs
- "Who Are You," Brown Derbies
- "Change in My Life," Harvard Opportunes
- "Sally in Our Alley," Yale Alley Cats
- "Danny Boy," Harvard Krokodiloes
- "Build Me Up Buttercup," Yale Spizzwinks(?)

Hop back in your car and continue in a southeasterly direction along I-95. Turn off the highway when you see signs for downtown New Haven and follow the arrows for about a half-mile until you reach the gorgeous gothic realm that is Yale University, America's third-oldest university. Head to the corner of Elm and Temple Sts to catch a free **⑫ Yale University Campus Tour** led by a current undergraduate. The tour does a good job of fusing historical and academic facts and passes by several standout architectural flourishes, including Yale's tallest building, **⑬ Harkness Tower**, a stunning bell tower and the preferred spot of some for a bit of late-night hanky-panky.

Although the walking tours overflow with tidbits about life at Yale, the guides refrain from mentioning the handful of tombs scattered around the campus. No, these aren't filled with corpses; in fact, it's quite the opposite – these tombs are the secret hangouts for a select group of senior students. The most notorious **⑭ Tomb**, located at 64 High St, is the HQ for the notorious Skull & Bones Club, founded in 1832. Its list of members reads like a *Who's Who* of high-powered politicos and financiers over the last two centuries. Members keep mum, letting rumors fly about the artifacts hidden deep within the crypt like Geronimo's skull and Hitler's fine china.

With all those "Type A" personalities milling about, one might think that the competition is fierce; however, the biggest rivalry on campus actually takes place beyond the classroom. It all revolves around pizza, and two greasy joints have been battling it out for the crown ever since Roosevelt was president (the second one). **⑮ Frank Pepe Pizzeria Napoletana**, known simply as Pepe's, is the original don of the dough. Then there's **⑯ Sally's Apizza**, which sprang up down the street a couple of years later. Yale's heated two-(pizza)-party politics will undoubtedly rage on for centuries to come. Take a break between slices and head to 306 York St and try smooth-talking your way into **⑰ Mory's Temple Bar**, a private dining club and Yale institution, which seats around 100. If you're lucky, you might catch a homemade melody sung by the Whiffenpoofs, the oldest collegiate a cappella troupe in the country.

Brandon Presser

TRIP INFORMATION

GETTING THERE
From Boston, cross over the Charles River to Cambridge and make your way down I-95.

DO

Brown University Campus Tours
Offers free tours of the campus and heaps of academic information. ☎ 401-863-2378; www.brown.edu; 45 Prospect St, Providence, RI; ◷ 8:30am-5pm Mon-Fri

Harvard University Campus Tours
Guided by members of the Crimson Key Society, focusing on history and humorous anecdotes. ☎ 617-495-1573; www.harvard.edu; Holyoke Center Arcade, 1350 Massachusetts Ave, Cambridge, MA; ◷ tours 10am & 2pm Mon-Fri, 2pm Sat

Leavitt & Peirce
A remnant of old-school Harvard, L&P sells an endless selection of tailor-made tobacco. ☎ 617-547-0576; 1316 Massachusetts Ave, Cambridge, MA; ◷ 9am-6pm Mon-Sat, to 8pm Thu, noon-5:30pm Sun

Yale University Campus Tours
Free campus maps and a self-guided walking-tour pamphlet ($1). ☎ 203-432-2300; www.yale.com.visitor; cnr Elm & Temple Sts, New Haven, CT; ◷ 9am-4:30pm Mon-Fri, 10am-4pm Sat & Sun, tours 10:30am & 2pm Mon-Fri, 1:30pm Sat

EAT & DRINK

Bartley's Burger Cottage
Kitschy paraphernalia smothers the walls while patrons devour juicy burgers. Cash only. ☎ 617-354-6559; www.mrbartley.com; 1246 Massachusetts Ave, Cambridge, MA; burgers from $9.25; ◷ 11am-9pm Mon-Sat

Daedalus
Slap on a beret and join the fray of anonymous jetsetters brazenly swigging their designer cocktails, and enjoy the roof deck in summer. ☎ 617-349-0071; www.daedalus harvardsquare.com; 45 Mt Auburn St, Cambridge, MA; cocktails from $9; ◷ 11am-2am

Darwin's Ltd
Highly evolved sandwiches fuse regional produce with savory meats. ☎ 617-354-5233; www.darwinsltd.com; 148 Mt Auburn St, Cambridge, MA; sandwiches from $7.10; ◷ 6:30am-9pm Mon-Sat, 7am-9pm Sun

Frank Pepe Pizzeria Napoletana
Immaculate pizza fired in a coal oven, just as it has been since 1925. ☎ 203-865-5762; www.pepespizzeria.com; 157 Wooster St, New Haven, CT; small pizza from $6.30; ◷ 11:30am-10pm Mon-Sat, noon-10pm Sun

Pinocchio's
Famous for square Sicilian slices, Pinocchio's is popular late at night with procrastinating Harvardites. ☎ 617-876-4897; www.pinocchiospizza.com; 74 Winthrop St, Cambridge, MA; Sicilian slice $2.40; ◷ noon-midnight Sun, 11am-1am Mon-Wed, to 2:30am Thu-Sat

Sally's Apizza
Giving Pepe's a run for its money since 1938. The white clam pie is legendary. ☎ 203-624-5271; www.sallysappiza.net; 237 Wooster St, New Haven, CT; white clam pie $10; ◷ 5-10pm Tue-Sun, closed Sep

SLEEP

Harvard Faculty Club
Bedrooms swathed in floral prints and covered in a blizzard of doilies. Open to members and friends of the Harvard community. ☎ 617-495-5758; www.hfc.harvard.edu; 20 Quincy St, Cambridge, MA; s/d from $199/$224

USEFUL WEBSITES
www.harvard.edu
www.brown.edu
www.yale.edu

www.lonelyplanet.com/trip-planner

LINK YOUR TRIP

Literary New England

WHY GO From Edith Wharton to Edward Gorey, Herman Melville to Harriet Beecher Stowe, the writers of New England have inspired generations with their poignant prose. Make this trip a mea culpa to your English teacher for not having read the great American classics you were assigned in school.

The ❶ Boston Public Library is a fitting place to begin the ultimate literary tour. Constructed in 1852, the eye-catching structure lends credence to Boston's reputation as the "Athens of America." After thumbing through fragile tomes containing some of the region's greatest published works (including John Adams' personal library), pick up a free brochure and take a self-guided tour through the sumptuous neoclassical space. Note the hard-to-miss murals by John Singer Sargent. If you get lost among the volumes, take a break at the ❷ Map Room Café. Swig a smooth cappuccino while memorizing bits of Robert Frost (it'll come in handy later), and enjoy the calm atmosphere in the enchanting Italianate courtyard.

If you don't have the courage to confront Boston's post–Big Dig concrete jungle, retreat to the opulent ❸ Omni Parker House. The nation's longest continuously operating hotel (it opened in 1855) was once a veritable sea of velvet drapes and floral prints, but today, after a hefty refurbishment, the rooms are thoroughly modern. Charles Dickens frequented the hotel (check out the oak-framed "Dickens Mirror" on the mezzanine level); it was here that he gave his first reading of *A Christmas Carol*.

When you're ready to hit the road, drive along I-93 (heading north) and take Hwy 1, then Rte 107 until you arrive in the quiet seaside town of Salem. Known for its bevy of spell-spewing witches, this little colonial haven also features the ❹ House of the Seven Gables. The

TIME
3 – 4 days

DISTANCE
610 miles

BEST TIME TO GO
Jun – Aug

START
Boston, MA

END
Middlebury, VT

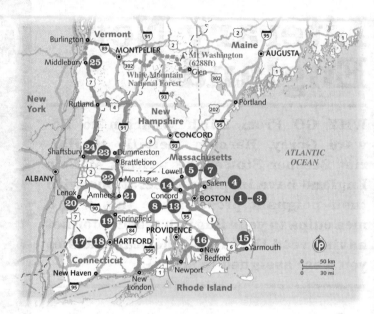

house was made famous by Nathaniel Hawthorne's novel of the same name, which used the manse as a metaphor to explore the gloomy Puritanical way of life in early New England. There are four historic buildings to be explored and a luscious waterfront garden to remind ourselves that New England is much less dour than Hawthorne's depictions.

For something a bit more modern, hop back on the highway and take I-95 to I-93 until the turnoff for I-495. Here you will find the grumbling industrial town of Lowell, home to the Beat Generation's beloved Jack Kerouac. A small landscaped path on Bridge St, known as the **5 Jack Kerouac Commemorative**, makes for a lovely place to stretch your legs and read several passages from his best-known works. His grave at **6 Edson Cemetery**, on the corner of Gorham and Saratoga Sts, has become an unofficial pilgrimage site for free spirits. Try a **7 Jack Kerouac Walking Tour**, compiled by the Jack Kerouac Subterranean Information Society. The fantastically detailed route stops at various sites throughout Lowell featured in five of his novels.

Woodsy Concord, just a short jaunt down Rte 3, is another step back in time. Nestled within the quaint collection of pitches and gables are the former residences of two of New England's most beloved authors. Check out the **8 Ralph Waldo Emerson Homes**, which boasts most of the original furnishings purchased by the writer, and a luscious organic garden planted by Henry David Thoreau for Nathaniel Hawthorne (he also inhabited the estate).

Louisa May Alcott wrote her famous semiautobiographical *Little Women* in her home Orchard House, which is now part of a small estate of historical buildings called **9 Louisa May Alcott Homes**. Complete Concord's literary hat-trick with a stay at **10 Wayside Inn**, made famous by Longfellow's poems *Tales from a Wayside Inn*.

After a day in the life of some of Concord's finest, check out their final resting place at **11 Sleepy Hollow Cemetery** (no relation to Ichabod Crane). Sleepy Hollow's wooded grounds challenge the stereotype of a spooky graveyard with towering evergreens, rolling hills, and plenty of space to gleefully spread a checkered tablecloth for a shady afternoon picnic. Head to the oft-visited Author's Ridge to visit the graves of Thoreau, Hawthorne, Emerson and two Alcotts, all quietly buried in the stunning setting that inspired each of their oeuvres.

"I went to the woods because I wished to live deliberately, to front only the essential facts of life, and see if I could not learn what it had to teach, and not, when I came to die, discover that I had not lived." Follow Henry David Thoreau's inspirational words from the nonfiction success *Walden; or, Life in the Woods* and enjoy an early-morning trip to nearby **12 Walden Pond**. It was here that Thoreau put Transcendentalism's naturalist beliefs into practice and built himself a rustic cabin on the shores of the pond. Beat the crowds and delight in crunching freshly fallen leaves underfoot while taking in the serene setting orbiting the quiet glacial shore. Today, tombstone-like boulders mark the site of Thoreau's cabin, and its original furnishings are now preserved at the **13 Concord Museum**, which also features other important pieces of "New Englandiana" such as Emerson's desk and chair, and Paul Revere's "one if by land" lantern.

OH! THE PLACES YOU CAN'T GO!

If Dr Seuss' inspirational words have you jonesing for your own literary adventure, beware of New England's literary decoys. Although they sound like honest-to-goodness New England towns, the following spots are figments of the authors' imaginations:

- Starkfield, Massachusetts – in *Ethan Frome* by Edith Wharton, supposedly located in the Berkshires.

- Arkham, Massachusetts – in several works by HP Lovecraft, home of the faux Ivy-League Miskatonic University.

- Castle Rock, Maine – in *The Dead Zone* by Stephen King, one of many made-up towns in King's scary state.

For a double dose of divinity, stop for lunch at the **14 Fruitlands Tearoom**, in the nearby town of Harvard. The restaurant sits on a former vegetarian commune founded by Louisa May Alcott's father, Bronson Alcott, who aspired to set up a place for Transcendentalists to thrive.

After some contemplative kumbaya-ing, it's time to blaze a trail down I-95 for something a little more light-hearted. Follow the turnoff on Rte 3 for

Cape Cod and switch to Rte 6 as you approach Yarmouth, home to weirdo wordsmith Edward Gorey (yes, that is actually his real last name.) His former home has since been transformed into the ⓕ **Edward Gorey House**, a museum featuring exhibits about his life and work. Don't forget to stop by the gift shop to grab some wickedly twisted bits of Gorey-ana.

If Gorey's gory stories of impaled children give you nightmares, calm your nerves at the plush, Victorian ⓠ **Melville House** in New Bedford. Herman Melville often visited his sister here, and his memory has been preserved in the aptly named Herman Melville room, which features a handsome portrait of the writer.

Start the day with a drive along I-195, I-395, and Rte 2 until you reach Connecticut's capital, Hartford. For 17 years, Samuel Langhorne Clemens (better known as Mark Twain) and his family called Hartford home and lived in a stunning orange-and-black brick Victorian home on Farmington Ave. His years here were known to be the most productive of his life and the most tragic (two of his children died here), and the ⓠ **Mark Twain House & Museum** carefully illustrates his history through photos, films, artifacts and manuscripts. He penned some of his most famous works here, including *The Adventures of Tom Sawyer, The Adventures of Huckleberry Finn* and *A Connecticut Yankee in King Arthur's Court.*

"The squat figure of the Lorax looks beseechingly up at passersby"

Next door to the Twain residence is the former home of the esteemed author Harriet Beecher Stowe. Now a museum in the ⓠ **Harriet Beecher Stowe Center**, the sun-drenched manse pays tribute to the author of *Uncle Tom's Cabin,* which bolstered the antislavery movement. Built in 1871, the Stowe house reflects the author's strong ideas about decorating and domestic efficiency, as expressed in her bestseller *American Woman's Home,* which sold almost as many copies as her ubiquitous novel.

As you head towards the rolling Berkshires, make a quick stop in Springfield to see the ⓠ **Dr Seuss National Memorial Sculpture Garden** before turning off of I-91. Born in Springfield in 1904, Theodor Seuss Geisel passed through the gates of Dartmouth College and worked as a political cartoonist before earning his doctorate in gibberish and settling down to write his first children's book. The sculpture garden, created by his stepdaughter Lark Grey Dimond-Cates, features large-scale incarnations of his literary oeuvre. There's a 10ft-tall 'book' displaying the entire text of *Oh! The Places You'll Go!* and an impish-looking Geisel sitting at his drawing board, the Cat standing by his shoulder. In the opposite corner of the quad, the squat figure of the Lorax looks beseechingly up at passersby, his famous environmental warning engraved at his feet: "*Unless.*"

HISTORY & CULTURE

Follow I-90 west of Springfield and head to Lenox just before the highway crosses the state border into New York. Almost 50 years after Nathaniel Hawthorne left his home in this quaint hamlet (now part of Tanglewood), another writer found inspiration in the pine-scented Berkshires. Pulitzer Prize–winner Edith Wharton came to Lenox in 1899 and proceeded to build her palatial estate, the ㉒ **Mount**. When not immersed in her craft, she would entertain a colorful array of guests including Henry James. Wharton summered at the Mount for a decade before moving permanently to France.

From patricians to poets – move along Rte 7 to Rte 8a and finally Rte 9 until you reach the birch-clad college town of Amherst, once home to the

> **DETOUR**
>
> If you're tired of the backseat peanut gallery screaming "Are we there yet?!" then make a bee-line to the tiny town of Glen for a visit to **Story Land** (www.storylandnh.com). This refreshingly non-Disneyfied theme park caters to the three-to-nine-year-old crowd with miniature rides and activities.

reclusive Emily Dickinson. During her lifetime, Emily Dickinson published only seven poems, but after her death, more than 1000 were discovered and published, and her verses on love, death, nature and immortality have made her one of the most important poets of her time. It is not known why she was so hermitic as she aged, although some say she fell in love (unrequitedly) with a married clergyman and withdrew from the world into a private realm of pain, passion and poignancy. Her home is now the ㉑ **Emily Dickinson Museum**, which features a tour of her house and the one next door, which belonged to her brother Austin. Continue north along Rte 63 and slip through the sleepy town of Montague to the find the ㉒ **Montague Bookmill**, a converted cedar gristmill from 1842 that has multiple rooms containing stacks of used books ripe for the picking.

Travel north into Vermont to find the ultimate place for a lit lover to hang their hat. ㉓ **Naulakha**, in Dummerston, offers guests the chance to spend the night in Rudyard Kipling's home – a truly unique experience closely guarded and maintained by the Landmark Trust USA. Kipling penned the ubiquitous *Jungle Book* here in little Naulakha, tucked in a valley that dimples the

NOT HALF BAKED

The **Bread Loaf Writers' Conference**, usually held in August, is the oldest writers' conference in America, having started long before 'creative writing' became a college course. Robert Frost inaugurated the idea in the 1920s, and today a mix of famous and aspiring writers still gather in the hill above Middlebury. Many events are open to the public; check out www.middlebury .edu/~blwc for more information.

state's mountainous spine. He dreamed up Mowgli and his mates as a child in colonial India, but used the quiet hideaway in the thick Vermont forests to bring his critters to life on the page. Kipling also wrote *Captains Courageous* here.

In Shaftsbury, Vermont, west along Rte 9, Frost fanatics will get their fill at the ㉔ **Robert Frost Stone House Museum**. It was here, in this modest country home, that Frost composed some of his most memorable works. In fact the guides will tell you that the beloved *Stopping by Woods on a Snowy Evening* was actually composed at the dining room table on a sweltering summer night. The poem was featured in his fourth volume of poetry, *New Hampshire*, which earned him his first coveted Pulitzer Prize.

> "At the end you'll find Frost's ubiquitous fork in the road… decide which way you want to go."

Let a stroll along the ㉕ **Robert Frost Interpretive Trail**, further north along Rte 7 (near Middlebury), be the final stop on your journey. As you wend your way through a picturesque thicket, pause to read the plaques featuring memorable quotes from his poetry. At the very end you'll find Frost's ubiquitous fork in the road. Now it's up to you to decide which way you want to go. The rest of the journey is yours.

Brandon Presser

TRIP INFORMATION

GETTING THERE
Start your trip in the heart of downtown Boston.

DO

Boston Public Library
A beautiful neoclassical structure affirming Boston's reputation as the "Athens of America." ☎ 617-536-5400; www.bpl.org; 700 Boylston St, Boston, MA; admission free; ⊙ 9am-9pm Mon-Thu, 9am-5pm Fri & Sat year-round, 1-5pm Sun Oct-May; ♿

Edward Gorey House
This museum in Gorey's former home has exhibits about his life and work, and a gift shop. ☎ 508-362-3909; www.edwardgoreyhouse.org; 8 Strawberry Lane, Yarmouth, MA; adult/child $5/2; ⊙ mid-Apr–mid-Dec; ♿

Emily Dickinson Museum
This museum details the reclusive and introspective life of poet Emily Dickinson. ☎ 413-542-8161; www.emilydickinsonmuseum.org; 280 Main St, Amherst, MA; adult/child $8/4; ⊙ 9am-5pm May-Oct

Harriet Beecher Stowe Center
The manse here pays tribute to the author of Uncle Tom's Cabin, which bolstered the antislavery movement. ☎ 860-525-9317; www.harrietbeecherstowe.org; 77 Forest St, Hartford, CT; adult/child $9/6; ⊙ 9:30am-4:30pm Tue-Sat, noon-4:30pm Sun Jun-Oct, closed Tue Nov-May

House of the Seven Gables
The house made famous by Nathaniel Hawthorne's novel of the same name. ☎ 978-744-0991; www.7gables.org; 54 Turner St, Salem, MA; adult/child $12/7.25; ⊙ 10am-5pm Nov-Jun, 10am-7pm Jul-Oct

Jack Kerouac Walking Tour
This fantastically detailed route stops at various sites throughout Lowell featured in five of his novels. Tour times fluctuate with demand. Self-guided maps are also available. http://ecommunity.uml.edu/jklowell; Lowell, MA

Louisa May Alcott Homes
The setting of bestselling Little Women, Alcott's home is now a museum detailing her life surrounded by Transcendentalism. ☎ 978-369-4118; www.louisamayalcott.org; 399 Lexington Rd, Concord, MA; adult/child $9/5; ⊙ 10am-4:30pm Mon-Sat, 1-4:30pm Sun Apr-Oct, reduced winter hours; ♿

Mark Twain House & Museum
This museum carefully illustrates Mark Twain's life in Hartford through photos, films, artifacts and manuscripts. ☎ 860-247-0998; www.marktwainhouse.org; 351 Farmington Ave, Hartford, CT; adult/child $14/8; ⊙ 9:30am-5:30pm Mon-Sat, noon-5:30pm Sun, closed Tue Jan-Mar

Montague Bookmill
This bookstore is a converted cedar gristmill from 1842 with many rooms of used books on offer. ☎ 413-367-9206; www.montaguebookmill.com; 440 Greenfield Rd, Montague, MA; ⊙ 10am-6pm

The Mount
Award-winning writer Edith Wharton came to Lenox in 1899 and built this palatial estate where she entertained a colorful array of guests. ☎ 413-551-1111; www.edithwharton.org; 2 Plunkett St, Lenox, MA; adult/child $18/free; ⊙ 9am-5pm May-Oct

Ralph Waldo Emerson Homes
Emerson's home boasts original furnishings and a luscious organic garden planted by Henry David Thoreau for Nathaniel Hawthorne. ☎ 978-369-2236; www.rwe.org/emersonhouse; 28 Cambridge Turnpike, Concord, MA; adult/child $7/free; ⊙ 10am-4:30pm Thu-Sat, 1-4:30pm Sun mid-Apr–Oct

Walden Pond
This stunning, silent glacial pond made famous by Henry David Thoreau and surrounded by multicolored trees was the epicenter of Transcendental thought. ☎ 978-369-3254; www.mass.gov/dcr/parks/northeast/wldn.htm; 915 Walden St, Concord, MA; admission free, parking $5; ⊙ dawn-dusk; ♿

EAT & DRINK

Fruitlands Tearoom

This restaurant sits on a former Transcendentalist commune founded by Louisa May Alcott's father. ☎ 978-456-3924; 102 Prospect Hill Rd, Harvard, MA; lunch $11-14; ☽ Apr-Oct

Map Room Café

A quaint coffee shop in the heart of the Boston Public Library. Grab a coffee and curl up with a borrowed book. ☎ 617-536-5400; www.bpl.org; 700 Boylston St, Boston, MA; coffee $2; ☽ 9am-9pm Mon-Thu, 9am-5pm Fri & Sat year-round, 1-5pm Sun Oct-May; ♿

SLEEP

Melville House

Herman Melville often visited his sister at this 1855 Victorian manse. Check out his portrait in the aptly named Herman Melville bedroom. ☎ 508-990-1566; www.melvillehouse.net; 100 Madison St, New Bedford, MA; d $130-175

Naulakha

Catch your Zs in the former cottage of Rudyard Kipling. ☎ 802-254-6868; www.landmarktrustusa.org/naulakha/about.html; 707 Kipling Rd, Dummerston, VT; r $275-425

Omni Parker House

The nation's longest continuously operating hotel anchors the heart of historical downtown Boston. Dickens loved to stay here. ☎ 617-227-8600; www.omnihotels.com; 60 School St, Boston, MA; r $199-599

Wayside Inn

This lovely 10-room inn, made famous by Longfellow's poems *Tales from a Wayside Inn*, has an extensive archive of the history of the inn, which has been operating since 1700. ☎ 978-443-1776; www.wayside.org; 72 Wayside Inn Rd, Sudbury, MA; d $125-175

USEFUL WEBSITES

www.bpl.org

LINK YOUR TRIP

www.lonelyplanet.com/trip-planner

The Great Rhode Island Bicycle Tour

WHY GO While driving between Massachusetts and Connecticut, many speed demons might not realize they've passed through an entire state. However, those who stop for a closer look will uncover a treasure trove of useless oddities and factoids that are somehow only salient in a state the size of a pinprick.

Any themed road trip in teeny Rhode Island, be it history or schlock, would only take three or four hours – one wrong turn and, oops, you're in Massachusetts! So, we've decided that for this trip, all you drivers must swap your Prius for pedals. Yes, that's right folks: leave your car in the driveway, it's time to blow the dust off your bicycle. This transport switcheroo will hopefully keep wayward wanderers from sneaking off to one of Rhode Island's bigger neighbors. And, of course, there's nothing wrong with "going green" and giving a shout out to our melting polar ice caps. Heck, if global warming continues, our poor little Ocean State is gonna get even smaller!

For those of you who don't have your own wheels – nice try, we're not letting you off the hook – there are plenty of places around Providence that offer daily rentals. Try ❶ **Providence Bicycle** on Branch Ave, or ❷ **East Providence Cycle** in (yeah, you guessed it) East Providence. If you can't snag a tandem, then at least score a ride sporting one of those cheesy wicker baskets dangling off the front – that'll really set the tone for our crap-tacular adventure.

The first stop on our tacky trek is the ❸ **Culinary Arts Museum at Johnson & Wales University** on Harborside Blvd in Providence. A shrine to Rhode Island's kitschy yesteryears, the museum features 25,000 sq ft of gallery space stuffed with everything from presidential

TIME
1 - 2 days

DISTANCE
40 miles

BEST TIME TO GO
Apr – Oct

START
Providence, RI

END
Newport, RI

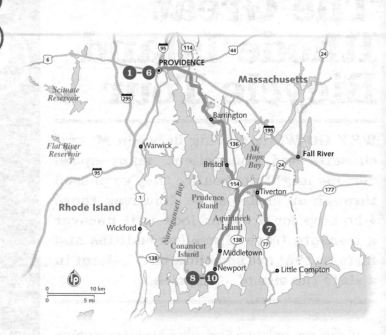

inaugural menus to a perfectly reassembled diner from the 1920s – there's even a special exhibit on Rhode Island's curious cuisine.

"one wrong turn and, oops, you're in Massachusetts! "

If the kitchen gadgets and recipe tomes got your tummy in a grumble, then hop back on your wheels and pedal down toward City Hall. Providence's most beloved tribute to heart-clogging Americana, the infamous **4 Haven Bros Diner**, is housed in a shiny steel truck. This heart-attack-on-wheels parks along Washington St every afternoon around 4:30pm and dishes out the calories until the wee hours of the morning. For a place with a bit more atmosphere (and by atmosphere we mean crayon doodles, cereal boxes and curling, faded pictures taped to the walls), try **5 Louis'**, Brown University's favorite greasy spoon, serving breakfast to bleary-eyed students while random fits of classical music waft through the air.

While the diner is Rhode Island's most familiar contribution to America's lunching lexicon, the wee state has an entire repertoire of bizarre recipes known only to its residents. Quench your thirst with a frosty plastic cup of frozen lemonade at **6 Del's** on Wickenden St (or at one of the 20 other locations within the state's borders). For years this franchised refreshment stand has been trying to establish its product as Rhode Island's beverage of choice, but the state legislature put the kibosh on these dreams by naming coffee milk the Official State Drink. This simple concoction of milk and coffee syrup is available almost everywhere, but it's best savored after an arduous bike ride down to Tiverton's historic four corners. Here you'll find **7 Gray's Ice Cream**, a Rhode Island institution. Enjoy your coffee milk with a couple of scoops of out-of-this-world ice cream made daily at the on-site dairy. Choose from over 40 flavors including Butter Krunch, Ginger, Frozen Pudding and Peach Brandy.

Capitalize on your sugar rush and cycle down to posh Newport. Skip the big-ticket mansions and make your way to **8 Belcourt Castle**, along opulent Bellevue Ave. From the exterior, this elegant Louis XIII–style hunting lodge seems rather similar to the other displays of wealth along the shoreline; however, a peculiar floor plan lurks behind the ornate facade. The original design scheme featured but a single bedroom, and the entire 1st floor was designed for the owner's beloved horses. Luxurious stables accommodated 30 coaching horses, each with their own monogrammed satin sheets. When Mr Belmont's dearest equine passed away, he had the brown beast stuffed and mounted in his study. It seems like Catherine the Great wasn't the only one with a bizarre horse fetish…

RAILS TO TRAILS

The old industrial train tracks that scar Rhode Island's verdant countryside are gradually being transformed into scenic bike paths along the coast and throughout the inner part of the state. Check out www.dot.state.ri.us/bikeri for more information on how to scope out these rail trails.

If you have enough energy to tackle one last attraction, head to **9 Aardvark Antiques**, home to the ultimate collection of unnecessary displays of wealth. Aardvark is like an orphanage of unwanted objets d'art – think giant copper seahorses, to-scale replicas of Michelangelo's *David* and fountains decked with satyrs spewing water from their mouths (and other less appropriate areas).

At the end of the day, do not pass go, do not collect $200 – go directly to jail, the **10 Jailhouse Hotel**, that is. This charming hotel, with its classical facade, was once the spot in town where drunks and derelicts spent the night. Today, guests have to fork over big bucks to sleep behind bars. But don't worry, the entire building has been completely redone – the strategically placed wrought-iron barricades are only used for show.

Brandon Presser

TRIP INFORMATION

GETTING THERE
Jump on I-95 from Boston and head south to the heart of downtown Providence.

DO

Aardvark Antiques
An orphanage of unwanted objets d'art – think giant copper seahorses and to-scale replicas of Michelangelo's *David*. ☎ 401-849-7233; www.aardvarkantiques.com; 9 JT Connel Hwy, Newport; ⏲ 9am-5pm Mon-Sat

Belcourt Castle
A stunning seaside castle with a bizarre horse history. ☎ 401-846-0669; www.belcourt castle.com; 657 Bellevue Ave, Newport; ⏲ 10am-4pm

Culinary Arts Museum at Johnson & Wales University
A shrine to Rhode Island's kitschy yester-years, this museum features 25,000 sq ft of gallery space stuffed with everything from presidential inaugural menus to diner memorabilia. ☎ 401-598-2805; www.culinary.org; 315 Harborside Blvd, Providence; adult/child $7/2; ⏲ 10am-5pm Tue-Sun

East Providence Cycle
A top spot in Providence to pick up a set of wheels. ☎ 401-434-3838; www.east providencebicycle.com; 414 Warren Ave, Providence; hybrid bicycle/tandem per day $25/50; ⏲ 9am-6pm Mon, 9am-8pm Tue-Fri, 9am-5:30pm Sat, 11am-5pm Sun; ♿

Providence Bicycle
A friendly shop offering bike rentals. ☎ 401-331-6610; www.providencebicycle.com; 725 Branch Ave, Providence; hybrid bicycle per day $30; ⏲ 9:30am-8pm Mon-Thu, 9:30am-6pm Fri, 9:30am-6pm Sun, shorter hours in winter; ♿

LINK YOUR TRIP
TRIP
21 Weird Vermont p199

EAT

Del's
This franchised lemonade stand serves up its signature recipe of frozen lemons. There are over 20 locations throughout the state. ☎ 401-463-6190; www.dels.com; 227 Wickenden St, Providence

Gray's Ice Cream
A Rhode Island institution serving out-of-this-world ice cream made daily at an on-site dairy. Choose from over 40 flavors, including Butter Krunch, Ginger, Frozen Pudding and Peach Brandy. ☎ 401-624-4500; www .graysicecream.com; 16 East Rd, Tiverton; ice cream $3-5; ⏲ 6:30am-9pm late May-Aug, to 7pm Sep-late May; ♿

Haven Bros Diner
This is the ultimate joint for anyone who wants to pack an artery. Washington & Spruce Sts, Providence; meals $5-10; ⏲ 4:30pm-4am

Louis'
Brown University's favorite greasy spoon serves breakfast to bleary-eyed students while random fits of classical music waft through the air. ☎ 401-861-5225; 286 Brook St, Providence; breakfast $3-7; ⏲ 5am-3pm; ♿

SLEEP

Jailhouse Hotel
This charming hotel, with its classical facade, was once the spot where drunks and derelicts spent the night. Today, guests have to fork over big bucks to sleep behind bars. ☎ 800-427-9444; www.jailhouse.com; 13 Marlborough St, Newport; r $179-239; ⏲ Apr-Nov

USEFUL WEBSITES
www.dot.state.ru.us/bikeri

www.quahog.org

www.lonelyplanet.com/trip-planner

Leaf Peeps & Harvest Eats

WHY GO Vermont is radiantly beautiful in autumn, its farmstands overflowing with freshly harvested produce and leaves sparkling with brilliant bursts of yellow and red. Chug fresh-pressed cider, pluck a patch of berries, and wander through the vivid streamers of seasonal foliage before the earth goes to sleep under thick blankets of snow.

Food and foliage – two of Vermont's biggest draw cards – are best appreciated in splendid harmony during the awe-inducing autumn months. After toiling in the fields, locals get to (literally) savor the fruits of their labor when their forested backdrop transforms into an enchanting blend of rusty hues. Then, as the palette of colors intensifies, the annual pilgrimage begins: legions of so-called "leaf-peepers" trek through the blazing thickets in search of the ultimate photo-op. But this trip isn't solely for arbor-holics; we've stocked the itinerary full of straight-off-the-farm eating options to celebrate the region's time-honored agricultural traditions.

Kick off your leaf hunt with a quick nosh at the ❶ Farmer's Diner in Quechee. This epicenter of the locavore movement is the brainchild of Tod Murphy, who years ago envisioned a restaurant that would buy direct from farmers, similar to what happened in his grandmother's day. Today roughly 65% of the diner's menu is sourced within a 70-mile radius. A board above the counter proudly lists dozens of ingredients and their origins: chicken from Misty Knoll, yogurt from Butterworks Farm, bacon from Vermont Smoke and Cure. Whatever you do, don't miss the incredible milkshakes made with ice cream from Strafford Creamery!

TIME
3 – 4 days

DISTANCE
275 miles

BEST TIME TO GO
Sep – Nov

START
Quechee, VT

END
Norwich, VT

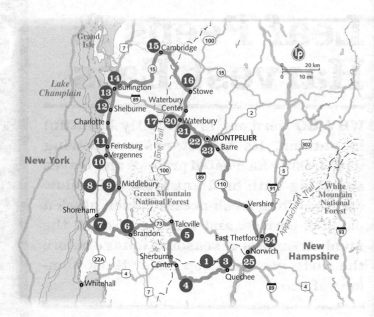

Work off those slabs of locally sourced bacon with a hike to the bottom of ② **Quechee Gorge**, which some have nicknamed Vermont's Grand Canyon. It's a few thousand feet too shallow to compete with the Arizona version, but the 15-minute descent on the south side of Hwy 4 is a memorable jaunt through the leafy curtains of an autumnal tapestry. Park at the gorge visitor center, half a mile west of the diner.

Next, it's on to ③ **Simon Pearce** in downtown Quechee, sited in an old woolen mill cantilevered out over the Ottauquechee River. Pearce, an Irish glassblower, immigrated to Quechee in 1981, drawn by a vision of running his entire operation self-sufficiently with hydro power. Three decades later, he has built a small empire, with his flagship Quechee store displaying two floors of pottery and glassware and offering glassblowing demonstrations daily. When lunchtime (or brunchtime on Sundays) rolls around, angle for a window seat at the riverview restaurant upstairs, where you can drink from Pearce-made stemware while appreciating the stunning views of a raging waterfall and a covered bridge flanked by shimmering trees.

After following the tree-lined Ottauquechee a few miles upstream along Hwy 4, stop in at the ④ **Long Trail Brewing Company**, Vermont's number-one producer of craft beer. On a sunny day, it's delightful to sit in its riverside beer garden – modeled after Munich's Hofbräuhaus – and admire the changing seasons.

Dinner tonight is on the farm, **5** **Liberty Hill Farm** in Rochester, to be precise. Located 30 miles northwest of the brewery, this eco-haven sits along one of Rte 100's prime patches of leaf-peeping territory. Thanks to its owners' efforts to conserve the surrounding stripes of blazing forest, Liberty Hill features one of Vermont's best barn-and-mountain vistas, especially in autumn. Overnight farm stays here include dinner and breakfast, served family style and making ample use of produce from the owners' garden. Other highlights include lounging on the front porch, snapping photographs of the leaf-strewn horizon and sampling the ultrafresh dairy products you might expect from a herd of over 100 cattle.

Next morning, head west on Rte 73 to cross Brandon Gap. Near the summit, a pristine wetland popular with moose, beavers and waterfowl sits at the foot of the lovely (and oxymoronically named) Mt Horrid. From the gap itself, a 1-mile hike north on the Long Trail leads to an overlook with spectacular panoramas of brilliant orange.

The pretty town of Brandon sits on the far side of pine-studded gap. In recent years the little burg has garnered a reputation across the state for its colorful street fairs and quirky art festivals. Another welcome addition to the town's landscape is **6** **Café Provence**, whose French cuisine lives up to its name. Founded by graduates of the New England Culinary Institute in Montpelier, this fabulous eatery cranks out croissants that could hold their own in any Parisian patisserie, and serves a seasonally changing menu sourced heavily from local farms.

BOTANY BRUSH-UP

So why exactly do the leaves change color? Good question. During spring and summer, trees transform sunlight into nourishment (photosynthesis), but when daylight begins to wane in autumn, the trees store up their photosynthetic energy like a hibernating bear. Chlorophyll, an integral chemical to the photosynthetic process, is responsible for a leaf's green color, so when photosynthesis stops the chlorophyll vanishes, allowing the dormant colorants – carotenoids (yellow) and anthocyanins (red) – to burst through.

A postcard-worthy meander west along Rte 73 follows the lazy curves of Otter Creek for a couple of miles before breaking into wide open farm country cascading toward Lake Champlain. Just shy of the lakeshore, double back eastward on Rte 74 to **7** **Champlain Orchards**, where you can pick two dozen varieties of apples (including many New England heirlooms) amid crimson-hued trunks or watch the pressing and bottling of ultrafresh cider. The orchard is famous for its free "while-you-pick" acoustic concerts and an annual autumn celebration in October, where barbecue pork, apple sauce and fresh-baked pies are served in leafy surrounds.

Speaking of pie, the orchard recently partnered with the Vermont Mystic Pie Company to create the world's tastiest and most butter-laden frozen apple pie, available in stores such as the ❽ **Middlebury Natural Foods Co-op**. Continue 17 miles northeast back toward the Green Mountains along Rte 74 and Rte 30 and you'll find Vermont Mystic pie sharing the freezer with its soul mate, Strafford Creamery's scrumptious cinnamon ice cream. A must-see for microbrew fans in Middlebury is ❾ **Otter Creek Brewing**, on Exchange St north of town. Tours three times daily (except Sunday) give you a chance to clamber amid vats of barley and hops, then taste samples to your heart's content. In addition to its many fine namesake brews, Otter Creek brews Wolaver's, one of America's oldest certified organic ales.

Continue your descent into decadence 10 miles north along leafy Hwy 7 in the picturesque little city of Vergennes, home to the ❿ **Daily Chocolate**. This sinfully seductive basement hole-in-the-wall, just opposite Vergennes' town square, specializes in weird but exquisitely tasty concoctions such as green-chile pistachio chocolate bark. Ride your chocolate buzz 5 miles further north along Hwy 7 through Ferrisburg. Just north of town, look for the round barn and camel – yes, a real live camel peacefully coexisting with alpacas and sheep – at Round Barn Merinos. Sighting the camel means you're nearing ⓫ **Starry Night Café**, a romantic little restaurant with intimate indoor seating plus a pond and patio out back for firefly-watching.

Head for the lakeshore just south of Burlington, where the century-old estate of the Vanderbilt-Webb family, Shelburne Farms, has been converted into a magnificent nonprofit working farm and environmental education center. The ⓬ **Inn at Shelburne Farms**, a stunning on-site mansion, is worth a look in fall. Visitors can savor high tea while appreciating the fiery foliage out the antique windows. We recommend staying overnight for the chance to attend a dusk concert or roam the 1400-acre grounds next morning, watching the making of the farm's excellent cheddar cheese and visiting the architecturally magnificent 19th-century outbuildings, including the twin-turreted, castlelike Farm Barn.

A couple of miles north in South Burlington, ⓭ **Magic Hat Brewery** exudes an infectious creative energy. Tours and tastes at the "Artifactory" are free and plentiful, with over 20 beer varieties flowing from four-dozen taps at the brand-new bar billed as Vermont's largest. Must-trys are the trademark No 9 (pale ale with a hint of apricot), the Orlio organic brews and Odd Notion, a whimsically changing seasonal creation.

Here, in the midst of Vermont's most urban corridor, you'd scarcely expect to discover foliage-filled farmland. Surprise! Five miles north on Hwy 7, tucked between the hubs of Burlington and Winooski, the Intervale Center is a bucolic complex of community gardens and farms hugging the fringes of the Winooski River. Descending from Hwy 7, Intervale Rd turns to dirt and passes through a lush tunnel of technicolor trees to **14** **Adam's Berry Farm**, where pick-your-own strawberry, blueberry and raspberry operations run straight through the peak of leaf-looking season till the first frost.

When autumn leaves crinkle shut and tumble to the frozen earth, local berries become flavorful dessert wines at **15** **Boyden Valley Winery**, 20 miles north in the stunningly beautiful Lamoille River valley at the foot of Mt Mansfield. Breathe in the bursting fall vistas and check out the award-winning (and appropriately named) Gold Leaf, a Vermont-inspired concoction that uses maple syrup straight from the farm combined with local apples.

You won't need to be tipsy to appreciate the curves of Smugglers Notch, the prettiest and narrowest paved mountain pass in the state. On the far side of the notch, as you drop down into Stowe, Sunday visitors should look for the **16** **Stowe Farmers Market** on the left side of Rte 108 shortly before its junction with Rte 100.

When the searing sunset matches the seasonal blooms of scarlet and gold, head to **17** **Waterbury** for an eclectic assortment of evening eats. On Hwy 2 just west of town, **18** **Cider House BBQ & Pub** crosses the Mason-Dixon Line with panache, incorporating food

VERMONT FRESH NETWORK

Fresh local food is never far away in the Green Mountain State, thanks to the **Vermont Fresh Network**, a partnership between the state's restaurants and farmers. Restaurants commit to supporting local producers by buying direct from the farm, while "farmers' dinners" throughout the year allow diners to meet the people who put the food on their table. For a full list of participating restaurants and upcoming events, see www.vermontfresh.net/vfnfarmerdinner.

from local producers into its Southern-influenced menu of barbecue, hush puppies and fried green tomatoes. Alternatively, kick back by the fire with a mint julep, or taste the wide range of hard and not-so-hard Vermont apple ciders.

Closer to downtown, a beautiful setting in a 19th-century grist mill at **19** **Hen of the Wood** complements a menu of fresh, ever-changing seasonal cuisine featuring local meat and produce, wild mushrooms and over a dozen artisanal cheeses. For a nightcap, or a lighter meal, **20** **Alchemist Pub & Brewery** is a laid-back alternative with a friendly bartender who offers free tastes of the in-house brews.

Wake up next morning and zip over to **21** **Red Hen Bakery**, east on Hwy 2 in Middlesex. Famous for its bread, Red Hen also makes amazingly buttery pastries – from sticky buns to offerings such as strawberry Danish with pistachios. The dining area is dotted with homey touches – a couch, a carpet and a wood stove – plus a viewing window into the bakery and photos of local growers such as Ben Gleason, whose organic wheat figures prominently in Red Hen's crusty loaves.

With 9000 residents, Montpelier (8 miles east on Hwy 2) is not only America's smallest capital city, it's also the only one without a McDonald's. Home to the prestigious New England Culinary Institute, it has an amazing crop of good eateries. A congenial spot is ㉒ **Kismet**, which balances its commitment to locavore- and vegetarian-friendly dining with a fun-loving spirit by offering quirky goodies like green eggs and maple hot chocolate.

EPEEPING

No creepy internet stalking here – ePeeping is the newest craze among fall foliage enthusiasts. Although once a game of chance, tracking down the most radiant trees has been considerably eased thanks to modern technology. During the height of autumn, there are several websites dedicated to the search for the most luminous leaf. Local and tourists tweet, text and blog their up-to-the-minute reports on viewing conditions. Check out www.foliage-vermont.com and www.yankeefoliage.com for details.

A different model for uniting farmers and community is ㉓ **LACE** (**Local Agricultural Community Exchange**), 6 miles east in Barre. Here Ariel Zevon has launched a market-café-deli that stocks local products and sells soups and sandwiches at great prices. Zevon's efforts to "lace people back into the land that feeds them" also include participation in the Barre City Street Market, a Wednesday afternoon event featuring local produce, crafts and entertainment.

Next, head southeast on Rte 110 and Rte 113 to the Connecticut River, where you'll find ㉔ **Cedar Circle Farm**. Like a roadside farmstand on organic steroids, it offers endless opportunities to appreciate Vermont's harvest bounty under a canopy of bright orange leaves. After plucking a pack of berries or wrestling an oblong pumpkin, up your java intake at the in-house café (don't forget to add Strafford Creamery's rich organic half-and-half into your cup of joe). Cedar Circle hosts myriad events throughout the year, but the annual pumpkin festival is the biggest draw. Held during prime leaf-peeping season, this bash draws in over a thousand visitors with hayrides, fresh nibbles and a multicolored backdrop.

As the dusky haze mutes the vibrant seasonal tones, meander downstream to the ㉕ **Norwich Inn**, a grand old establishment with rockers perched on its front porch overlooking Norwich's architecturally distinguished Main St. The best part about staying here is the built-in brewery right downstairs, with a patio offering views of the home-grown hops in the backyard. Jasper Murdock's Ale House brews its beers in such small batches that they're only available at the source. And the food's good too! By the time you finish breakfast the next morning, you should be ready to (literally) roll down the interstate back home.

Gregor Clark & Brandon Presser

TRIP INFORMATION

GETTING THERE
From Boston, take I-93 to I-89 northbound. At the first Vermont exit (Quechee-Woodstock), take Hwy 4 westbound to Quechee.

DO

Adam's Berry Farm
A mile north of downtown Burlington, descend into the lush Winooski Valley for pick-your-own organic blueberries, strawberries and raspberries. ☎ 802-578-9093; Intervale Rd, Burlington, VT; ⊙ late May–first frost; ♿

Cedar Circle Farm
Cedar Circle offers everything from dinners in the field to annual strawberry and pumpkin festivals. ☎ 802-785-4737; www.cedarcircle farm.org; Pavillion Rd, East Thetford, VT; ⊙ 10am-6pm Mon-Sat, 10am-5pm Sun May-Oct; ♿

Champlain Orchards
This lovely orchard near Lake Champlain specializes in pick-your-own apples, fresh-milled cider, and organic cherries, raspberries, peaches, plums and pumpkins. ☎ 802-897-2777; www.champlainorchards.com; 2955 Rte 74 W, Shoreham, VT; tours $5; ⊙ 8am-6pm Jul-Oct; ♿

EAT

Café Provence
Dine at the restaurant, or pop round the corner for French pastries at its Gourmet Provence bakery. ☎ 802-247-9997; www .cafeprovencevt.com; 11 Center St, Brandon, VT; mains $8-26; ⊙ 11:30am-9pm Tue-Sat, 9am-9pm Sat & Sun

Cider House BBQ & Pub
Hard and sweet cider mix intriguingly with barbecue and Southern fare. ☎ 802-244-8400; www.ciderhousevt.com; 1675 Hwy 2, Waterbury, VT; mains $10-24; ⊙ 11:30am-9pm Fri & Sat, 4-9pm Tue-Thu & Sun

Daily Chocolate
Using Vermont cream, butter and maple syrup, these creative chocolatiers make amazing stuff; watch them work while you order. ☎ 802-877-0087; www.dailychoco late.net; 7 Green St, Vergennes, VT; chocolate per lb $28; ⊙ 10:30am-5:30pm Tue-Fri, 11am-4pm Sat

Farmer's Diner
The "buy local" concept here is as old-fashioned as the diner itself. ☎ 802-295-4600; www.farmersdiner.com; 5573 Woodstock Rd (Hwy 4), Quechee, VT; mains $5-11; ⊙ 7am-8pm Thu-Mon, 7am-3pm Tue & Wed

Hen of the Wood
The menu changes with the seasons; the old mill setting remains beautiful year-round. ☎ 802-244-7300; www.henofthewood.com; 92 Stowe St, Waterbury, VT; mains $16-31; ⊙ 5-9pm Tue-Sat

Kismet
Serious about locavore dining, Kismet provides links on its website for suppliers of everything it serves. ☎ 802-223-8646; www.kismetkitchen.com; 207 Barre St, Montpelier, VT; mains $5.75-11.50; ⊙ 8am-2:30pm Wed-Sun

LACE (Local Agricultural Community Exchange)
This community-minded market sources virtually everything from surrounding farms. ☎ 802-476-4276; www.lacevt.org; 159 N Main St, Barre, VT; soups & sandwiches $4.65-7.95; ⊙ café & market 8.30am-6pm Mon-Fri, 9am-5pm Sat, 10am-4pm Sun

Middlebury Natural Foods Co-op
A true community enterprise, the co-op displays pictures of the many Addison County farmers whose food fills the shelves. ☎ 802-388-7276; www.middleburycoop.com; 9 Washington St, Middlebury, VT; ⊙ 8am-7pm

Red Hen Bakery
From ciabatta to olive bread to morning pastries, Red Hen's baked goods are exceptional. ☎ 802-223-5200; www.redhenbaking.com; 961B Hwy 2, Middlesex, VT; ⊙ 7am-6pm Mon-Sat, 8am-6pm Sun

Simon Pearce
Reserve ahead for a table overlooking the river in this renowned restaurant near Quechee's covered bridge. ☎ 802-295-1470; www .simonpearce.com; 1760 Main St, Quechee, VT; mains $12-30; ⊙ 11:30am-2:45pm & 6-9pm

Starry Night Café

From local strawberry salad to asparagus-cheddar soup, Starry Night's menu is as enticing as its intimate atmosphere. ☎ 802-877-6316; www.starrynightcafe.com; 5371 Hwy 7, Ferrisburg, VT; mains $17-26; ☽ 5:30-9pm Wed-Sun

DRINK

Alchemist Pub & Brewery

The ever-popular Alchemist emphasizes the organic in its ales, pub food and vegetarian fare. ☎ 802-244-4120; www.alchemistbeer.com; 23 S Main St, Waterbury, VT; ☽ 4-10pm Sun-Thu, 3-10pm Fri & Sat

Boyden Valley Winery

Boasting one of Vermont's prettiest settings, Boyden Valley specializes in fruity creations, including cassis made with local black currants. ☎ 802-644-8151; www.boydenvalley.com; cnr Rte 15 & Rte 104, Cambridge, VT; ☽ 10am-5pm daily May-Dec, 10am-5pm Fri & Sat Jan-Apr

Long Trail Brewing Company

Few beer-garden settings can rival Long Trail's deck overlooking the Ottauquechee River. ☎ 802-672-5011; www.longtrail.com; cnr Hwy 4 & Rte 100A, Bridgewater Corners, VT; ☽ visitor center & pub 10am-7pm

Magic Hat Brewery

With 48 taps and a penchant for creative experimentation, Magic Hat is just plain fun. ☎ 802-658-2739; www.magichat.net; 5 Bartlett Bay Rd, South Burlington, VT; ☽ 10am-6pm Mon-Sat, noon-5pm Sun

Otter Creek Brewing

Otter Creek offers free samples all day, plus brewery tours three times each afternoon. ☎ 802-388-0727; www.ottercreekbrewing.com; 793 Exchange St, Middlebury, VT; ☽ 10am-6pm Mon-Sat, tours 1pm, 3pm & 5pm

SLEEP

Inn at Shelburne Farms

No place in Vermont can match the elegance of Shelburne's lakefront setting or its afternoon teas. ☎ 802-985-8498; www.shelburnefarms.org; 1611 Harbor Rd, Shelburne, VT; r $155-465; ☽ early May–mid-Oct

Liberty Hill Farm

With its magnificent red barn and White River Valley panoramas, this working farm is a Vermont classic. ☎ 802-767-3926; www.libertyhillfarm.com; 511 Liberty Hill Rd, Rochester, VT; r incl dinner & breakfast per adult/child/teen $90/50/70; ☒

Norwich Inn

This inn in Norwich's village center has old-fashioned parlors, rocking chairs on the porch and a brand new annexe. ☎ 802-649-1143; www.norwichinn.com; 325 Main St, Norwich, VT; r $129-239, 2-night minimum in summer

USEFUL WEBSITES

www.foliage-vermont.com
www.vermontfresh.net

LINK YOUR TRIP

TRIP

21 Weird Vermont p199
22 Maine Lobster Tour p205

www.lonelyplanet.com/trip-planner

Weird Vermont

WHY GO If the Department of Tourism has convinced you that Vermont is all about fudge, fall leaves and teddy bears, think again. The Green Mountain State hides a host of quirkier attractions, each reflecting Vermont's longstanding tradition as a refuge for iconoclasts, artists and creative thinkers.

TIME
1 – 2 days

DISTANCE
125 miles

BEST TIME TO GO
Jun – Oct

START
Waterbury, VT

END
Beebe Plain, VT

It all begins with ice cream for breakfast. Yes, Ben & Jerry's Waterbury factory opens at 10am sharp (9am in summer) and yes, the staff will be happy to serve you whatever flavor you like. Just don't go asking for Bovinity Divinity, Dastardly Mash, Makin' Whoopie Pie or any of the other ex-flavors put out to pasture over the past two decades. To see these, you'll have to head up the hill to ❶ Ben & Jerry's Flavor Graveyard.

Quaintly perched on a knoll overlooking the parking lot, neat rows of headstones pay silent tribute to 27 flavors that flopped. Each memorial is lovingly inscribed with the flavor's brief lifespan on the grocery shelves of this earth and a poem in tribute. Rest in Peace Holy Cannoli, 1997–98! Adieu Miss Jelena's Sweet Potato Pie, 1992–93!

Twenty miles southeast in Barre, ❷ Hope Cemetery is a resting place of another sort. Names such as Bilodeau, Corti and Chiaravalli reflect Barre's heyday as the immigrant capital of Vermont. The headstones of Barre granite, some carved into whimsical forms such as a racing car, a soccer ball or a cube standing on end, celebrate the rock-carving tradition that's continued unabated here since the 1800s.

For an awe-inspiring look at the modern quarrying process, follow Rte 14 and Middle Rd 5 miles southeast of Barre to Graniteville, where massive granite blocks are liberated from the mountainside daily at ❸ Rock of Ages Quarry. Estimated to be 10 miles deep, the

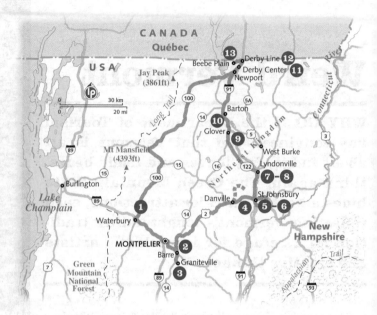

Barre granite field – one of the world's largest – yields a high-quality gray granite that supplies most of the nation's memorials. Quarriers have been working the same seam for over 100 years, literally digging themselves into a 620ft-deep pit. Guided bus tours whisk you to an observation platform high above, where on weekdays you can gaze down on the ant-sized workers cutting 1400-ton slabs of rock and hoisting them to the surface with gigantic derricks. Back down the hill, self-guided tours provide a glimpse of the factory floor where the cut stone is polished and carved.

For a more hands-on experience, test your industrial sandblasting skills at the newly opened Cut-in-Stone Center, or visit the adjacent outdoor bowling alley. Constructed from pure granite, this prototype never quite got off the ground commercially, but you can still roll a few frames if you don't mind setting up the pins yourself!

The landscape grows wilder as you follow Hwy 2 north into the Northeast Kingdom, an untamed domain of moose and dark pines. If the sight of so many trees makes you feel like climbing one – or even sleeping in one – the folks at ❹ **Twin Pines** can help. On their scenic 35-acre hillside horse ranch just east of Danville, they offer three-hour classes in recreational tree climbing, an exhilarating zip-line, plus a state-of-the-art tree house set in a forest full of chirping birds. Adventurous souls who don't mind heights or rustic living will appreciate the elegant hand-hewn stairway and deck, burl furniture, picture windows, Vermont Castings wood stove and a fire pole for dramatic exits. Advance reservations are essential. Note that there's limited, generator-powered electricity and no indoor plumbing, although guests have access to a bathroom with running water at the base of the tree. Those seeking a more traditional sleeping experience can continue 7 miles east to St Johnsbury.

Smack in the heart of "Saint J" (as it's known to the locals) stands the impressively Romanesque **⑤ Fairbanks Museum & Planetarium**. First opened in 1891, the museum is packed to the rafters with an eclectic mix of history and nature exhibits, many from founder Franklin Fairbanks' original "cabinet of curiosities."

DETOUR Late-summer travelers with a weakness for weird should check out the **Great Vermont Corn Maze** (www.vermontcornmaze.com), a seasonal operation 9 miles north of Hwy 2, reached from the town of Danville west of St Johnsbury. Attractions include a meticulously planned and seriously challenging corn maze, a barnyard golf game involving neither golf balls nor clubs and the ever-popular "Dead North: Farmland of Terror," a pre-Halloween event in a haunted cornfield. See the website for directions and photos of past years' mazes.

Seekers of the truly unusual should make a beeline for the bug art display upstairs. Bug art? Yes, eccentric Victorian John Hampson meticulously assembled his "mixed-media pieces" from thousands of dead bugs. Seen from a distance these weird masterpieces artfully depict familiar themes such as the American flag and George Washington. Step a little closer and you can see – eeew! – nothing but dead beetles and moths!

Two miles east of town, clearly signposted on Spaulding Rd just off Hwy 2, is another unique tribute to the animal kingdom, built by internationally acclaimed artist Stephen Huneck, who passed away in early 2010. The captivating **⑥ Dog Chapel** perches on a grassy hillside, its sign proclaiming: "Welcome All Breeds, All Creeds; No Dogmas Allowed." The chapel was inspired by a

BYOD (BRING YOUR OWN DOG)

When's the last time you went to a party and found yourself surrounded by dogs? At Stephen Huneck's semiannual **Dog Fest**, that's the whole point. In early August and October, Huneck invites the general public and their pets to his hillside farm for a day of free dog biscuits, Frisbee throwing and good-natured canine competitions. Humans will appreciate the apple pie and the superb views over the mountains of Vermont's Northeast Kingdom. For dates, see www.dogmt.com/events.php.

near-death experience Huneck survived in 1994: he awoke from a coma with a vision of a chapel that would celebrate the enduring spiritual bond between humans and animals. From the doggie weather vane crowning the steeple to the carved dog angel in the entryway, to the lovingly rendered stained-glass representations of dogs swimming after a ball or licking an ice-cream cone,

Huneck's affection for animals is readily felt. What makes this place doubly memorable is his invitation to visitors to commemorate their own pets through writings and photos. Thousands of heartfelt mementos from animal lovers are plastered on the walls throughout the chapel. Next door you'll find Huneck's gallery, where several happy hounds roam freely among the paintings and other artworks.

Ten minutes north of St Johnsbury (just off the I-91 Exit 24 in Lyndonville), take a gander at the parking lot of ❼ Bob's Welding, where propane tanks have been transformed into sculptures of moose, dinosaurs, a totem pole and other expressions of inspired lunacy. A stone's throw further north is ❽ Miss Lyndonville Diner, a great place to recharge your batteries and continue the dessert-for-breakfast tradition. The fresh strawberry pie (in season) is a local favorite.

Fifteen miles further north along Rte 122, near the town of Glover, the ❾ Bread & Puppet Theater is a tour de force of avant-garde art. For nearly 50 years, the internationally renowned Bread & Puppet Theater has been staging theatrical spectacles with a political twist. While the company can be seen both nationally and internationally, Vermont performances take place on weekends throughout the summer, starring gigantic puppets (some up to 20ft tall) borne through the fields on the company's hilltop farm. Even when no show is going on, you can visit the treasure trove of papier-mâché angels, devils, horses and other fantastic creatures from past performances, hauntingly displayed in a cavernous old barn.

If you've worked up an appetite, this may or may not be a good time to visit ❿ Currier's Quality Market in Glover, 2 miles north of Bread & Puppet on Rte 16. This community general store has a post office, a deli and shelves full of food and drink, but what's likelier to catch your attention are the dozens of animal trophies scattered throughout the store. Taxidermists gone wild have stuffed everything from moose to bear to a lynx tangling with a deer. As store patron Nancy Cressman puts it, "You reach for a box of Ritz crackers and suddenly you're petting a dead raccoon." Note that photos are encouraged but touching the stuffed animals is not.

"You reach for a box of Ritz crackers and suddenly you're petting a dead raccoon."

More animal-themed eating awaits 15 miles north off I-91, Exit 28. Near the corner of Routes 5 and 5A in Derby Center, an enormous archway of elk and deer antlers ushers you into the ⓫ Cow Palace, a steakhouse serving fresh elk venison from the adjoining ranch. Several not-yet-burgerized elk can be seen grazing in the adjacent field, while a stuffed polar bear presides over the tables inside.

To reach the trip's last two attractions, head north on Hwy 5. Here in the towns of Derby Line and Beebe Plain lie a pair of unusual points where you can stand with one foot in New England and one in Canada. In 1901 the cornerstone for Derby Line's ornate Queen Anne Revivalist library was laid squarely on the Vermont–Québec border, at a time when international boundaries were more porous than today. Seven years later, the US Congress passed legislation prohibiting new construction on the border, but the library was allowed to stand. Today a painted diagonal line indicates which country is which. The children's room is in Québec, the front entrance in Vermont. Bilingual staff from both countries work the reception desk. It's worth a stroll through just to see the gorgeous cherry, golden birch and bird's-eye maple details. However, the star attraction is the **⑫ Haskell Opera House** on the 2nd floor. In earlier times, this miniature theater regularly hosted traveling performers working the Boston–New York–Montréal circuit but fell into disuse when WWI spelled vaudeville's doom. Benign neglect, coupled with a strictly preservationist board of trustees, has left the original theater almost perfectly preserved, with its original painted curtain, dome, chandelier, ornamental plasterwork and stage backdrops still intact. The opera house hosts weekend performances throughout the summer, some in French and some in English.

If you enjoy this kind of borderline schizophrenia, continue west 3 miles along Elm St and Beebe Rd to the town of Beebe Plain, where you can stroll along the aptly named **⑬ Canusa Street**. Houses on the north side of the street are in Canada, while those on the south side are in the USA. A quick check of license plates in the local driveways will let you know where you stand. The sidewalk is on the Canadian side, so US citizens need to visit customs on both sides of the border before exploring this international oddity.

For a scenic return trip to Ben & Jerry's, with no backtracking, follow Hwy 5 to Newport, then Vermont Rtes 105 and 100 southwest to Waterbury.

Gregor Clark & Brandon Presser

TRIP
21

TRIP INFORMATION

GETTING THERE
From Boston, take I-93 northbound to I-89. At Exit 10 (Waterbury), follow Rte 100 north 1 mile to Ben & Jerry's.

DO

Ben & Jerry's Flavor Graveyard
With 27 tombstones, this faux graveyard crowns a hilltop above the ice-cream factory. ☎ 802-882-1240; www.benjerry.com; 1281 Waterbury-Stowe Rd, Waterbury; 30-minute tours adult/child $3/free; ☿ 9am-9pm Jul & Aug, 10am-6pm Sep-Jun; ♿

Bread & Puppet Theater
A funky old barn, stuffed to the rafters with giant puppets, showcases the artistic genius of Peter Schumann and his troupe. ☎ 802-525-3031; www.breadandpuppet.org; 753 Heights Rd, Glover; ☿ 10am-6pm Jun-Oct

Dog Chapel
The Dog Chapel is Stephen Huneck's most personal and striking work of art. ☎ 800-449-2580; www.dogmt.com; 143 Parks Rd, St Johnsbury; ☿ 10am-4pm Mon-Sat, 11am-4pm Sun; ♿ 🐾

Fairbanks Museum & Planetarium
This striking pink sandstone building houses Franklin Fairbanks' wide-ranging collection. ☎ 802-748-2372; www.fairbanksmuseum .org; 1302 Main St, St Johnsbury; adult/child $6/5; ☿ 9am-5pm Mon-Sat, 1-5pm Sun, closed Mon Nov-Mar; ♿

Haskell Opera House
A gift from lumber baron Martha Stewart Haskell, this early-20th-century gem straddles the US–Canada border. Take your passport if you want to park on the Canadian side! ☎ 802-873-3022; www.haskellopera.org; 93 Caswell Ave, Derby Line; tours adult/child $3/free; ☿ 10am-5pm Wed & Fri-Sun, 10am-8pm Thu May-Oct

Hope Cemetery
The final resting place of many a quarrier. Displays the carving skills of generations of immigrants. ☎ 802-476-6245; 262 E Montpelier Rd, Barre; ☿ dawn-dusk

Rock of Ages Quarry
The world's largest deep-hole granite quarry has operated continuously for over a century. ☎ 802-476-3119; www.rockofages.com; 558 Graniteville Rd, Graniteville; guided tours adult/child $5/2.50; ☿ 9:15am-3:35pm Mon-Sat late May–mid-Sep, daily mid-Sep–mid-Oct

EAT

Cow Palace
Eschew the golden arches in favor of Cow Palace's arch of antlers, the gateway to Vermont's freshest local elk venison. ☎ 802-766-4724; www.derbycowpalace.com; Main St, Derby; mains $9-21; ☿ 4-9pm Mon, 11am-9pm Tue-Thu & Sun, 11am-10pm Fri & Sat

Currier's Quality Market
Grab a deli sandwich or run the gauntlet of stuffed animals in the grocery department. ☎ 802-525-8822; 2984 Glover St, Glover; ☿ 6am-9pm Mon-Sat, 9am-6pm Sun

Miss Lyndonville Diner
This friendly local hang-out specializes in hearty breakfasts and other American classics. ☎ 802-626-9890; 686 Broad St, Lyndonville; mains from $5; ☿ 6am-8pm Sun-Thu, to 9pm Fri-Sat

SLEEP

Twin Pines
Sleep among the birds in a rustic tree house. Advance reservations are essential. Acrophobes need not apply! A three-hour "fun climb" is $60. ☎ 802-684-9795; www.new englandtreeclimbing.com/vermont.html; Maple Lane, Danville; tree house $100

USEFUL WEBSITES
www.travelthekingdom.com

LINK YOUR TRIP
TRIP

www.lonelyplanet.com/trip-planner

Maine Lobster Tour

WHY GO Maine's amazingly fresh lobster is so ubiquitous that if you ask 10 Mainers where to find the best lobster, you'll probably get 20 different answers. Taste-test your way across the state enjoying the various lobster incarnations: lobster roll, lobster salad and the traditional steamed lobster.

TIME
2 – 3 days

DISTANCE
200 miles

BEST TIME TO GO
Year-round

START
Wells, ME

END
Bar Harbor, ME

When humans first ate lobster, it was surely an act of desperation. The crops must have failed and the fish stopped biting, so some poor soul was forced to trudge through thick strands of seaweed in search of anything remotely edible. This unfortunate would have stuck a hand deep into a dark crevice and pulled out a wretched, googly-eyed creature with pincers wildly waving and furiously snapping shut. Eureka! This ghastly creature is delicious! Who'd have guessed this hideous arachnoid would wind up topping the price lists at fancy restaurants?

As you cross the state line into Maine, signs littered with superlatives crowd the streets attempting to lure those with lobster on the brain. Get some tail at ❶ **Mike's Clam Shack** in Wells. Mike's is definitely a tourist trap (the menus have detailed instructions about tipping in America), but its midsized lobster rolls, with a helping of unusually tasty fries, are delish. Those looking for a side order of sand and sun should try ❷ **Forbes Self Service Restaurant** along Wells Beach. The large, bright-blue-and-yellow hut offers a scrumptious lobster/mayo combo to go, so customers can chow down under the shade of their beach umbrella.

Before venturing deep into the heart of Maine's main lobster territory, make a pit stop in Portland, the state's largest city. The ❸ **Downeast Duck Tours**, aboard an amphibious bus/boat, is a unique way to learn about the region's vivid maritime history. The tour ambles around town then plunges into Casco Bay for a whole different perspective.

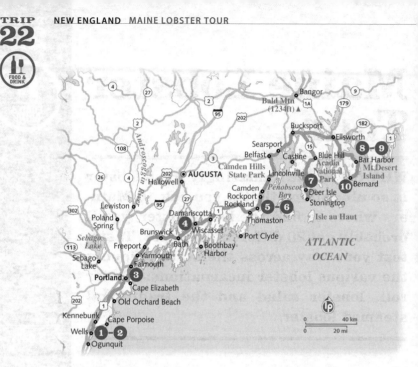

Hop back on Hwy 1 and continue your northward journey in search of an afternoon snack at ④ **Red's**, in little Wiscasset. The throngs of lip-licking tourists make this wobbly lobster stand very hard to miss. The lobster-roll recipe is simple: take a toasted hot-dog bun and cram it with one lobster's worth of meat. There's a small plastic bowl of melted butter for dipping, and *voilà* – no gobs of mayo, just juicy red meat and a plastic fork shoved in the middle like a pioneer's flag.

A stop in Rockland, further north on Hwy 1, is a must for any true lobster junkie. This little port teems with crustacean-related events throughout the year including lobster-boat racing and the annual Maine Lobster Festival (www.mainelobsterfestival.com). A trip with ⑤ **Captain Jack Lobster Boat Adventure** is a great way to get a behind-the-scenes look at lobster hunting in Maine. Spend an hour cruising the open seas on an authentic 30ft lobster boat while Captain Hale hauls his traps. Lunch and dinner cruises are also available for those who want some instant gratification. Sample some exqui-

YOU'VE GOT MAIL

The times they are a-changin'. Fresh Maine lobster used to be a luxury available only to those who made the pilgrimage. These days you can have the critters delivered to your doorstep with a click of your mouse and a quick call to FedEx. If you're too lazy to get off your keister and taste-test your way up the coast, then get in touch with **Browne Trading** (www.browne-trading.com) or **Maine Lobster Direct** (www.mainelobsterdirect.com).

sitely prepared seafood at Rockland's favorite restaurant, **6 Primo**, if you don't want your dishes rocking back and forth. Feast on modern twists of Italian faves like fresh vine-ripe antipastos and a heavenly espresso dessert float topped with vanilla and chocolate gelato.

To digest the lifetime's worth of lobster consumed earlier on in the day, settle for the night at the handsome **7 Pilgrim's Inn**, on the rugged, rock-strewn shores of Deer Isle. Built in 1793, the post-and-beam inn offers refined seaside charm in its 12 rooms and cottages.

Start the new day by continuing north to Bar Harbor, on Mount Desert Island (pronounced "dessert," for all you New England neophytes), where you can take a morning ride with the affable Captain John on **8 Lulu Lobster Boat**. Enjoy the postcard-worthy scenery around Acadia National Park while listening to colorful local legends and the faint claw-clicking of recently caught creatures. After a tour with Lulu, swing by the **9 Thirsty Whale**, a favorite hang-out for local lobster catchers. Try an amber brew while eavesdropping on the conversations of gruff sailors as they swap exaggerated stories of whale sightings, rip tides and catching a lobster THIS BIG. For the best lobster on

YOU'VE GOT MALE

Show your skills at the dinner table and wow those surrounding you by identifying the gender of your steamed seafood. The secret lies in the swimmerets (the small, leafy limbs dangling on the underside of the tail). If the first pair of swimmerets are hard, then you've caught yourself a male – female lobsters' swimmerets feel more featherlike.

Mount Desert Island, locals turn to **10 Thurston's Lobster Pound** out in Bernard, overlooking Bass Harbor. Park yourself on the rickety plastic patio furniture, strap on a bib and savor some of the juiciest crustaceans around while watching fishing boats unload their daily catch.

Brandon Presser

TRIP INFORMATION

GETTING THERE
From Boston, take I-95 north, passing the New Hampshire and Maine state lines before arriving in Wells Beach.

DO

Captain Jack Lobster Boat Adventure
Experience life as a lobster catcher aboard an authentic downeaster lobster vessel. ☎ 207-542-6852; www.captainjacklobstertours .com; 130 Thomaston St, Rockland; adult/child $25/15; ☻ 9am-dusk mid-May–mid-Oct; ♿

Downeast Duck Tours
This 70-minute amphibious bus putters through the Old Port, before plunging into the bay for a waterside tour. ☎ 800-979-3370; www.downeastducktours.com; 177 Commercial St, Portland; adult/child $24/19; ☻ mid-May–late Oct; ♿

Lulu Lobster Boat
A tour aboard a traditional lobster boat intermixed with local legends, great photo ops and traps full of lobster. ☎ 207-963-2341; www.lululobsterboat.com; Harborside Hotel and Marina, Bar Harbor; adult/child $30/17; ☻ 9am-6pm early May-late Oct; ♿

EAT

Forbes Self Service Restaurant
A bright-blue-and-yellow bastion of seafood serving beach bums some of the best lobster around. ☎ 207-646-7620; Wells Beach; lobster roll $15-18; ☻ breakfast, lunch & dinner late May-Aug

Mike's Clam Shack
An institution along the highway, Mike's is a bit touristy but serves up a great lobster roll with a tasty side of French fries. ☎ 207-646-5999; www.mikesclamshack.com; 1150 Post Rd, Wells; lobster roll $12.50; ☻ 11:30am-9:30pm; ♿

Primo
Set in a Victorian home and featuring expertly prepared seafood, Primo remains one of the top restaurants in the Northeast. ☎ 207-596-0770; 2 S Main St (ME 73), Rockland; mains $25-48; ☻ dinner Thu-Sun May & Sep-Dec, Thu-Mon Jun-Aug

Red's
A small stand overflowing with hungry tourists yearning for a lobster roll. ☎ 207-882-6128; cnr Main & Water Sts, Wiscasset; lobster roll $16-19; ☻ 11:30am-11pm Jun-Aug, 11:30am-9pm Sep-May

Thirsty Whale
Head here to mingle with locals and lobstermen over a pint of ale. ☎ 207-288-9335; 40 Cottage St, Bar Harbor; beer $2.50-4.50; ☻ 11am-1am, kitchen closes 9pm

Thurston's Lobster Pound
Overlooking Bass Harbor in Bernard, this casual waterside spot with superb views serves amazingly fresh lobster. ☎ 207-244-7600; Steamboat Wharf, Bernard; lobster roll $10.75; ☻ 11am-8:30pm late May–mid-Oct

SLEEP

Pilgrim's Inn
Sitting along the Northwest Harbor, this handsome post-and-beam inn was built in 1793 and offers refined seaside charm in its 12 rooms and cottages. ☎ 207-348-6615; www.pilgrimsinn.com; 20 Main St, Deer Isle Village; r incl breakfast $139-259

USEFUL WEBSITES
www.meliving.com/lobster/index.shtml
www.visitmaine.com

LINK YOUR TRIP
www.lonelyplanet.com/trip-planner

60 Lighthouses in 60 Hours

WHY GO In the early freight and fishing days of Maine, lighthouses were vital to ship safety. Today, the 60 looming shafts of brick and steel from Kittery to Calais are charming and photogenic reminders of a bygone era.

After eons hidden under thick, frozen sheets of ice, the melting glaciers gave birth to Maine's rugged coastline. The stunning expanse would one day prove to be a big moneymaker for the tourism industry, but first this jagged realm of granite and sand would be a great hazard to the burgeoning community of sailors and fishers. In order to protect the seagoers and their ships from a watery grave, many lighthouses were erected along the coast, casting their beams into the night sea. Today, over 60 lighthouses are peppered along the shoreline, and although many of them are no longer in use, they've become monuments to an earlier era and the perfect maritime Kodak moment.

Take a long weekend and wind your way up along the coast from Kittery to Calais clicking your camera at the dozen lights along the shore and the four-dozen lighthouses set adrift in the sea on wee islets. You will also learn about the difficult lives of keepers who sat in the towers all night long making sure the light burned brightly to warn passing ships. It was a lonely and tiresome life – the pay was poor and the extended periods of isolation often led to insanity. Eerie tales of shipwrecks, ghosts and murder will surely add some flavor to the journey.

Below you'll find the names of almost every light in the state, and a handful of other cool things to see along the way.

Start the trip in little Kittery, just over the border from New Hampshire. Here you'll find the first lighthouse on the trip, the ❶ Whaleback Ledge. Built in 1831, the light earned its name because it looks like it was constructed on the back of some mammoth sea

TIME
2 – 3 days

DISTANCE
375 miles

BEST TIME TO GO
Jun – Aug

START
Kittery, ME

END
Calais, ME

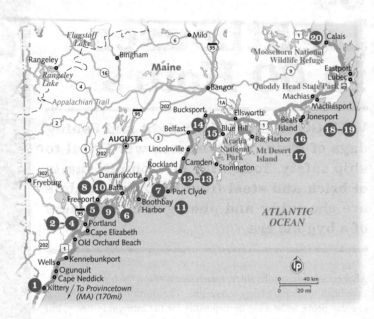

creature. Although it is not possible to visit the light, there are great views from Fort Foster.

As you wander up the coast you'll pass a half-dozen lighthouses before reaching Portland, including Boon Island Light, Cape Neddick (Nubble) Light, Goat Island Light, Wood Island Light, Cape Elizabeth Light and Spring Point Ledge Light. Portland, Maine's largest city and port, is graced with a handful of handsome lights including ❷ **Portland Breakwater (Bug) Light**, a veritable Greek temple with Corinthian columns, and just outside the city in Cape Elizabeth you will find ❸ **Portland Head Light**, Maine's oldest functioning lighthouse. During the American Revolution, the town of Cape Elizabeth posted soldiers at a rocky outcropping to warn locals of an eminent attack by the British.

> *"Today, over 60 lighthouses are peppered along the shoreline… monuments to an earlier era."*

Afterwards, a lighthouse was built in the same location and was completed in the winter of 1791. Today, the keeper's house has been passed into service as the ❹ **Museum at Portland Head Light**, which traces the maritime and military history of the region. There is also a small on-site artist's studio featuring local paintings and photography of the surrounding area's topography.

For a unique vantage point of the bay, try a two-and-a-half-hour kayak tour with ❺ **LL Bean**. The tours depart from the LL Bean store in Freeport, just 30 minutes north of Portland.

For an eerie tale, make your way to the turtle-shaped Seguin Island to visit a lighthouse with the same name. The state's first offshore station, the **6 Seguin Island Lighthouse**, was built to guide sailors through one of the foggiest areas in the country. After months of complaining that there was nothing to do, the keeper's wife convinced her husband to buy her a player piano. Unfortunately, the piano played only one song, which soon drove the keeper crazy. He strangled his wife and took an axe to the baby grand. Locals claim that the creepy tune rides the fog on particularly dismal evenings.

Cross another dozen lighthouses off the list, including Ram Island Ledge Light, Halfway Rock Light, Pond Island Light, Fort Popham Light, Perkins Islands Light, Squirrel Point Light, Doubling Point Light, Kennebec River Range Lights, Cuckold Light (yes, actually named for a man whose wife left him for another lover), Burnt Island Light, Hendricks Head Light, Ram Island Light and Monhegan Island Light. Give yourself some extra time to explore **7 Pemaquid Point Light**, Maine's most famous lighthouse after being featured on the front of the special edition Maine quarter. The stone tower was constructed in 1835 and today the keeper's house has been transformed into a small museum and a one-bedroom apartment available for weekly vacation rentals. Don't miss the detailed map of the Maine coast in the museum. This nautical chart features every lighthouse in the state.

SEEN FROM SPACE?

Only a few human-made items on the planet can be seen from space, so would you believe us if we told you that one of Maine's lighthouses could be viewed by extraterrestrials? Well, it's true...sorta. When NASA compiled an image database of photographs from around the world to identify earth should the space shuttle make alien contact, they included a picture of **Nubble Lighthouse** in York.

Sneak back to the industrial town of Bath, home to the **8 Maine Maritime Museum & Shipyard**, which preserves the rich tradition of shipbuilding in the Kennebeck region. The museum features mostly paintings and models, but if you check out the Percy & Small Shipyard, you'll find scores of locals working to restore antique watercrafts. In the summer, tourists can link up with a three-hour lighthouse tour offered by knowledgeable museum workers. As the evening shadows dance on the bobbing dinghies offshore, venture deep into the Harpswells for a sunset lobster dinner at **9 Cook's Lobster House** on Bailey Island. Stay in Bath for the night at **10 Popham Beach B&B**, which used to be a US Coast Guard station. Today, the four bright bedrooms sit directly on the sands of Popham Beach.

In the morning, stop in Boothbay Harbor for a leisurely cruise out to the lights on Monhegan Island and Burnt Island with **11 Balmy Days Cruises**. Then add tick marks to another 10 lights: Franklin Island Light, Marshall

Point Light, Matinicus Light, Tenants Harbor Light, Whitehead Light, Two Bush Island Light, Heron Neck Light, Browns Head Light, Goose Rocks Light and ⑫ **Owls Head Light**, where, according to local legend, the keeper's dog saved the day by continuously barking through a bad storm when the light couldn't penetrate the clouds and the foghorn was broken. Take a well-deserved break in Rockland to check out the ⑬ **Maine Lighthouse Museum**. Perched over Rockland harbor, the museum contains an array of nautical artifacts like lighthouse lights, foghorns and model ships. There's even a hands-on exhibit to keep young ones entertained.

Maine's biggest collection of mariner art and artifacts can be found in Searsport at the ⑭ **Penobscot Maritime Museum**. The center is spread throughout several historical buildings and is a stone's throw from the port to Sears Island, the largest uninhabited island on the East Coast.

Cross off Rockland Harbor Southwest Light, Rockland Breakwater Light, Indian Island Light, Grindle Point Light, Fort Point Light, Dice Head Light, Eagle Island Light and Blue Hill Bay Light, and continue on to Blue Hill to have a look at the current maritime conditions documented at the ⑮ **Marine Environmental Research Institute**. Members of the institute study the relationship between pollution and marine life. Visitors can learn about MERI's activities in a series of changing exhibitions in the main gallery, often with hands-on exhibits for children. In the summer, a variety of tours taking tourists to small, scrubby islands just off the coast are on offer.

DETOUR

In Provincetown, Massachusetts, you can have the chance to be a lightkeeper while staying at **Race Point Lighthouse** (www.racepointlighthouse .net). This 19th-century lighthouse sits amid unspoiled sand dunes in a remote corner of the National Seashore. Solar energy and gas run the lights and kitchen and your nearest neighbors are miles away…well, unless you count the seals and the dolphins just offshore.

For a look at life along the Maine coast before European colonization, have a peek at the ⑯ **Abbe Museum** in the town of Bar Harbor in Acadia National Park. The fascinating collection of over 50,000 artifacts from Maine's Native American heritage includes pottery, combs and fishing implements that span the last 2000 years. Contemporary pieces include finely wrought woodcarvings, birch-back containers and baskets. Campsites are available around the park on a first-come basis for those who decide to hang their hat for the evening. Lighthouses orbiting Acadia National Park include Burnt Coast Harbor Light, Great Duck Island Light, Baker Island Light and Bear Island Light.

A trip out to ⑰ **Mt Desert Rock Light**, Maine's most remote lighthouse, is not for the faint of heart; it's a challenge even to see this concrete conical shaft from a boat. Located on a scrubby little islet 20 miles from Mt Desert

Island, the lonely light gets battered and beaten throughout the year – even the smaller storms ravage the little island, leaving most of it submerged for the colder months of the year. Despite the harsh weather, the light has been burning strong since 1830.

After Acadia National Park, you've officially entered what Mainers call "Far Down East," a stretch of land far more rugged and unspoiled than any other rocky expanse you've seen thus far. Stop at ⑱ **Quoddy Head State Park**. The 531-acre park boasts a walking trail that passes along the edge of towering, jagged cliffs. The tides here are similarly dramatic, fluctuating 16ft in six hours. Follow the fantastic 4-mile loop trail and keep an eye on the sea for migrating whales (finback, minke, humpback and right whales), which migrate along the coast in the summer. The park also boasts intriguing subarctic bogland and the much-photographed red-and-white-banded ⑲ **West Quoddy Light**, built in 1858, which looks like a barber's pole.

After passing the last dozen lighthouses (Winter Harbor Light, Egg Rock Light, Crabtree Light, Prospect Harbor Light, Petit Maman Light, Narraguagus Island Light, Nash Island Light, Moose Park Light, Libby Island Light, Machias Seal Island Light, Little River Light, Lubec Channel Light), end the trip in Calais at ⑳ **Whitlocks Mill Light**, Maine's northernmost lighthouse. After checking off your 62nd lighthouse on the list, have a quick look around the grounds, which kiss the Canadian border.

Brandon Presser

HISTORY & CULTURE

TRIP INFORMATION

GETTING THERE
Follow I-95 north out of Boston and pass through New Hampshire until you reach the exit for Kittery in Maine.

DO

Abbe Museum
This fascinating museum contains a collection of artifacts related to Maine's Native American heritage. ☎ 207-288-3519; www.abbe museum.org; 26 Mt Desert St, Bar Harborm, ME; adult/child $6/2; ⊗ 10am-6pm late May-early Nov, 10am-4pm Thu-Sat early Nov-late May

Balmy Days Cruises
Takes day-trippers to Monhegan Island and Burnt Island. ☎ 207-633-2284; www.balmy dayscruises.com; Pier 8, Boothbay Harbor, ME; adult/child $32/16; ⊗ late May-Oct

LL Bean
This well-known outfitter offers "walk-on" 2½-hour kayak tours around the bay; tours depart from LL Bean's main store. ☎ 888-552-3261; www.llbean.com/ods; 95 Main St, Freeport, ME; adult/child $29/19; ⊗ Jul-early Sep

Maine Lighthouse Museum
Collections here include lighthouse artifacts like enormous jewel-like prisms, foghorns, marine instruments and ship models, with hands-on exhibits for children. ☎ 207-594-3301; www.mainelighthousemuseum.com; 1 Park Dr, Rockland, ME; adult/child $5/4; ⊗ 9am-5pm Mon-Fri, 10am-4pm Sat & Sun, closed Sun-Tue Nov-May

Maine Maritime Museum & Shipyard
This museum preserves the Kennec's long shipbuilding tradition. In summer, the museum offers a variety of cruises leading out to nearby islands. ☎ 207-443-1316; www.mainemari timemuseum.org; 243 Washington St, Bath, ME; adult/child $12/9; ⊗ 9:30am-5pm

Marine Environmental Research Institute
An important center studying the relationship between pollution and marine life. ☎ 207-374-2135; www.meriresearch.org; 55 Main St, Blue Hill, ME; admission free; ⊗ 9am-5pm Mon-Sat Jul-Aug, 9am-4pm Sep-Jun

Museum at Portland Head Light
The keeper's house has been transformed into a museum, which traces the maritime and military history of the region. ☎ 207-799-2661; www.portlandheadlight.com; 1000 Shore Rd, Portland, ME; adult/child $2/1; ⊗ 10am-4pm Jun-Oct, 10am-4pm Sat & Sun Apr-May & Nov–mid-Dec

Penobscot Maritime Museum
This superb museum houses Maine's biggest collection of mariner art and artifacts, which are spread through a number of historic buildings. ☎ 207-548-2529; www.penob scotmarinemuseum.org; 5 Church St (US 1), Searsport, ME; adult/child $8/3; ⊗ 10am-5pm Mon-Sat, noon-5pm Sun May–mid-Oct

Quoddy Head State Park
This 531-acre park boasts a walking trail that passes along the edge of towering, jagged cliffs. ☎ 207-733-0911; 973 S Lubec Rd, Lubec, ME; adult/child $2/1

EAT

Cook's Lobster House
A great spot for some lobster at sunset. ☎ 207-833-2818; 68 Garrison Rd, Bailey Island, ME; mains $12-29; ⊗ 11:30am-8pm

SLEEP

Popham Beach B&B
Formerly a US Coast Guard station, this upscale 1880s B&B has four bright rooms directly on the sands of Popham Beach. ☎ 207-389-2409; www.pophambeach bandb.com; 4 Riverview Ave, Phippsburg, ME; r incl breakfast $185-235

LINK YOUR TRIP
www.lonelyplanet.com/trip-planner

THE SOUTH TRIPS

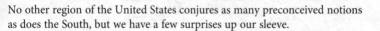

No other region of the United States conjures as many preconceived notions as does the South, but we have a few surprises up our sleeve.

We'll take you past ancient Native American burial sites as old as the Caesars on the Natchez Trace drive, and introduce you to a self-proclaimed hard-core Civil War reenactor who's also a Zen-minded historical preservationist. We'll take you through a tour of the South's musical roots, antebellum mansions, bluegrass and horse trails, Civil War history, natural beauty and urban hot spots.

You'll go down to the crossroads in Clarksdale, Mississippi, birthplace of the blues; out to Raleigh, Durham and Chapel Hill, North Carolina, where Southern hospitality meets university culture; and up to Lexington, Kentucky, for a mint julep and a day at the races. And we will, of course, spend plenty of time in New Orleans.

And you will eat. Barbecue (the noun, not the verb), po'boys, locavore Asian-Southern fusion and all the fried food one could ever want, served in plantations, catfish hotels, former train depots and pink mansions.

PLAYLIST 🎵 If it's American-born and you can hum to it, chances are its roots are in the South – from ragtime to rock and roll, jazz to country, and the blues to bluegrass. And if you want an education about new music tune into New Orleans' musician-supported WWOZ at 90.7FM (or streamed live from www.wwoz.org).

- "Hound Dog," Elvis Presley
- "Georgia on My Mind," Ray Charles
- "Cross Road Blues," Robert Johnson
- "Sweet Home Alabama," Lynyrd Skynyrd
- "Coat of Many Colors," Dolly Parton
- "Coal Miner's Daughter," Loretta Lynn
- "Rocky Top," The Osborne Brothers
- "Ring of Fire," Johnny Cash

THE SOUTH TRIPS

48 Hours in New Orleans

WHY GO Few destinations have as many sensational ways to kill time as the Crescent City. Its history runs deep, the colonial architecture is exquisite, there's mouthwatering Cajun and Creole food, historic dive bars, a gorgeous countryside, and lashings of great free live music.

The Vieux Carre, or ❶ French Quarter, is a good place to start your trip. At first it was just a tiny settlement on the river, surrounded by swamps and plantations. After the Louisiana Purchase prompted an influx of Anglo Americans, the French Quarter remained the heart of the Creole city, while white Americans settled Uptown. By the early 20th century the Quarter was a run-down working-class neighborhood and home to 12,000 people. But a 1930s preservation movement polished the old town houses and saved it from demolition. About 5000 people live here today.

Navigation remains a snap even though the grid was laid out in 1722. The narrow streets are lined with 19th-century Creole town houses and Victorian-era shotgun houses. You'll see wooden shutters, ornate cast-iron balconies and courtyards as you explore an endless lineup of appealing restaurants, bars, shops and galleries.

Begin your Nawlins adventure with a tipple at ❷ Lafitte's Blacksmith Shop, set in one of the few 18th-century cottages to survive the French Quarter fires during the Spanish era. This candlelit hole-in-the-wall is purported to have been smuggler Jean Laffite's workshop and French Quarter hideout. In the 20th century it became the favored watering hole of Tennessee Williams. Dine at ❸ Felix's Restaurant & Oyster Bar. It's been serving fresh-shucked oysters and boiled crawfish (in season) for 55 years. Or head to ❹ Coops, a Decatur St bar serving fantastic Cajun and Creole dishes. The fried chicken is particularly good.

TIME
2 days

BEST TIME TO GO
Feb – May

START
New Orleans, LA

END
New Orleans, LA

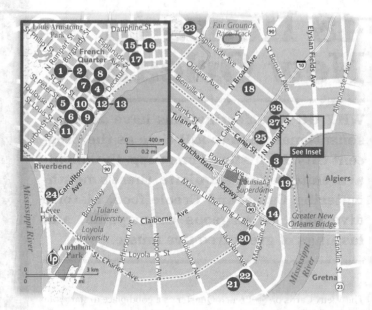

Take 30 minutes and experience the cheesy go-go bars and mid-grade meat market scene that have colonized Bourbon St, one of the oldest streets in town. Then quickly seek some cleansing night music. **5** **Preservation Hall** is the place to hear authentic New Orleans jazz played by local masters. The hall is cramped and sweaty, plus there's no bathroom, booze or snacks, so you'll likely just take in one of the three 50-minute nightly sets. But when the seven-piece band blows, the roof rocks and the crowd goes wild. **6** **One Eyed Jacks** offers a hip, local scene attracting bands that vary from punk to gypsy jazz. The front bar room is swanky, but the main theater is absolutely stunning with early-20th-century chandeliers, an oval bar and tables topped with miniature lamps. It's the perfect setting for the venue's burlesque shows.

Bed down at the traditional **7** **Andrew Jackson Hotel**, set on the same property of the former courthouse where the beloved general and future president, who saved the city from British invaders during the War of 1812, was famously held in contempt of court in 1815. You'll love the 18th-century courtyard, furnishings and gas lamp courtyard. Ask for one of the front 2nd-floor rooms with access to the veranda. It's next to the Cornstalk Hotel, so you'll hear horses trot by on occasion, which just adds to the charm.

In the morning swing by **8** **Croissant D'Or** for a breakfast of exquisite fresh-baked pastries. This is another locals' joint hidden in plain sight and the perfect place to recalibrate after a long New Orleans evening. Then stroll over to **9** **Jackson Square**, where you'll see a garden surrounding a monument to Andrew Jackson, the hero of the Battle of New Orleans, and the seventh president of the USA. But the real stars are the magnificent St Louis Cathedral and **10** **Presbytere**, designed in 1791 as the cathedral's rectory. It now holds a permanent exhibit of vibrant masks and costumes, parade floats and historic photos called "Mardi Gras: It's Carnival Time in New Orleans."

Royal St is a fun scene on Saturdays, when motorized traffic is blocked and pedestrians rule. In addition to the weekly influx of street musicians, magicians and puppeteers there are elegant antique shops, art galleries and vintage dress and hat boutiques. Chartres St is another great shopping lane for ladies looking for dresses and another pair of heels. **11** **Napoleon House** makes for a cozy lunch spot. Rumor has it that after Napoleon was banished to St Helena, a band of New Orleans loyalists plotted to snatch him and set him up on the 3rd floor here (didn't happen). An attractive bar set in a courtyard building erected in 1797, it has a back patio, crumbling stucco walls and extraordinary service.

After lunch walk to the **12** **French Market**. New Orleanians have been trading goods for over 200 years from this spot on the Mississippi's riverbanks. In addition to **13** **Café Du Monde** (famous for serving beignets 24 hours a day for decades), where you can snack on fried and sugared beignets, there's a flea market, permanent gift stalls geared to tourists and a produce market. Dine on spectacular Cajun fare at **14** **Cochon** in the Warehouse District, owned and operated by the reigning James Beard Southern Chef of the year (at the time of research), Donald Link. He serves a spectacular oyster roast and tasty *cochon* (Cajun spiced rice and sausage balls).

When darkness deepens, head to Frenchman St in the Faubourg Marigny District. This is where the

ART ANYONE?

New Orleans' Warehouse District, once a 19th-century industrial district where grain, coffee and produce were stored, fell into disrepair in the mid-20th century. But in 1976 the **Contemporary Arts Center** opened and launched a neighborhood revival. Artists rented lofts on the cheap, dozens of galleries sprang up, and the Warehouse District became known as the Arts District. Care to explore? Join the well-lubricated herd on Julia St for a district art walk on the first Saturday of every month.

locals party, and if you are staying in the Quarter, you can easily walk here. **15** **Snug Harbor Bistro** offers nightly live jazz. Sometimes it's an authentic brass band augmented with West African drummers, but you'll also find funky acid jazz and straight-ahead bop. The bar has an incredible selection of bourbon, tequila and rum. The **16** **Spotted Cat** is famous for "gypsy jazz": electric guitar, clarinet and a rhythm section. If you're lucky you'll see some hot local dancers swing. If you crave a late-night meal, order the pulled pork po'boy at **17** **13 Monaghan**. It's not just an extraordinary sandwich, but an effective hangover vaccine.

If you feel like a new place to rest your head, consider the ⑱ **Degas House** on Esplanade Ridge. When Edgar Degas lived here he also produced the city's most famous painting, *The Cotton Exchange In New Orleans*. The ⑲ **W New Orleans** in the Central Business District (CBD) is another fine choice. It's modern and stylish, walking distance to countless restaurants and art galleries in the CBD, and just a streetcar ride away from the Garden District.

The ⑳ **St Charles streetcar** will take you up and down this famous avenue, through the CBD, to the Garden District and Uptown mansions. Peer through the gates on Prytania and Coliseum Sts (you'll like Anne Rice's house on First St) before walking up and down Magazine St. There are tremendous snacking and shopping opportunities here. ㉑ **Agora Galleries** has a sexy collection of retro 1940s-inspired dresses and jewelry. ㉒ **Parasol's**, a neighborhood bar in the Garden District, has terrific roast beef po'boys.

If you make it all the way to Uptown, you can peruse the ㉓ **New Orleans Museum of Art & Besthoff Sculpture Gardens**, which has a permanent collection of over 40,000 pieces (paintings, sculpture, photography) from France, Africa, Japan and, of course, New Orleans, as well as edgy rotating exhibits and films, or just stroll beneath the old, mossy oaks in City Park. Before heading back to the CBD, stop into ㉔ **Jacques Imos Café**, one of the best-loved Creole and Cajun kitchens in the city.

THE TRAGIC TOUR

It's impossible to come to New Orleans without remembering Katrina and those caught in the floods. If you want a deeper view, take Grayline's Hurricane Katrina tour. You'll explore the vital Port of New Orleans, see the "breached" levee, and roll through the devastated Lower Ninth Ward. But you can also tour these neighborhoods by car on your own, or get a feel for ongoing reconstruction by visiting Habitat for Humanity's Musicians Village and Global Green's Eco Home.

You can also hop the Cemeteries streetcar from the CBD and take it to the above-ground tombs at the end of Canal St. The oldest, most famous and easiest to find is ㉕ **St Louis Cemetery #1**. But if it's Sunday consider brunch at ㉖ **Lil Dizzy's**, a laid-back neighborhood soul-food joint where you'll find delicious waffles, buttery biscuits, savory shrimp omelettes and spicy hot sausage, in the working-class, predominantly African American Tremé District, which was hit hard by the Katrina floods.

Nearby the ㉗ **Backstreet Cultural Museum** documents African American cultural traditions such as Mardi Gras Indians, Jazz Funerals and Social Aid & Pleasure Clubs; you can find out where that Sunday's Second Line Parade (Mardi Gras–style marching bands) might be. Or you may discover it in full bloom as you stroll through gritty Tremé.

Adam Skolnick

TRIP INFORMATION

GETTING THERE
From Mississippi take Hwy 61 to the I-10. From the east take I-20 to I-59 to New Orleans.

DO

Agora Galleries
An elegant, fun and rambling antiques showroom. ☎ 504-525-2240; 2240 Magazine St; ◷ 11am-6pm

Backstreet Cultural Museum
This private, nonprofit museum in the Tremé District documents New Orleans African American cultural traditions. www.backstreetmuseum.org; 1116 St Claude Ave; admission $8; ◷ 10am-5pm Tue-Sat; ♿

New Orleans Museum of Art & Besthoff Sculpture Gardens
The city's preeminent museum. The sculpture garden is free. ☎ 504-658-4100; www.noma.org; 1 Collins Dibol Circle; adult/senior/child $8/7/3, out-of-state admission $16/15/10; ◷ 10am-5pm Thu-Sun, noon-8pm Wed, closed Mon & Tue; ♿

One Eyed Jacks
One of the Quarter's younger, hipper scenes presents everything from burlesque theater to punk rock bands. ☎ 504-569-8361; www.oneyedjacks.net; 615 Toulouse St; cover $5-15; ◷ 2pm-6am

Presbytere
The old St Louis rectory houses a terrific Mardi Gras museum. ☎ 504-568-6968; 751 Chartres St; adult/senior & student/under 12yr $6/5/free; ◷ 9am-5pm Tue-Sun; ♿

Preservation Hall
Traditional, and consistently great, live New Orleans jazz in a cramped, sweaty music hall in the Quarter. ☎ 504-522-2841; www.preservationhall.com; 726 St Peter St; admission $10; ◷ 8am-11pm; ♿

Snug Harbor Bistro
At the time of writing, this was the best jazz club on Frenchman. And that's saying something. ☎ 504-949-0696; www.snugjazz.com; 626 Frenchman St; cover $5-25; ◷ 5pm-3am

Spotted Cat
The early-days jazz always delivers, and it's free. ☎ 504-943-3887; 623 Frenchman St; ◷ 4pm-late

St Louis Cemetery #1
New Orleans' oldest cemetery is where all the city's original luminaries, like Marie Laveau, are buried. *Easy Rider*'s acid trip was shot here. ☎ 504-525-3377; www.saveourcemeteries.org; 501 Basin St; admission free; ◷ 8am-3pm; ♿

Trashy Diva
The rebellious name doesn't do these retro-designer dresses justice. ☎ 504-299-3939; www.trashydiva.com; 2048 Magazine St; ◷ noon-6pm Mon-Sat, 1-5pm Sun

EAT & DRINK

Café Du Monde
The floors are coated with powdered sugar from the famous beignets at this 24-hour French Quarter café. ☎ 504-525-4544; www.cafedumonde.com; 800 Decatur St; beignets $1.75; ◷ 24hr

Cochon
This James Beard–approved hot spot serves up succulent Cajun cuisine. The *cochon* (fried rice balls mixed with sausage) and the wood-fired oysters rock! ☎ 504-588-2123; www.cochonrestaurant.com; 930 Tchoupitoulas St; dishes $7-22; ◷ 11am-10pm Mon-Fri, 5:30-10pm Sat; ♿

Coops
Insanely good regional pub grub. The fried chicken and redfish dinners with red beans and rice are fantastic. ☎ 504-525-9053; www.coopsplace.net; 1109 Decatur St; mains $10-15; ◷ 11am-late

Croissant D'Or
A quiet French-run patisserie with wonderful stuffed croissants (sweet and savory) and exquisite quiche. ☎ 504-524-4663; 617 Ursulines Ave; pastries $2-5; ◷ 7am-5pm; ♿

Felix's Restaurant & Oyster Bar
Has the best freshly shucked oysters in the Quarter. ☎ 504-522-4440; www.felixs.com; 739 Iberville St; mains $7-18; ◷ 10am-10pm Mon-Thu, 10am-midnight Fri & Sat, 10am-9pm Sun; ♿

Jacques Imos Café
Superb Creole and Cajun cooking in Uptown. The steaks are exceptional, and enjoy the deep-fried po'boy if you dare. ☎ 504-861-0886; www.jacquesimoscafe.com; 8324 Oak St; mains $15-29; ☺ 5:30-10pm Mon-Thu, 5:30-10:30pm Fri & Sat, closed Sun

Lafitte's Blacksmith Shop
Bourbon St's most historic and soulful watering hole. ☎ 504-523-0066; 941 Bourbon St; ☺ noon-late

Lil Dizzy's
This classic New Orleans soul food haunt is famous for its lunch buffets and Sunday brunch. ☎ 504-569-8997; 1500 Esplanade Ave; mains $12; ☺ 7am-2pm; ♿

Napoleon House
Wonderfully timeworn French Quarter institution just off Jackson Sq. ☎ 504-524-9752; 500 Chartres St; mains $9-15; ☺ 11am-5pm Mon, 11am-midnight Tue-Thu, 11am-1am Fri & Sat, 11am-7pm Sun

Parasol's
This neighborhood bar and eatery in the Garden District has a dozen po'boys on the menu. Order the roast beef. ☎ 504-899-2054; www.parasols.com; 2533 Constance St; po'boys $6-9; ☺ 11am-late; ♿

SLEEP

Andrew Jackson Hotel
A comfortable hotel in the Quarter. Rooms on the 2nd floor with balcony access are best. ☎ 800-654-0224; www.frenchquarterinns.com; 919 Royal St; r from $100; ♿

Degas House
The famous French artist lived here in the 1870s. Rooms are older but large and comfortable, and suites have fireplaces and balconies. ☎ 504-821-5009; www.degashouse.com; 2306 Esplanade Ave; r from $149; ♿

W New Orleans
Rooms on the upper reaches and the rooftop pool have insane Mississippi River views. ☎ 504-525-9444; www.whotels.com; 333 Poydras St; d from $210

USEFUL WEBSITES
www.experienceneworleans.com

LINK YOUR TRIP
www.lonelyplanet.com/trip-planner

Music City to Dixieland: A Musical Roots Run

WHY GO Waylon Jennings once said, "I've always felt that blues, rock and roll, and country are just about a beat apart." And a few miles. Get your motor runnin' on this musical tour of the South, where country, rock and roll, blues and jazz were all born within 500 miles of each other.

TIME
8 days

DISTANCE
660 miles

BEST TIME TO GO
Mar – May

START
Nashville, TN

END
New Orleans, LA

There isn't a spot on planet earth that has seen a soundtrack as influential as the American South. Go on – just try and name a region, anywhere in the world, that can sing a sweeter song than this: blues, rock and roll, country and jazz were all born here; gospel, bluegrass, soul, funk and R&B all grew up here; alternative and indie rock came here for college; and hip-hop settled here after graduation. Ethnically, politically and economically diverse, the sounds of the Southland cut through lines of race, color and creed and, in fact, owe a mound of debt to the composition of the South as a racially mixed land of milk and honey. How sweet it is.

Fire up a good road-trip mix tape and make your way to Music City, ❶ Nashville, home to country music and the most musicians per capita than any other city in the US (two for every 1000 residents, and those are just the serious ones). Drop your bags at ❷ Loews Vanderbilt Hotel, a chain hotel anywhere else, a spot steeped in local music memorabilia here. Toss some funds in the jukebox and get your dancing shoes on.

Nashville's honky-tonk history begins at the ❸ Country Music Hall of Fame & Museum, a straight shot east on West End Ave from the hotel. This 40,000-sq-ft facility will teach you everything you need to know about the origins of country music, from its humble beginnings in rural Tennessee to where we're at today: if you don't live in Nashville and are trying to make it in country music, well, you're gonna find a lot of tears in your beers.

Just down the road is the historic ❹ **Ryman Auditorium**, originally built as a church in 1892, though preaching nothing but the country music gospel these days. The *Grand Ole Opry,* the longest running radio show in the world, lived here from 1943 to 1974, but the venue fell into neglect when the *Opry* jumped ship to Music Valley. In 1994, a renovated and revitalized Ryman opened its doors and has never looked back. You can take a self-guided tour or, better yet, check out who's playing and catch a show. It's gonna be a long night, so you might want to fill up on a "Cheeseburger in Paradise" at ❺ **Rotier's**, rumored to be the burger Jimmy Buffet was singing about, served here on French bread.

Nashville is home to countless live-music venues but two stand out. Garth Brooks and Kathy Mattea were discovered at the ❻ **Bluebird Cafe**, where aspiring songwriters, talent scouts, tourists and wannabe Tim McGraws all converge among tightly spaced tables and a whole lot of hootin' and hollerin'. The musicians here perform right in your face. Early performances by aspiring musicians are often free and there is some real talent. The other spot to drown your sorrows in some tell-it-like-it-is sonic therapy is ❼ **Tootsie's Orchid Lounge**, where Willie Nelson, Waylon Jennings and Kris Kristofferson found their careers nurtured by legendary owner Tootsie Bess, a den mother of country music who died in 1978. Hank Williams, Patsy Cline and Waylon Jennings have all been famously drunk here. Aspiring talents show up at 10am in hopes of discovery (and you thought Los Angeles was bad).

It's located on the stretch of Broadway known as the Honky Tonk Highway for its plethora of bars and live-music venues.

Trade in your Stetsons for Stratocasters and leave country in the dust on I-40 (west bound) to **8** **Memphis**, the birthplace of rock and roll. When Elvis Presley walked into Memphis Recording Services, part of the now legendary **9** **Sun Studio**, in 1954, he was little more than a truck driver for an electric company. When he walked out that July, with a $4, 10-inch acetate carrying the songs "I Love You Because," "Blue Moon of Kentucky," and "That's All Right" in hand, he was days from becoming the world's first true rock and roll star, and is still its biggest.

They say timing is everything and nobody knows that better than Elvis. Though rock and roll had begun to take shape in the beginning of the decade, it lacked sex appeal and soul. Bill Haley & His Comets are most often credited with charting the first rock and roll song ("Rock Around the Clock") in 1955, but it wasn't exactly rough around the edges, nor sexy. It was right around that time that record producer Sam Phillips uttered the very un-PC, and now infamous, quote: "If I could only find a white boy who could sing like a Negro." In walked Elvis. There's so much history in that one simple room at Sun Studio, it has been known to bring grown men to tears, including this author. There's a free shuttle between here and **10** **Graceland** that runs every hour.

Don't be shocked at the green shag carpet that lines the walls and ceiling in the Jungle Room; the 350 yards of multicolored fabric that covers nearly everything in the Pool Room; and the mirrored ceiling in the TV room – Graceland is star-studded grandiosity, and it's obvious *Queer Eye for the Straight Guy* hasn't been anywhere near it. Elvis Presley's 1939 Colonial Revival–style mansion and 14-acre estate is a pilgrimage even a gay interior designer could love. You'll want to spring for the Platinum Package tour, which also includes Elvis' automobile museum and his two airplanes.

> **DETOUR**
>
> When the Grand Ole Opry departed from its former home in Ryman Auditorium, it moved to the 4400-seat **Grand Ole Opry House** (www.opry.com) east of Nashville in Music Valley. This squarish modern building hosts the Opry Friday and Saturday from March to November. Guided backstage tours are offered daily by reservation. Out this way, you'll want to hang your hat at the 2881-room **Gaylord Opryland Hotel** (www.gaylordhotels.com), a tourist attraction in itself.
>
> From Nashville, exit 215 on I-40 to Briley Parkway and follow the signs – it's just over 11 miles (about 20 minutes).

If Graceland doesn't suck the charmed life out of you, begin your evening with burgers at former brothel **11** **Ernestine's & Hazel's**, once a hangout of Stax recording folk like Otis Redding and Booker T & the MGs' Steve Cropper. Yes, Elvis ate here too. From here it's a quick trolley ride along Main St to

⑫ Beale St. Back in the 1860s, African American traveling musicians would perform here; in the early 20th century it was a debauched thoroughfare of gambling, drinking, prostitution, murder and voodoo; today, it is home to the blues (and lots of drunks). These days it is perhaps a little too Bourbony, but there are still plenty of good live-music venues to get your groove on along this historical stretch of 30 nightclubs. The most authentic of the lot is classic juke joint **⑬ Mr Handy's Blues Hall**, which is attached to the Rum Boogie Café.

Stumble like a rock star back to **⑭ Madison Hotel**, a whimsical boutique hotel with soulful tunes pumped right into the lobby inside a renovated 100-year-old bank building. If you're on an Elvis pilgrimage, you're sleeping out by Graceland at **⑮ Heartbreak Hotel**, where B&W photos of the King don the walls, and four themed suites evoke the true spirit of Presley's gaudiness.

Stop at the **⑯ Memphis Rock 'n' Soul Museum**, done up by the excellent Smithsonian Institute, before skipping town. This seven-gallery museum covers rock and roll, and soul, from rural roots to modern-day hit makers. It's here at this corner of Beale and 3rd that your adventure continues: head south from here and you are on the legendary Blues Highway, otherwise known as **⑰ Hwy 61**. It's a 70-mile drive from here to **⑱ The Crossroads**, the intersection of Hwy 61 and Hwy 49 just north of **⑲ Clarksdale, Mississippi**. This is where legend says Delta blues henchman Robert Johnson sold his soul to the devil at midnight in exchange for mastery of the guitar. Johnson went on to become one of America's first guitar heroes and one of the most influential blues musicians of all time, but the devil don't play that: he cashed in on his side of the deal when Johnson was just 27 years old. Three blue guitars mark the spot.

ASK A LOCAL

"If you come to Memphis and want to see something Elvis but don't necessarily want to see the iconic figure buried in his backyard, try a place called the **Hi-Tone**. It was once Elvis' karate studio but has long since been turned into a bar and fabulous venue for concerts. On any night of the week you can see acts like Elvis Costello and the Imposters and local rockers Lucero."
Kyle Blair, Memphis

The awesomely named **⑳ Shack Up Inn** is the place to stay (B&B here meaning Bed & Beer as opposed to Bed & Breakfast) as much for its renovated shotgun shacks as for proclamations like, "The Ritz we aint!" and "If you like 5-star shit, go somewhere else." It's 3 miles from the Crossroads on the old Hopson Plantation. A few miles north in downtown Clarksdale, everything old is becoming new again, all in the name of paying homage to the blues. **㉑ Delta Blues Museum**, in the old train depot, hosts an impressive collection of blues memorabilia.

But Clarksdale's blues heritage is hardly a thing of the past – stop in at the ㉒ **Cat Head Delta Blues & Folk Art, Inc** for kitschy blues memorabilia and CDs, but also to pick owner Roger Stolle's brain about what music to take in during your visit. He owns a blues record label and is also the booking agent for actor Morgan Freeman's blues club, ㉓ **Ground Zero,** a must-stop but not nearly as authentic as ㉔ **Red's,** a nitty-gritty, smoked-out juke joint rubbed with the kind of musical spices that makes the blues the sonic equivalent of a 60-day dry aged porterhouse. Speaking of which, ㉕ **Abe's** does the kind of gut-sticking bar-

"Clarksdale's blues heritage is hardly a thing of the past."

becue that will have you singing the blues on the toilet, but you won't much care at this stage, they are teeth-pickin' good. Save some room, though; ㉖ **New Orleans** may be the birthplace of jazz, but it's not a bad spot to chew the bone, either.

From Clarksdale, take Hwy 6 (east bound) to Batesville and catch I-55 (south bound) to I-10 (east bound) straight into the heart of the ㉗ **French Quarter.** You are now in jazz country, where jazz has been wizzled and spit out here dating back to the days when African and Caribbean slaves pounded out their rhythmic postcards home on Sunday in Congo Square (now ㉘ **Armstrong Square,** named after jazz great Louis Armstrong). Once European instruments and ragtime piano ditties in brothels were stirred into the pot, jazz was born like an improvised stew. Shockingly, New Orleans does not have a jazz museum, so you must resort to listening to music – not a bad deal at all, actually.

3 DOORS DOWN'S MISSISSIPPI – BRAD ARNOLD

"As a musician, there are not many places you can be more proud to be from than Mississippi. It all started right here on a little rural road in the middle of nowhere Mississippi. I can't put my finger on what it is in that area that breeds the music that comes from there, but it's something special. It cannot be replicated. People in Mississippi are very set in their ways, and believe what they believe. I've always believed myself if you're going to sing something, you better believe it and live it yourself. Those old blues guys down there, they live those blues.

I was in a bar down in Pascagoula not too long ago and there were a few guys onstage playing covers. An old African American man came in the door, 75 or 80 years-old – he'd been hitting the bottle – and asked the band, 'Do y'all mind if I play a song or two?' The guys reluctantly agreed. This old man never got through a full song, and the band went up there a few times to stop him, but I said, 'Don't you dare take the guitar away from that guy. That man stumbled in here off the street, asked nicely to borrow your guitar, and played something sincere. You ain't taking that guitar away from him until he puts it down. You're looking at the blues.'"

Brad Arnold, vocalist, 3 Doors Down

The genre has since branched off on numerous notes since inception, but traditional New Orleans–style jazz is preserved vehemently at ㉙ **Preservation Hall** on St Peter St, a muggy, dirty, Prohibition-inspired hothouse with no air conditioning and no beverages (although you are welcome to BYO *water*). Of course, as the name implies, all of this preserves the throwback feel – you think folks were comfortable back then? Um, no. They got their comfort from food.

For the quintessential Nola meal with a soundtrack to boot, head to the jazz brunch at ㉚ **Commander's Palace** and save room for the bread-pudding soufflé. With your ears still ringing, lay yourself to sleep at ㉛ **The Columns**, a lovely and quieter spot in the Garden District (though there's live music there nightly, too).

Elvis once said, "I don't know anything about music. In my line you don't have to." Now you know a little more than he did.
Kevin Raub

TRIP INFORMATION

DO

Cat Head Delta Blues & Folk Art, Inc
This kitschy, blues-themed shop is full of regional folk art and, more importantly, knowledge. ☎ 662-624-5992; www.cathead.biz; 252 Delta Ave, Clarksdale, MS; ⏱ 10am-5pm Mon-Sat; ♿

Country Music Hall of Fame & Museum
A $37 million slap on country music's ass. Historic Studio B tours also leave from here. ☎ 615-416-2001; www.countrymusichalloffame.org; 222 Fifth Ave S, Nashville, TN; adult/child $20/12; ⏱ 9am-5pm Mon-Fri, 10am-6pm Sat; ♿

Delta Blues Museum
The top blues museum in the region, housed inside the old train depot in Clarksdale. ☎ 662-627-6820; www.deltabluesmuseum.org; 1 Blues Alley, Clarksdale, MS; adult/child $7/5; ⏱ 9am-5pm Mon-Sat; ♿

Graceland
The King's home is the king of all decorating nightmares, but you gotta see it. ☎ 800-238-2000; www.elvis.com; 3765 Elvis Presley Blvd, Memphis, TN; platinum package tour adult/child $34/16; ⏱ 9am-5pm Mon-Sat, 9am-4pm Sun, 10am-4pm Wed-Mon winter; ♿

Memphis Rock 'n' Soul Museum
Immerse yourself in the origins of rock and roll and soul music at this excellent museum from the Smithsonian folks. ☎ 901-205-2533; www.memphisrocknsoul.org; 191 Beale St, Memphis, TN; adult/child $10/7; ⏱ 10am-7pm; ♿

Ryman Auditorium
Tour this venue of biblical importance to country music (the Grand Ole Opry stayed here for 31 years) or catch a show if you can. ☎ 615-889-3060; www.ryman.com; 116 Fifth Ave N, Nashville, TN; adult/child $12.50/6.25; ⏱ 9am-4pm

Sun Studio
The birthplace of rock'n'roll is still rockin'. A 1½-hour tour covers the studio memorabilia and all things Elvis. No children under five allowed. ☎ 800-441-6249; www.sunstudio.com; 706 Union Ave, Memphis, TN; adult/child $12/free; ⏱ 10am-6pm

EAT

Abe's
Bone-sticking good barbecue is the calling at this road-food classic immortalized everywhere from blues tunes to Mississippi Delta novels. ☎ 662-624-9947; 616 State St, Clarksdale, MS; mains $3-12; ⏱ 10am-9pm Mon-Thu, 10am-10pm Fri & Sat, 10:30am-2pm Sun; ♿

Commander's Palace
A Nola classic with a weekend jazz brunch and the best bread-pudding soufflé in town. ☎ 504-899-8221; www.commanderspalace.com; 1403 Washington Ave, New Orleans, LA; mains $27-38; ⏱ 11:30am-2pm Mon-Fri, 11:30am-1pm Sat, 10:30am-1:30pm Sun, 6:30-10pm nightly

Rotier's
A classic meat-and-three joint, the thick milkshakes are almost as famous as the cheeseburgers. ☎ 615-327-9892; www.rotiers.com; 2413 Elliston Pl, Nashville, TN; mains $5-18; ⏱ 10:30am-10pm Mon-Sat

DRINK

Bluebird Cafe
This divey institution is the place to get discovered in Nashville (just ask Garth Brooks). ☎ 615-383-1461; www.bluebirdcafe.com; 4104 Hillsboro Rd, Nashville, TN; admission free-$20; ⏱ 5:30-11:30pm Mon-Thu, 5:30pm-midnight Fri-Sun

Ernestine's & Hazel's
Former brothel-turned-juke joint serving up memorable "Soul Burgers." Otis Redding, James Brown and Elvis Presley would concur were they alive. ☎ 901-523-9754; 531 S Main St, Memphis, TN; mains $4-7; ⏱ 5pm-3am; ♿

Ground Zero
Actor and owner Morgan Freeman's take on an old-school juke joint inside a former cotton warehouse. ☎ 662-621-9009; www.groundzerobluesclub.com; 0 Blues Alley, Clarksdale, MS; ⏱ 11am-2pm Mon & Tue, 11am-11pm Wed & Thu, 11am-1am Fri & Sat

Mr Handy's Blues Hall
A classic juke joint, stale from the scent of 100 years of cigarettes and hard times. ☎ 901-528-0150; 182 Beale St, Memphis, TN; cover weekends $5; ⏱ 6pm-12:30am

Preservation Hall
The Preservation Hall Jazz Band holds court in this sonic museum of traditional Dixieland jazz. ☎ 504-522-2841; www.preservation hall.com; 726 St Peter St, New Orleans, LA; cover $10; ⏱ 8-11pm

Red's
Sure, it might look like a semi-abandoned building, but it's one of the foremost blues institutions in the Delta. ☎ 662-627-3166; 395 Sunflower Ave, Clarksdale, MS; cover $5; ⏱ 8pm-late Fri & Sat

Tootsie's Orchid Lounge
There's enough purple here to make Prince sick, but the talent and history make it a must-stop. Live music starts at 10am. ☎ 615-726-0463; www.tootsies.net; 422 Broadway, Nashville, TN; no cover; ⏱ 9:30am-2:30am

SLEEP

The Columns
A lovely 1883 Victorian choice in the Garden District, with live music nightly and jazz on Friday and Sunday. ☎ 504-899-9308; www. thecolumns.com; 3811 St Charles Ave, New Orleans, LA; r from $120

Heartbreak Hotel
Elvis-themed hotel steeped in '50s kitsch and chic, just steps from Graceland. ☎ 901-332-1000; www.heartbreakhotel.net; 3677 Elvis Presley Blvd, Memphis, TN; r from $112

Loews Vanderbilt Hotel
Its lobby jukebox is stocked with tunes from past VIP guests and its walls are lined with impressive music memorabilia. ☎ 615-320-1700; www.loewshotels.com; 2100 W End Ave, Nashville, TN; r from $150

Madison Hotel
This music-themed boutique hotel is where rock stars stay in Memphis. ☎ 901-333-1200; www.madisonhotelmemphis.com; 79 Madison Ave, Memphis, TN; r from $175

Shack Up Inn
Shotgun sharecropper shacks run by a straight-talking owner, and cozy retro rooms inside an authentic cotton gin on Hopson Plantation. You need to be over 25 to sign for a room. There's a two-night minimum on weekends. ☎ 662-624-8329; www.shackup inn.com; 1 Commissary Circle, off Hwy 49, Clarksdale, MS; r from $65

USEFUL WEBSITES
www.clarksdaletourism.com
www.neworleanscvb.com

LINK YOUR TRIP

TRIP
24 48 Hours in New Orleans p217

www.lonelyplanet.com/trip-planner

Cajun Country Road Trip

WHY GO Hidden in the maze of bayous, lakes, swamps and prairies that unfurl south and west of New Orleans is a wild and jubilant French-speaking culture punctuated by crawfish boils, all-night jam sessions and dance parties. You'll enjoy a small taste by looping through Cajun Country to Lafayette and back.

TIME
4 days

DISTANCE
370 miles

BEST TIME TO GO
**Mar – Jun &
Sep – Nov**

START
**New Orleans,
LA**

END
**New Orleans,
LA**

Most folks view Louisiana through a prism called New Orleans, but to experience Cajun Country is to know another side of one of America's most fun, and funky, states. In the South eras, cultures and fortunes collide, overlap and intermingle. Which is why in addition to legendary music halls and Cajun kitchens you'll also experience Louisiana's Creole culture and plantation history as you make this glorious trek.

Depart New Orleans on Hwy 90 through Westwego, then detour on Hwy 1 north to Thibodaux, where you'll find the ❶ **Wetlands Cajun Cultural Center.** Take a boat tour through the bayous and swamps with rangers who will detail Cajun history and discuss their traditional lifestyle. You'll learn that Cajuns came from rural France and settled in the Acadie region of Nova Scotia. When Great Britain took over, the Acadians refused to swear allegiance to the crown. Tempers flared until the British forcibly removed Acadians from their land in the mid-18th century. Many came to these wetlands in South Louisiana. Most hunted, fished and trapped, while others moved to the prairies to grow rice and beef. Over time their dialect crystallized, and so did their music and food, but they remained true to their own French heritage. If you're lucky you'll land here during a boat-building demonstration, or better yet, on a Monday evening when Cajun musicians jam (5pm to 7pm).

Next double back to Hwy 90W and go south on Hwy 182, the Old Spanish Missionary Trail, to ❷ **Houma,** the economic hub of the

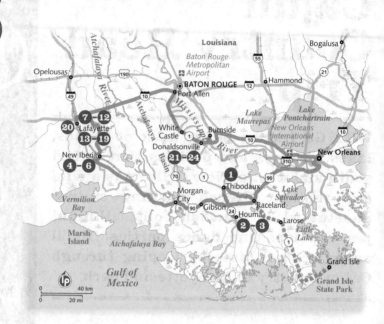

Cajun Wetlands. Like many towns and counties in the USA, it was named for the Native Americans whom the white settlers replaced. Carved by bayous, channels and waterways, you can understand their self-anointed title "Venice of America." But this isn't a tourist town, so you'll likely just pass through on your way to ❸ **Annie Miller's Son's Swamp & Marsh Tours**. Take an entertaining two-hour tour aboard a flat-bottom boat to see swamp life, plus some massive gators.

> *"Carved by bayous, channels and waterways, you can understand their self-anointed title 'Venice of America.'"*

Follow Hwy 182 to Gibson, where you'll link back onto Hwy 90W, Cajun Country's commercial lifeline. You'll roll past too many swamps, bayous, rivers and lakes to count, and eventually you'll reach ❹ **New Iberia**, a plantation town founded in 1779 on sugar and slaves, on Bayou Teche. Echoes of its plantation past are still on display. ❺ **Shadows on the Teche** is a palatial Greek-revival mansion with gorgeous grounds. Massive oaks drip with Spanish moss and a dark green lawn rolls to the brown banks of the bayou. Order a traditional Creole plate lunch at ❻ **Brenda's Diner**. The menu rotates, but there's always a selection of meats (such as smothered liver, fried pork chops, turkey wings and meatloaf) and sides (creamy, tangy mustard greens).

Next turn onto Hwy 31, a two-lane country road that leads to ❼ **Breaux Bridge**, a charming small country town outside of Lafayette. If you are in the area on a Saturday do not miss the zydeco brunch at ❽ **Café Des Amis**. From 8:30am some of the best zydeco bands in Louisiana jam as guests dance like mad. Stay the night nearby at ❾ **Maison Madeleine**, an 1830s Creole cottage set on a dirt road just off Lake Martin. The lake is known as the biggest white ibis rookery on earth. When dinner calls, head to ❿ **Pat's Fisherman's Wharf**, just 15 minutes away by car. It's a legendary Cajun seafood house built on a levee above the river and serving up boiled crawfish, fried gator tail, and terrific crawfish and lump crab étouffée.

On Sunday afternoon, ⓫ **Angelle's Whiskey River Landing** rocks to zydeco and Cajun tunes. It's a small house, and it gets packed. Locals dance on tables, on the bar and in the water. If you want to really experience a night or two on the water, rent a houseboat at ⓬ **Cypress Cove**. You don't even have to drive it. They'll pilot the boat out into the middle of Lake Henderson and lend you a little johnboat to get back to land for more beer.

⓭ **Lafayette** is the grooviest town in Cajun Country. It's home of the University of Louisiana, full of beautiful people, tasty Cajun cuisine and an abundance of live music. If you're looking for a young scene, check into the ⓮ **Blue Moon Guesthouse**. Part outdoor saloon, part hostel, you will not be bored, but don't expect early

TERRANCE SIMIEN'S LAFAYETTE

Louisiana-based musician Terrance Simien is considered a master of the zydeco genre and proud ambassador of Creole culture. Here are some of his favorite Lafayette haunts.

- Blue Moon Saloon (www.bluemoon presents.com) "It's a real down-home place where local people go to hear local music," says Terrance of the roots, honky-tonk, Creole and Cajun music bar nestled on the back porch of the Blue Moon Guesthouse. "It's about good times, good people coming together, dancing and having a good time."

- McGee's Café & Bar (www.mcgees landing.com) "It's right on the banks of the Atchafalaya Basin, so you have a beautiful view while you eat your meal," Terrance says of the family-owned marina restaurant renowned for some of the city's most authentic Cajun cooking. "They have real great crawfish, everything you order is done great."

- Old Tyme Grocery (www.oldetymegrocery .com) Terrance loves bringing out-of-towners to this old-fashioned white-and-red shack, which serves up some of Louisiana's finest po'boys. "They're some of the best I've ever had," he raves. "My favorite is the half-shrimp, half-oyster; they do these jumbo shrimps and huge oysters, and the bread is baked fresh in a local bakery."

Interview by Simona Rabinovitch

shut-eye. Crave more sophisticated sleep? Check into ⓯ **La Maison de Belle B&B**, a converted 1898 house with a lavish downstairs suite (including its own parlor and sitting room), and a rustic cabin out back where John Kennedy Toole penned *Confederacy of Dunces,* adjacent to the park.

On Wednesday mornings stop by ⓰ **Dwyer's** for a breakfast biscuit and listen in as old Cajun codgers hold court in their local French patois. The best plate lunches in town can be found at ⓱ **Antlers**, an old pool hall turned

Cajun rice and gravy lunch counter, dishing up stuffed and smothered pork chops, terrific stewed chicken and rice, and killer soft-shell crab po'boys. Dinner at ⑱ **Don's Seafood and Steakhouse**, a legendary local seafood house, is always tasty. The crawfish bisque is superb and comes with the heads stuffed with breadcrumbs and ground crawfish.

DETOUR

Once you are in Lafayette, detour northwest to **Eunice** (46 miles) and you'll land in Cajun music central. Musician Mark Savoy builds accordions at his **Savoy Music Center**, where you can also pluck some CDs and catch a Saturday morning jam session. Saturday night means the Rendez-Vous Cajuns are playing the **Liberty Theater**, which is just two blocks from the **Cajun Music Hall of Fame & Museum**.

If you're looking for something regional yet upscale, sample the Cajun fusion at ⑲ **Charley G's**. All ingredients come from local fishermen and farmers, and their smoked duck and andouille gumbo, and bluepoint crab cakes come highly recommended. If you're hungry for Cajun snack food between meals, take the short drive west to Scott and pick up some *boudin* (pork, rice, gravy and green onions) sausage from the

⑳ **Best Stop**, a third-generation Cajun butcher. Eat it with cracklin' (fried pork fat sprinkled with salt and pepper). When the moon shines, patrol the many buzzing bars on Jefferson Ave in Lafayette or head over to Blue Moon Saloon (attached to the guesthouse) for some live and local Cajun music.

You'll take the I-10 back to New Orleans, but make sure to turn off on Hwy 70 to historic ㉑ **Donaldsonville**. Although 632 buildings were burned and bombed during the Civil War, there remain dozens of antebellum homes in the area. But one of the city's most interesting attractions is the ㉒ **River Road African American Museum**, a private museum that tells the story of local African Americans from slave ships to the vicious toils and abuse of slavery to slave revolts and the Underground Railroad, to freedom and Jim Crow. This is a place to learn about African American Louisiana's unsung heroes and pioneers.

DETOUR

While you are in Thibodaux consider heading further south on Hwy 1 before heading toward Houma. You'll roll along the bayou through traditional shrimp fishing towns before the wetlands unfurl and roll onto **Grand Isle State Park** and the Gulf of Mexico. There's oil production (and oil money) here, but it's still a beautiful stretch of coastline, and has long been Louisiana's favored beach destination. Jean Lafitte and his crew once set up camp on the golden sand.

Hit ㉓ **Grapevine Café** for lunch or dinner, or for a dynamite Sunday brunch. It's owned by one of the founders of Café Des Amis in Breaux Bridge. Bed down in one of the large suites at ㉔ **Cabahanosse B&B**, which open onto a 2nd-story veranda shaded by an oak canopy. From here, return to the I-10 and follow it back to Nawlins.

Adam Skolnick

TRIP INFORMATION

GETTING THERE

Take Hwy 90W from New Orleans to Hwy 1 and Thibodaux. Double-back to Hwy 90W, turn onto Hwy 182S to Houma. Back on the 90W stop in New Iberia, take Hwy 31 to Breaux Bridge and I-10 to Lafayette.

DO

Angelle's Whiskey River Landing

Get wild on Sunday evenings at this long-beloved Cajun juke joint. Bar- and table-dancing is recommended. ☎ 337-228-2277; www.whiskeyriverlanding.net; 1365 Henderson Levee Rd, Breaux Bridge, LA; cover varies; ☾ 4-8pm Sun

Annie Miller's Son's Swamp & Marsh Tours

A classic two-hour Cajun gator tour. ☎ 985-868-4758; www.annie-miller.com; 3718 Southdown Mandalay Rd, Houma, LA; ☾ seasonal hrs, call ahead; ♿

Cypress Cove

Rent a houseboat and cruise beautiful Lake Henderson. ☎ 337-228-7484; www.houseboat-adventures.com; 1399 Henderson Levee, Henderson, LA; houseboat per day from $135; ☾ 8am-5pm Mon-Sat; ♿

River Road African American Museum

Details the harsh reality, and the heroes and triumphs of Louisiana's African American history. ☎ 225-474-5553; www.african americanmuseum.org; 406 Charles St, Donaldsonville, LA; admission $4; ☾ 10am-5pm Wed-Sat, 1-5pm Sun; ♿

Shadows on the Teche

New Iberia's most famous and accessible antebellum plantation home. Stroll the grounds and watch gentle Bayou Teche roll by. ☎ 337-365-5213; www.shadowsonthe teche.org; 317 E Main St, New Iberia, LA; adult/senior/student $10/8/6.50; ☾ 9am-4:30pm Mon-Sat, noon-4:30pm Sun; ♿

Wetlands Cajun Cultural Center

Enjoy ranger-guided boat tours of Bayou Lafourche where you'll learn about the natural and cultural history of Cajun Country.

Has live Cajun music every Monday night. ☎ 985-448-1375; www.nps.gov/jela; 314 St Mary St, Thibodaux, LA; admission free; ☾ 9am-7pm Mon & Tue, 9am-6pm Wed & Thu, 9am-5pm Fri & Sat; ♿

EAT

Antlers

Hands-down the best plate lunch in Lafayette. ☎ 337-234-8877; 555 Jefferson St, Lafayette, LA; mains $7-15; ☾ 11am-2pm Mon-Fri, dinner Fri and 2nd Sat; ♿

Best Stop

It's worth a drive from Lafayette just for the smoked boudin, a Cajun pork, rice and gravy sausage. ☎ 337-233-5805; www.thebest stopsupermarket.com; 615 Hwy 93, Scott, LA; ☾ 6am-3pm Mon-Fri; ♿

Brenda's Diner

Brenda serves heaping portions of delicious soul food. ☎ 337-367-0868; 409 W Pershing St, New Iberia, LA; mains $6-12, plate lunches $8; ☾ 7am-3pm Mon-Fri; ♿

Café Des Amis

The Creole and Cajun menu is good, but the real hit is the live zydeco breakfast every Saturday morning. ☎ 337-332-5273; www .cafedesamis.com; 140 E Bridge St, Breaux Bridge, LA; mains $12-22; ☾ 11am-2pm Tue, 11am-9pm Wed & Thu, 7:30am-9:30pm Fri & Sat, 8am-2:30pm Sun; ♿

Charley G's

This popular dining room serves upscale Cajun fusion, with live music from 6pm to 9pm Wednesday to Saturday. ☎ 337-981-0108; www.charleygs.com; 3809 Ambassador Caffrey Parkway, Lafayette, LA; mains $10-39; ☾ 11:30am-2pm & 5:30-9pm Mon-Thu, 5:30-10pm Fri & Sat

Don's Seafood and Steakhouse

A vintage seafood and steak house in downtown Lafayette. Don't miss the crawfish bisque. ☎ 337-235-3551; 301 E Vermilion St, Lafayette, LA; mains $12-25; ☾ 11am-9pm Sun-Thu, 11am-10pm Fri & Sat; ♿

Dwyer's

This family-owned joint is especially fun on Wednesday mornings when local Cajuns shoot the breeze in their old-school French dialect.

☎ 337-235-9364; 323 Jefferson St, Lafayette, LA; mains $5-12; ☻ 7am-3pm; ♿

Grapevine Café
The former owner of Café Des Amis serves up scrumptious Creole and Cajun dishes. The brunch is spectacular. ☎ 225-473-8463; www.grapevinecafeandgallery.com; 211 Railroad Ave, Donaldsonville, LA; mains $7-27; ☻ 11am-2pm & 5-9pm Tue-Thu, 5-9.30pm Fri, 11am-9.30pm Sat; ♿

Pat's Fisherman's Wharf
A delicious and authentic Cajun seafood joint perched above the river. ☎ 337-228-7512; www.patsfishermanswharf.com; 1008 Henderson Levee Rd (Hwy 352), Henderson, LA; mains $13-22; ☻ 11am-10pm; ♿

SLEEP

Blue Moon Guesthouse
There's a backyard nightclub and hostel environs (dorms, with a few private rooms) in this tidy old Lafayette home. ☎ 877-766-2583; www.bluemoonhostel.com; 215 E Convent St, Lafayette, LA; dm $18, r $70-90

Cabahanosse B&B
The four suites are large and comfortable with a fantastic 2nd-floor veranda, claw-foot bathtubs and a grill out back. ☎ 225-474-5050; www.cabahanosse.com; 602 Railroad Ave, Donaldsonville, LA; r $159; ♿

La Maison de Belle B&B
Overnight where John Kennedy Toole dreamed up *Confederacy of Dunces*. The grounds and adjacent park are lovely. ☎ 337-235-2520; 610 Girard Park Dr, Lafayette, LA; r $110-150

Maison Madeleine
Overnight in this gorgeous, historic Creole cottage surrounded by luscious gardens, just up the dirt road from Lake Martin. ☎ 337-332-4555; www.maisonmadeleine.com; 1015 John D Hebert Rd, Breaux Bridge, LA; r $125-180

USEFUL WEBSITES
www.epiculinary.com
www.theind.com

LINK YOUR TRIP
www.lonelyplanet.com/trip-planner

TRIP
24 48 Hours in New Orleans p217

HISTORY &
CULTURE

Antebellum South

WHY GO The Civil War decimated the South, but several elegant plantation homes built in the 30 years leading up to the war avoided the Union's fiery wrath. Referred to as antebellum, they not only represent some of the most astounding architecture on American soil, but also offer a glimpse into a bygone era.

TIME
8 days

DISTANCE
1100 miles

BEST TIME TO GO
Mar – Jun

START
Charleston, SC

END
Vacherie, LA

Many people's idea of antebellum architecture, whether they realize it or not, is Tara Plantation, the fictional abode of Scarlett O'Hara in Margaret Mitchell's 1946 novel, *Gone with the Wind* – but you can only visit that one in your own fantasyland. In the book, Tara is spared the fiery wrath of the Union's matchbook warfare, surviving untorched while its neighbors are burnt to the ground. That's pretty much how it went, and why antebellum architecture is so vehemently preserved today: there just isn't very much of it left.

Antebellum refers to a time and place in history – the 30 years leading up to the Civil War, from 1831 to 1861 – not an architectural style as some people think. Most antebellum homes are actually one of three styles: Greek Revival, Classical Revival, Tidewater or Federal style. They are boxy, grand mansions with central entrances in the front and back, impressive columns and sizable covered porches made for lazily watching the days go by while sipping on homemade lemonade or backyard hooch (as the case may be). These are typical architectural features introduced by Anglo Americans who settled in the area after the Louisiana Purchase in 1803. Today, antebellum homes conjure up romanticized images of Southern opulence, owned by folks with so much money, they'd gladly give you some (just ask nicely, hon); but in reality, folks with this much money usually "owned" slaves, so most of these antebellum homes aren't without their dark side.

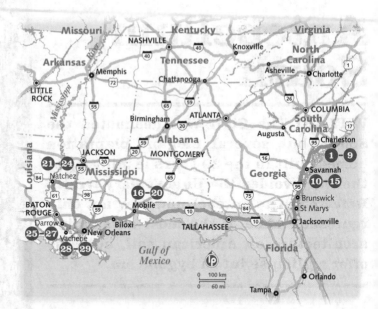

Bookending this trip are two evocative river roads – Ashley in Charleston, South Carolina and the Great Mississippi in Vacherie, Louisiana – that together represent the most picturesque destinations to take in the refined elegance of antebellum architecture in a concentrated area. But there is no shortage of impressive stops along the way – small patches of the Deep South, like the fictional Tara, were left untouched, while others suffered damage but not irreparably so, leaving behind one of America's most endearing architectural legacies.

① Charleston, South Carolina offers its visitors an unparalleled continuum of classical American architecture, ranging from early colonial through Federal, antebellum and Victorian styles, unmatched anywhere else in the United States. Despite being the cradle of the Civil War and its succession movement, a surprising amount of buildings here eluded destruction or irreversible damage. The **② Aiken-Rhett House** is the only surviving urban plantation. Built in 1818, it was described in a 19th-century newspaper ad as: "Twelve upright rooms, four on each floor, all well finished, the material of the piazzas and fences all of cypress and cedar; underneath the house are large cellars and storerooms." Confederate President Jefferson Davis slept here on a visit to Charleston in 1863.

Everywhere you turn in Charleston, an historic inn or hotel beckons. Try the **③ Mills House Hotel**, which is slightly hipper than most. Owned by Holiday

Inn, it's anything but a typical highway-exit haunt. An ornate $17 million restoration has returned it to the glory of its original opening date (1853). The staircases and chandeliers are original. Inside a 19th-century shipping warehouse a few blocks west, you'll find ❹ **S.N.O.B.** which stands for Slightly North of Broad, but order the Carolina quail breast over cheese grits and your graduation to food snob will be complete.

A few miles west of town is the impossibly scenic ❺ **Ashley River Road**, a picturesque glimpse into once-thriving South Carolina Lowcountry wealth. The oldest *preserved* plantation in the US is the pre-revolutionary ❻ **Drayton Hall**, built in 1738 and unique here for its Georgian-Palladian architecture. If it all goes down while you're in the area, this is a good place to seek shelter; it has survived the American Revolution, the Civil War, the earthquake of 1886, and Hurricane Hugo. A few clicks northwest is the ❼ **Magnolia Plantation** (1676), known for its exquisite formal gardens – said to be the origin of azaleas in the US – and 19th-century slave cabin.

Your bed for the night is at the ❽ **Inn at Middleton Place** on the sprawling ❾ **Middleton Place Plantation**, another 4 miles or so down Ashley River Road. The main house (c 1730) is home to the oldest landscaped gardens in the US. Several generations of influential Middletons stomped these gorgeous grounds, including the president of the first Continental Congress (Henry), a signer of the Declaration of Independence (Arthur) and a governor of South Carolina (Henry). The inn is cozy, and noted for its wide plantation shutters, hardwood floors and braided rugs. The whole property has also been designated a National Wildlife Federation (NWF) Backyard Wildlife Habitat site and offers memorable kayaking and birding. Allow a few hours to visit the plantations on Ashley River Road.

Leave Ashley River Road on Hwy 61, which takes you to Hwy 17 Alt (south bound) and I-95 (south bound) on to

ASK A LOCAL

"Beloved in Southern history, the **Olde Pink House** is my favorite of Savannah's antebellum structures. Today, as a fine-dining restaurant, the graceful dining rooms are dressed in white tablecloths and candles, while the grandeur and pioneering adventures of the 18th century seem to hover gracefully. My vivid imagination has often taken me on a time travel to the Planters Tavern, at basement level, to watch and listen as Liberty Boys plotted and put in motion Georgia's role in the united colonies' fight for independence from England."
Sandy Traub, Savannah

❿ **Savannah**, Georgia's Belle of the Ball. For a good comparison of middle-class versus high falutin' antebellum life, two good examples spell it out for you here. The ⓫ **Davenport House Museum**, a 200-year-old mansion built in Federal style is credited with spawning Savannah's historical preservation movement when it avoided demolition in 1955. Built by Isaiah Davenport in the 1820s, the simply appointed home boasts an impressive entrance hall with two iconic columns, a spiral staircase and Palladian window. There is, however, questionable – though period-perfect – wallpaper.

A block away, but worlds away in social status, one of the wealthiest men in America, cotton merchant Richard Richardson, built the ⑫ **Owens-Thomas House** between 1816 and 1819. This ornate English Regency mansion features rare Haint Blue ceiling paint, made from crushed indigo, buttermilk and wine, in the slave quarters. *Haint* means "haunt" in the Gullah language (still spoken by some Lowcountry African Americans), and the paint was used to ward off spirits. The home also boasts a gorgeous upstairs bridge connecting two sides of the house, impressive curved doors in the dining room and a beautiful Russian harp belonging to Isabella Habersham. The home is part of Savannah's ⑬ **Telfair Academy**, the oldest public museum of art in the Southeast.

MO-BEEL'S HISTORIC HOMES

Residents of Alabama's oldest city throw open the doors to their most preciously preserved historic homes for two days every March for the **Mobile Historic Homes Tour** (*Mo-beel,* not a bunch of trailers!). Mobile's diverse architectural styles are all represented on the tours: Creole cottages, Greek Revival mansions, Victorian and neoclassic residences, among others. It's a one-shot chance to get inside some of the country's best antique abodes.

Savannah is an ideal spot for a sleepover. Dine on the signature crispy scored flounder at ⑭ **Olde Pink House**, a 1771 National Landmark that turned from white to Jamaican pink after the original bricks "bled" through the plastered walls. The ⑮ **Kehoe House**, a romantic Renaissance Revival B&B built in 1892 and said to be haunted, is where you'll find your historic bed. Twins are said to have died in a chimney here, so they are boarded up. The skittish should steer clear of rooms 201 and 203!

Continue on I-95 (south bound) to Jacksonville, Florida, where you'll pick up I-10 (west bound) across the entity of the Florida Panhandle all the way to ⑯ **Mobile, AL**. It's risky to stop first and drop your bags at the ⑰ **Kate Shepard House**, historic Mobile's must-sleep. Innkeeper Wendy James is as gracious a host as humanly possible. The meticulous restoration of this gorgeous 1897 Queen Anne–style home by Wendy and her husband deserves the museum treatment itself. You won't want to leave. But it's the pecan praline French toast that ensures this wonderful find won't soon be forgotten. Ask about the long-lost Civil War papers found in the attic. This surely must be where the phrase "Southern hospitality" was first uttered. The house is across the street from Katharine Philips, who played a role in the Ken Burns documentary, *The War*.

Located in one of Mobile's eight National Register Historic Districts, the main T-shaped Greek Revival mansion at the ⑱ **Oakleigh Historic Complex** dates back to 1833. Its distinct cantilevered front staircase and grand double parlors offer a peek in to the Gulf Coast's high society lifestyle, while the Cook's House (1850), originally built for slaves, and Cox-Deasy Cottage (1850), built by a brick mason for his wife and 11 kids, show how the working and servant classes lived. Spend your evening in the classic ⓱ **Pillars** restaurant; they do wonderful things with blackened cow.

Before hopping on I-10 (west bound) towards Natchez, stop off at the ⓴ **Bragg-Mitchell Mansion** (1855), one of the most splendid Greek Revival mansions on the Gulf Coast. It closes without notice for special events though, so call ahead. From there, it's a 4½-hour drive to southwest Mississippi, where ㉑ **Natchez, Mississippi**, the oldest civilized settlement on the Mississippi River (beating out New Orleans by two years), stands perched on a bluff. Settled by the French in 1716, it remains a living antebellum museum (when it's not getting pounded by hurricanes) and boasts more antebellum homes than any other US city. If you can get here during spring and fall pilgrimage, many private residences are open to the public – but there is plenty to do and see here year-round.

㉒ **Longwood Plantation**, a six-story, 30,000-sq-ft, Greek Revival monster is considered the grandest octagonal house in America (rumor has it a sassy hexagonal number from Tallahassee is looking to unseat Longwood for most striking geometric dwelling). When the Civil War broke out during construction, the workers hightailed it out of here (damn straight), leaving the home unfinished. It's still unfinished (not cool, yet fascinating). You can sleep in Natchez most well-known antebellum attraction, the Federal-style ㉓ **Monmouth Plantation** (1818). Union soldiers almost took this one out, due to the succession cries of its original owner, Mexican War hero General John A Quitman. He died before war broke out, but if it weren't for his two daughters pleading with Union

ASK A LOCAL

"The historic homes are certainly the main attraction, but we also have a vineyard and winery, Old South Winery, and a great exhibit of photographs of life in Natchez from the mid-1800s to about 1920 at the Stratton Chapel. We have seasonal pilgrimages in the spring and fall, when more of the homes are open to the public for tours than usual, and that's when we enjoy more visitors because the seasons are milder."
Charles Burns, Natchez

soldiers on their way to declaring allegiance to the United States, Monmouth would have been a smoldering mess in no time. Toast to the daughters' quick-thinking resilience over mint juleps at the ㉔ **Carriage House** on the grounds of Stanton Hall (1857). It's famous for fried chicken and tiny buttered biscuits.

A little over two hours' travel south along the Mississippi River's scenic ㉕ **Great River Road** lands you in Darrow, Louisiana, worth a stop for the ㉖ **Houmas House Plantation** and its excellent restaurant, ㉗ **Latil's Landing**. The former is a grand mansion so unmistakably *Cribs*-worthy, it sold for

$1 million in 1857, and is notable as one of the few antebellum homes that remain an active residence (no, Snoop Dogg doesn't live here). The restaurant is set inside the 230-year-old French House on the same grounds, complete with original beamed ceilings, cypress mantels, wood-burning fireplaces and original wood floors. It's the foodie highlight of the trip.

Continue east along Great River Rd to the Louisiana's two most adored plantations. **28 Laura Plantation**, built in 1805, stands out for its whimsical exterior (canary yellow with a bright-red roof, pine-green shutters, and mauve and grey trim) and its fascinating tour – far and away the most interesting along the road for its deep-rooted Creole past, its slave quarters and the slaves' affiliation with the West African folktale of Br'er Rabbit (the American version of which was said to have originated here among slaves). The backbone of the tour is based on 5000 pages of documents related to the plantation found archived in Paris, plus the memoirs of Laura Locoul Gore, for whom the house is named. These written accounts from generations of the Creoles who lived here (the women who ran the plantation and the slaves who lived here) will inspire laughter one minute, tears the next, but it's never boring.

"A grand mansion so unmistakably Cribs-worthy, it sold for $1 million in 1857."

The easiest plantation on the eyes is **29 Oak Alley Plantation**, with its 28 perfectly symmetrical live oak trees naturally framing the 28-column entrance corridor to this majestic Greek Revival beauty from 1837. Arrive early or stay late for that postcard-perfect shot without a bunch of gawking tourists mucking up your photos. Like elsewhere on Great River Rd, countless movies have been filmed here, most notably *Primary Colors* and *Interview with the Vampire*. It runs a B&B, so you can sleep here, too, dreaming of a simpler time, wondering if the South were to rise again, what would become of its most treasured possessions?

Kevin Raub

HISTORY &
CULTURE

TRIP INFORMATION

GETTING THERE
From Atlanta, take I-20 (east bound) to I-26 (east bound) into Charleston.

DO
Aiken-Rhett House
Charleston's most intact antebellum mansion. Many pieces are still sitting in the same rooms for which they were purchased. ☎ 843-723-1159; www.historic charleston.org; 48 Elizabeth St, Charleston, SC; adult/child $10/5; ⏱ 10am-5pm Mon-Sat, 2-5pm Sun; ♿

Bragg-Mitchell Mansion
This Greek-Italianate mansion (1855) is the grandest of the surviving Gulf Coast antebellum homes. It does close sporadically though. ☎ 251-471-6364; www.braggmitchell mansion.com; 1906 Springhill Ave, Mobile, AL; adult/child $5/3; ⏱ 10am-4pm Tue-Fri; ♿

Davenport House Museum
This 200-year-old Federal-style mansion kicked off Savannah's preservation movement. ☎ 912-236-8097; www.davenport housemuseum.org; 324 E State St, Savannah, GA; adult/child $8/5; ⏱ 10am-4pm Mon-Sat, 1-4pm Sun; ♿

Drayton Hall
The oldest surviving Georgian Palladian structure in the US and the only originally intact plantation along the Ashley River. ☎ 843-769-2600; www.draytonhall.org; 3380 Ashley River Rd, Charleston, SC; adult/child $14/8; ⏱ 9:30am-4pm Nov-Feb; ♿

Houmas House Plantation
Exquisite 1828 Greek Revival mansion originally owned by Houmas Indians. There's a fantastic restaurant here too. ☎ 225-473-9380; www.houmashouse.com; 40136 Hwy 942, Darrow, LA; adult/child $20/10; ⏱ 9am-5pm Mon & Tue, 9am-7pm Wed-Sun; ♿

Laura Plantation
This 1805 Creole plantation runs exceptional tours of the colorful manor house, formal French gardens and historic outbuildings. ☎ 225-265-7690; www.laura

plantation.com; 2247 Hwy 18, Vacherie, LA; adult/child $18/5; ⏱ 10am-4pm; ♿

Longwood Plantation
The Civil War interrupted the construction of Longwood (1861), the grandest octagonal house in the US. ☎ 601-442-5193; www.natchezpilgrimage.com; 140 Lower Woodville Rd, Natchez, MS; adult/child $10/8; ⏱ 9am-4:30pm; ♿

Magnolia Plantation
Exquisite gardens (some parts as old as 325 years) and main home dating back to 1676. ☎ 843-571-1266; www.magnolia plantation.com; 3550 Ashley River Rd, Charleston, SC; adult/child incl house tour $22/17; ⏱ 9am-5:30pm; ♿

Middleton Place Plantation
Sprawling 18th-century Lowcountry plantation and America's oldest landscaped gardens. ☎ 843-556-6020; www.middleton place.org; 4300 Ashley River Rd, Charleston, SC; adult/child $25/5; ⏱ 9am-5pm; ♿

Oakleigh Historic Complex
A three-home museum highlighted by the main Greek Revival house (1833) and its 1840 rosewood piano with mother-of-pearl keys. ☎ 251-432-6161; www.historicmobile .org; 300 Oakleigh Pl, Mobile, AL; adult/child $7/3; ⏱ 10am-4pm Thu-Sun; ♿

Owens-Thomas House
Ornate English Regency mansion that's part of Savannah's Telfair Museum of Art. ☎ 912-233-9743; www.telfair.org; 124 Abercorn St, Savannah, GA; adult/child $15/5; ⏱ noon-5pm Mon, 10am-5pm Tue-Sat, 1-5pm Sun

Telfair Academy
Three unique buildings make up the Telfair, which isn't antebellum, but dates back to 1886. ☎ 912-790-8800; www.telfair.org; 121 Barnard St, Savannah, GA; adult/child $15/5; ⏱ noon-5pm Mon, 10am-5pm Tue-Sat, 1-5pm Sun

EAT
Carriage House
Southern fried chicken, tiny buttered biscuits and mint juleps top the fare at this restaurant on the grounds of 1857 Greek Revival Stanton

Hall. ☎ 601-445-5153; www.stantonhall .com; 401 High St, Natchez, MS; mains $10-15; ⊙ 11am-2pm Thu-Mon

Latil's Landing
Inside the 1770 French House on the grounds of Houmas House, chef Jeremy Langlois' discriminating cuisine will leave you feeling like a sugar baron. ☎ 225-473-9380; www .houmashouse.com; 40136 Hwy 942, Darrow, LA; mains $25-35; ⊙ 6-10pm Wed-Sat, 2-9pm Sun

Olde Pink House
This 1771 pink mansion on Reynolds Square epitomizes antebellum romance. The nouveau Southern cuisine ain't bad, either. ☎ 912-232-4286; 23 Abercorn St, Savannah, GA; mains $17-29; ⊙ 5-10:30pm Sun & Mon, 11am-10:30pm Tue-Thu, 11am-11pm Fri & Sat, closed 3-5pm daily

Pillars
Historic 1904 mansion-turned-restaurant, serving up excellent steaks (the Queen filet, blackened – trust us) and seafood, served in a space boasting picturesque original checkerboard-tile floors. ☎ 251-471-3411; www .thepillarsmobile.com; 1757 Government St, Mobile, AL; mains $16-34; ⊙ 11am-3pm Mon-Fri & 5pm-10pm Mon-Sat

S.N.O.B.
An eclectic menu, and decor carved from a 19th-century shipping warehouse. ☎ 843-723-3424; 192 E Bay St, Charleston, SC; mains $10-34; ⊙ 11:30am-3pm Mon-Fri, 5:30-10pm Sun-Thu, 5:30-11pm Fri & Sat

SLEEP

Kate Shepard House
This 1897 Queen Anne–style B&B isn't antebellum, but don't fret. The only thing more gorgeous than the home is the pecan praline French toast. ☎ 251-479-7048; www .kateshepardhouse.com; 1552 Monterey Pl, Mobile, AL; r from $145; 🐾

Kehoe House
An intimate, 13-room Renaissance Revival B&B on beautiful Columbia Square. ☎ 912-232-1020; www.kehoehouse.com; 123 Habersham St, Savannah, GA; r from $229

Inn at Middleton Place
Inviting cypress paneling, warm hardwood floors and wood-burning stoves are a highlight of this romantic inn at Middleton Place. ☎ 843-556-0500; www.theinnatmiddleton place.com; 4290 Ashley River Rd, Charleston, SC; r $170-285

Mills House Hotel
Originally opened just before the Civil War, this hotel features an opulent marble lobby and gilded elevators. ☎ 843-577-2400; www.millshouse.com; 115 Meeting St, Charleston, SC; r from $148

Monmouth Plantation
A night at this regal Federal-style 1818 mansion and eight outbuildings is like sleeping *on* history. Good restaurant, too. ☎ 601-442-5852; www.monmouthplantation.com; 36 Melrose Ave, Natchez, MS; r from $195

Oak Alley Plantation
Slip into slumber in century-old plantation cottages on the grounds of Oak Alley Plantation (1841) and its famously photographed 28 classic columns. ☎ 225-265-2151; www .oakalleyplantation.com; 3645 Hwy 18, Vacherie, LA; r from $130

USEFUL WEBSITES
www.charlestoncvb.com
www.visitnatchez.com

LINK YOUR TRIP
www.lonelyplanet.com/trip-planner

Driving the Natchez Trace Parkway

WHY GO With emerald mounds, jade swamps, hiking trails, opulent mansions, riverside saloons, and layer upon layer of American history, the Natchez Trace Parkway is the richest drive in the South. It winds 442 gorgeously wooded miles from Nashville all the way to Natchez in southern Mississippi.

TIME
3 days

DISTANCE
442 miles

BEST TIME TO GO
**Apr – Jun &
Sep – Nov**

START
Nashville, TN

END
Natchez, MS

America grew from infancy to childhood then adolescence in the late 18th and 19th centuries. That's when we explored and expanded, traded and clashed with Native Americans, and eventually confronted our own shadow during the Civil War. Evidence of this drama can be found along the Natchez Trace, but before you begin, enjoy a little night music.

You'll begin in ❶ Nashville, where amateur musicians descend in the hopes of becoming country music stars. There are boot-stomping honky-tonks, the country music hall of fame and a sweet historic district to explore. Don't miss ❷ Bluebird Cafe, tucked away in a suburban strip mall. This is a singer-songwriter haven. While you eat and sip cocktails, souls will be bared on the tiny stage. No midshow chitchat, mind, or you will get bounced.

If you'd like to enjoy a less controlled musical environment, head over to ❸ Tootsie's Orchid Lounge. In 1960, when Hattie "Tootsie" Bess bought the joint, she began nurturing up-and-coming country stars like Waylon Jennings and Faron Young on two stages. It remains a glorious dive smothered with old photographs and handbills from the Nashville Sound glory days, while the music (still country) has evolved with the times.

Grab dinner at ❹ Swett's, a family-owned, cafeteria-style Nashville institution that's been around for 53 years. It's all about Southern food

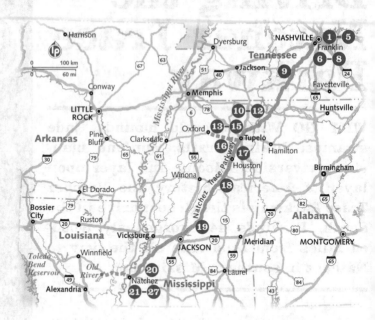

here, covering everything from BBQ chicken and pig's feet to turnip greens and baked apples. Snooze at the **5** **Union Station Hotel** on Broadway. If the 65ft vaulted lobby and 100-year-old timetables remind you of a train station, that's because this was the Nashville rail depot once upon a time.

"It remains a glorious dive smothered with old photographs and handbills from the Nashville Sound glory days."

The next day head south, and you will traverse the Double-Arch Bridge, 155ft above the valley, before settling in for a pleasant country drive. You'll notice dense woods encroaching and arching elegantly over the smooth highway for the next 442 miles.

Although it's just 10 miles outside of Nashville, it's worth stopping in the tiny historic hamlet of **6** **Franklin**. The Victorian-era downtown is charming and the nearby artsy enclave of Leiper's Fork is fun and eclectic. But you're in the area to check out one of the Civil War's bloodiest battlefields. On November 30, 1864, 37,000 men (20,000 Confederates and 17,000 Union soldiers) fought over a 2-mile stretch of Franklin's outskirts. Nashville's sprawl has turned much of the battlefield into suburbs, but the **7** **Carter House** property is a preserved 8-acre chunk of the Battle of Franklin. The house is still riddled with 1000 bullet holes.

At mile-marker 403.7 (don't mind the "backward" mile-markers, we think a north–south route works best), you'll find the first of several sections of the

8 Old Trace. In the early 19th century, Kaintucks (boatmen from Ohio and Pennsylvania) floated coal, livestock and agricultural goods down the Ohio and Mississippi Rivers aboard flat-bottom boats. Often their boats were emptied in Natchez, where they disembarked and began the long walk home up the Old Trace to Nashville, where they could access established roads further north. This walking path intersected Choctaw and Chicasaw country. In fact, indigenous travelers were the first to beat this earth. You can walk a 2000ft section of that original trail at this turnout.

Just under 20 miles later, at mile-marker 385.9, you'll come to the **9 Meriwether Lewis Site**, where the famed explorer and first governor of the Louisiana territory died of mysterious gunshot wounds at nearby Grinders Inn. Lewis' good friend, Thomas Jefferson, was convinced it was suicide, though his family begged to differ. Continue on and you will

> **DETOUR** If you plan on driving the entire Natchez Trace from Nashville to Natchez, you may want to detour at Tupelo along Hwy 6 to **Oxford**, Mississippi (about 50 miles), a town rich in culture and history. This is Faulkner country, and Oxford is a thriving university town with terrific restaurants and bars. Don't miss the catfish dinner at Taylor Grocery, 15 minutes south of Oxford.

cross into Alabama at mile-marker 341.8, and Mississippi at mile-marker 310 where you'll also find **10 Bear Creek Mound**, an ancient indigenous ceremonial site built between 1200 and 1400.

The highway bisects **11 Tishomingo State Park** at mile-marker 304.5. If you're taking it slow, you may want to camp here among the sandstone cliffs, fern gullies and waterfalls of Bear Creek canyon. Hiking trails abound and canoes are available for rent. The **12 Phar Mounds**, a 2000-year-old, 90-acre complex of eight indigenous burial sites, are worth braking for at mile-marker 286.7, and at mile marker 269.4 you'll contemplate the Civil War once again, this time at the **13 Confederate Gravesites** for 13 unknown soldiers.

At mile-marker 266 you'll roll into Tupelo and the **14 Natchez Trace Parkway Visitors Center**. Peruse natural and American history displays, grab maps and pick the brains of local rangers behind the counter. While you're in town consider visiting the **15 Elvis Presley Birthplace**. The original structure has a new roof and furniture, but Elvis grew up, learned to play the guitar and dreamed big in these humble rooms.

South from Tupelo, the trace winds past **16 Chicasaw Village**, where displays document how the Chicasaw lived, and the 2100-year-old **17 Bynum Mounds**, before reaching **18 French Camp**. If you plan on driving the trace in two days, you should overnight here in log cabins on the site of a former French pioneer settlement. You can tour a cute antebellum two-story home, built by Revolutionary War veteran Colonel James Drane. The table is set for dinner, aged leather journals are arranged on the desk and Drane's original US flag is in an upstairs bedroom along with a cool antique loom.

At mile-marker 122, tour the **19 Cypress Swamp**. The 20-minute trail snakes through an abandoned channel and continues on a boardwalk over the milky green swamp shaded by water tupelo and bald cypresses. Look for turtles on the rocks and gators in the water.

At mile-marker 10.3 is **20 Emerald Mound**, the best of the indigenous mound sites. Using stone tools, pre-Columbian ancestors to the Natchez Indians graded this 8-acre mountain into a flat-topped pyramid. It is now the second-largest mound in America. There are shady, creekside picnic spots here too.

KAYAKING THE OLD RIVER

According to Keith Benoist, a photographer, landscaper and co-founder of the **Phatwater Challenge** marathon kayak race, the Mississippi has more navigable river miles than any other state in the union. Natchez-born Benoist trains for his 44-mile race by paddling 10 miles of the Old River, an abandoned section of the Mississippi fringed with cypress and teeming with gators. If you're lucky enough to meet him at Under the Hill, he may just take you with him.

When the woods part, revealing historic antebellum mansions, you have reached **21 Natchez**, Mississippi. In the 1840s, Natchez had more millionaires per capita than any city in the world (because the plantation owners didn't pay their staff). Yes, old cotton money built these homes with slave labor, but they are graced all the same with an opulent, *Gone With the Wind* charm. "Pilgrimage season" is in the spring and fall, when the mansions open for tours, though some are open year-round. The redbrick **22 Auburn Mansion** is famous for its freestanding spiral staircase. Built in 1812, the architecture here – a pediment roof supported by thick columns – influenced countless mansions throughout the South.

Care to taste mansion life? **23 Monmouth Plantation** will do just fine. This 26-acre mansion property has 30 guest rooms within the mansion and in outlying buildings, done up with old Southern antiques. There are original Waterford chandeliers and luxurious canopy beds. Service and food are impeccable, as well. **24 The Castle**, a restaurant set at Dunleith mansion (also turned B&B), is widely considered the best in town, while **25 Magnolia Grill** is a casual spot for tasty salads and grilled fish, shrimp and steaks.

Natchez has dirt under its fingernails too. When Mark Twain came through town, he crashed in a room above the local saloon. **26 Under the Hill Saloon** remains the best bar in town, with terrific (and free) live music on weekends. And you can still crash upstairs at **27 Mark Twain Guesthouse**, where rooms on the riverside have a balcony overlooking the Mississippi River.

Adam Skolnick

TRIP INFORMATION

GETTING THERE
Catch the Natchez Trace Parkway in Nashville and follow it 442 miles until it ends in Natchez. Or vice versa.

DO

Auburn Mansion
An antebellum Natchez mansion open for year-round tours. ☎ 800-647-6742; www.natchezpilgrimage.com; Duncan Park, Natchez, MS; ⏰ tours 11am-2:30pm Tue-Sat; ♿

Bear Creek Mound
One of several ceremonial mounds along the Natchez Trace Parkway. ☎ 800-305-7417; www.nps.gov/natr; mile marker 310 Natchez Trace Parkway, MS; ♿ 👶

Bluebird Cafe
Obscure talents come to this suburban strip-mall café hoping to be discovered. ☎ 615-383-1461; www.bluebirdcafe.com; 4104 Hillsboro Pike, Nashville, TN; admission free-$20; ⏰ 5:30-11:30pm Mon-Thu, 5:30pm-midnight Fri-Sun

Bynum Mounds
Another interesting mound site with information detailing native life. ☎ 800-305-7417; www.nps.gov/natr; mile-marker 232.4 Natchez Trace Parkway, MS; ♿ 👶

Carter House
A preserved, 8-acre swath of the Franklin Battlefield. ☎ 615-791-1861; www.carterhouse1864.com; 1140 Columbia Ave, Franklin, TN; adult/senior/child $12/10/6; ⏰ 9am-5pm Mon-Sat, 1-5pm Sun; ♿ 👶

Chicasaw Village
An old indigenous village site just off the Trace. ☎ 800-305-7417; www.nps.gov/natr; mile-marker 261.8 Natchez Trace Parkway, MS; ♿ 👶

Confederate Gravesites
Thirteen unidentified Confederate soldiers were buried here just off the parkway. ☎ 800-305-7417; www.nps.gov/natr; mile-marker 269.4 Natchez Trace Parkway, MS; ♿ 👶

Cypress Swamp
This 20-minute walk around a gorgeous jade swamp is an ideal stretch break. ☎ 800-305-7417; www.nps.gov/natr; mile-marker 122 Natchez Trace Parkway, MS; ♿ 👶

Elvis Presley Birthplace
Elvis freaks descend to see where the king learned to walk then play guitar then thrust his pelvis. ☎ 662-841-1245; www.elvispresleybirthplace.com; 306 Elvis Presley Dr, Tupelo, MS; adult/child $12/6; ⏰ 9am-5pm Mon-Sat, 1-5pm Sun; ♿

Emerald Mound
These two massive grassy pyramids still buzz with ancient energy. ☎ 800-305-7417; www.nps.gov/natr; mile-marker 10.3 Natchez Trace Parkway, MS; ♿ 👶

Meriwether Lewis Site
The explorer Lewis died in these woods from mysterious gunshot wounds. ☎ 800-305-7417; www.nps.gov/natr; mile-marker 385.9 Natchez Trace Parkway, TN; ♿ 👶

Natchez Trace Parkway Visitor Center
The parkway visitors center is just outside Tupelo. ☎ 800-305-7417; www.nps.gov/natr; mile-marker 286.7 Natchez Trace Parkway, MS; ⏰ 8am-5pm, closed Christmas; ♿ 👶

Old Trace
Remnants of the Old Trace walking trail are preserved at various points in the woods along the parkway. ☎ 800-305-7417; www.nps.gov/natr; mile-marker 403.7 Natchez Trace Parkway, MS; ♿ 👶

Phar Mounds
This 2000-year-old complex includes eight mound sites scattered over 90 acres. ☎ 800-305-7417; www.nps.gov/natr; mile-marker 286.7 Natchez Trace Parkway, MS; ♿ 👶

Tootsie's Orchid Lounge
This purple glazed honky-tonk has hosted good live country music since 1960. ☎ 615-726-0463; www.tootsies.net; 422 Broadway, Nashville, TN; admission free; ⏰ 10am-late

Under The Hill Saloon
Historic bar that was once a favorite haunt of Mark Twain. ☎ 601-446-8023; www.underthehillsaloon.com; 25 Silver St, Natchez, MS; ⏰ 10am-late

EAT

Castle
Upscale continental cuisine served on the sensational Dunleith Plantation. ☎ 601-446-8500; www.dunleith.com; 84 Homochitto St, Natchez, MS; mains $18-34; ☽ 7:30-10am, 11am-2pm & 6-9pm Mon-Thu, 11am-10pm Fri, 6-10pm Sat

Magnolia Grill
Delicious, fresh, grilled fare served with fabulous Mississippi River views. ☎ 601-446-7670; www.magnoliagrill.com; 49 Silver St, Natchez, MS; mains $9-32; ☽ 11am-9pm, 11am-10pm Fri & Sat; ☝

Swett's
Tasty traditional Southern cooking has been served up cafeteria-style at this Nashville institution since 1954. ☎ 615-329-4418; www.swettsrestaurant.com; 2725 Clifton Ave, Nashville, TN; mains $9; ☽ 11am-8pm; ☝

SLEEP

French Camp B&B
Stay the night in a log cabin built on a former French pioneer site that was further developed by a Revolutionary War hero. ☎ 662-547-6835; www.frenchcamp.org; mile-marker 180.7 Natchez Trace Parkway, MS; cabins $75-150; ☝

Mark Twain Guesthouse
Riverboat captain Samuel Clemens used to drink till late at the saloon and pass out in one of three upstairs bedrooms (room 1 has the best view). Can be noisy until after 2am. ☎ 601-446-8023; www.underthehillsaloon.com; 25 Silver St, Natchez, MS; r $65-85

Monmouth Plantation
If you've ever wanted to make like Scarlett O'Hara and collapse into the luxurious shade of your veranda, you can do so at this historic plantation turned boutique hotel and divine restaurant. ☎ 800-828-4531; www.monmouthplantation.com; 36 Melrose Ave, Natchez, MS; r from $199

Tishomingo State Park
Campers can rent canoes and paddle Bear Creek. ☎ 662-438-6914; www.mississippistateparks.reserveamerica.com; mile-marker 304.5 Natchez Trace Parkway, Tishomingo, MS; campsite $16; ☝ ☺

Union Station Hotel
Once the Nashville train station and now a grand and elegant modern hotel. ☎ 615-726-1001; www.unionstationhotelnashville.com; 1001 Broadway, Nashville, TN; r from $149; ☝

USEFUL WEBSITES
www.scenictrace.com

LINK YOUR TRIP

www.lonelyplanet.com/trip-planner

Historic Battles of the Civil War

WHY GO The Civil War shaped the South and the rest of the United States in ways unmatched by any other period in American history. Civil War expert and Zen-minded self-proclaimed "hard core" reenactor Robert Lee Hodge leads us on a visit through some of the most influential Civil War sites in the South.

TIME
5 – 7 days

DISTANCE
741 miles

BEST TIME TO GO
Apr – Jun

START
Vicksburg, MS

END
Atlanta, GA

"I've been wearing the funny clothes and shooting guns for 27 years," says Robert Lee Hodge, about his lifelong fascination with the Civil War. "My brother named me after Robert E Lee. My favorite book growing up was *The Golden Book of the Civil War*. I'd say my prayers with my mom and she'd ask, 'What battle do you want me to read from tonight?'"

For Hodge, visiting battlefields and Civil War sites is not about celebrating war but about creating a connection with the land and with the past. "For me," says Hodge, "it's kind of a low-key spiritual thing. It's respectful and almost Zen-like. I go to these places now and they're places of peace. There's this weird juxtaposition between war and death and the brutality that people can do to each other and the land, and then you have birds chirping and quiet fields and the sun shining. People who go to battlefields can relate to this."

Although it's not one of Hodge's favorite battlefields, ❶ **Vicksburg National Military Park** is first on the list of anyone who studied the Civil War in eighth-grade history class. The Vicksburg campaign came in the middle of the war, and was a turning point of sorts, especially for the beleaguered Union troops. For over six months, starting in December of 1862, Grant and his army staged 11 battles with the Confederate army, many of them naval battles along the Mississippi River. After Grant's final decisive victory on July 4, 1863, the Mississippi

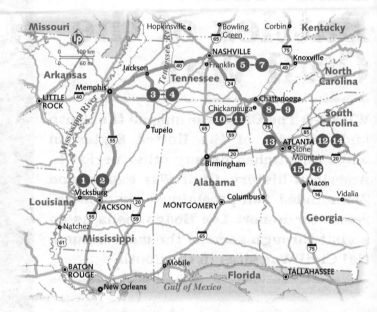

River was once again controlled by the Union forces, beginning a sea change in the direction of the war. Once you enter the battlefield grounds, you can drive along a 16-mile road that takes you past marked sites including trenches, a restored Union gunboat and a cemetery.

"'The battlegrounds are some of the best preserved in the United States."

Stay the night at the historic ❷ **Cedar Grove Mansion Inn & Restaurant**. Feel like a Southern belle when you sip wine and nibble cheese in the parlor's afternoon reception or as you tuck yourself in under a romantic canopied bed. (Hint: history fans will want to stay in Rhett's Penthouse Suite, where you can still see a patched-up hole from where a Union cannonball crashed through the wall during the Civil War.) The restaurant serves dinner only, but what a dinner it is. Taste 200 years of Southern culinary history with updated dishes like crab martini, pan-seared catfish on a bed of okra, and peppered risotto or quail with crawfish corn-bread dressing.

One of Hodge's favorite spots is ❸ **Shiloh National Military Park** in Hardin County, Tennessee. In one of the first of the ensuing mega-battles of the Civil War, over 109,000 Union and Confederate troops met near the Pittsburg Landing on the Tennessee River on April 6, 1862, resulting in a casualty rate of about 25%. The battlegrounds are some of the best preserved in the United States, partly because the area was designated a national landmark back in 1894. "Shiloh was one of the first preserved national military parks," says Hodge. "It's probably about 85% pristine. All these people of pedigree – senators, politicians – felt a strong desire to memorialize and interpret these places." After picking up a map at the visitors center, take a tour of the cemetery (eternal home to 4000 soldiers who died at the battle), Indian Mound and the site of the Methodist church that gave the battle its name.

"If you go to Shiloh," Hodge says, "you've got to go to Hagy's. They serve old-school Dr Pepper in bottles and have these pictures on the wall of old-time farmers plowing with mules, plus they serve all-you-can-eat catfish." Officially known as the ❹ Catfish Hotel, the original 1825 shack on the park grounds burned down in 1975, but the third generation of the Hagy family rebuilt the institution. It is one of the oldest continually operating restaurants in the country. After eating a plate full of breaded frogs legs, fried oysters and hush puppies, or smoked baby back ribs, relax in a catfish-shaped Adirondack chair overlooking the Tennessee River.

ASK A LOCAL

"We can't change history, nor should we be ashamed of it, but we should learn from it and not repeat its errors. My reenactor friends yearn to know American history as told by all of its participants. The African American perspective is still unique, but there are some of us in 'the hobby,' as reenactors call it. It's a joy to be with like-minded people who are just as passionate about history as I am."

Daniel J Johnson, aka Thomas Morris Chester, the only African American war correspondent hired by a major daily newspaper during the war

Take Hwy 22 north for about 40 miles until you hit I-40, which will take you toward Nashville. Detour south to ❺ Franklin, where the Battle of Franklin was fought and where, these days, a new battle for preservation is being waged. The historic downtown has many preserved buildings, but suburban sprawl has put the site of the Battle of Franklin on the Civil War Preservation Trust's most-endangered-sites list for several years in a row. First, head to the ❻ Carter House, which holds the dubious record of sustaining more bullets (over 1000) than just about any other building during the Civil War. The Carter family went to sleep on November 29, 1864, only to be woken in the middle of the night by a brigadier army general, who turned the house into a Union command center for the battle that was about to occur. What was to become known as the "five bloodiest hours in the Civil War" killed or wounded over 8500 mostly Confederate soldiers on and around the Carter farm. While 23 Carter family members and neighbors hid in the basement, Union and Confederate troops clashed, sometimes hand to hand, on their front porch. One of the arriving Confederate soldiers was Tod Carter, who was thrilled to see his home for the first time in three years. However, he later died inside after being mortally wounded (some say he never left and his ghost, along with dozens of others, still lingers).

The next stop in Franklin is ❼ Carnton Plantation. On the New York *Times* best-seller list for months, *The Widow of the South* was based on the life of Carrie McGavock, the mistress of the plantation during the Civil War. After the Battle of Franklin, the plantation – like many other large houses near battlefields – became an impromptu army hospital. McGavock cared for hundreds of wounded and dying men from both sides of the war, and in 1866, enlarged her own family's cemetery to bury 1500 troops. Tours now showcase the family's portraits and furnishings, much unchanged since the war.

BATTLEFIELD VISTAS

According to Robert Lee Hodge, "You've got to hit a battlefield early in the morning. Sunrise to 8am is best. It's beautiful with the fog in the morning, or at twilight with the fading light. I'm a filmmaker, so I'll take my tripod and camera out and I'll film the historic vistas I'm enamored with. That's when the spiritual vibe gets me more."

"On the floor, you can see imprints of bloody shoes from the Civil War," says Hodge. "They had tests done to make sure it wasn't oil from the 1950s, but no, it was blood."

On the anniversary of the battle, Franklin hosts thousands of die-hard Civil War reenactors, who spend days dressed in woolen shell jackets, camping out in A-frame canvas tents and eating Civil War rations from tin mess plates. Hodge had never much thought about the environment before he began spending time in historic locations that were being swallowed up by suburban sprawl, or ignored out of budget constraints or apathy. But then he found reenacting and, "the Confederate flag made me an environmentalist," he says. "It's about being at Franklin, Tennessee, on November 30, and preferably on a Wednesday, because the battle was on a Wednesday. It's about knowing that you're stepping on the same ground at the same time where people you've read about stepped." Years ago, a Pizza Hut was built over soldiers' graves, but preservation groups have raised $2.5 million and reclaimed the area as a public green space, open to visitors.

If you'd like to bed down for the night somewhere a tad more comfortable, head into **8** Chattanooga and the **9** The Inn at Hunt Phelan, a stately 1889 home with as many modern comforts as antique touches. Set your alarm to rise before dawn to head down Hwy 1/US-27 to the expansive **10** Chickamauga and Chattanooga National Military Park. Chattanooga was a major railroad thoroughfare at the start of the Civil War, so whichever side claimed it would be able to boast a clear transportation advantage. The park was the first battlefield made into a national military park, back in 1890. From September 18 to 20, 1863, over 60,000 Union troops and 43,000 Confederate troops fought at Chickamauga. At the end of the battle, there were 34,000 soldiers wounded, killed or taken prisoner. The Union troops had retired to Chattanooga, where they gathered supplies. One month later, under the direction of General Ulysses S Grant, Union and Confederate forces once again fought, this time resulting in a clear Union victory, paving the way for

Union General William Tecumseh Sherman to start his eastward march to the sea from Chattanooga the following spring. Be sure to stop in at ⑪ **Lookout Mountain**, the site of much fighting. "I haven't been able to find it yet," says Hodge, "but there's an interpretive marker [somewhere on the mountain] where my ancestors fought with the Fourth Alabama Calvary."

Head toward ⑫ **Atlanta**, to the ⑬ **Kennesaw Mountain National Battlefield Park**, located just before the city beltline. It's surrounded by suburbs, but is easily accessible. Considered one of the events with the most needless waste of troops, the series of battles led by General Sherman saw 3000 Union and 1000 Confederate soldiers die without any ground gained. In the city, Hodge recommends the ⑭ **Atlanta History Center**. For him, museums are about the "stuff" that make the history books and battlefields real, and the history center is filled with enough "stuff" to bring a tangible connection to the history of the war. "There are all sorts of relics from the army – guns, uniforms, IDs from everyone who did heroic deeds to unknown soldiers. It gives you an idea of: what did the guns look like? What were the blankets like? What were their letters like?"

A WAR BY ANY OTHER NAME

In the South, one conflict comes by many names.

- The Civil War: what the federals called it, simply a term for fighting within a country.

- War Between the States: used primarily by those in Confederate states, as states broke away and began fighting for independence.

- War of Northern Aggression: the South had the right to secede and the North attacked.

- War for Southern Independence: ditto.

- The Recent Unpleasantness: first used by Charlie Weaver on Jack Paar's *Tonight Show* in the 1960s, when the events of the 1800s weren't a too distant memory.

- The War: across the South and in Charleston, everyone will know what you mean.

Jack Thomson, Civil War historian

Don't miss sleeping in the ⑮ **Village Inn B&B**, one of only a handful of inns in the Southeast with a direct connection to the Civil War. It's 15 minutes east of downtown Atlanta. The only reason it wasn't burned down during Sherman's march was because it served as a Confederate hospital (there are a few reputed ghosts left over from days past). The inn was built in the 1840s and is as romantic as it gets – in-room spa tubs and fireplaces, homemade cookies waiting for you each afternoon and a veranda overlooking nearby ⑯ **Stone Mountain**. If you enjoy the breakfast so much you want to be able to make the raspberry-stuffed French toast or flaky biscuits at home, you're in luck; the B&B publishes its own recipe book so you can take some of the South home with you.

Alex Leviton

TRIP INFORMATION

DO

Atlanta History Center
See hundreds of artifacts from the Civil War, including uniforms, ID tags and letters home. ☎ 404-814-4000; www.atlantahistorycenter .com; 130 West Paces Ferry Rd, Atlanta, GA; adult/child$15/10; 🕑 10am-5:30pm Mon-Sat, noon-5:30pm Sun

Carnton Plantation
A mansion that became a makeshift Confederate hospital during the Battle of Franklin. ☎ 615-794-0903; www.carnton.org; 1345 Carnton Ln, Franklin, TN; adult/child $12/5; 🕑 9am-5pm Mon-Sat, 1-5pm Sun

Carter House
Over 1000 bullet holes riddled this mansion, next to where the Battle of Franklin raged. ☎ 615-791-1861; www.carterhouse1864. com; 1140 Columbia Ave, Franklin, TN; adult/child $12/6; 🕑 9am-5pm Mon-Sat, 1-5pm Sun

Chickamauga & Chattanooga National Military Park
Site of the second deadliest battle in Civil War history. ☎ 423-752-5213; www.nps .gov/chch; 3370 S. Lafayette Rd, Fort Oglethorpe, GA; admission free; 🕑 8:30am-6pm Apr-Sep, 8:30am-5pm Oct-Mar

Kennesaw Mountain National Battlefield Park
A full-scale battlefield with a scenic mountain and hiking trails. ☎ 770-427-4686; www .nps.gov/kemo; 905 Kennesaw Mountain Dr, Kennesaw, GA; admission free; 🕑 8:30am-6pm Apr-Oct, 8:30am-5pm Nov-Mar

Shiloh National Military Park
Near the Corinth Civil War Interpretive Center, with a driving tour of a historic battlefield. ☎ 703-689-5696; www.nps.gov/shil; 1055 Pittsburg Landing Rd, Shiloh, TN; admission free; 🕑 8am-5pm Apr-Sep, 8am-6pm Oct-Mar

Vicksburg National Military Park
A 16-mile driving tour of the USS *Cairo* museum, Civil War ironclad gunboat display and national cemetery. ☎ 601-636-0583; www.nps.gov/vick; 3201 Clay St, Vicksburg, MS; vehicle $8; 🕑 8am-5pm

EAT

Catfish Hotel
A catfish "palace" right on the Tennessee River, serving dishes and tradition for almost 200 years. ☎ 731-689-3327; www.catfish hotel.com; 1005 Pittsburg Landing, Shiloh National Military Park, TN; mains $9-12; 🕑 11am-9pm Tue-Thu & Sun, 11am-10pm Fri & Sat

Cedar Grove Mansion Inn & Restaurant
Decorated with furnishings brought back from an 1842 European honeymoon. The elegant mansion was once used as a Union hospital. ☎ 601-636-1000; www.cedar groveinn.com; 2200 Oak St, Vicksburg, MS; mains $18-32, r $100-215; 🕑 5-10pm dinner

SLEEP

The Inn at Hunt Phelan
The antebellum mansion is a registered historic landmark, as well as a gracious inn and four-star restaurant. ☎ 901-525-8225; www.huntphelan.com; 533 Beale St, Memphis, TN; r $165-295

Village Inn B&B
It doesn't get any more authentic than having a patched hole in your room from a Civil War cannon blast. ☎ 770-469-3459; www .villageinnbb.com; 992 Ridge Ave, Stone Mountain, GA; r from $145

USEFUL WEBSITES
www.civilwar.org
www.civilwartraveler.com

LINK YOUR TRIP

www.lonelyplanet.com/trip-planner

Eclectic Americana in the Triangle

WHY GO The Triangle – Raleigh, Durham and Chapel Hill – may be one of the most livable places in the country. The rare blend of Southern hospitality, university culture, rural charm and big-city life, however, also makes it a spectacular place to visit…if you know where to look.

Downtown ❶ **Raleigh** is filled with all the usual capital city offerings – excellent museums, professional sports venues, historic homes, impressive governmental buildings and so on – but we trust our readers can find these on their own. Instead, we start our tour with a good, swift kick in the pants.

But first, spend a day absorbing culture at the ❷ **North Carolina Museum of Art**. Bring your picnic blanket on summer evenings, as outdoor concerts (from jazz to world music), films and events grace every weekend from May to September. Next head west on Hwy 70 to ❸ **Angus Barn**, a storied local steakhouse with several agents of death beckoning. Guns and taxidermied heads line the wall heading up to the Wild Turkey cigar lounge (cigars are for sale in the gift shop's walk-in humidor), while butter-smooth marbled steaks adorn most diners' plates. The legendary wine list is thicker than the Oxford American dictionary (unabridged). If you've ever uttered "I could just kick myself" drop by the parking lot's 1937 kicking machine for a self-booting.

The liveliest area at night in Raleigh is ❹ **Glenwood South**, a formerly gritty warehouse district turned bustling cultural mecca of restaurants, pubs, clubs, art galleries, shops, wine bars and coffeehouses where you're encouraged to stay out past your bedtime. The neighborhood is bordered by Peace St to the north and Hillsborough St to the south, running along Glenwood Ave for half a mile of more than 100 businesses. Pull into ❺ **518 West**, an Italian restaurant housed in a former train depot, now in

TIME
5 days

DISTANCE
128 miles

BEST TIME TO GO
Year-round

START
Raleigh, NC

END
Siler City, NC

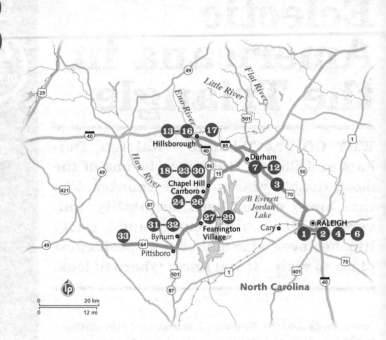

the heart of the fine dining scene. Venetian plaster walls and a boldly offbeat wine list bring a taste of the good life to the gentrified neighborhood. Cap off your late-night adventure with the most local of treats, the North Carolina–born and bred hot glazed doughnut from **6 Krispy Kreme**, whose 1950s sign glows on the edge of the historic Oakwood district of jaw-dropping Victorian beauties.

Start your second day in **7 Durham**, whose past is inextricably tied to the tobacco that made the Duke family one of the wealthiest in North Carolina history. Up until the 1990s, town residents say the smell of the sweet tobacco curing in downtown's brick warehouses would fill the streets. Just after the Civil War, Washington Duke planted several acres of the local Bright Leaf tobacco on his farm north of town. Millions of lung cancer diagnoses later, the **8 American Tobacco Historic District** is now an entertainment complex, exhibition space and outdoor concert venue with five restaurants (all, ironically, smoke-free). Next door is the most famous minor league ballpark in the country, the **9 Durham Bulls Athletic Park**, where, in between innings, mascot Wool E Bull shoots T-shirts from his miniature race car or referees wrestling matches between fans in inflatable sumo costumes.

Today science, medicine and art have replaced tobacco and farming as Durham's most prolific exports, and the Triangle has one of the most educated populations in the US, nowhere more apparent than in downtown Durham.

The city went through an ill-found "urban renewal" effort in the 1960s and '70s, but preservationists (including one woman who chained herself to the about-to-be-destroyed downtown theater, ensuring its survival to this day) eventually won out. These days, the "Durham Love Yourself" movement devotees (look for the T-shirts and bumper stickers everywhere) have an almost militant love for the city's revitalization of art galleries and restaurants. Join grad students, filmmakers and yoga teachers at the morning epicenter of the good fight, the ⑩ **Guglhupf Bakery and Patisserie**, a favorite for its European pastries and bread, outdoor patio, free wi-fi and inexpensive meals. If you want to go more upscale in the evening, the internationally recognized ⑪ **Magnolia Grill**, just north of Duke University's student hangout zone, ⑫ **Ninth Street**, has been wowing critics for the past decade with its Southern take on California-style cuisine.

FARMERS MARKETS

The Triangle's weather and agricultural roots make for spectacular farmers markets, some with traditional bluegrass or old-time entertainment, including:

- Durham: Saturday 8am to noon and Wednesday 3:30pm to 6:30pm in Central Park at 501 Foster St.

- Carrboro: Saturday 7am to noon and Wednesday 3:30pm to 6:30pm at 301 W Main St.

- Raleigh: Monday to Saturday 6am to 5pm and Sunday 8am to 6pm at 1201 Agriculture St.

From Durham, take Hwy 85 northwest to the historic town of ⑬ **Hillsborough**, whose heyday was around the Revolutionary War. The entire downtown is on the National Registry for Historic Places with more than 100 buildings from the 18th and 19th centuries. It's no wonder that dozens of writers have made it their home, including novelist Lee Smith and the late Doug Marlette, creator of the "Kudzu" comic strip. If you're here on the last Friday of the month from April to September, downtown turns into an art walk, with open studios, wine and cheese receptions and live music. If you're looking for lodging that's historical and charming, Hillsborough has several, including the ⑭ **Webb House B&B**, a 200-year-old Colonial home in downtown with claw-foot tubs, four-post beds and filling breakfasts. Start the next day at ⑮ **Ayr Mount**. The stately brick Federal-style home still has some of the original family furnishings from almost 200 years ago. The serene ⑯ **Poet's Walk** past the woodsy Eno River really shows off the beauty of the area. The ⑰ **Historic Occoneechee Speedway Trail**, off exit 165 from I-85, is, surprisingly, exactly as it sounds. It's not often you get to call a hiking trail "eclectic," but this one leads to the Occoneechee Speedway, used in Nascar's inaugural 1949 season. The overgrown track and surrounding area, blanketed with pines and weepy thickets, has been turned into a 44-acre nature preserve, accessible to day hikers. The original oval track dates back to the early 1900s, when it was used to train horses, and backs up against the Eno River, the unexpected final resting place of many an out-of-control stock car.

From Hillsborough, head back to the I-40 and take exit 265 for Hwy 86 to dine and drink in collegiate ⑱ **Chapel Hill**. The University Tour of the Triangle trip will introduce you to university life, but the noncollege crowd will appreciate one of *Gourmet* magazine's top 50 restaurants in the country, ⑲ **Lantern**. The chef and owner heads up a local Slow Food convivium and many of her ingredients are grown within a 50-mile radius. The sake- and tea-cured salmon bento box appetizer is like an edible toy set where adults are encouraged to play with their food. Stick with child-friendly food with dessert at ⑳ **Locopops**, a few doors down historic Franklin St. With flavors like Nilla wafer, mojito, plum black pepper and cherry hibiscus, you'll understand why obsessed locals are fiercely loyal to their gourmet Mexican popsicle parlor.

LIVING IN A TOBACCO WAREHOUSE

"In 2003, I bought a loft condo in the first tobacco warehouse converted after Durham's cigarette industry died out in the 1980s. Next to the elevators, signs read: "Ironically, the hallways and common areas in this former tobacco warehouse are smoke-free." My neighbors and I still hear stories from teary-eyed visitors about how they loved the smell of cured Bright Leaf tobacco when visiting their dads or granddads at work here in the 1940s."

Alex Leviton, guidebook author, San Francisco, CA & Durham, NC

Sleep off dessert at ㉑ **Siena Hotel**, an upscale Tuscan-inspired hotel where the restaurant, ㉒ **Il Palio**, marries all that is holy about Italian cuisine with a few Southern touches – fried green tomatoes on *mozzarella di bufala* or fennel-crusted tuna with watermelon. Start the next morning fresh at ㉓ **A Southern Season**, a football field–sized gourmet food store that sells everything, and we mean everything, from Le Creuset cookware and imported prosciutto to artisanal North Carolina organic cheeses and 500 different types of candy bars on its "Wall of Chocolate." Book the restaurant or legendary cooking classes in advance, and bring your credit card; the wine department is easily the top in the state.

"Open Barn weekends, a feast of goat cheese, farm lessons and baby goat cuddles."

Bordering Chapel Hill is the quirky town of ㉔ **Carrboro**, whose most famous resident dances to his own beat...literally. The center of town is the Triangle's version of the village green, the lawn at ㉕ **Weaver Street Market**, which now has an "Open Space Policy" to make sure dancing alone (and, um, shirtless, with no music) isn't a crime. During the day, wi-fi users and fans of the organic salad bar and hot bar congregate at picnic tables to nosh, read Umberto Eco novels or discuss the nearby biodiesel fuel pumping station. Events run throughout the week, including Sunday morning jazz concerts, Thursday evening After Hours concerts, and Friday night wine tastings. Hula-hoop clinics pick up during the summer.

For a more rocking evening at one of the South's most venerable venues for eclectic music, check out **26** **Cat's Cradle**. The Cradle exemplifies the Triangle's split personality (North Cackalacky's coolest club is currently housed in a strip mall), but indie legends Sonic Youth sang about it and bands like Superchunk and Ben Folds Five rose to fame in it. Fans are indoctrinated early; many shows are all ages.

Head west on Hwy 15/501 toward Pittsboro until a grain silo and colorful whirligigs welcome you to **27** **Fearrington Village**, home to the famed belted cows (the bovine version of the Oreo cookie). These black and white three-stripe cows, and goats, have been at this farm's location for generations. The tiny village deserves an afternoon wander through shops that sell books, garden supplies and gifts, but the night belongs to the famed **28** **Fearrington House Restaurant** – there's not an award it hasn't won. With dishes like duck breast and foie gras in a cherry cinnamon sauce or pork belly and lobster with shellfish cappuccino, it's no wonder. Get in touch with your inner Southern belle next door at **29** **Fearrington Inn**, where the exercise in sumptuous hospitality includes canopied beds, English high-tea finger sandwiches each afternoon and in-room massages. For lunch in the village, dine at the Old Granary Restaurant, where lighter fare like salad with cornmeal-fried oysters or sea scallops on cauliflower risotto have an equally gourmet feel. If you feel a sudden urge to retire here, you're not alone; Fearrington caters to well-heeled and active older folks (the housing wing of the village advertises in the back of *New Yorker* magazine).

ASK A LOCAL

"I like to go where the wild things are: like **Bynum**, a Chatham County mill village, home of stilt-walking puppeteers (www.paperhand.org) and famous artist, Clyde Jones. Among a frenzy of new construction in the Triangle, this oasis protrudes like an extra 5lb on a supermodel. Get to the Bynum General Store music series by 6:30pm to grab a seat, and you'll get to see the fireflies spring to life. Plus, it offers jam sessions and art shows on Saturdays."

Molly Matlock, director, Chatham County Arts Council, Bynum, NC

If Fearrington is exquisite sophistication overlaid on farm fields, **30** **Allen & Son Barbecue** is as plain and genuine as North Carolina red clay. Here, before sunrise, owner Keith Allen loads hand-chopped hickory logs into a barbecue pit, lays out a pig and cooks his homemade sauce from scratch to maintain one of the last bastions of genuine pit cooking. Believe your waitress – who might or might not have a beehive hairdo and call you "Hon" – when she tells you to order the peanut butter pie.

Keep going down the road towards **31** **Bynum**, a tiny former mill village where intellectuals and artsy types dwell alongside longtime residents all in humble front-porch cottages. Lazed up against the Haw River, Bynum is perhaps best known for artist Clyde Jones and his colorful, chain saw–cut wooden critters. There's no museum or store, as Jones refuses to sell his creations for money (though he's given one away to Mikhail Baryshnikov), but it just takes a quick stroll through town to see dozens gracing front yards.

SUNDAY SUPPER

On the third Sunday of each month, the **Sunday Dinner at the Celebrity Dairy** kicks off at 1:30pm with an all-afternoon Slow Food feast. Local farms contribute sustainably raised meats and fresh produce to create four mouthwatering courses, shared with 35 new friends over BYO wine in between tours of the dairy facilities, lazing on the tire swing and, in February's kidding season, cuddling baby goats in the barn.

On Friday nights in summer, mosey on down to the ❸❷ **Bynum General Store** whose "Front Porch Music Series" draws an astoundingly wide variety of artists, including folk/country goddess Tift Merritt, who got her start hereabouts. The store provides the plastic chairs and hot-dog vendor, you provide the toe tappin'.

The tour ends at the ❸❸ **Inn at Celebrity Dairy**, the culmination of all that is good and right about the Triangle's eclectic side. If you liked the goat cheese at Lantern, Weaver Street Market, Fearrington House Restaurant, the Carrboro farmers market or Magnolia Grill, you can thank Celebrity Dairy, a working organic goat dairy farm. Each spring and fall, the dairy welcomes all to its Open Barn weekends, a feast of goat cheese, farm lessons and baby goat cuddles. The inn's seven rooms are antiqued but comfortable – there's a bay window seat in the 3rd-floor attic room (shared bath), and an 1887 log cabin cottage with a private front porch. In the winter, curl up with Wordsworth in front of the fireplace; in summer, take Kerouac out to the front porch, shared with the farm kittens and chickens.

Alex Leviton

TRIP INFORMATION

DO

American Tobacco Historic District
Five restaurants, including sushi, pub food and pizza; Friday evening summer concerts; temporary art exhibits and history, next door to the Athletic Park. ☎ 919-433-1566; www .americantobaccohistoricdistrict.com; 318 Blackwell St, Durham, NC; ♿

Ayr Mount and Poet's Walk
A homage to Revolutionary era homes and gardens. ☎ 919-732-6886; www.classical american.org; 376 St Mary's Rd, Hillsborough, NC; admission $10; ☉ tours 11am Wed-Sat & 2pm Thu-Sun, closed Jan & Feb

Bynum General Store
Old-time summer front porch music series with events throughout the year. www .bynumfrontporch.org; 950 Bynum Rd, Bynum, NC; suggested donation $3-7; ☉ 7pm Fri; ♿

Durham Bulls Athletic Park
In 2008, Kevin Costner returned to this iconic stadium to jam with his band. ☎ 919-956-2855; www.durhambulls.com; 409 Blackwell St, Durham, NC; baseball tickets $6-16; ♿

Historic Occoneechee Speedway Trail
A historic Nascar speedway that's now a 3-mile walking trail reclaimed by nature (and Preservation North Carolina). www .presnc.org; 320 Elizabeth Brady Rd, Hillsborough, NC; admission free; ☉ 7am-8pm Jun & Jul, 7am-7pm Apr, May, Aug & Sep, 8am-6pm Mar & Oct, 8am-5pm Nov-Feb; ♿

North Carolina Museum of Art
An international art collection inside, a deluge of films, concerts and events outside. ☎ 919-839-6262; www.ncartmuseum.org; 2110 Blue Ridge Rd, Raleigh, NC; museum free, events $3-40; ☉ 10am-5pm Tue-Thu & Sat, 10am-9pm Fri; ♿

A Southern Season
Sixty thousand square feet of the world's best culinary finds, with a popular cooking school and restaurant. ☎ 800-253-3663; www. southernseason.com; 201 S Estes Dr, Chapel Hill, NC; ☉ 9am-9pm Mon-Sat, 11am-6pm Sun; ♿

Weaver Street Market
Weaver Street is not only an expansive coop, but the "town square" of Carrboro with weekly entertainment. ☎ 919-929-0010; www.weaverstreetmarket.com; 101 E Weaver St, Carrboro, NC; ☉ 7:30am-9pm Mon-Fri, 8am-9pm Sat & Sun; ♿

EAT

518 West
Trendy Italian in the heart of Raleigh's nightlife district. ☎ 919-829-2518; www.518west.com; 518 W Jones St, Raleigh, NC; mains $7-18; ☉ 11:30am-9:30pm Mon, 11:30am-10pm Tue-Thu, 11:30am-10:30pm Fri & Sat, 10:30am-2pm & 5-9pm Sun

Allen & Son Barbecue
Slow-cooked BBQ and ribs over real hickory wood with all the fixin's. ☎ 919-942-7576; 6203 Millhouse Rd, Chapel Hill, NC; mains $4-9; ☉ 10am-5pm Tue & Wed, 10am-8pm Thu-Sat; ♿

Angus Barn
Special occasion steakhouse with a gift and cigar shop and a "Wild Turkey" lounge. ☎ 919-781-2444; www.angusbarn.com; 9401 Glenwood Ave, Raleigh, NC; mains $19-57; ☉ 5:30-10:30pm Mon-Fri, 5-10:30pm Sat, 5-10pm Sun; ♿

Fearrington House Restaurant
A reclaimed village with a romantic inn and surrounding shops and farmlands. ☎ 919-542-2121; www.fearrington.com; 2000 Fearrington Village Rd, Pittsboro, NC; mains $18-42; ☉ 6pm-9pm Tue-Sat, 6-8pm Sun

Guglhupf Bakery and Patisserie
A full selection of omelettes, small plates and pastries, but the bread basket is everyone's favorite. ☎ 919-401-2600; www.guglhupf .com; 2706 Durham-Chapel Hill Blvd, Durham, NC; mains $4-20; ☉ 8am-9:30pm Tue-Thu, 8am-10pm Fri & Sat, 9am-5pm Sun; ♿

Il Palio
Upscale Italian delicacies paired with top-notch wine in an elegant setting. ☎ 919-929-4000; www.sienahotel.com/ilpalio; 1505 E Franklin St, Chapel Hill, NC; mains $12-32; ☉ 5:30-9pm Sun-Thu, 5:30-10pm Fri & Sat

Krispy Kreme
Have a late-night doughnut in the state that brought the world the treat. ☎ 919-833-3682; www.krispykreme.com; 549 N Person St, Raleigh, NC; doughnut $1; ☾ 24hr; ⚐

Lantern
Asian-Southern fusion known for its cocktails, Slow Food–inspired menus and sophistication. ☎ 919-969-8846; www.lanternrestaurant.com; 423 W Franklin St, Chapel Hill, NC; mains $14-26; ☾ from 5:30pm

Locopops
Beloved gourmet Mexican popsicles; also in Raleigh, Durham and Hillsborough. ☎ 919-286-3500; www.ilovelocopops.com; 128 E Franklin, Chapel Hill, NC; popsicle $2-3; ☾ noon-9pm; ⚐

Magnolia Grill
An internationally award-winning neighborhood restaurant with desserts to die for. ☎ 919-286-3609; www.magnoliagrill.net; 1002 Ninth St, Durham, NC; mains $22-31; ☾ from 6pm Tue-Thu, 5:30pm Fri & Sat, closing around 9:30pm or 10pm

DRINK

Cat's Cradle
Headquarters for the indie rock and live-music scene in the Triangle, and beyond. ☎ 919-967-5053; www.catscradle.com; 300 E Main St, Carrboro, NC; shows $10-20; ☾ around 8pm on show nights

SLEEP

Fearrington Inn
A reclaimed village with an inn, restaurant and surrounding shops and farmlands. ☎ 919-542-2121; www.fearrington.com; 2000 Fearrington Village Rd, Pittsboro, NC; r $275-575

Inn at Celebrity Dairy
The most peaceful spot in the Triangle, with roaming farm animals, an inviting B&B and a third Sunday of the month supper. ☎ 919-742-5176; www.celebritydairy.com; 144 Celebrity Dairy Way, Siler City, NC; r $90-150; ⚐

Siena Hotel
Just outside the main Franklin St strip, the Tuscan-inspired hotel has professional rooms and a *bellissimo* restaurant. ☎ 919-929-4000; www.sienahotel.com; 1505 E Franklin St, Chapel Hill, NC; r $125-259; ⚐

Webb House B&B
The centrally located bed and breakfast offers early-19th-century panache with decidedly modern amenities. ☎ 919-732-8466; www.webbhousebb.com; 117 Queen St, Hillsborough, NC; r $95-195; ⚐

USEFUL WEBSITES
www.durham-nc.com
www.visitchapelhill.org

LINK YOUR TRIP   www.lonelyplanet.com/trip-planner

TRIP
25 Music City to Dixieland: A Musical Roots Run p223

The Great Smokies

WHY GO The Cherokee Indians fell in love with these ancient, mist-shrouded mountains, which they named Shaconage (Place of the Blue Smoke). Lose yourself in their lush valleys and mossy, shaded trails. But lest you overdose on trees, there's plenty of man-made fun (hello, Dollywood!) on either side of the park.

The Great Smoky Mountains, a subrange of the Appalachians, straddle the North Carolina–Tennessee border. On a map, the southwestern corner of North Carolina looks like a lump of taffy being flattened by the rollers of Tennessee and Georgia. This "tail" – geographically part of the Tennessee Valley – is crisscrossed with thundering mountain rivers, and dotted with lakes and hidden waterfalls.

The terrain, unsurprisingly, is fantastic for whitewater rafting, kayaking and tubing. The ❶ **Nantahala Outdoor Center** (NOC) launches trips on the class II and III rapids of the Nantahala River from their main outpost west of Bryson City. Ride a group raft or a two-person ducky through the wide, brown river gorge, spinning through a dizzying whirlpool and splish-splashing over the Nantahala Falls. The NOC also offers whitewater trips for all ages and skill levels on a half-dozen other rivers in the Appalachians. Experienced paddlers can brave the 9-mile trip down the roiling class IV–V Cheoah, launching from nearby Robbinsville. After a long day on the river, put your sore muscles to bed at the NOC's ❷ **Nantahala Inn**, a rustic, pine-paneled motor lodge tucked into the trees.

Trips on the historic ❸ **Great Smoky Mountains Railroad** depart from Bryson City and plow through the dramatic Nantahala Gorge and across the Fontana Trestle. The former Murphy Branch Line, built in the late 1800s, brought unheard of luxuries like books, factory-spun cloth and oil lamps to these mountains, making rural Appalachian life a little

TIME
5 days

DISTANCE
180 miles

BEST TIME TO GO
Apr – Jun, Sep & Oct

START
near Bryson City, NC

END
Knoxville, TN

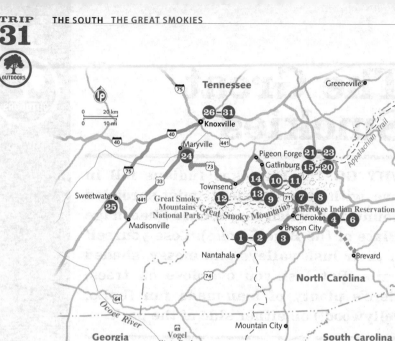

less tough. Themed trips on the red-and-yellow trains include a beer tasting, a Thomas the Tank Engine–themed ride for kids, and a mystery dinner theater.

Half an hour to the northeast is the town of ❹ **Cherokee**, the major North Carolina gateway to the Great Smoky Mountains National Park. The Cherokee people have lived in this area since the last ice age, though many of them died on the Trail of Tears. The descendents of the people who escaped or returned are known as the Eastern Band of the Cherokee, about 12,000 of whom live on the Qualla Boundary reservation near town. Seeing contemporary Cherokee can feel a bit sad, with "chiefs" hawking plastic headdresses on Tsali Blvd and elderly locals playing the one-armed bandits in the dim, smoky depths of Harrah's Cherokee Casino.

But several sights transcend the kitsch and stereotypes, and actually teach a thing or two about Cherokee culture and history. The cool, earth-colored halls of the ❺ **Museum of the Cherokee Indian** have displays filled with artifacts such as pots, deerskins, woven skirts, eerie life-sized dioramas and a new animated exhibit on Cherokee myths.

In the summer, catch ❻ **Unto These Hills**, an outdoor play dramatizing the Trail of Tears. Performed at the Mountainside Theater since 1950, it's the second longest–running outdoor drama in America (the oldest is *The Lost Colony*, in the North Carolina coastal town of Manteo).

Pick up any last minute supplies at the mini-mart and head into the vast, cool wilderness of Great Smoky Mountains National Park. Established in 1934, the park attracts as many as 10 million travelers a year, making it the most-visited national park in America. To beat high-season crowds, merely wander off the main trails to find yourself deep in the damp, earth-scented wilderness.

Newfoundland Gap Rd/Hwy 441 is the only thoroughfare crossing the entire 521,000-acre park. And what a drive it is, traversing 33 miles of deep oak and pine forest, and wildflower meadows. Stop first at the **7 Oconaluftee Visitor Center**, with interactive exhibits on the park's history and ecosystems. Pick up a map and stroll the Oconaluftee River Trail, which leaves from the center and follows the river for 1.5 miles to the boundary of the Cherokee reservation. Don't forget to pick up a free backcountry camping permit if you plan to go off-trail.

Also near the park entrance is the **8 Mountain Farm Museum** and **Mingus Mill**. The museum, located next to the visitor center, is a 19th-century farmstead assembled from buildings from various locations around the park. The worn, wooden structures, including a barn, a blacksmith shop and a smokehouse, give you a peek into the hardscrabble existence of early Appalachian settlers. A half-mile north, the 1886 Mingus Mill still grinds corn and wheat.

THE TRAIL OF TEARS

In the late 1830s, President Andrew Jackson ordered more than 16,000 Native Americans removed from their southeastern homelands and resettled in what's now Oklahoma. Thousands died of disease, exposure and exhaustion on the forced march west, now known as the "Trail of Tears." In Gatlinburg, see a **monument to Tsali**, the Cherokee hero who, according to legend, was executed for his part in an anti-relocation rebellion.

Further down the road, 6643ft **9 Clingmans Dome** is the third-highest mountain east of the Mississippi. You can drive almost all the way to the top via Clingmans Dome Rd, then walk the rest of the way to the Jetsons-like concrete observation tower. From here you can see over the spruce- and pine-covered mountaintops for miles around.

Climbing 6593ft **10 Mt LeConte** is probably the park's most popular challenge, sure to give some serious hamstring burn. The Alum Cave Trail, one of five routes to the peak, starts out from the Alum Cave parking area on the main road. Follow a creek, pass under a stone arch and wind your way steadily upward past thickets of rhododendron, myrtle and mountain laurel. **11 LeConte Lodge**, a collection of rough-hewn log cabins near the summit, is the park's only non-camping accommodation. There's no electricity, no real showers and all the food – beef and gravy for dinner, grits and ham for breakfast – is packed in by llamas three times a week. But you'll be amply rewarded by glowing purple sunrises from the eastern-facing cliffs at Myrtle Point.

Continuing on Newfound Gap Rd, turn left on Little River Rd, which becomes Laurel Creek Rd, running right into the 11-mile loop around ⑫ **Cades Cove**. This secluded (except for the glut of cars in summer) valley contains the remnants of a 19th-century settlement. Park your car to see the old churches and farmhouses up close, and to hike trails through postcard-perfect meadows filled with deer, wild turkeys and the occasional bear. Cyclists take note – cars are banned from the loop road until 10am every Wednesday and Saturday from May through September.

DETOUR

In the Pisgah National Forest, one hour southeast of Cherokee, you'll find **Sliding Rock**, a 60ft-long natural waterslide. In summertime visitors wait their turn to swoosh down the slick rock face into the 7ft-deep pool below. The ride can be painful on the tailbone and the water is freezing, but you'll line up to do it again anyway. Nearby **Brevard** is a cute mountain town of B&Bs and candy shops.

Doubling back to Little River Rd, you'll find the ⑬ **Elkmont Campground**. The 220 wooded sites can fill up quickly in high season. Back at the juncture of Little River and Newfound Gap Rds is the ⑭ **Sugarlands Visitor Center**, park headquarters. There's a bookstore, exhibits on plant and animal life, and seasonal ranger-led talks and tours.

Driving out of the park on the Tennessee side is a bit disconcerting. All at once you pop out of the tranquil green tunnel of trees and into a blinking, shrieking welter of cars, motels and minigolf courses, all blaring Christmas music and smelling of fried dough. Welcome to ⑮ **Gatlinburg**. It's Heidi meets Hillbilly in this vaguely Bavarian-themed tourist wonderland, catering to Smokies visitors since the 1930s. Turn off your cynical side and let the kitsch work its magic. Most of the tourist attractions are within the compact, hilly little downtown.

Pancakes are to Gatlinburg what pizza is to New York. Though there's a different pancake house on every corner proclaiming itself the best in town, ⑯ **Pancake Pantry** is the granddaddy of them all. Chow down on 24 varieties of pancake, cheese-swollen omelettes or whipped cream–smothered waffles in a building that looks like an overgrown Smurf house.

The Ripley's franchise operates seven shock-and-awe-style attractions in town. The gargantuan ⑰ **Ripley's Aquarium of the Smokies** features sea turtles, piranhas and stingrays far, far from their homes. A 340ft-long moving sidewalk shunts you through the clear tunnel on the floor of the Shark Lagoon, where you can watch long, sinister shapes glide by overhead. Though the original ⑱ **Ripley's Believe It or Not!** burned down in 1992, taking with it nearly all the exhibits, the popular odditorium rose from the ashes twice as large. Join the crowds to gawk at the shrunken heads, the 6583.5ft-long gum-wrapper chain and the 1840s vampire-killing kit.

The ⑲ **Gatlinburg Sky Lift**, a repurposed ski-resort chair lift, whisks you high over the Smokies. You'll fill up your camera's entire memory card with panoramic snapshots. At night, take your pick of a plethora of Appalachian-themed motels and lodges. ⑳ **Buckhorn Inn** is a tasteful bed and breakfast with views of Mt LeConte, and a flagstone terrace with rocking chairs.

A few miles north of Gatlinburg is the dismal stretch of chain motels, ye olde kountry shoppes and discount cigarette warehouses known as ㉑ **Pigeon Forge**. This town exists for one reason only: the worship of that big-haired, big-busted angel of East Tennessee, Dolly Parton. Dolly was born in a one-room shack in the nearby hamlet of Locust Ridge, started performing on Knoxville radio at the age of 11 and moved to Nashville at 18 with all her worldly belongings in a cardboard suitcase. She's made millions singing about her Smoky Mountain roots and continues to be a huge presence in her hometown, donating money to local causes and riding a glittery float in the annual Dolly Parade.

The ㉒ **Dollywood** theme park is an enormous, gushy love letter to mountain culture. Minivans full of families pour in each morning to ride the hee-haw themed thrill rides like the Mystery Mine Coaster and the Tennessee Tornado; see demonstrations of traditional Appalachian crafts such as wagon-making; and browse a plethora of shops hawking Christian-themed T-shirts and pink taffy. You can also tour the bald eagle sanctuary, attend Sunday services at the country chapel or worship at the altar of Dolly in the Chasing Rainbows life-story museum. The adjacent ㉓ **Dollywood's Splash Country** takes the same themes and adds water. Ride the Mountain Scream waterslides and the "whitewater rafting adventure" of Big Bear Plunge.

WATERFALLS OF THE SMOKIES

The Smokies are full of waterfalls, from icy trickles to roaring cascades. Here are a few of the best:

- Grotto Falls: you can walk behind these 25ft-high falls, off Trillium Gap Trail.
- Laurel Falls: this popular 80ft fall is located down an easy 2.6-mile paved trail.
- Mingo Falls: at 120ft, this is one of the highest waterfalls in the Appalachians.
- Rainbow Falls: on sunny days, the mist here produces a rainbow.

ASK A LOCAL

"Any real Dolly fan must make a pilgrimage to **Dollywood**. But there are also several less well-known stops in the area. Many fans visit the **Sevier County Courthouse** in Sevierville and get their picture made at the statue of her on the courthouse lawn. In Pigeon Forge you'll pass the **Little House of Prayer**, where her 'holy roller' Pentecostal grandfather preached, and **Caton's Chapel School**, one of the schoolhouses Dolly attended as a child."

Duane Gordon, webmaster, www.dollymania.net

Head out of town via Hwy 321. This rural highway gives you an idea of what a Tennessee road trip was like before I-40 sliced its way through the state.

Watch as the tree-covered peaks of the Smokies mellow into grassy green hills dotted with farmstands and flea markets; stop for an ice-cream cone as you pass through the time-warp town of **24** **Maryville**, where it still looks like 1955.

About two hours southwest of Pigeon Forge is the town of Sweetwater, home to America's largest underground lake. **25** **The Lost Sea** is a genuine country roadside attraction, where families and elderly couples with guidebooks queue up for hour-long tours. Before the modern tourist era, the caves were used as a dance hall, as a venue for cockfighting and as a hiding place for moonshine stills. Descend into Craighead Caverns via a long metal tunnel and ride a glass-bottom boat across the eerie greenish lake, illuminated from below by underwater lights. If you're lucky you'll spot a silvery cave trout gliding through the murky depths.

"Ride a glass-bottom boat across the eerie greenish lake, illuminated from below by underwater lights."

Double back northeast for 45 minutes to hit **26** **Knoxville**. This funky little gem of a city is one of those places where, despite the lack of specific tourist attractions, you come away feeling like you might want to live there one day. Driving in, note the giant gold orb towering over the city skyline. That's the **27** **Sunsphere**, a relic of the 1982 World's Fair. You can walk up to the observation deck for free. Downtown Knoxville is full of splendid 19th-century warehouses and storefronts turned lofts and boutiques. Pedestrian-only **28** **Market Square** is the center of the action, with outdoor cafés and a public green that hosts summertime concerts and plays.

Grab a table in the crowded, art-filled dining room of the **29** **Tomato Head**, where tattooed hipsters will serve you a gorgonzola and free-range chicken calzone. Right around the corner, the **30** **Hotel St Oliver** is like something out of a Tennessee Williams play. The 28 rooms have the eccentric elegance of a slightly dotty Southern belle, with Victorian wingback armchairs and thick Persian carpets. Sit for a spell in the dim downstairs library with its crumbling leather tomes and gilt-framed oil paintings. Wind down with a night of music at the impeccably restored **31** **Bijou Theatre**. Built in 1909, the Bijou has hosted luminaries of the bygone era like Dizzy Gillespie and Groucho Marx. These days, Knoxville's old guard comes for the ballet, while the whippersnappers from the University of Tennessee bobble their heads to indie rock performers such as Bright Eyes.

Emily Matchar

TRIP INFORMATION

GETTING THERE

From Charlotte, NC, take I-85 South to I-26 West to I-40 W. Turn onto the Great Smoky Mountains Expressway and continue for 40 miles toward Bryson City.

DO

Bijou Theatre

Downtown Knoxville's opulent 19th-century theater hosts big-name rock acts, ballet and theater. ☎ 865-656-4444; www.knoxbijou .com; 803 S Gay St, Knoxville, TN; ⏱ show times vary

Dollywood

Revel in the Appalachian-themed kitsch at this family-friendly amusement park, owned by East Tennessee's own darlin' Dolly. ☎ 865-428-9488; www.dollywood.com; 1198 McCarter Hollow Rd, Pigeon Forge, TN; adult/child $53/42; ⏱ hrs vary by season, closed Jan-Mar; ♿

Dollywood's Splash Country

Cool off in the Mountain Waves pool at Dolly's 25-acre water park. ☎ 865-428-9488; www.dollywoodssplashcountry.com; 1198 McCarter Hollow Rd, Pigeon Forge, TN; adult/child $46/40; ⏱ 10am-6pm, 10am-7pm high season; ♿

Gatlinburg Sky Lift

Ride this chairlift high into the mountains for incomparable views. ☎ 865-436-4307; www.gatlinburgskylift.com; 765 Parkway, Gatlinburg, TN; adult/child $12/9; ⏱ 9am-10pm, 9am-5pm winter

Great Smoky Mountains Railroad

Choose from a variety of scenic train tours, including dinner and wine trips and kid-friendly rides. ☎ 800-872-4681; www.gsmr .com; 226 Everett St, Bryson City, NC; adult/child from $34/19; ♿

The Lost Sea

Descend into Craighead Caverns and sail across a 4.5-acre underground lake. ☎ 423-337-6616; www.thelostsea.com; 140 Lost Sea Rd, Sweetwater, TN; adult/child $16/7.50; ⏱ 9am-5pm, until later spring & summer; ♿

Mountain Farm Museum and Mingus Mill

Be transported to the 19th century at this replica farm (next to Oconaluftee Visitor Center) and working grist mill (a half-mile up the road). ☎ 423-436-1200; www.nps .gov/grsm; ⏱ 9am-5pm Mar-Nov

Museum of the Cherokee Indian

Artifact-filled exhibits trace the long, proud and often sad history of Native Americans in these mountains. ☎ 828-497-3481; www .cherokeemuseum.org; 589 Tsali Blvd, Chero-kee, NC; adult/child $9/6; ⏱ 9am-5pm

Nantahala Outdoor Center

This trusted river outfitter has whitewater trips for all levels, with several outposts throughout the Appalachians. ☎ 828-488-2176; www .noc.com; 13077 Hwy 19 W, Bryson City, NC; guided rafting trips from $38; ♿

Oconaluftee Visitor Center

Pick up maps and camping permits at North Carolina's gateway to the Smokies. ☎ 423-436-1200; www.nps.gov/grsm; Hwy 441, near Cherokee, NC; ⏱ 8am-4:30pm, until later spring & summer

Ripley's Aquarium of the Smokies

Take a walk through the shark tunnel and play with stingrays at this massive fish tank. ☎ 865-430-8808; http://gatlinburg .ripleyaquariums.com; Parkway light 5, Gatlinburg, TN; adult/child $19/10; ⏱ 9am-9pm Sun-Thu, 9am-11pm Fri, Sat & daily in high season; ♿

Ripley's Believe It or Not!

The shrunken heads are a crowd pleaser at this house of oddities. ☎ 865-436-5096; www .ripleys.com; Parkway light 7, Gatlinburg, TN; adult/child $17/9; ⏱ 10am-11pm; ♿

Sugarlands Visitor Center

Tennessee's main park entrance has a book-store and ranger tours in summer. ☎ 865-436-1291; www.nps.gov/grsm; Hwy 441, TN; ⏱ 8am-4:30pm, until later spring & summer

Unto These Hills

This outdoor play dramatizing Cherokee his-tory has been performed at the Mountainside Theater since 1950. ☎ 866-554-4557; www .cherokee-nc.com; Drama Rd, Cherokee, NC; adult/child $18/8; ⏱ 8:30pm Mon-Sat Jun-Aug

EAT

Pancake Pantry

Dig into an extra-tall stack at this beloved all-day breakfast joint. ☎ 865-436-4724; 628 Parkway, Gatlinburg, TN; mains $4-9, ⏱ 7am-4pm, 7am-3pm Nov-Mar; ♿

Tomato Head

Fill your belly with pizza and tofu burritos at this quirky locals spot. ☎ 865-637-4067; 12 Market Sq, Knoxville, TN; mains $5-9; ⏱ 11am-9:30pm Tue-Thu, 11am-3pm Mon, 11am-10:30pm Fri & Sat, 11am-9pm Sun

SLEEP

Buckhorn Inn

Curl up by the fire and gaze out at the misty mountains from the parlor of this gracious bed and breakfast. ☎ 865-436-4668; www .buckhorninn.com; 2140 Tudor Mountain Rd, Gatlinburg, TN; r from $115

Elkmont Campground

The park's largest campground has 220 sites on the banks of the Little River. ☎ 865-436- 1200; www.nps.gov/grsm; Little River Rd, TN; campsites from $17; ⏱ Mar-Nov; ♿

Hotel St Oliver

Sleep amid quirky Southern antiques in this eccentric old downtown hotel, with a grand piano in the tiny lobby. ☎ 865-521-0050; www.hotelstolivertn.com; 407 Union Ave, Knoxville, TN; r from $100

LeConte Lodge

Hike up to these rustic cabins at the summit of Mt LeConte and enjoy a group meal and a stunning sunrise. ☎ 865-429-5704; www .leconte-lodge.com; cabins per adult/child from $79/60, meals $37/25; ⏱ Mar-Nov

Nantahala Inn

Rafters crash at this simple wooden lodge amid the pines after a day on the river. ☎ 828-488-2176; www.noc.com; Hwy 19, 12 miles west of Bryson City, NC; r from $59

USEFUL WEBSITES

www.gatlinburg.com
www.nps.gov/grsm

LINK YOUR TRIP
www.lonelyplanet.com/trip-planner

TRIP
4 Skyline Drive to the Blue Ridge Parkway p75

Kentucky Bluegrass & Horse Country

WHY GO A trip through the sunlight-dappled hills and meadows of Bluegrass Country is like a massage for your tired brain. Drive the scenic byways from Louisville to Lexington and beyond, stopping to tour storybook-like country estates, ride horses through the poplar forests and sip the region's famous bourbon.

TIME
3 days

DISTANCE
140 miles

BEST TIME TO GO
Apr – Sep

START
Louisville, KY

END
Harrodsbug, KY

Kentucky's Bluegrass Region encompasses the north-central part of the state, including the cities of Lexington, Frankfort and Louisville, and is home to half the state's population. Though Lexington is the capital of Horse Country, cheerful, solid ❶ **Louisville** has the racing world's most iconic building: the white spires of ❷ **Churchill Downs**. The Run for the Roses, as the Kentucky Derby is known, happens here on the first Saturday in May. Though most seats are reserved years in advance, if you're around on Derby Day you can pay $40 to get into the Paddock area, though don't expect to see much. But from April through November you can get ultra-cheap seats for warm-up races and simulcasts of racing events worldwide.

Wander over to the riverfront downtown, with its well-preserved 19th-century brick buildings. Have a mint julep while listening to live piano music in the ❸ **Lobby Bar** of the gilded Brown Hotel, where starlets and ambassadors got up to no good during the Roaring Twenties. Clear your head with a stroll around the ❹ **Old Louisville** neighborhood south of downtown, with America's largest collection of Victorian homes.

Head out of Louisville and into the Arcadian countryside, where – sorry to disappoint – but the grass is not actually blue. Poa pratensis, or Kentucky Bluegrass, gets its name from the bluish-purple buds it sprouts in early summer which, from a distance, can give fields of the grass a slightly sapphire cast.

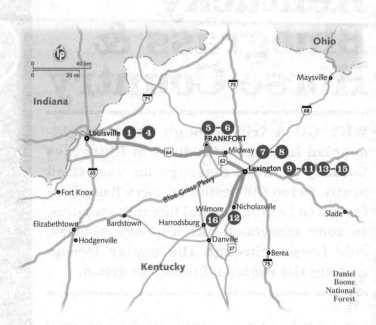

About an hour east of Louisville is Kentucky's tiny capital, **5 Frankfort**. This well-tended bluffside city has a gracious, all-American downtown – good for a leg-stretching stroll. A scenic overlook on Hwy 60 offers a sweeping view over the capital buildings, a popular photo op. Stay the night at the **6 Meeting House**, a 168-year-old Federal-style mansion in the historic district. Have a tall glass of tea on the veranda and sleep in one of four bedrooms, each decorated with quirky, hand-picked antiques.

The next day, have a decadent lunch near the village of **7 Midway**, at the **8 Holly Hill Inn**. This winsome 1845 Greek Revival estate, nestled beneath the oaks, houses one of the best restaurants in Kentucky. The married chef-owners serve a simple but elegant multi-course feast of handmade pastas, locally raised meats and farmstead cheeses. Diminutive Midway is the state's first railroad town and home to Kentucky's only all-female college, Midway College.

"This well-tended bluffside city has a gracious, all-American downtown."

Drive the scenic oak-lined Old Frankfort Pike into stately **9 Lexington**, once known as the "Athens of the West" for its architecture and culture. The area surrounding Lexington, known as the Inner Bluegrass (or Horse Country), has been a center of horse breeding for three centuries. The region's ancient limestone deposits are natural fertilizers, feeding the lush meadows that in turn nourish grazing thoroughbreds.

Outside the city is the 1200-acre ❿ **Kentucky Horse Park**, an equine theme park and sports center. The park is home to about 50 different horse breeds, from the Akhal-Teke to the Welch Cob. Catch the daily Parade of Breeds or, in springtime, watch mares and new foals nuzzle in the paddock. The park's Museum of the Horse has life-sized displays on horses through history, from the dog-sized prehistoric eohippus to modern polo ponies. Here you learn just how deep the human–horse relationship runs – Cro-Magnon man painted horses on cave walls as far back as 17,000 years ago.

To tour a working stable and training facility, visit the ⓫ **Thoroughbred Center**, where visitors get to see a day in the life of Derby hopefuls, from morning workouts to cool-down currying. You'll see exactly why blue-blooded Kentucky horses get reputations as divas. In the afternoon get even more up-close-and-personal with the horses with a guided ride at ⓬ **Sunburst Horsemanship Center**. This picturesque Lexington farm offers lessons for all levels, from basic safety to advanced jumping.

In the evening, put your money on an old-school harness race, where jockeys are pulled behind the horses in two-wheeled carts called sulkies, at the ⓭ **Red Mile**. Fans have been cheering from the grandstands at this red dirt track since 1875. Though live races are in the fall only, simulcasts are offered year-round.

ASK A LOCAL

"The American Saddlebred horse was developed primarily in Kentucky and was often used to ride around the plantations. It was showy and high-stepping and pretty, and could be hitched to the wagon and go to church and show off. It was developed from a riding horse into a show horse – we have quite a strong showing contingent around here, They're beautiful horses, with long flowing manes and tails – very aristocratic."

Kathy Hopkins, Lexington

For dinner, try quirky ⓮ **a la Lucie** in Lexington's grand historical district. The funky bistro decor could have been scrounged from a Parisian flea market, but the menu is all over the map – lobster corn dogs, Mediterranean stuffed eggplant, bourbon pork. Spend the night in restored 19th-century style at the ⓯ **Gratz Park Inn** around the corner. Its leather and dark wood-paneled library makes you just itch to smoke a pipe.

If you have time in the morning, drive 30 miles through scenic pasturelands dotted with horse barns along Hwy 68 to ⓰ **Shaker Village of Pleasant Hill**. In the early 1800s these softly rolling hills were home to a communal society of 500 peace-loving men and women. Though the Shakers worshipped God through uninhibited ecstatic dancing, they practiced strict celibacy (probably why there aren't any left). See their remarkable craftsmanship in dozens of restored buildings and learn about their history at the Shaker Life Exhibit.

Emily Matchar

TRIP 32

ROUTE

TRIP INFORMATION

GETTING THERE
From Nashville, take I-65 north for 170 miles, exit at 137 for I-64, and then at 4 for Louisville.

DO
Churchill Downs
The world's most famous horseracing track is home to the Kentucky Derby and various other races. ☎ 502-636-4400; www.church illdowns.com; 700 Central Ave, Louisville; admission from $10; ⊙ race times vary

Kentucky Horse Park
This horse-theme park has 50 breeds and two equine history museums. ☎ 859-233-4303; www.kyhorsepark.com; 4089 Iron Works Parkway, Lexington; adult/child Mar-Oct $15/8, Nov-Mar $9/6; ⊙ 9am-5pm, closed Mon & Tue Nov-Mar; ⌖

Red Mile
This 1875 track has live harness racing and simulcasts. ☎ 859-255-0752; www.theredmile .com; 1200 Red Mile Rd, Lexington; ⊙ simulcasts afternoon & evening, live racing Aug-Oct

Shaker Village of Pleasant Hill
America's largest restored Shaker village, outside the town of Harrodsburg, has an inn, restaurant and historical displays. ☎ 800-734-5611; www.shakervillageky.org; 3501 Lexington Rd, Harrodsburg; tours adult/child Apr-Oct $15/5, Nov-Mar $7/3; ⊙ 10am-5pm Apr-Oct, 10am-4pm Nov-Mar

Sunburst Horsemanship Center
This school and training facility has lessons for riders of all levels. ☎ 859-224-8480; www. sunbursthorsemanshipschool.com; 1129 Durham Lane, Lexington; intro lesson $60; ⌖

Thoroughbred Center
Watch champion horses go through their paces at this working farm. ☎ 859-293-1853; www.thethoroughbredcenter.com; 3380 Paris Pike, Lexington; adult/child $10/5; ⊙ tours 9am Mon-Sat, closed Sat Nov-Mar

EAT & DRINK
a la Lucie
This bohemian bistro has vintage furniture and an eclectic international menu. ☎ 859-252-5277; www.alalucie.com; 159 N Limestone St, Lexington; mains $8-28; ⊙ 11:30am-2pm Mon-Fri & 4:30-10pm Mon-Sat

Holly Hill Inn
This stately old country manse is just the place for a special dinner. ☎ 859-846-4732; www.hollyhillinn.com; 426 N Winter St, Midway; mains $18-30; ⊙ 5:30-10pm Wed-Sat, 11:30am-2pm Sat & Sun

Lobby Bar
Sip bourbon in the opulent, marble-floored lobby of the Brown Hotel, an Old Louisville institution. ☎ 502-583-1234; www.brown hotel.com; 335 West Broadway, Louisville; ⊙ 4pm-2am

SLEEP
Gratz Park Inn
Draw the brocade curtains and fall asleep on a 19th-century poster bed in Lexington's historic district. ☎ 859-231-1777; www.gratzparkinn .com; 120 W Second St, Lexington; r from $179

Meeting House
The quirky antiques at this Federal-style bed-and-breakfast speak of the owners' fascination with local history. ☎ 502-226-3226; www.themeetinghousebandb.com; 519 Ann St, Frankfort; r from $115

USEFUL WEBSITES
www.bluegrasskentucky.com
www.visitlex.com

LINK YOUR TRIP
www.lonelyplanet.com/trip-planner

TRIP 4 Skyline Drive to the Blue Ridge Parkway p75

FLORIDA TRIPS

Florida will cast a spell on you. Spanish explorers saw manatees and imagined they were mermaids. Ponce de León found the fabled Fountain of Youth after Native Americans showed him a sacred spring. Latter-day developers dug up mucky swampland and tangled mangrove forests, and sold paradise for a pretty penny to snowbird retirees.

In its history, Florida has inspired as much madness and murder as it has fantasies of a magical kingdom where dreams really do come true. But the Sunshine State is also a kitschy, fun-loving vacationland made for spring breakers, lovebird couples and minivan-driving families. Florida claims 1800 miles of coastline – amazingly, two-thirds of that is sandy beaches. Cold beer, a basket of peel-and-eat shrimp, waving palms trees, gentle surf and hypnotic sunsets are never far away.

PLAYLIST ♫ Florida has got booty-shakin' Latin rhythms and pop sounds, deep veins of Southern blues and folk, the twang of country guitars, and rebellious rock and hip-hop. For Sunshine State road-tripping, download:

- "Cheeseburger in Paradise," Jimmy Buffet
- "Free Bird," Lynyrd Skynyrd
- "It's Five O'Clock Somewhere," Alan Jackson
- "Ramblin' Man," Allman Brothers
- "I Won't Back Down," Tom Petty
- "Hands Down," Dashboard Confessional
- "Miami," Will Smith
- "Bella," Los Primeros

But wait, there's more. Savor Miami's heady Latin American cultural mix, inviting for foodies and nightclub mavens alike. Paddle around pristine bays and go gator spotting in the Everglades. Follow the epic Overseas Highway all the way out to kooky Key West.

Welcome to Florida. The adventure starts now.

FLORIDA TRIPS

48 Hours in Miami

WHY GO Miami is all about Latin flavor, especially when it comes to cuisine. Lee Klein, food critic for the *Miami New Times* newspaper, shares some of his favorite Latin American eateries in Little Havana and beyond, plus offbeat hideaways and culinary gems in his own bohemian neighborhood, Miami Beach.

TIME
2 days

BEST TIME TO GO
Nov – Apr

START
El Palacio del los Jugos

END
Miami International Airport

While you get ready to jump in and explore Miami's toothsome side, be prepared to speak *un poquito español* (a little Spanish). Or just smile, point politely and ask *por favor, quiero esto* (I'd like, please). But don't let any language barriers get in the way of your mission: to try the most authentic Latin tastes Miami has to offer. "Miami has always been strong on ethnic holes-in-the-wall," Klein opines. "Cuban, Haitian, Central American, South American – the list goes on and on." Many Latin American eateries stay open after midnight, too – convenient in a city where *la vida nocturna* is key.

For a first taste of Miami's melting pot, head out to ❶ El Palacio de Los Jugos. This open-air marketplace, with food stands like you'd find all over Latin America, is at the intersection of where Havana and Miami shake hands. Klein recommends: "Walk over to where the guy is whacking the tops off of coconuts for fresh juices. Buy a plate of pork *asada* with fried plantains, black beans and rice, and devour it on a bench in the corner while you watch all the activity going on." As for the juices, you can experiment with more exotic flavors like melon, mamey or *guarapo* (pressed sugarcane).

❷ Little Havana is Miami's best-known Cuban community. ❸ Calle Ocho (aka SW 8th St) doesn't just cut through the heart of the neighborhood – it *is* the heart of the neighborhood. "It's not commercial. It's not a tourist attraction," Klein points out. "This is where you'll see

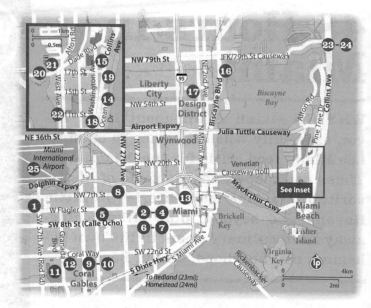

old Cuban men smoking cigars and playing chess." That's especially true in ④ **Máximo Gómez Park**, named for a late-19th-century Cuban independence fighter. Another Little Havana landmark is ⑤ **Versailles** restaurant, where politicians (even US presidents) drop by to take the pulse of the community. "When something important happens," Klein says, "this is where Cuban Americans go to debate and discuss it." Order a *café Cubano* (nicknamed a *cafecito*), sweetened espresso brewed with sugar, at the walk-up window.

Don't stop your explorations of Little Havana yet. Klein gives us a great tip: "At almost any Cuban supermarket," he reveals, "they sell great authentic Cuban food to go." Pick up roast chicken, *vaca frita* (crispy beef) or *churrasco* (grilled meat kabobs) at ⑥ **El Nuevo Siglo**. Get there early in the day before they run out of anything, then scarf it down at the basic counter seats and tables. Klein's pick for Cuban fast food is nearby: ⑦ **El Rey de Las Fritas**. "I love their pork burgers with sautéed onions, loads of seasonings and potato sticks on top," he says.

Off Little Havana's main drag, ⑧ **Salmon & Salmon** proves that, even in this Cuban community, other Latin American groups have their own lively gathering spots. Klein recommends this Peruvian hole-in-the-wall for authentic seafood, like *ceviche mixto* (raw seafood marinated in citrus juices usually with chiles, garlic, onion and cilantro). The small storefront dining room is always packed with locals, so expect a wait for a table.

Likewise, Cuban comfort food isn't limited to Little Havana. Drive south to **9** **Coral Gables**, a wealthy Mediterranean-style enclave, to find another one of Klein's picks: **10** **Sergio's**. This retro-licious restaurant plates up Cuban comfort food just like mama used to make at airy outdoor tables, or swing inside and sink into a booth. Then spend the afternoon strolling around town,

to walk off everything you've feasted on so far. Don't miss seeing Coral Gables' lavish **11** **Biltmore Hotel**, a splendid Jazz Age survivor, and the spring-fed **12** **Venetian Pool**, a wonderland of cascading waterfalls and coral-rock grottos.

Just across the river from Little Havana, **14** **Garcia's Seafood Grille & Fish Market** is like pirates' hidden treasure. "Here you can sit overlooking an undeveloped stretch of the Miami River," Klein says. Yes, it's seedy and ramshackle, but in a cinematic way.

DETOUR To see where all those fresh fruit and veggies on Miami restaurants' top tables come from, drive out to Redland, where organic farms and vineyards rub sun-kissed shoulders. Book ahead for a chef-prepared **Dinner in Paradise** (www.paradisefarms.net). In Homestead, stop by the long-running farm stand **Robert Is Here** (www.robertishere.com) for a strawberry milkshake. This agricultural region, an hour's drive southwest of Miami Beach, has authentic Mexican food, too – try out some of those roadside taco trucks.

"They used to film *Miami Vice* here," he amusingly adds. Don't let the simple ambience of Garcia's downstairs fish market deter you. Climb the narrow stairway up to the classy bar and grill sporting a riverside deck, where some of Miami's movers and shakers fork into conch steaks and grouper fillets and wolf down dolphinfish (mahimahi) sandwiches.

At long last, Miami Beach. You've already been fantasizing about dreamy **15** **South Beach**, right? Part beach bum, part A-list glamour girl, SoBe is where the carnivalesque action never stops. "You can't ignore the beach," Klein, a neighborhood denizen, admits. "Especially not topless Haulover Beach." Chic outdoor cafés and restaurants line Ocean Dr, but for upscale plates, pick standard-bearing **16** **OLA** (Of Latin America, get it?) for chef David Rodriguez's innovative pan–Latin American cuisine. "It's worth going just to try the ceviche menu," Klein says. Fork into traditional Peruvian *mixto*, or go bold with whole lobster tail marinated in coconut milk and citrus juices, served with sage sorbet.

Detour across the bay to **17** **Michy's**, the love child of chef Michelle Bernstein and husband David Martinez. "The menu is half Latin America, half continental American," Klein remarks. To wit: white gazpacho and *jamon*–blue cheese croquettes appear alongside steak frites and duck confit. Bordering Miami's Design District, **18** **Little Haiti** has plenty of holes-in-the-wall serving true island specialties like *ragout* (cow's feet), *queue de boeuf* (oxtail), *foie* (liver) and *griot* (spicy fried pork). It's one of Miami's most flavorful

CITY

neighborhoods, where young men in tank tops listen to Francophone rap while matrons wearing bright headscarves gossip in front of *botanicas* (ie *vodou* shops).

Back in South Beach, Collins Ave is a trove of historic art-deco hotels such as the **19** **Hotel Astor** and fashionable modern high-rises such as the **20** **Delano Hotel**, designed by Ian Schrager, which Klein calls "a little Alice-in-Wonderlandish." On the oasis of Lido Island, **21** **The Standard** "really nails that 1950s Miami vibe," Klein enthuses. This hip urban hotel lets guests play bingo as DJs spin, take holistic yoga classes or drift away in the spa's Turkish hammam. For drinks, head back across the causeway to the comfortably unpretentious **22** Purdy Lounge or hit the Mondrian's **23** **Sunset Lounge**, overlooking the bay, for high-flying cocktails. Klein points out the hotel's gob-stopping vending machine, where you can put down a deposit on anything from a Bentley to a brand-new house.

ART BEYOND THE BEACH

Miami's **Design District** is for foodies and art lovers alike. Here a contemporary gallery scene thrives, neatly bounded by NE 38th and 41st Sts and NE 2nd and N Miami Aves. Culture vultures can also head north to the **Museum of Contemporary Art** (MOCA; www.mocanomi.org) or time their trip for December's international **Art Basel** (www.artbaselmiamibeach.com) event. Back in SoBe, peruse the eccentric all-media collections of the unique **Wolfsonian Museum** (www.wolfsonian.org), inside a historic art-deco movie palace.

For a sweet ending to a hot night of clubbing, northern Miami Beach's **24** **La Perrada de Edgar** doles out Columbia hot dogs with kookily delicious toppings (bacon, eggs, potato sticks, pineapple and/or whipped cream, anyone?). Wait until the next morning to swing by **25** **Buenos Aires Bakery**. "By everyone's opinion," Klein says, "this is the place to go for stuffed empanadas and *alfajores* (confections) made with *dulce de leche* (caramel)."

Finally, if you find yourself back at the airport craving one last Cuban meal, Klein gives the thumbs-up to **26** **La Carreta**, a city-wide chain. Get your *arroz con pollo, ropa vieja* and other Cuban classics done right here. The cafeteria set-up makes for quick getaways, especially once you've refueled with a *cafecito* or two for the long flight home.

Sara Benson

TRIP INFORMATION

GETTING THERE
Miami is 235 miles southeast of Orlando or 25 miles south of Fort Lauderdale/Hollywood International Airport via I-95.

DO
Máximo Gómez Park
Aka Domino Park, here Little Havana's board game–playing retirees while away the mornings and afternoons. ☎ 305-285-1684; 801 SW 15th Ave, Miami; admission free; 🕙24hr; ♿ 👹

Venetian Pool
Take the plunge at this stunning public water park, just as Olympian-swimmers-turned-movie stars Esther Williams and Johnny "Tarzan" Weissmuller once did. ☎ 305-460-5306; www.coralgablesvenetianpool.com; 2701 De Soto Blvd, Coral Gables; adult/child $10.50/6; 🕙 11am-5:30pm Tue-Fri, 10am-4:30pm Sat & Sun, extended hr Jun-Aug; ♿

EAT & DRINK
Buenos Aires Bakery
Little Argentinean sidewalk café and coffee shop gets big applause for its meat and vegetable empanadas. ☎ 305-861-7887; www.buenosairesbakeryandcafe.com; 7134 Collins Ave, Miami Beach; items $2-6; 🕙7am-9pm; ♿

El Nuevo Siglo
Never mind the blindingly bright lights: this Little Havana *supermercado* has tasty take-out and a bakery for dessert. ☎ 305-854-1916; 1305 SW 8th St, Miami; dishes $2-10; 🕙7am-7pm; ♿

El Palacio de Los Jugos
Instantly addictive *jugos naturales* (fruit juices), *batidos* (tropical milkshakes), Cuban sandwiches, roast chicken and other succulent take-out. ☎ 305-264-4557; 5721 W Flagler St, Miami; dishes $3-8; 🕙7am-9pm Mon-Sat, to 8pm Sun; ♿

El Rey de Las Fritas
Miami's mini chain of Cuban fast-food joints, serving burgers, *batidos* and hot pressed sandwiches. ☎ 305-644-6054; 1821 SW 8th St, Miami; dishes $2-6; 🕙 9am-10:30pm Mon-Sat; ♿

Garcia's Seafood Grille & Fish Market
Though it may feel like a smuggler's shack, the blackboard specials and table service are sophisticated; complimentary valet parking. ☎ 305-375-0765; 398 NW River Dr, Miami; mains $9-22; 🕙 11am-3pm & 5:30-9:30pm

La Carreta
Don't worry, it's not your usual airport fare, folks. Fill up on fried pork, shredded beef and steamed tamales. www.lacarreta.com; Miami International Airport, 4200 NW 21st St, Miami; mains $7-12; 🕙 6am-10:30pm; ♿

La Perrada de Edgar
Columbian hot dogs with all the extra topping will almost ensure a heart attack. Wash 'em down with tart lemonade. ☎ 305-866-4546; 6976 Collins Ave, Miami; items $3-6; 🕙 10am-2am; ♿

Michy's
Dramatic dining room for Latin American fusion fare on modish northern Biscayne Blvd. ☎ 305-759-2001; http://michysmiami.com; 6927 Biscayne Blvd, Miami; mains $17-34; 🕙 6:30-11pm Tue-Thu, 6:30-11:30pm Fri & Sat, 6-10pm Sun

OLA
Nuevo Latino cooking from ground-breaking city chef Douglas Rodriguez, along with a standout Spanish and South American wine list. ☎ 305-695-9125; www.olamiami.com; Sanctuary Hotel, 1745 James Ave, Miami; mains $16-40; 🕙 6:30-11pm Sun-Thu, 6:30pm-1am Fri & Sat

Purdy Lounge
No-attitude neighborhood bar where laid-back couches and reggae nights rebel against SoBe's velvet-roped, see-and-be-seen

nightclub scene. ☎ 305-531-4622; www.
purdylounge.com; 1811 Sunset Harbor Rd,
Miami Beach; ☾ 3pm-5am Mon-Fri, 6pm-
5am Sat & Sun

Salmon & Salmon
Peruvian house specialties include *tacu-
tacu* (Creole-style fried beans and rice) and
anything with octopus. Just overlook the
tacky strip-mall location. ☎ 305-649-5924;
2907 NW 7th St, Miami; mains $12-25;
☾ noon-10pm

Sergio's
Every home-style Cuban sandwich, pork or
seafood dish comes heaped with *maduros*
(fried plantains). ☎ 305-529-0047; www.
sergios.com; 3252 Coral Way, Coral Gables;
mains $6-15; ☾ 10am-midnight Sun-Thu,
10am-2am Fri & Sat; ♿

Sunset Lounge
Inventive tropical cocktails, breathtaking
bayside views, poolside cabanas, labyrinthine
gardens with "kissing corners" and a sandbox
strictly for grown-ups. ☎ 305-514-1941;
www.mondrian-miami.com; 1100 West Ave,
Miami Beach; ☾ 11am-2am

Versailles
Step inside this old-school Little Havana
Cuban restaurant for *vaca frita* (crispy beef),
lechon asado (marinated pork), croquettes
and other traditional dishes. ☎ 305-444-
0240; 3555 SW 8th St, Miami; mains $6-25;
☾ 8am-2am Mon-Thu, 8am-3:30am Fri,
8am-4:30am Sat, 9am-1am Sun; ♿

SLEEP

Biltmore Hotel
Sleep in the lap of luxury at this grand 1920s
hotel, ornamented with Italian, Spanish and
Moorish architectural accents. ☎ 305-445-
1926; www.biltmorehotel.com; 1200 Anastasia Ave, Coral Gables; r & ste $200-5000;
♿ ⛲

Delano Hotel
"Still cool and classy after all these years,"
says Klein. Step inside just to see the multimillion-dollar contemporary art collection.
☎ 305-672-2000; www.delano-hotel.
com; 1685 Collins Ave, Miami Beach; r & ste
$310-5000

Hotel Astor
Small but sleek rooms made over with earth
tones, with mod cons. Free beach gear to
borrow. ☎ 305-531-8081; www.hotelastor.
com; 956 Washington Ave, Miami Beach; r &
ste $130-570

The Standard
This tongue-in-cheek boutique hotel rates
its rooms by size, from "Missionary" to "Full
Spread." Don't be thrown off by the vintage
mid-century modern sign that says "Lido
Spa Hotel" outside. ☎ 305-673-1717; www.
standardhotels.com/miami; 40 Island Ave,
Miami Beach; r $189-539; ⛲

USEFUL WEBSITES
www.miamiandbeaches.com
www.miaminewtimes.com

LINK YOUR TRIP
www.lonelyplanet.com/trip-planner
TRIP

Cruisin' Florida's East Coast

WHY GO Go on, just admit it. This is exactly why you came to Florida: partyin' beach towns, panoramic coastal drives and lazy sunny days of swimming, surfing and margaritas by the pier. We've got the ultimate beach-bum's itinerary, from Jax Beaches all the way south to Miami.

There's no really bad time to take this classic road trip down Florida's east coast. Summer sees more rain, but the ocean waters are balmy. March and April are overrun with college students on spring break; then again, the weather is so awesome, maybe it's worth fighting the crowds. Fall brings hurricanes, but you might get lucky and evade the storms. Winter is drier, and also colder, yet it warms up the further south you go. So just hit the road whenever you feel like it, and optimistically whistle "Here Comes the Sun."

Start your beach-bum's journey up north in Jacksonville. Get into the spring-break spirit of things at ❶ Anheuser-Busch Brewery, which produces over eight million barrels annually, now using ecoconscious practices. Guided tours are equal parts history and propaganda, ending with free samples. Dude! Afterward, let your designated driver whisk you down to ❷ Jax Beaches. Beside the sand dunes, the beach's fishing pier is the place to bring drinks, cast your line and wait for a nibble. Hidden inland in a strip mall, the funky ❸ Beach Hut Cafe is the kind of place where plastic palm trees and flip-flops fit right in. All day it dishes up Southern-style breakfasts such as country ham with red-eyed gravy. Spaced along Hwy A1A heading north are quieter Neptune Beach and Atlantic Beach, if you want to possibly have some white sand all to yourself.

Take the long way southbound via coastal Hwy A1A. Slow down for ❹ Cap's on the Water, a raw bar and seafood house inhabiting an authentic 1940s fishing camp, where you can sit and shuck

TIME
6 days

DISTANCE
475 miles

BEST TIME TO GO
Nov – Apr

START
Jacksonville, FL

END
Miami, FL

oysters on the creaky back deck. Before you know it, you'll be motoring into **5 St Augustine Beach**, with its fishing pier and merrily black-and-white-striped lighthouse. Go beachcombing, swimming, paddling, hiking and cycling or pitch your tent overnight at **6 Anastasia State Park**, famous for its unbroken ocean horizons. Or head across the Bridge of Lions into downtown St Augustine, Florida's oldest European settlement, riddled with narrow cobblestone alleyways, to the no-frills, tongue-in-cheek **7 Pirate Haus Inn**. Yo-ho-ho, me hearties!

Synonymous with spring-break madness, **8 Daytona Beach** keeps a carnivalesque atmosphere going on its vintage 1950s boardwalk year-round. Take a gondola ride on Main Street Pier, then hit the miles of white-sand beaches for anything from swimming and boogie boarding to surfing and parasailing. (Shh, don't disturb the sea turtles that lay their eggs in the sand here between mid-May and October.) Meander south to **9 Ponce Inlet Light Station**, the tallest lighthouse on Florida's east coast, which is gorgeously lit up after sunset.

Nearby, **10 Down the Hatch Seafood Restaurant** is a waterfront seafood galley where hot live bands and Floribbean cuisine go hand-in-hand. Back on Daytona Beach's main drag, we can't resist the **11 Aku Tiki Inn** for its tropical kitsch appeal and fabulously divey tiki bar downstairs, where disco has never died. Just inland, the Daytona International Speedway attracts even bigger crowds than the beach, especially when Nascar comes to town during "Speed Weeks." (In the old days, drivers actually used to race on the beach.) At the speedway, the ⑫ **Daytona 500 Experience** lets you admire stock cars, take a tram tour of the steeply banked track, and virtually experience all the thrills of auto racing – even take a ride-along with a professional driver.

THE ROAD LESS TAKEN

From Daytona, it's about 200 miles of pokey-slow coastal driving (or cheat by taking faster I-95) down to Palm Beach. Break up your journey at ⑬ **Indialantic Beach**, one of those oft-forgotten, off-the-beaten-path beach towns that are almost too cool a secret to reveal. Sandy shores, great surfing, a boardwalk and cycling paths by the sea await. Follow the surfers north up Hwy A1A to ⑭ **Da Kine Diego's Insane Burrito** shop, with its outdoor patio plastered with graffiti and surf-brand stickers. Can't tear yourself away from the wide-open ocean horizons? Then pretend you're living in your own private beach house at the unforgettably relaxing ⑮ **Oceanfront Cottages**.

Florida's Hwy A1A, celebrated in pop culture and sung about by Jimmy Buffet and Vanilla Ice, traces a perilous path along the Atlantic Coast barrier islands. Apart from its National Scenic Byway designation (www.scenica1a.org), however, Hwy A1A often lacks ocean views, with wind-blocking vegetation growing on both sides of the road. Unless you're just moseying up or down the coast to the next beach town, Hwy 1 or I-95 are often better choices for driving long distance.

Back on the road, detour to Jupiter Island's ⑯ **Blowing Rocks Preserve**. When the surf's up, the sea breaks against a rocky limestone coastline, sometimes spouting 50ft into the air – pretty impressive! Perched on the water with lighthouse views, ⑰ **Square Grouper Tiki Bar** is a classic Florida dive that starred in Alan Jackson's music video "It's Five O'Clock Somewhere" with Jimmy Buffet. For creative seafood with a twist, head to ⑱ **Little Moir's Food Shack**, a popular strip-mall roadside café that feels more like the laid-back Keys than the hoity-toity Gold Coast.

"a waterfront seafood galley where hot live bands and Floribbean cuisine go hand-in-hand."

South Florida's answer to Beverly Hills, ⑲ **Palm Beach** lets the hoi polloi (that's you) laze on its white-sand municipal beach, kept immaculately free of seaweed. Or cycle alongside the Intracostal Waterway on the Lake Trail, aka the "Trail of Conspicuous Consumption," and gawk at the multimillion-dollar mansions. They say that JFK liked to slip away to ⑳ **Green's Pharmacy**, where everyone from trust-fund babies to bikini-clad college girls gorges on plates of biscuits-and-gravy, omelettes and tasty burgers at an old-fashioned lunch counter. Heading south, ㉑ **Delray Beach** is a lot less stuffy. Its main drag, Atlantic Ave, is chock-a-block with cafés and bars full of those bronzed bods that you'll see taking a dip along the sandy beachfront. Join the cool cats at lantern-lit ㉒ **Dada**, a two-story bungalow, for sipping cocktails and groovin' to live bands.

Your last stop before Miami, ㉓ **Fort Lauderdale Beach** is not the spring-break bacchanalia destination it once was, although you'll find outposts of beach-bummin' bars and motels in between the swanky boutique hotels and multimillion-dollar yachts. The beach itself stretches for 7 miles next to a diamond-white promenade, nearby where swimmers, surfers, jet skiers and beach volleyball players all worship the sun. Not far from the beach, ㉔ **Ask Me Inn** is a homey apartmentlike place with sweet little balconies and beach chairs for guests to borrow. Drive inland to try the famous garlic crabs at the ㉕ **Rustic Inn**, where locals slam down wooden mallets on newspaper-covered tables just to get at the delicious stuff inside. Alternatively, follow the coast south to bewitching Hollywood Beach to chow down on brontosaurus-sized burgers among the junkyard antiques and jungle greenery of ㉖ **Le Tub**, where you can toast the sunset with a cold beer and watch boats sail by.

> **DETOUR** Just east of the Everglades, **Biscayne National Park** is a protected marine sanctuary harboring amazing tropical coral reef systems, most within sight of Miami's skyline. It's only accessible by water: take a glass-bottomed-boat tour; a snorkel or scuba-diving trip; or rent a canoe or kayak to lose yourself in this 300-sq-mile system of islands, underwater shipwrecks and mangrove forests. Get oriented at the park's Convoy Point visitor center, about an hour's drive south of Miami Beach.

Finally, say *bienvenidos a* ㉗ **Miami Beach** as you cruise down glam Ocean Dr. For the hottest clubs and most beautiful beaches, head straight to ㉘ **South Beach**, a kaleidoscopic circus of humanity, from A-list Hollywood celebrities to hormone-crazed 20-something college students. Chic boutique hotels are scattered around SoBe's charming art-deco historic district, but expect to drop some serious coin to stay here. For deco style on a budget, check out the shagalicious ㉙ **Hotel Chelsea**, just a heartbeat from all the action on the happening beachfront promenade. Rising above SoBe's overhyped eating gambles, ㉚ **Joe's Stone Crab** ain't cheap, but you'll never forgive yourself if you don't try what it's famous for. (Tip: the take-out window is less expensive, then you can tote your fresh catch over to the beach for a picnic.) By now you're probably broke, so end your beach bum's trip at ㉛ **Zeke's Roadhouse**, a dive bar with a heady collection of microbrews, right on Lincoln Rd's posh pedestrian mall.

Sara Benson

TRIP INFORMATION

GETTING THERE
From downtown Jacksonville, it's a 30-minute drive east to the beach, which is about 25 miles southeast of the airport.

DO

Anheuser-Busch Brewery
Make reservations for behind-the-scenes brewmaster tours. ☎ 904-696-8373; www.budweisertours.com; 111 Busch Dr, Jacksonville; basic tours free, brewmaster tour adult/child $25/10; ☺ 10am-4pm Mon-Sat

Blowing Rocks Preserve
Explore the lagoon boardwalk, butterfly garden and nature trail alongside a sea-turtle nesting beach. ☎ 561-744-6668; www.nature.org; 574 S Beach Rd, Hobe Sound; adult/child $2/free; ☺ 9am-4:30pm; ♿

Daytona 500 Experience
A shrine to all things Nascar; call ahead to double-check track tour times. ☎ 386-681-6800; www.daytona500experience.com; 1801 W International Speedway Blvd, Daytona; adult/child from $25/20; ☺ 10am-6pm, with seasonal variations; ♿

Ponce Inlet Light Station
Painstakingly restored, with a fine collection of Fresnel lenses. ☎ 386-761-1821; www.ponceinlet.org; 4931 S Peninsula Dr, Ponce Inlet; adult/child $5/1.50; ☺ 10am-6pm, 10am-9pm Memorial Day-Labor Day; ♿

EAT & DRINK

Beach Hut Cafe
Don your board shorts and flip-flops for oh-so-filling breakfasts and lunch specials. ☎ 904-249-3516; 1281 3rd St S, Jacksonville Beach; mains $4-8; ☺ 6am-2:30pm; ♿

Cap's on the Water
Gobble down fresh shrimp and Floridian gumbo on a sunset-view deck. ☎ 904-824-8794; www.capsonthewater.com; 4325 Myrtle St, St Augustine; mains $10-27; ☺ 11:30am-3:30pm & 4:30pm-close Fri-Sun

Da Kine Diego's Insane Burrito
Hawaiian-style surf shack dishes up Cal-Mex fusion burritos and tacos with eclectic salsas. ☎ 21-779-8226; 1360 Hwy A1A, Satellite Beach; mains $5-9; ☺ 11am-9pm; ♿ 🐾

Dada
Detour west of downtown for drinks (skip the dinners, though), eclectic tunes and boho vibes. ☎ 561-330-3232; www.dada.closer magazine.com; 52 N Swinton Ave, Delray Beach; ☺ 5pm-2am

Down the Hatch Seafood Restaurant
Overlooking mangroves and the river, this casual marina eatery serves up killer surf-and-turf with sunset views. ☎ 386-761-4831; www.down-the-hatch-seafood.com; 4894 Front St, Ponce Inlet; mains $16-25; ☺ 11:30am-9pm

Green's Pharmacy
At this vintage diner with mint-green linoleum, be prepared for sticker shock on the blue-plate specials. ☎ 561-832-4443; 151 N County Rd, Palm Beach; mains $9-15; ☺ 6am-3pm Mon-Sat, to 2pm Sun; ♿

Joe's Stone Crab
Opened as a 1913 lunch counter, this swanky seafood and chophouse where the city's movers and shakers dine is tops. ☎ 305-673-0365; www.joesstonecrab.com; 11 Washington Ave, Miami Beach; mains $16-66; ☺ 11:30am-2pm Tue-Sat, 5-10pm Sun-Thu, 5-11pm Fri & Sat, with seasonal variations

Le Tub
Sirloin burgers, barbecue rubs and seafood salads take time to make, so don't be in a hurry, dude. ☎ 954-921-9425; www.theletub.com; 1100 N Ocean Dr, Hollywood Beach; mains $9-21; ☺ noon-4am

Little Moir's Food Shack
Strip-mall café with high-flying seafood fusion dishes like yucca-encrusted corvina or grouper cheeks. ☎ 561-741-3626; www.littlemoirsfoodshack.com; 103 S Hwy 1, Jupiter; mains $15-25; ☺ 11am-9pm Mon-Sat; ♿

Rustic Inn
Weekday seafood lunch specials and the weighty "Admiral's Platter" combo are deals. ☎ 954-584-1637; www.rusticinn.com; 4331 Ravenswood Rd, Fort Lauderdale; mains $7-45; ⏱ 11:30am-10:45pm Mon-Sat, noon-9pm Sun; ♿

Square Grouper Tiki Bar
Grab a bottle of brew and let your troubles float away at Castaways Marina. ☎ 561-575-0252; www.squaregrouper.net; 1111 Love St, Jupiter; ⏱ noon-midnight Sun-Thu, to 1am Fri & Sat

Zeke's Roadhouse
Squeeze inside the bar for cheap pours, then head outside for people-watching: fashionista hotties, Rastafarian bohemians and the downright weird denizens. ☎ 305-672-3118; 625 Lincoln Rd, Miami Beach; ⏱ 4pm-2am

SLEEP

Aku Tiki Inn
Chain-motel standard rooms and kitchenettes by the beach; rates spike during spring break and "Speed Weeks." ☎ 386-252-9631; www.bwakutiki.com; 2225 S Atlantic Ave, Daytona Beach; r $90-200; ♿

Anastasia State Park
Campsite reservations are recommended. Pick up supplies or lunch from Island Joe's camp store. ☎ 904-461-2033; www.floridastate parks.org/anastasia; 1340 Hwy A1A S, St Augustine; per vehicle $8, campsite $28; ⏱ 8am-sunset; ♿ ☺

Ask Me Inn
Side-street apartment complex has a hospitable owner renting eclectic rooms and suites, some with full kitchens. ☎ 954-760-4211; www.askmeinn.com; 300 N Birch Rd, Fort Lauderdale; r $110-150; ♿

Hotel Chelsea
Vintage (read: slightly worn) art-deco rooms with minimalist panache, boudoir lighting and spa bathrobes. Complimentary cocktail hour nightly. ☎ 305-534-4069; www. thehotelchelsea.com; 944 Washington Ave, Miami Beach; r $180-399

Oceanfront Cottages
Simple, tidy kitchenette suites, some with whirlpools and ocean-view decks, near the beach. ☎ 321-725-8474; www.oceanfront cottages.com; 612 Wavecrest Ave, India-lantic; ste $160-350

Pirate Haus Inn
Multilingual, family-friendly hostel in the Old City; breakfast is all-you-can-eat pancakes. ☎ 904-808-1999; www.piratehaus.com; 32 Treasury St, St Augustine; dm $20, r $65-95; ♿

USEFUL WEBSITES
www.miamiandbeaches.com
www.visitflorida.com

LINK YOUR TRIP

www.lonelyplanet.com/trip-planner

Doing Disney & More

WHY GO Let your inner child loose at Mickey's Magic Kingdom, but don't stop there. Orlando has amusements galore for kids of all ages. NASA's Kennedy Space Center is an easy day trip, too, near the wildlife havens and surf-friendly beaches of the Space Coast.

Florida's most popular vacationland destination, Orlando revolves around its theme parks designed for kids, but also anyone who ever wished upon a star and whispered, "I want to go to Disney World." Even if you're not a huge fan of that dang mouse, you'll find a lot more to entertain you in Orlando, including thrill-a-minute water parks. A quick escape from the city, Florida's Space Coast has even more places to play outside: go surfing the waves at Cocoa Beach or watching manatees outside Titusville.

Start your trip in the belly of the magical beast, ❶ **Walt Disney World**. The dream of building the self-proclaimed "Happiest Place on Earth" started in the 1960s, when ol' Walt bought almost 30,000 acres of swamp and woodlands here. Nowadays 16 million people from around the globe visit his famous creation each year. The resort revolves around the ❷ **Magic Kingdom**, where kids, grandparents, honeymooners and everyone in between skips down Main St together toward Cinderella's Castle. Classic rides like Space Mountain, Pirates of the Caribbean and It's a Small World are unbelievably popular, so get in line early. Without any character parades or screaming roller coasters, Disney's ❸ **Epcot** is a less frantic experience. Slow down for the international theme pavilions, or zoom into Future World near Epcot's iconic geodesic dome (yes, it looks just like a golf ball). When it gets too hot to stand in any more lines, take the whole family to cool off at Disney's ❹ **Typhoon Lagoon**, with an abundance of palm trees and a beckoning white-sand beach, plus a snorkeling reef with

TIME
5 – 7 days

DISTANCE
250 miles

BEST TIME TO GO
Sep – Nov &
Jan – Feb

START
Orlando, FL

END
Cocoa Beach,
FL

291

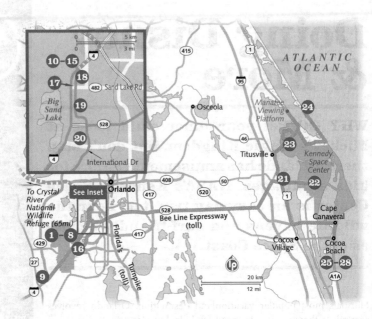

kaleidoscopic tropical fish, Orlando's biggest wave pool and water tubes and slides aplenty.

Staying and eating inside Walt Disney World may save you time but not money. Of all Disney's theme hotels, **5 Disney's Wilderness Lodge** – a homage to Yosemite's Ahwahnee and other great American national-park lodges – and **6 Disney's Fort Wilderness Resort** both provide a little green space for relaxing, plus in-park transportation by boat (slow but tons of fun). Don't expect gourmet kitchens at any of the hotels, but Disney character–hosted dining events are beloved by starry-eyed kids. At Disney's Contemporary Resort, the **7 California Grill** has coveted rooftop views of the Magic Kingdom's nightly fireworks. Foraging further afield, Disney's Animal Kingdom Lodge has standout dining options, from a family-friendly buffet to African-spiced **8 Jiko**, with its sunset-colored dining room. If you'd rather escape all the hullabaloo, the condo-style **9 Omni Orlando Resort at ChampionsGate** is less than half an hour's drive from Walt Disney World.

Just a bit smarter, funnier and faster than dear old Disney, modern **10 Universal Orlando** gets your adrenaline pumping with its revved-up rides and entertaining shows. Divide your time between **11 Universal Studios**, with its movie-themed revues and rides, like the Revenge of the Mummy special-effects roller coaster or seeing Shrek 4-D, and the no-holds-barred **12 Islands of Adventure**, where superheroes race by on motorcycles and thrill rides will either get you soaked or start some rad barf-o-rama. Connecting both parks, ⑬ **Universal Citywalk** is kinda cheesy, but it's an after-dark destination for crankin' live-music clubs to theme restaurants and bars to suit every taste, from Jimmy Buffet Parrotheads to Nascar fans. More than just a restaurant that's a mouthful to say, ⑭ **Bob Marley: A Tribute to Freedom** has an actual recreation of the Rastafarian musical legend's Jamaican home, complete with memorabilia and live reggae bands jammin' nightly in an open-air veranda courtyard. The ⑮ **Hard Rock Hotel** has the most va-va-voom of Universal's resorts; guests get free water-taxi rides and skip-the-line privileges at theme parks. Or you can keep the movie-and-TV-character madness going nonstop at the ⑯ **Nickelodeon Suites Resort**, where suites designed with kids in mind feature SpongeBob Squarepants, Jimmy Neutron and the Rugrats.

Running alongside Universal Orlando, tacky ⑰ **International Drive** is one long traffic-jammed strip of classic tourist traps and American chain restaurants that you might have thought had gone the way of the dinosaurs. For daredevil teenagers,

> **ASK A LOCAL**
>
> "Our best tip for doing Disney right is to: arrive 30 minutes before opening; stay at the park through lunch, and for another hour or so; leave around 2pm or 3pm (when it's hottest and most crowded); take a nap back at the hotel (kids *and* parents), then eat dinner and return to the park at 6pm (lots of people will be leaving then, with screaming, tired children who didn't get a nap); and stay until closing."
>
> *Daniel Boland, Orlando*

⑱ **Wet 'n' Wild** water park delivers high-speed thrills with menacing names like Storm, Mach 5 and Brain Wash – yeowch. A tamer place to while away an afternoon, ⑲ **Pirate's Cove** "adventure" minigolf course has sunken ships, waterfalls and a cannon shot by a skeleton. Ahoy, mateys! At the southern end of I-Dr are Orlando's mega aquatic theme parks, headed up by ⑳ **SeaWorld Orlando**. What everyone comes to see are the spectacular animal shows, but ask yourself: is it right to keep highly intelligent dolphins and orcas (killer whales) captive just so they can perform acrobatic tricks to a rock'n'roll soundtrack? (Watch the controversial documentary *The Cove* for more food for thought.) Look for the manatee exhibit, where endangered "sea cows" rescued by SeaWorld staff are rehabilitated for return to the wild.

When you're ready to escape the concrete jungle and nonstop crowds of Orlando, it's a little over an hour's drive east to the Atlantic Ocean – ah, fresh air! – and Florida's ㉑ **Space Coast**. NASA was founded here in the late 1950s. It was from Cape Canaveral that the first humans to successfully land on the moon launched. Although NASA's space-shuttle program has ended, the ㉒ **Kennedy Space Center** is still a gob-stoppingly cool place. Devote most of your day to the science exhibits and historical museum, IMAX theaters, shuttle-launch simulator and outdoor rocket park. But first take the hop-on, hop-off bus tour of working NASA facilities, walk underneath a real rocket

OUTDOORS

and touch a piece of the moon. Don't be surprised if your bus driver points out alligators hauled out by the roadside or bald eagles nesting in nearby trees.

> **DETOUR** Between December and March, **Crystal River National Wildlife Refuge** (www.fws.gov/crystal river) offers one of the surest bets for seeing Florida's endangered manatees in the wild. It's an unforgettable thrill to take a glass-bottomed-boat cruise, paddle a kayak or go snorkeling and scuba diving while encountering these "sea cows" at home in their natural habitat. The refuge is only accessible by boat. Make reservations with tour-boat operators in the town of Crystal River, about a two-hour drive west of Orlando.

That's because NASA is surrounded by **23** **Merritt Island National Wildlife Refuge**, also a prime stop on the Atlantic Flyway for migratory birds. Stop at the refuge's visitors center east of Titusville for maps and information, then take the 7-mile Black Point Wildlife Drive and head out to the manatee-viewing platform. **24** **Canaveral National Seashore** protects the longest stretch of undeveloped dunes on Florida's east coast. It's split between the wilder southern section, Playalinda Beach (east of Titusville), and family-friendly Apollo Beach further north, which has a helpful visitors center and nature trails for hiking alongside the seemingly endless dunes.

If you're too seduced by the waves to return to Orlando just yet, backtrack south of Titusville to **25** **Cocoa Beach**, where the whimsical 1960s TV show *I Dream of Jeannie* was set. Its beautiful white-sand beaches

"walk underneath a real rocket and touch a piece of the moon."

attract surfers like sharks to a chum slick these days. Plenty of local outfitters can teach you the tricks of the ancient Hawaiian art of wave-riding, including **26** **Cocoa Beach Surf Company**. The town's funky fishing pier is crowded with touristy seafood joints and beachy bars, but hands down the best end-of-the-day views are dockside at **27** **Sunset Waterfront Cafe and Bar**. If you want to hang around the Space Coast overnight, the irresistibly kitschy (and pink!) **28** **Fawlty Towers** is a family-friendly motel with a poolside tiki bar.

Sara Benson

TRIP INFORMATION

GETTING THERE
Walt Disney World is a 25-mile drive southwest of Orlando's airport via Hwy 528 and I-4 to Epcot Center Dr.

DO
Canaveral National Seashore
Barrier island with blissful beaches for swimming, surfing, fishing, hiking and camping. ☎ 321-267-1110; www.nps.gov/cana; Hwy 402, Titusville; adult/child $3/free; ⏲ 6am-6pm Nov-Apr, to 8pm May-Oct, visitors center hr vary; ♿

Cocoa Beach Surf Company
Private and group lessons, weekend clinics and surf camps. ☎ 321-868-8966; www.cocoabeachsurfcompany.com; 4001 N Atlantic Ave, Cocoa Beach; 1hr surfing lesson $40-50; ⏲ by reservation; ♿

Kennedy Space Center
Part historical museum, astronaut tribute and memorial, educational center and theme park; reserve ahead for lunch with an astronaut. ☎ 321-449-4444; www.kennedyspacecenter.com; Orsino; adult/child from $38/28; ⏲ 9am-6pm; ♿

Merritt Island National Wildlife Refuge
Abundant wildlife watching in multiple habitats, including mangrove swamp and hardwood hammock. ☎ 321-861-6667; www.fws.gov/merrittisland; Hwy 402, Titusville; admission free; ⏲ sunrise-sunset, visitors center 8am-4:30pm Mon-Fri, 9am-5pm Sat, plus 9am-5pm Sun Nov-Mar; ♿

Pirate's Cove
In a sea of minigolf courses, this swashbuckler rises to the top. Try Blackbeard's Challenge course, if ye dare. ☎ 407-352-7378; www.piratescove.net; 8501 International Dr, Orlando; adult/child from $11/10; ⏲ 9am-11:30pm; ♿

SeaWorld Orlando
IMAX movies, kiddie rides at Happy Harbor, aquariums and live shows amuse huge crowds. ☎ 407-351-3600; www.seaworld

orlando.com; 7007 SeaWorld Dr, Orlando; adult/child from $79/69; ⏲ daily, with seasonal variations; ♿

Universal CityWalk
Pedestrian shopping mall with a 20-screen cineplex, restaurants and late-night bars and clubs with live music; after 9pm, under 21s not allowed. ☎ 407-363-8000; www.universalorlando.com/citywalk; 6000 Universal Blvd, Orlando; admission free, parking $14; ⏲ 11am-2am; ♿

Universal Orlando
More high-tech than Disney, with plenty of rides and shows for short-attention-span-theater types. ☎ 407-363-8000; www.universalorlando.com; 6000 Universal Blvd, Orlando; adult/child from $80/70; ⏲ daily, with seasonal variations; ♿

Walt Disney World
Spread-out theme parks and attractions are all touched by the magic of Mickey Mouse. ☎ 407-939-6244; http://disneyworld.disney.go.com; off I-4, exit 67, Orlando; adult/child from $79/68; ⏲ daily, with seasonal variations; ♿

Wet 'n' Wild
Twisted water slides, chutes, whirlpools and toboggan rides will scare the bejeezus out of kids, but probably not teens. ☎ 407-351-1800; www.wetnwildorlando.com; 6200 International Dr, Orlando; adult/child $48/42; ⏲ daily, with seasonal variations; ♿

EAT & DRINK
Bob Marley: A Tribute to Freedom
Jerk-spiced chicken, monk stew and veggie patties with yucca fries will fill your soulful belly, mon. ☎ 407-224-3663; www.universalorlando.com; Universal Citywalk; mains $8-16; ⏲ 4-10pm Sun-Thu, to 11pm Fri & Sat

California Grill
Come for the California fusion fare, above-par wine list and spectacular fireworks views; reservations essential. ☎ 407-939-3463; http://disneyworld.disney.go.com; 4600 World Dr, Lake Buena Vista; mains $28-44; ⏲ dinner daily, with seasonal variations; ♿

Jiko
Sophisticated dining room draws inspiration from the African diaspora, with a top-drawer South African wine list; reservations essential. ☎ 407-939-3463; http://disneyworld. disney.go.com; 2901 Osceola Pkwy, Lake Buena Vista; mains $26-41; ☾ dinner daily, with seasonal variations; ⚐

Sunset Waterfront Cafe and Bar
Nothing-special seafood, but outdoor dockside tables have incredible views. ☎ 321-783-8485; www.sunsetwaterfrontcafe andbar.com; 500 W Cocoa Beach Causeway, Cocoa Beach; mains $8-26; ☾ 11:30am-10pm Mon-Sat, 4-10pm Sun; ⚐

SLEEP

Disney's Fort Wilderness Resort
Old West–styled cabins and campsites nestle among pine and cypress trees. ☎ 407-824-2900; http://disneyworld.disney.go.com; 4510 N Fort Wilderness Trail, Lake Buena Vista; campsite $45-120, cabin $270-410; ⚐ ⚐

Disney's Wilderness Lodge
A lodgepole-pine lobby, fireplace and minigeysers welcome you at this imitation Arts and Crafts grand hotel. ☎ 407-824-3200; http://disneyworld.disney.go.com; 901 Timberline Dr, Lake Buena Vista; r $240-495; ⚐

Fawlty Towers
Retro motel rooms near the beach, including some kitchen suites; rates include free movie rentals and fitness-club access. ☎ 321-784-3870; www.fawltytowersresort.com; 100 E Cocoa Beach Causeway, Cocoa Beach; r $75-120; ⚐ ⚐

Hard Rock Hotel
Righteous rock-and-roll party pads and a gigantic white-sand pool complex for 20-somethings, but also fun, family-friendly themed suites. ☎ 407-503-2000; www. universalorlando.com; 5800 Universal Blvd, Orlando; r $235-500; ⚐ ⚐

Nickelodeon Suites Resort
Complete with character breakfasts, nightly TV-themed live shows, a backyard water park with slides and a kids' spa. ☎ 407-387-5437; www.nickhotel.com; 14500 Continental Gateway, Orlando; r $120-290; ⚐

Omni Orlando Resort at ChampionsGate
Luxury multi-bedroom villas, perfect for families, plus a sprawling pool complex with a lazy river ride. ☎ 407-390-6664; www. omnihotels.com; 1500 Masters Blvd, ChampionsGate; r $110-400; ⚐

USEFUL WEBSITES
www.mouseplanet.com
www.orlandoinfo.com

LINK YOUR TRIP
www.lonelyplanet.com/trip-planner

Overseas Highway to Key West

WHY GO Welcome to South Florida's lotusland, where snowbird retirees, proudly self-proclaimed rednecks, Cuban and Bahamian immigrants and rum – lots of rum – make a potent mix. Add sugary white-sand beaches, protected coral reefs and wildlife habitat, endless plates of conch fritters and key lime pie – who can resist?

TIME
3 days

DISTANCE
150 miles

BEST TIME TO GO
Dec – Apr

START
Key Largo, FL

END
Key West, FL

This sun-baked Caribbean archipelago called the Florida Keys is an escape from urban Miami. Here in the "Conch Republic," the motto seems to be "do whatever the hell you want." It's equal parts tacky, trippy and tempting. Hang out for a while, and you may find yourself turning into a "Freshwater Conch" – a mainland transplant – right quick. Wherever and whenever the crazy spirit of these islands moves you, just pull off the highway for biker bars, seafood grills and blissful beaches.

Start in wild eastern Key Largo. Near the causeway toll bridge, kick up your heels at ❶ **Alabama Jack's**. It's a quintessential Keys watering hole: a shack on a mangrove bay full of guys in sleeveless tees ready to get their fish on. On weekend afternoons, live country-and-western bands play. Drive west through sedate Crocodile Lake National Wildlife Refuge and join the Overseas Highway (Hwy 1), which streams for 127 miles all the way to Key West. ❷ **John Pennekamp Coral Reef State Park** is an ocean sanctuary with an aquarium, hiking and paddling trails, glass-bottomed catamaran tours, and snorkel and dive trips that let you glimpse the underwater beauty, as well as the odd *Christ of the Deep,* a sunken 4000lb bronze statue gifted by Italy. Back on dry land, ❸ **Mrs Mac's Kitchen** roadside diner exhibits hick flair: just look at those license plates hanging on the wall. Besides, you know it's gonna be good when the seafood specials list is longer than the

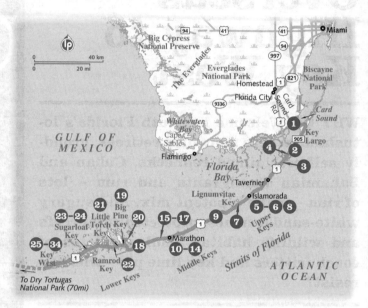

regular menu of good ol' home cooking. For a unique sleep, climb aboard the floating ④ **Key Largo Boatel**.

When you reach Islamorada, you'll finally feel like you're in the islands. Here at last are unbroken horizons of sea and sky, one perfect shade of blue mirroring the other. The ramshackle waterfront building may not look like much, but you'll be surprised how damn good the peel-and-eat shrimp and cracked conch are at the ⑤ **Island Grill**. Near mile marker 73.5, sandy ⑥ **Anne's Beach** opens upon a sky-bright stretch of calm waters for splashing about beside a tunnel of hardwood hammock. Kids will love getting stuck in the tidal mud flats. Down the road, ⑦ **Robbie's Marina** is a combo tourist shop, fishing marina and cruise-boat operator. From here, you can kayak over to the virgin tropical rain forest of Lignumvitae Key, tour Indian Key's historical ruins or get happily buzzed on a party boat. Don't forget to look in on the fearsome tarpon fish before you leave. If the sun is setting and your soul is aching for a romantic hideaway, ⑧ **Casa Morada** is a clean-lined modern boutique hotel by the water that's sweet relief from all the Keys kitsch. If you'd rather pitch a tent, head for ⑨ **Long Key State Park**, where hiking and canoe trails circle a tidal lagoon and a wildlife observation tower.

> "Here at last are unbroken horizons of sea and sky, one perfect shade of blue…"

The Middle Keys are anchored by Marathon. Take heart: you're more than halfway to Key West by now. Stop and stretch your legs at ⑩ **Crane Point**, a nature center with walking trails through a hardwood hammock and wild-life exhibits for kids, including marine touch tanks. Detour south to pretty little ⓫ **Sombrero Beach**, a white-sand playground backed by palm trees where you can swim to your heart's delight. Wet your whistle at the ⓬ **Hurricane Bar & Grille**, where the ambience is right for rednecks, mad fishers, flip-flop–wearing tourists and local bands. Marathon's laid-back ⓭ **Keys Fisheries Market & Marina** is that rare thing in the islands: a nontouristy, unfussy and authentic seafood spot. Heading west, the endearing yet also wonderfully educational ⓮ **Turtle Hospital** is dedicated to helping injured sea turtles return to the wild.

Take a deep breath because next up on the horizon is the gasp-worthy ⓯ **Seven Mile Bridge**. Florida is full of head-spinning causeways, but none longer than this beauty soaring over the Gulf of Mexico. (Never mind that it's actually a bit shorter than 7 miles long.) Walk out onto the parallel ⓰ **Old Seven Mile Bridge**, a hurricane-battered railway and auto causeway no longer used except as the Keys' longest fishing pier. Below the old bridge, about 2 miles from the mainland, ⓱ **Pigeon Key** is a National Historic District. Hop a ferry over to the island to amble around an early-20th-century railroad workers' village built by real-estate tycoon Henry Flagler, or come just for the snorkeling and sun-splashed beach.

The Lower Keys are even more beautifully remote. Picturesque ⓲ **Bahia Honda State Park** has a heart-stopping white-sand beach, albeit sometimes strewn with seaweed.

ASK A LOCAL

"When is the best time to visit Key West? If you don't want hot, come after mid-October. As for big events, Fantasy Fest is amazing and a lot of fun. If you don't need to be here for the big parade, visit during the week before, when hotel rates are lower, but there are still events going on every day, like the **Goombay Festival** (www.goombay-keywest.org) in Bahama Village, where vendors sell food and all kinds of crafts."
Shelby Betz, Key West

Drop by the park's nature center, hike atop an old rail bridge or go snorkeling at Looe Key Reef. On Big Pine Key, ⓳ **National Key Deer Refuge** is a sanctuary for those endangered miniature white-tailed deer that you might see hopping around the flatlands, especially on ⓴ **No Name Key**. To really get away from it all, indulgent ㉑ **Little Palm Island Resort & Spa** is an exclusive private island where Caribbean idyll dreams really do come true. On Ramrod Key, down-home ㉒ **Boondocks Grille & Draft House** has a tiki bar, a karaoke machine, a minigolf course, charbroiled burgers and special treats for your four-legged canine companions. On Sugarloaf Key, take the side road near mile marker 17 next to the airport out to ㉓ **Perky's Bat Tower**, where a 1920s real-estate developer's dream went awry. To eliminate pesky mosquitoes from his planned vacation resort, Richter Perky built this 35ft-high tower and moved in a colony of bats, who promptly flew off, never to return. The mosquitoes stayed. Further west, stop at ㉔ **Baby's Coffee** for fresh-roasted java and truly heavenly key lime pie.

Hurly-burly ㉕ **Key West** is where the Overseas Highway ends and the party really begins. Settle into the island's laid-back lifestyle at the historic ㉖ **Mermaid & the Alligator** bed-and-breakfast or the ㉗ **Orchid Key Inn**, a design-savvy boutique hotel. Catch a Caribbean sunset at ㉘ **Mallory Sq**, then join the parade of freaks (honey, we mean that with love) bar hopping along Duval St. Stumble over to the venerable ㉙ **Green Parrot**, the oldest bar on an island crammed with drunken dives, where you can expect to hear blues bands howling through the clouds of cigarette smoke. With an understandably massive hangover the next day, chow down on deep-fried conch fritters at ㉚ **B&O's Fish Wagon** as you perch on wooden stools and gaze slack-jawed at the mishmash of kitschy found art.

DETOUR ▶ Think you've reached land's end at Key West? You haven't seen **Dry Tortugas National Park** (www.nps.gov/drto), a 2¼-hour ferry ride or 40-minute seaplane flight out into the Gulf of Mexico. This small cluster of coral reefs, named "The Turtles" by Spanish explorer Ponce de León, is a hot spot for diving, snorkeling, bird-watching, fishing and looking longingly out to sea from atop Fort Jefferson. Getting here isn't cheap, but it's worth it just for the unpeopled beaches.

So, what else is there to do in Key West besides eat, drink and be merry? Well, you can pay your respects to Florida's ㉛ **Southernmost Point** (technically, a misnomer, but who's really paying attention by now?) and the bizarre six-toed cats who rule the roost at the ㉜ **Hemingway House**, where "Papa" once lived and wrote – that is, when he wasn't out fishing or drinking Cuba libres. For a more authentic slice of Keys culture, stroll through ㉝ **Bahama Village**, an artsy, colorful Caribbean neighborhood that's only a bit tattered around the edges, or venture inside the ㉞ **Museum of Art & History**, inhabiting a grand 19th-century customs house.

Sara Benson

TRIP INFORMATION

GETTING THERE

From Miami, it's a 60-mile drive southwest to Key Largo partly via toll roads, taking over an hour.

DO

Bahia Honda State Park

Take a cool dip in the sea, rent kayaks or hop on a snorkel boat. ☎ 305-872-2353; www.bahiahondapark.com; 36850 Overseas Hwy, Big Pine Key; per vehicle $8; ☼ park 8am-sunset daily, nature center 9am-noon & 1-5pm Thu-Mon; ⛎

Crane Point

Kids will love this ecofriendly nature center; don't miss the historic Bahamian and Cracker houses. ☎ 305-743-9100; www.cranepoint. net; 5550 Overseas Hwy, Marathon; adult/ child $11/7; ☼ 9am-5pm Mon-Sat, noon-5pm Sun; ⛎

Hemingway House

Gorgeous Spanish-colonial home shows off antiques and the famous novelist's memorabilia. ☎ 305-294-1136; www.hemingway home.com; 907 Whitehead St, Key West; adult/child $12/6; ☼ 9am-5pm

John Pennekamp Coral Reef State Park

Get wet at the USA's original underwater park. ☎ 305-451-1202; www.pennekamp park.com; 102601 Hwy 1, Key Largo; per vehicle $8, 2½hr boat tour adult/child $24/17; ☼ 8am-sunset; ⛎

Museum of Art & History

It's filled with folk art, Caribbean artifacts and videos about pirates and Papa Hemingway. ☎ 305-295-6616; www.kwahs.com; 281 Front St, Key West; adult/child $10/5; ☼ 9:30am-4:30pm

National Key Deer Refuge

Pick up information and maps and browse the displays at headquarters. ☎ 305-872-2239; www.fws.gov/nationalkeydeer; Big Pine Key Plaza, 28950 Watson Blvd, Big Pine

Key; admission free; ☼ park 24hr daily, office 8am-4:30pm Mon-Fri; ⛎

Pigeon Key

Island ferries depart four or five times daily; call for schedules and reservations. ☎ 305-743-5999; www.pigeonkey.net; 1 Knights Key Blvd, Marathon; adult/child $11/8.50; ☼ 10am-4pm; ⛎

Robbie's Marina

Reservations recommended for boat tours and snorkeling trips. ☎ 305-664-9814, tickets 800-979-3370; www.robbies.com; 77522 Overseas Hwy, Islamorada; tours adult/child from $20/15; ☼ hours vary; ⛎

Turtle Hospital

Daily schedules for behind-the-scenes tours of this wildlife-rehabilitation facility vary (reservations advised). ☎ 305-743-2552; www.turtlehospital.org; 2396 Overseas Hwy, Marathon; adult/child $15/7.50; ☼ 9am-6pm; ⛎

EAT & DRINK

Alabama Jack's

Waterfront biker bar has been dishing up homemade fare like crab cakes and fried grouper sandwiches since 1947. ☎ 305-248-8741; www.alabamajacks.com; 58000 Card Sound Rd, Key Largo; mains $4-15; ☼ 11am-7pm

Baby's Coffee

"Dark & stormy" Cuban roasts, rich "Sexpresso" and top-shelf key-lime pie to go. ☎ 305-744-9866; www.babyscoffee.com; MM 15.1, Overseas Hwy, Sugarloaf Key; items $3-6; ☼ 6:30am-6pm Mon-Fri, 7am-5pm Sat, 8am-5pm Sun

Boondocks Grille & Draft House

Live entertainment almost nightly at the Keys' biggest tiki hut. ☎ 305-872-4094; www.boondocks.us.com; MM27.5 Overseas Hwy, Ramrod Key; mains $10-20; ☼ 11am-1am; ⛎ 👶

B&O's Fish Wagon

Roly-poly conch fritters, fried-fish sandwiches and bottles of Bud, ahoy. ☎ 305-294-9272;

www.bosfishwagon.com; 801 Caroline St, Key West; mains $5-18; ☺ 11am-9pm; ♿

Green Parrot
At this rogues cantina, check out the Hieronymus Bosch—like painting over the urinals. ☎ 305-294-6133; www.greenparrotbar.com; 601 Whitehead St, Key West; ☺ 10am-4am Mon-Sat, noon-4am Sun

Hurricane Bar & Grille
Sassy staff will bring you bacon sliders and butt-kickin' house cocktails. ☎ 305-743-2220; www.thehurricanegrille.com; 4650 Overseas Hwy, Marathon; mains $8-19; ☺ 11am-2am

Island Grill
Casual, contemporary Floribbean fare with breezy ocean views and lotsa live bands. ☎ 305-664-8400; www.keysislandgrill.com; 85501 Overseas Hwy, Islamorada; mains $8-25; ☺ 7am-10pm Sun-Thu, 7am-11pm Fri & Sat

Keys Fisheries Market & Marina
Famous for its lobster Reuben sandwiches, Cajun-fried fresh fish and colossal stone-crab claws (in season). ☎ 305-743-4353; www.keysfisheries.com; 3502 Gulfview Ave, Marathon; mains $8-15; ☺ 11am-9pm; ♿

Mrs Mac's Kitchen
Serving honest-to-goodness Keys seafood and key-lime freezes inside a crowded, coral-pink house. ☎ 305-451-3722; www.mrsmacskitchen.com; 99336 Overseas Hwy, Key Largo; mains $4-18; ☺ 7am-9:30pm Mon-Sat; ♿

SLEEP

Casa Morada
Sea-view suites mix Mexican antiques with mod cons; complimentary breakfast and yoga classes. Kayaks and bicycles available for rent. ☎ 305-664-0044; www.casamorada.com; 136 Madeira Rd, Islamorada; ste $249-659

Key Largo Boatel
Relaxing, yet slightly cramped and aging houseboats enjoy sun-soaked views over Largo Sound. ☎ 305-766-0871; www.keylargohouseboat.com; 47 Shoreland Dr, Key Largo; r $75-200; ♿

Little Palm Island Resort & Spa
This romantic adults-only, all-suites hotel is only accessible by boat or seaplane. Skip the full meal plan or else you might burst. ☎ 800-343-8567; www.littlepalmisland.com; 28500 Overseas Hwy, Little Torch Key; ste $600-1300

Long Key State Park
Come for picnicking, beachcombing, paddling, and tent and RV camping (reservations essential). ☎ 305-664-4815; www.floridastateparks.org/longkey; 67400 Overseas Hwy, Long Key; per vehicle $5, campsite $36; ☺ 8am-sunset; ♿ 🅿

Mermaid & the Alligator
Devour a full breakfast poolside at this breezy two-story Victorian mansion and cigar-maker's Conch-style cottage. ☎ 305-294-1894; www.kwmermaid.com; 729 Truman Ave, Key West; r $200-320

Orchid Key Inn
Tailored "tropical deco" rooms come with kitchenettes and luxurious extras like Egyptian-cotton robes and plasma TVs. ☎ 305-296-9915; www.orchidkeyinn.com; 1004 Duval St, Key West; r $160-290; 🅿

USEFUL WEBSITES
www.fla-keys.com
www.floridakeys.org

LINK YOUR TRIP
TRIP
www.lonelyplanet.com/trip-planner

33 48 Hours in Miami p279
37 Go Wild in the Everglades p303
39 Freaky Florida p313

Go Wild in the Everglades

WHY GO Exchange the urban jungles of Miami for South Florida's iconic ecosystem, the 'Glades. Wade into its vast "river of grass," where alligators float through mangrove swamps, flocks of birds soar across flooded horizons and endangered manatees perform elegant underwater ballet in the bays.

TIME
2 – 3 days

DISTANCE
210 miles

BEST TIME TO GO
Nov – Apr

START
Homestead, FL

END
Everglades City, FL

Don't you dare visit Miami without taking time for a day trip out to the Everglades. Starting just a little over an hour's drive from South Beach, this ecological wonderland is the USA's largest subtropical wilderness, flush with myriad endangered and rare species, from alien-looking "sea cows" (manatees), gnarly alligators and tawny panthers, to delicate orchid and water-nymph plants. Despite rampant over-development and agricultural run-off that has shrunk and polluted the 'Glades since the early 1900s, unique biotic "islands of life" where wildlife still thrive have been restored, both inside and around Everglades National Park.

After enduring Miami metro traffic, stop off at the famous 1950s farm stand ❶ Robert Is Here. Wander around the petting zoo while you sip a sweet key-lime-pie shake. On weekends, check out the antique cars and jive to live bands. The flat farmland becomes more wild and tangled, studded with pine and cypress trees, as you drive southwest toward ❷ Everglades National Park. Duck inside the Ernest Coe Visitor Center for a quick, painless lesson about 'Glades ecology, including those all-important differences between gators and crocs.

From the park's entrance station, it's a 38-mile winding drive down to Florida Bay. Along the way, detour on the 0.8-mile Ahniga Trail, a popular boardwalk where you're almost guaranteed to spot alligators and diverse bird life. Beyond the sunset-worthy Pa-hay-okee Overlook,

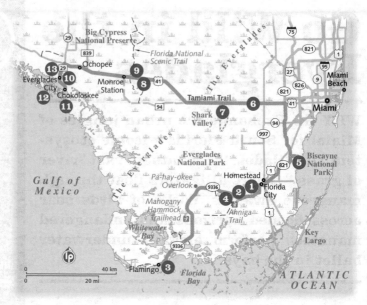

the 0.5-mile Mahogany Hammock Trail is a more secluded boardwalk stroll through junglelike vegetation. Here just a few inches of elevation makes all the difference, creating a flood-resistant biodiverse island. At the end of the main park road in Flamingo, hop aboard a boat tour or rent a canoe or kayak for backcountry exploration at ❸ **Flamingo Marina**. Since there's no lodge here, you'll need to bring along your own tent to pitch back at ❹ **Long Pine Key Campground**.

Both Homestead and Florida City have run-of-the-mill motels, *taquerías* and seafood shacks, if you'd rather stay in town. Heading north, it's a quick detour to ❺ **Black Point Marina**. The park has beautiful bayside hiking trails (just ignore "Mt Trashmore" dump marring the background), but what everyone comes to see on weekends are inebriated owners trying to haul their boats into and out of the water. Catch the free show from the deck of the park's bar and grill, where you can feast on conch fritters, lobster bisque and damn decent burgers.

Roughly where Little Havana's Calle Ocho ends, the ❻ **Tamiami Trail** begins. This modern highway cuts straight west through the 'Glades all the way to the Gulf of Mexico. At first, you'd be forgiven for thinking it's nothing but a corridor of Old Florida kitsch, with gator farms, roadside seafood shacks and tribal-run casinos. Pass by the ecologically questionable airboat and swamp-buggy tour outfitters. Instead, take a tram safari through ❼ **Shark**

Valley, Everglades National Park's northern outpost. Or rent a bike and cycle along the valley's 15-mile paved, mostly flat loop trail, pausing to climb the panoramic observation tower. Shorter nature trails through hardwood forest and sawgrass slough start near Shark Valley's visitors center.

Further west along the Tamiami Trail (aka Hwy 41 here), pull off at ❽ **Big Cypress Gallery**. In the tradition of Ansel Adams, gallery owner Clyde Butcher prints large-format black-and-white photography that elevates the 'Glades and South Florida's swamps to a spiritual level. A little further down the highway is the Oasis Visitor Center for the swampy ❾ **Big Cypress National Preserve**, home to scenic loop drives and challenging hikes along the Florida Scenic Trail. The latter can be flooded waist-deep during the rainy season (roughly, from May to October). You'll find a handful of first-come, first-served primitive and developed campgrounds signposted off Hwy 41.

For fresh seafood (y'all are starvin' by now, right?), keep trucking west to Ochopee, then turn south toward the tiny pit-stop of Everglades City. Pop open a cold beer at the raw bar overlooking the marina or grab a table inside the ❿ **Oyster House Restaurant** for conch fritters, steamed shrimp and fried grouper. The place even has its own 'Glades observation tower. Further along, in the end-of-the-road fishing village of Chokoloskee, the ⓫ **Smallwood Store**, built on stilts by the water's edge, is a time capsule of Old Florida. Once a Native American trading post, today this general store is a museum. Once you've come this far, you're back inside Everglades National Park. Boat tours of the park's ⓬ **10,000 Islands**, which float temptingly just offshore, depart from back in Everglades City. You can rent canoes and kayaks or join a guided paddling tour at ⓭ **Ivey House**, an eco-friendly B&B owned by a 'Glades naturalist.

Sara Benson

> **ASK A LOCAL**
>
> "I always look forward to heading down to Flamingo and getting in a kayak. It's only two hours from Miami city, but it's a world away. It's so soulful, and relaxed. If you paddle out into the bay, you're often able to bump into something – whether a sting ray, a shark or a flock of wading birds. Very lucky visitors might see manatees, or if they really go out of their way, a flamingo."
>
> *Greg Litten, Everglades National Park ranger*

"black-and-white photography that elevates the 'Glades and South Florida's swamps to a spiritual level."

TRIP INFORMATION

GETTING THERE
Homestead is a 40-mile drive southwest of the metro Miami area, mostly via toll roads.

DO

Big Cypress Gallery
Make reservations for Clyde's private swamp walks in mid-February. ☎ 239-695-2428; www.clydebutcher.com; 52388 Tamiami Trail, Ochopee; admission free; ⊙ 10am-5pm

Big Cypress National Preserve
Swamps and forests are home to adventurous hiking trails, scenic drives and roadside campgrounds. ☎ 239-695-1201; www.nps.gov/bicy; 33100 Tamiami Trail, Ochopee; admission free; ⊙ 24hr, visitors center 9am-4:30pm; &

Everglades National Park
About 1.5 million acres of wilderness open for wildlife watching, hiking, boating and fishing. ☎ 305-242-7700; www.nps.gov/ever; 40001 SR-9336, Homestead; per vehicle $10; ⊙ 24hr, visitor center 9am-5pm; &

Flamingo Marina
Boat tours typically depart daily, weather permitting; reservations recommended, especially in winter. ☎ 239-695-3101; Everglades National Park; 90min boat tours adult/child $27/13; ⊙ hours vary; &

Shark Valley
Park concessionaire runs narrated tram tours and rents bicycles. ☎ 305-221-8455; www.sharkvalleytramtours.com; Tamiami Trail; 2hr tours adult/child $18/11, bicycle rental per hr $8; ⊙ daily tour schedules vary; &

Smallwood Store
Yesteryear trading post and general store now operates as a small historical museum. ☎ 239-695-2989; www.florida-everglades

.com/chokol; Chokoloskee; admission free; ⊙ 10am-5pm daily Dec-Apr, 10am-4pm Fri-Tue May-Nov; &

EAT

Black Point Marina
At the bar-and-grill, stick with seafood classics and cold beer; bring mosquito repellant. ☎ 305-258-3918; www.miamidade.gov/parks; 24775 SW 87th Ave, Cutler Bay; mains $8-20; ⊙ 11am-10pm; &

Oyster House Restaurant
Serves hush puppies in every seafood basket and stone-crab claws in season. ☎ 239-695-2073; www.oysterhouserestaurant.com; Chokoloskee Causeway, Hwy 29 S, Everglades City; mains $5-23; ⊙ 11am-9pm Sun-Thu, to 10pm Fri & Sat; &

Robert Is Here
An unmissable family-run fruit stand vending fresh produce, ice-cream shakes and alligator jerky. ☎ 305-246-1592; www.robertishere.com; 19200 SW 344th St, Homestead; shakes $5; ⊙ 8am-7pm Nov-Aug; & ⊛

SLEEP

Ivey House
Beautifully renovated 1920s lodge with Old Florida atmosphere offers spick-and-span rooms and a hideaway cottage. ☎ 239-695-3299; www.iveyhouse.com; 107 Camellia St, Everglades City; r $70-145; ⊛

Long Pine Key Campground
First-come, first-served campground with tidy drive-in tent and RV sites. ☎ 305-242-7700; www.nps.gov/ever; 6 miles west of Ernest Coe Visitor Center, Everglades National Park; campsite $16; & ⊛

USEFUL WEBSITES
www.evergladestrail.org
www.florida-everglades.com

www.lonelyplanet.com/trip-planner

LINK YOUR TRIP

High Life Down on the Gulf Coast

HISTORY & CULTURE

WHY GO It's all about the sybaritic lifestyle on Florida's other coast, from rolling your own cigars in Tampa's Ybor City to lazing around ritzy beach towns like Naples to finding Jimmy Buffet's cheeseburger in paradise. If you're lucky, you might find your own private island hideaway, too.

TIME
3 – 4 days

DISTANCE
350 miles

BEST TIME TO GO
Oct – Apr

START
Tampa, FL

END
Naples, FL

This is the flip side of Florida. Like a gorgeous half-sister to the Atlantic Coast, the state's western Gulf Coast (ie not the Panhandle) is the stuff of tropical dreams: pearly sands dipped into turquoise seas, fiery red sunsets and more than 100 barrier islands just waiting for you to get your feet wet. Whether you hang out in bohemian beach towns, or mix with the rich and famous in exclusive seaside resorts, you can't fail to uncover the good life here.

Set beside a mesmerizingly blue bay, Tampa is a metro hub. But it has small-town roots – just amble through ❶ **Ybor City**. Along the cobblestone streets of this reborn 19th-century Spanish and Cuban historic district are chic nightlife and eateries. But the best reason to come is to learn how to roll cigars at the ❷ **Gonzalez y Martinez Cigar Company**. It's next door to the beautifully ornate 1920s Columbia Restaurant building, a local landmark. Other historic cigar factories and storefronts along 7th Ave, which also sell mostly Honduran and Dominican blends (fie upon that Cuban import ban!), let you watch cigar-rolling masters at work. Cuban restaurants are a dime a dozen around here, but partyin' crowds favor ❸ **Mema's Alaskan Tacos**. Afterward, hit the bars (include the city's first microbrewery) inside the double-decker ❹ **Centro Ybor**, which gets even livelier on the first Saturday evening of every month during Artwalk events at local galleries, artists' studios and fine-arts performance spaces.

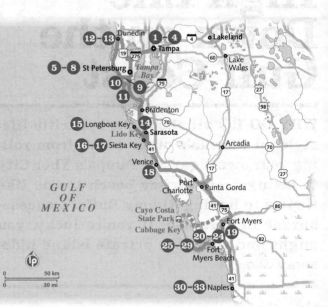

Speaking of art, downtown St Petersburg, with its historical waterfront district facing Tampa Bay, claims two top-notch art museums. At the **5** **Salvador Dalí Museum**, you'll find the largest collection of this surrealist master's paintings outside Spain. Not far away, the globe-spanning **6** **Museum of Fine Arts** exhibits everything from Greco-Roman antiquities and modern American paintings to contemporary photography and risk-taking installation art. Feel like a million bucks yourself at the **7** **Vinoy Renaissance**, a national historic hotel and the choice of celebrities, socialites and politicians since the Jazz Age. This showplace is at the southern edge of the charming **8** **Coffee Pot Bayou** neighborhood, known for its Mediterranean revival–style homes.

You won't really feel like you're living the high life until you hit the beach. First make a quick detour and fearlessly elbow the crowds aside at **9** **Ted Peters Famous Smoked Fish** for down-home seafood delights, best munched atop salty crackers. Then sail across the causeway over to the funky seaside town of **10** **St Petersburg Beach**, the start of a seductive strand of barrier beaches stretching north for over 30 miles. Its southernmost point is **11** **Fort De Soto Park**, a tranquil stretch of soft white sand with a perfectly swimmable shoreline, plus cycling and canoe trails. Then slowly drive north along the gulf, passing kitschy old motor hotels, beach bars, fishing marinas and seafood shacks, all the way to escapist **12** **Honeymoon Island**, which starred in a 1940s *Life* magazine contest for newlyweds. Today this state-park gem is a magnet for swimming, bird-watching, surfing and kayaking. For even more unspoiled natural beaches, hop a ferry over to ⑬ **Caladesi Island**.

Cruise south along I-275 toward Sarasota, an affluent beach resort. In the Roaring Twenties, its fame soared after John Ringling made Sarasota the winter home for his traveling circus. The Ringlings were also great patrons of the arts and avid collectors. Be wowed by the family's priceless acquisitions and tour their Cà d'Zan mansion at the ⑭ **Ringling Museum Complex**, north of downtown. Don't overlook the tiny circus-history museum, with its calliopes, sequined costumes and vintage posters. Just offshore, Sarasota's barrier islands are beatific bayside escapes, tempting with their powdery

HELLO, SUNSHINE!

Wave goodbye to Tampa as you soar over the epic **Sunshine Skyway Bridge**. It measures an astounding 5.5 miles long and rises over 430ft above the bay at its highest point. As the world's longest cable-stayed concrete bridge, it's a dizzying sight, especially at twilight. It's not Florida's longest bridge, however; that honor goes to the Keys' Seven Mile Bridge (actually just 6.79 miles long, but who's counting?).

white sands. Cross the bay to Longboat Key, where locals swear by the stiff drinks and fresh catch at the marina's ⑮ **Moore's Stone Crab Restaurant**. Further south, lazy-daisy ⑯ **Siesta Key** has a low-key, alternative vibe. Show up on Sunday around sunset to join the drum circle or just toast the end of another beautiful day at the beach with chilled margaritas. Groove midway down the key to bed down at the ⑰ **Tropical Shores Beach Resort**, only a short walk from the sands. Just south of Sarasota, ⑱ **Venice** has another blessedly long, sun-kissed stretch of sand, surf enough to bump a boogie board on, and a fishing pier with killer sunset views and a tiki bar.

Keep going with the lifestyles-of-the-rich-and-famous theme at Fort Myers' ⑲ **Edison & Ford Winter Estates**. Inspect inventor Thomas Edison's botanical laboratory, which is still chock-full of gizmos as if he'd just stepped away to refill his coffee pot, and stroll around the bountiful gardens that provided scientific research fodder. Edison's one-time business partner, the auto maker Henry Ford, moved in next door in 1916, and you can tour both of these self-made men's homes today. A 30-minute drive southwest, ⑳ **Fort Myers Beach** is one of the Gulf Coast's rowdiest, most redneck beach towns. It's worth the drive out to solitary ㉑ **Lovers Key State Park** for peaceful swimming, paddling, hiking or bird-watching.

"escapist Honeymoon Island, which starred in a 1940s Life *magazine contest for newlyweds."*

Sunsets over the gulf are phenomenal there. At the beach's Fish Tail Marina, ㉒ **Fish House Restaurant** is where you'll often see boat captains chowing down on the killer grouper sandwiches outside with cold beers in hand. The beach's main drag, Estero Blvd, is chock-a-block with cookie-cutter condo hotels and retro motels. The dazzlingly white ㉓ **Best Western Beach Resort** stands out, not just for its soothingly clean-lined, contemporary rooms but also its sparkling swimming pool fronting the gulf. Budget-savers take refuge at the family-run ㉔ **Sun Deck Inn & Suites** – just look for the hand-crafted miniature lighthouses out front.

South of Fort Myers, paradisiacal ㉕ **Sanibel & Captiva Islands** are a perfect hideaway for reclusive millionaires, but also give the hoi polloi a chance to comb the beaches for souvenir seashells (learn everything you need to know at the ㉖ **Bailey-Matthews Shell Museum**). Dig in at one of the islands' chic seafood eateries along the main road, or fuel up for a day of exploration at the country-kitsch ㉗ **Over Easy Café**. Many visitors rent bicycles to scoot around the islands, or even just to cycle the 5-mile scenic loop through ㉘ **JN "Ding" Darling National Wildlife Refuge**, past fishing holes, canoe trails and hiking paths. Expect to spot alligators and abundant bird life here, especially during winter on the tidal mud flats. Back in Old Town Sanibel, the modest, neat-as-a-pin ㉙ **Tarpon Tale Inn** is just a short walk from bayside beaches.

> **DETOUR**
>
> Among Florida's largest undeveloped barrier islands, **Cayo Costa State Park** (www.floridastateparks.org/cayocosta) is a do-it-yourself adventure. It's worth bringing your own everything just to experience the crystal-clear waters, shady palms and gumbo-limbo hammocks. Just south is **Cabbage Key** (www.cabbagekey.com), where Jimmy Buffet found his cheeseburger in paradise, and Ernest Hemingway once slept in these 1930s wooden cottages. The only way to reach the islands is by boat, with departures from Bolkeelia or Pineland, about a 45-minute drive from downtown Fort Myers.

Wind up your high-life tour down in romantic ㉚ **Naples**, where ornate houses with manicured gardens have peek-a-boo views of the gulf. The white-sand beaches are lovely and less crowded here. For culture vultures, the ㉛ **Philharmonic Center for the Arts** supports a forward-thinking art museum. Downtown in Old Naples, swanky 5th Ave is awash in citrus-colored storefront boutiques, Italianate cafés and the Old World–style ㉜ **Inn on Fifth**. Closer to the pier, ㉝ **Campiello** is the solution to a foodie's dilemma: will it be seafood or Italian tonight? (Answer: both.)

Sara Benson

HISTORY & CULTURE

TRIP INFORMATION

GETTING THERE
Tampa is an 85-mile drive southwest of Orlando via I-4, taking about 1½ hours without traffic.

DO

Bailey-Matthews Shell Museum
Explore the wide world of mollusks, from rare fossils to South Florida's colorful native species. ☎ 239-395-2233; http://shellmuseum.org; 3075 Sanibel-Captiva Rd, Sanibel; adult/child $7/4; ⊙ 10am-5pm; 🚻

Caladesi Island
White-sand beaches, wildlife watching, bayside kayak trails and a snack bar. ☎ 727-734-5918, ferry info 727-734-1501; www.floridastateparks.org/caladesi; 1 Causeway Blvd, Dunedin; round-trip adult/child $10/6; ⊙ ferry departures hourly 10am-3pm; 🚻

Edison & Ford Winter Estates
Tour two gracious homes and botanical gardens, and peek into the inventor's lab. ☎ 239-334-7419; www.efwefla.org; 2350 McGregor Blvd, Fort Myers; adult/child $20/11; ⊙ 9am-5:30pm

Fort De Soto Park
For family-friendly swimming beaches, hiking and paddling nature trails and a historic fort. ☎ 727-893-9185; www.pinellascounty.org.park; 35000 Pinellas Bayway S, Tierra Verde; admission free; ⊙ 8am-sunset; 🚻

Gonzalez y Martinez Cigar Company
Cuban-American family of cigar makers has been rollin' 'em by hand since the late 19th century. ☎ 813-247-2469; 2025 E 7th Ave, Ybor City; admission free; ⊙ 10am-5pm Mon-Sat

Honeymoon Island
Climb the nature center's observation deck and kayak through Pelican Cove. ☎ 727-469-5942; www.floridastateparks.org/honeymoonisland; 1 Causeway Blvd, Dunedin; per vehicle $8; ⊙ 8am-sunset; 🚻

JN "Ding" Darling National Wildlife Refuge
It's free to visit the refuge's educational center, which keeps shorter hours. ☎ 239-472-1100; www.fws.gov/dingdarling; MM2, Sanibel-Captiva Rd, Sanibel; per vehicle/cyclist $5/1; ⊙ wildlife drive 7am-½hr before sunset, closed Fri; 🚻

Lovers Key State Park
Sweet relief from spring-break party central; bicycle, canoe and kayak rentals available. ☎ 239-463-4588; www.floridastateparks.org/loverskey; 8700 Estero Blvd, Fort Myers Beach; per vehicle $8; ⊙ 8am-sunset; 🚻

Museum of Fine Arts
Startling broad collection pulls together everything from European masterworks to pre-Columbian artifacts. ☎ 727-896-2667; www.fine-arts.org; 225 Beach Dr NE, St Petersburg; adult/child $14/8; ⊙ 10am-5pm Tue-Sat, 1-5pm Sun; 🚻

Philharmonic Center for the Arts
Modern-art masters and thought-provoking rotating exhibitions of contemporary works, as well as orchestral performances. ☎ 239-597-1900; www.thephil.org; 5833 Pelican Bay Blvd, Naples; adult/child $8/4; ⊙ 10am-4pm Tue-Sat, noon-4pm Sun

Ringling Museum Complex
Explore the circus baron's Gilded Age mansion, art collections and secret gardens. ☎ 941-359-5700; www.ringling.org; 5401 Bay Shore Rd, Sarasota; adult/child $25/10; ⊙ 10am-5pm Thu-Tue, 10am-8pm Wed

Salvador Dalí Museum
An impressive collection covers the mad-genius artist's entire range. ☎ 727-823-3767; www.salvadordalimuseum.org; 1000 3rd St S, St Petersburg; adult/student/child $17/12/4; ⊙ 10am-5:30pm Mon-Wed, Fri & Sat, 10am-8pm Thu, noon-5:30pm Sun; 🚻

EAT & DRINK

Campiello
Posh wine list complements the Floridian seafood and seasonal Italian cooking;

HISTORY &
CULTURE

reservations recommended. ☎ 239-435-1166; www.campiello.damico.com; 1177 3rd St S, Naples; mains $23-34; ⊙ 11:30am-3pm & 5-10pm

Fish House Restaurant

Savor the waterfront views, hot crab dip, hush puppies and frozen rum runners. ☎ 239-765-6766; 7200 Estero Blvd, Fort Myers Beach; mains $10-30; ⊙ 11am-10pm; ♿

Mema's Alaskan Tacos

Fish, gator, red-meat and veggie tacos, plus homemade tamales and dozens of micro-brews. ☎ 813-242-8226; http://memas alaskantacos.com; 1724 E 8th Ave, Ybor City; items $3-8; ⊙ 11am-1am Sun-Wed, 11am-3am Thu-Sat; ♿

Moore's Stone Crab Restaurant

Only come for the stone crabs in season (October to March). ☎ 941-383-1748; www.stonecrabstoyourdoor.com; 800 Broadway St, Longboat Key; mains $12-25; ⊙ 11:30am-9:30pm, with seasonal variations; ♿

Over Easy Café

Omelettes and eggs Benedict all kinds of ways (breakfast served until 2:30pm daily), fresh salads and grilled sandwiches, and blue-plate dinner specials. ☎ 239-472-2625; www.overeasycafesanibel.com; 730 Tarpon Rd, Sanibel; mains $6-18; ⊙ 7am-8pm; ♿ 🐾

Ted Peters Famous Smoked Fish

Local dive is always jam-packed for its smoked-fish spread and salmon dinners; cash only. ☎ 727-381-7931; 1350 Pasadena Ave S, South Pasadena; mains $6-19; ⊙ 11:30am-7:30pm Wed-Mon

SLEEP

Best Western Beach Resort

Low-slung beauty, just steps from beach bars and seafood restaurants, almost makes you forget it's a chain. ☎ 239-463-6000; www.bestwestern.com; 684 Estero Blvd, Fort Myers Beach; r $145-210; ♿ 🐾

Inn on Fifth

Cocoon inside this classy Mediterranean-inspired boutique hotel with plush ameni-ties, all right downtown. ☎ 239-403-8777; www.innonfifth.com; 699 5th Ave S, Naples; r $150-220

Sun Deck Inn & Suites

Amiable hosts rent nothing-fancy but still comfy apartment studios and suites. ☎ 239-463-1842; www.sundeckresort.com; 1051 3rd St, Fort Myers Beach; r $85-160; ♿

Tarpon Tale Inn

Cute cluster of contemporary cottage bun-galow studios and suites on the island's east end. ☎ 239-472-0939; www.tarpontale.com; 367 Periwinkle Way, Sanibel; r $100-255; ♿

Tropical Shores Beach Resort

Beachy at-home contemporary studios and suites; some have kitchens and shared sun-decks. ☎ 941-349-3330; www.tropical shores.com; 6717 Sara Sea Circle, Siesta Key; r $100-220; ♿ 🐾

Vinoy Renaissance

Candy-pink waterfront palace that's ineffably posh offers beach-chic bay-view rooms and a gigantic outdoor pool. ☎ 727-894-1000; www.marriott.com; 501 5th Ave NE, Tampa; r $200-500; ♿

USEFUL WEBSITES

www.fortmyers-sanibel.com
www.visittampabay.com

LINK YOUR TRIP

www.lonelyplanet.com/trip-planner

TRIP

Freaky Florida

WHY GO Florida overflows with wacky, oddball roadside Americana. Take a wild ride along the Atlantic Coast; detour inland to hunt ghosts, gators and even mermaids; and experience kooky, end-of-the-world Key West. Then you'll get a taste of what the Sunshine State offers lovers of the bizarre and the strange.

TIME
5 days

DISTANCE
750 miles

BEST TIME TO GO
Year-Round

START
St Augustine, FL

END
Key West, FL

Alligator wrestling, mermaids and coral castles: Florida has so much weirdness, it's hard to know where to begin. So, let's take it from the top – of the state, that is.

Perched on the northern Atlantic Coast, the city of St Augustine is the oldest occupied European settlement in North America. Ransacked by pirates, its old colonial village is allegedly rife with ghosts, especially after dark, or so say fans of the paranormal. By day, entertain equally fanciful stories at the ❶ Fountain of Youth. In 1513, Spanish explorer Ponce de León supposedly drank from this natural spring revered by Timucuan tribespeople. The Spaniard lived to a ripe old age, and so the apocryphal legend was born. Go on, take a drink – test out the magical theory for yourself.

From Daytona Beach, then let the road signs (or the spirits) guide you inland along county back roads to ❷ Cassadaga Spiritualist Camp, founded in the 1890s, when a global fever for spiritualism peaked. Today 40-odd mediums work to help visitors communicate with beings on a higher plane, including departed loved ones; half-hour readings cost at least $40. If you dare, take a walk around spooky, mist-laden Spirit Lake afterward, then check out the 1920s ❸ Cassadaga Hotel, assuredly haunted by "friendly" ghosts.

Get ready for Orlando, home to more freaky kitsch than you can throw a pair of Mickey Mouse ears at. But even before Walt Disney built his Magic Kingdom, there was ❹ Gatorland. Trumpeting itself as the "Alligator Capital of the World," this old-fashioned 1940s theme park stages amusing shows like "Gator Jumparoo" and the always popular human-versus-alligator wrestling matches. Snap a photo of yourself standing fearlessly inside the giant-sized gator jaws by the entrance. Meander west over to the Gulf Coast to ❺ Weeki Wachee Springs State Park. Since the 1950s, vacationing families and celebrities alike have been hypnotized by the underwater mermaid shows, viewed from a submerged theater built by an ex-Navy frogman. Today, both sexes perform in the park's hokey submarine revues, which actually require quite a lot of stamina and determination, as the mermaids and mermen don't get to wear scuba gear.

From Orlando, it's a long haul south to Miami. But you'll know it's worth it when you roll into ❻ Miami Beach, simultaneously the city's most glamorous and yet hang-loose bohemian neighborhood. Watching the constant parade of supermodels, bodybuilders, freaks and weirdoes on South Beach (SoBe) is entertainment enough, but you can always step inside the ❼ World Erotic Art Museum for some more, um, stimulation. The artworks and artifacts arc from classical to contemporary, but overall it's more giggle-inducing than titillating. Admit it: you want to see that giant golden phallus, right?

Out on Miami's Virginia Key, far from the neon-lit nightclubs of SoBe, **8** **Jimbo's** is the kind of redneck watering hole you'd expect to find in the Panhandle. Originally built as a movie set, it has starred in movies and on TV in everything from *Ace Ventura* to *CSI Miami*, and even on a Mariah Carey album cover. This Old Florida haunt sells delish smoked fish and cold beers, and its bocce-ball court gets pretty packed on weekends. Further from the city near the Everglades, Homestead's **9** **Coral Castle** is one man's kitschy do-it-yourself testament to lost love. While it might not exactly be the "American Stonehenge," it's still mighty impressive: Latvian immigrant Ed Leedskalnin dug up over 2.2 million tons of coral rock to build this mock castle. Its engineering was once a bit of mystery, especially since the broken-hearted Romeo worked secretively at night without using any mortar.

> **DETOUR**
>
> Beyond the "Redneck Riviera" of Florida's far-out Panhandle, the **Interstate Mullet Toss** is a quirky tradition. In late April, contestants gather at the Flor-Bama Lounge & Package liquor store (www.florbama.com) to see who can toss a mullet (that is, a dead fish, not the ponytail haircut) furthest across the state line into Alabama. It's about a seven-hour round-trip from St Augustine.

Hop on the Overseas Highway down and out to the Florida Keys. It's where everyone too crazy for the mainland winds up: Harley bikers, sun-addled fishermen and scandalously ill-clad grannies crowd the roadhouses all along the highway, which passes over freakishly long causeways. In Key Largo, sleeping under the sea is not just for the fishes anymore. Originally designed as an underwater marine laboratory, **10** **Jules' Underseas Lodge** offers the Keys' most unique accommodations, where you can slumber five fathoms down and dig into dinner prepped by a "mer-chef." Keep going to the end of the highway in **11** **Key West**, aka the "Conch Republic." Once a hotbed for pirates and smugglers, today the island keeps the raucous celebration

"the kooky Key West Cemetery, filled with unusual epitaphs like 'I told you I was sick.'"

of outlandishness going strong nightly on Duval St and for Halloween's riotous Fantasy Fest. Wander around the kooky **12** **Key West Cemetery**, filled with unusual epitaphs like "I told you I was sick." Maybe you've heard of the freakish six-toed cats at the Hemingway House? Yes, they're definitely odd, but touring the gardens of Papa Hemingway's first house in Key West, **13** **Casa Antigua**, offers even more for kitsch lovers. Trust us: you'll bust a gut laughing.

Sara Benson

TRIP
39

OFFBEAT

TRIP INFORMATION

GETTING THERE
From Jacksonville, take I-95 south, then Hwy 16 east toward the coast; it's a 40-mile trip to St Augustine.

DO
Casa Antigua
Pay for your self-guided garden tour inside the Pelican Poop Shoppe. ☎ 305-296-3887; www.pelicanpoopshoppe.com; 314 Simonton St, Key West; admission $2; ☼ 10am-5pm

Cassadaga Spiritualist Camp
Get oriented and ask about guided tours (including orb photography) at the bookstore information center. ☎ 386-228-2880; www.cassadaga.org; 1112 Stevens St, Cassadaga; tours $15-25; ☼ 10am-5pm Mon-Sat, 11:30am-5pm Sun

Coral Castle
Marvel at a jilted lover's obsessive monument to his sweet Agnes. ☎ 305-248-6345; www.coralcastle.com; 28655 S Dixie Hwy, Homestead; adult/child $10/5; ☼ 8am-6pm Sun-Thu, to 8pm Fri & Sat

Fountain of Youth
Ticky-tacky tourist attraction built upon an actual archaeological site visited by Native Americans and Spanish colonists. ☎ 800-356-8222; www.fountainofyouthflorida.com; 11 Magnolia Avenue, St Augustine; adult/child $8/5; ☼ 9am-5pm

Gatorland
PETA would not approve of the crazy animal antics here. ☎ 800-393-5297; www.gatorland.com; 14501 S Orange Blossom Trail, Orlando; adult/child $23/15; ☼ 9am-5pm; ♿

Key West Cemetery
Pick up a free self-guiding map or make walking-tour reservations in advance. ☎ 305-292-8177, tours 305-292-6718; www.keywestcity.com; 701 Passover Lane, Key West; admission free, tours $10; ☼ 7am-6pm

Weeki Wachee Springs State Park
Call ahead for show times at this retro aquatic theme park. ☎ 352-592-5656; http://weekiwachee.com; 6131 Commercial Way, Spring Hill; adult/child $13/5; ☼ 10am-4pm, with seasonal variations; ♿

World Erotic Art Museum
One old woman's eccentric collection of all things sexual and sensual. ☎ 866-969-9326; www.weam.com; 1205 Washington Ave, Miami Beach; admission $15; ☼ 11am-10pm Mon, Wed & Thu, to midnight Fri-Sun

EAT & SLEEP
Cassadaga Hotel
Like your great-aunt's house, complete with doilies and creaky stairs. Inexpensive vittles are found at the Lost in Time Café. ☎ 386-228-2323; www.cassadagahotel.net; 355 Cassadaga Rd, Cassadaga; r $55-155; ☼ hours vary

Jimbo's
Hang out at the riverside shacks and reminisce about Florida's good ol' days. ☎ 305-361-7026; www.jimbosplace.com; Duck Lake Rd, Virginia Key; admission $5 (may be refundable); ☼ hours vary

Jules' Underseas Lodge
Certified divers can skip training ($150). ☎ 305-451-2353; www.jul.com; 51 Shoreland Dr, Key Largo; r per person $475; ♿

USEFUL WEBSITES
http://unx3.tripod.com/strange.html
www.roadsideamerica.com

LINK YOUR TRIP
www.lonelyplanet.com/trip-planner

North Florida Backwaters & Byways

WHY GO To find genuine "Old Florida" haunts these days, you'll have to traverse back roads through the state's northernmost reaches, from the Atlantic Coast all the way west along the skinny Panhandle. Centuries-old Spanish forts, colonial plantations, hoary lighthouses, forgotten fishing villages, blues clubs and barbecue and seafood shacks await.

TIME
6 – 7 days

DISTANCE
650 miles

BEST TIME TO GO
Apr – Nov

START
Fort George Island, FL

END
Pensacola, FL

Maybe it's something in the aquifer, but all Floridians, even those who arrived here just yesterday, are afflicted with a sentimental yearning for "Old Florida" – meaning, what life used to be like here 50, 100 or even 300 years ago. Folks often mourn disappearing Deep South towns dripping in Spanish moss; ramshackle fishing villages rife with raw oyster bars and creaky piers; and Cracker-style houses where you can sip long, cool, sweet tea on the veranda. To experience Old Florida for yourself, just let your inner serendipity loose to follow forgotten coastal roads and dusty country lanes. Don't rush it, honey.

Start tripping back in time at ❶ **Fort George Island Cultural State Park**, where Native Americans first set foot over 7000 years ago. Now part of Timucuan Preserve, these swampy wetlands feel ancient. Almost swallowed up by wild trees, the dirt-road Saturiwa Trail circles the island. Pick up a self-guided driving tour map and CD at the 1928 Ribault Club, a Gatsby-esque testament to the Jazz Age. Further along the trail, ❷ **Kingsley Plantation** preserves another side of Florida's past: its slaveholding days. Here you'll find Florida's oldest standing plantation house, once owned by Zephaniah Kingsley and his wife, Anna, herself a freed slave. North on Amelia Island, eight different sovereign flags have flown throughout history. A wealthy retreat during the Victorian era, the island's Fernandina Beach later became a shrimping port. In its quaint walkable downtown, ❸ **España** stands

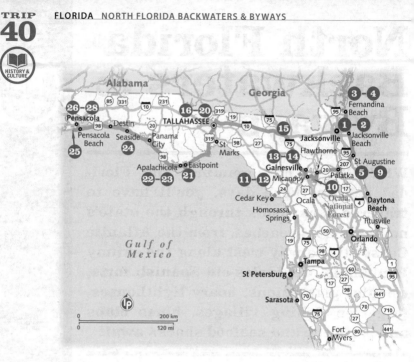

out for seafood, Spanish tapas-style or heaped in steaming plates of paella. Nearby, ❹ **The Addison** B&B inhabits a Victorian-era merchant's house.

In the morning, take Hwy A1A south and board the historic St John's River Ferry to continue south to Jacksonville Beach and beyond. Before arriving in St Augustine, stop off Hwy A1A at ❺ **Cap's on the Water** seafood restaurant and oyster bar, built atop a 1940s Old Floridian fishing camp. The heart of St Augustine proper is its inland ❻ **Old Town**, where narrow cobblestone laneways abound with touristy shops and restaurants. But at the authentic ❼ **Colonial Spanish Quarter Museum**, living-history guides bring the 18th century to life, including at a bawdy tavern. Beside the monumental Old City Gate, ❽ **Castillo de San Marcos National Monument** has been standing guard since 1695, and re-enactors may fire the fort's resounding cannons for you. Just further north in St Augustine's antiques district, ❾ **Our House** B&B is a tranquil escape.

Now it's time to kiss the ocean goodbye. Follow Hwys 207, 20 and 200 inland, then veer off onto lyrical County Rd 235, which winds around to lakeside ❿ **Marjorie Kinnan Rawlings Historic State Park**. The Pulitzer Prize–winning novelist's 1930s Cracker-style home and farm has been beautifully restored, nestled among citrus groves and woodlands. After taking a tour, keep driving to sleepy ⓫ **Micanopy**, once a Native American trading post. Florida's oldest inland settlement charms with its antiques shops and cafés.

HISTORY & CULTURE

⑫ **Mosswood Farm Store** lets you drink organic coffee in rocking chairs on a shady front porch and munch on fresh-baked goodies while you listen to fast-pickin' bluegrass music. Ah, bliss.

Not far away, the university town of Gainesville comes alive after dark, especially in its downtown bars and live-music venues. Fuel up at ⑬ **Chunky T's BBQ**, famous for its mustardy special sauce. After all, what could be more Old Florida than smoked brisket or ribs? For an atmospheric night's sleep, ⑭ **Magnolia Plantation B&B** is a short walk from the downtown hubbub. The next day, it's a long haul to Tallahassee. En route, get off the interstate for ⑮ **Stephen Foster Folk Culture Center State Park**. Named after the composer who immortalized Florida's Suwannee River, this nature center offers canoe and hiking trails, along with demonstrations of traditional crafts like quilting and stained-glass making. Act like you're not startled when the 97-bell carillon tower rings.

Closer to Atlanta than Miami, Florida's capital is far more Southern, culturally speaking, than most of the state it administrates. Downtown the 1845 ⑯ **Tallahassee Historic Capitol** is fetchingly draped by candy-striped

WHO Y'ALL CALLIN' A CRACKER?

Across the US, the word "cracker" is usually pejorative slang for white people. The term is thought to have derived from how slave drivers would crack their whips. But in Florida, the term "cracker" is often used with pride by those who have lived here for generations. Historically speaking, a Florida cracker refers to an American colonial settler who arrived here after the Spanish ceded control to the British in 1763.

awnings and topped by a glass dome. (It's grander than the dull modern highrise that replaced it.) Get a quick civics lesson inside, then feel like a power broker yourself when checking into the dignified ⑰ **Governor's Inn**. North of downtown, eclectic ⑱ **Kool Beanz Café** is a neighborhood institution beloved for its seasonally inspired Southern cooking. Rising on a hillside, the city's ⑲ **Mission San Luis** digs deep into colonial Floridian history, with living-history exhibits about the Spanish and American mission periods, including how colonization impacted the lives of the Apalachee tribespeople. After dark, follow rural back roads north of I-10 to ⑳ **Bradfordville Blues Club**, where the beers are ice cold, and the bonfire and the live acts are cracklin' hot. Tap your feet as famous bluesmen and women play their hearts and souls out.

South of Tallahassee sprawls the "Forgotten Coast," where laid-back fishing villages and sugar-white beaches kiss the Gulf of Mexico. From Eastpoint, duck over the 4-mile-long causeway to St George Island. Originally dating from 1852, the ㉑ **St George Lighthouse** dramatically toppled over in 2005 but since has been faithfully rebuilt. Back on the mainland, ㉒ **Apalachicola** harbors several historic 19th- and 20th-century buildings, all stationed along a self-guided historical walking tour whose stops include Southern mansions, a former general store and an old-fashioned ships' chandlery. Downtown, don't miss the classic Old Florida images exhibited at Richard Beckel's photography gallery. Raw bars serving oysters from the rich beds of Apalachicola Bay are everywhere, but foodies flock to **23** **Tamara's Café Floridita** for fresh seafood with a Latin twist. Outdoor tables are perched on a busy corner, perfect for people-watching. After you've had your fill, keep driving west, following coastal highways that move as slowly as molasses pours. Take a breather in almost too picturesque **24** **Seaside**. This planned community, a 1980s laboratory for New Urbanism, may feel strangely like a movie set. That's because it was – remember *The Truman Show*? Airstream trailers parked by the all-American town square sell everything from fresh-juice smoothies to grilled kabobs for picnicking at the beach.

> **DETOUR** Jutting into the Gulf of Mexico, windswept **Cedar Key** (www.cedarkey.org) is a charmingly unpretentious ensemble of ramshackle buildings, fishing boats and bird-inhabited bayous. Known for its clam farming, this historical island accesses a national wildlife refuge where manatees swim. Hire boats for pleasure cruises at the harbor, or rent a kayak for estuary exploration. The island's annual seafood festival happens in October. Cedar Key is a 60-mile drive southwest of Gainesville via Hwy 24.

At the far western tip of the Panhandle, Pensacola is just a fishing line's throw from 'Bama. Get your thrills from that end-of-the-world feeling by driving past Pensacola Beach along the Gulf Islands National Seashore, here a barrier island dotted with dazzling diamond-white sand dunes, all the way out to **25** **Fort Pickens**. This pre–Civil War Navy fort has a unique pentagonal shape and is infamous for being the place where Apache chief Geronimo and his warriors were once imprisoned. Downtown, take a wander around the city's waterfront district, where the compact **26** **Historic Pensacola Village** has a tidily well-preserved collection of 19th-century houses, including a fine French Creole home, and tiny university-run historical museums. Grab a bite of Pensacola Bay's bounty at the **27** **Fish House**, most popular for its harbor-view deck. Or walk inside the cute-as-a-button **28** **Happy Pig Cafe** for family-style barbecue with all the Southern fixin's like mac 'n' cheese and banana pudding for dessert.

"the 'Forgotten Coast,' where laid-back fishing villages and sugar-white beaches kiss the Gulf of Mexico."

Sara Benson

TRIP INFORMATION

GETTING THERE
From I-95 north of Jacksonville, take Hwy 9A east to Hwy 105 (Heckscher Dr) east, then follow the signs to Fort George Island Cultural State Park.

DO

Castillo de San Marcos National Monument
Bring quarters for the metered parking lot. ☎ 904-829-6506; www.nps.gov/casa; 1 S Castillo Dr, St Augustine; adult/child $6/free; ⊙ 8:45am-5:15pm, last entry 4:45pm; ⬤

Colonial Spanish Quarter Museum
Chat with a blacksmith, carpenter or soldier's wife re-enacting the 1740s. ☎ 904-825-6830; www.historicstaugustine.com; 53 St George St, St Augustine; adult/child $7/4; ⊙ 9am-5:30pm, last entry 4:45pm; ⬤

Fort George Island Cultural State Park
Ranger-led educational programs take place at Ribault Club. ☎ 904-251-2320; www.floridastateparks.org/fortgeorgeisland; 11241 Fort George Rd, Fort George Island; admission free; ⊙ park 8am-sunset, visitor center 9am-5pm Wed-Sun; ⬤

Fort Pickens
Due to frequent flooding, call ahead to check road conditions. Ranger-guided tours usually depart at 2pm daily. ☎ 850-934-2600; www.nps.gov/guis; Fort Pickens Rd, Pensacola; per vehicle $8; ⊙ 9:30am-4pm Nov-Feb, to 5pm Mar-Oct; ⬤

Historic Pensacola Village
Explore independently, or time your visit for a tour led by costumed guides. ☎ 850-595-5985; www.historicpensacola.org; 120 Church St, Pensacola; adult/child $6/3; ⊙ 10am-4pm Tue-Sat; ⬤

Kingsley Plantation
Nineteenth-century cotton and citrus plantation has a haunting history. ☎ 904-251-3537; www.nps.gov/timu; 11676 Palmetto Ave, Fort George Island; admission free; ⊙ 9am-5pm; ⬤ ⬤

Marjorie Kinnan Rawlings Historic State Park
Take a stroll by yourself, or call ahead for guided-tour schedules. ☎ 352-466-3672; www.floridastateparks.org/marjoriekinnanrawlings; 18700 S CR-325, Cross Creek; per vehicle $3, tours adult/child $3/2; ⊙ 9am-5pm; ⬤ ⬤

Mission San Luis
Costumed interpreters demonstrate colonial crafts and show off a reconstructed Native American council house. ☎ 850-245-6406; www.missionsanluis.org; 2100 W Tennessee St, Tallahassee; adult/child $5/2; ⊙ 10am-4pm Tue-Sun; ⬤

St George Lighthouse
Tours start from the maritime museum downstairs. ☎ 850-927-7744; www.stgeorgelight.org; 2 E Gulf Beach Dr, St George Island; adult/child $5/3; ⊙ 10am-5pm Mon-Wed, Fri & Sat, noon-5pm Sun; ⬤

Stephen Foster Folk Culture Center State Park
Live-music events and folk-craft workshops are often held here. ☎ 386-397-2733; www.floridastateparks.org/stephenfoster; Hwy 41, White Springs; per vehicle $5; ⊙ 9am-5pm; ⬤ ⬤

Tallahassee Historic Capitol
Inspect the ballyhooed butterfly ballot from the 2000 US presidential election. ☎ 850-487-1902; www.flhistoriccapitol.gov; 400 S Monroe St, Tallahassee; admission free; ⊙ 9am-4:30pm Mon-Fri, 10am-4:30pm Sat, noon-4pm Sun; ⬤

EAT & DRINK

Bradfordville Blues Club
This juke joint is tricky to find, so call ahead for tickets and directions. ☎ 850-906-0766; www.bradfordvilleblues.com; 7152 Moses Lane, Tallahassee; admission $15-30; ⊙ usually Fri & Sat evenings

Cap's on the Water
Peel fresh shrimp on the waterfront deck, or step inside for fried gator tail with citrus sauce. ☎ 904-824-8794; www.capsonthe water.com; 4325 Myrtle St, St Augustine; mains $10-27; ☒ 11:30am-3:30pm & 4:30pm-close Fri-Sun

Chunky T's BBQ
An institutional atmosphere doesn't deter 'cue enthusiasts from sampling the stripped-down menu of meats and sides. Cash only. ☎ 352-284-4862; www.chunkytsbbq.com; 918 NE 16th Ave, Gainesville; mains $5-20; ☒ 11am-8pm Thu-Sat

España
Tucked-away tapas bar with an outdoor garden and Old and New World wine list. ☎ 904-261-7700; www.espanadowntown. com; 22 S 4th St, Fernandina Beach; small plates $4-10, mains $19-28; ☒ 5-10pm

Fish House
Order spicy shrimp atop cheesy gouda grits à Ya Ya, along with other blackened and fried gulf seafood specialties. ☎ 850-470-0003; www.goodgrits.com; 600 S Barracks St, Pensacola; mains $9-28; ☒ 11am-10pm

Happy Pig Cafe
Combos of smoked turkey, beef brisket and succulent ribs will leave you wanting more. ☎ 850-912-8480; 200 S Alcaniz St, Pensa-cola; mains $7-12; ☒ 11am-9pm; &

Kool Beanz Café
Always buzzing with friendly folks; stop by for classic blackened shrimp with kale or pan-fried frog legs. ☎ 850-224-2466; www. koolbeanz-café.com; 921 Thomasville Rd, Tallahassee; mains $7-19; ☒ 11am-2:30pm Mon-Fri, 5:30-10pm Mon-Sat

Mosswood Farm Store
An organic country bakery and earth-friendly general store stocking picnic supplies. ☎ 352-466-5002; http://mosswoodfarm store.com; 703 NE Cholokka Blvd, Micanopy; items $2-10; ☒ 10am-6pm Tue-Fri, 9am-6pm Sat & Sun

Tamara's Café Floridita
For South American and Caribbean spins on locally caught seafood; try the fried oysters with jalapeño sauce. ☎ 850-653-4111; www.tamarascafe.com; 71 Market St, Apalachicola; mains $12-30; ☒ 8am-9pm Mon-Fri, to 10pm Sat & Sun

SLEEP

The Addison
Ecoconscious inn mixes modern luxuries with genteel Old Florida ambience; some shared baths. ☎ 904-277-1604; www.addisonon amelia.com; 614 Ash St, Fernandina Beach; r $165-265

Governor's Inn
At this businesslike boutique hotel, over three dozen airy rooms and suites all have inviting four-poster beds. ☎ 850-681-6855; www.thegovinn.com; 209 S Adams St, Tal-lahassee; r $135-319

Magnolia Plantation B&B
An adorable, homey and welcoming inn with fireplace Victorian rooms and bungalow cot-tages. ☎ 352-375-6653; www.magnoliabnb. com; 309 SE 7th St, Gainesville; r $135-175, studios $190-350; & 🐾

Our House B&B
Choose from kitchenette studios in the garden or tasteful rooms in the main Victo-rian home; full gourmet breakfast included. ☎ 904-347-6260; www.ourhouseofstaug ustine.com; 7 Cincinnati Ave, St Augustine; r $149-199

USEFUL WEBSITES
www.nps.gov/nr
www.visitflorida.com

LINK YOUR TRIP
www.lonelyplanet.com/trip-planner

GREAT LAKES TRIPS

We know what you're thinking: the Midwest is flat. And boring. Why would anyone want to road-trip through a cornfield?

Now, now, there's no need for that, especially when you have red-cliffed Hwy 61 hugging Lake Superior's shore in Minnesota. And the Great River Rd rising and twisting along the Big Muddy in Illinois. And county roads snaking through cow-dappled hills in southern Wisconsin.

The Great Lakes themselves are huge, like inland seas, offering beaches, islands, dunes, resort towns and lots of lighthouse-dotted scenery. Dairy farms and orchards blanket the region, meaning fresh pie and ice cream await trip-takers, too. The Midwest's big cities – Chicago, Detroit and Cleveland – provide the entertainment. Each rocks in its own special way, with the cultural sights to back up the Stratocasters.

PLAYLIST ♫ Nasty blues, smooth Motown, chest-thumping rock and tender punk make up our Midwest mix.

- "Highway 61 Revisited," Bob Dylan
- "Wang Dang Doodle," Koko Taylor
- "Skyway," Replacements
- "My City was Gone," Pretenders
- "Via Chicago," Wilco
- "ABC," Jackson Five
- "Fever," Buddy Guy
- "Seven Nation Army," White Stripes

And when the Midwest does flatten out? There's always a goofball roadside attraction, like the meaty Spam museum or world's biggest ball of twine, to revive imaginations. So buckle up, why doncha?

GREAT LAKES TRIPS

48 Hours in Chicago

WHY GO The Windy City will blow you away with its cloud-scraping architecture, lakefront beaches and world-class museums. Want to bike by Obama's house? Eat a gourmet hot dog? See a play before it exports to Broadway? Chicago's blend of high culture and earthy pleasures delivers the goods.

TIME
2 days

BEST TIME TO GO
May – Sep

START
Chicago, IL

END
Chicago, IL

First things first: ditch the car. Exploring Chicago by foot and the elevated train system is the hassle-free way to go. In summertime, water taxis ply the river and lakefront, too.

Energize for the day ahead with a rocket-fuel cup of ❶ **Intelligentsia Coffee**. The local chain roasts its own beans, and the baristas know how to percolate them (staff won the US Barista Championship in 2009). Sip by the window and watch the crowds pass by – they're likely headed to ❷ **Millennium Park**, one block east.

Where to start amid the mod designs? Pritzker Pavilion, Frank Gehry's swooping silver band shell, on which the park centers? Crown Fountain, Jaume Plensa's splashy water work, where images of locals spout gargoyle-style? Or "the Bean" (officially *Cloud Gate*), Anish Kapoor's 110-ton, silver-drop sculpture? That's the one. Join the visitors swarming it to see the skyline reflections. The park also offers free guided tours, free yoga classes (Saturday morning, on the Great Lawn) and free classical and world-music concerts – all in summertime, of course, Chicago's snow-free season.

A silvery pedestrian bridge rises from the park's center and arches over to the ❸ **Art Institute of Chicago**. Damn, there's a lot of stuff hanging on the walls. It's the second-largest museum in the country, with masterpieces aplenty, especially Impressionist and

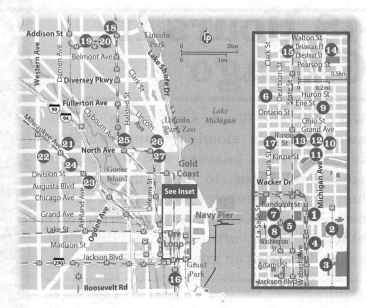

Postimpressionist works. Georges Seurat's pointillist *Un Dimanche Après-Midi à l'Île de la Grande Jatte* (A Sunday Afternoon on the Island of La Grande Jatte) is here; so is Grant Wood's *American Gothic*. The Modern Wing puts up Picassos and Mirós by the roomful. You'll be gawking for at least few hours, and needing a repast by the time you leave.

CHICAGO BY BOAT, BIKE OR HOT DOG

Delve deeper into the city with a tour:

- The **Chicago Architecture Foundation** (www.architecture.org) has boat and walking jaunts to various lofty monuments.

- **Bike Chicago** (www.bikechicago.com) pedals to the South Side past Obama's house and hot spots.

- **Weird Chicago Tours** (www.weirdchicago.com) takes buses to ghost, gangster and red-light sites.

- **Chicago Food Planet Tours** (www.chicagofoodplanet.com) goes by foot to neighborhood pizza, pastry and hot-dog joints.

Fortunately, **4 The Gage** sits across the street. The gastropub dishes Irish-tinged grub with a fanciful twist, like Guinness-battered fish and chips or fries smothered in curry gravy. The booze rocks, too, including a solid whiskey list and small-batch beers that pair with the food.

By now it's hotel check-in time. Architecture buffs can key in at the **5 Hotel Burnham**, housed in the landmark 1890s Reliance Building, the precedent for the modern skyscraper. Eco-guests can curb their carbon footprint at LEED-certified **6 Hotel Felix** (free parking if you're driving a hybrid).

Walk west a block from Hotel Burnham to see ❼ **The Picasso**, a sculpture created by Mr Abstract himself and ensconced in Daley Plaza. Bird, dog, woman? Picasso couldn't decide either, which is why it's officially titled *Untitled*. Across Washington St is another head-scratcher, this one by Joan Miró called ❽ **The Sun, the Moon and One Star**. More big-name public artworks pop up throughout downtown.

Make your way north on Michigan Ave, aka the ❾ **Magnificent Mile**. Bloomingdales, Saks and other swanky department stores are nothing you haven't seen before, but it's convenient to have them all in a row. The ❿ **Tribune Tower** raises its Gothic head on Michigan Ave's east side soon after you cross the river. Check out chunks of the Taj Mahal, Parthenon and further famous structures embedded in the lower walls. Across the street, the ⓫ **Wrigley Building** glows as white as the Doublemint Twins' teeth, and a few paces north, stairs lead to the underground ⓬ **Billy Goat Tavern**. *Tribune* and *Sun-Times* reporters have guzzled in the scruffy lair for decades. It's also the place that spawned the Curse of the Cubs. Order a burger and Schlitz, then look around at the newspapered walls, and you'll get the details.

Blues- and jazzheads will want to detour west a few blocks to ⓭ **Jazz Record Mart** and flick through the thousands of CDs and LPs. Otherwise, it's time to get high. The ⓮ **John Hancock Center** is Chicago's third-tallest building, after the Willis Tower (née Sears) and the Trump Tower, but it has the sweetest views thanks to its lakeside locale. Those needing a city history lesson should ascend to the 94th-floor observatory, and get the edifying audio tour that comes with admission. Those secure in their knowledge can shoot straight up to the 96th-floor lounge, where the view is free if you buy a drink.

Now we come to a complicated issue: what pizza to devour for dinner. Everyone has an opinion, including Oprah. And she likes ⓯ **Pizano's Pizza**. It's a good recommendation for deep-dish newbies, since it's not jaw-breakingly thick. Plus it's just two blocks west of the Hancock.

> **ASK A LOCAL**
>
> "All the free stuff is what keeps us in town! The **Lincoln Park Conservatory** has desert, jungle, orchids – it's a free trip around the world. The **Cultural Center** puts on awesome free concerts during lunchtime. Events like **Blues Fest** and **Jazz Fest** fill downtown most summer weekends, with acts like Stevie Wonder for free. **SummerDance** is every Thursday – free dance lessons, followed by a great local band, and always a crazy, integrated mix of people."
> *Miki Greenberg, Lake View, Chicago*

Grab a cab and finish the night at ⓰ **Buddy Guy's Legends**, 2 miles south. The location and facade are a bit rough around the edges, but the acts are consistently good. Mr Guy himself usually plugs in the ax in January.

Start the next day with breakfast at ⑰ Xoco, Rick Bayless' Mexican street-food restaurant. Crunch into warm churros (spiraled dough fritters) and accompany with chile-spiked hot chocolate. Ah, sweet comfort. What could be wrong in the world?

Take the train north to ⑱ Wrigley Field and find out. The ivy-walled 1914 ballpark hosts the woefully cursed Cubs, who've racked up more than 100 years of World Series futility. No tickets? Peek in the "knothole," a garage-door-sized opening on Sheffield Ave, to watch for free. Or practice your swing (and beer drinking) at ⑲ Sluggers, one of many high-fiving bars that circle Wrigley. It's 10 pitches for a dollar at the upstairs batting cages. Save some dough, though, for a T-shirt at ⑳ Strange Cargo, on Clark St a block south. Staff will iron-on Harry Caray, Mike Ditka or other local sport-hero decals, as well as Obama, Smurfs and more.

"mingle with beautiful people and grizzled regulars, seated pint by pint under the nude-politician paintings."

If the weather stinks, plan B is to hop the Blue Line train to the Wicker Park neighborhood. Get off at the Damen stop, and spend the afternoon poking through hipster record stores, fashion boutiques and thrift shops along North, Milwaukee and Division Sts. ㉑ Quimby's shows the local spirit; the bookstore stocks 'zines and graphic novels, and is a linchpin of Chicago's underground culture. ㉒ Handlebar wafts a similar vibe. The bike-messenger hangout dishes eclectic, vegetarian-skewed meals and pours a well-curated beer list.

That's the new Wicker Park. The old Wicker Park was home to working-class European immigrants, particularly from Poland. In fact, Division St used to be called "Polish Broadway" for all the polka bars that lined it. Experience the old world at ㉓ Podhalanka, a hole-in-the-wall pierogi and borscht restaurant that's like eating at your grandma's house c 1984. The cook ensures you're well fed – to the point you'll need to lie down after the onslaught. The ㉔ Wicker Park Inn, a B&B in a classic brick row house, sits a half-mile away.

For evening entertainment, see what's on at ㉕ Steppenwolf Theatre. John Malkovich, Gary Sinise and other now-famous actors started the drama troupe in a church basement, and paved the way for Chicago's theater scene. If you'd rather yuck it up, catch a show at ㉖ Second City, the launching pad of jokesters from John Belushi to Stephen Colbert. Quaff a nightcap where they used to, across North Ave at the ㉗ Old Town Ale House. The unpretentious favorite lets you mingle with beautiful people and grizzled regulars, seated pint by pint under the nude-politician paintings.

See? Chicago is your kind of town.
Karla Zimmerman

CITY

TRIP INFORMATION

GETTING THERE
Chicago has two international airports (O'Hare and Midway), and it's a hub for Amtrak and Megabus. I-90 and I-94 speed through downtown.

DO

Art Institute of Chicago
Masterpieces galore. ☎ 312-443-3600; www.artic.edu/aic; 111 S Michigan Ave; adult/student $18/12, admission free 5-8pm Thu; ☻ 10:30am-5pm Mon-Fri, 10:30am-8pm Thu, 10am-5pm Sat & Sun, with seasonal variations incl Fri evenings Jun-Aug; ♿

Buddy Guy's Legends
Real-deal blues acts wail on Buddy's stage. ☎ 312-427-1190; www.buddyguys.com; 700 S Wabash Ave; cover usually $10-15; ☻ restaurant 11am-midnight, club from 9:30pm Sun-Thu, 5:30pm Fri, 6pm Sat

Jazz Record Mart
It's the one-stop shop for jazz and blues CDs, vinyl and souvenirs. ☎ 312-222-1467; www.jazzmart.com; 27 E Illinois St; ☻ 10am-8pm Mon-Sat, noon-5pm Sun

John Hancock Center
Tour the 94th-floor observatory, or drink in the 96th-floor lounge. ☎ 888-875-8439; www.hancock-observatory.com; 875 N Michigan Ave; adult/child $15/10; ☻ 9am-11pm; ♿

Millennium Park
Modern designs and free concerts, fitness classes and tours make Millennium ground zero for cool culture. ☎ 312-742-1168; www.millenniumpark.org; cnr Michigan Ave & Randolph St; ☻ sunrise-sunset; ♿

Quimby's
See and be 'zine at this groovy bookstore. ☎ 773-342-0910; www.quimbys.com; 1854 W North Ave; ☻ noon-9pm Mon-Thu, noon-10pm Fri, 11am-10pm Sat, noon-6pm Sun

Second City
It's the improv theater where Bill Murray, Tina Fey and others honed their wit. ☎ 312-337-3992; www.secondcity.com; 1616 N Wells St; tickets $20-50

Sluggers
Practice your swing at the bar's batting cages. ☎ 773-472-9696; www.sluggersbar.com; 3540 N Clark St; 10 pitches $1; ☻ 3pm-2am Sun-Thu, 11am-2am Fri & Sat

Steppenwolf Theatre
Malkovich, Sinise and other Hollywood stars started the drama group in a local basement. ☎ 312-335-1650; www.steppenwolf.org; 1650 N Halsted St; tickets $20-55

Strange Cargo
The retro store stocks wigs, platform shoes and a mind-blowing array of kitschy iron-on T-shirts. ☎ 773-327-8090; www.strange-cargo.com; 3448 N Clark St; ☻ 11:30am-6:30pm Mon-Sat, 11:30am-5:30pm Sun

Wrigley Field
Beautiful historic baseball park, cursed team. Plan ahead or over-pay street hustlers on game day. ☎ 773-404-2827; www.cubs.com; 1060 W Addison St; tickets $16-100

EAT & DRINK

Billy Goat Tavern
Chips, "cheezeborgers" and cheap beer go down in this dive. ☎ 312-222-1525; www.billygoattavern.com; lower level, 430 N Michigan Ave; burgers $3-6; ☻ 6am-2am Mon-Fri, 10am-2am Sat & Sun

The Gage
It's a rarity downtown: a happenin' gastro-pub serving good food and beer. ☎ 312-372-4243; www.thegagechicago.com; 24 S Michigan Ave; mains $16-32; ☻ 11am-11pm, 11am-midnight Fri

Handlebar

Local cyclists congregate around the eclectic, vegetarian-friendly menu (ie African groundnut stew) and summertime patio. ☎ 773-384-9546; www.handlebarchicago. com; 2311 W North Ave; mains $9-14; 🕑 11am-11pm Sun-Thu, 11am-midnight Fri & Sat

Intelligentsia Coffee

The local chain roasts its own beans and brews strong stuff. ☎ 312-920-9332; www. intelligentsiacoffee.com; 53 E Randolph St; 🕑 6am-8pm Mon-Thu, 6am-9pm Fri, 7am-9pm Sat, 7am-7pm Sun

Old Towne Ale House

This neighborhood watering hole has slaked Second City's thirst for decades. ☎ 312-944-7020; www.oldtownalehouse.net; 219 W North Ave; 🕑 8am-4am Mon-Fri, 8am-5am Sat, noon-4am Sun

Pizano's Pizza

Heft a slice of tangy-tomato deep-dish pie; the thin crust wins raves, too. ☎ 312-751-1766; www.pizanoschicago.com; 864 N State St; small pizzas $12-17; 🕑 11am-11pm Sun-Thu, 11am-2am Fri & Sat

Podhalanka

Devour potato pancakes, pierogies and other Polish fare on red vinyl seats as the Pope stares from the wall. ☎ 773-486-6655; 1549 W Division St; mains $4-10; 🕑 9am-8pm Mon-Sat, 10am-7pm Sun

Xoco

Churros for breakfast, *tortas* (sandwiches) for lunch, *caldos* (soups) for dinner, compliments of celebrity chef Rick Bayless. ☎ 312-334-3688; www.rickbayless.com; 449 N Clark St; mains $8-12.50; 🕑 7am-9pm Tue-Thu, 7am-10pm Fri, 8am-10pm Sat

SLEEP

Hotel Burnham

Lodged in the landmark Reliance Building, Burnham's super-slick decor woos architecture enthusiasts. ☎ 312-782-1111; www. burnhamhotel.com; 1 W Washington St; r from $179; ♿

Hotel Felix

The 225-room Felix is silver LEED certified; its earth-toned, mod-furnished rooms are small but efficiently and comfortably designed. ☎ 312-447-3440; www.hotelfelixchicago. com; 111 W Huron St; r $139-189

Wicker Park Inn

This B&B is in a classic brick row house in the Wicker Park neighborhood, a 10-minute train ride from downtown. ☎ 773-486-2743; www.wickerparkinn.com; 1329 N Wicker Park Ave; r $149-199; ♿

USEFUL WEBSITES

www.chicagoreader.com
www.explorechicago.org

LINK YOUR TRIP
TRIP

www.lonelyplanet.com/trip-planner

A Moveable Feast

WHY GO Loosen the belt for this foodie-fueled trip between Minneapolis and Milwaukee, where back roads roll by fish fries and supper clubs, creamy pies and frozen custard, a mustard museum and an organic farming mecca. Local breweries help wash it all down.

Did we mention cheese? Because there's lots of that, too, in cow-speckled southern Wisconsin, where the route meanders. The nation's largest concentration of cheese makers lives in the region. And they offer plenty of hunky goodness to nibble along the way.

Take your first bite at ❶ Matt's Bar, a few miles south of downtown Minneapolis. The unadorned building belies its profound contribution to world cuisine: the Jucy Lucy. That's a burger stuffed with a molten core of American cheese, made by pinching two patties around the yellow slices and grilling to greasy perfection. Just make sure to let the gooey cheese cool before chomping down; a scalded tongue is the mark of a greenhorn. The spelling is no misprint, by the way. Staff wrote "Jucy Lucy" on the sign the day it was invented in 1954, and it stuck.

Drive south to get on I-494 east around St Paul, then drop onto Hwy 10 heading southeast into Wisconsin. About 17 miles beyond the border you'll come to Ellsworth, the state's "Cheese Curd Capital." We could explain that curds are milk solids that separate from whey (aka liquid) when milk is coagulated, but it's not important. All you need to know is that fresh curds squeak when you bite into them, and you can practically hear the ❷ Ellsworth Cooperative Creamery – curd maker for A&W, Dairy Queen and baseball's Miller Park – before you see it. Arrive at 11am to savor curds hot off the press.

TIME
4 days

DISTANCE
500 miles

BEST TIME TO GO
May – Sep

START
Minneapolis, MN

END
Milwaukee, WI

Continue on Hwy 10 to Osseo. Motor a few blocks south to 7th St and the ❸ Norske Nook, where "Pie Fixes Everything," according to the sign inside. Fork into the restaurant's banana cream, blueberry crunch and pecan cream cheese varieties, and you'll believe it. They've all won blue ribbons at the National Pie Championships. So have the chocolate mint and raspberry white chocolate confections. Thank the thick, hand-rolled crust for the honors.

Wipe the crumbs from your mouth, then hop on I-94 south for 30 miles to Hwy 27 south. It meets up with Hwy 14/61 and becomes Main St in Viroqua, an earthy little town that has one of the country's densest populations of organic farmers, including many Amish. Munch on their wares, and maybe even meet the growers themselves, at the ❹ Viroqua Food Cooperative. The surrounding countryside is also a trout-fishing haven, with more than 60 creeks to cast a line, and dotted with distinctive round barns.

Stay on Hwy 14 southeast through Richland Center, Frank Lloyd Wright's birthplace, and into Spring Green. ❺ Taliesin, Wright's home for most of his life and the site of his architectural school, lies 3 miles south via Hwy 23. Take a tour and learn how Wright incorporated the local landscape into his work, making him organic before its time. Back in town, drop by the ❻ Spring Green General Store for sandwiches and eclectic lunch specials like pumpkin curry stew, and snooze in Wright style at the ❼ Usonian Inn, designed by one of the master's acolytes.

For a more urban night's rest, keep on truckin' to Madison, 40 miles east on Hwy 14. Wisconsin's beloved capital wins kudos for everything from most ecofriendly city to most walkable, best road-biking and most vegetarian city in the US. But before entering town, pull over in the suburb of Middleton at the ❽ **National Mustard Museum**. Born of one man's ridiculously intense passion, the building houses 5200 mustards, kooky condiment memorabilia and a mustard bar to sample the spreads. Tongue-in-cheek humor abounds, especially if CMO (chief mustard officer) Barry Levenson is there to give you the shtick.

> *"the building houses 5200 mustards, kooky condiment memorabilia and a mustard bar to sample the spreads."*

While dreams of Dijon dance in your head, curl under the covers at ❾ **Arbor House**, an 1853 tavern that's now a wind-powered, vegetarian-breakfast-serving B&B. The owners even provide bikes to zip around Madison's bountiful trails. It's off the Midvale Blvd exit from Hwy 14, about 3 miles southwest of Capitol Sq, the city's epicenter.

Speaking of which, the ❿ **Dane County Farmers' Market** takes over the square every Saturday from April to November. It's one of the nation's largest markets, famed for its artisanal and farmstead cheeses. Arriving on a nonmarket day? Walk around the corner to ⓫ **Fromagination**, which specializes in hard-to-find local hunks. Gastronomes should also pay a visit to ⓬ **L'Etoile and Cafe Soleil**. Slow-Food pioneer Odessa Piper offered farm-to-table dinners here for 30 years. These days, chef Tory Miller does the cooking with seasonal ingredients sourced at the farmers market.

Take Hwy 18 west out of Madison to Hwy 69 south, and you're back in dairy-farm land. There's no better place to see a Spotted Cow than hilltop ⓭ **New Glarus Brewery**, where it's the flagship ale. Wander through on a self-guided tour, chat with the brewers and slurp samples in the tasting room.

ASK A LOCAL

"The towns around Lake Geneva (between Beloit and Milwaukee) host tons of food events. There's nothing like a hot brat and cold beer amid a fun crowd at the **Corn & Brat Fest**. Williams Bay also has a **Pancake Day**. Fontana has a big **lobster boil**. The **Bash on the Bayou**, at Kirsch's on Lake Como, is the coolest thing going; it runs every Sunday from 3pm to 6pm all summer long. There's a website that has all the info: www.lakegenevawi.com."

J O'Leary, Williams Bay

Stay on Hwy 69 south to Monroe. Things get really cheesy around these parts, as a guided tour through the old milking machines, churns and copper kettles at the ⓮ **Historic Cheesemaking Center** proves (right off the highway at 21st St). Snap the requisite photo with Honey Belle the cow statue, then head downtown to the old-school Swiss tavern ⓯ **Baumgartner's** for a fresh limburger-and-raw-onion sandwich. Ask the staff about the dollar on the ceiling trick (but carefully – mind your breath!).

Continue on Hwy 69 south out of town to County Rd P, Wisconsin's south-ernmost strip of pavement. Turn right (west) and mosey for 4 miles to ⓰ **Inn Serendipity**, a two-room, carbon-negative B&B on a working organic farm. See what's baking in the solar oven, look for owls with the inn's binoculars, and watch stars smudge the night sky.

Make your way to Hwy 11/81 heading east to Beloit. When Hwy 81 ends, merge onto I-43 north and take exit 2 for Hart Rd. Turn right, and then left on County Rd X to the ⓱ **Butterfly Club**. With its woodsy location, radish-and-carrot-laden relish trays, and mile-long, unironic cocktail list, the Butterfly is a quintessential supper club, a type of time-warped establishment common in the upper Midwest. Order an old-fashioned and prepare to spend the evening carving into chicken Oscar and prime rib.

Cruise up I-43 to Milwaukee, our final destination. After resting your weary belly at the ⓲ **Iron Horse Hotel**, with biker-friendly rooms by the Harley Museum, and browsing the nearby ⓳ **Milwaukee Public Market**, redolent with spices, wines and cooking demos, you're ready for ⓴ **Kopp's**, cus-tard purveyor par excellence. For the uninitiated, frozen custard is like ice cream, only smoother and richer thanks to extra egg yolks being whipped in. Take I-43 north to subur-ban Glendale and brake at exit 78 for Kopp's kitschy, retro building.

DETOUR
Adults and kids alike learn to compost, beekeep, make goat-milk soap and build solar water heaters at **Angelic Organics** (www.learngrow connect.org), a large farm 5 miles south of the Wisconsin border in Caledonia, Illinois. Work-shops typically cost $10 to $80 and must be booked in advance.

Let's assume it's Friday, the hallowed day of the "fish fry." This communal meal of beer-battered cod, French fries and coleslaw came about years ago, providing locals with a cheap meal to socialize around and celebrate the workweek's end. The tradition is still going strong at ㉑ **Lakefront Brewery**, a stone's throw north of downtown. Festivities include a polka band, bubble machine and 16 house-crafted beers. If it's not the magic day, make do with Lakefront's daily brewery tour and toast the region's bounty over an Organic Extra Special Bitter. Bottoms up!

Karla Zimmerman

TRIP INFORMATION

GETTING THERE
I-94 and I-35 converge in Minneapolis. Near the junction on downtown's east side, get on Hiawatha Ave for 2.5 miles, go right on E 35th St, then left on Cedar Ave S. Matt's Bar is on the corner of 35th and Cedar.

DO
Dane County Farmers' Market
All the cheeses, veggies, flowers and breads are made by the folks behind the 150 vendor tables. ☎ 608-455-1999; www.dcfm.org; Capitol Sq, Madison, WI; ⏱ 6am-2pm late Apr-early Nov; ♿

Ellsworth Cooperative Creamery
It's one of Wisconsin's biggest cheese-curd producers; get your squeaks at the co-op's store. ☎ 715-273-4311; www.ellsworthcheesecurds.com; 232 N Wallace St, Ellsworth, WI; ⏱ 8am-5pm Mon-Fri, to 2pm Sat

Fromagination
This amazing cheesemonger specializes in artisanal and farmstead hunks from local dairies. ☎ 608-255-2430; www.fromagination.com; 12 S Carroll St, Madison, WI; ⏱ 9:30am-6pm Mon-Fri, 8am-4pm Sat

Historic Cheesemaking Center
Take a guided tour through the cheesy tools of yesteryear; the building also holds Green County's visitors center. ☎ 608-325-4636; www.nationalhistoriccheesemakingcenter.org; 2108 6th Ave, Monroe, WI; suggested donation $2; ⏱ 9am-4pm Apr-Oct

Lakefront Brewery
The microbrewery churns out groovy ales and lagers; the Friday fish fry is a must. ☎ 414-372-8800; www.lakefrontbrewery.com; 1872 N Commerce St, Milwaukee, WI; tours $6, fish fry $10; ⏱ tours 3pm Mon-Sat, fish fry 4:30-9pm Fri; ♿

Milwaukee Public Market
Wine and ethnic-food vendors fill the sprawling warehouse; big-name chefs do cooking demonstrations, too. ☎ 414-336-1111; www.milwaukeepublicmarket.org; 400 N Water St, Milwaukee, WI; ⏱ 10am-8pm Mon-Fri, 8am-6pm Sat, 10am-6pm Sun

National Mustard Museum
The wacky sight holds shelf after shelf of the yellowy condiment and weird containers from around the globe. ☎ 800-438-6878; www.mustardmuseum.com; 7477 Hubbard Ave, Middleton, WI; admission free; ⏱ 10am-5pm

New Glarus Brewery
Learn about Fat Squirrel and Road Slush on the self-guided tour, then swill them. ☎ 608-527-5850; www.newglarusbrewing.com, 2400 Hwy 69, New Glarus, WI; tours free, tastings $3.50; ⏱ 10am-4pm

Taliesin
It's the Frank Lloyd Wright mega-sight, with a wide range of guided tours. ☎ 608-588-7900; www.taliesinpreservation.org; Hwy 23, Spring Green, WI; tours $16-80; ⏱ visitors center 9am-5:30pm May-Oct

Viroqua Food Cooperative
Green and proud of it, the co-op stocks local meats, cheeses and produce. ☎ 608-637-7511; www.viroquafood.coop, 609 N Main St, Viroqua, WI; ⏱ 7am-9pm Mon-Sat, 9am-8pm Sun

EAT & DRINK
Baumgartner's
Cheese sandwiches and local brewskis rule the tables at this timeless Swiss tavern. ☎ 608-325-6157; www.baumgartnercheese.com; 1023 16th Ave, Monroe, WI; sandwiches $4-7; ⏱ 8am-11pm

Butterfly Club
It's a real-deal supper club with classic American fare and crooning entertainment. ☎ 608-362-8577; www.butterflyclub.us; 5246 E County Rd X, Beloit, WI; mains $15-24; ⏱ 5-9:30pm Tue-Thu, 4:30-10pm Fri, 5-10pm Sat, noon-8pm Sun

Kopp's
Kopp's perennially wins Milwaukee's best frozen custard award, and has a huge variety of rich flavors. ☎ 414-961-2006; www.kopps.com; 5373 N Port Washington Rd, Glendale, WI; ⏱ 10:30am-11:30pm

L'Etoile and Cafe Soleil

Slow-Food institution L'Etoile serves dinner; Soleil slings daytime's organic croissants and sandwiches. ☎ 608-251-0500; www.letoile-restaurant.com; 25 N Pinckney St, Madison, WI; café mains $8-10, restaurant mains $29-42; ☺ cafe 7:30am-1:30pm Mon-Thu, 7:30am-2:30pm Fri & Sat, restaurant varies Tue-Sat

Matt's Bar

Bare-bone Matt's birthed the Jucy Lucy. Fries and beer round out the menu. Cash only. ☎ 612-722-7072; www.mattsbar.com; 3500 Cedar Ave S, Minneapolis, MN; burgers $3.50-5; ☺ 11am-10:45pm Mon-Wed, 11am-11:45pm Thu-Sat, noon-10:45pm Sun

Norske Nook

The Nook bakes 30-plus varieties of award-winning pie, alongside Norwegian and American mains. ☎ 715-597-3069; www.norskenook.com; 13804 7th St, Osseo, WI; pie slices $3-4; ☺ 6am-8pm Mon-Sat, 8am-4pm Sun

Spring Green General Store

Chomp deli sandwiches or inventive daily specials like sweet potato stew. ☎ 608-588-7070; www.springgreengeneralstore.com; 137 S Albany St, Spring Green, WI; mains $5-7; ☺ 9am-6pm Mon-Fri, 8am-6pm Sat, 8am-4pm Sun

SLEEP

Arbor House

Arbor House is a sustainably focused, eight-room B&B by Madison's arboretum; free wi-fi and bike use. ☎ 608-238-2981; www.arbor-house.com; 3402 Monroe St, Madison, WI; r weekday $110-175, weekend $150-230

Inn Serendipity

Eco-authors John Ivanko and Lisa Kivirist own this two-room B&B, wonderfully situated in the middle of nowhere. ☎ 608-329-7056; www.innserendipity.com; 7843 County Rd P, Browntown, WI; r $105-120

Iron Horse Hotel

Classy, loft-style rooms fill the old factory building; motorcycle riders get special perks. ☎ 888-543-4766; www.theironhorsehotel.com; 500 W Florida St, Milwaukee, WI; r $159-239; ♿

Usonian Inn

One of Frank Lloyd Wright's students designed this no-frills motel, located near Taliesin. ☎ 877-876-6426; www.usonianinn.com; E5116 Hwy 14, Spring Green, WI; r $65-135

USEFUL WEBSITES

www.eatwisconsincheese.com
www.travelwisconsin.com

LINK YOUR TRIP

www.lonelyplanet.com/trip-planner

Michigan's Gold Coast

WHY GO They don't call it the Gold Coast for nothing. Michigan's western shoreline features endless stretches of beach, dunes, wineries, orchards and B&B-filled towns that boom during the summer. Hemingway hangouts and hanging ten are part of the package, too.

Hit the waves first in New Buffalo. While it looks like a typical resort town, it's also the Midwest's surfing hub. You heard right. You can surf Lake Michigan, and the VW-bus-driving dudes at ❶ **Third Coast Surf Shop** will show you how. They rent wetsuits and boards, and for novices they offer 1½-hour lessons from the public beach right out the front door.

"Those are *big* waves," says a wide-eyed 50ish woman, in from her first go. They're not really, especially in low-wind summertime, but it's a kick to get wet and learn your longboard from your swivel leash. The shop also gives skimboarding, paddleboarding and sandboarding lessons (the latter on local dunes).

Hungry from all the activity? Devour a wax-paper-wrapped cheeseburger, spicy curly fries and cold beer at ❷ **Redamak's**, an old roadhouse half a mile northeast on Buffalo St/Hwy 12. Follow Hwy 12 as it curves inland for 6 miles to the wee town of Three Oaks, where Green Acres meets Greenwich Village in a funky farm-and-arts blend. By day, rent bikes at ❸ **Dewey Cannon Trading Company** and cycle lightly used rural roads past orchards and vineyards. By eve, catch a provocative play or art-house flick at Three Oaks' theaters.

Retrace your path on Hwy 12, and turn right on the Red Arrow Hwy. Drop your bags under the animal heads at the 1920s ❹ **Lakeside Inn** and clear your palate for a drink. By now you've noticed all the wineries around. Connoisseurs often regard ❺ **Tabor Hill Winery** as

TIME
4 days

DISTANCE
475 miles

BEST TIME TO GO
Jul – Oct

START
New Buffalo, MI

END
Mackinaw City, MI

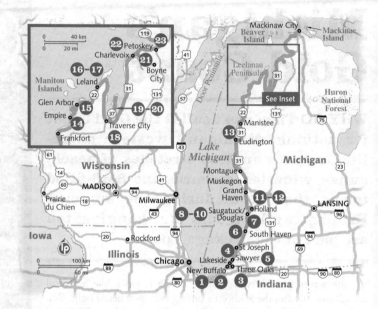

the region's best. Pull off the highway past Sawyer on Browntown Rd and go right. When it ends at Hills Rd turn left, and then right on Mt Tabor Rd. The vintner provides tours and lets you belly up in the tasting room for swigs of its blood-red cabernet franc and crisp sparkling wines. There's also a grape-encircled restaurant.

Return to the Red Arrow Hwy and head north until it intersects with I-94 and Business I-94. Follow Business I-94 through downtown St Joseph. Soon it converges with the Blue Star Hwy (Hwy 63), a scenic thoroughfare that'll carry you 25 miles to South Haven and **6 Sherman's Dairy Bar**. The Moose Tracks, Malt Supreme and 48 other scoops can't get any fresher, since they're whipped up in Sherman's onsite factory. And they are *huge*. Get your licks by taking Phoenix Rd off the highway and going east for 3 miles.

The next stretch of the Blue Star Hwy, up to Saugatuck, is superbly spattered with odd antique shops and fruitful farm stands. A few miles before Saug-atuck turn right (east) on Hwy 89 and motor inland 4 miles to **7 Crane's Pie Pantry**. Pick your own raspberries, apples and peaches at the orchard – or say to hell with that, and sprint across the road to the tchotchke-filled restaurant for a bulging slice of fruit pie.

When the Blue Star Hwy reaches Saugatuck, you'll know it by the crowds. The strong arts community and gay-friendly vibe draw boatloads of vacationers.

Make your base at the retro-cool ❽ **Pines Motorlodge**, with rooms amid the firs, and set out to explore. Galleries of pottery, paintings and glasswork proliferate downtown along Water and Butler Sts. At the foot of Mary St, climb aboard the clackety ❾ **Saugatuck Chain Ferry**, and the operator will pull you across the Kalamazoo River. On the other side, walk to the dock's left and you'll come to Mt Baldhead, a 200ft-high sand dune. Huff up the stairs to see the grand view, then race down the north side to Oval Beach. Back downtown, check the ❿ **Saugatuck Center for the Arts** to see who's performing in the evening.

Next stop: Holland. You don't have to cross the ocean for tulips, windmills and clogs; just drive north 11 miles on Hwy 31. Luckily, an excellent brewery and ecohotel hide in the kitsch. They sit a block apart, making it way too easy to raise another Dragon's Milk ale at the ⓫ **New Holland Brewing Company Pub** before stumbling into your bamboo sheets at the ⓬ **City Flats Hotel**.

FRUITED PLAINS

Western Michigan is ripe with U-pick farms and orchards signposted from the main roads. Pull over, put in an hour of labor and reap the sweet rewards. In general, these are the best pluckin' times.

- Strawberries: June
- Cherries: early July
- Blueberries: July and August
- Raspberries: July and August
- Peaches: early August
- Apples: September and October

Lake Shore Ave is the back-road alternative to Hwy 31 from Holland to Grand Haven. Pick it up from Ottawa Beach Rd just before entering Holland State Park on Lake Macatawa's north side, and you're golden (as in sandy beaches) for 22 miles. After Grand Haven, filter back onto Hwy 31 and blow north for 30 miles. The first exit north of Montague is County Rd B15, another shore-hugger that's prettier than the highway. It meanders for 35 miles and then connects to Business Hwy 31.

After a bit more driving, it's time to stretch the legs at ⓭ **Ludington State Park**, beyond the same-named city limits on Hwy 116. People simply pull over on the roadside and make a break for the beautiful stretches of beach. There's also a top-notch trail system and a renovated lighthouse to hike to (or live in, as the volunteer lighthouse keeper).

Get back on Hwy 31 and head to Manistee. Three miles beyond hop on Hwy 22, which clasps the coast for the next 115 miles. Inland lakes, clapboard towns and historic lighthouses flash by, and soon you're in ⓮ **Sleeping Bear Dunes National Lakeshore**. Stop at the park visitors center in Empire for hiking information and trail maps, then steer north for 2 miles to Hwy 109 and the Pierce Stocking Scenic Drive. The 7-mile, one-lane, picnic-grove-studded loop is one way to absorb the stunning lake vistas. The other is the Dune Climb, which entails trudging up a 200ft-high sand pile. It's also on Hwy 109.

The road ends in Glen Arbor, where the ⑮ **Glen Arbor B&B** brightens up a century-old farmhouse. Rejoin Hwy 22 and swing north to ⑯ **The Cove** in Leland for whitefish and chowder. Tables overlook atmospheric Fishtown and its weather-beaten shacks-cum-shops. To meet the folks who put the food on your plate, sign up with ⑰ **Learn Great Foods** and tour local farms, fisheries and vineyards; some jaunts include alfresco dinner among the greens.

> **DETOUR** Several islands float off Michigan's shore. Car-free **Mackinac Island** (www.mackinacisland.org) is the most touristed; park and take a ferry from Mackinaw City. For a quieter alternative, sail to **Beaver Island** (www.beaverisland.org), an Irish-influenced enclave of 600 people; ferries depart from downtown Charlevoix. **South Manitou Island** (www.leelanau.com/manitou), with boats leaving from Leland, is another wilderness winner.

Hwy 22 rides up and down the Leelanau Peninsula and eventually rolls into Traverse City, the region's "big" city, with an unabashed love for cherries. It's a happenin' place with kiteboarding and sailing, music and movie festivals, and brewpubs like ⑱ **North Peak Brewing Company**, tapping seven swell beers.

From here, energetic road-trippers can opt to veer up Hwy 37 through the grape- and cherry-planted Old Mission Peninsula. Stop in a winery – ⑲ **Peninsula Cellars**, in an old schoolhouse, is a fine one that makes whites – and take your new purchase to Lighthouse Park beach to sip at the land's tip. Many vineyards double as B&Bs, including intimate ⑳ **Grey Hare Inn**.

Pick up Hwy 31 back in Traverse City. North of yacht-riddled Charlevoix, look for Boyne City Rd, which skirts Lake Charlevoix and eventually arrives at the ㉑ **Horton Bay General Store**. Ernest Hemingway fans will recognize the building, with its "high false front," from his short story "Up in Michigan." Papa Hemingway idled away some youthful summers telling fish stories on the big porch, as his family had a cottage on nearby Walloon Lake. Continue the literary theme by tossing back a drink at ㉒ **City Park Grill**, a Hemingway hangout further up Hwy 31 in Petoskey.

"Papa Hemingway idled away some youthful summers telling fish stories on the big porch..."

Time for a choice on this final stretch: take the "fast" way to Mackinaw City via Hwy 31, or dawdle on narrow Hwy 119. The latter lets you hunt for Petoskey stones (honeycomb-patterned fragments of ancient coral) at ㉓ **Petoskey State Park**, then dip and curve through thick forests and along bluffs as part of the Tunnel of Trees scenic route. You probably can guess our choice.

Karla Zimmerman

TRIP INFORMATION

GETTING THERE
I-94 whizzes by New Buffalo. Take exit 1 from the Michigan border, then go left on LaPorte Rd into town.

DO

Dewey Cannon Trading Company
Rent two-wheelers and get a Backroads Bikeway Map. ☎ 269-756-3361; www.applecidercentury.com; 3 Dewey Cannon Ave, Three Oaks; bike hire per day $15; ☯ 10am-4pm Sun-Fri, to 9pm Sat, with seasonal variations; ♿

Horton Bay General Store
Ernest Hemingway memorabilia packs this old-fashioned shop. ☎ 231-582-7827; www.hortonbaygeneralstore.com; 05115 Boyne City Rd, Boyne City; ☯ 7am-6pm Mon-Thu, to 8pm Fri & Sat, to 4pm Sun late May-early Sep

Learn Great Foods
It leads culinary tours to local farms, including cooking demos and alfresco dinners on-site. ☎ 231-758-3407, 866-240-1650; www.learngreatfoods.com; Leelanau Peninsula, Petoskey & other locations; tours $50-105

Ludington State Park
Miles of shoreline, three campgrounds and cool hiking trails fill Ludington's 5300 acres. ☎ 231-843-8671; www.michigan.gov/dnr; Hwy 116, Ludington; vehicle fee $8, campsites $16-29; ☯ year-round; ♿

Peninsula Cellars
Sample wines in the red-and-white schoolhouse; they're known mostly for whites. ☎ 231-933-9787; www.peninsulacellars.com; 11480 Center Rd, Old Mission Peninsula; admission free; ☯ 10am-6pm Mon-Sat, noon-6pm Sun May-Oct, reduced hrs Nov-Apr

Petoskey State Park
Trails lace forested dunes, and famed Petoskey stones lie on the beach at this well-used park. ☎ 231-347-2311; www.michigan.gov/dnr; 2475 Hwy 119, Petoskey; vehicle fee $8, campsites $27-29; ☯ year-round; ♿

Saugatuck Center for the Arts
See what's gigging: live music performances, art exhibits and art classes compose the mix. ☎ 269-857-2399; www.sc4a.org; 400 Culver St, Saugatuck; tickets free-$35

Saugatuck Chain Ferry
The indescribably cool, hand-cranked little vessel is the Great Lakes' last. departs from the foot of Mary St; one way $1; ☯ 9am-9pm late May-early Sep; ♿

Sleeping Bear Dunes National Lakeshore
Pick up hiking information and trail maps at the visitors center. ☎ 231-326-5134; www.nps.gov/slbe; 9922 Front St, Empire; vehicle fee $10; ☯ 8:15am-6pm Jun-Aug, 8:15am-4pm Sep-May; ♿

Tabor Hill Winery
The dry reds and whites are often considered south Michigan's best. ☎ 800-283-3363; www.taborhill.com; 185 Mt Tabor Rd, Buchanan; tours & tastings free; ☯ tours noon-4:30pm May-Oct, weekends only Nov-Apr, tastings from 10am Mon-Sat, from noon Sun

Third Coast Surf Shop
Learn to surf, paddleboard and sandboard via group or private lessons. ☎ 269-932-4575; www.thirdcoastsurfshop.com; 22 S Smith St, New Buffalo; lessons $50-70; ☯ 10am-6pm Jun-Aug, reduced hrs spring & fall, closed Jan-Mar

EAT & DRINK

City Park Grill
This historic restaurant-bar (Hemingway was a regular) plates solid American fare. ☎ 231-347-0101; www.cityparkgrill.com; 432 E Lake St, Petoskey; mains $11-22; ☯ 11:30am-11pm Sun-Thu, 11:30am-midnight Fri & Sat, reduced hrs Nov-Apr

Cove
The Cove offers whitefish (prepared four ways), seafood chowder and a good-time, waterside location. ☎ 231-256-9834; www.thecoveleland.com; 111 River St, Leland; mains $18-26; ☯ 11am-10pm, closed Nov-Apr

Crane's Pie Pantry
Buy a sweet slice at the restaurant, or pick fruit in the orchard. ☎ 269-561-2297; www.cranespiepantry.com; 6054 124th Ave, Fennville; pie slices $3.75; ⊗ 9am-8pm Mon-Sat, 11am-8pm Sun May-Oct, reduced hrs Nov-Apr; ⊛

New Holland Brewing Company Pub
Swill robust beers (around 10% alcohol) or house-made rums. ☎ 616-355-6422; www.newhollandbrew.com; 66 E 8th St, Holland; pints $4-5; ⊗ 11am-midnight Mon-Thu, 11am-1am Fri & Sat, noon-10pm Sun

North Peak Brewing Company
Munch pizzas, mussels and pretzel-crusted walleye with fresh suds. ☎ 231-941-7325; www.northpeak.net; 400 W Front St, Traverse City; mains $9-18; ⊗ 11am-11pm Mon-Thu, 11am-midnight Fri & Sat, noon-10pm Sun

Redamak's
This burgers-and-beer roadhouse dates from the 1940s; the curly fries reign supreme. Cash only. ☎ 269-469-4522; www.redamaks.com; 616 E Buffalo St, New Buffalo; burgers $4.50-10; ⊗ noon-10:30pm, closed Nov-Feb

Sherman's Dairy Bar
Beloved Sherman's scoops massive cones in 50 flavors; lines can be lengthy. ☎ 269-637-8251; www.shermansicecream.com; 1601 Phoenix Rd, South Haven; single-dip cones $2.50; ⊗ 11am-11pm Mon-Sat, noon-11pm Sun, closed Nov-Feb; ⊛

SLEEP

City Flats Hotel
The 56 rooms in this gold-LEED-certified ecohotel vary by decor, but all use sustainable materials. ☎ 616-796-2100; www.cityflatshotel.com; 61 E 7th St, Holland; r $119-219; ⊛

Glen Arbor B&B
The owners renovated the antique building into a sunny, French country inn with six themed rooms. ☎ 231-334-6789; www.glenarborbnb.com; 6548 Western Ave, Glen Arbor; r $95-185; ⊗ closed Dec-Apr

Grey Hare Inn
An intimate, three-room B&B on a working vineyard, in French style with bay views. ☎ 231-947-2214; www.greyhareinn.com; Carroll St, Old Mission Peninsula; r $150-250

Lakeside Inn
Thirty-one simple rooms spread over three floors in this atmospheric lodge with a private beach. ☎ 269-469-0600; www.lakesideinns.com; 15251 Lakeshore Rd, Lakeside; r summer $115-200, winter $90-175; ⊛

Pines Motorlodge
Retro tiki lamps, pinewood furniture, free wi-fi and breakfast, and communal lawn chairs add up to a fun, social ambience. ☎ 269-857-5211; www.thepinesmotorlodge.com; 56 Blue Star Hwy, Douglas; r $129-189

USEFUL WEBSITES
www.michigan.org
www.michiganhemingwaysociety.org

LINK YOUR TRIP
www.lonelyplanet.com/trip-planner

An Amish Country Ramble

WHY GO Life slows waaay down in north-eastern Ohio, home to the nation's largest Amish community. Learn to quilt, boogie at a barn dance and maybe even buy a cow at auction along the slowpoke roads, where buggies have the right of way.

While the area is idyllic, it's a bit of an anachronism, too. Tour buses roar up beside long-bearded men in horse-drawn buggies. Visitors chat on cell phones next to bonneted women churning butter. The Amish of Wayne and Holmes Counties are happy to package their lifestyle to make money from tourism – but they're also serious about staying true to the *ordnung* (way of life), which for many means no electricity, telephones or motorized vehicles. Somehow it all clicks together.

Start in Kidron, where ❶ **Lehman's** sells non-electric products to locals in a 32,000-sq-ft barn. Stroll through to ogle wind-up flashlights, wood-burning stoves and hand-cranked meat grinders. If those are too off-the-grid, try the ecofriendly wooden toys or organic gardening books.

Once you find your way out, head to the strip mall next door. The ❷ **Hearthside Quilt Shoppe** stocks locally made quilts, as well as fabric, patterns and notions for do-it-yourself types. Uninitiated in the patchwork ways? Take a class or join the chitchat during the monthly Tuesday-night Quilt Guild.

If it's Thursday, another opportunity awaits. Follow the buggy lineup a short way south on Hwy 52/Kidron Rd to the ❸ **Kidron Auction**. Amish men in white shirts and suspender-hitched trousers fill the barn's benches alongside local farmers. Everyone looks hard at the pigs, cows and lambs that parade around the dirt floor. The auctioneer talks fast into the crackling microphone, prices volley back and forth,

TIME
2 days

DISTANCE
50 miles

BEST TIME TO GO
May – Oct

START
Kidron, OH

END
Millersburg, OH

HISTORY &
CULTURE

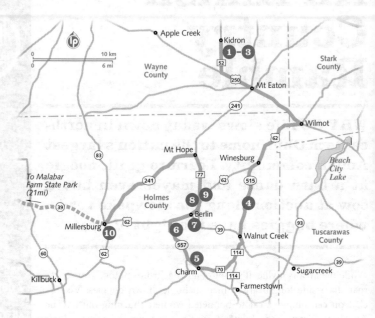

and by early afternoon scores of animals hoof it home with their proud new owners. A flea market rings the barn for folks seeking non-mooing merchandise. Similar auctions take place in Sugarcreek (Monday and Friday), Farmerstown (Tuesday) and Mt Hope (Wednesday).

Continue south on Hwy 52/Kidron Rd a few miles to Hwy 250. Take it east to Mt Eaton and Wilmot. At the latter get on scenic Hwy 62 west to B&B-laden Winesburg. At the outskirts, jump on Hwy 515 south toward Walnut Creek.

Before reaching town you'll see ④ **Yoder's Amish Home**. It may be touristy, but where else will you get to peek into a local home and one-room schoolhouse, and take a buggy ride through a field? Guides provide tours and explain Amish culture.

After Walnut Creek zig left on Hwy 39 east (toward Sugarcreek), zag right on Hwy 114, then keep an eye out for Hwy 70 veering off to the right (the Guggisberg Cheese sign marks the spot).

Twisty Hwy 70 takes you far from the madding crowd. Instead of the usual veggies and eggs, farms here sell heifers, beekeeping supplies and windmills from their front porches. The road dead-ends in Charm, a sweet spot to spend the night since it's small enough to be peaceful yet big enough to have a couple of inns and restaurants. Turn right on Hwy 557 and soon you'll arrive at the **5 Guggisberg Swiss Inn**. Staff dress in Alpine garb and make cheese at the factory across the street. They also arrange horseback rides at the inn's stables.

It's embarrassing to be in Amish country this long without stopping for pie. So pull over at **6 Hershberger's Farm & Bakery** a few miles further up Hwy 557. More than 25 kinds of flaky goodness waft from the racks; the 6in mini-pies are key for those who can't commit to a single flavor. Hershberger's also offers great-looking seasonal produce, homemade ice-cream cones and Big Ben, a mondo Belgian horse.

DETOUR What do Bogie, Bacall and Johnny Appleseed have in common? They've all spent time at **Malabar Farm State Park** (www.malabarfarm.org). There's a lot going on here: hiking and horse trails; pond fishing (ask for a free rod at the visitors center); tours of Pulitzer-winner Louis Bromfield's home (where Bogie and Bacall got married); monthly barn dances; a farmhouse hostel; a spring-cooled produce market (Mr Appleseed's favorite watering hole); and a fine restaurant. Malabar is 30 miles west of Millersburg via Hwy 39.

More pie ahead. Follow Hwy 62 east into Berlin, the area's tchotchke-filled core. Park at home-style **7 Boyd & Wurthmann Restaurant**. "There's enough food here to choke a horse," says an overalls-clad local when the bonneted waitress brings his country-fried steak, noodles and grape cream pie. Amen, brother.

Just beyond Berlin's center at the flashing light turn left (north) onto Hwy 77, and within a mile is **8 Heini's Cheese Chalet**. Watch cheese makers cut curds through the factory window, or take a free tour. You'll learn how Amish farmers hand-milk their cows and spring-cool (versus machine-refrigerate) the output before delivering it each day. Then grab a handful of samples and peruse the kitschy History of Cheese Making mural. Of course fresh cheese calls for fresh bread, so follow your nose across the street to **9 Kauffman's Country Bakery**, where 200 loaves bake daily.

> *"There's enough food here to choke a horse,' says an overalls-clad local..."*

Continue on hilly, horse-doo-dotted Hwy 77 to Mt Hope, and turn left on Hwy 241 to Millersburg. This is the region's largest town, more antique-y than Amish. It holds old bookshops, a pretty rail-to-trail path and **10 Hotel Millersburg**, an 1847 stagecoach inn that still provides lodging today. The tavern is one of Amish country's rare places to get a drink, and a swell spot to finish the drive.

Karla Zimmerman

HISTORY &
CULTURE

TRIP INFORMATION

GETTING THERE
Kidron is about 80 miles south of Cleveland.
Take I-77 to Canton's outskirts, then Hwy 30
west to Kidron Rd.

DO

Hearthside Quilt Shoppe
Buy a finished quilt or DIY supplies, or take
a class (check the schedule online). ☎ 330-
857-4004; www.hearthsidequiltshoppe.com;
13110 Emerson Rd, Kidron; 2hr classes $20;
🕑 9:30am-5pm Mon-Sat

Heini's Cheese Chalet
The store sells more than 70 types. To see
the cheese makers in action, come before
11am weekdays (except Wednesday).
☎ 800-253-6636; www.heinis.com; 6005
Hwy 77, Berlin; tours free; 🕑 8:30am-5pm
Mon-Sat

Kidron Auction
Hay gets auctioned at 10am, cows at 11am,
pigs at 1pm, while the flea market goes
on throughout. ☎ 330-857-2641; www.
kidronauction.com; 4885 Kidron Rd, Kidron;
admission free; 🕑 from 10am Thu

Lehman's
The community's main purveyor of modern-
looking products that use no electricity.
☎ 888-438-5346; www.lehmans.com; One
Lehman Circle, Kidron; 🕑 8am-5:30pm
Mon-Sat, 8am-8pm Thu; ♿

Yoder's Amish Home
Look inside an Amish home and school, pet
barnyard animals and take a buggy ride.
☎ 330-893-2541; www.yodersamishhome.
com; 6050 Hwy 515, Walnut Creek; tours
adult/child $11/7; 🕑 10am-5pm Mon-Sat
mid-Apr–late Oct; ♿

EAT

Boyd & Wurthmann Restaurant
Hubcap-sized pancakes, 23 pie flavors, fat
sandwiches and Amish specialties draw
crowds. Cash only. ☎ 330-893-3287; Main
St, Berlin; mains $5-10; 🕑 5:30am-8pm
Mon-Sat

Hershberger's Farm & Bakery
Gorge on pie, produce and preserves from
the market inside. Pet the farmyard animals
(free) and take pony rides ($3) outside.
☎ 330-674-6096; 5452 Hwy 557, Millersburg; baked goods $2-7; 🕑 bakery 8am-
5pm Mon-Sat, farm from 10am but closed
Nov–mid-Apr; ♿

Kauffman's Country Bakery
Grab a deli sandwich or fresh-baked bread to
go with your purchases from nearby Heini's
Cheese Chalet. ☎ 330-893-2129; www.
kauffmanscountrybakery.com; 4357 Hwy 62,
Berlin; baked goods $2-6; 🕑 7am-5:30pm,
closed Sun Dec-Apr

SLEEP

Guggisberg Swiss Inn
The 24 tidy, compact rooms are bright with
quilts and light-wood furnishings; free wi-fi
and breakfast add to the sweetness. ☎ 877-
467-9477; www.guggisbergswissinn.com;
5025 Rte 557, Charm; r $79-110; ♿

Hotel Millersburg
This homey, historic hotel provides 26 casual
rooms above a modern tavern and dining
room. ☎ 330-674-1457, 800-822-1457;
www.hotelmillersburg.com; 35 W Jackson
St, Millersburg; r $79-139; 🐾

USEFUL WEBSITES
www.thebudgetnewspaper.com
www.visitamishcountry.com

LINK YOUR TRIP
www.lonelyplanet.com/trip-planner

TRIP
3 The Lincoln Highway p65
46 Rockin' the Midwest p353

OUTDOORS

Lake Lovers' Trail

WHY GO It's all about the water in Michigan's Upper Peninsula, where three of the Great Lakes lap the lonely, forested shoreline. Explore the Shipwreck Coast, watch freighters leap the Soo Locks and hike the wave-bashed cliffs of Pictured Rocks National Lakeshore.

TIME
3 – 4 days

DISTANCE
350 miles

BEST TIME TO GO
Jul – Sep

START
Mackinaw City, MI

END
Ishpeming, MI

Start in Mackinaw City, at the Lower Peninsula's tip, to make the grand entrance. Motor past the fudge shops and ferry docks (the town is the jump-off point for popular Mackinac Island) – you're here for the ❶ Mackinac Bridge, a 5-mile beauty that connects the state's upper and lower parts. The $3.50 toll is worth every penny, providing views of Lake Michigan to the west, Lake Huron to the east, and oodles of islands that freckle both. Oh, that wind whipping around your car 200ft above the roiling straits? Fear not: only one vehicle has ever blown off in the bridge's 50-plus-year history (a Yugo, in a gale).

After crossing, you're officially in the Upper Peninsula (UP). As residents – or "Yoopers" – will tell you, this rural, heavily forested region is distinct from the rest of Michigan. Only 45 miles of interstate slice through the trees, and you're now driving them on I-75 north to Sault Ste Marie. When you arrive, take exit 394 (Easterday Ave), and head to the waterfront to the ❷ Soo Locks Park & Visitors Center. The impressive canals act as an "elevator" between Lake Huron and Lake Superior, which is 21ft higher. From the observation deck, you'll see the gates swing open, the huge freighters glide in, and the locks transport the vessels up or down before squirting them out the other side.

Retrace your path on I-75, heading south to Hwy 28. Take it west for 30 miles to Hwy 123, a scenic road that loops north. When you reach the village of Paradise, veer north on Whitefish Point Rd for 11 miles to the ❸ Great Lakes Shipwreck Museum. Dozens of vessels – including the *Edmund Fitzgerald* that Gordon Lightfoot crooned

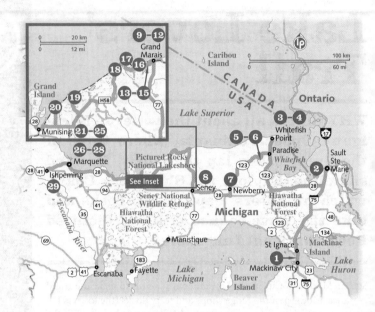

about – have sunk off the area's storm-battered shore. The museum tells their stories, and the *Fitz's* bronze bell stars among the haunting displays. The grounds also include a lighthouse President Lincoln commissioned and a bird observatory that 300 species fly by. To have the foggy place to yourself, spend the night at ④ **Whitefish Point Light Station B&B**, five rooms in the old Coast Guard crew quarters onsite.

Return to Paradise and pick up Hwy 123 where you left off, continuing westward to ⑤ **Tahquamenon Falls State Park**. The Lower Falls are a series of small cascades that swirl around an island; many visitors rent a rowboat and paddle out to it. The Upper Falls, 200ft across with a 50ft drop, wow onlookers with their mighty rush – including Longfellow, who mentioned them in his *Song of Hiawatha*. The park also has camping, great hiking and the rustic ⑥ **Tahquamenon Falls Brewery**, maker of Black Bear Stout and meaty sandwiches and main courses.

The ⑦ **Tahquamenon Logging Museum** crops up just before Newberry on Hwy 123. Swing in for a lumberjack breakfast in the mess hall and to examine old logging tools. Soon you'll meet Hwy 28 again. Take it west to ⑧ **Seney**, a town Ernest Hemingway made famous as the setting for his Nick Adams story "Big Two-Hearted River." (Note, though, Hemingway took poetic license – it's the Fox River that runs through Seney, while the more lyrical-sounding Two-Hearted lies several miles northeast.)

From Seney, turn north on Hwy 77 to Grand Marais. This speck on the map rocks harder than you'd think. We mean it literally, as you'll see at the ❾ Gitche Gumee Agate and History Museum, a block west of the highway on Brazel St (look for the green-trimmed, handmade fishing tug dry docked next door). The owner, Karen, has stuffed the museum-shop with color-swirled stones, many found on local beaches. Toast them with an Agate Amber and whitefish sandwich at nearby ❿ Lake Superior Brewing Company. Or cruise around the bay (past the pickle-barrel house!) to retro ⓫ West Bay Diner for mountainous all-day breakfasts with slab bacon. ⓬ Hilltop Cabins and Motel, on a bluff a mile east, offers a peaceful night's slumber.

Grand Marais also is the eastern gateway to ⓭ Pictured Rocks National Lakeshore, a series of freaky-shaped cliffs and caves where blue and green minerals have streaked the red and yellow sandstone into a kaleidoscope of color. County Rd 58 (Alger County Rd) spans the park; pick it up downtown. It's 52 slow miles to the other end in Munising, though most of the way is now paved. Then again, you could ditch the car and hike through the park on the shore-clasping ⓮ North Country Trail.

The park's ⓯ Grand Sable Visitor Center, a few miles west of Grand Marais on County Rd 58, provides maps, backcountry permits and other details. As you drive onward you'll see various access points to ⓰ Grand Sable Dunes and the 1874 ⓱ Au Sable Point Lighthouse – reached via a 3-mile round-trip walk beside shipwreck skeletons (the trailhead is at Hurricane River Campground). Next is driftwood- and agate-strewn

THE SHIPWRECK COAST

Congested shipping lanes, thick fog, and volatile early-spring and late-fall storms have littered the waters around Whitefish Point with the highest concentration of shipwrecks in Lake Superior – hence its ominous nicknames of "Shipwreck Coast" and "Graveyard of the Great Lakes." The vessels, from wooden schooners to modern steel freighters, now comprise the **Whitefish Point Underwater Preserve** (www. whitefishpoint.net).

⓲ Twelvemile Beach, then hike-rich ⓳ Chapel Falls. Eventually you'll see the turnoff to ⓴ Miners Castle Overlook, perhaps the park's most iconic formation. It looks different now from the stock photos, since one of the "turrets" broke off in a 2006 rockslide.

County Rd 58 winds up in downtown Munising, the park's western gateway, which does a brisk trade in boat tours. The classic is ㉑ Pictured Rock Cruises, departing from the city pier downtown and zipping along the shore past Miners Castle and back. ㉒ Shipwreck Tours, a mile west on Munising Ave (aka Hwy 28), sets sail in glass-bottom boats to hover over sunken schooners and steamers. Or leave the motor behind: ㉓ Northern Waters guides day-long kayak trips to Pictured Rocks and Grand Island. Afterward, feast on sandwiches, ice cream and free wi-fi at downtown's artsy **24** **Falling Rock Cafe and Bookstore**, then turn in at tidy **25** **Alger Falls Motel**.

DETOUR Rugged **Grand Island** (www.grandislandmi. com) floats a half-mile offshore from Munising and is part of Hiawatha National Forest. Visitors can day-trip over to hike and mountain bike, or spend the night in one of 17 rustic campsites. Watch for black bears. Bike rentals and a three-hour bus tour are available on-island, but otherwise amenities are limited. The Grand Island Ferry makes the trip between late May and mid-October; the dock is on Hwy 28 about 4 miles west of Munising.

Hop on Hwy 28 heading west, a beautiful stretch of road brushed by beaches, parks and rest areas where you can pull over and enjoy the scenery. After 45 miles you'll reach outdoorsy Marquette. Stay on Front St into downtown, and check into the mahogany-and-marble-bedecked **26** **Landmark Inn**. There's lots of action on the waterfront here. Stroll to Lower Harbor Park, punctuated by a huge, abandoned ore dock. Pop into **27** **Thill's Fish House** in a Quonset hut at Main St's foot. Awash in ropes and anchors, Thill's is Marquette's last commercial fishing operation, and it hauls in fat catches daily; try the smoked whitefish sausage. To continue the nautical theme, keep east on Lakeshore Blvd a half-mile to the **28** **Marquette Maritime Museum**. Besides a shiny lens collection and replica fishing shack, visitors can tour the picture-perfect red lighthouse dotting the point.

"how best to commemorate your trip. A Yoopanese dictionary? Polyester moose tie? Beer-can wind chimes?"

We've taken our water-bound route seriously thus far. Now it's time to add Big Gus, the world's largest chainsaw. And Big Ernie, the world's largest rifle. Kitsch runs rampant at **29** **Da Yoopers Tourist Trap and Museum**, 15 miles west on Hwy 28/41, past Ishpeming. Browse the store and decide how best to commemorate your trip. A Yoopanese dictionary? Polyester moose tie? Beer-can wind chimes? The possibilities – like the UP's lakeshore – are endless.

Karla Zimmerman

TRIP INFORMATION

GETTING THERE
I-75 and Hwy 31 are the main routes from Detroit and southern Michigan to Mackinaw City.

DO

Da Yoopers Tourist Trap and Museum
Brake for Yooper gag gifts and outdoor oddities. ☎ 800-628-9978; www.dayoopers.com; Hwy 28/41, Ishpeming; admission free; 🕑 9am-6pm Mon-Thu, to 8pm Fri, to 7pm Sat, 10am-6pm Sun, with seasonal variations

Gitche Gumee Agate and History Museum
Colorful rocks, local artifacts and lore fill the museum shop. ☎ 906-494-3000; www.agatelady.com; E21739 Brazel St, Grand Marais; admission $1; 🕑 afternoon only, hours vary, mid-May–early Sep

Grand Sable Visitor Center
Pick up trail maps and backcountry permits at this Pictured Rocks park info center. ☎ 906-494-2660; www.nps.gov/piro; E21090 County Rd 58, Grand Marais; 🕑 9am-5pm late May-early Sep

Great Lakes Shipwreck Museum
Evocative relics from sunken ships prove the Great Lakes' power. ☎ 888-492-3747; www.shipwreckmuseum.com; 18335 N Whitefish Point Rd, Paradise; adult/child $12/8; 🕑 10am-6pm May-Oct; ♿

Marquette Maritime Museum
Peruse the museum in the old waterworks building; staff also offer tours through the swell-viewing lighthouse. ☎ 906-226-2006; www.mqtmaritimemuseum.com; 300 Lakeshore Blvd, Marquette; adult/child $7/5; 🕑 10am-5pm mid-May–mid-Oct; ♿

Northern Waters
Guides lead kayak trips to Pictured Rocks or Grand Island; beginners welcome. ☎ 906-387-2323; www.northernwaters.com; 712 W Munising Ave, Munising; full-day tours adult/child $125/95; 🕑 9am late May-Sep

Pictured Rock Cruises
Boats with both deck-top and enclosed seating hug the shore for 18 miles. ☎ 906-387-2379; www.picturedrocks.com; 100 W City Park Dr, Munising; 2½hr tours adult/child $33/10; 🕑 10am-5pm with seasonal variations, mid-May–mid-Oct; ♿

Pictured Rocks National Lakeshore
Wild-looking, multi-hued cliffs and sea arches form the 71,000-acre park. ☎ 906-387-3700; www.nps.gov/piro; btwn Munising & Grand Marais; admission free; 🕑 24hr; ♿ 🐾

Shipwreck Tours
Set sail in a glass-bottom boat and see three ships in their watery graves. ☎ 906-387-4477; www.shipwrecktours.com; 1204 Commercial St, Munising; 2hr tours adult/child $30/12; 🕑 10am & 1pm with seasonal variations, mid-May–mid-Oct; ♿

Soo Locks Park & Visitors Center
Watch massive freighters get raised or lowered between Lakes Huron and Superior. ☎ 906-253-9101; www.soolocksvisitorscenter.com; Portage Ave, Sault Ste Marie; admission free; 🕑 9am-9pm mid-May–mid-Oct

Tahquamenon Falls State Park
Michigan's second-largest public play lot has tea-colored waterfalls, trails, camping, paddling and more. ☎ 906-492-3415; www.michigan.gov/dnr; Paradise; vehicle fee $8, campsites $16-23; 🕑 year-round; ♿

Tahquamenon Logging Museum
Learn about logging, the region's big business, in this down-home museum on an old farmstead; the cook shack hosts lumberjack breakfasts. ☎ 906-293-3700; www.superiorsights.com/loggingmuseum; Hwy 123, Newberry; adult/child $3/1.50; 🕑 May-early Sep; ♿

EAT & DRINK

Falling Rock Cafe and Bookstore
Enjoy new and used books, live music and wi-fi with your sandwich. ☎ 906-387-3008; www.fallingrockcafe.com; 104 E Munising Ave, Munising; mains $5-9; ☻ 9am-8pm Sun-Fri, to 10pm Sat, with seasonal variations

Lake Superior Brewing Company
Whitefish sandwiches, pasties (meat-and-veg pies) and pizzas go down the hatch with house-made brewskis and root beer. ☎ 906-494-2337; N14283 Lake Ave, Grand Marais; mains $7-13; ☻ noon-11pm

Tahquamenon Falls Brewery
Carve into steaks and pasta and/or sip beer in the lodge-like ambience; by the Upper Falls. ☎ 906-492-3300; www.tahquamenonfalls brewery.com; Hwy 123, Paradise; mains $10-20; ☻ 11am-8:30pm, closed Apr & Nov

Thill's Fish House
Buy fresh-caught trout or whitefish in various forms (smoked, pickled, sausage) right on the dock. ☎ 906-226-9851; 250 E Main St, Marquette; items $4-9; ☻ 8am-5:30pm

West Bay Diner
This classic stainless-steel diner serves big breakfasts and sandwiches on homemade bread. ☎ 906-494-2607; E21825 Veteran St, Grand Marais; mains $7-12; ☻ 7:30am-4pm

SLEEP

Alger Falls Motel
Snowmobilers, in particular, love this mom-and-pop motel, with 16 rooms and free wi-fi; located 2 miles east of town. ☎ 906-387-3536; www.algerfallsmotel.com; E9427 Hwy 28, Munising; r $50-70; ☻

Hilltop Cabins and Motel
Eight cabins and a five-unit motel rise a mile east of downtown; follow Veteran/Grand Marais/Everett Aves. ☎ 906-494-2331; www.hilltopcabins.net; N14176 Ellen St, Grand Marais; r & cabins $75-150; ☻ ☻

Landmark Inn
The elegant, six-story Landmark fills a historic building on the harbor front, and has resident ghosts. ☎ 906-228-2580; www.thelandmarkinn.com; 230 N Front St, Marquette; r $139-229

Whitefish Point Light Station B&B
Operated by the Shipwreck Museum's historical society, the five rooms are in a 1923 Coast Guard lifeboat station, with water views. ☎ 888-492-3747; www.shipwreckmuseum.com/overnight.phtml; Whitefish Point; r $150; ☻ Apr–mid-Nov

USEFUL WEBSITES
www.hunts-upguide.com
www.uptravel.com

LINK YOUR TRIP
www.lonelyplanet.com/trip-planner

TRIP
43 Michigan's Gold Coast p337
47 Dylan, Moose & More on Highway 61 p359

Rockin' the Midwest

WHY GO Music fans know that "Cleveland Rocks" and Detroit is "Rock City." Chicago's got the power-chord mojo, too. But where can you plug into the best rock, rap, jazz and blues? Josh Chicoine, musician and co-director of the Chicago International Movies and Music Festival, guides us through the Midwest's scene.

As lead singer and guitarist for the M's – indie rockers whom *Pitchfork* described as "as fine a purveyor of vintage British glam-pop as any Midwestern band" – Josh Chicoine toured the country multiple times before the band went on hiatus in 2009. Nowadays he works on CIMM Fest. The four-day event each March spotlights global films in which music plays a central role. Screenings and concerts bring together the two disciplines "in a headlock of love." Chicoine is CIMM's music person, so he knows his psycho-surf-rockabilly from punk-lounge – and the top venues to hear them.

We start in Cleveland, rock's unlikely mecca thanks to the ❶ **Rock & Roll Hall of Fame and Museum**. How did such a world-renowned sight end up in rust-belt Ohio? Because Cleveland is the hometown of Alan Freed, the disk jockey who popularized the term "rock and roll" in the early 1950s. The memorabilia impresses – Jimi Hendrix's Stratocaster, Keith Moon's platform shoes, Ray Charles' sunglasses – but it goes beyond that, with multimedia exhibits tracing rock's history and social context. Plan on spending the afternoon (and c'mon, stop trying to touch Neil Peart's drum set).

When darkness falls, Chicoine recommends the ❷ **Grog Shop** in funky, alternative Coventry, a neighborhood 7 miles east of downtown. It's a sweaty, cheap-beer club, the kind of place where buzz bands thrash before hitting it big. A block away, ❸ **Tommy's** provides the requi-

TIME
4 days

DISTANCE
450 miles

BEST TIME TO GO
Year-Round

START
Cleveland, OH

END
Chicago, IL

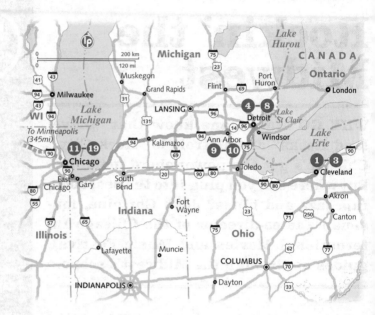

site fuel-up. The old hippie haven has served tofu, sprouts and spinach pies since 1972.

Detroit is up next. Roadies know it's I-90 west to I-280 north around Toledo, and then I-75 north into Motown. "Detroit is tough," Chicoine says. "It's a rough town for acts who don't live there. Detroiters really support their own" – and that includes quite an assortment through the years. Motown Records and soul music put Detroit on the map in the 1960s. Fans can check out the ❹ **Motown Historical Museum** in a modest house where Berry Gordy launched the company – and the careers of Stevie Wonder, Diana Ross, Marvin Gaye and Michael Jackson – with an $800 loan. Alas, everyone split for the glitz of LA by 1972.

Around the same time, the Stooges and MC5 started Detroit on its hard-edged, garage-rock way. By 1976 Motown was officially crowned "Rock City," thanks to KISS's tune. Chicoine suggests the ❺ **Lager House** to catch the vibe today: "It's not very big, but it books lots of indie and local stuff. It's a rock bar for sure – a little seedy, a little dirty, and don't expect the prettiest bathrooms." He advises the ❻ **Magic Stick** for a similarly loud but larger venue. Neo-rockers the White Stripes rose from the ranks of its Stroh's-splattered floor. So did fellow garage rockers the Von Bondies. In fact, the frontmen from the two bands got into an infamous brawl at the Stick, solidifying its street cred forevermore.

If you want to stay on the White Stripes' trail, but fancy something mellower than a live show, head to ❼ **The Bronx**, where Jack and Meg used to hang. There's not much inside the dimly lit dive besides a pool table and couple of jukeboxes filled with ballsy rock and soul. But that's the way the neighborhood regulars and local musicians like it. They're also fond of the beefy burgers fried up late at night. A mile north, the ❽ **Inn on Ferry Street** provides deliciously soft bedding to rest your noggin after all the head-banging.

Refreshed? It's on to Ann Arbor, 40 miles west via I-96 and Hwy 14. Chicoine says the ❾ **Blind Pig** is the must-do venue here – and everyone from John Lennon to Nirvana to the Circle Jerks seems to agree, since they've all played the storied stage. Before leaving town, take the short walk over to ❿ **Zingerman's Delicatessen** to stock up on responsibly sourced sandwiches and absurdly decadent brownies. They'll keep you company on the long, flat drive to Chicago, 250 miles west on I-94 and I-90.

"It's a rock bar for sure – a little seedy, a little dirty, and don't expect the prettiest bathrooms."

It's a burden of riches in the Windy City, where indie clubs slouch on almost every corner. Could Chicoine possibly pick a favorite? "⓫ **Schuba's**," he says. "It's renowned across the country. The room is intimate, and has great sound because it's all wood. My Morning Jacket, the Shins and lots of other bands have played it. There's also the ⓬ **Hideout**," Chicoine continues. "The owners have nursed a very outsider, underground, alt-country vibe. It feels like the downstairs of your grandma's rumpus room. Hipsters flock there, bands on tour want to play there – it has a lot of indie, do-it-yourself cachet. Not far away is the ⓭ **Double Door**," he rolls on. "It's hit or miss in what you'll see, but it's booked a lot. And it's in Wicker Park, a former artists' enclave that's now a popular and trendy boutique-ville."

PLAYLIST ♪   The Midwest offers it all, from upbeat Motown to indie classics, with some blues greats along the way.

• "C'mon C'mon," Von Bondies
• "Kiss," Prince
• "Turn on the News," Husker Du
• "300 Pounds of Joy," Howlin' Wolf
• "Where Did Our Love Go," Supremes
• "Champagne and Reefer," Muddy Waters

For a post-show cocktail, Chicoine points to nouveau speakeasy ⓮ **The Violet Hour**, around the corner from the Double Door. It's not marked, so look for the poster-covered, wood-paneled building and door topped by a yellow light bulb. U2 found it for their recent record-release party. "There are high-backed booths for privacy, chandeliers, long velvet drapes and lots of mixology going on," Chicoine says.

Speaking of speakeasies, Al Capone's favorite one lingers as a top-regarded Chicago jazz club. The ⓯ Green Mill, in the northern Uptown neighborhood, was part-owned by Capone's bootlegging pal Machine Gun McGurn.

MUSICAL FAIRS

The Midwest hosts several blowout music fests. Foremost are **Lollapalooza** (www.lollapalooza.com) in early August, when 130 bands take over Chicago's Grant Park; **Pitchfork Music Festival** (www.pitchforkmusicfestival.com), also in Chicago, a sort of Lollapalooza Jr for indie bands in mid-July; the **Movement/Detroit Electronic Music Festival** (www.myspace.com/detroitmusicfest), in techno's birthplace over Memorial Day weekend; and **Summerfest** (www.summerfest.com), which brings hundreds of bands to Milwaukee for 11 days in late June or early July. The **Chicago International Movies and Music Festival** (www.cimmfest.org) is also gaining momentum.

The tunnels where they hid the booze still lie underneath the bar. Low-lit, loungey and famed for its martinis, the Green Mill today is Chicoine's jazz pick for its consistently good acts and diverse crowd.

Several more jazz clubs dot the city, a legacy from the early 20th century when Louis Armstrong, Benny Goodman and other musicians swung around town. But Chicago's greatest claim to musical fame came in the 1940s. That's when Muddy Waters, Howlin' Wolf and friends plugged in their amps and birthed the electric blues.

To see the old Chess Records studio, where the bluesmen cut their first tracks and paved the way for rock and roll with their screaming guitars, visit ⓰ Willie Dixon's Blues Heaven, which occupies the building. It's modest as an attraction, but blues fans will thrill to walk the halls where Etta James, Bo Diddley, Chuck Berry and even Mick Jagger once roamed. Head north to ⓱ Kingston Mines when you're ready to hear the live version. "This is Chicago blues in a juke-joint atmosphere," Chicoine says. "Two stages host bands nightly." The frets bend on through the wee hours.

DETOUR ▶ **Minneapolis** (www.minneapolis.org) is another rock hot spot, 410 miles west of Chicago via I-90 and I-94. Prince and post-punkers Hüsker Dü and the Replacements cut their chops in downtown's influential **First Ave & 7th Street Entry** (www.first-avenue.com). Prince filmed *Purple Rain* at the club, and local mayors have been known to stage-dive for votes here. For more music, check the **Triple Rock Social Club** (www.triplerocksocialclub.com), **400 Bar** (www.400bar.com) and **Electric Fetus** (www.electricfetus.com) record shop.

You're probably beat from all the, well, beats. Chicoine says indie bands stay at the ⓲ Days Inn Chicago – one of the few hotels on Chicago's north side, where most clubs are located. The slick ⓳ James hotel downtown also has housed a musician or two. It's a full-on luxury property with custom beds, commissioned artworks and gracious staff who'd probably remove all the brown M&M's from the minibar if asked.

Karla Zimmerman

HISTORY & CULTURE

TRIP INFORMATION

GETTING THERE
To reach rock's hall of fame take I-90 into downtown Cleveland; get off at exit 174B and turn right on E 9th St.

DO

Blind Pig
The Pig grabs the coolest rock and blues groups passing through. No band? No problem. Swill in the attached bar. ☎ 734-996-8555; www.blindpigmusic.com; 208 S 1st St, Ann Arbor, MI; tickets $5-20

Double Door
Just-under-the-radar alt-rock bands get loud here, but the cachet is such that groups like the Rolling Stones have plugged in, too. ☎ 773-489-3160; www.doubledoor.com; 1572 N Milwaukee Ave, Chicago, IL; tickets free-$20

Green Mill
Local and national jazz artists perform seven nights per week; Sunday is also popular for the nationally acclaimed poetry slam. ☎ 773-878-5552; www.greenmill jazz.com; 4802 N Broadway Ave, Chicago, IL; tickets $4-12

Grog Shop
Up-and-coming rockers yowl at this longtime music house in the Coventry neighborhood. ☎ 216-321-5588; www.grogshop.gs; 2785 Euclid Heights Blvd, Cleveland, OH; tickets free - 15

Hideout
Alt-rock, folk and country bands twang each night in Chicago's most laid-back venue, hidden behind a factory. ☎ 773-227-4433; www.hideoutchicago.com; 1354 W Wabansia Ave, Chicago, IL; tickets $5-10

Kingston Mines
Noisy, hot, sweaty and conveniently located in Lincoln Park, Kingston Mines is a popular nightly blues draw. ☎ 773-477-4646; www. kingstonmines.com; 2548 N Halsted St, Chicago, IL; tickets $12-15

Lager House
Scrappy bands or DJs play most nights in this dingy, atmospheric punk/underground club. ☎ 313-961-4668; www.pjslagerhouse. com; 1254 Michigan Ave, Detroit, MI; tickets free-$10

Magic Stick
It's Detroit's top address for indie rockers and rap DJs; the complex also holds the larger Majestic Theater, a bowling alley and a pizza restaurant. ☎ 313-833-9700; www.majestic detroit.com; 4120 Woodward Ave, Detroit, MI; tickets $5-17

Motown Historical Museum
It offers a simple look at Motown Records' hit-making studios; guides tell tales and show old photos. ☎ 313-875-2264; www. motownmuseum.com; 2648 W Grand Blvd, Detroit, MI; adult/child $10/8; ☺ 10am-6pm Tue-Sat, plus Mon Jul & Aug

Rock & Roll Hall of Fame & Museum
As-cool-as-expected memorabilia and multimedia exhibits overwhelm the senses. ☎ 216-781-7625, 888-764-7625; www. rockhall.com; 751 Erieside Ave, Cleveland, OH; adult/9-12yr $22/13; ☺ 10am-5:30pm, to 9pm Wed year-round, to 9pm Sat Jun-Aug

Schuba's
A friendly bar pours microbrews in front, while indie bands play nightly in the cozy back-room club. ☎ 773-525-2508; www. schubas.com; 3159 N Southport Ave, Chicago, IL; tickets $5-25

Willie Dixon's Blues Heaven
The old Chess Records Studio holds a no-frills collection of blues memorabilia. ☎ 312-808-1286; www.bluesheaven.com; 2120 S Michigan Ave, Chicago, IL; tours $10; ☺ 11am-4pm Mon-Fri, noon-2pm Sat

EAT & DRINK

The Bronx
It's the quintessential dive bar: dark, smoky, with cheap burgers and booze, and Detroit's best jukebox. ☎ 313-832-8464; 4476

HISTORY &
CULTURE

2nd Ave, Detroit, MI; mains $4-8;
☯ 11:30am-2am

Tommy's
Tofu, seitan and other old-school veggie
dishes emerge from the kitchen, though
carnivores have multiple options, too. ☎ 216-
321-7757; www.tommyscoventry.com; 1823
Coventry Rd, Cleveland, OH; mains $6-10;
☯ 9am-9pm Sun-Thu, to 10pm Fri, 7:30am-
10pm Sat

Violet Hour
It's like a highbrow speakeasy, with an
unmarked door and elaborate cocktails.
☎ 773-252-1500; www.theviolethour.com;
1520 N Damen Ave, Chicago, IL; cocktails
$12; ☯ 6pm-2am Sun-Fri, to 3am Sat

Zingerman's Delicatessen
A local institution with nationwide acclaim,
Zingerman's piles local and organic ingredients onto big-ass sandwiches. ☎ 734-663-
3354; www.zingermansdeli.com; 422 Detroit
St, Ann Arbor, MI; sandwiches $10-15.50;
☯ 7am-10pm

SLEEP

Days Inn Chicago
The well-kept hotel is uniquely located
in Lincoln Park, close to the lakefront and
various music venues. ☎ 773-525-7010;
www.daysinnchicago.net; 644 W Diversey
Parkway, Chicago, IL; r $120-180; ♿

Inn on Ferry Street
Forty guestrooms fill a row of Victorian
mansions by the Detroit Institute of Arts; free
wi-fi and hot breakfast included. ☎ 313-
871-6000; www.innonferrystreet.com; 84 E
Ferry St, Detroit, MI; r $129-229

The James
This mod boutique hotel attracts a suave
crowd who appreciates top-notch service
and comfortable luxury. ☎ 312-337-1000,
877-526-3755; www.jameshotels.com; 616 N
Rush St, Chicago, IL; r $159-359; ♿

USEFUL WEBSITES
www.chicagoreader.com/music
www.motorcityrocks.com

LINK YOUR TRIP
TRIP

www.lonelyplanet.com/trip-planner

Dylan, Moose & More on Highway 61

WHY GO Mention Hwy 61 and many folks hum Bob Dylan. But this North Shore road is not about murder, poverty or any other mean-street mumblings from his *Highway 61 Revisited*. Instead it's a journey along Lake Superior's glinting shore, tucked between red-tinged cliffs and boreal forest from Duluth to Canada.

Let's clarify one thing first. "Hwy 61" is also used to reference the fabled Blues Highway that clasps the Mississippi River en route to New Orleans. That road is actually US Hwy 61, and it starts near St Paul, Minnesota. Our Hwy 61 is a state scenic road, and it starts in Duluth – which is where we'll start (as did Dylan, who was born here).

Dramatically spliced into a cliff that tumbles down to Lake Superior, Duluth is one of the busiest ports in the nation, sporting over 40 miles of wharf and waterfront. Check in at ❶ **Fitger's Inn**, which carved its 62 classy rooms from an old brewery on the waterfront. Hop on Superior St and head a mile south to Canal Park. You can't miss the ❷ **Aerial Lift Bridge**, Duluth's landmark that raises its mighty arm to let horn-bellowing ships into port. About a thousand leviathans a year glide through. Check the computer screens outside the ❸ **Maritime Visitors Center** to learn when the big ones come and go. The first-rate center also has exhibits on Great Lakes shipping and shipwrecks.

Up for stretching the legs? It's about a 1.5-mile mosey along the lakefront trail to ❸ **Leif Erikson Park** by 14th Ave E. A rose garden, a replica of Leif's Viking ship and free outdoor movies each Friday eve in summer reward the effort. Plus you can say you hiked the ❺ **Superior Trail**, which traverses this stretch. It's a lot easier than the rest of the 205-mile path along the ridgeline to Canada – though you'll miss out on the occasional moose and black bear.

TIME
2 – 3 days

DISTANCE
150 miles

BEST TIME TO GO
Jul – Sep

START
Duluth, MN

END
Portage, MN

Back downtown on Superior St, vegetarian-friendly ⑥ **Pizza Luce** cooks locally sourced breakfasts and gourmet pizzas, with lots of booze to help down the latter. It's plugged into the local music scene and hosts bands, too. Across the road, indie ⑦ **Electric Fetus** sells a whopping selection of CDs, vinyl and local arts and crafts, including Dylan buttons. Get 'em while you can: Duluth is pretty laid-back when it comes to its famous son. Yes, there are signs on Superior and London Sts for "Bob Dylan Way," pointing out places associated with the legend (like the armory where he saw Buddy Holly in concert, and decided to become a musician). But you're on your own to find ⑧ **Dylan's birthplace**. Take Superior St northeast a few blocks to 3rd Ave E; turn left and go up the hill about a half-mile to No 519. Dylan lived on the top floor until age six, when his family moved inland to Hibbing. It's a private residence, so all you can do is stare from the street – no ringing the doorbell.

Before leaving Duluth, drive up to ⑨ **Hawk Ridge Observatory**, 600ft above Lake Superior. The view is grand, especially between mid-August and November, when 94,000 raptors swing by as part of the autumn hawk migration. The site is about 15 minutes from downtown. Take Superior St northeast to 45th Ave E; turn left and go to Glenwood St. Turn left and within a mile you'll reach Skyline Parkway; the observatory is a mile onward.

Now the action begins. Retrace the route from Hawk Ridge, except continue on 45th Ave E to the waterfront and London Rd – aka Hwy 61 – and turn left. Follow the signs for the North Shore Scenic Dr (also called Scenic 61 or Old Hwy 61). There's a Hwy 61 expressway that also covers the next 20 miles, but steer clear and dawdle on the curvy, time-hewn, two-lane route instead. Unspoiled shoreline and fisherfolk casting at river mouths will be your companions until you reach ⑩ **Russ Kendall's Smoke House** in Knife River. Four generations of Kendall folk have fired up the locally plucked trout and line-caught Alaskan salmon. Buy a brown-sugar-cured slab, and you're set for picnics for miles to come.

"Unspoiled shoreline and fisherfolk casting at river mouths will be your companions..."

OK, so the fish is demolished by Two Harbors, a couple of miles up the road. Luckily, ⑪ **Betty's Pies** wafts serious flaky goodness here. Consider the five-layer chocolate tinful, stacked with dark chocolate, cinnamon meringue, regular whipped cream and chocolate whipped cream. Fork in 2 miles north of town. For a view-worthy bed, tuck in at Two Harbors' ⑫ **Lighthouse B&B**, if you can snag one of the four rooms.

⑬ **Gooseberry Falls State Park** spills 13 miles onward. The five cascades, scenic gorge and easy trails draw carloads of visitors. ⑭ **Split Rock Lighthouse State Park** lies 6 miles beyond. The shiner itself is a state historic site with a separate admission fee. If you don't mind stairs, say 170 or so each way, tramp down the cliff to the beach for incredible views of the lighthouse and surrounding shore.

Ten miles later, not long after cruising by taconite-crazed Silver Bay, watch for the sign to ⑮ **Palisade Head** and turn down the narrow, windy road to look out from the rust-red cliff top. On a clear day you can see Wisconsin's Apostle Islands. Rock climbers love the Head. Though it's not contiguous, it's part of ⑯ **Tettegouche State Park**, whose main span begins 2

DETOUR ➤ The **Gunflint Trail** (www. gunflint-trail.com), aka Hwy 12, slices inland from Grand Marais to Saganaga Lake. The paved, 57-mile-long byway skirts the **Boundary Waters Canoe Area Wilderness** (www.fs.fed.us/r9/forests/superior/bwcaw), the legendarily remote paddlers' paradise. For Boundary permits and information, visit the **Gunflint Ranger Station**, just south of Grand Marais on Hwy 61. Even if you're not canoeing, the road has excellent hiking, picnicking and moose viewing. It takes 1½ hours to drive one way, but you'll want longer to commune with your new antlered friends.

miles up-road. Like almost all the parks dotting the North Shore, Tettegouche offers fishing, camping, paddling and hiking trails to waterfalls and little lakes, plus skiing and snowshoe trails in winter. The idyllic swimming hole at the Baptism River's mouth is a warm-weather bonus.

Hwy 61 rolls by more birch trees, parks and cloud-flecked skies for the next 60 miles. When you finally pull in to happenin' little Grand Marais, you'll need sustenance. Take your pick: ⑰ **World's Best Donuts**, where staff nobly arrives at 3am each morning to fry and glaze; ⑱ **Sven and Ole's**, a classic for sandwiches and pizza, plus beer at the attached pub; or the ⑲ **Angry Trout Cafe**, an upscale, sustainably focused restaurant in a converted fishing shanty. A stone skip east of the Trout, do-it-yourselfers can learn to build boats, tie flies or brew beer at the ⑳ **North House Folk School**. The course list, which strives to preserve local traditions, is phenomenal – as is the school's two-hour sailing trip aboard the Viking-esque schooner *Hjordis*.

DETOUR

Isle Royale National Park (www.nps.gov/isro) is technically part of Michigan, but it's easily accessed from Grand Portage by daily ferries between May and October. The 210-sq-mile island is totally free of vehicles and roads, and gets fewer visitors in a year than Yellowstone gets in a day – which means the packs of wolves and moose creeping through the forest are all yours. There's one lodge; otherwise prepare to camp backcountry-style.

Spend the night in town at plain-and-simple ㉑ **Harbor Inn**. Or head 14 miles further up Hwy 61 to trail-encircled ㉒ **Naniboujou Lodge**. The rustic, TV-less property was once a private club for Babe Ruth and contemporaries, though it looks a bit different today with its mind-blowing Great Hall and psychedelic Cree Indian designs.

The final stretch of highway passes through the Grand Portage Indian Reservation and casino, and, finally, ㉓ **Grand Portage National Monument**, where the early voyagers had to carry their canoes (hence the name) around the Pigeon River rapids. This was the center of a far-flung fur-trading empire, and the reconstructed 1788 trading post and Ojibwe village show how the little community lived in the harsh environment. It's impressively lonely and windblown – the type of place Bob Dylan might write about – and fitting for the end of the road. Because with that, Hwy 61 stops cold at the Canadian border.

Karla Zimmerman

TRIP INFORMATION

GETTING THERE
Take I-35 into Duluth. The city also has a decent-sized airport and Greyhound service from Minneapolis.

DO

Electric Fetus
The uber-cool record shop stocks local arts and crafts in addition to tunes. ☎ 218-722-9970; www.electricfetus.com; 12 E Superior St, Duluth; ⏱ 9am-9pm Mon-Fri, to 8pm Sat, 11am-6pm Sun

Gooseberry Falls State Park
The five cascades and easy trails make it a family favorite. ☎ 218-834-3855; www.dnr.state.mn.us; 3206 Hwy 61, Two Harbors; per vehicle $5, campsites $20; ⏱ 8am-10pm; ♿

Grand Portage National Monument
Ogle the reconstructed fur-trading post and Ojibwe heritage center. ☎ 218-475-0123; www.nps.gov/grpo; 170 Mile Creek Rd, Grand Portage; admission $3; ⏱ heritage center year-round, historic site mid-May–mid-Oct, call for hours; ♿

Hawk Ridge Observatory
At 600ft above the lakeshore it's a heckuva view, especially during the autumn hawk migration. ☎ 218-428-6209; hawkridge.org; 3980 E Skyline Pkwy, Duluth; admission free; ⏱ 6am-10pm

Leif Erikson Park
This lakefront sweet spot has a rose garden, a Viking ship and outdoor movies on Friday night in summer. **cnr London Rd & 14th Ave E, Duluth; admission free;** ⏱ 24hr

Maritime Visitors Center
Learn about Great Lakes shipping; the monitor tracks when the next freighter arrives. ☎ 218-720-5260; www.lsmma.com; 600 Lake Ave S, Duluth; admission free; ⏱ 10am-9pm Jun-Aug, reduced hour Sep-May; ♿

North House Folk School
The center teaches traditional crafts, like Native American basket weaving, canoe carving and schooner sailing. ☎ 218-387-9762; www.northhouse.org; 500 Hwy 61, Grand Marais; classes from $35, 2hr sailing tour $45

Split Rock Lighthouse State Park
The beaming centerpiece has a separate fee from the park. ☎ 218-226-6377; www.dnr.state.mn.us; 3755 Split Rock Lighthouse Rd, Two Harbors; per vehicle $5, campsites $12, lighthouse $8; ⏱ 10am-6pm

Tettegouche State Park
Fishing, camping, swimming and hiking (the Shovel Point path wins raves) are all part of the package. ☎ 218-226-6365; www.dnr.state.mn.us; 5702 Hwy 61, Silver Bay; per vehicle $5, campsites $20; ⏱ 9am-8pm

EAT & DRINK

Angry Trout Cafe
This sustainably focused restaurant serves Lake Superior fish alongside local wild rice and produce. ☎ 218-387-1265; www.angrytroutcafe.com; 416 Hwy 61, Grand Marais; mains $12-25; ⏱ 11am-8:30pm, closed mid-Oct–Apr

Betty's Pies
Rackfuls of pie are Betty's claim to fame, though there's a lengthy menu of sandwiches, burgers and omelets, too. ☎ 218-834-3367; www.bettyspies.com; 1633 Hwy 61, Two Harbors; sandwiches $5-9; ⏱ 7am-9pm, reduced hr Oct-May

Pizza Luce
Locals love it for the gourmet pizzas, vegetarian options, full bar and bands. ☎ 218-727-7400; www.pizzaluce.com; 11 E Superior St, Duluth; large pizzas $20-22; ⏱ 8am-1:30am Sun-Thu, to 2:30am Fri & Sat

Russ Kendall's Smoke House
Point to your favorite salmon; staff will wrap it in newspaper, and you're on your picnicking way. ☎ 218-834-5995; 149 Scenic Dr, Knife River; salmon per pound $15; ⏱ 9:30am-5:30pm

Sven and Ole's

It's a classic for sandwiches and pizzas. Go ahead: ask about the lutefisk pizza. ☎ 218-387-1713; www.svenandoles.com; 9 Wisconsin St, Grand Marais; sandwiches $4-8; 🕐 11am-8pm, to 9pm Thu-Sat

World's Best Donuts

Mmm, donuts. The elephant-ear-like skizzle also has a following. ☎ 218-387-1345; www.worldsbestdonutsmn.com; 10 E Wisconsin St, Grand Marais; items $0.50-1; 🕐 4:30am-4:30pm Mon-Sat, to 2pm Sun, closed mid-Oct–mid-May

SLEEP

Fitger's Inn

Located in an old brewery, many of the upscale rooms have water views; free breakfast and wi-fi included. ☎ 218-722-8826, 888-348-4377; www.fitgers.com; 600 E Superior St, Duluth; r $99-209; 🦽

Harbor Inn

The rooms may look plain-Jane, but they're comfy and well located and have free wi-fi. ☎ 218-387-1191; www.bytheharbor.com; 207 Wisconsin St, Grand Marais; r $95-135; 🦽

Lighthouse B&B

You can't beat this real-deal lighthouse for ambience and lake views. ☎ 218-834-4814, 888-832-5606; www.lighthousebb.org; 1 Lighthouse Point, Two Harbors; r $135-155

Naniboujou Lodge

Rooms at the historic property vary in decor, but each offers an away-from-it-all experience. ☎ 218-387-2688; www.naniboujou.com; 20 Naniboujou, Grand Marais; r $90-110; daily mid-May–mid-Oct, weekends only rest of yr

USEFUL WEBSITES

www.northshorevisitor.com
www.visitduluth.com

LINK YOUR TRIP

www.lonelyplanet.com/trip-planner

Rich in Kitsch

WHY GO A meaty Spam shrine, the resting place of the Frisch's Big Boy, a cow-doo-throwing contest – the quirks rise from the Midwest's backyards and back roads, wherever there are folks with a passion, imagination and maybe a little too much time on their hands.

We're not going to sugarcoat it: you'll have to drive hundreds of miles on yawning interstates through windblown towns to see these oddities. It's crazy. It's madness. Then again, the same can be said for each of our destinations.

We begin in Darwin, Minnesota, home to a very big stringed orb. That's right, kitschsters, it's the ❶ **World's Largest Ball of Twine Built by One Person** (not to be confused with the bulkier "Largest Built by a Town" in Cawker City, Kansas). Darwin-local Francis A Johnson wrapped the 17,400lb whopper on his farm over the course of 29 years. Gawk at it in the town gazebo. Better yet, visit the museum beside it and buy your own twine ball starter kit in the gift shop.

Get on Hwy 12 east and head toward the Twin Cities for 50 miles. On the outskirts hop on I-494 south for 17 miles. Exit on Hwy 77 south, then at Killebrew Dr a half-mile later.

By now you know we're steering to the ❷ **Mall of America**, the USA's largest shopping center. Yes, it's just a mall, filled with the usual stores, movie theaters and eateries. But there's also a wedding chapel inside. And an 18-hole minigolf course. And an amusement park with 24 rides, including a roller coaster. And sharks. You'll work up an appetite walking through (the mall's the length of 88 football fields), so grab a nosh at the ❸ **Magic Pan Crepe Stand** on the 1st floor.

TIME
2 – 3 days

DISTANCE
430 miles

BEST TIME TO GO
May – Sep

START
Darwin, MN

END
Green, WI

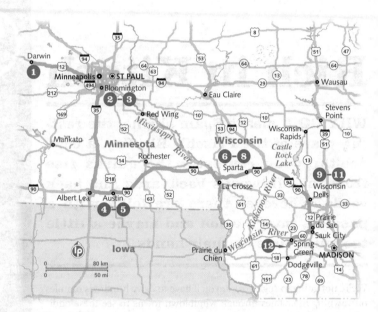

Swing onto I-35 going east and then south to Albert Lea. Merge onto I-90 east. After 18 miles, take exit 178A into Austin, Minnesota – the birthplace of Spam. The ❹ **Spam Museum** educates on how the blue tins have fed armies, become a Hawaiian food staple and inspired legions of haiku writers. What's more, you can chat up the staff (aka "spambassadors"), indulge in free samples, and try your hand at canning the sweet pork magic. Jonesing for tins of bacon Spam and cheese Spam? The gift store rocks all nine varieties.

To satisfy any lingering carnivorous urges, drive a half-mile south on Main St to ❺ **Piggy Blues Bar-B-Que**. Pull up a plate of dry-rubbed, hardwood-smoked ribs, squirt on hot-spice or bourbon sauce from the squeeze bottles, and wash it down with Schell's beer from nearby New Ulm, Minnesota. Piggy even serves a Spam burger.

Return to I-90 and motor east for 125 miles to Sparta, WI, a button-cute town amid swooping green hills. Loads of cyclists come to the self-proclaimed "bicycling capital of America," thanks to its miles of tunnel-laden, rail-to-trail paths and B&Bs that ooze homeyness on tree-shaded streets, like the ❻ **Franklin Victorian**.

Sparta is no stranger to kitsch – witness the ❼ **World's Largest Bicyclist**, a vintage, 32ft-tall statue in the park at Water and Wisconsin Sts – but it woefully under-promotes its most fabulous asset: the ❽ **FAST Mold Yard**. FAST stands for Fiberglass Animals, Shapes and Trademarks, and it's the company that sculpts the hulking jack-a-lopes, ax-wielding lumberjacks and other novelties seen so often during back-road travels. The Mold Yard is purgatory for the statues' casts, where FAST keeps them in case they're needed again. Gaze over the Frisch's Big Boy, life-size dinosaurs, truck-sized ice-cream cones and more bizarro creations rising in post-apocalypse style from the field behind the factory. It's about 7 miles northeast of Sparta. Take Angelo Rd/Hwy 21, then turn left onto Hwy Q.

"hulking jack-a-lopes, ax-wielding lumberjacks and other novelties seen during back-road travels."

Zip back to I-90 east for 65 miles to the **9** **Wisconsin Dells**. Every Midwest kid has done time in this mega-center of carny diversions. The 21 water parks, water-skiing thrill shows, torture museums and gumdrop shops combine to unleash a $1 billion tourism juggernaut. And those molds you saw in Sparta? Many of their spawn are right here. Drive up Hwy 12, the Dells' main vein, and you'll get the picture.

Embrace the scene and check into **10** **Kalahari Waterpark Resort**, a quintessential, 750-room Dells behemoth. Once you get past the jungle theme, the rooms are a perfectly pleasant place to chill when you're done mock-surfing in the pools. For eats, try **11** **Denny's Diner**, a red-white-and-blue greasy spoon with big sides of outlandishness (think Tasmanian devil with an arm falling out of its mouth, and lots o' Elvis).

DETOUR ▶ If you're in the Dells the first weekend in September, check out the annual **Cow Chip Throw** (www.wiscowchip.com) in Prairie du Sac, Wisconsin, where 800 competitors fling dried manure patties toward the horizon. The record is 248ft. The town is off Hwy 12, via County Rd Pf.

As eye-popping as it all is, our next stop makes the Dells look tame. Take Hwy 12 south for 20 miles, then Hwy 60 west near Sauk City for another 20 miles. At Spring Green, take Hwy 23 south and follow the signs to the **12** **House on the Rock**. Holy crazed genius! Alex Jordan built the structure atop a rock column in 1959 (some say as an "up yours" to neighbor Frank Lloyd Wright). He then stuffed the house to mind-blowing proportions with wonderments. The world's largest carousel, whirring music machines, freaky dolls and crazed folk art are but a fraction of the sensory-overloading sprawl. You can visit one, two or all three parts of the house. Those with kitsch stamina (and four hours to kill) should go the whole way.

Karla Zimmerman

②
OFFBEAT

TRIP INFORMATION

GETTING THERE
The fun starts in Darwin, Minnesota, about 60 miles west of Minneapolis via Hwy 12.

DO
FAST Mold Yard
The factory that makes giant novelty statues puts the Frisch's Big Boy and others out to pasture. ☎ 608-269-7110; 14177 Hwy Q, Sparta, WI; admission free; ☼ sunrise-sunset

House on the Rock
By turns beautiful and strange, nightmarish and dreamy. ☎ 608-935-3639; www.thehouseontherock.com; 5754 Hwy 23, Spring Green, WI; adult/child $28.50/15.50; ☼ 9am-5pm daily, 9am-6pm May-Aug, closed Tue-Thu Nov-Mar

Mall of America
The USA's biggest shopping center has its own zip code and indoor amusement park. ☎ 952-883-8800; www.mallofamerica.com; off I-494 at 24th Ave, Bloomington, MN; ☼ 10am-9:30pm Mon-Sat, 11am-7pm Sun; ♿

Spam Museum
Hormel Foods pays irreverent homage to its peculiar pork brand. ☎ 800-588-7726; www.spam.com; 1101 N Main St, Austin, MN; admission free; ☼ 10am-5pm Mon-Sat, noon-5pm Sun; ♿

World's Largest Ball of Twine
One man's obsession for 29 years: see the mondo stringed result in the gazebo. ☎ 320-693-7544; www.darwintwineball.com; 1st St, Darwin, MN; admission free; ☼ gazebo 24hr year-round, museum 1-4pm Apr-Sep, by appointment Oct-Mar

EAT
Denny's Diner
No-frills eggs, hash browns and cinnamon buns amid Dells kitsch (Elvis statue!) and overstimulated kids. ☎ 608-254-7647; 2 Munroe St at Hwys 12 & 23, South Dells, WI; mains $5-9; ☼ 6:30am-1:30pm; ♿

Magic Pan Crepe Stand
Take a break in the mega mall with turkey-and-cheese, Nutella-and-banana and other pancake styles. ☎ 952-853-0200; 1st floor, Mall of America, Bloomington, MN; crepes $3.50-7; ☼ 10am-9:30pm Mon-Sat, 11am-7pm Sun

Piggy Blues Bar-B-Que
Piggy plates ribs, pulled-pork sandwiches, cornbread and more near the Spam Museum. ☎ 507-434-8485; 323 N Main St, Austin, MN; mains $8-12; ☼ 11am-8pm Mon-Thu, 11am-9pm Fri & Sat

SLEEP
Franklin Victorian B&B
Four rooms with private baths spread across this wi-fi-rigged Queen Anne home; staff will deliver breakfast to your room. ☎ 608-366-1427; www.franklinvictorianbb.com; 220 E Franklin St, Sparta, WI; r $109-129

Kalahari Waterpark Resort
Families and conventioneers alike appreciate each room's comfy beds, small private deck and free wi-fi. ☎ 877-525-2427; www.kalahariresorts.com; 1305 Kalahari Dr, South Dells, WI; r $99-219; ♿

USEFUL WEBSITES
www.bikesparta.com
www.wisdells.com

LINK YOUR TRIP
www.lonelyplanet.com/trip-planner

GREAT PLAINS TRIPS

The Great Plains states are more than happy to transition you between east and west. But if you slow down for just a moment, they'll open the door, invite you in and share some of the country's finest history, scenery and carnivorous cuisine. You'll hear tales of outlaws and cowboys, restless men who targeted boomtowns from Dodge City north to Deadwood. Geronimo, Crazy Horse and the Five Civilized Tribes have their own stories to share at cultural centers and battlefields in Oklahoma, Nebraska and South Dakota. Video gamers can get their kicks in Nebraska, where Chimney Rock and Scottsbluff give life to the famous video game *The Oregon Trail*. Book lovers revel in literary landscapes, from Mark Twain's Hannibal to Laura Ingalls' *Little House* books, while beef con-

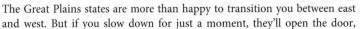 **PLAYLIST** 🎵 Big-sky ballads and cowboy songs are musical mainstays in the Great Plains. But every now and then you need a little jam with your bread and butter, and OKC's groovin' Flaming Lips are more than happy to oblige.

- "Do You Realize??," Flaming Lips
- "Amie," Pure Prairie League
- "The Execution of All Things," Rilo Kiley
- "Late Night Radio," Greg Brown
- "The Wind," Cat Stevens
- "Carry on Wayward Son," Kansas
- "Maple Leaf Rag," Scott Joplin
- "Cowboy Casanova," Carrie Underwood

noisseurs devour fried-onion burgers, spicy barbecue and Cattlemen's steak. All this, and we haven't mentioned Gateway Arch, Mt Rushmore or Fargo's Woodchip Marge. One required stop? The prairie. Vaulting grasshoppers, scratchy blue stems, unabashed birdsong, the smell of cut grass – by tickling the senses, it reinvigorates the soul. Pull over, leave the car, breathe deep. We think you'll see what we mean.

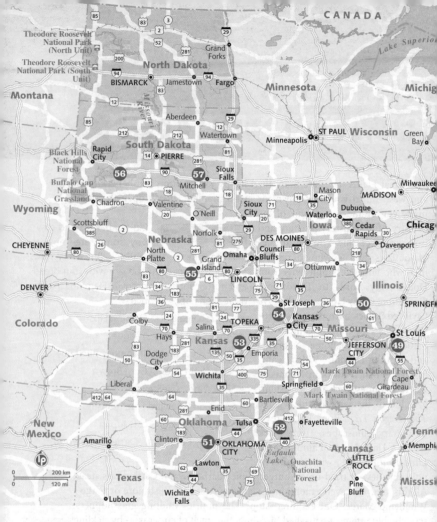

GREAT PLAINS TRIPS

48 Hours in St Louis

WHY GO Gateway Arch isn't just a portal to the West; it's also the front door to a vibrant city that's long inspired adventurers. Swoop up the Arch, sample a free brew, stretch for a fly ball and slurp frozen custard on this two-day tour that embraces the spirit of St Louis.

The city's joie de vivre sneaks up on you, not obvious at first, but there, waiting. It's got a musical bent, one that tickles your ear when you're strolling down Delmar Blvd. It floats past when the hipster pedals past, belting out a song. It dances through the air on the melodies of a sidewalk band. All this before sunset, before Chuck Berry takes the stage…

But wait. Let's not get ahead of ourselves. The city's confident charm first catches your notice when the white-haired lady at ❶ **Ted Drewes** hands you a cup of M&M's and swirled custard upside down. Why does she do it? Because it proves the thickness of the product – an ice-creamy vanilla custard mixed with the topping of your choice. These "concretes," along with sundaes, shakes and plain vanillas, have lured fans to the frosty white shack since 1930.

The charm keeps flowing at 1371-acre ❷ **Forest Park**, where the best attractions are free. They're also architecturally stunning, appropriate for a park that hosted the 1904 World's Fair. After passing through the column-flanked north entrance of the beaux arts ❸ **St Louis Art Museum**, built for the fair, get your bearings inside the cavernous Sculpture Hall. In the "Along the River" gallery, evocative regional paintings of rivers and prairies capture the spirit of Great Plains adventure and set an exploratory mood for the museum's wide-ranging collection.

Just east, bright flowers sparkle inside the aptly named ❹ **Jewel Box**. This glass-walled art-deco structure, built in 1936, is an oasis beloved by romantics and St Louis brides. When it comes to satisfying kids, the

TIME
2 days

BEST TIME TO GO
Year-round

START
Chippewa St, St Louis, MO

END
Lafayette Sq, St Louis, MO

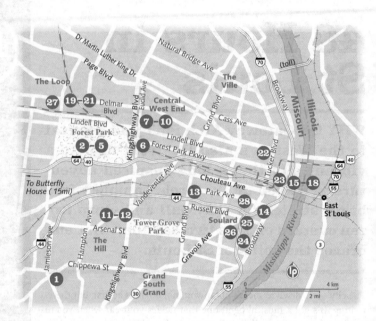

5 **St Louis Zoo** meets the Goldilocks standard: not too big; not too small. In fact, at 90 acres and 17,900 animals, it's just right for a no-fuss afternoon of animal-gazing. Penguins and puffins, as well as chimps, draw noticeable oohs and aahs.

For shut-eye, consider the **6** **Parkway Hotel**, an eight-story, 220-room indie property just east of the park. Unpack your bags, then explore the surrounding **7** **Central West End**. Mansions sit across from chocolate "lounges" in this chichi neighborhood where you can while away an afternoon flipping through the staff picks at friendly **8** **Left Bank Books** or surfing the web at scruffy **9** **Coffee Cartel**. As for that chocolate lounge, there's no better place to nibble sweets than **10** **Bissinger's, a Chocolate Experience**, where the bonbons are served with fine wine and fancy choc-tails.

You'll be hard-pressed to find a choc-tail in **11** **The Hill**, a 50-square-block Italian neighborhood zestily touting its ethnic heritage – as red, white and green fireplugs vividly attest. Narrow streets are lined with trim "shotgun" houses, but the big draw is the dense cluster of family-owned Italian restaurants. Join the buzzy crowds inside busy **12** **Cunetto's House of Pasta**. Convenient digs include the simple rooms at the **13** **Water Tower Inn** on the St Louis University campus.

The next morning, as you stroll past the apples, baguettes and sausages at the ⑭ **Soulard Farmers Market**, consider the history. The market opened here in 1838, the same year St Louis resident William Clark died. Clark, together with Meriwether Lewis, led the Lewis and Clark Expedition, commissioned by President Jefferson after the 1803 Louisiana Purchase. Their mission? To explore the country's newest acquisition and search for a waterway to the Pacific. Preparations took place in and around St Louis.

Just north, the ⑮ **Jefferson National Expansion Memorial** and its delicate calling card, the ⑯ **Gateway Arch**, honor Jefferson and the city for their role in the nation's push west. Glance up at the 630ft-tall arch as you approach. An elevator rises to the top of that? Not exactly. Picture a five-person pod gliding upward, tram-like, in a four-minute swoop. It's fun, and once on top you'll have sweeping views that can extend 30 miles on clear days. Visible below is the ⑰ **Old Courthouse & Museum**, where the Dred Scott slavery case was first tried.

Dioramas and murals provide an "impressionistic" overview of western history at the ⑱ **Museum of Westward Expansion** underneath the Arch. One tip? Don't follow the Jefferson statue's gaze as you enter or you'll end up in one of the least compelling exhibit areas (an overview of American Indian peace medals). Instead, follow the timeline to the left of Jefferson. It chronicles the taming of the West between 1800 and 1900. Just beyond, entries from Lewis and Clark's journals accompany stunning, mural-sized photographs of the landscapes described.

ASK A LOCAL If you're craving a burger, Molly Murphy recommends the super-thin patties at **Carl's Drive In** (9033 Manchester Rd). "It's like a little teeny drive-in shack," says Murphy. "People go bananas for the burgers." Add a side of fries and custom-made root beer, then settle in at one of the counter-side stools.

Jefferson's not the only president to turn his eye toward St Louis. Barack Obama fell for ⑲ **Pi Pizza** after a campaign stop. He subsequently invited the owners to whip up a few pizzas at the White House. The appeal? Pi's deep-dish pizzas have a cornmeal crust that cradles flavor-packed cheeses and gourmet toppings – a lip-smackingly satisfying combination. Waitstaff sport "No Provel" T-shirts, a not-so-subtle dis of traditional St Louis–style pizza: cracker-thin crusts slathered with processed Provel cheese.

Pi's saucy attitude is apt for ⑳ **The Loop**, a hustling, music-infused block that once served as the turn-around point for downtown streetcars. A rotating moon tops the ㉑ **Moonrise Hotel**, a whimsical beacon for this sleek hotel in the heart of the neighborhood.

Rooftop whimsy continues at ㉒ City Museum, where a yellow school bus perches precariously over the side of the building. What's going on? It's up to you to find out. Slides, ladders, caves, a rooftop Ferris wheel – it's a Wonka-esqe wonderland. Kids reign during the day, but weekend nights are for grown-ups (it's open until 1am) who wish life could always be this cool.

"Slides, ladders, caves, a rooftop Ferris wheel – it's a Wonka-esqe wonderland."

If your timing's right (April to early October), head back downtown for a baseball game at the Cardinals' retro-style ㉓ Busch Stadium. The Cardinals won the World Series in 2006, the year the stadium opened. No game? Drown your sorrows with two free beers during the hour-long factory tour at ㉔ Anheuser-Busch Brewery, the world's largest beer plant. Though Belgian InBev purchased the company in 2008, the tour keeps its focus on the company's roots, even swinging by stalls housing the famous Clydesdales. You'll use elevators, escalators, shuttles and foot power to see it all. Last stop? The hospitality room.

It's a short hop to cave-like Irish pub ㉕ John D. McGurk's. Within this red-brick warren, a generational mix of patrons consumes Guinness and hearty sandwiches. If you'd prefer more panache, ever-so-stylish ㉖ Sidney Street Cafe will embrace you with a lively intimacy perfect for couples or quartets of old friends. Menu descriptions border on over-the-top, but one look at passing mains – whiskey-sauced steaks, encrusted seafood – and hyperbole will be forgiven.

> **DETOUR**
>
> Snapping a photo of a quick-fluttering Common Blue Morpho in the **Butterfly House** (www.butterflyhouse.org) is about as easy as bottling a sunset. Nearly 2000 tropical butterflies representing 80 species swoop, nest and feed among lush, path-hugging plants in this oft-recommended wonderland 20 miles west of downtown. Most fun? Watching wide-eyed children go giddy among these darting, whisper-winged treasures. Education and conservation are key concerns. Near the entrance, you'll find information about efforts to preserve butterfly habitats.

But the night's not over yet. This is St Louis, home of Scott Joplin, Ike Turner and Nelly. Head back to the music-filled Loop and ㉗ Blueberry Hill, where the easygoing staff will fill you in on the night's entertainment – rock, jazz or blues – and encourage you to scope out the eatery and its engaging mishmash of rock memorabilia before committing. Chuck Berry rattles the rafters the second Wednesday of the month.

For one last smooch from this devil-may-care city, stop by ㉘ Park Avenue Coffee in the morning for gooey butter cake, a St Louis specialty whose name says it all. Park Avenue, in classy Lafayette Sq, makes 74 types of butter cake, but the flavor-packed plain, served with a smooth roast coffee, is really all the kiss that you need.

Amy C Balfour

TRIP INFORMATION

GETTING THERE
St Louis is 250 miles east of Kansas City and 300 miles south of Chicago.

DO

Anheuser-Busch Brewery
Each tank in the "aging house" holds 200,000 six packs. ☎ 314-577-2626; www.budweiser tours.com; 12th & Lynch Sts, Soulard; 9am-5pm Mon-Sat, 11:30am-5pm Sun Jun-Aug, slightly shorter hours rest of year

Busch Stadium
No game? Take a one-hour tour of the 2006 stadium. ☎ 314-345-9000 tickets, 314-345-9565 tours; www.stlcardinals.com; Broadway & Clark Ave, downtown; game tickets $20-200, tours adult/child $10/6; regular season Apr-early Oct

City Museum
Hands-on, climb-up, crawl-through exhibits are recycled urban castoffs. ☎ 314-231-2489; www.citymuseum.org; 701 N 15th St, downtown; general admission/including rooftop $12/17; 9am-5pm Wed & Thu, 9am-1am Fri & Sat, 11am-5pm Sun year-round, Mon & Tue mid-Mar–Aug;

Gateway Arch
Eero Saarinen's concrete-supported arch sits on the site of a former fur-trading post. ☎ 877-982-1410; www.gatewayarch.com; Gateway Arch Riverfront, downtown; tram adult/child $10/5; 8:20am-9:10pm Jun-Aug, 9:20am-5:10pm Sep-May;

Jewel Box
This 50ft cantilevered glass greenhouse earns its National Historic Register listing. ☎ 314-531-0080; www.stlouis.missouri.org; cnr Wells Dr & McKinley Dr, Forest Park; admission $1, 9am-noon Mon & Tue free; 9am-4pm Mon-Fri, to 11am Sat, to 2pm Sun

Left Bank Books
Magazines and bestsellers upstairs, travel and used books downstairs, bookstore cat –

underfoot. ☎ 314-367-6731; www.left -bank.com; 399 N Euclid, Central West End; 10am-10pm Mon-Sat, 11am-6pm Sun

Museum of Westward Expansion
The 1700-pound bison was part of a herd at Theodore Roosevelt National Park. ☎ 314-655-1700, 877-982-1410; www.nps.gov/jeff; Gateway Arch Riverfront, downtown; admission free; 8am-10pm Jun-Aug, 9am-6pm Sep-May;

Old Courthouse & Museum
Dred Scott and his wife sued their owner for their freedom in 1846. ☎ 314-655-1700, 877-982-1410; www.nps.gov/jeff; 11 N 4th St, St Louis; admission free; 8am-4:30pm;

St Louis Art Museum
Current expansion is adding skylights, overlooks and exhibit space to the World's-Fair-built museum. ☎ 314-721-0072; www.slam.org; 1 Fine Arts Dr, Forest Park; 10am-5pm Tue-Sun, to 9pm Fri;

St Louis Zoo
Big cats prowl the Red Rocks area, penguins preen in The Wild, and mothers take a breather by The Carousel. ☎ 314-781-0900; www.stlouiszoo.org; 1 Government Dr, Forest Park; admission free; 9am-5pm;

EAT & DRINK

Bissinger's, a Chocolate Experience
Cozy and stylish, Bissinger's is the place to reward yourself after a hard day of shopping. ☎ 314-367-7750; www.experiencebissing ers.com; 32 Maryland Plaza, Central West End; mains $3-11; noon-6pm Sun-Tue, to 10pm Wed, to midnight Thu-Sat

Blueberry Hill
Kids can enjoy a meal – try the famous burgers – before 8pm. ☎ 314-727-4444; www.blueberryhill.com; 6504 Delmar, The Loop; mains $5-14; 11am-1:30am Mon-Sat, to midnight Sun

Cunetto's House of Pasta
Bucatini, cannelloni, fettucine, linguini, ravioli, pennine, spaghetti, tortellini. 'Nuff said?

☎ 314-781-1135; www.cunetto.com; 5453 Magnolia Ave, The Hill; lunch $7-12, dinner $9-19; 🕑 11am-2pm Mon-Fri, 4:45-9:30pm Mon-Thu, 4:45-10:30pm Sun; ♿

John D. McGurk's
In addition to Guinness, enjoy Irish stew, the lush outdoor patio and nightly live music. ☎ 314-776-8309; www.mcgurks.com; 1200 Russell Blvd, Soulard; mains $7-20; 🕑 11am-1:30am Mon-Sat, 3pm-midnight Sun

Park Avenue Coffee
Gooey butter-cake slices may include blueberry, butter pecan, Snickers and peanut-butter-chocolate-and-banana Elvis. ☎ 314-621-4020; www.parkavenuecoffee. com; 1919 Park Ave, Lafayette Sq; pastries under $5; 🕑 6:30am-10pm Mon-Thu, 6:30am-11pm Fri, 7am-11pm Sat, 7:30am-10pm Sun

Pi Pizzeria
Pi is pronounced pie, but the name is short-hand for the infinitely delightful 3.14 math-ematical symbol. ☎ 314-727-6633; www. restaurantpi.com; 6144 Delmar, The Loop; pizzas $12-23; 🕑 11am-midnight Mon-Sat, to 11pm Sun; ♿

Sidney Street Cafe
Not up for a meal? Savor lobster turnovers or bleu cheese tarts at the cozy front bar. ☎ 314-771-5777; www.sidneystreetcafe. com; 2000 Sidney St, Soulard; mains $18-26; 🕑 5-9:30pm Tue-Thu, 5-10:30pm Fri & Sat

Soulard Farmers Market
For a morning pick-me-up, head into the Grand Hall for pastries and coffee. ☎ 314-622-4180; http://stlouis.missouri.org/citygov /soulardmarket; 730 Carroll St, Soulard; 🕑 8am-5pm Wed-Fri, 6am-5pm Sat; ♿

Ted Drewes
Swirl in one of 25-plus toppings – raspberry, caramel or M&M's? – to turn that vanilla cus-tard into "concrete." ☎ 314-481-2652; www. teddrewes.com; 6726 Chippewa St; mains under $5; 🕑 11am-11pm Feb-Dec; ♿

SLEEP

Moonrise Hotel
Nibble toasted ravioli and sip a cocktail under the moon on the Rooftop Terrace. ☎ 314-721-1111; www.moonrisehotel.com; 6177 Delmar, The Loop; r $229-279, ste $329; ♿

Parkway Hotel
An hourly shuttle runs guests to nearby at-tractions. ☎ 314-256-7777; www.thepark wayhotel.com; 4550 Forest Park, Central West End; r $122-200; ♿

Water Tower Inn
Do your laundry, work out in the fitness room or kick back in one of the lounges. ☎ 314-977-7500; www.slu.edu/x27017.xml; 3545 Lafayette Ave, St Louis University; r $79

USEFUL WEBSITES
www.explorestlouis.com
www.riverfronttimes.com

LINK YOUR TRIP
www.lonelyplanet.com/trip-planner

Twain Tour

WHY GO Tom and Huck don't just step off the page in Hannibal, Missouri. They sneak out of second-story windows, tout the glories of fence painting and scramble through treacherous caves. Cindy Lovell, Executive Director of Mark Twain's Boyhood Home & Museum, points us to the places that inspired the author and his characters.

TIME
2 days

DISTANCE
50 miles

BEST TIME TO GO
May – Oct

START
Hannibal, MO

END
Florida, MO

It's hard to separate fact from fiction in Hannibal. Mark Twain lived in the Mississippi-hugging town between 1839 and 1853, and he based many of his stories on real people and places in the community. "Anyone who's read *Tom Sawyer* or *Huckleberry Finn* will come here and their jaws will drop," says Lovell, "because it's all real."

The jaw-dropping starts the moment Hwy 79 swoops into downtown, plunking you one block west of ❶ Cardiff Hill, a towering riverside landmark mentioned in *The Adventures of Tom Sawyer*. Look for the bronze statue of Tom and Huck at the base of the hill. "It's the only statue in the US that honors two fictional characters," says Lovell. Left of the statue, 244 steps climb to the base of a small lighthouse and bird's-eye views of the Mississippi River and downtown.

Climb down to rejoin Tom and Huck, then cross North St to enter the engaging ❷ Mark Twain Boyhood Home & Museum, a seven-building complex dedicated to all things Twain. With its wall-sized photographs, family artifacts and Twain-written observations, the introductory Interpretive Center sets an upbeat, accessible tone for literary exploration. For details about the real people behind Huck, Jim and Injun Joe, Lovell recommends the displays in the adjoining octagon-shaped room, "an homage to the octagonal writing room where Twain wrote many of his books."

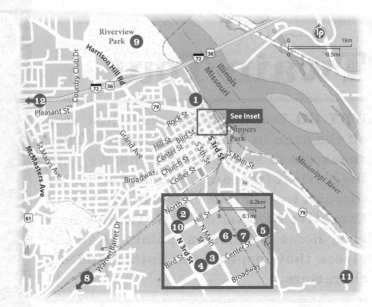

A short path leads to a low-ceilinged shack sitting on the spot where Tom Blankenship – son of the town drunk and the model for Huck Finn – was believed to have grown up with seven siblings. Though the original house was torn down in 1911, the current structure was rebuilt based on a photo of the original house. Displays inside the cramped structure discuss book banning and the depiction of African Americans in American literature.

TWAIN'S BEST TRAVEL QUOTES PART ONE

- "Travel is fatal to prejudice, bigotry, and narrow-mindedness, and many of our people need it sorely on these accounts. Broad, wholesome, charitable views of men and things cannot be acquired by vegetating in one little corner of the earth all one's lifetime."

- "I have found out that there ain't no surer way to find out whether you like people or hate them than to travel with them."

From here, stroll to the author's boyhood home, where he was known by his birth name, Sam Clemens. Here you'll wander past period furnishings in the kitchen, dining room and parlor. Upstairs, in the author's bedroom, "you'll see the famous window where young Sam Clemens would've sneaked out," says Lovell.

For a full Tom Sawyer immersion, step out onto Hill St and bask in the warmth of the Missouri sun as you pose beside Tom's infamous white fence. If your timing is especially good, the moment will be capped by the blare of a train chugging past the river just east. Directly across Hill St is the home of Twain's childhood sweetheart, Laura Hawkins, the inspiration for Becky Thatcher. The house is currently under renovation but should be completed by the end of 2010. Visitors will be given a token representing one of Twain's childhood friends and will learn from that person's perspective what it was like to grow up in Hannibal in the mid-1800s.

Next door to the Hawkins home is the Justice of the Peace Office where Twain's father worked as a peace officer. As a boy, Twain came across a dead body that had been "stored" in his father's office prior to burial. In his autobiography, Twain mentions this incident and describes his mad scramble out of the office window: "I took the sash with me; I did not need the sash, but it was handier to take it than to leave it, so I took it." Next door is Grant's Drug Store. This small but fascinating shop is filled with tonics, patent medicines, 1800s remedies and one horrid dental instrument known as a tooth hook.

TWAIN ON ANNIVERSARIES

The year 2010 marks the 175th anniversary of Twain's birth and the 100th anniversary of his death. Unfortunately, the author had an unfavorable opinion of such milestones: "What ought to be done to the man who invented the celebrating of anniversaries? Mere killing would be too light. Anniversaries are very well, up to a certain point." To satisfy Twain, this trip merely notes the occurrence of said anniversaries, leaving any celebrating to your discretion.

The last building in the complex is the Museum Gallery two blocks south. Here, a wobbly raft, a climbable stagecoach and other interactive displays highlight key scenes from Twain's best-known books. Water rats won't want to miss a turn at the giant captain's wheel, a reminder of Twain's early years as a Mississippi riverboat captain. An adjacent marker explains that the phrase "mark twain" was a riverboat term signaling safe water ahead. Not a bad pen name for an author who never forgot his youthful adventures on the Mississippi.

For an afternoon caffeine jolt, Lovell likes the nearby ❸ **Java Jive**. "Java Jive is the first coffee shop west of the Mississippi," she says. It's also Hannibal's hub, where locals gather to gossip, surf the web and solve all the world's problems. From there, take some time to wander the compact downtown, keeping an eye out for the office of the ❹ **Hannibal-Courier Post**. "It's the oldest newspaper in Missouri," says Lovell, and the spot "where Sam Clemens launched his newspaper career."

If you're strolling downtown on a Friday or Saturday in summer, take a moment to chat with the two young teens dressed as Tom and Becky. These local seventh-graders, sponsored by the chamber of commerce, are highly trained "mini-experts," says Lovell, and they'd love to answer your questions on all things Twain and Hannibal.

No visit to Hannibal is complete without time spent on the river. The best choice for road-trippers on a tight schedule is the ⑤ Mark Twain Riverboat, which docks at Center St landing off Main St. Its one-hour narrated cruise highlights river lore and local points of interest.

For a local point of prurient interest – and dinner – hustle over to ⑥ Lula Belle's Restaurant, where framed pantaloons pay homage to the restaurant's rowdy days as a house of ill repute. Although this former brothel was built after Twain's days in Hannibal, he'd surely appreciate the restaurant's saucy joie de vivre and generous menu. "A lot of people like the Mississippi Surf & Turf, which is barbecued ribs and fried catfish," says Lovell. "Every single dish is served with peel-and-eat shrimp, salad and baked bread."

CARTOON COYOTE

Animator Chuck Jones modeled Wile E. Coyote, Warner Brother's scrawny but determined roadrunner chaser, after the coyote described in Twain's 1872 travelogue *Roughing It*: "The cayote is a long, slim, sick and sorry-looking skeleton, with a gray wolf-skin stretched over it, a tolerably bushy tail that forever stays down with a despairing expression of forsakenness and misery, a furtive and evil eye, and a long sharp face, with slightly lifted lip and exposed teeth. He has a general slinking expression all over. The cayote is a living, breathing allegory of Want."

Low-maintenance travelers with a naughty sense of fun – and a tolerance for noisy trains – may enjoy one of the six rooms above the restaurant at ⑦ Lula Belle's B&B. Each of the six named rooms – think Gypsy Rose, Purple Passion – comes with an eclectic mix of Victorian-style decor. Decorative, guest-signed bars of soap add to the offbeat sense of fun.

To sleep in a room where Twain once slept – while savoring the charms of one of Missouri's top-rated B&Bs – follow Hwy 61 south to ⑧ Garth Woodside Mansion. In his memoirs Twain wrote, "I spent my night with John and Helen Garth three miles from town in their spacious, beautiful house." The description holds true today. Inside this well-appointed home, guests enjoy full breakfasts, antique-filled rooms, accommodating hosts and loads of Twain history. An inscribed photograph from Twain to Mrs Garth, following the death of her husband, hangs on the 2nd floor.

Guests can choose one of eight bedrooms inside the mansion or one of three cottages in back. For a romantic getaway, reserve the Dowager Cottage, a stone-and-glass wonder with two fireplaces, a king-sized featherbed, personally served breakfasts and a 10ft shower with 11, count 'em, 11 showerheads.

Start your second day with a reflective moment at the 100-year-old ⑨ Riverview Park just north of downtown. "This park presents two exceptional views of the Mississippi River," says Lovell and they "really put into perspective the vastness of the river. At the lookout points, you're about 100ft above the river, so it's really impressive." There's also an inspiring statue of Twain overlooking the river.

Hungry? For fried chicken and a healthy dose of Hannibal kitsch, pull into the **⑩ Mark Twain Dinette & Family Restaurant** on the corner of 3rd and Hill Sts; it's hard to miss. "They have a big root beer mug that says Mark Twain Dinette and revolves," says Lovell.

From town, a 2-mile drive south leads to **⑪ Mark Twain Cave**, the inspiration for Injun Joe's hideout in *Tom Sawyer*. Today, one-hour tours take visitors past a collection of unusual limestone formations along a level walkway. One of these formations is Aladdin's Palace – named by a young Sam Clemens after he read *One Thousand and One Nights*. Bring a sweater, Lovell advises, because the cave remains a cool 52°F year-round.

If you have time for a little more Twain, take Hwy 36 west to Hwy 24, following it west to Florida, Missouri, about 38 miles from Hannibal. "His birthplace is here and the original manuscript of *Tom Sawyer*," says Lovell. The cabin where he was born, and the manuscript, can be found at the **⑫ Mark Twain Birthplace State Historic Site** beside the 2775-acre Mark Twain State Park.

TWAIN'S BEST TRAVEL QUOTES PART TWO

- "The gentle reader will never, never know what a consummate ass he can become, until he goes abroad. I speak now, of course, in the supposition that the gentle reader has not been abroad, and is therefore not a consummate ass."

- "I was a traveler! A word had never tasted so good in my mouth before. I had an exultant sense of being bound for mysterious lands and distant climes which I never have felt in so uplifting a degree since."

From here, continue to St Louis or simply hit the highway for your next adventure, taking full advantage of Twain's advice to explore well beyond your little corner of the earth.
Amy C Balfour

TRIP INFORMATION

GETTING THERE
From St Louis, take I-70 west to Hwy 61 north. Follow it 85 miles to Hannibal.

DO

Mark Twain Birthplace State Historic Park
See a Twain 1st edition, furnishings from his Hartford home and the cabin where he was born. ☎ 573-565-3449; http://mostateparks. com/twainsite.htm; 37352 Shrine Rd, Florida; adult/child $2.50/1.50; ⏰ 10am-5pm Apr-Oct, to 4:30pm Nov-Mar

Mark Twain Boyhood Home & Museum
Set aside 1½ hours minimum to explore the seven buildings. ☎ 573-221-9010; www. marktwainmuseum.org; 120 N Main St, Hannibal; adult/senior/child $9/7.50/5; ⏰ 9am-5pm, with seasonal variations; ♿

Mark Twain Cave
This limestone playground became Injun Joe's lair in *Tom Sawyer*. ☎ 573-221-1656; www.marktwaincave.com; 300 Cave Hollow Rd, Hannibal; adult/child $16/10; ⏰ 9am-6pm, with variations; ♿

Mark Twain Riverboat
See Hannibal and the Mississippi from the breezy decks of a riverboat. ☎ 573-221-3222; www.marktwainriverboat.com; 100 Center St, Hannibal; sightseeing cruise adult/child $14/11; ⏰ 11am-4pm, with variations; ♿

Riverview Park
Look for non-native black squirrels, imported from Germany decades ago, inside the 465-acre park. ☎ 573-221-0154; www.hannibal parks.org; 2000 Harrison Hill, Hannibal; admission free; ⏰ dawn-dusk; ♿ 🐾

EAT & DRINK

Java Jive
Sip coffee, surf the net or peruse local pottery at this comfy coffee joint. ☎ 573-221-1017; www.ayerspottery.com; 211 N Main St, Hannibal; coffee & pastries under $5; ⏰ 7:30am-10pm Mon-Thu, 7:30am-10:30pm Fri & Sat, 8am-6pm Sun

Lula Belle's Restaurant
Former bordello offers seafood, pasta and steaks. ☎ 573-221-6662; www.lulabelles. com; 111 Bird St, Hannibal; mains $7-25; ⏰ 11am-2pm & 4-8:30pm Mon-Thu, 4-9:30pm Fri & Sat

Mark Twain Dinette & Family Restaurant
Breaded tenderloins, homemade root beer and friendly service. ☎ 573-221-5511; 400 S 3rd St (Hwy 79); mains under $10; ⏰ 6am-8pm; ♿

SLEEP

Garth Woodside Mansion
Birdwatch in the morning, nibble cookies in the afternoon, slumber on a featherbed at night. ☎ 573-221-2789; www.garth mansion.com; 11069 New London Gravel Rd, Hannibal; r $175-245, cottages $290-395

Lula Belle's B&B
The central sitting area encourages mingling with other guests. ☎ 573-221-6662; www. lulabelles.com; 111 Bird St, Hannibal; r $60-$100

USEFUL WEBSITES
www.pbs.org/marktwain
www.visithannibal.com

LINK YOUR TRIP

www.lonelyplanet.com/trip-planner

Here's the Beef

WHY GO Carnivores, grab your steak knives. This culinary tour is a nine-course romp through Oklahoma, Missouri and Iowa that's heavy on the heartland's finest export: beef. You'll find it char-grilled, barbecued, chicken-fried, even stuffed with onions. But vegetarians, never fear, pizza and gooey butter cakes will keep you sated too.

TIME
5 – 6 days

DISTANCE
1012 miles

BEST TIME TO GO
Year-round

START
El Reno, OK

END
Des Moines, IA

Cowboys drove more than six million longhorns from Texas north to Kansas between 1867 and 1886. These hardy beef animals were then loaded onto freight trains in railroad towns and shipped east for consumption. Two of the busiest cattle trails, the Chisholm Trail to Abilene and the Western Trail to Dodge City, crossed Oklahoma's open range. The state, with its miles of prime grazing land, soon became a top spot for cattle ranches. Today, Oklahoma ranks fourth in cattle and calf production in the US.

This is a very good thing for road-trippers in search of a burger. One Oklahoma specialty is the fried onion burger, a Sooner State favorite available at diners and dives statewide. This smashed-flat delicacy – ground beef mixed with onion then caramelized on the grill – allegedly got its start in El Reno, a Route 66 town that once bordered the Chisholm Trail. Today, sidle up to a stool at the L-shaped bar in ❶ Robert's Grill, a red-trimmed white box that's served fried onion burgers since 1926. The onion-filled patty – sizzled up in front of you – is best enjoyed with a basket of piping-hot fries.

In nearby Oklahoma City, there's an entire neighborhood dedicated to livestock: ❷ Stockyards City. This dining and shopping district, just south of I-40 via exit 148A, sits beside Oklahoma National Stockyards, the largest stocker and feeder cattle market in the world. The

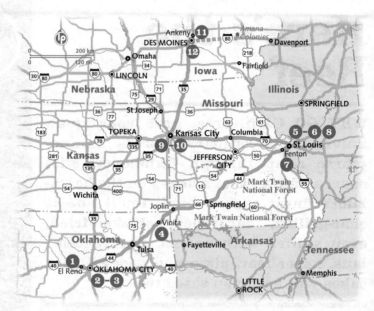

most famous steak restaurant in town, ❸ **Cattlemen's Steakhouse**, serves up sirloins for breakfast, lunch and dinner. The corn-fed, slow-aged beef in this century-old chophouse comes with salad, baked potato and roll. The adventurous may want to graze on the lamb fries, a testicular specialty of the house.

Oklahoma's state meal doesn't include a well-seasoned sirloin or a tender fillet. Nope, the official state meal, pursuant to House Concurrent Resolution 1083, includes black-eyed peas, fried okra, pecan pie and *chicken-fried* steak. What's chicken got to do with beef? Not much. This calorie-laden dish starts with a thin, tough cut of beef that's pummeled, tenderized, coated in flour and baking powder then fried to a golden brown. Aliases include country-fried steak, pan-fried steak, or, as more delicately named in *The Bride's Cook Book of Oklahoma City* in 1930, breaded steak. Ahem.

A popular version of the dish is served at beloved ❹ **Clanton's Café** in Vinita on Route 66 northeast of Tulsa. This family-run eatery (four generations since 1927) takes food seriously – just look at the one-word neon sign over the entrance: EAT. Clanton's chicken-fried steak is a tender piece of cube steak dunked in an egg-and-buttermilk batter, covered with flour then griddle-fried. This crispy delight is served with white or brown gravy, choice of potato, vegetable, soup or salad, and a roll. We recommend the salad. The heavenly ranch dressing is so well seasoned you might just forget yourself and slurp the remainder like soup. Not that we'd know anything about that.

From here, follow I-44 east to St Louis. Yes, the route becomes a bit circuitous here, but we believe anticipation is half the fun. (If you're simply dying for barbecue, by all means skip St Louis and shoot north to Kansas City on Hwy 71. We completely understand.) St Louis earns its beef cred because the hamburger made its debut here at the 1904 World's Fair.

River City is also known for taking traditional dishes – pizza, ravioli, butter cake – and adding a distinctive spin. Some say its distinctive spin on pizza is akin to a crime, but longtime residents will defend their unique pies to the grave. The problem? Provel cheese. This locally created pizza topper is a processed combination of provolone, mozzarella and white cheddar. Fans say it's creamy and a little bit buttery. Detractors use the word "filmy."

See for yourself at **5 IMO's Pizza**, a local chain open since 1964. It's the city's most famous purveyor of St Louis–style pizza. If you're heading to Forest Park, pull into the IMO's just south of the park's Hampton Rd entrance. This fast-paced outpost – green booths, a few tables, a fake-brick floor – bustles with families, seniors and solos, all chowing down on side salads and gooey pizzas. The square-cut slices have a thin, cracker-like crust topped with hot Provel and your choice of standard toppings – including hamburger for those not ready for a beef break.

Another St Louis creation is toasted ravioli, an appetizer that tops the menus of Italian restaurants in The Hill, a longtime Italian enclave southwest of downtown. These meat-filled ravioli are deep-fried then served with marinara sauce and a sprinkling of Parmesan. Though the restaurant behind the dish's creation hasn't been confirmed, one leading contender is **6 Charlie Gitto's**, a welcoming, dimly lit stalwart that fills up fast with an upbeat, well-dressed crowd on a Saturday night. According to restaurant lore, in 1947 a chef at Angelo's – Charlie Gitto's precursor – decided to deep-fry a ravioli after he'd accidentally dropped it in bread crumbs.

For good service, clean rooms and a name in keeping with our culinary theme, consider an overnight at the **7 Pear Tree Inn**, 14 miles southwest of The Hill. Yes, it's part of a Midwest chain, but nice touches include popcorn and lemonade in the afternoon and a hearty continental breakfast selection that includes Belgian waffles.

Not up for waffles? Sample a River City specialty instead, the accurately named gooey butter cake. To make the basic version of this longtime favorite, chefs fill a yellow cake crust with varying combinations of powdered sugar, eggs, cream cheese and butter. The result is a perfect morning storm of gooey, chewy and sweet. The only butter-cake dilemma within the chic, spare walls of ❽ **Park Avenue Coffee** is deciding which flavor to order: Park Ave makes 74 varieties, with 10 to 12 available by the slice on any given morning. From Almond Joy to Mango to White Chocolate Macadamia Nut Cookie Dough, there's a taste for every palate.

Getting full? Better cowboy up, pardner. The next stop is Kansas City, the barbecue capital of the Midwest. They take their barbecue serious here, and the sauced-up, piled-high slabs of beef – and pork – don't have time for no crybabies. Besides, from St Louis, Kansas City is an easy shot west on I-70.

STICK IT TO ME

About 50 types of food were available on a stick at the Iowa State Fair in 2009. These included meatballs, teriyaki beef, deep-fried HoHos, hard-boiled eggs, potato lollipops (deep-fried russet potatoes served with dipping sauce), fried pickles, chocolate-covered cheesecake and fudge puppies (waffles covered in chocolate syrup and topped with whipped cream). The best named? Chicken-lips-on-a-stick – breaded chicken breasts with hot sauce and a side of blue cheese.

The sandwich maestros at ❾ **Arthur Bryant's** keep the line moving with a booming "Who's next?!" – a no-nonsense bellow that inspires a thrilling combination of anticipation and fear in first timers. But these fast-serving barbecue folk see the line stretching to the door behind you, and they don't want to mess up the system. The indecisive should order the combo with beef and sliced pork and a side of fries. This towering sandwich, like all of them, is piled high on white bread then plopped on a plate and passed through a window. Pay at the end of the line.

Arthur Bryant's beef is good on its own, but it doesn't earn world-famous status until it's doused with one of the three knock-your-socks-off sauces perched on every table. Choices are original, sweet heat, and rich and spicy.

> *"With every smiling bite of the silky but kickin' original, an angel in heaven earns its wings."*

With every smiling bite of the silky but kickin' original, an angel in heaven earns its wings. Half the fun is chatting with your neighbors in line, looking at the black-and-white photos of famous guests and simply diving into the bustling scene. We met one couple back for a resupply of sauce – they'd been using two cases in their basement for the last 16 years!

For a less hectic scene and fewer tourists, follow 18th St east to Prospect St south, taking Swope Parkway east to Blue Parkway. Pull into the tiny lot fronting the brown-brick ❿ LC's. The sign outside this smoke-cured joint tells you all you need to know: Bar-B-Q-Ribs-Beef-Pork-Turkey-Ham-Sausage. A favorite here? The burnt ends – crispy shavings from the edges of smoked brisket.

No culinary tour through the plains is complete without a visit to Iowa. The state may rank a mere seventh when it comes to sheer number of cattle and calves (3,950,000 head in 2008; Texas leads with 13.6 million), but Iowans give connoisseurs of beef one of the country's heartiest welcomes.

Iowans are particularly fond of loose-meat sandwiches, and many sing the praises of ⑪ Maid-Rite, a regional chain that's credited with creating the sandwich in 1926. What is a loose-meat sandwich? We've heard it called a sloppy joe without the sloppy: seasoned ground beef piled onto a warm bun. Franchises share the recognizable red-and-white accents and 1950s vibe. Breaded tenderloins, onion rings, chocolate milk and maybe even Elvis share space beside the menu's loose-meat listings. Our Iowa sources were partial to the outlet in Ankeny.

Ankeny is also close to Des Moines, site of the annual ⑫ Iowa State Fair. And while Iowa's state fair isn't the biggest (that'd be the one in Texas) or the oldest (probably New York), this 11-day extravaganza is surely the most, well, all-American. In 2009 attendance surpassed one million. Beef-eating road-trippers will be glad to know that, out of nearly 200 food vendors, four sold barbecue beef sandwiches, 10 served steak sandwiches and 14 offered hamburgers and cheeseburgers.

Finally full? Walk off the calories with a stroll around the fairgrounds. One highlight is the 5.5ft butter cow, a 600-pound sculpture that's been whipped up every year since 1911. They say this charismatic dairy maid could butter 19,200 slices of toast. Top-model bulls and shorthorns are on display at the fair's livestock show, one of the largest in the world. End this trip with a satisfied smile, unbuttoned fat pants and a heartland view from the top of the fair's double Ferris wheel.

DETOUR The **Amana Colonies** (www.amanacolonies. com) are seven villages stretched along a 17-mile loop northwest of Iowa City. They were established as German religious communes in the mid-1800s. Until the Great Depression, members embraced a Utopian lifestyle, with no wages paid and all assets community owned. Today you can shop for arts, crafts, cheese and baked goods. There are several restaurants offering filling, home-cooked German meals.

Amy C Balfour

FOOD & DRINK

TRIP INFORMATION

GETTING THERE
From Oklahoma City, travel 30 miles west on I-40 to El Reno, Oklahoma.

DO
Iowa State Fair
To navigate the 400-acre fairgrounds, including campsites, download a walking tour from the website. ☎ 515-262-3111; www.iowastatefair.org; E 30th St & E University Ave, Des Moines, IA; adult/child $10/4; 🕐 7am-1am; ♿

EAT
Arthur Bryant's
The 18oz bottles of sauce sell for $3.50. ☎ 816-231-1123; www.arthurbryantsbbq.com; 1727 Brooklyn Ave, Kansas City, MO; mains $8.35-18; 🕐 10am-9:30pm Mon-Thu, 10am-10pm Fri & Sat, 11am-8pm Sun; ♿

Cattlemen's Steakhouse
According to lore, the owner won the restaurant in a 1945 craps game after rolling two threes, aka a "hard six." ☎ 405-236-0416; www.cattlemensrestaurant.com; 1309 S Agnew, Oklahoma City, OK; mains $11-26; 🕐 6am-10pm Sun-Thu, to midnight Fri & Sat

Charlie Gitto's
Beefy entrees include meat-stuffed tortellini, baked spaghetti with meatballs and char-grilled tenderloin. ☎ 314-772-8898; www.charliegittos.com; 5226 Shaw Ave, St Louis, MO; mains $14-40; 🕐 5-10pm Mon-Thu, 5-11pm Sat, 4-10pm Sun

Clanton's Cafe
Thoughtful waitstaff make you feel welcome without even looking like they're trying. ☎ 918-256-9053; www.clantonscafe.com; 319 E Illinois, Vinita, OK; mains $3-15;

🕐 6am-8pm Mon-Fri, 7am-2pm Sat, 11am-2pm Sun; ♿

IMO's Pizza
The $7 lunch special includes an 8in, one-topping pie, salad and drink. ☎ 314-644-5480; www.imospizza.com; 1000 Hampton Ave, St Louis, MO; mains $6-18; 🕐 10am-11pm Mon-Thu, to midnight Fri & Sat, to 10pm Sun; ♿

LC's
Thick, hand-cut fries help you swab up your sauce. ☎ 816-923-4484; www.lcsbar-b-que.nv.switchboard.com; 5800 Blue Parkway; mains $7.49-20; 🕐 11am-9pm; ♿

Maid-Rite
In-house variations on the Maid-Rite include the Cheese-Rite, the Chili-Rite, and the BBQ Texas-Rite. ☎ 515-963-0600; www.maid-rite.com; 802 SE Oralabor Rd, Ankeny, IA; mains $3-17; 🕐 11am-8pm Mon-Fri, 8am-8pm Sat, 8am-3pm Sun; ♿

Park Avenue Coffee
They mail gooey butter cakes worldwide. ☎ 314-621-4020; www.parkavenuecoffee.com; 1919 Park Ave, St Louis, MO; pastries under $5; 🕐 6:30am-10pm Mon-Thu, 6:30am-11pm Fri, 7am-11pm Sat, 7:30am-10pm Sun

Robert's Grill
It's 14 stools around the counter at this no-fuss burger joint. ☎ 405-262-1262; 300 S Bickford, El Reno, OK; mains under $6; 🕐 6am-9pm Mon-Sat, 11am-7pm Sun

SLEEP
Pear Tree Inn
Check the e-saver rates on the website for significant savings. ☎ 636-343-8820; www.druryhotels.com; 1100 S Hwy Dr, Fenton, MO; r $50-68; ♿ 🐾

USEFUL WEBSITES
www.saucemagazine.com
www.travelok.com

LINK YOUR TRIP
www.lonelyplanet.com/trip-planner

Oklahoma's Tribal Trails

WHY GO Oklahoma's state flag is the only flag in the union that honors Native Americans. The state is also the headquarters for 39 tribes. What's the history behind the tribal heritage? This trip uncovers the answers – and the ongoing story – at museums and tribal centers from Tahlequah to Washita.

TIME
3 – 4 days

DISTANCE
390 miles

BEST TIME TO GO
May – Sep

START
Tahlequah, OK

END
Anadarko, OK

Two of eastern Oklahoma's earliest known tribes, the Osage and the Quapaw, ceded millions of acres to the US government in the 1820s. The US then gave the land to five east-coast tribes, the Cherokee, Chickasaw, Choctaw, Creek and Seminoles. Because these five tribes had implemented formal governmental and agricultural practices in their communities, they were collectively called the Five Civilized Tribes.

The Five Civilized Tribes were forced to move to the Oklahoma area, known then as the Indian Territory, after settlers in the southern states decided they wanted the tribes' fertile farmlands for themselves. Between 1830 and 1850, the five tribes were forcibly relocated. Their routes are collectively known as the Trail of Tears.

Of these forced removals, perhaps none is more tragic than the relocation of the Cherokees. The history and horror behind the forced march is movingly traced at the six-gallery ❶ **Cherokee Heritage Center** outside Tahlequah. Interactive displays describe key events that preceded the forced removal – court battles, stockade imprisonment – then focus on the army-commanded marches that moved about 16,000 tribe members west between 1838 and 1839. Disease, cold and starvation killed 2000 to 4000 Cherokees on the 800-mile journey; their hardships are recounted in artistically powerful displays that highlight their suffering as well as their determination.

TRIP
52

GREAT PLAINS OKLAHOMA'S TRIBAL TRAILS

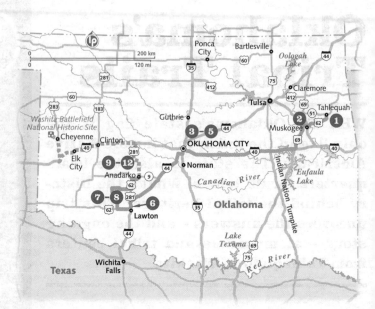

Outside, at the Ancient Village, visitors can learn what life was like in a Cherokee community before the arrival of Europeans. The one-hour guided tour includes pottery-making and blowgun demonstrations.

The Choctaws were skilled farmers living in brick and stone homes in Mississippi and Alabama in the early 1800s. They were relocated to Oklahoma in the 1830s – after 16 broken treaties with the US. Oklahoma's name derives from the Choctaw words for "red man," and the state flag is derived in part from a flag carried by Choctaw soldiers fighting for the Confederacy during the Civil War.

Learn more about the Choctaws and the other relocated tribes at the small but engaging ❷ **Five Civilized Tribes Museum** in Muskogee, 30 miles west of Tahlequah via the lake-crossing Hwy 62. Located in a former Indian Agency office, the museum dedicates one wall to each tribe. Displays cover an eclectic array of topics, from Choctaw code talkers in WWI to variations in lacrosse sticks. The gift shop sells pottery, painting and jewelry made by members of the five tribes.

As for the Indian Territory, the US government said it would belong to the five tribes "for as long as the stars shine and the rivers may flow." The reality? More like 70 years. In the mid-1800s the country was quickly expanding west, and white settlers wanted the land. Through legislative maneuvering, certain Indian-owned lands were deemed "unassigned." This opened them up for settlement. The Oklahoma Land Rush began on April 22, 1889, when 50,000 would-be settlers made a mad dash for their own 160-acre allotment.

Rancher Charles Colcord was one of the earliest land claimants in what is now downtown Oklahoma City (he arrived on April 23). The 12-story Colcord Building, built in 1910, was one of many properties developed by this entrepreneurial city father. It's known today as the ❸ **Colcord Hotel**. Fresh from an $18 million renovation, the hotel's 108 contemporary, black-framed rooms are splashed with forest greens and deep reds and come with Euro-top mattresses and 32in flat-screen HDTVs.

THE ABCS IN CHEROKEE

George Gist, son of a fur-trader father and Cherokee mother, is more commonly known as Sequoyah. Although he was unable to read English, Sequoyah recognized the importance of written language. After fighting for the US in the War of 1812, he developed a syllabary and writing system for the Cherokees. Based on 85 symbols, his written communication system is still used by tribe members today. Sequoyah is also the namesake for the towering redwood.

Bustling ❹ **Ted's Café Escondido** can't claim Native American heritage, but this longtime Okla-Mex hot spot north of downtown is worth your own small-scale land run. Complimentary starters include chips, warm tortillas and four accompaniments (two salsas, one queso, one veggie relish). But don't stop there. The wide-ranging menu includes spinach enchiladas, chicken chimirajas and tacos el carbon. Families, groups, couples, solos – all do just fine inside its hospitable, colorful walls. Expect a wait at peak hours.

In the morning, set aside an hour or two for the ONEOK gallery inside the impressive ❺ **Oklahoma History Center**, which opened in 2005. Videos, photographs and oral histories explore the heritage of the 39 tribes headquartered in the state. Artifacts include an 1890 cradleboard, a Kiowa pictorial calendar and an original letter from Thomas Jefferson that Lewis and Clark gave to the Otoe tribe. In it, Jefferson invites the tribe to the nation's capital. Be sure to look up before you leave – there's a Pawnee star chart on the ceiling.

"Step inside to see where Apache leader Geronimo was detained on three separate occasions."

Oklahoma isn't just home to eastern tribes. Numerous western and plains tribes, including the Apache, Comanche, Kiowa and Wichita, were also forced here as the US expanded west. An 80-mile drive southwest on I-44 (a toll road) leads to the still-active Fort Sill. The US Army built the fort in 1869 in Kiowa and Comanche territory to prevent raids into settlements in Texas and Kansas. By the 1880s and 1890s its role had changed, and the fort was serving as a protective sanctuary for many tribes. Today, Fort Sill is home to the US

Army Field Artillery School. It's the only southern plains fort built during the Indian Wars that's still in use as a military installation.

The ⑥ **Fort Sill Museum**, which fills several original buildings, explores the history of the fort. One gallery is dedicated to the work of the 10th Cavalry. This group of African American buffalo soldiers built many of the stone buildings on the fort's original quadrangle. They also constructed the 1872 Post Guardhouse, the center of law enforcement for the Indian Territory. Step inside to see where Apache leader Geronimo was detained on three separate occasions. Geronimo and other Apache warriors were brought here in 1894 as prisoners of war. Geronimo's grave, marked by an eagle-topped stone pyramid, is on fort grounds a few miles from the guardhouse.

Leave booming artillery in your wake as you roll west on Hwy 62 to state Hwy 115 north. Black-eyed susans, scrubby trees and barbed-wire fences line the two-lane byway as it unfurls from tiny Cache toward the hill-dappled ⑦ **Wichita Mountains Wildlife Refuge**. This 59,202-acre refuge protects bison, elk, longhorn cattle and a super-active prairie dog town. Wildlife is abundant; observant drivers might even see a spindly, palm-sized tarantula tiptoeing across the road. At the visitors center, informative displays highlight the refuge's flora and fauna. A massive glass window yields inspiring views of prairie grasslands. For a short-but-scenic day hike, rangers recommend the creek-hugging Kite Trail to the waterfalls and rocks at the Forty Foot Hole. It starts at the Lost Lake Picnic Area. For a bird's-eye view of the refuge, try the Elk Mountain Trail. Want the views without the hike? A short drive leads to the summit of 2464ft Mt Scott, a craggy peak popular with rock climbers.

Doris Campground, west of the visitors center, has drinking water and a central restroom with showers. Campsites come with fire pits, grills and picnic tables. Single-unit campsites, with or without electricity, are available first-come, first-served, as are 20 semi-primitive sites. Limited permits for backcountry camping are available by reservation or by walk-in at the visitors center.

Rode-hard-and-put-up-wet best describes ⑧ **Meers Store & Restaurant**, a ramshackle burger-and-beer joint hunkered at the end of a twisty, country-road junction north of the refuge. Its smashed-flat, 7in Meers burger – made from the beef of the restaurant's own Longhorns – is a "must-eat" in the region.

From here, Hwy 115 cruises north over low-rolling fields flanked by rock-and-tree-dotted hillsides. Bales of hay and grazing cows are a common sight, the view occasionally punctuated by the sleek, whirring windmills of the Blue Canyon Wind Farm. From Hwy 115, take state Hwy 19 east to Hwy 62/281, following it into ⑨ **Anadarko**. Eight tribal lands are located in the area, and students from 46 different tribes are enrolled in Anadarko schools. The town regularly hosts powwows and Native American events.

To mix a little shopping with your learning, visit the ⑩ **Southern Plains Indian Museum**. It houses a small but diverse collection of Plains Indian clothing, weaponry and musical instruments. There's also a small collection of American Indian dolls. The gift shop sells museum-quality crafts including jewelry, dolls and beadwork items (barrettes, purses and moccasins). About 85% of the store's customers are Native American.

Just east is the ⑪ **National Hall of Fame for Famous American Indians**. A short outdoor walk leads past the bronze busts of well-known Native Americans including Pocahontas, Geronimo and Sitting Bull. In 2009, a tornado swept through Anadarko, ripping two of the 42 busts from their pedestals.

Native American guides lead guests to seven reconstructed tribal dwellings at ⑫ **Indian City USA**, 2 miles south of town. During the 45-minute tour, you'll walk inside a Wichita grass lodge and a Pawnee earth lodge, learn facts about tribal customs and famous warriors (Geronimo was only 4ft 11in) and watch Native American dances. The adjoining museum displays headdresses, cradleboards and peyote paraphernalia. Indian City was also hit by the tornado, but the Kiowas, who purchased the complex in 2008, are working hard to repair damaged dwellings.

> **DETOUR**
>
> In the early morning hours of November 27, 1868, Lt Col George A Custer led a surprise attack on a Cheyenne camp beside the Washita River. Thirty to 60 Cheyenne, including their peace-promoting leader Black Kettle, were killed. How many women and children died? Was it a massacre or another battle in a back-and-forth series of retaliatory campaigns? Exhibits at the new **Washita Battlefield National Historic Site** (www.nps.gov/waba) examine the attack and the history behind it. An interpretive trail leads to the Cheyenne campsite.

Stay tuned for information on the much-anticipated American Indian Cultural Center and Museum (www.aiccm.org), scheduled to open in 2013 or 2014 in Oklahoma City. To gauge its progress, look for the promontory earth mound near I-40's junction with I-35. The cultural center will have interactive and multimedia displays, Native American pieces from the Smithsonian American Indian collection and a performance space.

For a weekend's worth of Native American artwork, food, music and dance, schedule your Oklahoma visit for mid-June. That's when the Red Earth Native American Cultural Festival erupts in Oklahoma City. Representatives of more than 100 tribes – dressed in full tribal regalia – kick off the four-day event with a Friday-morning parade through downtown.

Amy C Balfour

TRIP INFORMATION

GETTING THERE
From Tulsa, follow Hwy 412 east to Hwy 69 south; in Wagoner, take state Hwy 51 east.

DO
Cherokee Heritage Center
Three columns from the Cherokee National Female Seminary mark the entrance. ☎ 918-456-6007; www.cherokeeheritage.org; 21192 S Keeler Dr, Park Hill, OK; adult/child $8.50/5; ☾ 10am-5pm Mon-Sat, 1-5pm Sun, closed Jan; ♿

Five Civilized Tribes Museum
Between 1785 and 1902 there were 69 treaties between the US and the tribes. ☎ 918-683-1701; www.fivetribes.org; 1101 Honor Heights Dr, Muskogee, OK; adult/child $3/1.50; ☾ 10am-5pm Mon-Fri, 10am-2pm Sat

Fort Sill Museum
The Old Post Chapel held its first services on Christmas Eve 1875. ☎ 580-442-5123; http://sill-www.army.mil; 437 Quanah Rd, Fort Sill, OK; admission free; ☾ 8:30am-5pm Tue-Sat; ♿

Indian City USA
Dwellings include a tepee, wiki-up and adobe pueblo. ☎ 405-247-2063; www.anadarko.org; Rte 8, south of Anadarko, OK; adult/child $5/3; ☾ store 10am-6pm, tours 10am-3pm; ♿

National Hall of Fame for Famous American Indians
Humorist Will Rogers was of partial Cherokee descent. ☎ 405-247-5555; www.anadarko.org; Hwy 62, east of Anadarko, OK; admission free; ☾ 9am-5pm Mon-Sat, 1-5pm Sun

Oklahoma History Center
Look for the firefighting gear of the Cherokee Fire Dancers. ☎ 405-522-5248; www.okhistorycenter.org; 800 Nazih Zuhdi Dr, Oklahoma City, OK; adult/child $7/4; ☾ 10am-5pm Mon-Sat; ♿

Southern Plains Indian Museum
Contributing tribes include the Kiowa, Comanche, Southern Cheyenne, Wichita and Fort Sill Apache. ☎ 405-247-6221; www.doi.gov/iacb/museums/museum_s_plains.html; 715 E Central Blvd, Anadarko, OK; admission free; ☾ 9am-5pm Tue-Sat; ♿

EAT
Meers Store & Restaurant
Meersburger: grass-fed Longhorn, dill pickles, tomatoes, onions, lettuce, cheese. ☎ 580-429-8051; www.meersstore.com; Hwy 115, north of refuge; mains $4-11; ☾ 10:30am-8:30pm Sun, Mon, Wed & Thu, 10:30am-9pm Fri & Sat; ♿

Ted's Café Escondido
Efficient waitstaff deserve kudos. ☎ 405-848-8337; www.tedscafe.com; 2836 NW 68th St, Oklahoma City, OK; most mains $9-15; ☾ 11am-9:30pm Mon-Thu, 11am-10pm Fri & Sat, 11am-8:30pm Sun; ♿

SLEEP
Colcord Hotel
Tall guests can request a "Stretch King" bed. ☎ 405-601-4300; www.colcordhotel.com; 15 N Robinson Ave, Oklahoma City, OK; r from $159, ste $309; 🐾

Wichita Mountains Wildlife Refuge
Search for eagles on an interpretive tour. ☎ 580-429-3222; http://wichitamountains.fws.gov; 32 Refuge Headquarters, Indiahoma, OK; primitive sites $6, single units $8-16; ☾ visitors center 8am-6pm summer, 8am-4:30pm winter; ♿ 🐾

USEFUL WEBSITES
www.aiccm.org/oklahoma-indian-tourism
www.nativetimes.com

LINK YOUR TRIP
www.lonelyplanet.com/trip-planner

Plains, Cranes & Automobiles

OUTDOORS

WHY GO Prairie grasses once blew with abandon in the plains, untouched by the farmer's plow. Birds, elk and bison ranged free, their paths unhampered by fences and city sprawl. Today, back roads and byways link hardy pockets of wild frontier – nature preserves and wildlife refuges – in Kansas, Nebraska and South Dakota.

TIME
5 – 6 days

DISTANCE
782 miles

BEST TIME TO GO
May – Sep

START
Tallgrass Prairie National Preserve, KS

END
Wind Cave National Park, SD

The prairie's beauty doesn't really sink in until you're pushing through a chest-high swath of tallgrass, unsettling a few grasshoppers as you search for the perfect wildflower. Such beauty is easily yours at the **1 Tallgrass Prairie National Preserve** in the Flint Hills of eastern Kansas. Established in 1996, the 10,894-acre preserve is the one of the last remnants of tallgrass prairie. Tallgrass once covered 140 million acres in the Great Plains, but less than 4% is left. Most disappeared under the farmer's plow. The Flint Hills prairie was spared because farming is tough in the region's rocky soil, and locals turned to ranching instead. In the backcountry (open May to October), hike past lakes and limestone or hop a ranger-driven bus for a 90-minute tour. The preserve protects 30 mammal and nearly 500 bird species. Buffalo were introduced in 2009.

For local history, drive 15 miles north to **2 Council Grove**, a stop on the Santa Fe Trail. It's a friendly place, where rancher types say, "Welcome to our town." While the soda fountain at **3 Aldrich Apothecary** might seem old-fashioned, it's downright modern compared to 1857 **4 Hays House**, which claims to be the "oldest continuously operated restaurant west of the Mississippi River." But the burgers are nothing but fresh.

On I-70 west, you won't pass any signs for the **5 Konza Prairie Biological Station**. But this 8600-acre tallgrass stand, 4.5 miles north of exit 307, is one of the most breathtaking spots in Kansas (the state is named for the Konza tribe). Though most of the prairie is closed

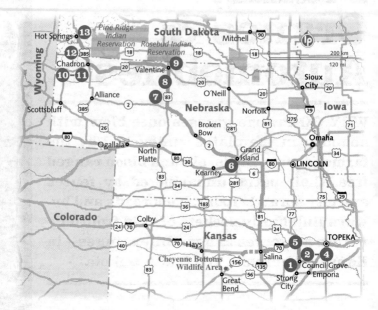

to visitors, three hiking trails are open. On the wonderful 2.5-mile Nature Trail, scurrying lizards, scratchy grasses and chirping birds keep your senses pleasantly alert. In early fall, your path may be framed by a prairie's bouquet of bright yellow compass flowers.

TORNADO ALLEY

Stormchasers and Weather Channel addicts know that Kansas and Nebraska are part of Tornado Alley, a tornado-prone swath of land stretching north from central Texas into Iowa and eastern South Dakota. Here, wet, tropical air from the Gulf of Mexico meets dry, high-flowing air from the Rockies – a perfect brew for supercells. In spring and summer, check local radio stations for weather updates and carry a map so you can track a storm's progress (www. spc.noaa.gov/faq/tornado; www.nssl.noaa.gov/edu/safety/tornadoguide.html).

Take your pick of country roads north to Nebraska's I-80. While each is unique, presume these commonalities: low hills, white silos, red Ford trucks and a cell tower every 20 miles. You'll shadow cranes migrating north during March and April, when 80% of the world's sandhill cranes – and millions of ducks and geese – recharge along the Platte River. The new **6 Nebraska Nature & Visitor Center** has trails and a 35ft observation platform. From Grand Island, Hwy 2 heads into Nebraska's distinctive **7 Sandhills**, 19,600 sq miles of sand dunes covered with mixed-grass prairie. The hills are better suited for ranching than farming; note the cattle brands listed on wooden signs beside Hwy 83. On windy days, rippling prairie grasses seem alive, their graceful undulations a distraction from less important things – like staying in your lane.

Gaping while driving is encouraged on the 9-mile Little Hay Rd Wildlife Drive in ⑧ **Valentine National Wildlife Refuge**. Look for muskrats, beavers and white-tailed deer. Almost 300 bird species converge on the refuge, many attracted to the numerous ponds and lakes. These marshy havens are fed by the underground Ogallala Aquifer. If it's April, settle into an observation blind. With luck, a prairie chicken will perform its dramatic courtship dance.

Landscapes collide in ⑨ **Fort Niobrara National Wildlife Refuge** just north, creating an ecological hot-spot protecting prairie grasses, sand dunes, coniferous forest, a canyon-carving river and limestone walls. And that's without mentioning the bison, elk and prairie dogs that call the 19,131-acre refuge home. A float down the bluff-flanked Niobrara River is a popular way to see the refuge in summer and early fall.

DETOUR The only problem with the 41,000-acre **Cheyenne Bottoms Wildlife Area** (www.kdwp.state.ks.us), 160 miles southwest of Council Grove, is the birds. They're so darn mesmerizing you want to stop and snap a picture every five seconds – not completely unexpected in the nation's largest interior wetlands and one of the country's most important stopovers for migrating shorebirds. The endangered whooping crane (fewer than 300 in the wild) recharges here between late October and early November.

It's barns, cows, ponds and windmills on the two-hour drive to welcoming Chadron. Here, the ⑩ **Westerner** is a model of indie motel perfection: welcoming staff, comfy rooms, free wi-fi, doubles under $50 and proximity to a free-chip-serving Mexican restaurant. The last can be found at ⑪ **Angela's Eatery**, recommended for its hearty combo platters and attentive waitstaff.

The 65-mile drive north from Chadron passes through South Dakota's ⑫ **Buffalo Gap National Grassland**. After curving through Hill City, the road breezes into ⑬ **Wind Cave National Park**. Best known for its sprawling cave system, Wind Cave is also a convergence point for short, mixed and tallgrass prairies.

ASK A LOCAL "There's so much wildlife in this area. It's fantastic," says Ericka Lans of Chadron, Nebraska. "I always tell people to go to Chadron State Park." According to Lans, you might see bighorn sheep, bald eagles, golden eagles and red-tailed hawks. For bison, antelope, deer and turkey, she recommends Fort Robinson State Park, west of Chadron (www.stateparks.com/chadron.html; www.stateparks.com/fort_robinson.html).

Like Fort Niobrara, Wind Cave harbors bison, elk and prairie dogs. Unlike Fort Niobrara, Wind Cave allows backcountry camping. Follow Wind Cave Canyon Trail to Highland Creek Trail: you'll pass limestone cliffs, mixed-grass prairie and maybe great horned owls and prairie dogs. Pitch your tent, gaze at stars and hope a bison doesn't smooch you in the morning.

Amy C Balfour

TRIP INFORMATION

GETTING THERE
From Topeka, Kansas, drive 80 miles south-west following I-335 south (toll road) to Hwy 50 west then Hwy 17 north.

DO

Fort Niobrara National Wildlife Refuge
A crossroads for migrating birds, the refuge attracts 230-plus species. ☎ 402-376-3789; www.fws.gov/fortniobrara; Valentine, NE; admission free; ☒ visitors center 8am-4:30pm daily Jun-Aug, Mon-Fri Sep-May, grounds dawn-dusk; ☒ ☒

Konza Prairie Biological Station
Most wildflowers bloom in June; tallgrass sways at its highest in fall. No pets. ☎ 785-587-0441; http://keep.konza.ksu.edu/visit; Manhattan, KS; donation $2; ☒ dawn-dusk; ☒

Nebraska Nature & Visitor Center
Fossils indicate sandhill cranes were in the area *nine million* years ago. ☎ 308-382-1820; www.nebraskanature.org; 9325 S Alda Rd, Alda, NE; admission free; ☒ 9am-5pm Mon-Sat year-round, 9am-5pm Sun Mar-early Apr, with variations; ☒

Tallgrass Prairie National Preserve
Thirteen bison arrived in 2009. ☎ 620-273-8494; www.nps.gov/tapr; Strong City, KS; admission free; ☒ visitors center 9am-4:30pm, grounds dawn-dusk; ☒ ☒

Valentine National Wildlife Refuge
The 1930s Civilian Conservation Corps helped build the refuge; their buildings are used today. ☎ 402-376-1889/3789; www.fws. gov/valentine; Hwy 83, NE; admission free; ☒ dawn-dusk; ☒ ☒

EAT & DRINK

Aldrich Apothecary
Enjoy root-beer floats, cherry phosphates and free wi-fi. ☎ 620-767-6731; www.apothecaryshops.com; 115-119 W Main St, Council Grove, KS; mains under $5; ☒ 9am-5:30pm Mon-Fri, 9am-5pm Sat; ☒

Angela's Eatery
Margaritas and cheap beer: conviviality starts early on Friday evening. ☎ 308-432-5500; 251 Main St, Chadron, NE; mains $5-15; ☒ 11am-8pm Mon-Thu, 11am-8:30pm Fri & Sat; ☒

Hays House
Amiable staff will let you explore the Santa Fe Trail–era digs. ☎ 620-767-5911; www.hayshouse.com; 112 W Main St, Council Grove, KS; mains $6-22; ☒ 11am-8pm Tue-Thu, 11am-9pm Fri, 6am-9pm Sat, 6am-8pm Sun; ☒

SLEEP

The Westerner
In the lobby, grab the free *Voices of the Sandhills* for fascinating frontier stories. ☎ 308-432-5577; www.westernerinns.com; 300 Oak St, Chadron, NE; r $40-50; ☒ ☒

Wind Cave National Park
Prairie here thrives when bison, elk and prairie dogs graze on dead leaves, allowing sunshine to reach young plants. ☎ 605-745-4600; www.nps.gov/wica; Hwy 385, Hot Springs, SD; admission free; ☒ visitors center 8am-7pm Jun-Aug, closes earlier rest of year; ☒

USEFUL WEBSITES
www.kansasflinthills.travel
www.nebraskaflyway.com

LINK YOUR TRIP
www.lonelyplanet.com/trip-planner

Wild West Legends

WHY GO The 1870s and 1880s were the West's wildest years. Jesse James was a bigger-than-life bad boy. Wild Bill paced the streets of Abilene. Cowboys caroused in the Wickedest Little City in America. This trip shoots from crime scenes to cattle towns in Missouri, Kansas and Oklahoma, hitting the West's most legendary hot-spots.

TIME
5 – 6 days

DISTANCE
935 miles

BEST TIME TO GO
Year-round

START
Coffeyville, KS

END
St Joseph, MO

Just after 8am on April 3, 1882, Jesse James decided to dust a picture hanging on his parlor wall. The 34-year-old outlaw, who went by the alias Thomas Howard, stepped onto a chair and started to clean. At that moment the young Bob Ford – a gang member – shot James in the back of the head, killing him. The reward for his well-aimed shot? Eternal infamy as "the dirty little coward who shot Mr Howard."

The bullet tunneled into the wall, leaving a jagged hole that's long enthralled visitors to ❶ Jesse James House in St Joseph, Missouri. The museum's newspaper clippings and artifacts provide an engaging round-up of James' outlaw past, but they never pinpoint the reason for his ongoing appeal. Was he Robin Hood? A selfish murderer? Or a romanticized symbol of the West – a lawless man staying one step ahead of the shackles of civilization?

To stroll the streets of a once anarchic city, take Hwy 59 south into Kansas, picking up I-70 west through the prairie-topped Flint Hills. The region is home to ❷ Abilene, the northern terminus of the Chisholm Trail and one of the West's most famous cow towns. Wild Bill Hickok, a marshal here in 1871, took two Colt revolvers, a Derringer and a rifle when he patrolled rowdy Texas Ave. Despite his gunslinger skills, Hickok lost his job after accidentally killing his partner in a gunfight. Watch shoot-outs in Old Town on summer weekends (www.abilenekansas.org).

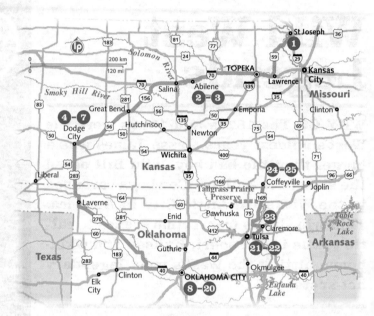

For civilized eats, make reservations at ❸ **The Brookville Hotel**. This fourth-generation restaurant has served skillet-fried chicken dinners since 1915. The owners moved the eatery from Brookville to its interstate-adjacent location in 1999, keeping the chicken but losing the hotel rooms.

I-70 leads west to Hwys 156 and 56, low-traffic roads rolling into ❹ **Dodge City**, a boom-and-bust railroad community that first gained fame as a buffalo trade center. The city survived the 1875 buffalo collapse by replacing bison with another commodity: longhorn steer. Between 1875 and 1886, cowboys drove five million steers to Dodge from Texas along the Western Trail. During the cattle boom, cowboys, gamblers and prostitutes flocked to the saloons and dance halls lining Front St, earning Dodge the nickname The Wickedest Little City in America. No-nonsense marshals like Wyatt Earp and Bat Masterson instilled law and order by the end of the 1870s.

The Wild West facade fronting the ❺ **Boot Hill Museum & Front Street** may look hokey, but inside you'll find informative exhibits spotlighting the soldiers, buffalo hunters, cowboys and settlers who made the region their home. And yes, you must press the button for the big-screen Buffalo Stampede – you won't soon forget the sensory blast. Dig into chips, salsa and chicken tacos at the no-frills but satisfying ❻ **Casa Alvarez** west of the museum. Gunslingers and cowboys dot the walls at the friendly ❼ **Boot Hill Bed and Breakfast**, where five Victorian-style rooms are named for Western heroes.

Motoring south on Hwy 283, picture cowboys, steers and chuck wagons stirring up dust on the region's Western Trail. South of Laverne, our horseshoe trail curves east, following Hwy 270 to I-40 and **8** **Oklahoma City**, the state's capital. This longtime cattle town, which sprang to life during the 1889 land run, has spiffed up its downtown with a glossy history center and a revitalized warehouse district, **9** **Bricktown**. Land Run Lagers and pub grub are the draw at the red-brick, vat-filled **10** **Bricktown Brewery**, while a comfy night's sleep is on tap at the new, 200-room **11** **Hampton Inn & Suites** beside AT&T Bricktown ballpark.

The **12** **National Cowboy & Western Heritage Museum** is like a chuckwagon dinner. You think you'll be full after a few bites, but once you dig in, well, git-along, little dogie, you're soon begging for more. From Charles M Russell's stunning Western landscapes to intriguing displays on cattle brands, barbed wire and boots-and-hats, it's endlessly compelling. Though one question remains unanswered: did cowboys ever smile? Absorbing photos of grim-faced wranglers suggest they never did. And as for that dogie, just know that's cowpoke talk for motherless calf.

NOBODY PUTS KITTY IN A CORNER

Gunsmoke's Miss Kitty was loosely based on Dodge City actress Dora Hand. Known for her beauty and kind manner, she was deeply beloved. In October 1878, a bullet meant for the mayor killed Dora as she slept. Outraged, a super-posse of famous lawfolk – including Wyatt Earp and Bat Masterson – tracked and captured her killer. Lack of evidence set him free, but the scoundrel was later felled, fatally, by a bullet. In Dodge, hundreds attended her funeral.

The compact Law & Order exhibit at the vast **13** **Oklahoma History Center** features a jailbird turned US marshal, the exploits of a hanging judge and the prison uniform of bank robber Emmett Dalton. Modern-day cowboys head to **14** **Stockyards City**, a shopping and dining district beside the **15** **Oklahoma National Stockyards**, the world's largest stocker and feeder cattle market. To watch the Monday auction, tread the catwalk over the pens starting at 8am (if you've ever been described as high maintenance, you may find this a less than enjoyable experience).

It's OK to handle the hats at affable **16** **Shorty's Ca'boy Hattery**, where the beaver-fur lids are custom-made. Complete the ensemble with cowboy duds from sprawling **17** **Langston's** one block south. For a saucy collection of western wear and gifts, wander the 35-plus booths at **18** **Stockyards Mercantile**. If someone hollers "All hat and no cattle!" show them who's boss by finishing a Presidential T-bone at red-boothed **19** **Cattlemen's Steakhouse**. Kids and solos will do fine at this famous, century-old eatery. Gobble empanadas, cookies and pastries at the welcoming **20** **Panaderia La Herradura**, a nearby Mexican bakery and grocery.

A 100-mile drive northeast ends in art-deco Tulsa. A green neon cactus marks the entrance to the ranch-style **㉑ Desert Hills Motel** where simple-but-clean accommodations welcome travelers on Route 66.

> DETOUR
>
> Hankering for a glimpse of the open prairie? Try the Nature Conservancy's **Tallgrass Prairie Preserve** (www.nature.org) north of Pawhuska, Oklahoma. Prairie grasses once covered 142 million acres in 14 Midwestern and Great Plains states, but development and farming reduced prairie-grass coverage more than 90%. The Nature Conservancy maintains the world's largest protected remnant – 39,100 acres – at the preserve. A total of 20,000 visitors come here annually, braving bumpy gravel roads, for bison, wildflowers, hiking and solitude.

Sun-dappled portraits of cattle drives, buffalo hunts and western landscapes by Thomas Moran, Frederic Remington and Albert Bierstadt capture the romance of the west at the **㉒ Gilcrease Museum**, an inspiring place to escape the city's sprawl. The museum's American western and Native American artwork was gathered by Thomas Gilcrease, an Oklahoman of Creek descent who discovered oil on his 160-acre tribal allotment.

Claremore is the resting place of legendary humorist Will Rogers (1879–1935), a genial, part-Cherokee cowboy who once said, "I never met a man I didn't like." The fascinating **㉓ Will Rogers Memorial Museum** traces his career from cattle-driving cowboy and trick roper to radio personality, journalist and actor, using quotes, radio snippets, a Jo Mora diorama and loads of artifacts. His movies are shown daily. As you leave, glance at a few photographs. Unlike his forebears, this Renaissance cowboy knew how to smile.

Take Hwy 20 west to Hwy 169, following it north to **㉔ Coffeyville**, Kansas. On October 5, 1892, the five-man Dalton Gang rode into this burg with an ingenious but risky plan: they would rob two banks at once, splitting their ranks to double their take. Twelve minutes and 500 gunshots later, four gang members lay dead. Four innocent citizens – the Dalton Defenders – were dead or dying beside them.

Coffeyville touts its Dalton-related sites – body outlines, wall-sized murals, the original jail – like a proud parent. Get the full story at the **㉕ Dalton Defenders Museum** then walk to Isham Hardware, open since 1870. From Isham's front door, peer into Death Alley. There, the trapped gang took fire from the exact spot where you're standing.

The failed robbery marked the end of an era. Railroad tracks linked the coasts, barbed wire blocked the open range and frontier lines were gone from government maps. The Wild West was tamed, only to live on in history books, legends and cowboy songs: roll on, little dogies, roll on.
Amy C Balfour

TRIP INFORMATION

GETTING THERE
From Kansas City, Missouri, drive 55 miles north on I-29 and I-229.

DO

Boot Hill Museum & Front Street
The *Gunsmoke* exhibit has memorabilia from the long-running Dodge-based drama. ☎ 620-227-8188; www.boothill.org; Front St & 5th Ave, Dodge City, KS; adult/child Jun-Aug $8/free, Sep-May $7/free; 🕑 8am-8pm daily Jun-Aug, 9am-5pm Mon-Sat, 1-5pm Sun Sep-May; 🚻

Dalton Defenders Museum
Emmett Dalton – shot 35 times – served 14 years, was pardoned, then moved to California. ☎ 620-251-5944; www.kansastravel.org/daltongang1.html; 113 E Eighth St, Coffeyville, KS; adult/child $3/1; 🕑 10am-4pm Mon-Sat, 1-4pm Sun

Gilcrease Museum
The collections include clothing, moccasins and tools made by Great Plains tribes. ☎ 918-596-2700; www.gilcrease.org; 1400 N Gilcrease Museum Rd, Tulsa, OK; adult/child $8/free; 🕑 10am-5pm Tue-Sun; 🚻

Jesse James House
The most eye-catching exhibit belonged to Jesse's brother Frank: a rattlesnake tie. ☎ 816-232-8206; www.ponyexpressjessejames.com; 12th & Penn Sts, St Joseph, MO; adult/child $3/1.50; 🕑 10am-5pm Mon-Sat, 1-5pm Sun Apr-Oct, weekends & varied weekday hrs Nov-Mar

Langston's
Looking for boots? There's a wall-full of choices here. ☎ 405-235-9536; www.langstons.com; 2224 Exchange Ave, Oklahoma City (OKC), OK; 🕑 9am-8pm Mon-Sat, noon-6pm Sun

National Cowboy & Western Heritage Museum
John Wayne, Glenn Ford and Tom Selleck are a few actors honored in the Western Performers Gallery. ☎ 405-478-2250; www.nationalcowboymuseum.org; 1700 NE 63rd St, OKC, OK; adult/child $12.50/6; 🕑 10am-5pm; 🚻

Oklahoma History Center
A land-run wagon anchors an informative display about Oklahoma's land rush. ☎ 405-522-5248; www.okhistorycenter.org; 800 Nazih Zuhdi Dr, OKC, OK; adult/child $7/4; 🕑 10am-5pm Mon-Sat; 🚻

Oklahoma National Stockyards
The stockyards celebrate their centennial in 2010. ☎ 405-235-8675; www.onsy.com; 107 Livestock Exchange Bldg, OKC, OK; admission free; 🕑 auctions start 8am Mon & Tue

Shorty's Ca'boy Hattery
Ladies and kids have plenty of choices too. ☎ 405-232-4287; www.shortyshattery.com; 1206 S Agnew Ave, OKC, OK; 🕑 8:30am-6pm Mon-Fri, to 5pm Sat

Stockyards Mercantile
Jewelry, home decor, baby T-shirts and cowboy-wear for Fido – it's here. ☎ 405-605-4390; www.stockyardsmercantile.com; 1312 S Agnew Ave, OKC, OK; 🕑 10am-6pm Mon-Thu, to 8pm Fri, 9am-8pm Sat, noon-4pm Sun

Will Rogers Memorial Museum
By age 55, Rogers had written 3500 newspaper columns, appeared in 71 movies and completed several globe-circling tours. ☎ 918-341-0719; www.willrogers.com; 1720 W Will Rogers Blvd, Claremore, OK; 🕑 8am-5pm; 🚻

EAT & DRINK

Bricktown Brewery
Toast the West with a barbecue burger, beer-battered fries and a Bison Hefeweizen. No Sunday lunch. ☎ 405-232-2739; www.bricktownbrewery.com; 1 N Oklahoma Ave, OKC, OK; mains $8-20; 🕑 11am-2am Mon-Sat, noon-2am Sun

Brookville Hotel
Dinner: one half-chicken, family-style servings of mashed potatoes and gravy, cream-style corn, biscuits. ☎ 785-263-2244;

www.brookvillehotel.com; 105 E Lafayette, Abilene, KS; meals $14; ⊙ vary, but generally 5-7pm Wed-Sun, 11:30am-2pm Sat & Sun; ♿

Casa Alvarez

Bring cash – no debit or credit cards accepted. ☎ 620-225-7164; 1701 W Wyatt Earp Blvd, Dodge City, KS; mains $6-12; ⊙ 11am-2pm, 5-9pm Mon-Thu, 11am-9:30pm Fri-Sun; ♿

Cattlemen's Steakhouse

Waitstaff watch you cut into your steak to ensure it's cooked to order. ☎ 405-236-0416; www.cattlemensrestaurant.com; 1309 S Agnew Ave, OKC, OK; mains $11-26; ⊙ 6am-10pm Sun-Thu, to midnight Fri & Sat

Panaderia La Herradura

Bakery procedure? Grab tongs, load up tray, carry it all to the counter. ☎ 405-232-3502; 2235 SW 14th St, OKC, OK; mains under $5; ⊙ 7am-9pm Mon-Sat, 8am-5pm Sun

SLEEP

Boot Hill Bed & Breakfast

Enjoy views of Boot Hill from the Matt Dillon Suite. ☎ 620-225-0111; www.boothill dodgecity.com; 603 W Spruce St, Dodge City, KS; r $99-175

Desert Hills Motel

Fifty rooms, free wi-fi and an on-site laundry. ☎ 918-834-3311; www.deserthillstulsa. com; 5220 E 11th St, Tulsa, OK; r from $38

Hampton Inn & Suites

Bad news? Parking is $8 a day. Good news? Two hot breakfast items included with the cereal and pastries. ☎ 405-232-3600; http://hamptoninn1.hilton.com; 300 E Sheridan Ave, OKC, OK; r $129-189

USEFUL WEBSITES

www.stockyardscity.org
www.visitdodgecity.org

LINK YOUR TRIP

www.lonelyplanet.com/trip-planner

On the Pioneer Trail

WHY GO The Oregon Trail isn't just an app on your iPhone. It's a real-life path, along with the California and Mormon trails, that channeled thousands of pioneers west. Follow in their wagon tracks on Nebraska's Great Platte River Rd then visit the windswept settlements that anchored the western migration.

An estimated 400,000 people trekked west across America between 1840 and 1860, lured by tales of gold, promises of religious freedom and visions of fertile farmland. They were also inspired by the expansionist credo of President James Polk and the rallying cry of New York editor John O'Sullivan, who urged Americans in 1845 to "overspread the continent allotted by Providence for the free development of our yearly multiplying millions."

These starry-eyed pioneers became the foot soldiers of manifest destiny, eager to pursue their own dreams while furthering America's expansionist goals. The movement's success depended on the safe, reliable passage of these foot soldiers through the Great Plains and beyond. The California, Oregon and Mormon pioneer trails served this purpose well, successfully channeling the travelers and their "prairie schooners" on defined routes across the country.

These trails overlap in Nebraska. All three track the Platte River on an east–west corridor known today as the Great Platte River Rd. You can follow it on I-80 or Hwy 30.

For a wide-ranging introduction to pioneer life, spend a few hours at the 200-acre ❶ Stuhr Museum of the Prairie Pioneer in Grand Island, Nebraska. In summer, period re-enactors go about their business in an 1890s railroad town, answering questions about their jobs

TIME
3 – 5 days

DISTANCE
466 miles

BEST TIME TO GO
May – Sep

START
Grand Island, NE

END
Chadron, NE

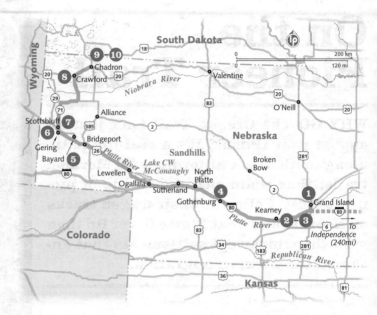

and home life. Also on view are an 1860s log-cabin settlement, a one-room schoolhouse and a Pawnee earth lodge.

On the 2nd floor of the museum's Stuhr Building, a covered wagon overflows with furniture and clothes – an inspiring symbol of the pioneers' can-do optimism. A few steps away, black-and-white photos of a primitive sod house and a prairie funeral depict the darker, harsher realities lurking behind the romance of the pioneer dream. Interesting fact? In 1880, 20% of Nebraska's population was foreign born, with most settlers emigrating from Germany, Sweden and Ireland.

Just west on I-80, a shimmering brown span swoops over four lanes of highway like an imposing medieval drawbridge. This horizon-breaking distraction – it depicts a setting Nebraska sun – is the ❷ **Great Platte River Road Archway Monument** (access it just ahead off exit 272). A little bit hokey, a little bit history, it's a rootin', tootin' ode to the west that puts a high-tech, glossy spin on the pioneer journey and western travel, sweeping in everything from stampeding buffalo to the gold-seeking '49ers. The mini-adventure begins with a dramatic escalator ride up to the enclosed, two-story bridge.

Modern pioneers searching for outdoor supplies will find a mother lode of clothing, gear and weapons at the 35,000-sq-ft ❸ **Cabela's** just east of Kearney. If you're planning on hunting, fishing, paddling or hiking, the store has got you covered – although you might need to buy a GPS unit to navigate the sprawling interior. Note: animal lovers may find the store unappealing, perhaps even horrifying. Every stuffed mount imaginable is on prominent display.

The Pony Express (1860–61) was the FedEx of its day, using a fleet of young riders and swift horses to carry letters between Missouri and California in an astounding 10 days. Each horseman rode full-bore for almost six hours – changing horses every 10 miles – before passing the mail to the next rider. Their route through Nebraska generally followed the Oregon Trail. In Gothenburg, step inside what some researchers think is an original **4** **Pony Express Station**, one of just a few still in existence. The engaging array of artifacts includes a mochila, the rider's mail-holding saddlebag.

Set your clocks to mountain time just west of Sutherland. In Ogallala, once known as the "Gomorrah of the Cattle Trail," pick up Hwy 26; it travels northwest beside the North Platte River. The Oregon and California trails turned north near here too, following the river toward Wyoming and the wild blue yonder. You'll experience a little "yonder" yourself as cornfields give way to untamed prairie grasses and desolate bluffs on this two-laner, known as Nebraska's Western Trails Historic & Scenic Byway. Look right soon after leaving Ogallala to glimpse sparkling Lake McConaughy through the low hills.

PIONEER TRAILS BY AUTO

About one in 10 travelers died on the arduous trek west. For a point-by-point listing of pioneer graves, massacre sites and abandoned buildings along the Oregon, California and Mormon trails, download or pick up a copy of the National Park Service's *National Historic Trails Auto Tour Route Interpretive Guide* (www.nps.gov/oreg/plan yourvisit/brochures.htm). This treasure trove of tragedy includes brief site descriptions as well as directions. But it's not all doom and gloom: there are also listings for wagon ruts and museums.

After Lewellen, cattle herds, passing trains and tumbleweed towns are the biggest distractions until Bridgeport. From there, centuries-old bluff formations rise up from the horizon, their striking presence a visual link connecting modern-day travelers (and Oregon Trail gamers) with their pioneer forebears. One of these links is Chimney Rock, located inside the **5** **Chimney Rock National Historic Site**. It's visible after Bridgeport on Hwy 92. Chimney Rock's fragile 120ft spire was an inspiring landmark for pioneers, and it was mentioned in hundreds of journals. It also marked the end of the first leg of the journey and the beginning of the tough – but final – push to the coast.

As you enter Gering, just south of the city of Scottsbluff, don't follow Hwy 92 when it joins Hwy 71 north. Continue straight onto Old Oregon Trail Rd. It follows the actual route of the trail and leads straight to **6** **Scotts Bluff**

National Monument. Spend a few minutes in the visitors center – there's a nice collection of western art in the William Henry Jackson Gallery – then hit the trail. You can hike the 1.6-mile Saddle Rock Trail (one-way) or drive the same distance up to the South Overlook for bird's-eye views of Mitchell Pass.

Before you leave, spend a few moments hiking the trail through Mitchell Pass itself. The covered wagons on display here look unnervingly frail as you peer through the bluff-flanked gateway, a narrow channel that spills onto the Rocky Mountain–bumping plains. For pioneers, reaching this pass was a significant milestone; it marked the completion of 600 miles of Great Plains trekking. The trailhead is just west of the visitors center.

"You'll experience a little 'yonder' yourself as cultivated cornfields give way to untamed prairie grasses..."

Too bad **7** **Emporium Coffeehouse & Café** wasn't around in the 1850s. The smooth roast coffee at this breezy, umbrella-fronted eatery in downtown Scottsbluff is a perfect afternoon pick-me-up. The menu includes a range of bistro fare, from My Big Fat Greek Salad to Wild Mushroom Ravioli to the Midnight Cubano sandwich with pork loin, ham and all the traditional fixin's. From here, we leave the Great Platte River Rd and head north to a historic military fort and a lonely trading post, important bastions of the frontier that paved the way for long-term settlers.

Nebraska's prairie is often described as a "sea of grass." This analogy proves true on the 75-mile drive north from Scottsbluff on Hwy 71. Prairie grasses bend and bob as strong winds sweep over 360 degrees of low-rolling hills, punctuated by the occasional wooden windmill or lonely cell-phone tower. Enjoy the drive. This is roll-down-your-window-and-breathe-in-America country. Traveling packs of motorcyclists seem to agree, sporadically blasting into view like riders unleashed from the gates of, well, heaven.

Hwy 71 passes through Sioux County, named for the Plains tribe that hunted and traveled throughout Nebraska. Sioux warrior Crazy Horse was fatally stabbed on the grounds of Fort Robinson, now **8** **Fort Robinson State Park**, on September 5, 1877, at the age of 35. The fort – in operation between 1874 and 1948 – was the area's most important military post during the Indian Wars.

In summer, visitors descend on the 22,000-acre park for stagecoach rides, steak cookouts, trout fishing and hiking. There are two museums on the grounds, the Fort Robinson Museum and the Trailside Museum, as well as the reconstructed Guardhouse where Crazy Horse spent his final hours. For a unique overnight stay, make reservations at the Fort Robinson Inn & Lodge. You might just find·yourself sleeping in officers' quarters built in 1874.

If you prefer your historic digs in an urban setting, drive 20 miles east to Chadron and book a room at the ❾ **Olde Main Street Inn**. This 1890s grand dame has lost a bit of her Victorian luster but none of her charm. The inn's nine rooms come with an eclectic mix of antiques, a resident ghost and loads of history. General Nelson Miles and his staff were headquartered here during Wounded Knee.

The pub grub whipped up by congenial owner Jeanne Goetzinger at the inn's Longbranch Saloon (open Wednesday to Saturday) is locally appreciated, and the snakebite pizza and green chili are favorites. While you wait, check out the old newspaper clippings and artifacts tucked here and there around the bar – and don't be afraid to talk to the locals. The Longbranch may look like a Wild West saloon but the easygoing barflies – from the guy on the laptop to the beer-swigging Cornhusker fan to the three old ladies gabbing in the corner – keep the vibe welcoming. At press time, Olde Main St's restaurant is open by reservation for fine-dining events.

End your journey at Chadron's ❿ **Museum of the Fur Trade**, a well-curated tribute to the mountain men and trappers who paved the way for the pioneers. For a small museum, it holds a fascinating array of artifacts: from 1820s mountain-man leggings and hand-forged animal traps to blankets, pelts and liquor bottles. Kit Carson's shotgun is displayed beside the world's largest collection of Native American trade guns.

> **DETOUR**
>
> Independence, Missouri, was a popular "jumping-off point" for pioneers preparing to follow the Oregon and California trails. For an accessible, straightforward history of these two trails and others, spend an hour or two at the city's **National Trails Museum** (www.frontiertrails museum.org). Exhibits include a wall-sized map of the major trail routes, a mock general store and diary entries from the pioneers.

In back, there's a reproduction of the Bordeaux Trading Post; it was in operation here from 1837 to 1876. The harsh reality of life on the plains is evident the moment you step inside the squat, unnervingly cramped building. Though it's not the original structure, the reproduction was so precisely done – based on eyewitness accounts – the building is listed on the National Register of Historic Places.

From here, all choices are good. Continue east to the Sandhills on Hwy 20, known as the Bridges to Buttes Byway, or head north for buffalo and more history in South Dakota's Black Hills.

Amy C Balfour

TRIP INFORMATION

GETTING THERE
From Omaha, Nebraska, follow I-80 west for 145 miles to Grand Island, Nebraska.

DO

Cabela's
Skilled at niche marketing, the company prints more than 100 different mail-order catalogs. ☎ 308-234-3933; www.cabelas.com; 3600 Hwy 30 E, Kearney, NE; ☾ 8am-8pm Mon-Sat, 10am-6pm Sun

Chimney Rock National Historic Site
Pioneers etched their names – now erased by erosion – on the clay, ash and sandstone rock. ☎ 308-586-2581; www.nps.gov/chro; Chimney Rock Rd, Bayard, NE; adult/child with parent $3/free; ☾ 9am-5pm; ♿

Great Platte River Road Archway Monument
One exhibit tracks the speed limit of cars on I-80. ☎ 308-237-1000; www.archway.org; 1 Archway Parkway, Kearney, NE; adult/youth/child $10/6/3; ☾ 9am-6pm late May-Aug, shorter hours rest of yr; ♿

Museum of the Fur Trade
"Mad as a hatter" is linked to rabbit-fur hat makers, often driven to dementia by mercury-based chemicals. ☎ 308-432-3843; www.furtrade.org; 6321 Hwy 20, Chadron, NE; adult/child $5/free; ☾ 8am-5pm May-Oct; ♿

Pony Express Station
The youngest rider was Charlie Miller, 11; he lived to be 105. www.ci.gothenburg.ne.us; 1500 Lake Ave, Gothenburg, NE; admission free; ☾ 8am-8pm Jun-Aug, shorter hours rest of yr; ♿

Scotts Bluff National Monument
The 1930s Civilian Conservation Corp built the three-tunneled Summit Rd. ☎ 308-436-9700; www.nps.gov/scbl; Gering, NE; per person/carload $3/5; ☾ 8am-7pm Jun-late Aug, 8am-5pm rest of yr; ♿

Stuhr Museum of the Prairie Pioneer
More than 60 buildings dot the grounds. ☎ 308-385-5316; www.stuhrmuseum.org; 3133 W Hwy 34, Grand Island, NE; adult/child May-Sep $8/6, Oct-Apr $6/4; ☾ 9am-5pm Mon-Sat, noon-5pm Sun, with variations; ♿

EAT & SLEEP

Emporium Coffeehouse & Café
The wine and spirits list has more than 100 selections. ☎ 308-632-6222; www.emporiumcoffeehouseandcafe.com; 1818 1st Ave, Scottsbluff, NE; mains $7-29; ☾ coffeehouse 7am-10pm, café 11am-2pm Mon-Sat, 5-10pm Mon-Fri, both with variations

Fort Robinson State Park
The fort held 500 to 600 POWs during WWII. ☎ park 308-665-2900, reservations 402-471-1414; www.stateparks.com/fort_robinson.html; Crawford, NE; r $45-230, campsites $7-12; ☾ lodge & modern camping Apr-Nov, primitive camping year-round; ♿

Olde Main Street Inn
The resident ghost is a prankster. ☎ 308-432-3380; www.chadron.com/oldemain; 115 Main St, Chadron, NE; r $60-85

USEFUL WEBSITES
www.visitnebraska.gov
www.westnebraska.com

LINK YOUR TRIP
www.lonelyplanet.com/trip-planner

Where the Buffalo Roam

WHY GO Shaggy bison lumber across the plains. Giant monuments praise great men. Windswept prairies unfurl below towering mountains. This Black Hills tour embraces the region's heritage in all its messy glory, swooping past Mt Rushmore, the Crazy Horse Memorial, three sprawling parks and a lasso's loop of gaudy billboards that ropes them all together.

TIME
4 – 5 days

DISTANCE
200 miles

BEST TIME TO GO
May – Sep

START
Badlands National Park, SD

END
Wind Cave National Park, SD

Picture a low-rolling plain. Prairie grass brushing against your knee. A few grasshoppers, a butterfly. All's quiet, tranquil. But then…a whisper. A low rumble just off the horizon. Dust rises from a nearby hill. In moments, the earth is rattling beneath your feet, the rumble rolling into a roar. Dust explodes into a matted, mud-splattering horde. The ground quakes. Dirt scatters. And chaos pounds past in one poetic, ephemeral moment.

Similar scenes played out regularly in the early 1800s when 60 million buffalo roamed the plains – plentiful, free-ranging but, unfortunately, not very fast. Rampant overhunting decimated their ranks and by 1889 fewer than 1000 remained. Today, their numbers have climbed to 250,000, and several Black Hills parks are managing healthy herds.

More than 600 buffalo, also known as North American bison, roam **❶ Badlands National Park**. The name originated with French trappers and the Lakota Sioux, who described the park's jagged spires and crumbling buttes as "bad lands." Today, an easy drive reveals a landscape more geologically fascinating than bad. In fact, this crumbling former floodplain is strangely inviting, its corrugated hillsides softened by an ever-changing palette of reds and pinks.

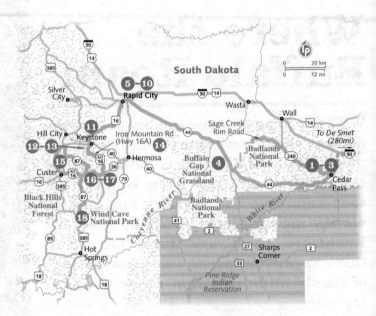

You can see the eroding rocks up close on the **❷ Notch Trail**, a 1.5-mile (round-trip) leg stretcher that twists through a canyon, scampers up a wooden ladder then curves along a crumbly ridgeline to an expansive view of grasslands and more serrated walls. At the **❸ Ben Reifel Visitor Center** just down the road, a visually stunning film captures the park's natural diversity with jaw-dropping close-ups of the plants and animals that thrive in the mixed-grass prairie.

The Badlands Loop Rd (Hwy 240) stretches west from the visitors center into the park's north unit, curving along a narrow ridge of buttes known as the Badlands Wall. The loop can be driven in an hour, but stopping at the numerous overlooks can easily fill a morning – and your digital card. Your best bet for glimpsing buffalo, called *tatanka* by the Sioux, is a drive on Sage Creek Rim Rd in the western section of the park.

To avoid I-90, double back to the visitors center and pick up Hwy 44. Badlands bluffs give way to rolling prairie on this made-for-convertibles byway that swings through the **❹ Buffalo Gap National Grassland** on its way to the Black Hills.

In bustling **❺ Rapid City**, the Black Hills' unofficial capital, bronze statues of 35 US presidents anchor downtown street corners (with the last few arriving by 2011). Good restaurants and bars cluster near the 700 block of Main St.

For a warm welcome and a bit of Black Hills charm, set aside an hour or two for supper at the airy, art-filled **6** **Corn Exchange**. Chef MJ Adams stirs up Slow Food meals from locally grown organic ingredients, complemented by a thoughtful selection of French wines.

With its golden microbrews and elbow-bumping good cheer, the **7** **Firehouse Brewing Co**, located inside a 1915 firehouse, is a fun place to regroup after a day on the road. On busy nights, expect a wait for the hearty pub grub, although we spotted a few spare seats at the bar.

Bird's-eye views and expansive breakfasts are highlights at comfy **8** **Big Sky Lodge**, just off Hwy 16A south of town. Cap your day with twinkling city views from the lodge's hill-topping hot tub. In the morning, return to town on Skyline Dr. This twisty route spins north on a narrow ridgeline that passes **9** **Dinosaur Park** and the seven enormous dinosaurs that congregate there. It's a scenic spot for letting the kids burn some energy.

From Skyline Dr, take Quincy St to Mt Rushmore Rd and turn right. Presidential profiles have nothing on the eye-catching sign fronting **10** **Black Hills Bagels**: a cowboy holding tight to a bucking bagel. Behind the eatery's Old West facade, lines start early for the crispy soft bagels. The white chocolate chunk is a crowd pleaser. We also recommend the vanilla nut. If you ate breakfast at Big Sky, stock up here for trail snacks.

DETOUR ➤ You won't find giant sculptures or galloping buffalo in **De Smet**, 280 miles east of the badlands. But this prairie village still packs a mighty punch. Bookworms know that Laura Ingalls Wilder based several *Little House on the Prairie* books on her adventures here. The Laura Ingalls Wilder Memorial Society's tour through key sites – the surveyor's house, the schoolhouse and Ma and Pa's home – is surprisingly moving (www .discoverlaura.org). Just be prepared for the hardcore Laura fans who know the books inside and out.

One indisputable fact about the Black Hills? It will always, always, always take longer than you think to reach a key attraction. Trust us. Slow-moving Winnebagos, serpentine byways and kitschy roadside distractions will ruin your pace. And the distractions start early on Hwy 16A: Bear City, Old Mac-Donald's Farm, Christmas Village. Kitsch reigns supreme in **11** **Keystone**, a gaudy town bursting with rah-rah patriotism, Old West spirit and too many fudgeries. The fuss is directly attributable to its proximity to Mt Rushmore 2 miles west.

The awesomeness of **12** **Mt Rushmore National Memorial** is tempered by a few Park Service missteps, most notably the toll booths at the cash-only ($10), blockade-like parking garage. Inspiration returns with your first full view of the 60ft mountainside visages: George Washington, Thomas Jefferson,

Theodore Roosevelt and Abraham Lincoln. Sculptor Gutzon Borglum chose these four presidents "to commemorate the founding, growth, preservation and development of the United States."

The narrow Avenue of Flags, lined with flags from 56 states and territories, funnels visitors to Grand View Terrace. You'll snap your best photos here. Just below is the visitors center, where exhibits geared to short attention spans highlight the Herculean efforts of Borglum and his team to blast and carve the memorial between 1927 and 1941. The half-mile ⑬ **Presidential Trail** offers pine-framed views (and a stroll under the noses) of the presidents.

"Driving the 66-mile Peter Norbeck Scenic Byway is like flirting with a brand-new crush…"

Driving the 66-mile ⑭ **Peter Norbeck Scenic Byway** is like flirting with a brand-new crush: always exhilarating, occasionally challenging and sometimes you get a few butterflies Named for the South Dakota senator who pushed for its creation in 1919, the oval-shaped byway is broken into four roads linking the most memorable destinations in the Black Hills (drivers of large RVs should call Custer State Park for tunnel measurements).

Iron Mountain Rd (Hwy 16A) is the most diverse of the four, beloved for its pigtailing loops, Mt Rushmore–framing tunnels and one gorgeous glide through sun-dappled pines. Tackle it early to avoid caravans of looky-loos. The adjoining 14-mile Needles Hwy (Hwy 87) swoops below granite spires, careens past rocky overlooks and slings though a supernarrow tunnel.

Six miles south of the Needles junction with Hwy 16, the formidable ⑮ **Crazy Horse Memorial** attempts to break free from a lofty Black Hills mountain. Begun in 1948 by Boston-born sculptor Korczak Ziolkowski, the 563ft work-in-progress honors the Lakota Sioux warrior who famously defended his homeland from the ever-encroaching US Cavalry. Fiercely independent – at a time when fellow Sioux were cooperating with the Indian Agencies – Crazy Horse refused to sign US treaties. As he succinctly explained, "One does not sell the earth upon which the people walk."

The sculpture – Crazy Horse astride a charging steed – will be the largest mountain carving in the world upon completion. At present, Crazy Horse's 87.5ft profile is visible (the Mt Rushmore profiles would all fit inside it), and there's an inkling of his outstretched arm. The project is financed solely by entrance fees and donations, meaning it may not be completed for decades. At the visitors complex, a sprawling assortment of vendors and cultural exhibits tends to obscure the memorial's meaning. Many Native Americans oppose the project as a desecration of sacred land. To get your bearings, start by reading the first-hand accounts of Crazy Horse in the exhibit area by the entrance.

From here, take Hwy 385 south to Hwy 16A. Follow it east to ⑯ **Custer State Park,** named for the golden-curled Civil War general and Indian fighter George A Custer. Custer led a scientific expedition into the Black Hills in 1874. The expedition's discovery of gold drew so many new settlers that an 1868 treaty granting the Sioux a 60-million-acre reservation in the area was eventually broken. Crazy Horse and the Lakotas retaliated, killing Custer and about 265 of his men at Wyoming's Battle of the Little Big Horn in 1876.

The park is a 71,000-acre wildlife bonanza, home to one of the largest free-roaming buffalo herds in the world (about 1500) as well as the handout-seeking "begging burros." Scan for elk, pronghorns, big horn sheep and prairie dogs from the 18-mile Wildlife Rd. Top hiking trails include the 111-mile prairie-and-mountain-traversing Centennial Trail and the 3.5-mile Harney Peak Trail to the 7242ft summit of Harney Peak, the highest point in the Black Hills (one-way distances). Mountain bikers, rock climbers and trout fisherman will also find plenty of distractions.

Woodsmen will weep – with joy – inside a comfy log cabin at the park's popular ⑰ **Blue Bell Lodge & Resort Cabins.** The rugged, tree-dotted complex has horse stables and trail rides, a general store, a playground and a cozy dining room ornamented with stuffed game trophies.

⑱ **Wind Cave National Park,** site of the fourth-longest cave in the world, is 30 miles south. For an introduction to the cave's history and geology, wander the exhibits at the visitors center prior to one of the ranger-led cave tours (most are one to 1½ hours). Short on time? Follow the path from the visitors center to the

BUFFALOS, ART & PANCAKES

For a sure-fire buffalo sighting, visit Custer State Park during its Buffalo Roundup on the fourth Monday in September. During this popular event, the park's buffalo are branded, sorted and vaccinated before the fall buffalo sale, which keeps the herd at manageable levels. Enjoy an early morning pancake breakfast at the corrals. An outdoor arts festival runs the preceding Saturday and Sunday across from the **Peter Norbeck Visitor Center** (www.custerstatepark.info).

cave entrance, built by the Civilian Conservation Corps in the 1930s. Although you can't enter the cave itself without a guide, you can push though the revolving door and glimpse the inky depths. Back outside, walk over to the stone-encircled natural entrance. Wind blasting from the small opening might just ruffle your hair.

Not all of the park's treasures are underground. Wind Cave's 28,295 above-ground acres abound with bison and prairie dogs. Climb the short Prairie Vista Trail for a final, windswept view of the majestic grasslands. A place where the buffalo once again roam.

Amy C Balfour

TRIP INFORMATION

GETTING THERE
From Sioux Falls, South Dakota, drive 280 miles west on I-90 to exit 131 for Badlands National Park.

DO

Badlands National Park
The rare black-footed ferret is staging a comeback here. ☎ 605-433-5361; www.nps.gov/badl; Hwy 240; 7-day pass per person/carload $7/15; ☽ Ben Reifel Visitor Center 7am-7pm summer, 8am-5pm spring & fall, 9am-4pm winter; ♿

Crazy Horse Memorial
Price includes evening laser-light show; buses to mountain's base are $4. ☎ 605-673-4681; www.crazyhorsememorial.org; 12151 Avenue of the Chiefs, Crazy Horse; per person/carload $10/27; ☽ 7am-after light show Jun–mid-Oct, 8am-dusk rest of yr; ♿

Custer State Park
Tepee-shaped branch clusters are slash piles, built to reduce forest-fire threats. ☎ 605-255-4515; Hwy 16A; www.custerstatepark.info; 7-day pass per person/carload $6/15; ☽ visitors center varies, generally 9am-5pm, closed Dec-Mar, grounds open year-round; ♿

Mt Rushmore National Memorial
Budding rock-carvers learn the craft during a one-week workshop. ☎ 605-574-2523; www.nps.gov/moru; admission free, parking $10; ☽ visitors center & viewing areas 8am-11pm summer, visitors center 8am-5pm, viewing areas generally until 10pm rest of yr; ♿

Wind Cave National Park
The wind, which allegedly blew off the cave founder's hat, is caused by differing in-side–outside atmospheric pressure. ☎ 605-745-4600; Hwy 385; www.nps.gov/wica; admission free, cave tours adult $7-23, child $3.50-4.50; ☽ visitors center 8am-7pm Jun-Aug, closes earlier rest of yr; ♿

EAT & DRINK

Black Hills Bagels
An eclectic crew arrives early for bagels, coffee and wi-fi. ☎ 605-399-1277; www.blackhillsbagels.com; 913 Mt Rushmore Rd, Rapid City; mains under $8; ☽ 6am-3pm Mon-Fri, 7am-3pm Sat & Sun; ♿

Corn Exchange
Solo diners do well at the attentive but easygoing bar. ☎ 605-343-5070; www.cornexchange.com; 727 Main St, Rapid City; mains $19-23; ☽ 5-9pm Tue-Sat

Firehouse Brewing Co
From Barely Blond to Smoke Jumper Stout, all brews are produced on-site. ☎ 605-348-1915; www.firehousebrewing.com; 610 Main St, Rapid City; mains $7-23; ☽ 11am-10pm Mon-Thu, 11am-11pm Fri & Sat, 4-9pm Sun; ♿

SLEEP

Big Sky Lodge
Just north of Rapid City, this'll give you a head start to Mt Rushmore. ☎ 605-348-3200; www.bigskylodge.com; 4080 Tower Rd, Rapid City; r $85-99, ste $99-145; ♿ 🐾

Blue Bell Lodge & Resort Cabins
Mountain men swoon for the sleeping cabin – a one-room log structure. ☎ 605-255-4772; www.custerresorts.com; 25453 Hwy 87, Custer State Park; cabins $140-260; ☽ May–mid-Oct; ♿

USEFUL WEBSITES
www.blackhillsbadlands.com
www.sdgfp.info/Publications/Parks/Tatanka.pdf

LINK YOUR TRIP

www.lonelyplanet.com/trip-planner

Offbeat Dakotas

WHY GO North and South Dakotans are good-hearted, stoic and salt-of-the-earth. But strange? Well, yeah. Need we mention the Corn Palace? Sue, the World's Largest Holstein Cow? The Minuteman missile silo hunkered beside a sod house? And we haven't even mentioned Wall Drug. Trust us, on this tour, weird is worth your time.

TIME
5 – 6 days

DISTANCE
930 miles

BEST TIME TO GO
May – Sep

START
Mitchell, SD

END
Fargo, ND

Eye-popping! A-maize-ing! As the Mitchell, South Dakota, visitor guide admits, the puns don't stop when it comes to the city's famous attraction, the 1892 **1 Corn Palace**. Each summer, hardworking teams cover its Moorish exterior with theme-based murals made from 275,000 naturally colored corncobs. Take a guided tour, buy corny souvenirs or study photographs of the palace in years gone by. Gaudy billboards dot the farms and hillsides surrounding I-90, disappearing momentarily as the interstate swoops over the magnificent Missouri River. Set your watch to mountain time at Murdo then look right for the **2 skeleton man walking a skeleton dinosaur** sculpture just east of exit 170's 1880 Town.

Forty miles west, a striking juxtaposition awaits: a 1909 sod house sits just down the interstate from a Minuteman missile silo. These two structures, built within 60 years of one another, reveal not only the rapid pace of 20th-century technological development but also the physical results of single-minded, can-do determination. The sod house slumps on the grounds of the engagingly hokey **3 Prairie Homestead**, south of exit 131. Rules are few at this scrappy slice of Americana, the only park we've visited where guests are allowed to feed the prairie dogs (all white!). They'll even sell you the feed. The gritty, low-slung house, built of buffalo-grass sod and native cottonwood logs, is tucked into a low hill on the 160-acre claim. One note: do not, under any circumstances, look inside the outhouse.

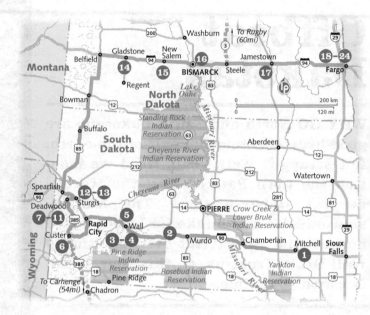

One mile north is the ❹ **Minuteman Missile National Historic Site**. During the Cold War, 150 underground missile silos dotted regional grasslands, placed here due to the region's sparse population and proximity to the Soviet Union. The silos were deactivated in the 1990s, but a representative launch-control facility and missile silo were preserved for public viewing. Guided tours to the Delta-01 control facility are available by reservation. The Delta-09 silo can be viewed – through a clear cover – without a reservation (half a mile south of exit 119). Rangers are usually on-site in the morning. But enough about juxtapositions. It's time to worship at ❺ **Wall Drug**. By our unofficial count, 62 Wall Drug billboards dot I-90 west between the Corn Palace and exit 110. After all that hype, only a curmudgeon could resist passenger pleas to pull over. Free ice water! Cowboy hats! Homemade ice cream! This 1931 warren of kitsch does have a few charms tucked behind its Old West facade: Native American jewelry, cowboy wear, a travelers' chapel, a climbable jackalope, the Hole in the Wall bookstore and, somewhere, a drugstore.

The ❻ **Flintstones Campground** keeps it kitschy in Custer, 100 miles southwest of Wall. The "modern stone age" setting honors Hanna-Barbera's cartoon family and includes a mini–theme park, Bedrock-y buildings and a drive-in selling brontoburgers. Grown-ups and gamblers may prefer ❼ **Deadwood**, a Wild West town made famous by Wild Bill Hickok, Calamity Jane and the lyrically foul-mouthed *Deadwood* series on HBO. The town, a National Historic Landmark, sprang to life in 1874 after George Custer's Black Hills

Expedition discovered gold in neighboring hills. As prospector Charlie Utter presciently predicted, "This rush is going to be a lallapaloozer!"

For your own lallapaloozer, sample the Victorian-era charms of the **8 Bullock Hotel**, opened in 1895 by sheriff Seth Bullock. Today, this three-story hotel is a stop for ghost hunters. A lobby notebook details paranormal shenanigans. Hustle down casino-lined Main St for a drink at **9 Saloon No. 10** (named for an 1876 mining claim), where sawdust floors, stuffed game, blackjack tables and old photographs recall rowdier days. Wild Bill Hickok was killed while playing cards at the bar's original location across the street. Legend says Calamity Jane claimed his fateful chair – now perched above the entrance.

> **DETOUR** Rising from a western Nebraska field, **Carhenge** (www.carhenge.com) is a faithful reproduction of Stonehenge assembled from 38 discarded cars. Other car-part art poses in the neighboring Car Art Reserve. Carhenge is 150 miles south of Rapid City. Follow Hwy 385 south into Nebraska, turn left at State Link 7A then turn south at Hwy 87. It's 5 miles north of Alliance, Nebraska.

In the morning, wander the fantastic **10 Adams Museum & House**. This treasure trove displays playing cards from Hickock's last game, Sol Starr's mayor badge and 1800s newspaper articles about local girls gone bad (soiled doves). There's even a Cabinet of Curiosities complete with a two-headed calf – the holy grail of offbeat. Deadwood's most notorious former residents rest at **11 Mt Moriah Cemetery**, known as Boot Hill. Wild Bill, Calamity Jane and Potato Creek Johnny, a colorful prospector, are buried within a few feet of each other.

"There's even a Cabinet of Curiosities complete with a two-headed calf…"

Follow Hwy 14A 30 miles east to **12 Sturgis**, where billboards tout abstinence, riding safe and personal injury attorneys. These harbingers of doom are not-so-subtle reminders that Sturgis rumbles to life once a year during the Sturgis Motorcycle Rally (www.sturgismotorcyclerally.com). This convivial festival (second week of August) draws 500,000 Harley-Davidson enthusiasts. Inside the fancy-cabin walls of **13 Sturgis Coffee Company**, order a pony espresso and an apple-cinnamon scone – the latter are delicious – then sidle out and saddle up for the lonely drive to North Dakota. After turning onto Hwy 85 north, it's 100 miles of low-rolling plains, intermittent dirt roads and unexpected antelope herds. Approaching Buffalo, South Dakota, look right. The spot unofficially designated as the furthest from a McDonald's in the Lower 48 is one hour east.

In North Dakota, follow I-94 east to *Geese in Flight*, a towering ode to art and nature at exit 72. It marks the northern end of the 32-mile **14 Enchanted Highway** (www.enchantedhighway.net). Hugging the highway is a series of whimsical metal sculptures by local artist Gary Greff, who wanted to attract travelers and business to adjacent communities. Don't miss *Grasshopper's Delight*.

OFFBEAT

⑮ Sue, the World's Largest Holstein Cow, keeps things udderly weird at New Salem, south of exit 127. Moored on a hill, the 38ft bovine is visible from the highway. Bismarck, 30 miles east and in the central time zone, isn't particularly offbeat, but it's well supplied with hotels. **⑯ Select Inn** has clean rooms, flat-screen TVs and strong wi-fi. Continue east on I-94, taking Jamestown's exit 258 to stand beside the **⑰ World's Largest Buffalo**. Erected in 1959, this colossal animal tops out at 26ft and weighs 60 tons. And don't try to set him up with Sue. They tried; it didn't work out. For all things buffalo, check out the Buffalo Museum (www.buffalomuseum.com) next door and look for the albino bison out back.

DETOUR

Good news! The **geographical center of North America** is just 110 miles north of North Dakota's I-90, in Pierce County, North Dakota. A 21ft pyramid-shaped cairn honors this achievement at the corner of Hwys 2 and 3 in the town of Rugby (www.rugbynorthdakota.com). Grab a burger and fries at wi-fi–offering **Cornerstone Café** (☎701-776-6528) next door. Across the street is a visitor center with brochures from every state. From Steele, North Dakota, follow Hwy 3 north until you get there.

Upbeat **⑱ Fargo** was just another midsized city on the plains until the Coen brothers arrived. Their quirky 1996 film *Fargo* (mostly filmed in adjacent Minnesota) made characters out of cold winters and flat accents. Speaking of wood-chippers, don't miss the 1926 **⑲ Fargo Theatre**. Midnight movies, indie festivals, music concerts and a Mighty Wurlitzer make it everything an independent theater should be. It's also home to Woodchip Marge, an MGM gift. Downtown's central artery, Broadway, is flanked by two active (but quiet) sets of railroad tracks and lined with indie-owned boutiques and restaurants – part of recent revitalization

ASK A LOCAL

"JL Beers (518 1st Ave N) is now open, and it's going great. It's a really fun place… It's got 32 kinds of domestic beer and 30 bottled imports," says Fargo resident Bob Stein. "It's only 13ft wide and not even 100ft deep, [but] they really move a lot of people. They specialize in hamburgers and homemade chips."

efforts. Brick-columned markers highlight noteworthy sites. To explore by bike, stop by **⑳ Island Park Cycles** inside the Great Northern Train Depot. With its pressed ceiling, used-book exchange and cozy red booths, the underground **㉑ Red Raven Espresso Parlor** exudes quirky – but welcoming – cool.

For lunch, savor a juicy, cheddar-topped bison burger with sweet-potato chips at **㉒ HoDo Lounge**. The adjoining **㉓ Hotel Donaldson** earns its offbeat cred with 17 luxurious rooms decorated by local artists. Most fun? The Sky Prairie, a stylish, prairie-and-wildflower-infused rooftop bar with sweeping city views. Finish with a delicious treat from **㉔ Nichole's Fine Pastry**, where croissants, scones and tartlets call out to be loved. And trust us, they will be.

Amy C Balfour

TRIP INFORMATION

GETTING THERE
From Sioux Falls, South Dakota, drive 75 miles west on I-90 to Mitchell, South Dakota.

DO

Adams Museum & House
Handy notebooks explain the origins of the artifacts. ☎ 605-578-1714; www.adams museumandhouse.org; 54 Sherman St, Deadwood, SD; donations welcome; ⏲ 9am-5pm May-Sep, to 4pm & closed most Sun & Mon Oct-Apr; ♿

Corn Palace
To see corn murals inside the gym, follow the corncob footprints. ☎ 605-996-6223; www.cornpalace.com; 604 N Main St, Mitchell, SD; ⏲ 8am-5pm, 8am-9pm Jun-Aug, closed Sun Dec-Mar; ♿

Fargo Theatre
Historic touches include the original marquee, a 1937 Art Moderne interior and a Wurlitzer organ. ☎ 701-239-8385; www.fargotheatre.org; 314 Broadway, Fargo, ND; movies $5-12; ⏲ vary; ♿

Island Park Cycles
The Metro Trail Map highlights Red River bike paths and shared roads downtown. ☎ 701-280-1796; www.gncycles.com; 425 N Broadway, Fargo, ND; bike rental 1st/2nd day $25/15; ⏲ 10am-7pm Mon-Sat, plus Sun spring & summer, with variations; ♿

Minuteman Missile National Historic Site
In 30 minutes a missile could hit the Soviet Union with 1.2 megatons of explosive force. ☎ 605-433-5552; www.nps.gov/mimi; 21280 Hwy 240, Phillip, SD; ⏲ visitors center 8am-4:30pm Mon-Sat Jun-Aug, closed Sat Sep-May, silo 8am-4pm May-Oct

Mt Moriah Cemetery
Grab a walking-tour guide for bios on famous inhabitants and gravesite locations. ☎ 605-578-2600; www.cityofdeadwood.com; Lincoln St, Deadwood, SD; adult/child $1/0.50; ⏲ 8am-8pm summer, 8am-5pm rest of yr

Prairie Homestead
Kitschy charms – animatronic greeters, white prairie dogs, roaming chickens – enliven the homesteading experience. ☎ 605-433-5400; www.prairiehomestead.com; Hwy 240, 2.5 miles south of I-90, Philip, SD; senior/child $7/5; ⏲ sunrise-sunset; ♿

Wall Drug
Opened in 1931, the lonely drugstore found success in 1936 with a highway sign offering free water. ☎ 605-279-2175; www.walldrug.com; 510 Main St, Wall, SD; ⏲ 6:30am-10pm summer, 7am-5:30pm winter; ♿

World's Largest Buffalo
Elmer Petersen created this shaggy beast from steel beaming, wire mesh and sprayed cement. ☎ 800-222-4766; http://tourjamestown.com; western end of 17th St, Jamestown, ND; ⏲ 9am-9pm Jun-Aug, 9am-7pm Sep–mid-Oct, 8am-5pm mid-Oct–May; ♿

EAT & DRINK

HoDo Lounge
Comfort food – fish and chips, Reubens, hanger steak – comes with a fashionable twist. ☎ 701-478-6969; www.hoteldonaldson.com; 101 Broadway, Fargo, ND; mains $7-12; ⏲ 11am-11pm Mon-Sat, 5-9pm Sun

Nichole's Fine Pastry
If red-velvet cupcakes are a sin, then we're going to hell with a frosting-dabbed smile. ☎ 701-232-6430; www.nicholesfinepastry.com; 13 S 8th St, Fargo, ND; most pastries under $5; ⏲ 8am-6pm Tue & Wed, 8am-10pm Thu-Sat

Red Raven Espresso Parlor
Architecture profs and Michael Pollan–reading students from North Dakota State keep this coffee shop up-to-the-minute. ☎ 701-478-7337; www.redravenep.com; 14 Roberts St, Fargo, ND; ⏲ 9am-midnight Mon-Fri, 11am-midnight Sat & Sun

Saloon No. 10
Named for a mining claim, this burger-serving saloon embraces its shoot-'em-up history with summer re-enactments of Wild Bill's demise. ☎ 605-578-3346; www.saloon10.com; 657 Main St, Deadwood, SD; ⏲ 8am-2am

Sturgis Coffee Company

This cavernous java joint has a bar-style counter popular with chit-chatters and newspaper readers. ☎ 605-720-1480; www.sturgiscoffeecompany.com, 2275 Lazelle St, Sturgis, SD; pastries under $5; ⏲ 6am-5pm Mon-Fri, 7am-noon Sat; ♿

SLEEP

Bullock Hotel

Party like it's 1895: vintage black-and-white photos, 24-hour slots, a creaky elevator and possibly a ghost. ☎ 605-578-1745; www.historicbullock.com; 633 Main St, Deadwood, SD; r $113-188; ♿

Flintstones Campground

Cartoon-themed campground convenient to Custer State Park, Mt Rushmore and Windcave National Park. ☎ 605-673-4079; www.flintstonesbedrockcity.com; Hwys 16 & 385, Custer, SD; campsites $21-27, cabins $43; ⏲ mid-May–early Sep; ♿ 🐾

Hotel Donaldson

Layout and artwork vary room to room, but all have heated tile floors, plush linens and Bose stereos. ☎ 701-478-1000; www.hoteldonaldson.com; 101 Broadway, Fargo, ND; r $179-330; 🐾

Select Inn Bismarck

Pluses: Hearty continental breakfasts and hefty discount coupons (check inside local travel guides). ☎ 701-223-8060; www.vistarez.com; 1505 Interchange Ave, Bismarck, SD; r $64-94; 🐾

USEFUL WEBSITES

www.deadwood.org
www.fargomoorhead.org

LINK YOUR TRIP

www.lonelyplanet.com/trip-planner

TEXAS TRIPS

With a state the size of Texas, you can pick and choose your adventures. If you're into the great outdoors you'll love Texas' Gulf Coast, where you can watch endangered birds and sea turtles at national parks or party down on South Padre Island. Out in west Texas there's more big fun to be had hiking, rafting and riding in the mountains of Big Bend.

If you like to travel on your stomach, central Hill Country, where the meat-market barbecue tradition dates back 100 years, is for you. Nearby San Antonio is the best place to sample Mexican food; while you're there, check out the city's vibrant Hispanic culture, music and history.

At rodeos and ranches across the state it's the traditional Texas cattle-country heritage that's on display. But if you're looking for something more offbeat, the state has that too: in roadside attractions, such as Cadillac Ranch, which pokes unexpectedly out of the northwest plains; and some Texans think that all of alternative Austin is out there. We think you'll enjoy the unusual shows, great music and eclectic shops. So, come on, waltz across Texas with us.

PLAYLIST 🎵 A list of country singers from Texas reads like a Hall of Fame, and numerous legendary rockers were born here too. Listen for modern "Texas Music" shows on radio stations across the state. And take along a sampling of these classic Texas tunes on your iPod:

- "Angel Flying too Close to the Ground," Willie Nelson
- "Me and Bobby McGee," Janis Joplin
- "El Paso," Marty Robbins
- "Waltz Across Texas," Ernest Tubb
- "Bob Wills Is Still the King," Waylon Jennings
- "Amarillo by Morning," George Strait
- "Only the Lonely," Roy Orbison
- "It's a Texas Thing," Gary P Nunn

TEXAS TRIPS

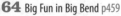

48 Hours in Austin

WHY GO Austin is pure fun. Airstream-trailer food courts, festival-like 6th St, eclectic SoCo shops, parks, lakes and music galore. Packing it all into 48 hours can be a challenge, so we sought out fun-and-funky-B&B owners Chris and Sylvia Mackey to give us the insider lowdown.

You can tell by the naive art that decorates ❶ Austin Folk House, one of two B&Bs Chris and Sylvia run near the University of Texas (UT), that this couple has a serious sense of humor. A painted wood relief of a cartoonish devil fishing for souls among beer cans is a favorite. The rooms are pretty traditional, but the "unromantic" package jokingly offers a six-pack and pizza to drown your break-up sorrows. Sylvia and Chris spend ample time seeking out local entertainment and are happy to share suggestions with guests.

"With just 48 hours, I'd start with something fairly typically Austin," Chris says. "Downtown is not overrated." For the first night, they suggest dinner and a show. Have a cab drop you at the corner of 5th St and N Congress Ave. From there you can't go in any direction and not find a bunch of good restaurants; downtown is thick with them. Almost every kind of food is represented, too. Then you'll be near ❷ Esther's Follies, a long-running local musical comedy revue that pokes fun at all sorts of subjects. Sylvia likes it because they keep it current – and very funny. "Obama" may be onstage thanking the almighty, Oprah, before a magician singing "Chic Chica Boom" merengues across the stage and turns a puppy into a ruffle-bedecked assistant. Think vaudeville for the 21st century. "It's always an excellent time at Esther's," says Chris.

Or if it's Monday night, there's ❸ DK Sushi and the sushi pimp's karaoke show. "We're the type that go out of our way to find strange stuff, and I've never seen anything like this karaoke show," says Chris. The Korean owner dresses up in a 1970s pimp suit and afro wig and

TIME
2 days

BEST TIME TO GO
**Mar – May &
Sep – Nov**

START
**University of
Texas**

END
Zilker Park

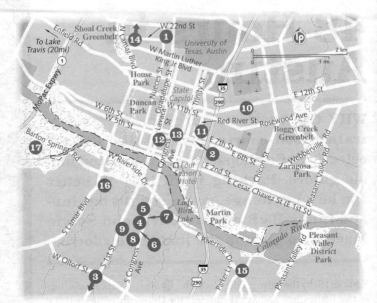

provides chauvinistic, not even remotely politically correct, comic banter. If the singers aren't excellent, he'll gong them off the stage and down a sake bomb with 'em. Inappropriate rowdiness is the order of the evening. Women, watch your rears. "Some people will leave hating it," Chris says. "You can go to Vegas and never see anything this outlandish."

The next morning wake up late, sip your java, watch as the people-parade goes by and become human again at ④ **Jo's Coffee**. The outdoor café is at the heart of the trendy S Congress Ave neighborhood, or SoCo, where even the places to stay are happenin'. In the 1950s this was the outskirts of town but, instead of knocking down the motor-court motels, people updated them.

> "You can go to Vegas and never see anything this outlandish."

Eclectic ⑤ **Austin Motel** has rooms with full waterfall murals, and some sporting giant retro polka dots – each guest quarter is more than unique. Their motto: "so close yet so far out." Singles are kind of small so pick a double by the pool if you want more space. Up the street, the ⑥ **Hotel San José** takes a more upscale, Zen-like approach to the motor court. Minimalist rooms of different shapes and sizes gather around soothing green spaces. There's no restaurant, but the small courtyard wine bar attracts local celebrities such as Sandra Bullock, and bento-box meals are available for delivery.

While you're here, you should definitely do some shopping. "⑦ SoCo is really exploding," says Sylvia. "There are a lot of unique shops, including one dedicated entirely to water pipes." Other eclectic options include a costume shop where you can get that special belly-dancing outfit year-round, a kitschy candy store selling novelties you remember from childhood, and vintage clothing outlets. After you've picked up a snazzy, snapfront 1950s Western shirt, make sure to look for a pair of fire-red lizard skins at ⑧ **Allen Boots**. In the 1600 block stop for a snack at the makeshift trailer park, an outdoor food court of sorts in a parking lot. The silver Airstream selling cupcakes was the originator of the trend, but you can also get pizza, crepes, sandwiches etc from about noon to 9pm, Tuesday through Sunday.

Over on S 1st St there's another gathering of classic trailers selling food-stuffs, this one with a canopy of shade and picnic tables. Among them, ⑨ **Torchy's Tacos** is the best option, according to Chris. Both he and Sylvia recommend the juicy pork tacos – and that you read the menu thoroughly. The owner's funny-bone pokes out on the names of items like the "Republi-can" taco, which has a "wiener" in it. "There's something known as 'Austin chic'," Chris explains. It's a trendy, yuppified aesthetic – with a quirky edge. "S Congress, S Lamar and S 1st St all have it."

Some locals resent the well-completed gentrification of formerly boho neigh-borhoods. "Keep Austin Weird" bumper stickers promote an individualism some fear may be lost amid the continued influx of newbies to the capital. Sylvia suggests that if you want to check out the still-up-and-coming, you have to head to ⑩ **East Austin**. A lot of little restaurants and art galleries are spread around the neighborhood, and new businesses are coming in all the time. In November there's a coordinated East Austin Studio Tour (www .eastaustinstudiotour.com). This used to be the neighborhood locals avoided for being a little dodgy, and it's still rather unconventional. According to Sylvia, it's what S Congress Ave was 10 years ago. Technically East Austin includes anywhere west of Hwy 290 downtown, but the largest concentra-tion of businesses branch out from 12th St.

In season watch the bats emerge from under the Congress Ave bridge at twilight. Otherwise, the second night

GOING BATTY

One of Austin's most original shows is all natural. Up to 1.5 million Mexican free-tailed bats fly out from beneath Congress Ave Bridge just before sunset nightly from March to November. Most spectators look on from the grassy, waterfront banks east of the bridge but we think a comfort-able chair on the balcony of the lobby lounge at the **Four Seasons Hotel** (www.fourseasons. com), "batini" drink in hand, is an even better vantage point. **Capital Cruises** (www.capital cruises.com) runs bat-watching cruises.

head straight for the nearest club. "Somewhere will have live music start-ing by 6:30 every night," says Chris. Near the intersection with E 7th St, it's tattoos and rock'n'roll on ⑪ **Red River St**. Harder-core and alternative clubs are most prevalent, but there are a few hip-hop options as well. The

⓬ Warehouse District (radiating from E and W 4th Sts and N Congress Ave) attracts a slightly older crowd with swing dancing, Latin rhythms, live jazz and gay dance clubs. Upscale rooftop bars seem to be all the rage there these days. As Chris says, you wouldn't be out of place if you wore a jacket in the Warehouse District.

SOUTH BY SOUTHWEST

The mecca of music festivals, **South by Southwest** (http://sxsw.com; passes from $165) attracts more than 1700 acts, representing every genre of music – metal funk, indie ska, baseline jazz, rock, acoustic, folk… And there are scads more bands playing at unofficial venues. The five days in mid-March when 10,000 fans converge on Austin is the best (for indie-music lovers) or worst (for crowd-haters) time to be in the city. Plan ahead; hotels are often booked a year in advance.

You would be laughed outta town if you dressed up for raucous **⓭ E 6th St** and its techno clubs, Irish pubs and dueling pianos. There are some good restaurants around, so you will see paunchy tourists early on. But after 11pm it's mostly a fall-down-drunk frat-boy crowd roaming the street. Bars here are stacked one on top of the other, so walk by the door of each and decide which music, and which type of crowd, you like. Heck, why stop at one, pick five.

There are free street performances on Friday and Saturday nights, too – a guy with a guitar, or people doing spray-paint art. If you're lucky, you'll run into the town's most famous and flamboyant transvestite, Leslie, who hangs out on the downtown streets having her picture taken and drinks bought by locals and tourists alike. At the end of your evening, flag down one of the petty cab cyclists or rickshaw runners to shuttle you back to your hotel.

AUSTIN CITY LIMITS

Since Willie Nelson played on the pilot episode in 1974, local PBS affiliate KLRU Studio has celebrated Texas music with its *Austin City Limits* (http://austincitylimits.org) TV show, broadcast Monday at 9:30pm. Big names such as Elvis Costello and Phish still share the stage with newer acts. In 2011 the production will move from UT to a $40 million theater in the W Hotel development on 2nd St. Until then, tickets are free. Check the website for giveaway info.

If you want to go all out before you leave town, Sylvia suggests the next day you have an extravagant brunch at **⓮ Fonda San Miguel**. Dishes like the pork pipian verde take three days to make. Central Mexican moles and meats are just part of the extensive spread that easily measures up to a fancy Friday-night dinner. Endless salads, ceviches, tres leches cake… When George W Bush was governor, he and Laura ate there every Sunday, Sylvia says.

A much more budget-friendly alternative, Chris's favorite chicken in the world comes from **⓯ Pollo Rico**, a beloved local chargrilling chain. Pick up a whole chicken with sides for less than $13, and head over to Lady Bird Lake (formerly Town Lake) to picnic. There's plenty of green space just off the 10-mile-long waterfront hike and bike trail that lines both sides of the shore. You might want to cruise by **16** **Bicycle Sport Shop** and get a rental for the afternoon.

A few miles further west, the city's **17** **Zilker Park** has even more excellent picnicking potential. A 46-acre "Great Lawn" is where all of Austin comes to hang out. The park also has springs for swimming and kayak rentals for paddling out on Lady Bird Lake. Sporty types throw the disc around on the disc golf course or play sand volleyball or soccer on the fields. A 30-acre botanic garden blooms with wildflowers in spring, roses in summer and Christmas lights in winter. Bring a blanket to enjoy a performance at the outdoor amphitheater, which stages Shakespeare, musicals and concerts throughout the warmer months. When you've finished your afternoon idyll, 48 hours will, sadly, have come to an end.

Hey, maybe you could sneak in at least one more night in town. LC Rocks, an awesome '80s cover band, could be playing, and local country crooner Dale Watson is sure to be somewhere. You still haven't been to Antone's, Continental Club or the Elephant Room for more local tunes... Two days isn't enough. "If you like music and clubs," says Chris. "You really need to spend a week."

Lisa Dunford

> **DETOUR** Little more than 20 miles northwest of downtown the Colorado River has been divided into a series of six Highland Lakes. The 19,000-sq-acre **Lake Travis** (www.laketravisguide.com), Austin's aquatic playground, is the largest. Fourteen public parks and many more marinas and hotels line the lakeside; one is even clothing-optional. Swim, rent a boat, water ski or just ogle the incredible mansions along the shore for an afternoon's diversion.

TRIP INFORMATION

GETTING THERE

Austin is 80 miles northeast of San Antonio, the region's largest air hub. Take I-35 all the way.

DO

Allen Boots

The thousands of attention-grabbin' boots often attract celebrity attention. ☎ 512-447-1413; www.allenboots.com; 1522 S Congress Ave; ⏱ 9am-8pm Mon-Sat, noon-6pm Sun

Bicycle Sport Shop

Reserve ahead. Qualified staff offer loads of route and trail suggestions. ☎ 512-477-3472; http://bicyclesportshop.com; 517 S Lamar Blvd; ⏱ 10am-7pm Mon-Fri, 9am-6pm Sat, 11am-5pm Sun; ♿

DK Sushi

Sushi, Korean and Japanese food is served with a side of karaoke and adult-only humor on Monday at 7:30pm. ☎ 512-326-5807; www.dksushi.com; 6400 S First St; mains $12-18; ⏱ 11am-9:30pm Mon-Fri, 4:30-9:30pm Sat

Esther's Follies

The musical comedy and magic show pokes fun at politicians – and life in general. ☎ 512-320-0553; www.esthersfollies.com; 525 E 6th St; tickets $20; ⏱ 8pm Thu-Sat, 10pm Fri & Sat

Zilker Park

More than 350 acres of parkland includes nature trails, gardens. ☎ 512-472-4914; www.ci.austin.tx.us/zilker; 2201 Barton Springs Rd; admission free; ⏱ 5am-10pm; ♿ ♻

EAT

El Pollo Rico

Locals obsess over the charbroiled chickens with green chile sauce, rice and tortillas. ☎ 512-326-1888; www.elpollorico.org; 1928 E Riverside Dr; mains $4-8; ⏱ 10am-10pm

Fonda San Miguel

Interior Mexican cuisine served in an upscale atmosphere. The collection of original Hispanic art is impressive. ☎ 512-459-4121; www.fondasanmiguel.com; 2330 W North Loop; mains $20-30; ⏱ 5:30-9:30pm Mon-Sat, 11am-2pm Sun

Torchy's Tacos

Other than the green chiles from New Mexico, Torchy's buys all its fresh ingredients locally. ☎ 512-366-0537; www.torchystacos.com; 1311 S 1st St; mains $3-8; ⏱ 7am-10pm Mon-Wed, 8am-11pm Thu-Sat, 8am-10pm Sun

DRINK

Jo's Coffee

The outdoor coffee bar is front and center on S Congress Ave. Perfect for people-watching. ☎ 512-444-3800; 1300 S Congress Ave; ⏱ 7am-9pm Sun-Fri, 7am-10pm Sat

SLEEP

Austin Folk House B&B

Funky folk-art gives this rambling B&B a fresh feel. The home-baked cookies and scones are delish. ☎ 512-472-6700; www.austinfolkhouse.com; 506 W 22nd St; r $95-140

Austin Motel

Savvy thrift-shopperesque furniture and varied room themes make this SoCo motorcourt motel extra eclectic. ☎ 512-441-1157; www.austinmotel.com; 1220 S Congress Ave; r $70-145; ♻

Hotel San José

The San José oozes a sleek, Zen sophistication, with cherry platform beds and meditation gardens. ☎ 512-852-2350; www.sanjosehotel.com; 1316 S Congress Ave; r $95-260

USEFUL WEBSITES

www.austintexas.org
www.austinchronicle.com

LINK YOUR TRIP

www.lonelyplanet.com/trip-planner

TRIP

59 San Antonio Mariachis & Machacado p431
60 Best of Hill Country BBQ p437

San Antonio Mariachis & Machacado

WHY GO Of all the cities in the state, San Antonio speaks with the strongest Spanish accent. Sure, you can sip a margarita on the Riverwalk. But in a town with such a vibrant Hispanic heritage, you can also explore history, try lesser-known tastes and hear live mariachi music nightly.

Roughly 60% of the 1.35 million residents in San Antonio claim Hispanic descent, so it's no wonder that this is a stellar city for exploring Tex-Mex culture. Historically the west side of town was predominantly Mexican-American and it's still the best place to start your journey. Number one on any itinerary should be ➊ **Market Sq**. Shopping the stalls for Talavera pottery, colorful paper flowers, woven blankets, silver jewelry, crazy wrestling masks and 100% vanilla is a fair approximation of visiting a Mexican border-town *mercado* (market). Buy a Tecate beer or a watermelon *aguas frescas* (literally "cold waters" – fruit-infused beverages) and listen to the Tejano musicians and singers that play weekends on the little outdoor stage among the shops and restaurants.

Watching the goings-on from an outdoor table at ➋ **Mi Tierra Café** is a hot ticket. There's almost always a wait for a table at the Market Sq landmark restaurant that the Cortez family has been operating since 1941. As touristy as it may seem, this is a not-to-miss local experience. Every room is a riot of colorful streamers and piñatas, multiple *trios* of Mexican troubadours walk around serenading the tables, and the smell of fresh hot sauce is in the air. A full *panderia* (bakery) at the front sells every kind of Mexican cookie and *pan dulce* (sweet bread) imaginable. Each evening in the Mariachi Bar section, much tequila is consumed in accompaniment to trumpeting musical ensembles.

The same family runs the comparatively sedate ➌ **La Margarita**. We prefer the grilled meats, including *cabrito* (goat), and the variety of

Trip Details

TIME
3 days

DISTANCE
10 miles

BEST TIME TO GO
Mar – May

START
Market Sq

END
King William District

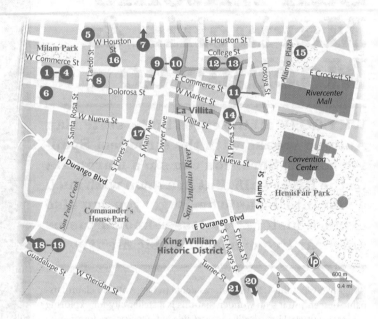

regional cuisine here to the standard, enchilada-rice-and-beans dinners two doors down. It seems as if the evening mariachi musicians – in their silver button–studded, traditional *charro* (horserider) outfits with wide-brimmed hats – are a little younger and fresher here too.

Also in Market Sq, the Smithsonian-affiliated ④ **Museo Alameda** can draw on any of the Washington collections for its changing exhibits. Recently, one focused on local painter Jesse Treviño, whose photo-realistic compositions often depicted the west-side barrio of his youth. Look for his 90ft-tall mural, ⑤ **Spirit of Healing**, on the Christus Santa Rosa Hospital at the corner of W Houston and N Santa Rosa Sts.

If you plan to head back to the Mariachi Bar for a *paloma* (literally "dove," a citrusy tequila-and-Squirt drink), consider staying at ⑥ **La Quinta Market Square**. The rustic orange rooms and Mexican prints are a step above the standard chain, and you can easily stumble to your room for the night. It's a drive, but breakfast at ⑦ **Blanco Cafe #1** is a good way to start the next day. *Menudo* (spicy tripe soup) is a known hangover cure, especially with chopped-up jalepeños. Locals have been coming back for that and all the other like-*mami*-made Mexican faves since 1974.

Sightseeing continues a few blocks from Market Sq at ⑧ **Casa Navarro**. Beginning in the 1700s, Mexican soldiers from the local *presido* (fort) inhabited many small area houses. Tour one of the few remaining Laredito neighborhood structures, the 1854 home of José Antonio Navarro, a *Tejano* (Texas-born Mexican). Navarro was one of only two native Texans to sign the 1836 Texas Declaration of Independence and he served in the Texas legislature under Mexico, the Republic of Texas and during statehood.

It's easy to imagine Navarro attending mass at nearby ❾ **San Fernando Cathedral**. In the early 1800s, San Antonio's missions had been secularized and their congregants swelled the San Fernando parish numbers. The corner stone for the current church was laid in 1868. Make sure you seek out the side door that leads behind the altar to the *retablos* (votive alter screen), a stunning gilt masterpiece depicting Christ and saints. If you're in town on Saturday, don't miss the rousing, bilingual ❿ **Mariachi Mass** at 5:30pm.

On any other day, continue to the ⓫ **Riverwalk**. Restaurant after restaurant after bar after restaurant lines the below-street-level waterfront promenade off Crockett St. Beautiful landscaping and a river view make ⓬ **La Mansión del Rio** a lovely place to stay. Heavy beamed ceilings and

> **ASK A LOCAL**
>
> "Mariachi music is embraced 24/7 in San Antonio in restaurants, schools, family gatherings and during the annual **Mariachi Vargas Extravaganza** (www.mariachimusic.com). The eight-day festival attracts more than 1000 musicians and 15,000 aficionados. Among local groups, look for Mariachi Oro y Plata, who perform at the Mariachi Bar (at Mi Tierra Café in Market Sq). You can count on them playing *mariachi loco* (crazy mariachi) for tourists, but you can also request traditional songs like *Cascabel* and *Las Bodas*."
>
> *Cynthia Muñoz, Mariachi Vargas Extravaganza producer, San Antonio*

hand-carved wooden doors are in keeping with the 1852 date of construction. Even if you don't sleep over, stop for a meal at ⓭ **Las Canarias**, where ingredients like roasted chiles and chorizo share the menu with foie gras. Book ahead for a patio table, as there are only a handful. ⓮ **Hotel Contessa**, also on the Riverwalk, is another sleeping option that shows a Spanish influence.

If you've never been to the ⓯ **Alamo**, now is the time. Ethnic Mexicans fought on both sides of the 1836 siege at this fortified mission. In one case at least, the battle pitted brother against brother. Gregorio Esparza was the only Texas fighter allowed the respect of burial, because his brother fought with the Mexican troops on the other side of the wall. The rest of the bodies were burned – an abomination at the time. Learn more in the long barracks museum before you head over to ⓰ **Penner's** to pick up a *guayabera* shirt or dress – you're going out. These traditionally linen shirts made in Oaxaca, Mexico, are ideal in balmy climes: worn untucked, they're dressy but cool.

Weekends the ⓱ **Cadillac Bar** often has bands playing Tejano polkas or accordion-based conjunto music. Or the ⓲ **Guadalupe Theatre** might be running a play such as *Las Nuevas Tamaleras,* about the family tradition of making tamales. The theater also hosts Mexican music festivals, dances and cinema nights. In the same west-side neighborhood as the theater, ⑲ **Segovia Candy** has been making pralines and coconut candies for three generations. The store is quite simple but you can find their tricolor confections at numerous Mexican restaurants around town as well.

San Antonio has so many Mexican restaurants, in fact, that you may have trouble deciding where to eat breakfast on day three. Fredericksburg Rd is known for little hole-in-the-walls, the Riverwalk has numerous alternatives, and the morning meal is our favorite at Mi Tierra. Wherever you go you'll likely have options such as *machacado* (a spiced, dried beef) in your omelets, or *barbacoa* (cow head meat) in your taco, eggs scrambled with crisp tortillas in *migas,* and tortillas-and-eggs topped with *ranchero* sauce (a thin, heated salsa) and melted cheese in *chilaquiles.* Branch out from the bacon-and-egg breakfast taco; you'll be doing plenty of walking today.

LITTLE CITY

The city's first neighborhood **La Villita** (www. lavillita.com), or little city, was a collection of huts housing Spanish officers stationed at the Alamo in the 1700s. More permanent brick and adobe structures grew up after the devastating 1819 flood. Today artisan shops and galleries fill the four-block historic district between the Riverwalk and Nueva St.

There are four missions spread out in the ⑳ **San Antonio Missions National Historical Park** system. Start at the visitor center at Missión San José, where exhibits and a film introduce the history of Spanish religious colonization. Built between 1731 and 1745, the missions flourished only until the 1780s. Rangers conduct free guided tours of each at varying times throughout the day. Pick up a map and ask for directions to the next site; the signage is not the best.

Afterwards, your drive back downtown will take you up S St Marys St in the King William District – perfect for stopping at ㉑ **Rosario's**. You've heard mariachis, you've tasted *machacado,* now it's time for a margarita. You can taste for yourself whether the version here deserves all the accolades it's received. Judging by the blockbuster crowds, it's not just the drinks that measure up. (The roasted salsa and grilled tilapia tacos are also extremely popular.) Sit back, enjoy the lively crowd and consider your crash course in local Tex-Mex culture complete.

Lisa Dunford

TRIP INFORMATION

GETTING THERE
San Antonio International Airport is an excellent hub, 8 miles north of downtown. Follow Hwy 281 to I-35 south, exit at W Commerce St for the Market Sq area.

DO
Alamo
The iconic mission church contains an Alamo defenders' shrine; the barracks holds a battle history museum. ☎ 210-225-1391; www.thealamo.org; 300 Alamo Plaza; admission free; ⏱ 9am-5:30pm Mon-Sat, 10am-5:30pm Sun Sep-May, 9am-7pm Mon-Sat, 10am-7pm Sun Jun-Aug

Casa Navarro
Tour three early Texan adobe and limestone structures that were once home to prominent Tejano political figure José Antonio Navarro. ☎ 210-226-4801; www.visitcasanavarro.com; 228 S Laredo St; adult/child $4/3; ⏱ 9am-4pm Tue-Sun

Guadalupe Theatre
Guadalupe Cultural Arts Center seeks to preserve Latino culture, putting on plays, movie nights and dances at this restored 1940s theater. ☎ 210-271-3151; www.guadalupeculturalarts.org; 1300 Guadalupe St; ticket prices vary; ⏱ performance times vary

Market Sq
Shop at a *mercado* without crossing the border. Frequent festivals, including Fiesta in April, are held here. ☎ 210-207-8600; www.marketsquaresa.com; 514 W Commerce St; ⏱ 10am-8pm Jun-Aug, 10am-6pm Sep-May

Museo Alameda
A Latin American–oriented adjunct to the Smithsonian Museum in Washington DC. Rotating exhibits examine everything from art to aerospace. ☎ 210-299-4300; www.thealameda.org; 101 S Santa Rosa St; adult/child $4/2; ⏱ noon-6pm Tue-Sun

Penner's
Since 1916 locals have been buying *guayabera* shirts imported from Mexico by the Penner family store. Opt for 100% linen; it's cooler. ☎ 210-226-2487; www.pennersinc.com; 311 W Commerce St; ⏱ 9am-6pm Mon-Sat

San Antonio Missions National Historic Park
Four missions built along the San Antonio River in the 1700s are part of this national park. ☎ 210-922-7152; www.nps.gov/saan; San José visitor center, 6701 San Jose Dr; admission free; ⏱ 9am-5pm

San Fernando Cathedral
The 1868 building incorporates an earlier Catholic church built in 1738. Seven of the 10 weekly masses are conducted in Spanish. ☎ 210-227-1297; www.sfcathedral.org; 115 Main Plaza; admission free; ⏱ 9am-5pm Mon-Sat

Segovia Mexican Candy
The owner's family has been making whipped confections and nutty sweets at this small shop and factory for nearly 100 years. ☎ 210-225-2102; 1837 Guadalupe St; ⏱ 9am-5pm Mon-Fri

EAT
Blanco Cafe #1
Authentic hole-in-the-wall Tex-Mex diner with homemade tortillas. Locals crowd the place for weekend breakfast and lunch. ☎ 210-732-6480; http://blancocafe.net; 1720 Blanco Rd; mains $4-8; ⏱ 6am-9pm Mon-Sat, 9am-2pm Sun

La Margarita
Regional Mexican cuisine including seafood dishes from Veracruz and a red mole from Oaxaca. Sizzling fajita plates are a favorite. ☎ 210-227-7140; www.lamargarita.com; 120 Produce Row; mains $12-20; ⏱ 11am-10pm

Las Canarias
Enjoy romantic, Spanish-inspired cuisine in a hacienda-like dining room or overlooking the

Riverwalk. ☎ 210-518-1000; www.laman sion.com; La Mansión del Rio, 112 College St; breakfast $12-16, mains $24-42; ⏱ 6:30am-10:30pm Mon-Sat, 10am-10pm Sun

Mi Tierra Café
Red leather booths and multihued streamers are just part of the colorful atmosphere at this landmark eatery, serving since 1941. ☎ 210-225-1262; www.mitierracafe.com; 218 Produce Row; breakfast $7-10, mains $10-18; ⏱ 24hr

Rosario's
Always lively Rosario's, in the King William District, makes a strong claim for the best Mexican in San Antonio. Live music Friday. ☎ 210-223-1806; http://rosariossa.com; 910 S Alamo St; mains $7-16; ⏱ 11am-10pm

DRINK
Cadillac Bar
Downtown worker bees buzz in for a drink on weekday evenings. On weekends live music alternates with DJs spinning. ☎ 210-223-5533; 212 S Flores St; ⏱ 11am-midnight Sun-Thu, 11am-2am Fri & Sat

SLEEP
Hotel Contessa
Mediterranean modern – the upscale Contessa is a bit more Spanish than Mexican. The restaurant and bar serve great tapas. ☎ 210-229-9222; www.thehotelcontessa.com; 306 W Market St; r $250-300; 🐾

La Mansión del Rio
Mexican-colonial era élan drips from every terracotta fountain at this Omni-run luxury hotel. Most river view rooms have balconies. ☎ 210-518-1000; www.lamansion.com; 112 College St; r $150-250

La Quinta Market Square
What an excellent location out the back door of Mi Tierra Café. Mexican agave photos and vibrant color schemes liven this motel up. ☎ 210-271-0001; www.lq.com; 900 Dolarosa St; r $70-$110

USEFUL WEBSITES
www.visitsanantonio.com
www.thesanantonioriverwalk.com

SUGGESTED READS
- *Woman Hollering Creek & Other Stories* – San Antonio resident Sandra Cisneros's stories reflect on the social role of Mexican and other Latin American immigrant women.
- *Exodus from the Alamo: The Last Stand Myth* – In light of scholarly research of Mexican accounts, Phillip Tucker re-examines the battle of the Alamo.

LINK YOUR TRIP

www.lonelyplanet.com/trip-planner

Best of Hill Country BBQ

WHY GO No forks, no sauce, no sides, no salads: that's how many central Texas barbecue joints started. And it's the meat – slow-smoked brisket, ribs and sausage – that's still revered. Join food pilgrims from across the state as they taste their way through small towns around central Texas in search of barbecue's best.

The meat-market barbecue tradition began here back when German and Czech settlers opened groceries with butcher shops in the early 1900s. Not all the cuts of meat sold, and proprietors would smoke the leftovers so they wouldn't spoil. The trimmings from what did sell went into sausage making. When itinerant farm workers came in hungry from the field, and with crackers and pickles from the shelves made a meal of the smoked meats out the back, a tradition was born.

Eventually store owners added lunch rooms and stopped selling dry goods altogether. Most even stopped selling uncooked meat. ❶ Lockhart, the legislature-proclaimed "Barbecue Capital of Texas," has several good examples of traditional meat-market joints. You can't drive into the population-12,000 town southeast of Austin and not know that ❷ Black's Barbecue has been in the same location since 1932. Billboards advertising Texas' longest-run family 'Q joint appear frequently. But of the three acclaimed eateries in town, Black's is probably the most progressive. Get in the cafeteria-style line and you're immediately confronted with a whole host of salads and side dishes: macaroni and cheese, green beans with bacon, corn bread…and desserts include some darn good, sticky-sweet peach cobbler. Edgar Black Sr and wife Myrtle started the place as a butcher shop outlet for a cattle-owning partner. Edgar Black Jr and wife Norma moved walls around, came up with a thick sauce recipe, and made the place more of a restaurant, open seven days a week.

TIME
4 days

DISTANCE
110 miles

BEST TIME TO GO
Mar – May & Oct

START
Lockhart, TX

END
Coupland, TX

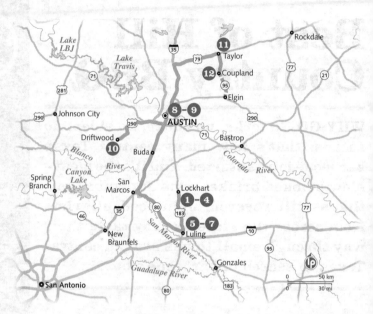

The Kreuz family had begun operating a market down the road in 1900. In 1948 the Schmidts bought the place and continued its evolution to barbecue joint. **③ Smitty's Market** has the most old-time, authentic feel in town. You walk through a hot-as-Hades, blackened pit room past a boss cutting thick slabs of meat on a much thicker butcher block. The eating area, where you get drinks and pinto beans or potato salad (your only choices), does indeed resemble an old general store. And in a side room you can see the wall chains where knives were attached, the only utensils until the 1970s. They still pile the meat, crackers, pickles and onions on butcher paper, but now they give you a plastic knife.

Here's where the story gets strange. Nina Schmidt runs this barbecue place in the same building her father did, but it's her brother Rick Schmidt that inherited the business name and most family recipes. A family feud erupted, lawsuits were filed and in 1999 Rick moved **④ Kreuz Market** (pronounced "krites") to the outskirts of town. A cavernous barn is the antithesis of the intimate old dining room, but wood picnic tables and a screened-in porch keep it rustic. With more room on a bigger pit, they began experimenting. Smoked prime rib, ham and jalapeño-and-cheese sausage got added to the menu. Shoulder clod, a leaner brisketlike cut, became a big hit with the cholesterol-conscious crowd. One thing hasn't changed – there's no sauce. As the sign says, they don't need it cause they ain't got "nothin' to hide." The pork ribs here are our favorite, with a peppery crust that tastes like good jerky and tenderloin-soft meat next to the bone.

Every five years *Texas Monthly* magazine stirs the great barbecue debate by printing its picks for the state's 50 best. Lockhart's places usually rank at least top 10, so locals know to expect an occasional Yankee or two clutching a tattered magazine in line. But at weekends, hoards of Austinites also descend, intending to eat at all three of the favorites. From personal, stomach-shattering experience, this author doesn't recommend it. For lunch, pick the place with the style and menu that suits you, because for dinner we have an even better suggestion.

"An RC cola and a pile of barbecue is more than plenty."

Just 15 miles south down Hwy 183, **5 Luling** is the kind of small town where everybody knows everybody and the annual Watermelon Thump Festival is the biggest event of the year. **6 City Market** has been serving barbecue downtown since 1957. Tables are mostly filled with families and local old-timers; you could definitely eavesdrop on town gossip here. For our money, City Market provides the best of the big three meats; we've never had a bad meal here. The well-marbled brisket is always juicy, ribs are tender and the site-made sausage has a tight, springy consistency. Push into the crowded pit room at the back to place your order. Then use the few extra sheets of pink butcher paper they give you as plates and pour a dab of the thin, vinegary-mustardy sauce from the bottle on the table to dip in. They do serve the now-ubiquitous pinto beans and potato salad, but forgo those. An RC cola and a pile of barbecue is more than plenty. Before you go, be sure to look at the oil boom–era photos lining the old walls.

ASK A LOCAL

"I remember coming to City Market with my father growing up. Back then it was mostly men. When we moved back after retirement, Saturday-afternoon barbecue became a habit. We get to eat well and catch up. Our friends from high school still come here."
George Springs, Luling

Aside from the flower and farmers markets at the intersection of E Davis St and Hwy 183/Rte 80, there's not a whole lot to see in Luling. After an early dinner, settle in for a quiet night at the **7 Francis-Ainsworth House**, which once belonged to the town doctor. The original 1890s home is barely visible under the 1916 enlargement that doubled the size and added full-length porches. Proprietor Ada Potts cooks up a mean breakfast. You'll have to walk it off on the hike and bike trails in **8 Austin** – so you can eat more barbecue, of course.

The state's capital has numerous temples to 'Q – Stubb's, Artz Rib House, Green Mesquite – but two stand out for their stories. The original **9 County**

Line BBQ sits high on Bee Cave Rd overlooking Hill Country. The building was a speakeasy during Prohibition, a place where Texan politicians could tipple in secret and women who weren't their wives could visit. Rumor has it that the hilltop view and a lookout posted nightly were why no raids were successful. Flash forward to the 1970s, when a few good ol' boys decided they could make a go of an "upscale" barbecue place (one with table service and forks, not fine china) at this site; a restaurant where you could order margaritas and eat late. Succeed they did – the County Line empire now has nine outlets. The state senate even recognized their "legendary" contribution in Resolution 867. We agree, the barbecue is pretty darn good. Try the brontosaurus-sized beef ribs, or the less traditional char-grilled rib-eye at the original.

MEAT BY MAIL

Can't get enough of Hill Country BBQ? Not to worry, several places ship brisket, sausage, ribs – even smoked turkeys – right to your door. Many also sell dry rubs, dipping sauces and the all-important apron. Check out these places:

- Black's Barbecue (www.blacksbbq.com)
- County Line BBQ (www.airribs.com)
- Kreuz Market (www.kreuzmarket.com)
- Salt Lick Bar-B-Queue (www.saltlickbbq.com)

Though **10** **Salt Lick Bar-B-Que** is technically 22 miles south of town, at a spot in the road called Driftwood, Austin is encroaching. In the 1960s, when Thurman Roberts started selling barbecue from a brick pit on the family's ranch, the place was a lot more remote. His first screened dining room sat eight. Today his son owns a restaurant that can serve more than 2000 on a busy summer afternoon. It's BYOB and, with so many people waiting beneath the trees with a cooler and folding chairs, often takes on the air of a county picnic. The original, hand-built open pit is heretical to some. Purists claim that the direct flame, slightly quicker cooking times and sweet-tangy sauce mopped on repeatedly *(gasp!)* mean that this is grilled meat, not barbecue. Not that it's stopped the crowds from coming – be prepared to wait.

If the barbecue joints in Austin were a little too "restaurant" for your taste, you'll love getting back to basics at **11** **Louie Mueller Barbecue** in Taylor, 37 miles northeast. Louie moved his barbecue joint here in 1959 and by then the building had already been a gymnasium and a grocery store. His son, the late Bobby Mueller, took over in 1974, expanding the menu and the building. Today Bobby's son Wayne carries on. While you stand in line contemplating whether to try smoked chicken or stay conventional, they give you a sample of a burnt end – the crispy, caramelized, fatty bits from a cooked brisket (you can order 'em at any real barbecue restaurant). The pit room is not separated, so even with two-story ceilings and neon beer signs, the main room is dark. Sitting on the attached screened porch with a full stomach and a cold longneck when a breeze blows in – that's a classic Texas afternoon.

FOOD &
DRINK

We'd be remiss when talking Texas 'Q if we didn't mention the Mikeska dynasty. Czech immigrants John and Francis Valis Mikeska settled on a farm near Taylor and raised nine children by growing crops and butchering meat. The first son to open a barbecue business did so in Taylor after WWII. Rudy Mikeska's is no longer operating, but you'll see the Mikeska name on establishments all over the center of the state. These aren't franchises, they're independent eateries – all run by descendents of John and Francis.

The downtown streets of Taylor are deserted even by small-town standards. So two-step down the road to the old ⑫ **Coupland Inn and Dancehall.** The hall has been operating since about 1910, but the bar dates back to the 1860s. Look for the bullet holes in the wood. If you book a package deal at the inn, you get a reserved table for the live country music on a Friday or Saturday night. Also attached is a restaurant that serves – guess what – barbecue. Can you ever have enough, really?

DETOUR Sausage lovers take note. A mere 8 miles south of Coupland is the hot-link capital of Texas. **Elgin** has not one but two family-owned barbecue places that specialize in this spicy meat. **Southside Market & Barbeque** (www.southsidemarket.com) and **Meyer's Elgin Sausage** (www.cuetopiatexas.com) both ship sausages to restaurants and supermarkets around the state. Try them at their home restaurants in town.

So which barbecue is best? Luling's City Market gets our vote but, in the end, it's a personal preference and you'll have to decide for yourself. Let the food critics fight. For us it's more about lingering in the slow country town, eating good food at rustic family joints where the stories and traditions are written in smoke.

Lisa Dunford

TRIP INFORMATION

GETTING THERE
Lockhart is 35 miles southeast of Austin. Follow Rte 71 east to Hwy 183 south.

DO
Coupland Inn and Dancehall
On Friday and Saturday nights two-step round the old wood floor to live Texas and country music. Period furnishings and bordello-esque decor dresses up each of the diminutive 1900s rooms. ☎ 512-856-2226; www.couplanddancehall.com; dancehall 101 Hoxie St, inn 103 Hoxie St, Coupland; dancehall tickets $10-15, r incl breakfast, shared bathroom $99; ☾ dancehall 8-11pm Thu, 8pm-midnight Fri, 8pm-1am Sat

EAT
Black's Barbecue
The same family has been cooking 'Q at Black's since 1932. ☎ 512-398-2712; www.blacksbbq.com; 214 N Main St; meat per lb $10; ☾ 10am-8pm Sun-Thu, 10am-8:30pm Fri & Sat
City Market
Our pick for small-town barbecue at its best. Generation after generation of Luling locals have eaten here regularly. ☎ 830-875-9019; 633 E Davis, Luling; meat per lb $7-11; ☾ 7am-6pm Mon-Sat
County Line BBQ
A full-service barbecue restaurant on a hill outside Austin; their smoked prime rib beats all. ☎ 512-327-1742; www.countyline.com; 6500 Bee Caves Rd; mains $11-20; ☾ 11am-2pm & 5-9pm Mon-Fri, 11am-9pm Sat & Sun

Kreuz Market
A modern, barnlike place with traditional recipes. You and two busloads of friends could eat here. ☎ 512-398-2361; www.kreuzmarket.com; 619 N Colorado St, Lockhart; meat per lb $7-11; ☾ 10:30am-8pm Mon-Sat

Louie Mueller Barbecue
The old blends seamlessly with the new in this expanded, but still rustic, open-pit eatery. ☎ 512-352-6206; www.louiemuellerbarbecue.com; 206 W 2nd St, Taylor; meat per lb $9-10; ☾ 10am-7:30pm Mon-Sat

Salt Lick Bar-B-Que
Massive open pits and a parklike setting entice Austinites to drive the 22 miles south to Salt Lick. ☎ 512-858-4959; www.saltlickbbq.com; 18300 FM 1826, Driftwood; mains $11-16; ☾ 11am-9pm

Smitty's Market
The blackened pit room has been a fixture since this place was a market in the 1900s. ☎ 512-398-9344; www.smittysmarket.com; 208 S Commerce, Lockhart; meat per lb $7-11; ☾ 7am-6pm Mon-Sat, 9am-3pm Sun

SLEEP
Francis-Ainsworth House
A restrained use of antiques and light colors keep this 1916 B&B feeling fresh. Full hot breakfasts and private baths included. ☎ 830-875-3435; www.ainsworthhouse.com; 214 S Pecan, Luling; r $125 incl breakfast

USEFUL WEBSITES
www.austintexas.org

LINK YOUR TRIP
www.lonelyplanet.com/trip-planner

Cattle Country Drive

WHY GO The heyday of epic cattle drives and enormous ranches may have been back in the late 1800s but the legacy lives on today. Attend a Fort Worth stockyard rodeo, go horseback riding on a Bandera dude ranch or tour a modern-day cattle ranch in Kingsville, and you're on the trail.

TIME
4 days

DISTANCE
485 miles

BEST TIME TO GO
**Mar – May &
Sep – Nov**

START
Fort Worth, TX

END
Kingsville, TX

After the end of the Civil War in 1865, working-age men drifted back to Texas looking for something to do. Many took advantage of a new opportunity when the Chisholm Trail longhorn cattle drives started in 1867 and a mere four years later, 5000 cowpokes per day were being paid to git those lil' doggies along – all the way from San Antonio to a railroad shipping yard in Abilene, Kansas. Operations such as that of Captain Richard King in south Texas and XIT Ranch in the Panhandle acquired more territory than some small countries. But a devastating blizzard spelled the beginning of the end when it killed most of the cattle in Kansas in 1886. By that time homesteaders had begun fencing off much of the open range, and the railroad network soon reached the furthest corners of the nation, making long drives unnecessary.

It's estimated that 10 million head of cattle tramped through ❶ **Fort Worth** when the Chisholm Trail was in use. Western-wear stores, cowboy doodad shops, steak houses and honky-tonks now fill the old buildings in the ❷ **Historic Stockyards**, surrounding the intersection of N Main St and E Exchange Ave, north of downtown. But a few of the pens still contain cattle. Every day at 11:30am and 4pm, wrangly old cowpokes with handlebar mustaches prod 16 to 20 longhorns down Exchange Ave in a minitrail drive. It's a goll-dang Kodak moment, pardner. Kids seem to love watching the steam train reverse direction on the roundhouse, too.

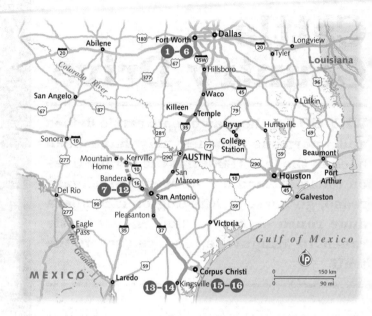

Rodeo events, such as the one at **3** **Cowtown Coliseum** in the stockyards, all grew out of ranch work. Steer roping and wrestling was needed so animals could be branded or given medicine; bareback riding came from breaking in new horses… Cowboys honed their skills competing with neighboring hands, or just blew off steam during the down time. A few got darn tricky with their rope work and riding and you can see examples of that at the Coliseum too. April through August, Pawnee Bill Wild West Shows are held in addition to the regular weekend rodeos.

"The grandparents of the current owners met as Western stunt doubles on the Hollywood back lots in the 1930s."

After you've walked around and bought your fill of bandanas and toy six-shooters, check into your room at the 1907 **4** **Stockyards Hotel**. Its Western rooms are the most in keeping with the district's pervasive Old West theme, but the Victorian rooms are historically accurate also. You won't be hurtin' for eating options if you stay right close by but there's also **5** **Reata**, downtown, which is co-owned by a real-life rancher. Decorative saddles hang on the walls and calf fries are on the menu.

Wherever you chow down, you just gotta end your evening at **6** **Billy Bob's Texas**. Once a cattle barn, this legendary Texas honky-tonk can contain 6000 two-steppers at once. Of course it has a mechanical bull you can ride, but on Friday and Saturday nights it also has live bull-riding in an on-site arena.

It's not just the stockyards whose use has evolved over time; so have many of the ranches themselves. You'll see for yourself after you drive the 280 miles south to the central Texas ranchland outside San Antonio. Today there are 14 spreads around **7 Bandera** that are run as dude ranches. Historically these were smaller in size than cattle operations in other areas and most range from a few hundred to a thousand acres today.

8 Dixie Dude Ranch has been in the same family since it began as a stock farm in 1901. The grandparents of the current owners met as Western stunt doubles on the Hollywood back lots in the 1930s. Seeing signs of things to come they turned the family property into a guest ranch way back in 1937. Today the ranch has the fifth generation of descendents working the place. They do still raise goats, and trap and sell wild hogs, but most of the time is spent entertaining guests. As at other area dude ranches, Dixie provides three meals and two horseback rides a day. You can stay in cabins or in more of a motellike bunkhouse: simple and rustic but superclean.

> **ASK A LOCAL**
>
> "Bandera backs up its claim to being the 'Cowboy Capital of the World' with Western activities and festivals all year long. The locals do indeed participate. There's even a weekly horseback ride on Sunday afternoon where folks gather at one of the honky-tonks around noon, make multiple stops through town, then return for some guitar pickin' later. Those like me who don't ride still adopt the swagger."
>
> *Linda Joiner, Bandera*

Each ranch has extra amenities, such as hay rides and swimming holes, that vary from place to place. Properties adjacent to the 5500-acre Hill Country State Natural Area, such as **9 Silver Spur Guest Ranch**, offer even more room to roam. Extended natural area rides are an add-on, but occasional Western demonstrations and weekend evening barbecues are part of Silver Spur's standard plan. Nonguests can reserve ahead for one-hour rides and cowpoke breakfasts. There's nothing quite like hearty camp bread cooked in a Dutch oven over an open fire.

Also open to everyone, the Friday-night rodeo at **10 Twin Elm Guest Ranch** (April through August) is quite the crowd-pleaser. Adults compete in the bull riding and calf roping, and kids get to do the "mutton bustin'." Decked out in pads and helmets, little ones clutch a running sheep's curly locks for as long as they can – always way less than eight seconds. The rodeo is just one of the many weekend events around. Saturdays when the weather is warm enough, cowboy poets, trick ropers and musicians entertain in the center of Bandera as part of Cowboys on Main St from 1pm to 4pm.

With its false-front Old West–era buildings and wooden boardwalks, the small town (population 947) itself is an attraction, It's not nearly as commercialized as the Fort Worth Stockyards, so you can still find some interesting old antiques at local stores. **⑪ OST Restaurant** has been dishing up good eats on Main St since the 1930s. A big breakfast of chicken-fried steak and eggs sounds like just the hearty grub you need before heading out on the trails. While you're there look for the row of saddles that double as barstools, and the old photos of the town and townsfolk.

Another Bandera town classic is **⑫ Arkey Blue's Silver Dollar Saloon**, also established in the 1930s. This basement honky-tonk ain't much to look at, but it does have history. Hank Williams Sr carved his name in the underside of one of the tables when he played here regularly, and Ernest Tubbs and Willie Nelson also came by quite often. Every Friday and Saturday night it still has live country-and-western bands, as do a number of places in town. Even the new coffee house has gotten into hosting acts. There might be a local pickin' circle somewhere to listen to or a restaurant steak night with local entertainment. The friendly Bandera County Visitors Bureau (www.banderacowboycapital.com) keeps a listing of all the goings on. In addition to Arkey and his Blue Cowboys, Art & Lisa are another regular country act worth listening out for.

DETOUR Take a day's detour and you could participate in an actual longhorn trail drive. Established in 1880 and located in Mountain Home, **YO Ranch** (www.yoranch.com) makes an event of rounding up 1600lb behemoths (with a 7ft horn span) every May and October. For groups of 10 people or more, it'll set up a smaller drive any time. It also runs numerous tours, exotic wildlife watching, a ranch hotel and a steak house on the property. Mountain Home is 50 miles northwest of Bandera.

Big cattle drives through little Bandera were never commonplace. The town was on the Old Spanish Trail, a feeder trail for the Chisholm that only local ranchers used. Similar spur routes existed all over the state. Drive 200 miles southeast and you'll come to the Texas coast to where Captain Richard King's men had to follow a secondary trail when they drove their first herd north in 1867. A riverboat captain and entrepreneur, King had gotten into ranching in the mid-1800s when he'd come across Santa Gertrudis Creek, an oasis in a wild, arid land south of Corpus Christi. The Mexican land grant he bought, and longhorns he found on the property, became the basis for the legendary **⑬ King Ranch**.

During the Civil War, blockade-running was a lucrative business for King and he poured his profits into his ranch. Not content to just gather strays and send them to market, he began a program of upbreeding to develop stock suited for the harsh climate. After his death in 1925, his widow Henrietta and son-in-law Robert Kleberg continued the practice. The ranch developed the first new breed of cattle in America, the Santa Gertrudis. Around that time, King Ranch holdings in Texas totaled about 1.2 million acres. Today the ranch boundaries incorporate about 825,000 acres, which is still larger than the state of Rhode Island. The 1½-hour **14** **King Ranch Tour** covers both agriculture and history. Find out more about the cattle and the prize quarter horses raised here, and about the *vaqueros* who in early days relocated from Cruellas, Mexico. Some families are raising their seventh generation on the ranch, which has its own school, fire truck and 401K plans.

Mosey into neighboring **15** **Kingsville** – much of what you see was at one time donated by or invested in by Henrietta King, including churches, the high school, a hospital and a university. E Kleberg Ave is the heart of old downtown, where you can still eat at drugstore lunch counters serving specials such as King Ranch chicken, a tasty enchilada casserole. The highlight of the block is undoubtedly **16** **King Ranch Saddle Shop**. The fine leather work done by the ranch was in such demand that years ago it branched out to selling not only hand-tooled saddles but exquisite leather bags, clothing, furniture even. A hunter's hunter wouldn't be caught dead, pardon the pun, without their King Ranch shooting vest or shell bags.

HOW BIG IS BIG?

King Ranch may loom large now – at its current size it's larger than Rhode Island – but in the 1970s the operation owned an estimated 11 million acres, with sites in Argentina, Australia, Brazil, Cuba, Morocco, Spain, Venezuela, Florida, Kentucky and Pennsylvania. Expanding and improving its registered cattle breed was part of the motivation. Interests change and those properties have been sold, but the hearty Santa Gertrudis is the most prevalent cattle breed raised in Australia today.

The shop's catalog company does a roaring worldwide business, which is not odd – few ranches support themselves by cattle alone these days. Adjunct interests such as oil royalties, citrus farming, hunting leases, guest lodges, movie-location site rental, publishing and shops are often what pay the bills. Times they may have changed, but ranching history in Texas has left a definite trail – one that's easy for modern-day cowpokes to follow.

Lisa Dunford

HISTORY & CULTURE

TRIP INFORMATION

GETTING THERE
Fort Worth is 30 miles from Dallas. Follow I-30 east from downtown to I-35W, which bisects Fort Worth.

DO
Cowtown Coliseum
Watch cowboys and cowgirls rope and ride at rodeo shows. ☎ 817-625-1025; www.stockyardsrodeo.com; 121 E Exchange Ave, Fort Worth; adult/child $15/10; ⏲ 8pm Fri & Sat; ♿

King Ranch
Take a history and livestock tour to find out more about the state's largest cattle ranch. ☎ 361-595-1344; www.king-ranch.com; Hwy 141 west, Kingsville; adult/child $8/4; ⏲ noon & 2pm Mon-Sat, 1pm & 3pm Sun

King Ranch Saddle Shop
Sought-after leather purses, bags and luggage attract patrons to this ranch shop. ☎ 877-282-5777; www.krsaddleshop.com; 201 E Kleberg Ave, Kingsville; ⏲ 10am-6pm Mon-Sat

Twin Elm Guest Ranch
Local ranch workers compete at steer wrestling, barrel racing and other rodeo events. ☎ 830-576-3049; www.twinelmranch.net; 810 FM 470, Bandera; admission $6; ⏲ 8pm Fri Apr-Aug

EAT
OST Restaurant
Everything chicken-fried and smothered in gravy is tasty. The all-you-can-eat lunch buffet is a bargain. ☎ 830-796-3836; 305 Main St, Bandera; mains $4-14; ⏲ 6am-10pm; ♿

Reata
The best place to enjoy this upscale cowpoke cuisine is on the 4th floor roof deck. ☎ 817-336-1009; www.reata.net; 310 Houston St, Fort Worth; mains $16-31; ⏲ 11am-2:30pm & 5:30-10:30pm

DRINK
Arkey Blue's Silver Dollar Saloon
Country legends have played this below-ground dance hall since it opened in the '30s. ☎ 830-796-8826; 308 Main St, Bandera; ⏲ 10am-2pm

Billy Bob's Texas
Texas' largest honky-tonk: regular bands, dance lessons, plates of barbecue and live bull rides. ☎ 817-624-7117; www.billybobstexas.com; 2520 Rodeo Plaza, Fort Worth; ⏲ 11am-2am Mon-Sat, noon-2am Sun

SLEEP
Dixie Dude Ranch
Family-owned and -operated since the 1930s; Dixie attracts many repeat guests. ☎ 800-375-9255; www.dixieduderanch.com; 833 Dixie Dude Ranch Rd, Bandera; per adult/child incl meals & activities $135/85; ♿

Silver Spur Guest Ranch
Horseback riding, hay rides, swimming and fossil digging keep you busy at this activity-oriented ranch. ☎ 830-796-3037; www.ssranch.com; 9266 Bandera Creek Rd, Bandera; per adult/child incl meals & activities $130/80; ♿

Stockyards Hotel
Cowboy bronzes and deep leather sofas hark back to the cattle-baron days. ☎ 800-423-8471; www.stockyardshotel.com; 109 E Exchange Ave, Fort Worth; r $189-229

USEFUL WEBSITES
www.kingsville.org

www.lonelyplanet.com/trip-planner

LINK YOUR TRIP

Gulf Coast Jaunt

WHY GO Birds, beaches and boats. Along more than 400 miles of coastline watch for endangered whooping cranes, surf pierside waves, walk for miles on undeveloped stretches of sand and sail out to reel in the next big catch. There's not a tumbleweed in sight on the other side of Texas.

TIME
4 days

DISTANCE
410 miles

BEST TIME TO GO
May & Oct

START
Galveston, TX

END
South Padre Island, TX

Cruise a mere 45 miles southeast of Houston and you're already at the beach. Miles of sugary sand front the Gulf Coast seawall and fried-fish emporiums crowd the bayside piers of ❶ Galveston. This island is part sunburned beach bum, part genteel Southern lady, with sizable Victorian districts that date to the city's heyday as a port of entry for immigrants heading west. In 2008 Hurricane Ike ravaged the grand old gal, causing $3 billion in property damage. But that hardly compares to the 1900 "Great Storm," which leveled the island and claimed 8000 lives. Look into the history of the port and its turbulent times at the ❷ Texas Seaport Museum and the adjacent ❸ Pier 21 Theatre. Survivor accounts narrate the Great Storm film, which is shown daily.

Galveston may show signs of Ike's impact for decades to come, but the historic ❹ Strand commercial district, surrounding the Mechanic and 22nd Sts intersection, rebounded fairly quickly. Old-fashioned brick-front buildings are spiffily refurbished, and boutiques, ice-cream parlors and general stores opened for the shopping masses. New restaurants there and beyond replaced those that closed; the former includes ❺ 901 Postoffice, which has made waves in foodie circles with its corn-crusted Gulf snapper, pomegranate-glazed ribs and laid-back bungalow setting.

Along the seashore truckloads of sand were brought in to replace the 50ft that was swept away. Spanish colonial ❻ Hotel Galvez (1911)

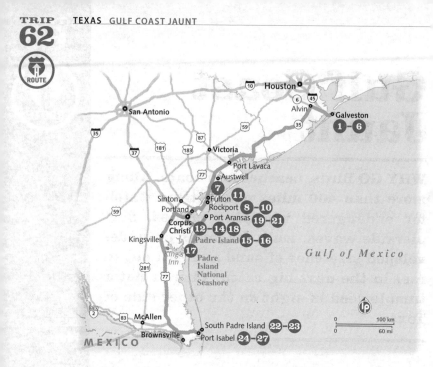

has fabulous views of the restored (and freely accessible) beachfront that lines most of the island. A cushy lounge chair beneath the palm trees on the pool deck provides an excellent vantage point for admiring the Gulf of Mexico.

When it's time to end your idyll, head south down the coastline along Rte 35. Traveling through small one-stoplight towns, over sparkling bays and past marshy estuaries that attract abundant birdlife, you get a good sense of coastal living Texas-style. Your first turnoff, 170 miles south, is ⑦ **Aransas National Wildlife Refuge**. This 115,000-acre wetland park protects the wintering ground of 240 or so whoopers, the most endangered of the planet's cranes. All 500 of the majestic white birds living in the wild or captivity are descendents of the 15 that remained in the 1940s. Standing nearly 5ft tall, with a 7ft wingspan, whooping cranes are an impressive sight. But even from the Aransas viewing platforms they can be hard to spy in the distance.

> "Standing nearly 5ft tall, with a 7ft wingspan, whooping cranes are an impressive sight."

To get closer sign up for one of the whooping crane boat tours (November through March) run out of ⑧ **Rockport**, 35 miles south. Top choice is Captain Tommy with ⑨ **Rockport Birding & Kayak Adventures**. His boats hold fewer people than the big tourist vessels but they're custom made for whooper-spotting in the shallows outside the refuge. It's not uncommon to spot 60 bird species on a half-day excursion.

Spending some time in town is a good idea, as the creative little community is known for its galleries and shops. Most line Austin St, where you can buy both knick-knacky shell sculptures and oil paintings. ❿ **Latitude 2802** combines fine art with fine eating: the restaurant-gallery uses the freshest catches, and its local paintings often reflect a coastal theme.

Back up the road Rockport runs into Fulton, which is more of a working fishing village with seafood restaurants in and around the harbor. Spend the night at ⓫ **Inn at Fulton Harbor** and you'll have a front-row seat for the shrimp-boat activity. The inn's dusty blue clapboard siding and white washed shutters harmonize perfectly with the seaside setting.

The next morning calls for an easy 30-mile drive further south on Rte 35, ending at ⓬ **Corpus Christi**. In addition to a large marina and strollable waterfront with *miradores* (observation pavilions), the "City By the Sea" has a small downtown strand and the much more expansive Padre Island beaches close by. Anchored at bay, in front of the beach-bum restaurants and T-shirt shops, is the ⓭ **USS Lexington Museum**. The 900ft naval carrier, the "Blue Ghost," is outfitted much as it would have been during its nearly 50 years at sea (it was commissioned

ASK A LOCAL

"The Intercoastal waterway produces best in the spring and fall seasons. Many a fisherperson has scored the 'Texas triple crown,' a red drum, a sea trout and a flounder, all during the same morning. I am not much of an off-shore fisherman, but have caught king mackerel, Spanish mackerel, bonito and grouper on the same day."
Fred Marshall, Fulton

from 1943 to 1991). Explore what's under the waves next door at the ⓮ **Texas State Aquarium**. The jellyfish in the huge tank look ethereal and poetic, until you remember the pain they inflict. (Locals all know that meat tenderizer takes the sting right out.)

Still part of town, but 20 miles east, the prime sunning and surfing spots are on ⓯ **Padre Island**. Cross the long and low JFK Causeway bridge over the Laguna Madre bays to the only island road and follow any access road north to the public beach. So many miles of coastline stretch forth that you can legally drive and park on the sand. No environmental groups seem to be protesting, but concerned folk can use the free parking lot at ⓰ **Bob Hall Pier**, off Park Rd 22. It's also a popular local hang-out, where you can watch the wannabe surfers catch very small waves near the pilings.

If you're looking for more solitude, 5 miles further south is ⓱ **Padre Island National Seashore**. Here the tidal flats, shifting dunes and shallow waters provide endless opportunities for hiking, swimming and windsurfing. Most of the 70 miles of this island refuge are accessible by 4WD only. Hike a mile or two and you'll likely have the place to yourself.

No matter which beach you pick, anytime you're on the island it's a good excuse to stop at **18** **Snoopy's Pier** for lunch. Smell the sea air, hear the seagulls crying and dig into fresh fried shrimp, oysters, tilapia or catfish at a rambling, open-air shack overlooking the bay. True a-fish-ianados will in-stead want to travel 19 miles north up the island to the fishing village of **19** **Port Aransas**, a base for deep sea excursions. Here you can charter pri-vate boats with guides, or go as part of a group with regular fishing trips on boats such as the *Wharf Cat* and *Scat Cat* of **20** **Fisherman's Wharf**. They have all the equipment and expertise to help first-timers get their sea legs. The waterfront by the Port A marina is crazy with seafood restaurants, all bearing names like Fin's, Hook's,

> **DETOUR**
>
> Travelling Hwy 77 at meal-time? There's a two-hour detour you have to make. Thirty miles past Corpus follow FM 628 east 9 miles to County Rd 2270, **King's Inn** (11am to 10pm) restaurant and the best fried seafood in the state. Tues-day through Saturday it serves shrimp, scallops, oysters and fish family-style on Baffin Bay – and have been since 1945. The onion-and-jalapeño tartar sauce is so tasty people dip crackers in it. A true coastal Texas experience.

Trout Street, Shell's… And the classic **21** **Tarpon Inn** is just a block away. The covered breezeways outside your room have been the perfect place to rock away an evening watching the water for more than 100 years.

Get up early the next day, as your next stop is a ways away. Though it has a similar name and related geography, there's no coastal road plying the 180 miles to **22** **South Padre Island**. You'll have to follow Hwy 77 to get to spring-break central. A whole 'nother side of the Texas Gulf Coast reveals itself at this resort: condo after condo line the Gulf-side beaches, where wave-runner rental and parasailing opportunities abound. The only educational thing on the island is **23** **Sea Turtle Inc**, a rescue facility that offers tours and feeding presentations every half hour.

For more authenticity, you may want to stay just across the mainland bridge in **24** **Port Isabel**. Built in 1852, the atmospheric **25** **lighthouse** sets the smaller-town tone. Climb up for a good look around. Many of the low-lying buildings were once private fishing "camps."

Lodging for the night at **26** **Marchan's White Sands Motel** is a chance to live like the fishingfolk do today. Rooms are basic, but the boat slips and marina bustle. On site there's both a place to clean fish and a restaurant that fries them. But if you'd rather embrace the kitsch, you can do that in Port Isabel too. **27** **Pirate's Landing** is not only a themed paradise with a full-scale 17th-century Spanish galleon floating outside, it's a surprisingly good restaurant. Go ahead, order a tropical drink in a parrot-shaped glass, matey. You've completed your coastal cruise, you've earned it.

Lisa Dunford

TRIP INFORMATION

GETTING THERE
Take I-45 from Houston to Galveston, 50 miles southeast. Follow it across the causeway to 61st St on the island.

DO

Aransas National Wildlife Refuge
Endangered whooping cranes winter in this 70,000-acre marshland park. You may also see alligators. ☎ 361-286-3559; www.fws.gov; FM 2040, Austwell; per vehicle $5; ☾ park sunrise-sunset, visitor center 8:30am-4:30pm

Fisherman's Wharf
Runs regular five-hour, deep-sea fishing excursions. Bait, rods, reels and reeling-in assistance provided. ☎ 361-749-5448; www.wharfcat.com; 900 N Tarpon St, Port Aransas; adult/child $60/30; ☾ 8am & 2pm May-Sep

Padre Island National Seashore
Seventy miles of protected shoreline and dunes, and Kemp Ridley sea turtles nest here. ☎ 361-949-8068; www.nps.gov/pais; Park Rd 22, North Padre Island; per vehicle $10; ☾ park 24hr, visitor center 9am-5pm; ♿

Pier 21 Theatre
A multimedia presentation about the 1900 "Great Storm" is narrated with entries from survivors' diaries; screenings are on the half-hour. ☎ 409-763-8808; www.galveston.com/pier21theatre; 2nd floor, Pier 21, Galveston; adult/child $5/4; ☾ 10am-5pm Wed-Mon

Port Isabel Lighthouse
Seventy-five steps lead up to an excellent view of the Laguna Madre and the coastline. The lighthouse was decommissioned in 1905. ☎ 956-943-7602; www.portisabelmuseums.com; 414 E Queen Isabella Blvd, Port Isabel; adult/child $3/1; ☾ 9am-5pm

Rockport Birding & Kayak Adventures
The smallest whooping crane tour boat in town can take you further afield, and uses four-stroke engines to minimize pollution. ☎ 877-892-4737; www.whoopingcranetours.com; Rockport Marina, off Cactus St, Rockport; birding tour $45; ☾ mid-Nov–Mar

Sea Turtle Inc
Hear a talk about the rescued animals and get up close with six different sea turtle species. ☎ 956-761-4511; www.seaturtleinc.org; 6617 Padre Blvd, South Padre Island; adult/child $3/1; ☾ 10am-4pm Tue-Sun; ♿

Texas Seaport Museum
Find out about the town's 19th-century shipping heyday and tour a 1877 Scottish tall ship. ☎ 409-763-1877; www.tsm-elissa.org; cnr Harborside Dr & 21st St, Galveston; adult/child $8/5; ☾ 10am-5pm; ♿

Texas State Aquarium
Highlights include exhibits on local marine life, including jellyfish, and a benign touch pool with lightning whelks. ☎ 361-881-1200; www.texasstateaquarium.org; 2710 N Shoreline Blvd, Corpus Christi; adult/child $16/10; ☾ 9am-5pm; ♿

USS Lexington Museum
Fold-wing planes still cover the deck of the first US naval carrier to train women – still afloat as a museum. ☎ 361-888-4873; www.usslexington.com; 2914 N Shoreline Blvd, Corpus Christi; adult/child $13/8; ☾ 9am-5pm

EAT

901 Postoffice
Relaxed island dining at its finest. The food is upmarket, but the restored house setting is just so laid-back. ☎ 409-762-1111; 901 Postoffice St, Galveston; mains $29-40; ☾ 6-10pm Thu-Sat

Latitude 2802
Get your freshly caught Gulf fish steamed in a paper bag and topped with crabmeat dressing. ☎ 361-727-9009; www.latitude2802.com; 105 N Austin St, Rockport; mains $16-20; ⏱ 5-10pm Tue-Sun

Pirate's Landing
Specializes in wild-caught fish and costume-wearing silliness. Kids love the goofy hats and pirate games. ☎ 956-943-3663; http://pirateslandingrestaurant.com; 110 S Garcia St, Port Isabel; mains $16-20; ⏱ 11am-10pm; ♿

Snoopy's Pier
Waterfront seafood shack with open-air seating and some of the best hand-breaded fried shrimp in town. ☎ 361-949-8815; www.snoopyspier.com; 13313 S Padre Island Dr, Corpus Christi; mains $7-12; ⏱ 11am-10pm

SLEEP

Hotel Galvez
Bask in palm-fringed, Spanish-colonial luxury at this c 1910 property. Even the pool has a great view of the Gulf of Mexico. ☎ 409-765-7721; www.galveston.com/galvez; 2024 Seawall Blvd, Galveston; r $150-250

Inn at Fulton Harbor
A casual, seaside lodging with crisp white trim and dusky blue clapboards fits right in across from harbor shrimp boats. ☎ 361-790-5888; www.innatfultonharbor.com; 215 N Fulton Beach Rd, Fulton; r $80-110

Marchan's White Sands Motel
It's a fisherperson's life at this spick-and-span motel with full service marina and boat slips on site. ☎ 956-943-2414; www.the-white-sands.com; 418 W Hwy 100, South Padre Island; r $50-90

Tarpon Inn
Since 1866 guests have been coming to this Texas Historic Landmark inn. Note that it's still TV- and phone-free. ☎ 361-749-5555; www.thetarponinn.com; 200 E Cotter Ave, Port Aransas; r $90-150

USEFUL WEBSITES
www.galveston.com
www.sopadre.com

SUGGESTED READS
- *Through a Night of Horrors: Voices from the 1900 Galveston Storm,* by Case Edward Green
- *Walking Historic Galveston,* by Jan Johnson
- *Crane Music: A Natural History of American Cranes,* by Paul Johnsguard
- *Fishing the Texas Gulf Coast: An Angler's Guide to More than 100 Great Places to Fish,* by Mike Holmes
- *Gulf Breeze,* coastal Texas fiction by Gerri Hill

LINK YOUR TRIP
www.lonelyplanet.com/trip-planner

Oddball Art & Aliens

WHY GO What is it about the desolation and wide open spaces of north and west Texas that seems to attract eccentrics? Driving this lonely way you'll see Cadillacs planted nose down in dirt, a giant jackrabbit, modern art in the middle of nowhere – and maybe even an alien or two.

Outside the towns, there's often a whole lotta nothin' on the endlessly flat Panhandle plains of Texas. The great wide open is punctuated only by the occasional windmill, and the distinct odor of cattle feedlots in the distance. Maybe that's why late local millionaire Stanley Marsh planted the shells of 10 Cadillacs in the deserted ground west of **1** **Amarillo** – just to give you something to look at. He said he created the installation that's come to be known as **2** **Cadillac Ranch** in 1974 as a tribute to the golden age of car travel. Kids clambering over the cars today think it's all for fun. Come prepared: accepted practice is to leave your own mark by spray painting on the cars.

Even more auto art is on display 18 miles east, in Conway, where in tribute to the aforementioned tribute (and to attract business), owners of a souvenir stand upended five Volkswagen Beetles. The stand's long gone, but you can still see the graffiti-covered cars, dubbed **3** **Bug Ranch**, freely accessible on the south side of I-40 east access road.

Any oddity hunt in Amarillo has to include dinner at the **4** **Big Texan Steak Ranch and Motel**. Outside, white stretch limos with longhorn hood ornaments wait beneath blinking marquee lights. Inside, the shooting arcade pings and cowboy troubadours sing as you dig into some seriously big steaks. The whole place is done up to look like a Victorian-era saloon – spindle-railed balconies, animal trophies,

TIME
4 days

DISTANCE
630 miles

BEST TIME TO GO
Apr – May

START
Amarillo, TX

END
El Paso, TX

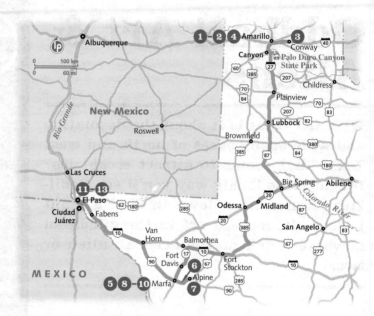

Western-dressed waiters and all. Even the associated hotel masquerades as an Old West town.

Turn your car southwest and more open spaces await. On a stormy evening the sky becomes a show when angry black clouds approach slowly across the vast expanse, exploding in thunder and lightning that's a darn good imitation of judgment day. Of course, regular ol' sunsets ain't bad either.

"stop by to see the fabulous and funky boots, including the Guinness-recognized 'Largest Cowboy Boots'"

Your next stop, the tiny town of ⑤ **Marfa**, wins the prize for most far out in Texas, and not just because it's 430 miles far out of Amarillo. Ever since the first recorded sighting of the famous "Marfa Lights" way back in the 1800s, folks have been speculating about extraterrestrials. Numerous studies have been conducted – to prove the blinking orbs are distorted headlights, heat-related or due to the curvature of the earth…

The only thing scientists all agree on? They have no idea what the heck causes the apparition. Check the night-time sky yourself at the freely accessible ⑥ **Marfa Lights Viewing Platform**, 8 miles east of town. Of course, the lights may not appear. A surer bet is to watch the warbly documentary at the ⑦ **Apache Trading Post**, in Alpine, and to pick up a few conehead stretchy figurines to commemorate your visit.

Oh, but that's not all Marfa offers – there's art here, too. Bafflingly, well-known modern artist Donald Judd chose a barren local patch to set up his abstract "Boxes" installation. The ⑧ **Chinati Foundation** today sprawls over several buildings and exhibits like-minded artists. Through the years Marfa has accumulated a surprising number of artists and galleries. Apparently if you build it, they will come. Pick up a walking map from the chamber of commerce (www.marfacc.com; corner W Lincoln St and N Highland Ave); the main concentration of galleries is on San Antonio St. Dining later on one of the creative meals at ⑨ **Cochineal** only seems appropriate. A global gourmet restaurant in the middle of a desert? Makes perfect sense in Marfa.

This desert outpost first came to fame when James Dean, Elizabeth Taylor and Rock Hudson filmed *Giant,* a Texas movie classic, here in 1955. The cast and crew stayed at the Spanish mission revival–style ⑩ **Hotel Paisano**, and you should too. Look for the memorabilia and movie playing in a room off the lobby.

It's 200 miles to your last stop, ⑪ **El Paso,** but they will fly by once you reach I-10, where the speed limit is 80mph. Make sure to get fuel when you can. Gas stations are few and far between. As you reach town, Mexican curio warehouses and discount cowboy boot emporiums welcome you on both sides of the highway. Save yourself for the real deal: ⑫ **Rocketbuster Boots**, where handmade leather is art for your feet. Hawaiian dolls, dancing Day of the Dead skeletons and stylized initials are just a few of the design options. Even if you can't shell out $800 to $3000 for a custom pair, stop by to see the fabulous and funky boots, including the Guinness-recognized "Largest Cowboy Boots" (4ft tall by 3.5ft wide). Who knows, you might not be able to pass up a Christmas-stocking boot or an artistic leather pillow while you're there.

> **DETOUR** There are more entertaining diversions en route. **Palo Duro Canyon** (www.palodurocanyon.com, 27 miles south of Amarillo), the country's second-largest hole in the ground, is impressive and the *Texas* musical melodrama staged there is truly over the top. The Buddy Holly Center in **Lubbock** (www.visitlubbock.org, 120 miles south of Palo Duro) honors native son and rock'n'roller…and is shaped like a guitar. In **Odessa** (www.odesssacvb.com, 116 miles south of Lubbock) meet 8ft-tall Jack the Rabbit and don't miss the rabbit-and-dumplings recipe printed nearby.

And with the giant pair of cowboy boots, a long, strange Texas trip has come to an end. Sitting in El Paso, you are closer to Los Angeles than Houston. Have your last breakfast at ⑬ **H&H Car Wash**, a hole-in-the-wall Mexican diner attached to a hand car wash, and watch the dusty road go down the drain.

Lisa Dunford

OFFBEAT

TRIP INFORMATION

GETTING THERE

Amarillo airport receives flights from Dallas, Denver, Houston and Las Vegas. Oklahoma City is 260 miles east on I-40.

DO

Apache Trading Post

Missed the Marfa lights? This gift shop, 14 miles east of the viewing platform, shows a short documentary on demand. ☎ 432-837-5506; www.apachetradingpost.com; 2701 W Hwy 90, Alpine; film $2; 🕑 10am-6pm Mon-Sat

Cadillac Ranch

Pull up roadside and hike from the gate to the field studded with the shells of 10 Cadillacs. **Eastbound I-40 feeder, btwn exits 60 & 62, Amarillo; admission free;** 🕑 dawn-dusk; ♿

Chinati Foundation

The morning tour takes in Judd's original modern art installation; the afternoon tour highlights changing exhibits. ☎ 432-729-4362; www.chinati.org; off Hwy 67, Marfa; adult/child $10/5; 🕑 tour 10am & 2pm Wed-Sat

Rocketbuster Boots

More than a custom boot shop, Rocketbuster is a virtual museum of vintage Americana. ☎ 915-541-1300; www.rocketbuster.com; 115 S Antony St, El Paso; admission free; 🕑 9am-5pm Mon-Fri, custom fittings by appt

EAT

Big Texan Steak Ranch

Consume the 72oz steak, plus all the fixin's, in an hour and it's free; otherwise you pay $72. ☎ 800-657-7177; www.bigtexan.com; 7700 I-40 east, Amarillo; mains $18-40; 🕑 7:30am-10:30pm; ♿

Cochineal

Foodies love the global cuisine served in a minimalist setting appropriate to the town that modern art built. ☎ 432-729-3300; 107 W San Antonio St, Marfa; mains $22-34; 🕑 6-10pm Tue-Sun

H&H Car Wash

Go for the egg, bacon, potato and cheese breakfast tacos; stay to get your car cleaned. ☎ 915-533-1144; 701 E Yandell Ave, El Paso; mains $3-7; 🕑 7am-3pm

SLEEP

Big Texan Motel

Sleep in the pseudo–Old West surrounds of a false-front town. The cement pond (aka swimming pool) is Texas shaped. ☎ 800-657-7177; www.bigtexan.com; 7700 I-40 east, Amarillo; r $60-80; 🐾

Hotel Paisano

Historic rooms at this 1929 hotel are definitely small, but James Dean slept here. Rock Hudson also booked a suite. ☎ 800-657-7177; www.hotelpaisano.com; 207 N Highland Ave, Marfa; r $99-149, ste from $160

USEFUL WEBSITES

www.visitamarillotx.com

LINK YOUR TRIP

www.lonelyplanet.com/trip-planner

TRIP

Big Fun in Big Bend

WHY GO Looking for some Texas-sized adventure? Way far west Texas has as much mountain-hiking, river-rafting, four-wheel-drivin' fun as you can handle. During four days in the Big Bend area, you'll explore one national and three state parks – plus adjacent wilderness areas. Yee-haw!

Ever wondered about the western elbow of land poking into Mexico on a map of Texas? Well, that's Big Bend. The area is named for the meandering Rio Grande, which also serves as a natural, national border. North of the river's canyons, the Chihuahua desert landscapes give way to a series of rugged mountain chains. Towns here are small, gasoline expensive, and cell-phone service nonexistent. This is as wild as Texas gets.

Start your adventure in the tallest town in Texas, ❶ Fort Davis (5000ft), which was established in 1854. The old courthouse, Hotel Limpia, a few shops and a caboose selling ice cream will hold your interest for a time. But most visitors use this as a base for further exploration. If you stay at ❷ Indian Lodge in Davis Mountain State Park, 3 miles west, you can hike trails that lead to a historic fort site or drive up steep switchbacks to an overlook. The lodge itself is a landmark, built in 1933 by the Civilian Conservation Corps to resemble a Native American adobe settlement. The stark white buildings cut a dramatic line among the desert succulents.

Winding your way up to ❸ McDonald Observatory atop Mt Locke (6791ft), 16 miles northwest, you'll pass several pull-outs for picture-taking. In the daytime the observatory plays solar-spotting videos in the theater and has star-watching exhibits on view. It's worth returning at 9pm for a Star Party: circle in the outdoor amphitheater as

---

TRIP 64

OUTDOORS

TIME
5 days

DISTANCE
240 miles

BEST TIME TO GO
Feb – Mar &
Oct – Nov

START
Fort Davis, TX

END
Alpine, TX

459

researchers tell stories about the constellations and locate them overhead with a hand-held laser pointer. The night sky this far from civilization is amazing. Afterwards you get to line up and look through six to eight high-powered telescopes that bring stellar objects right down to earth. You can also book a tour of the giant telescopes housed in buildings further up the mountain.

Enjoy the temperature up here while you can, the mountains are a good 10°F to 20°F cooler than the desert valley where you're headed. Driving south along Hwys 17 and 67 to Presidio (80 miles), you'll pass **4** **Shafter**, a little ghost town and cemetery where a few sandstone brick ruins are all that remain of a silver-mining community. Presidio isn't much, but it is the nearest official Mexican border crossing and a good starting point for a scenic drive. East of there **5** **Rte 170** hugs the Rio Grande, taking you up and down through the remote terrain of low desert arroyos, sweeping vistas and stony mountains. At one point there's a 15% grade, the maximum allowable but, unlike other scenic routes in the area, this one is paved.

Past the town of Redford, you're cruising in **6** **Big Bend Ranch State Park**, which has free picnic spots overlooking the river. Spring wildflowers vary depending on rainfall and elevation, but late February is a good time to start looking for the 2ft-tall bluebonnets that grow along the roadsides. In late March or April you'll usually start seeing the vibrant red blooms of the choyo cactus and the peachy-yellow hues of prickly pears.

About 50 miles (1½ hours) along, ❼ **Lajitas Golf Resort & Spa** appears a bit like a mirage. The Wild West look-alike buildings are meant to resemble a town. In fact, the resort does have its own zip code. Horseback rides, posh camp-outs, "Billy the Kid" Colt 45 target practice and river rafting are all big fun. After checking in, rejuvenate at the spa, dine on upscale Tex-Mex, or listen to live music on weekends at the Thirsty Goat saloon.

Another option is driving the 12 miles east into ❽ **Terlingua** ghost town for dinner. Unlike at Shafter, many of the ruined clay-brick shanties here have been reinhabited. Before the mercury mines dried up in the 1940s, 2000 people lived here. Today hippies and hardcore desert dwellers form an interesting, off-the-grid community. The ❾ **Starlight Theatre** now plays host to both locals and tourists at dinner. Dishes like chicken fried antelope and pork with chipotle sauce star, and Thursday through Sunday there's live music. Happy hour at the bar has a following, but those in the know usually just pick up a beer at the ❿ **Ter-**

> **DETOUR** Native Americans have known about the springs at modern-day **Balmorhea State Park** (www.tpwd.state.tx.us), 37 miles north of Fort Davis, since ancient times. In the 1930s the Civilian Conservation Corps came along and created a mighty fine swimming hole by walling off some of the flow to make a 72°F to 76°F pool. It's a perfect temperature for a cooling dip on your way down to Big Bend.

lingua Trading Company next door and hang out on the benches lining the long front porch to watch the sun go down. The Trading Company sells a historic ghost town walking-tour map ($0.50) in addition to a large local book selection, Western art, Native American artifacts and the aforementioned adult beverages.

Leave the pavement behind on day three. First, stop for breakfast burritos al fresco at ⓫ **Kathy's Kosmic Kowgirl Kafe**, about 3 miles east of Terlingua. The hot-pink school bus and travel trailer with colorful signage are as much roadside attraction as they are eatery. Pull a folding chair up to a card table outside or grab one of the Adirondacks in front of the fire pit. Occasional events include movies shown on weekend evenings, flea markets and benefit cook-offs.

After breakfast, rendezvous with the local outfitter of your choice for an outdoor adventure. There are several to choose from along Rte 170 where Terlingua meets Study Butte, near the intersection with Hwy 118. Operators including ⓬ **Big Bend River Tours** run anything from a gentle two-hour float to two days of rapid running. Longer trips such as those to Bouquillas Canyon may include side hikes to Native American sites. Of course, much depends on the weather. You're most likely to have high enough water (and warm enough weather) for serious river running in September and October, after the summer rainy season. Rafting and horseback-riding combos are available, too. If you'd rather be dusty than wet, outfits including ⑬ **Far Flung Outdoor Center** also offer Jeep and ATV tours.

If you have a high-clearance 4WD vehicle of your own, the book to get is *Road Guide to Backcountry Dirt Roads* from ⑭ **Big Bend National Park**. The park boundary starts just 2.5 miles south of Study Butte, on Hwy 118, but the main visitor center is at Panther Junction, 26 miles further on. Rangers there are great about helping you plan hikes. You have several different terrain options within the 800,000-plus acres. Down in the desert at 2200ft, ⑮ **Santa Elena Canyon Trail** (40 miles southwest of Panther Junction) is one of the most popular treks due to stunning rock and river views. It's rated easy, but you have to wade through a stream and climb stairs in the canyon wall. Avoid it at all costs during the devil's playground–like summer heat.

SOME LIKE IT HOT

Every year in the first weekend in November the **Terlingua International Chili Cook-Off** (www. abowlofred.com) attracts more than 5000 visitors. That's a whole heapa people for a town with a population of fewer than 300. Word must have spread during the 44 years this has been going on. In addition to chili tasting, great Texas entertainment like Gary P Nunn, an ugly hat contest and other food contests are all part of the spicy fun.

Most of the park's 150 miles of hiking paths are in the cooler Chisos Mountains, at 5400ft and above. Begin in Chisos Basin, eight switchback-laden miles southwest of Panther Junction. The flat ⑯ **Window View Trail**, only a third of a mile in length, leads you to a view of a picturesque opening in the rocks that photographers love at sunset. The trail to the window itself is much more challenging, with an 800ft descent. The park's basic, motellike lodgings at Chisos Basin are where most people stay: not for the sound-leaking rooms ($110 to $150), but for the view.

"As you're walking you may be serenaded by a guitarist over in Mexico, literally a stone's throw away"

Back on the desert floor, 28 miles southeast of Chisos, is ⑰ **Hot Spring Trail**. Get there early – to beat the heat and to improve your chances of having the place to yourself. The hike is less than a mile along the riverbank to the former foundations of a bath house, which now serve as an outdoor tub, full of hot spring water. As you're walking you may be serenaded by a guitarist over in Mexico, literally a stone's throw away, or see little crafts "for sale" on the path with seemingly no-one attending. Watch long enough and you'll spy the salesperson hidden on the other bank. You could sit partially submerged in the hot water with the effervescent spray in your face and the rushing sounds of the Rio Grande below all day, but you have a dinner reservation.

Take a quick look at ⓲ **Rio Grande Village** on your way out of the park. The surprisingly green stand of cottonwood trees there comes from an irrigation system set up by homesteading farmers. Grab some road snacks at the campground store (8am to 5pm), but don't fill up. Your next adventure is a culinary one. Ninety miles north, the tiny town of ⓳ **Marathon** (population 400) is little more than a main street with a few cafés, stores – and a historic hotel with a destination restaurant.

Foodies from around the state make sure they put ⓴ **Cafe Cenizo** on any Big Bend itinerary. Here classic techniques are applied to Texas ingredients (think mole-rubbed tenderloin, or gingered peaches in pureed sweet potato soup) and served in rustic comfort. Make a night of it and stay at the associated ㉑ **Gage Hotel**. First opened in 1902, the original building comes straight out of a dime-store Western. A lazy fan whirs above the high four-poster bed as light streams in through wooden shutters onto a pile of saddle blankets. In the authentically creaky, wooden-floored building, rooms can be quite noisy; we prefer the hacienda-style suites organized around tropical courtyards. The best of the bunch have kiva fireplaces; all have timber ceilings and hand-painted folk art. Open the top half of the handcrafted wood door and listen to the doves splashing in the fountain outside. The fragrant roses and vibrant bougainvillea are the last you'll see of lush vegetation for a while.

Hwy 90 skirts through the mountain ranges but flattens out shortly after you pass ㉒ **Alpine**, the largest town in the region. It's a good place to fill up on fuel and food. Plus, Sul Ross State University is here, and they put on a heck of a cowboy poetry gathering in February. Might be just the event to schedule your next big fun around…we know you'll be back.
Lisa Dunford

TRIP INFORMATION

GETTING THERE
Fort Davis is 200 miles from El Paso. Follow I-10 to Hwy 118, a scenic route.

DO

Big Bend National Park
More than 800,000 acres of remote mountains, rivers and desert valleys. ☎ 432-477-2251; www.nps.gov/bibe; off Hwys 118 or 385, Big Bend; 7-day pass per vehicle $20; ☷ park 24hr, visitor center 9am-6pm

Big Bend River Tours
Experienced guides and equipment rental. ☎ 800-545-4240; www.bigbendrivertours. com; Box 317, Rte 170, Terlingua; half-day tour $75; ☷ office 9am-5pm

Far Flung Outdoor Center
Jeep and ATV tours take you off-road to great views and Native American sites. Rafting also available. ☎ 800-839-7238; www.farflungoutdoorcenter.com; Box 377, Rte 170, Terlingua; tours $50-150; ☷ office 9am-5pm

McDonald Observatory
Learn about the stars, tour the telescopes and see a solar viewing. ☎ 432-426-3640; http://mcdonaldobservatory.org; Hwy 118, Fort Davis; adult/child $8/7; Star Party $10/8; ☷ 10am-5:30pm; ☷

Terlingua Trading Company
Shop for area arts and crafts, or just grab a beer and hang out on the porch with the locals. ☎ 432-371-2234; www.historic-terlingua.com; 100 Ivey Rd, Terlingua; ☷ 10am-9pm

EAT

Cafe Cenizo
Gourmet renditions of Texas faves are casual and classy, like the restaurant itself. ☎ 432-386-4205; www.gagehotel.com; Gage Hotel, 101 Hwy 90, Marathon; mains $24-39; ☷ 6-9pm Sun-Thu, 6-10pm Fri & Sat

Kathy's Kosmic Kowgirl Kafe
You can't miss this neon-pink trailer serving breakfast and barbecue in the middle of a desert. ☎ 432-371-2164; www.kosmic kowgirl.com; Rte 170, Terlingua; mains $4-8; ☷ 6am-3pm Thu-Sun

Starlight Theatre
This ghost-town restaurant has quite the stage presence, with Western murals and twinkly overhead lights. ☎ 432-371-2326; www.starlighttheatre.com; 631 Ivey Rd, Terlingua; mains $15-20; ☷ 5-10pm

SLEEP

Gage Hotel
A 1902 brick-front hotel and adobe suites are part of an Old West oasis with a tropical pool and gardens. ☎ 800-884-4243; www.gageho tel.com; 101 US 90, Marathon; r $115-260; ☷

Indian Lodge
The 1930s stucco rooms have recently renovated pine ceilings and Southwestern hues. ☎ 512-389-8982; www.tpwd.state. tx.us; Davis Mountain State Park, Hwy 118, Fort Davis; r $90-110

Lajitas Golf Resort & Spa
The resort resembles a town, each building with a theme – from Old West boardwalk hotel to Texas cavalry officers' quarters. ☎ 877-525-4827; www.lajitas.com; Rte 170, Lajitas; r $150-300

USEFUL WEBSITES

www.visitbigbend.com

LINK YOUR TRIP
www.lonelyplanet.com/trip-planner

ROCKY MOUNTAINS TRIPS

Supremely beautiful, rugged and wild and free, the Rockies seem invented for road trips: drifting down the byways of Colorado, Wyoming, Montana and Idaho and getting lost in the region's natural beat. Big blue skies stretch forever, and roads slip through alpine valleys, past windswept prairies, between lofty snowcapped peaks and into small towns where the old West's heart still throbs.

Everything about the Rockies – from the bears to the beers – feels big, larger than life. There's an adventure for each season waiting around every turn – be it broncs and bulls at the Cody Nite Rodeo in summer or champagne powder skiing in Vail, Aspen or Sun Valley in winter – guaranteeing you'll never be bored.

The truth is, wherever in the Rockies you may wander, you're in for a hell of a good trip. Whether you're wandering the streets of big-city Denver, summiting a 14er or geyser gawking and big bear stalking in mighty Yellowstone, it doesn't take long to slip right into that sweet, pine-scented nirvana they call the Rocky Mountain high.

PLAYLIST ♫ The Rocky Mountain states have been rocking to their own tunes for decades now – heck, Colorado's official state song is John Denver's most famous anthem, "Rocky Mountain High." The songs here come from genres as different as the mountains are from the prairie, but when played in combination, make the perfect Rockies road-trip soundtrack.

- "How to Save a Life," The Fray
- "A Mile High in Denver," Jimmy Buffett
- "I Can Still Make Cheyenne," George Strait
- "Half Moon Rising," Yonder Mountain String Band
- "Rocky Mountain Music," Eddie Rabbitt
- "Idaho," Train
- "Wild Montana Skies," John Denver

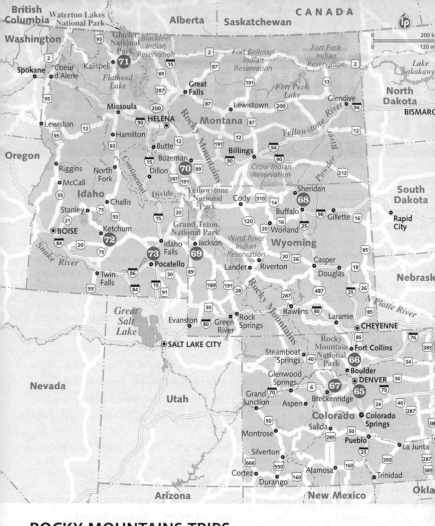

ROCKY MOUNTAINS TRIPS

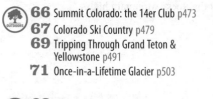

48 Hours in Greater Denver

WHY GO Sitting at exactly 5280ft, this city has sunshine, culture and 300 blue-sky days of cosmopolitan attitude. Get to know the cow-gone-to-pot town in a whole new light – with more medical-marijuana dispensaries than Starbucks, the Mile High City's nickname has taken on a whole new meaning.

TIME
2 days

BEST TIME TO GO
May – Nov

START
State Capitol Building

END
Denver I-25, north of Denver

Start your weekend in the Mile High City off right, climbing to the 15th step of the domed ❶ State Capitol building. Engraved with the words "one mile above sea level," the step is where Denver's official height measurement is taken – the building sits on slightly higher ground than the rest of the city.

Designed by Elijah E Myers to resemble the national capitol building, the Colorado statehouse was constructed out of white granite in the 1890s. In 1908 it received a facelift: the original copper dome was replaced with one made from 200oz of real gold plating to commmerate the 1880s gold rush that built Denver. Make sure to wander inside – Congress is in session between January and May and the public is welcome to sit in the impressive galleries and watch the debates on the floor. Even if you're not into politics, it is well worth wandering inside for nothing more than aesthetic purposes – this is one of the most impressive state capitals we've seen; stained-glass windows and hand-painted murals tell the story of Colorado against a backdrop of rare multicolored marble and gold-plated bannisters. Sherlock Holmes types will want to inspect the interior carefully – bizarre history lessons can be gleaned from obscurely placed plaques, while subtle graffiti, including an image resembling George Washington, covers portions of walls and floor, secretly etched into the soft stone over the years. (Don't try this yourself, you will be arrested.)

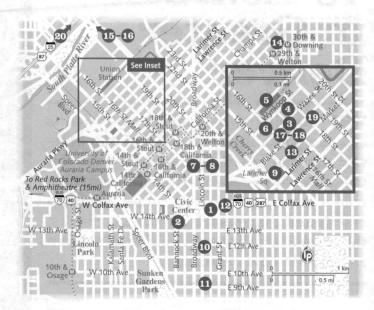

West of the capitol, around the green expanses of the civic-center park, is the city's most abstract attraction, the ❷ **Denver Art Museum**. Designed by Daniel Libeskind of World Trade Center memorial fame, the museum's Frederic C Hamilton wing, its newest and most expensive, looks like the Sydney Opera House stuck inside a mammoth fan; at once mesmerizing and torturous. Love it or hate it, you can't not dig the museum's permanent collections, all of which are top quality – its Native American art collection is one of the country's largest, featuring pieces from tribes across America.

After a morning of museum hopping, your stomach is probably growling. Luckily you're just a few blocks from Denver's most happening gourmet-eating strip, historic ❸ **LoDo**. Walk northwest on 14th St to hit Denver's original city center. It's home to blocks of tidy red-brick buildings dating back more than a century; once manufacturing warehouses, today they've been converted into sidewalk cafés and big-city bistros, swanky lounges, retro furniture shops and designer boutiques. Turn right on Wynkoop St, at LoDo's northern edge, and inhale the smell of frying meat and hops as you walk into the city's beloved homegrown tap house, the ❹ **Wynkoop Brewing Company**. The brainchild of city mayor John Hickenlooper (who was famous for his successful microbreweries long before he succeeded in politics, and is now running unopposed on the Democratic ticket for governor), it serves juicy burgers and award-winning microbrews in big and breezy environs. There are more than 20 billiard tables should you care to indulge in an après-lunch game.

Just across the street from the Wynkoop, ❺ **Union Station** is worth a peek. Constructed in 1881 to consolidate gold-rush traffic, the station once carried more than a million passengers a year. By 1954 service was decreased by half, and today only one Amtrak passenger train passes through Union's impressive arches each day.

Two blocks south of the brewery on Wynkoop is Denver's best literary shop, the well-loved ❻ **Tattered Cover Bookstore**. The massive store, covering all genres in varying degrees of detail, has an entire corner devoted to armchair travel, and plenty of overstuffed chairs to curl into. Want to write your story? The journal selection is fantastic, with creative and unique offerings for all tastes and ages.

Also in the neighborhood, tonight's sleeping spot: the swank ❼ **Brown Palace Hotel**. This distinguished historic landmark is *the* place to stay in Denver. Within walking distance of restaurants and nightlife, it has hosted everyone from the Beatles to Winston Churchill. Have afternoon tea in the impressive lobby then head to the award-winning ❽ **Palace Arms** for dinner. The patriotic pioneer decor dates back to the 1700s – check out the silver centerpiece the British royal family commissioned. The food is as impressive as the old-world ambience. Signature dishes include Kobe rib-eye steak and seared bison tenderloin.

Afterwards, leave your car at the hotel and return to LoDo on foot, to sample the nightlife, martinis and…champagne. Opulent ❾ **Corridor 44**, in Larimer Sq, is Denver's only champagne bar, offering more than 100 selections of champagne and sparkling wine by the glass, split or bottle. Chic, white-leather banquettes coupled with exposed red-brick walls give it a Western-meets-NYC ambience.

With a champagne buzz, catch a cab to ❿ **Church**. There's nothing like ordering stiff drinks in a cathedral to really mess with your mind. Lit by hundreds of altar candles and flashing blue strobe lights, the Church has three dance floors, a couple of lounges and even a sushi bar! Arrive before 10pm Friday through Sunday to avoid the cover charge. Just two blocks away, ⓫ **Watson's Liquor and Grocery** is an old-fashioned corner store, in operation since the 1950s. It used to be a straight-up booze and sundry outlet but started stocking famous Western DVDs a couple of years ago – the owner may have figured nothing kills depression faster than bourbon and Roy Rogers or John Wayne.

Come morning, have breakfast at the ⓬ **Walnut Café**, which has been the city's breakfast spot du jour for decades now. It's perfect for hangover recovery, offering a diverse range of American standards like waffles and eggs

CITY

cooked any way you like. Walk the meal off window-shopping the pedestrian-only **13 16th Street Mall**, Denver's most recognized attraction. Closed to traffic for an entire 12 blocks (and with its own ecofriendly free hop-on, hop-off shuttle should you tire of walking), the al fresco mall features dozens of shops.

At the southern end of the mall, grab Denver's one-line downtown light rail north, then jump on the bus, taking it north to the last stop at 30th and Downing Sts. Here you'll find the most unique museum in the Rockies, the **14 Black American West Museum & Heritage Center**. It's dedicated to "telling history how it was," and provides an intriguing look at the contributions of African Americans (from cowboys to rodeo riders) during the pioneer era – according to museum statistics one in three Colorado cowboys were black.

> **DETOUR**
>
> Denver's most unique concert venue, **Red Rocks Park & Amphitheatre** is set between 400ft-high red-sandstone rocks 15 miles southwest of Denver. Acoustics are so good that many artists record live albums here. The 9000-seat theater offers stunning views and draws big-name bands all summer. Even if you can't take in a show (concerts from $30), visit the park to hike through the bizarrely placed rocks.

Afterwards, grab your car and head to the Highlands neighborhood. Here you'll find the discombobulating **15 Urbanistic Tea and Bike Shop**, which sells exactly what it advertizes – tea and cycles. The smells alone are weird enough (think bike-chain grease mixed with spicy fruit aromas) to merit a wander. But the brother-sister team of Ethan and Michelle Bontrager also know their subjects well. Ethan is a bike mechanic who can fix just about any unmotorized wheeled vehicle, while you can tell from her catch-the-subtleties descriptions that Michelle has tasted every one of the 140 teas she sells. Plus, she usually keeps a pot of something delicious-smelling brewing behind the counter. It's a totally only-in-Colorado shopping experience.

MILE-HIGH SPORTS

Denver is known for manic sports fans, and boasts five pro teams, including the Colorado Rockies (baseball), Colorado Avalanche (hockey) and the most hallowed team of all, the beloved (not to mention record-holding) four-time Super Bowl champs, the Denver Broncos football team, who fill their legendary **INVESCO Field @ Mile High Stadium** nearly every game day – watch out, Raiders fans. Check out the signature white stallion sculpture on the arena's exterior wall.

16 Rosa Linda's Mexican Café is a good lunch pick. For more than 20 years the Aguirre family has been serving Denver reasonably priced authentic Mexican comfort fare with a side of old-fashioned hospitality. Winner of numerous awards, including status as one of the *Wall Street Journal*'s top 15 nachos in the nation (we agree; they were mouth-watering), Rosa Linda's also does excellent *chile rellenos* and *mole*. The menu includes plenty of vegetarian and health-conscious choices (check out the whole-wheat grilled cactus burrito).

Spend night two in the heart of LoDo, at the **17** **Jet Hotel**. Priced for partying, this slick minimalist boutique in the heart of LoDo is all about fun, especially on weekends. That's when Denver's beautiful people come for the slumber party with bottle-service experience. Rooms are Zen humble, with thick white comforters and dark shades to block out the light and noise. Lobby bar the **18** **Jet Lounge** is where you should have predinner drinks. It features a bedroom-meets-house-party vibe, especially late at night – think candles, couches and weekend DJs. If you're not into all-night ragers come during the week, when the hotel attracts a quieter, more business-oriented crowd who come for the cheap rooms.

Eat dinner just down the street at longtime favorite the **19** **Vesta Dipping Grill**. Pick a type of meat, then choose from 30 sauces to dip it into. It's a simple concept that works exceedingly well, creating melt-in-your mouth dishes – many Asian inspired – served in relaxed and funky environs. Afterwards it's time to hit up the **20** **Grizzly Rose**, a legendary country-music club just north of city limits on I-25 that makes for a fitting rowdy and authentic ending spot to this Mile High adventure. It is one kick-ass honky-tonk, attracting real cowboys from as far as Cheyenne. The Country Music Association and *Playboy Magazine* have both named it the best country bar in America. If you've never experienced line dancing, there's no better place to put on the boots, grab the Stetson and let loose.

Becca Blond

TRIP INFORMATION

GETTING THERE
Denver is on I-25, 100 miles south of Cheyenne, Wyoming.

DO

Black American West Museum & Heritage Center
African American contributions in the West during the 1800s are often overlooked. ☎ 303-292-2566; 3091 California St; adult/student $8/6; ⏱ 10am-2pm Mon-Fri, 10am-5pm Sat & Sun, closed Mon & Tue winter

Colorado State Capitol
Free 45-minute tours: meet at the north (Colfax) entrance. ☎ 303-866-2604; cnr Broadway & E Colfax Ave; ⏱ 7am-5:30pm Mon-Fri

Denver Art Museum
One of the USA's largest Native American art collections. ☎ 720-865-5000; www.denverartmuseum.org; 100 W 14th Ave; adult/student $13/10; ⏱ 10am-5pm Tue-Sat, 10am-9pm Wed, noon-5pm Sun

Tattered Cover Bookstore
Massive and bursting with books. ☎ 303-436-1070; 1628 16th St; ⏱ 6:30am-9pm Mon-Fri, 9am-9pm Sat, 10am-6pm Sun

Urbanistic Tea and Bike Shop
More than 140 teas plus cycles galore. ☎ 303-561-3025; 3215 Lowell Blvd; ⏱ 9am-7pm Mon-Fri, 9am-5pm Sat, 11am-5pm Sun

Watson's Liquor and Grocery
Looking for whiskey and an old Western? This homegrown business sells both. ☎ 303-837-1366; 900 Lincoln St; ⏱ 8am-midnight Mon-Fri, 10am-midnight Sat, 10am-8pm Sun

EAT & DRINK

Church
There's nothing like ordering a smart cocktail inside an old cathedral. ☎ 303-832-3538; 1160 Lincoln St; cover $10

Corridor 44
Denver's only champagne bar serves 100 types of bottled sparkling grape along with savory bits and small-plate dishes. ☎ 303-893-0044; 1433 Larimer Sq; mains $9-25; ⏱ 3pm-2am

Grizzly Rose
This kick-ass honky-tonk is famous for bringing in huge industry stars – Willie Nelson, LeAnn Rimes – and only charging $10. ☎ 303-295-1330; 5450 N Valley Hwy; cover $5-10

Rosa Linda's Mexican Café
Mexican comfort staples and old-fashioned hospitality. ☎ 303-455-0608; 2005 W 33rd Ave; mains $6-12; ⏱ 11.30am-10pm; 🐾

Vesta Dipping Grill
Choose a meat then one of 30 dipping sauces. Funky Vesta is a favorite date spot. ☎ 303-296-1970; 1822 Blake St; mains $15-25; ⏱ 5-10:30pm

Walnut Café
Denver's top breakfast/hangover-recovery joint. ☎ 303-832-5108; 338 E Colfax Ave; mains $5-10; ⏱ 7am-1pm

Wynkoop Brewing Company
Juicy burgers and award-winning microbrews. ☎ 303-297-2700; 1634 18th St; mains $7-20; ⏱ 11am-2am

SLEEP

Brown Palace Hotel
This distinguished historic landmark is *the* place to stay in Denver. ☎ 303-297-3111, 800-321-2599; www.brownpalace.com; 321 17th St; r $150-500

Jet Hotel
Slick minimalist boutique, priced for partying. ☎ 303-572-3300; www.thejethotel.com; 1612 Wazee St; r $100-200

USEFUL WEBSITES
www.denver.org

www.lonelyplanet.com/trip-planner

LINK YOUR TRIP
TRIP

Summit Colorado: The 14er Club

WHY GO Colorado has 52 mountains over 14,000ft, and to join the state's most exclusive climbing group, the 14er club, you'll need to summit at least one. This trip introduces four fantastic 14ers, and the best places to pop the champagne and toast the ultimate Rocky Mountain high post ascent.

TIME
4 days

DISTANCE
320 miles

BEST TIME TO GO
Jul – Sep

START
Boulder, CO

END
Colorado Springs, CO

Summiting all of Colorado's mountains over 14,000ft (14ers) is a lifetime achievement for many. But with more than 50 of these giants to climb – some quite easy, others grueling and technical – getting started can be the hardest part of joining this elite club. This trip makes the goal a tad easier, by outlining routes up four flagship peaks.

Begin the ascent in (The People's Republic of) ❶ **Boulder**, a liberal university town with a yuppie-stoner vibe and a mad crush on the outdoors. The first US city to specifically tax itself to preserve open space, way back in 1967, it's ground zero for Colorado's pro-cycling, running and climbing crowd. The area's best rock climbing is found in ❷ **Eldorado Canyon State Park**, southwest off Hwy 93. With Class 5.5 to 5.12 routes, it's a good place to warm up if you plan to tackle technical routes up any of the 14ers. Hikers can acclimate to the altitude on one of the gorgeous canyon trails.

Back in Boulder, grab lunch, or afternoon tea, at the ❸ **Boulder Dushanbe Teahouse**, a model example of this unique community's character. A gift from sister city Dushanbe, Tajikistan, the building is a work of art inside and out. Check out the vibrant hand-carved and painted ceiling, the meticulous work of 40 artisans. The teahouse was created in Tajikistan, then deconstructed and shipped to Boulder. The food tastes as good as the place looks, featuring international fare incorporating the Amazon, the Mediterranean and, of course, Tajikistan.

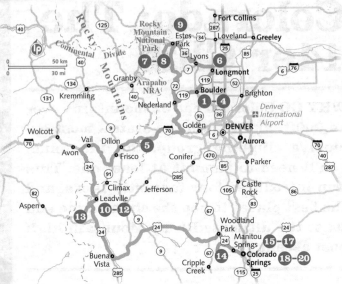

Dushanbe's menu lists more than 100 types of loose-leaf tea, many created by the house blender. Traditional afternoon tea must be booked 24 hours in advance but is a delightful experience.

In keeping with the climbing theme, spend the night at the ④ **Boulder Outlook Hotel & Suites**. Calling itself the "cure for the common hotel," the totally green hotel isn't just colorful and energetic; it also features an 11ft-high rock-climbing boulder (plus heated chlorine-free pool) inside! Grab a beer, and perhaps catch a live act at the hotel bar, before retiring early. You're going up the mountain tomorrow.

Just 50 miles from Boulder, ⑤ **Grays Peak** is one of Colorado's favorite 14er peaks. The trail is only 3.5 miles each way, making it popular with the family crowd. You'll likely see couples summiting this peak with nearly newborns swaddled on their backs – it's a top pick for baby's first 14er among the mountaineering mom-and-dad set. The 14,270ft mountain's other claim to fame is being the tallest point on the Continental Divide. (There are higher summits in Colorado, but none sitting directly atop the east–west watershed). The 3054ft ascent, climbing almost 1000ft per mile, is steep, but the hike is swift; plus, the views from the top are sweet and losing your 14er summit virginity, priceless. The trailhead begins at Stevens Gulch Rd – take I-70 west to exit 221.

Celebrate the big event at ➏ **Oskar Blues Liquids & Solids**, facing the next 14er challenge, Long's Peak. A brewpub famous for canning extra-strength microbrews (they don't call one beer "TenFidy" for nothing: it's 10.5% alcohol), it's located 10 miles north of Boulder on Hwy 119 in Longmont. The restaurant serves better-than-average barbecue and Cajun classics – we love the black-and-blue burger, washed down with a cold canned Gordon's. There's live music and it's usually packed nightly. You have to be up at 3am tomorrow so this probably isn't the best night for a no-drive pub crawl, but for future reference a bus runs between the Longmont brewpub and the original venue in the mountains in nearby Lyons on some nights; check online for details.

> "plus, the views from the top are sweet and losing your 14er summit virginity, priceless."

Inside Colorado's most famous natural attraction, ➐ **Rocky Mountain National Park**, ice-cream-cone-shaped ➑ **Long's Peak** stands 14,255ft tall and has only one trail that doesn't require ropes to summit. Called the Keyhole Route, it can only be accessed during a short summer window after the snow melts, usually around July. Begin super early – we're talking around 3am here, no joke. It's an 8-mile climb to the top, which you'll want to reach by 10am to be off the mountain before the first of the afternoon thunderstorms rolls in. Long's location, where the mountains hit the plains, makes it attractive to lightning. Massive electrical storms are an almost daily reality in summer. The first 6 miles of hiking aren't too strenuous, but save some reserves for the final 1.5 miles, which includes an intense 4850ft scramble through a field of small boulders to the top.

SMALL-SCREEN BOULDER

Best known as *Mork & Mindy*'s home town, Boulder has actually logged quite a bit of small-screen airtime over the decades, most recently starring in the ABC Family Channel hit *Make It or Break It*, about teenage gymnasts. Speaking of teens, the grandmother of teen lit, Judy Blume, set one of her adult novels, *Smart Women*, in the city; while Stephen King used Boulder as the final battle location in his apocalyptic novel *The Stand* – the TV miniseries shot scenes at the Hwy 36 pull-out 9 miles south.

If you've ever seen the movie *The Shining* then tonight's lodging pick, the ➒ **Stanley Hotel**, should look familiar. Stephen King was inspired to pen his psychotic horror story after staying at this sprawling white resort above Estes Park. The hotel, which is believed to be haunted, was the original creation of Freelan O Stanley, co-inventor of the famous Stanley Steamer. He built the place in 1909 to get people using his steam-powered automobiles, rather than the railway system, for holiday travel. Grab dinner at the hotel restaurant, have a glass of whiskey at the gorgeous old bar for courage, and embark upon an after-dark building ghost tour.

From Estes Park it's 160 miles to Colorado's highest incorporated city, ❿ Leadville, at 10,200ft. The air is thin but delectably crisp and clean in Leadville, a down-to-earth, nostalgic town where the local pharmacy is still called the drugstore and run by its sole owner rather than a national chain. The "city in the clouds" comes with a century and a quarter's worth of mining history, including a stake in the Wild West gold rush that included a short reign as Colorado's second-largest city. Spend the night at the ⓫ Delaware Hotel. Right downtown, it's a carefully restored building with Victorian rooms and suites, plus attentive service. Load up on carbs at the cheerful, spotless ⓬ Tennessee Pass Café. It serves delicious pizza and pasta and plenty of fresh and savory veggie fare to keep all eaters' appetites stimulated.

THE LEADVILLE TRAIL 100

Held over a late August weekend, the Leadville Trail 100 is the city's premier outdoor event, featuring two grueling 100-mile races. Run on parallel dirt-road courses that rarely dip lower than 2 miles above sea level, the ultra-marathon and mountain-bike race are considered ultimate tests of willpower and lung power. In 2009 Lance Armstrong made mountain-bike course history when he shattered previous records, finishing in an astounding six hours, 28 minutes and 51 seconds. Visit www.leadvilletrail100.com for more info.

Colorado's tallest mountain, and the second-highest peak in the Lower 48, ⓭ Mt Elbert stands a proud 14,443ft tall. The North Mt Elbert Trail is one of the most popular summit routes, beginning just under 3 miles south of Leadville off Hwy 24 to Hwy 300 (a local road) and even smaller Hwy 11 (a county road) for about a mile to the Halfmoon Campground sign. Turn right onto a dirt road, and follow it 5 miles to the trailhead on the left. There's plenty of parking and even a toilet. The 8.75-mile route to the top takes about four hours up (less down). You'll pop up above the tree line at 11,900ft (this is another mountain that you need to leave early to hike), where you'll have a first glimpse of a false summit on the horizon – sorry, you've got another two miles and 2500ft of elevation to go. Still, it's worth the effort: after you've reached the summit, you'll have climbed to the very top of Colorado!

Mt Elbert is 130 miles, as the crow flies, from 14,110ft ⓮ Pikes Peak. The final mountain in the fantastic four is the state's most famous and the only summit accessible by road and train.

The 12.5-mile Barr Trail is the main route up the peak. This is the longest and most strenuous hike, climbing 7300ft. It is imperative to leave early enough (3am again here, people) to get back below the tree line before the summer thunderstorms.

Luckily, Pikes Peak is the only mountain with both a paved toll way and train running up and down it, so if nasty weather threatens catch a ride down on the ⑮ Pikes Peak Cog Railway. Katherine Lee Bates was inspired to pen "America the Beautiful" after riding the Swiss-built trains to the top in 1893. The trailhead, and the train, both depart from quirky ⑯ Manitou Springs. Practically falling into a crumbly red-rock canyon, Manitou is well worth a stroll post summit. Surely one of the nation's quirkiest small towns, hosting a slew of unusual festivals – from a Christmas fruit-cake catapult contest to Halloween-costumed coffin races down the main street. There's even a marathon to the top of Pikes Peak! The games still work at the historic ⑰ Penny Arcade in the heart of downtown. The old-fashioned emporium is truly worth a wander, no matter your age, for the goosebump-worthy nostalgia it elicits.

This trip's final sleeping spot is located 6 miles west on Hwy 24 in ⑱ Colorado Springs. The state's second-largest city is home to a bizarre amalgamation of evangelical Christians, military families and ultra-liberal college students (not to mention the hollowed-out mountain where the president would weather a nuclear strike). The Cold War–era downtown is packed with top-quality restaurants, bars and interesting shops, including the excellent ⑲ Mountain Chalet, where you should purchase a 14er T-shirt. They come in a variety of shapes, sizes and designs but all feature a mapped layout of the 52 mountains and the words, "Don't trust anyone under 14,000ft." It's a proper souvenir ending.

In a picture-perfect location against the blue-green slopes of Cheyenne Mountain, everything about the ⑳ Broadmoor Resort is exquisite: acres of lush grounds and a shimmering lake to stroll past, world-class golf, ornately decorated grandiose public spaces, myriad bars and restaurants, a fantastic spa, and uber-comfortable European-style guest rooms. On a warm summer afternoon there's no better spot for a drink with a view than the hotel's al fresco bar overlooking a private lake. Order a bottle of bubbly and a cigar and celebrate summiting these four fantastic mountains with true-blue, old-fashioned Wild West hospitality and style.

Becca Blond

RACE TO THE TOP

Think hiking to the top of Pikes Peak is challenging? Try running! The **Pikes Peak Marathon**, held the third weekend in August, challenges athletes with an 8000ft elevation gain in 13 miles; the last 2000ft of which come during the final 3-mile sprint to the summit. Or…you could try the half-marathon going down. Word of warning: we've seen the first-aid tent after runners come in. Expect to painfully shed the skin of your soles. Still, saying you've completed a 14er marathon is a priceless conversation opener.

TRIP INFORMATION

GETTING THERE
Boulder is 30 miles northwest of Denver via I-25 to Hwy 36, which turns into 28th St.

DO

Eldorado Canyon State Park
Fantastic technical climbing in a gorgeous location; look for the park entrance west of Hwy 93. ☎ 303-494-3943; Eldorado Springs Dr, Boulder; ☺ visitors center 9am-5pm

Mountain Chalet
This locally owned outdoor store sells a unique collection of 14er T-shirts. ☎ 800-346-7044; www.mtnchalet.com; 226 N Tejon St, Colorado Springs; ☺ 10am-6pm; ♿

Pikes Peak Cog Railway
Trains depart from the Manitou Springs depot; the round-trip ride takes 3¼ hours. One-way tickets are only available on the day's first and last trains, and not on Saturday or holidays. ☎ 719-685-5401; www.cograilway.com; 515 Ruxton Ave, Manitou Springs; tickets $20-33; ☺ Apr-Jan; ♿

Rocky Mountain National Park
For current climbing conditions and info on various routes up Long's Peak, visit the main ranger station. ☎ 970-586-1206; www.nps.gov/room/planyourvisit/longspeak.htm; admission per car $20

EAT

Boulder Dushanbe Teahouse
This Tajik work of art serves creative international fare and a 100-variety-strong loose-leaf tea menu. ☎ 303-442-4993; www.boulderteahouse.com; 1770 13th St; mains $8-20; ☺ 8am-10pm

Oskar Blues Liquids & Solids
Serving the best canned microbrews in Colorado, Oskar Blues is revered among Boulderites. Order a burger and Gordon's brew. ☎ 303-485-9500; 1555 S Hover Rd, Longmont; mains $7-15; ☺ 11am-close

Tennessee Pass Café
A cheerful and spotless place serving a little bit of everything from Italian to Thai. ☎ 719-486-8101; 222 Harrison Ave, Leadville; mains $8-15; ☺ 11am-close

SLEEP

Boulder Outlook Hotel & Suites
Travelling with dog? Book one of the designated "Fido rooms" at this zero-waste hotel. ☎ 303-443-3322; www.boulderoutlook.com; 800 28th St, Boulder; r from $100; ♿

Broadmoor Resort
One of the USA's top five-star resorts, everything about the property, from the golf greens to the Euro-style guestrooms, is just so. ☎ 719-634-7711; www.broadmoor.com; 1 Lake Ave; r from $250; ♿

Delaware Hotel
Victorian rooms and a suite, attentive service and a locally lauded restaurant in the heart of downtown. ☎ 719-486-1418; www.delawarehotel.com; 700 Harrison Ave, Leadville; r & ste $75-200; ♿

Stanley Hotel
Rooms are posh modern with 42in flat-screen TVs, neutral colors and plush duvets. ☎ 970-586-4964; www.stanleyhotel.com; 333 Wonderview Ave; r from $159, ghost tours $13

USEFUL WEBSITES
www.14ers.com

LINK YOUR TRIP
www.lonelyplanet.com/trip-planner

OUTDOORS

Colorado Ski Country

WHY GO From Aspen and Vail's world-class glitz to family and ski-bum favorite Breckenridge and local pick never-summer A-Basin (it's not called the highest resort in northern America for nothing), this trip takes you slope-side to toast the best of central Colorado ski country with much champagne (powder).

TIME
5 days

DISTANCE
140 miles

BEST TIME TO GO
Jan – Mar

START
Breckenridge, CO

END
Aspen, CO

The Colorado Rockies are synonymous with riding waxed plastic objects down snow-slicked mountains in winter, but ❶ Breckenridge takes passion for skiing and snowboarding to a whole new level. Nowhere else in Colorado is the state's coming-of-age ritual, affectionately called 'ski-bumming,' practiced by recent college graduates with such rigorous devotion as in Breck (the town's local abbreviation). As a result, Breck has a low-key, lived-in vibe missing from more sterile Vail, and a serious reputation for hard partying.

The ❷ Breckenridge Ski Area, sitting right downtown, covers four different mountains and all skill sets. Peak 8 is the local pick for riding, serving up a number of terrain parks and a giant half-pipe. From here you catch the T-bar up to the ❸ Imperial Express Superchair, which at 12,840ft is the highest chairlift in the USA. From the top, the Snow White area offers 150 acres of above-tree-line double-black backcountry bowls, the best of which can be reached only after hiking. Arrive early on a fresh-powder morning to score new tracks through deep snow, and you won't notice how long you've been walking. Not an expert? Beginners should know Breckenridge's green runs – of which there are plenty on Peak 8 and Peak 9 – are some of the state's easiest and most flat.

Make Breckenridge your Summit County base. Check into the ❹ Fireside Inn B&B & Hostel for three nights. Rooms are more than

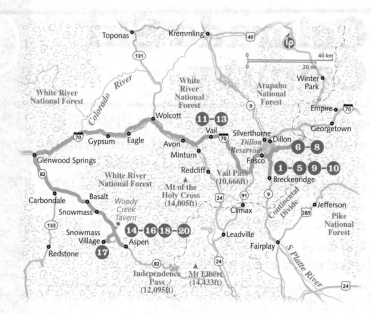

comfortable, and there's a hot tub to soak away sore muscles. Have dinner at ⑤ **Downstairs at Eric's**, a Breckenridge institution locals flock to for pitchers of microbrews, juicy burgers and delicious mashed potatoes. There are more than 120 beers to choose from. The basement joint also features a full-on video-gaming area, in a room separate from the restaurant.

Ski unpretentious ⑥ **A-Basin Ski Area**, 15 miles from Breckenridge, the next day. With its bottom at 13,000ft, it's North America's highest-base-elevation ski resort (more than likely winning on more than one level) and the local pick to ride. This is especially true in spring, when temps warm up enough for large tailgate cookouts and parties in the big parking lot – known universally as "the Beach" – to start in earnest. FYI, April is one of Colorado's snowiest months, and there is something very alluring about skiing in less-than-sub-zero temperatures.

Filled with steeps, chutes and walls, A-Basin isn't beginner friendly but can't be beat for thrilling backcountry descents. Ride the Zuma lift to access ⑦ **Montezuma Bowl**. Here you'll find 36 thrilling backcountry (but still in bounds) intermediate-to-expert runs. The Jump is the biggest, baddest run on Montezuma, beginning with a 10ft drop off the mountain's ledge into a 35-degree-angle steep trail. The ⑧ **East Wall**, which includes the only-accessible-by-foot Shit for Brains run, is A-Basin's other legendary backcountry area. A-Basin's elevation usually keeps it open until mid-June.

The outdoor bar is a great place to kick back with a cold microbrew after a day on the slopes.

Back in Breckenridge, locals in the know don't miss happy hour at the **9** **Hearthstone Inn**. The fine-dining restaurant – known for its elk tenderloin and trout dishes – offers the best deal around between 4pm and 6pm daily. Of course many start with happy-hour shrimp and cocktails, then move on to the romantic Victorian dining room for the main course. Ski bums love to rag on **10** **Cecilia's**, but this doesn't stop them from flocking to this long-established party spot nightly. After dinner, head to the basement martini bar with a big dance floor to jive the night away. There's even a corner couch for making out.

NORDIC VAIL

You don't need to pay big bucks – or scare yourself silly flying downhill – to enjoy all the snow sports around Vail and Aspen. Cross-country skiers can get their fix at the **Cordillera Nordic Center** (www.cordillera-vail.com), 15 miles west of Vail in Edwards. Check with the White River National Forest Holy Cross Ranger District for details on nearby backcountry ski routes such as Shrine Pass.

Just under 40 miles west of Breckenridge on I-70, **11** **Vail Mountain Resort** is Summit County's most famous swanky winter playground. This is where the movie stars and tycoons ski, and it's not odd to see Texans in 10-gallon hats and ladies in mink coats zipping down the slopes. If you're a Colorado ski novice it's worth paying to take your first run here. Vail lives up to its hallowed vertical reputation. Stretching 6 miles, the area is famous for its wide-open **12** **Back Bowls**, offering 2734 acres of choose-your-path riding for intermediate and advanced skiers and boarders. On a blue-sky powder day, this is as close to heaven as we've gotten. Speaking of blue sky, for a slightly less vertical backcountry experience visit **13** **Blue Sky Basin**, where the intermediate trails are solitary and powder packed.

"On a blue-sky powder day, this is as close to heaven as we've gotten."

If you liked Vail, you'll love **14** **Aspen**, just around 100 miles southwest. The town rivals Vail for star power, and kicks it into another stratosphere when it comes to architectural charm. There is no condo-and-coffee-shop cluster of businesses constructed to resemble a French Alps village here. Nope, Aspen is the real deal: an authentic silver-mining town with a true-blue Wild West pedigree that doubles as a high-octane winter resort, hosting some of the world's wealthiest riders.

The Aspen Skiing Company runs the area's four resorts, and it's OK to mountain hop on a single lift ticket. **15** **Aspen Mountain** (or Ajax) is the signature peak. Open since 1847, and bumped right up with the city, it serves up a smorgasbord of trails – from easy groomers to moguls and double-black shoots – accessed via shiny gondolas you might very well be sharing with a famous face. At the end of the day fly down the Little Nell run right up to the eternally chic ⑯ **Ajax Tavern** for oysters on the half-shell, truffle fries and steaming Irish coffees with the celebrity fur-boot-wearing crowd. Inside the historic Little Nell hotel, one of the city's premier sleeping spots, it's been Aspen's favorite après-ski spot for years now.

Just a short drive down Hwy 82, ⑰ **Snowmass** is the Aspen Ski Company's other main squeeze. The recent recipient of a $1 billion facelift meant to bring the village to Aspen glamour standards by adding swank hotels, bars and restaurants, Snowmass remains a skier's and snowboarder's mountain at heart, boasting the USA's longest vertical drop at 4400ft and champagne powder terrain for all levels and riding styles.

Head back to Aspen for the night, where the personable and unpretentious ⑱ **Hotel Jerome** exudes historic elegance. Rooms feature period antiques, marble baths with big tubs and thick down comforters on the beds. A ski concierge and a heated outdoor pool help round out the reasons to sleep here, but one of the best is easy access to the onsite ⑲ **J-Bar**, which has served as Aspen's premier saloon since 1889. Full of historic charm, it's always packed with everyone from local shopkeepers to Hollywood stars. Order the signature Aspen Crud cocktail if you're in the mood for something sweet. It's a delicious blend of bourbon and ice cream! The more tart J-Rita is equally delicious. The menu features gourmet American pub fare that's nearly as tasty as the drinks.

> **DETOUR** A local haunt for decades now, and the late Hunter S Thompson's favorite watering hole, **Woody Creek Tavern** is well worth the 8-mile winding trek from Aspen: take Hwy 82 west to Smith Way, turn right into Woody Creek Canyon, make a left on Upper River Rd, a sharp right on Woody Creek Dr and then a left onto Little Woody Creek Dr. Covered in Thompson paraphernalia, this is where Johnny Depp and the gonzo journalist became friends. The tavern is open for dinner only, and serves excellent burgers.

Aspen's handsome, historic red-brick downtown is full of unique boutiques, classy saloons and gourmet eating establishments – no other Colorado town (not even Denver) can boast standalone Louis Vuitton, Gucci, Prada and Chanel stores. In early 2010 Aspen's attitude was considered glamorous enough to merit its own reality show, the locally controversial *Secrets of Aspen*. Most of the haute-couture shopping is found on Galena St, Aspen's version of Rodeo Dr. Visit Hopkins Ave, dubbed Restaurant Row, for posh eateries like ⑳ **Jimmy's**, the perfect place to bid your Colorado ski trip goodbye with top-shelf tequila. Aspen's top spot for dinner and dancing, Jimmy's is a steak and crab shack with an attitude, attracting a very A-list crowd. Settle into a well-loved booth, order your favorite cut of meat and check out the writing on the wall. No, we're not being cryptic: Jimmy's idea of decorating is covering the walls with guest graffiti. Bring a pen. You're paying a king's ransom to dine with the rich and famous, so you may as well leave your mark! Or you could just eat in the perpetually packed bar, which has a less expensive menu and serves 105 types of tequila and mescal.

Becca Blond

OUTDOORS

TRIP INFORMATION

GETTING THERE

Breckenridge is 100 miles from Denver via I-70 west to Hwy 9 south. Colorado Mountain Express runs shuttles from Denver International Airport.

DO

A-Basin Ski Area

North America's highest-elevation resort, Arapahoe Basin usually stays open until mid-June. ☎ **970-468-0718; www.arapahoebasin.com; 28194 Hwy 6, Keystone; lift ticket $65;** 🕑 **hours vary**

Aspen & Snowmass Mountains

Aspen's four mountains are operated by Aspen Skiing Company and lift tickets are interchangeable. ☎ **970-925-1220; www.aspensnowmass.com; lift ticket $96;** 🕑 **hours vary**

Breckenridge Ski Area

Spanning four mountains, Breck has some of the region's best beginner and intermediate terrain and a renowned snowboard park. ☎ **800-789-7669; www.breckenridge.snow.com; Hwy 9, Breckenridge; lift ticket $92;** 🕑 **hours vary**

Vail Mountain Resort

It's not just glam; the mountain also serves up some of the country's best back-bowl powder skiing. ☎ **970-476-9090; www.vail.com; I-70, Vail; lift ticket $97;** 🕑 **hours vary**

EAT & DRINK

Ajax Tavern

Inside the historic Little Nell, it's been voted best après-ski bar and dining spot in Aspen. ☎ **970-920-6334; 685 E Durant Ave, Aspen; mains $10-30;** 🕑 **11:30am-10pm**

Cecilia's

A long-established après-dark club, Cecilia's comes with all the essential party fixings, including a big dance floor. ☎ **970-453-2243; 520 S Main St, Breckenridge;** 🕑 **2pm-2am**

Downstairs at Eric's

This basement institution serves pitchers of microbrews and delicious burgers, sandwiches and pizzas. ☎ **970-453-1401; 111 S Main St, Breckenridge; mains from $6;** 🕑 **11am-10.30pm**

Hearthstone Inn

Fantastic happy-hour specials as well as gourmet dinners inside a cozy, antique-filled Victorian inn. ☎ **970-453-1148; 130 S Ridge St, Breckenridge; mains $15-40;** 🕑 **5:30-10pm**

J-Bar

Down an Aspen Crud at this fantastically happening watering hole. ☎ **877-412-7725; 330 E Main St, Aspen; mains $8-15;** 🕑 **11.30am-1am**

Jimmy's

Aspen's dinner and dancing spot du jour attracts a very A-list crowd and, specializes in tequila and surf and turf. ☎ **970-925-6020; 205 S Mill St, Aspen; mains $15-50;** 🕑 **11.30-10pm**

SLEEP

Fireside Inn B&B & Hostel

A clean, welcoming hostel and B&B with friendly staff; there's a hot tub for après-ski soaking and easy downtown access. ☎ **970-453-6456; www.firesideinn.com; 114 N French St, Breckenridge; dm $28-38, r incl breakfast $90-160**

Hotel Jerome

A posh, historic ski hotel so luxuriously comfy you'll want to snuggle in and never leave. ☎ **877-412-7725, 330 E Main St, Aspen; r from $200**

USEFUL WEBSITES

www.aspenchamber.org

www.gobreck.com

LINK YOUR TRIP

www.lonelyplanet.com/trip-planner

TRIP

6 The Great Divide Treasure Hunt p95

65 48 Hours in Greater Denver p467

66 Summit Colorado: The 14er Club p473

Wild West Wyoming

WHY GO From broncs and bulls at rodeo to cowboys riding the wind-whipped range, galloping with legends and pageantry, central Wyoming can feel like a blockbuster country ballad. Follow this trail through the heart of beef, bull and Buffalo Bill territory for the best of Wyoming's Wild West, past and present.

TIME
5 – 6 days

DISTANCE
550 miles

BEST TIME TO GO
Jun – Aug

START
Sheridan, WY

END
Cheyenne, WY

The pioneer spirit is alive and rocking in the Cowboy State's cultural heartland, blowing as hard and true as the region's famous winds. Whether you are craving a big steak, a stay at a dude ranch or to follow in the footsteps of the Wild West's ultimate No 1 fan, Buffalo Bill Cody, you'll find an adventure on the plains between Sheridan and Cody, Lander, Laramie and Cheyenne.

Begin in ❶ Sheridan. The cattle-on-the-prairie town with a pedigreed past is one of Wyoming's hottest weekend-adventure destinations, with nouveau West attitude that's authentic rather than campy. Comprising about 50 meticulously restored two-story brick buildings dating back a century, the historic Main St district is one of the state's best preserved. Visit ❷ King's Saddlery & Don King Museum at the southern end; it's where locals shop for boots and bridles. The Western tack shop is renowned for its hand-tooled leather. Three generations of the King family dedicated themselves to collecting Native American artifacts and Wild West memorabilia the world over – you can see the collection in the museum adjacent to the saddlery. After purchasing the correct gear, it's time to pony up, cowboy, and hit the range. ❸ South Fork Mountain Lodge & Outfitters runs hourly and overnight guided horseback-riding trips, including a good-length four-hour lunch ride into the Bighorn National Forest.

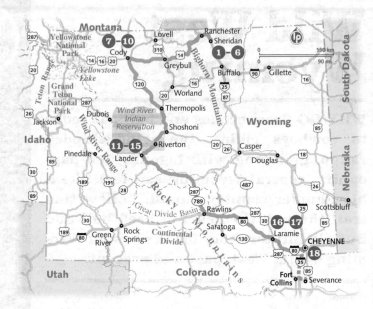

One of 17 National Historic Landmarks in Wyoming, the ④ **Sheridan Hotel** is Buffalo Bill Cody's old place – he used to audition his Wild West show performers from its front porch. Built with B&M Railway money in 1893, it once attracted the likes of Ernest Hemingway, Will Rogers and presidents Theodore Roosevelt and William Howard Taft. The hotel stopped taking overnight guests in 1965, when the park service bestowed on it historic status, but not before the place acquired one permanent resident: 89-year-old hotel housekeeper and hostess Kate Arnold. Arnold had lived and worked here for 64 years, right up until her death just three years before the hotel closed. For some only-in-Wyoming reason (or maybe it's the hotel; its ornately gabled roof made it into *Ripley's Believe It or Not!* in 1949 as the "House of 69 Gables"), Arnold's cremated ashes were placed in the wall of her 3rd-floor bedroom, which it's said her ghost still haunts.

Sleeping is no longer permitted at the Sheridan, but the ⑤ **1893 Grill & Spirits** still serves a mean cut of beef amid equally delicious old-fashioned ambience. Before dining, grab a "ditch" (that's Wyoming-speak for whiskey and water) from the same mahogany wood bar where Buffalo Bill and Hemingway used to linger. It's said Cody always sat on the third stool from the left and paid with a $20 coin when drinking at his own establishment. During the Wild West days, reputable women wouldn't set foot in the Sheridan's bar and card room; however, quite a few horses did. Equines entered with their riders after races across the plains – the winning human was responsible for buying everyone a round of drinks. Walk off dinner in Sheridan's former red-light district. Main St just south of the inn once housed the city's brothels, seedy hotels and true-blue Western shoot-out watering holes: the building at 304 N Main St wasn't called the Bucket of Blood Saloon for no reason.

Bunk at ❻ **Spahn's Big Horn Mountain Bed & Breakfast**, 15 miles west of town. Wyoming's oldest B&B features ecofriendly solar-powered rooms with patchwork quilts and claw-foot tubs in a four-story log cabin. The big deck is a great asset. Highlights of staying include evening wildlife safaris, where guides take guests on a search for moose and elk before serving a chuck-wagon-style supper in the prairie.

From Sheridan it's a 147-mile streak west over the Bighorn Mountains on Hwy 14 to ❼ **Cody**, the final Buffalo Bill–related pit stop on this trail. The "Wild West and proud of it" town, named for Mr Cody himself, has a prime location just 52 miles east

RODEO TIME IN THE ROCKIES

The Rockies' biggest rodeo, **Cheyenne Frontier Days**, has been rocking the state capital for 10 days at the end of July since 1919. The mega event has no fewer than nine daily rodeos with more than 40 bucking bulls and 70 bareback-bronc riders. The **Buffalo Bill Cody Stampede Rodeo** isn't quite as big, but it's just as old. Held over five days in early July, it's unique in its incorporation of spectacles from Cody's Wild West shows into the modern pageantry.

of Yellowstone National Park. Gorgeous distant Teton views, coupled with Cody's enthusiastic efforts to preserve and dramatically re-tell its storied past, make it one of Wyoming's top roadside attractions. The superb ❽ **Buffalo Bill Historical Center** showcases everything Western: look for posters, grainy films and other lore pertaining to Buffalo Bill's world-famous Wild West shows and museums dedicated to Native Americans.

Spend the night at the ❾ **Irma Hotel**, built by ol' Mr Bill himself in 1902. It offers historic rooms in the main building or more modern, less expensive motel-style rooms next door. Don't miss the ornate cherrywood bar at the on-site Silver Saddle Saloon. It was a gift from Queen Victoria. Gunfights break out at 6pm in front of the hotel June through September.

Cody calls itself the "Rodeo Capital of the World," and with the country's longest continuously running rodeo, it just might be. The ❿ **Cody Nite Rodeo** runs for 87 nights straight, from June through August. Started in 1939, it has its roots in ranch contests and games, and began as an outlet for ranchers, working huge, isolated plots of land, to come together and socialize during the short summers. Seventy years later, it's still going strong, and many of the young competitors are Wyoming cowboys and girls, who come to Cody in summer to race barrels and rope calves in the night rodeo. Grab a turkey leg, burrito or funnel cake from the lit-up vendors and have a county-fair-style dinner before the main show.

Refreshingly unpretentious ⑪ **Lander** is a hippie-cowboy mountaineering town just a stone's throw from the glacier-pocked Wind River Range, 163 miles south of Cody. It's the kind of place where twentysomething boys and girls wearing dreads *and* Stetsons talk rock climbing and cattle with local ranchers and Arapahoe Indians at the Wild West saloon turned microbrewery. It's also locked in hot competition with Sheridan for Wyoming's best adventure town. Try ⑫ **Sinks Canyon State Park** for a fresh-air, blood-circulating fix. Six miles south of Lander on Sinks Canyon Rd (Hwy 131), it's the area's premier rock-climbing spot, but it's worth visiting for the perplexing natural features alone: the Middle Fork of the Popo Agie River flows through the narrow canyon and disappears into the soluble Madison limestone mountain. The river pops up faster and warmer a quarter of a mile downstream in a pool called the Rise. If you know how to climb, and want to, Sinks features the best rocks in the region. Outdoor shops in Lander can point you in the right direction.

> "twentysomething boys and girls wearing dreads and Stetsons talk rock climbing and cattle..."

Lander is also home to the coolest bar-and-restaurant row in Wyoming. Exactly one block long, the four establishments making up the Colter Row Block are all under the same ownership, but hey, we're not going to knock this energizing development. The businesses are eye-catching, renovated with historic accuracy and connected by series of decks that create a European-café-meets-college-party-hopping vibe. Begin with a before-dinner pint at the legendary ⑬ **Lander Bar**, which has been around long enough to have a horse-hitching post out front. Its barnlike interior pays tribute to Wyoming's Western history, with memorabilia from its mining, ranching, Native American and mountain-climbing past gracing its walls, and the classic Wyoming saloon hosts live bands on weekends. The Rock Chuck Rye is what to order – it's a Great American Beer Festival gold medal winner. Wander two doors down for dinner at ⑭ **Cowfish**, which serves cow cooked four different ways, as well as fish – hence the moniker. The environs are posh comfortable, with high tin ceilings and exposed-brick walls. Order the "CowCrustacian" for something different; it's the restaurant's version of surf and turf. For sleeping, try the ⑮ **Pronghorn Lodge**. It has faultless spacious rooms, plus a hot tub, just one block from downtown.

It's 225 miles south from Lander to the windswept prairie town of ⑯ **Laramie**. In the heart of the flat grasslands, Wyoming's legendary winds blow strong and steady here. Wind aside, Laramie is Wyoming's cultural hub, infused with a lively energy thanks to the student population attending the state's only four-year university here. Stretch your legs with a stroll and a window shop around the compact downtown before continuing 21 miles west on Hwy 130 to the **⑰ Vee Bar Guest Ranch**, this trip's final sleeping destination. If you have a few extra vacation days at your disposal, we'd suggest booking in for more than one night. Most guests stay a week at this authentic dude ranch, but even two nights allows a taste of the experience – and enough time to partake of more of the included activities, from horseback rides across the range to fly fishing, river tubing and overnight campouts. Single-night stays are possible on Saturday in summer and other nights the rest of the year. Digs are in comfortable, rustic and old-fashioned cabins. Dinners are steak-and-seafood affairs.

It's a quick 50-mile dash east on I-80 to this trip's finish line, **⑱ Cheyenne**. Sitting at the crossroads of two major highways, I-80 and north–south route I-25, in the spot where the Rocky Mountains crash into the prairie, it's Wyoming's state capital and largest city, but other than during two weeks in July when the rodeo comes to town, it doesn't offer much for travelers, especially considering big-smoke Denver is just 100 miles south. To get back to where you started, in Sheridan, head north on I-25 for 325 miles.

Becca Blond

> **DETOUR**
>
> No Wyoming beef-and-bull trip would be complete without tasting the ultimate local delicacy, Rocky Mountain oysters – like their cousin-by-name-only relatives, they're purported to have aphrodisiac qualities. Luckily, **Bruce's Bar**, the establishment responsible for starting the fried-testicle-eating phenomenon (original owner Bruce Ruth cooked the first ball basket in 1959), is just 54 miles from Cheyenne, across the Colorado line in oh-so-appropriately named Severance. Take I-25 south to Hwy 14 east to get here. The restaurant is at 123 First St.

TRIP INFORMATION

GETTING THERE
Sheridan is 425 miles north of Denver and 325 miles north of Cheyenne on I-25.

DO

Buffalo Bill Historical Center
A sprawling complex of five museums; the main showcase is devoted to Buffalo Bill. ☎ 307-587-4771; www.bbhc.org; 720 Sheridan Ave, Cody; adult/child $15/6; ⏰ 7am-8pm Jun-Aug, 10am-3pm Tue-Sun Sep-May

Cody Nite Rodeo
Held for 87 nights straight; gates open at 7pm. ☎ 307-587-2992; www.codystampede rodeo.com; Stampede Park, 421 W Yellowstone Ave, Cody; adult/child from $18/8; ⏰ 8pm Jun 1-Aug 31

King's Saddlery & Don King Museum
One of the region's largest collections of Native American artifacts and cowboy memorabilia is found here. ☎ 307-672-2702; www.kingsropes.com; 184 N Main St, Sheridan; admission free; ⏰ 8am-5pm Mon-Sat

Sinks Canyon State Park
The park is open year round from dawn to dusk. In summer a visitors center also opens. ☎ visitors center 307-332-3077; 3079 Sinks Canyon Rd, Lander; ⏰ 9am-6pm Jun-Aug

South Fork Mountain Lodge & Outfitters
Does guided horseback-riding trips into the Bighorn Mountains, including a four-hour ride with lunch. ☎ 307-267-2609; www.southfork-lodge.com; Hwy 16 W, Sheridan; lunch trip $90

EAT & DRINK

1893 Grill & Spirits
Inside the Sheridan Inn, it's known for delicious cuts of Wyoming beef and a bar Ernest Hemingway once favored. ☎ 307-673-2777; www.1893grill.come; 866 N Broadway, Sheridan; lunch $6-10, dinner $15-40; ⏰ 11am-9pm, bar open later

Cowfish
This restaurant serves cow four different ways, along with seafood. Order its version of surf and turf, the "CowCrustacian." ☎ 307-332-7009; 128 Main St, Lander; mains $10-30; ⏰ 11am-late

Lander Bar
There's live music many nights at this landmark big-barn bar serving local microbrews. ☎ 307-332-8228; 126 Main St, Lander; mains $6-10; ⏰ 11am-late

SLEEP

Irma Hotel
Book Buffalo Bill's old suite at this historic 1902 hotel. ☎ 307-587-4221; www.irmahotel.com; 1192 Sheridan Ave, Cody; r $100-150

Pronghorn Lodge
Good value, central and clean, it has a hot tub onsite. Rates include breakfast. ☎ 307-332-3940; www.pronghornlodge.com; 150 Main St, Lander; r $65-150

Spahn's Big Horn Mountain Bed & Breakfast
Wyoming's oldest B&B, 15 miles west of Sheridan, also does nightly wildlife safaris and cookouts for $40. ☎ 307-674-8150; www.bighorn-wyoming.com; Hwy 335, Sheridan; r & cabins $115-175

Vee Bar Guest Ranch
Offers a true-blue Wyoming dude ranch experience, 21 miles west of Laramie. A two-night minimum applies for all nights except Saturday June through August. ☎ 307-745-7036; www.vee-bar.com; 2081 Hwy 130; r day/week incl all meals & activities $150/1450

USEFUL WEBSITES
www.wyomingtourism.org

LINK YOUR TRIP
www.lonelyplanet.com/trip-planner

Tripping Through Grand Teton & Yellowstone

WHY GO For an Alice-in-Wonderland outdoor adventure, pay Yellowstone and Grand Teton National Parks a visit. From a hallucinogenic landscape of sulfur-burping hot pots and mammoth mountains to half the world's geysers and the whole must-see animal line-up, everything about these blockbuster natural treasures is super-sized surreal.

TIME
7 days

DISTANCE
250 miles

BEST TIME TO GO
Jun – Sep

START
Jackson, WY

END
Yellowstone National Park, WY

Filled with trippy geothermal features, safari-worthy wildlife and gargantuan mountains, the nearly conjoined (just 8 miles apart) national parks conjure up the au-naturel-meets-psychedelic American Dream. Enter the looking glass through a portal in Wyoming's northwest corner. **①** **Jackson**, sitting just south of Grand Teton National Park's southern entrance, is more than a park gateway. It's a chic destination on its own, Wyoming's most cosmopolitan town, where cowboy meets couture. Wander into the venerable **②** **Million Dollar Cowboy Bar** to get a true taste of its character. Once the regional center for illegal gambling, today the bar is a melting pot of ski bums and tourists, hipsters, ranchers and movie stars. Spend the night at the **③** **Anvil Motel**, which has a great location, in a red barnlike building, just a block from the hopping central square. Rooms have a Western motif, and the best perk to sleeping here is the available passes to the nearby rec center, which has an indoor pool, a waterslide, a hot tub, a workout room and our personal favorite, the dry sauna.

Wake early. Grab breakfast at the **④** **Harvest Bakery & Cafe**. The natural-foods store – filled with organic produce, fresh breads and baked goods – also features a sit-down café that's a bit of a Jackson eating institution, serving a cornucopia of yummy breakfast choices, from blue-corn pancakes to challah French toast. **⑤** **Grand Teton National Park** is just 12 miles north of Jackson on Hwy 89, but drive

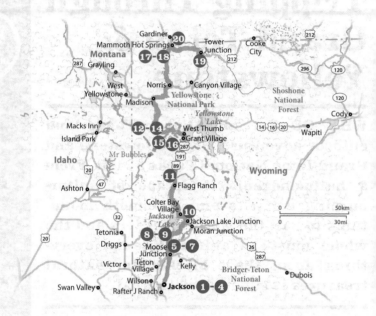

slow. Whether this is visit number one or 10, the view approaching these craggy peaks is so dramatic it elicits gasps each time. The Tetons' dozen highest peaks seem to surge straight up, like a demented 12,000ft granite-and-glacier-capped monster, blocking the end of the pavement rolling out front of your car. The youngest chain of the Rocky Mountains, the Teton Range was formed about nine million years ago, the result of a 40-mile-long earthquake. The Shoshone, the region's original human inhabitants, called the strange-looking mountains Teewinot (meaning many pinnacles). But it was the name bestowed by bohemian French trappers in the early 19th century that stuck. They dubbed the most prominent peaks (including the showcase 13,7700ft Grand Teton) "Les Trois Tetons" for their ostensible resemblance to female breasts.

Enter the park through Moose Gate and pause at nearby **6** **Craig Thomas Discovery & Visitor Center** for backcountry permits, trail guides and the scoop on where to look for bear and moose. It also has good natural-history exhibits and a well-produced film that introduces the park. Just north of the visitors center is the turn-off for Antelope Flats Rd, leading to **7** **Mormon Row**, your next stop. Here, in a gorgeous sage-and-wildflower-encrusted tundra locale, against a picture-perfect Teton backdrop, are a series of original homesteader barns and cabins built by early Mormon settlers. It's a beautiful photo op.

When you've finished playing Ansel Adams in the meadow, head north to **8** **Jenny Lake Lodge**, your destination for the next two nights. The most exclusive park lodging, it's our favorite guilty Teton pleasure, and one of those once-in-a-lifetime memories worth paying top dollar for. With the exception of lunch, rates include meals and activities like horseback riding and mountain biking. Take advantage of both this afternoon, as the next day is fully booked. Dress up for dinner (men, this means a jacket). It's a romantic, candlelit, five-course affair.

"It's a chic destination on its own, Wyoming's most cosmopolitan town, where cowboy meets couture."

Get a good night's sleep, and eat hearty at breakfast. Your second day in Grand Teton involves an epic hike. Gaining nearly 3000ft in elevation, the **9** **Amphitheater Lake Trail** is a strenuous 9.6-mile round-trip lung buster. If you can handle the uphill assault, this is one of the few hikes in the park that takes you into and out of the backcountry in a single day. The trail ascends through wildflower-carpeted meadows and dense forests – keep an eye out for foraging bears who consider the whitebark pine here a delicacy – before dumping you out on a monstrous rocky plateau. Here, under the imposing granite guard of Disappointment Peak, and within view of the two tallest Tetons, two shimmering glacier lakes await. Plunge into the first, called Surprise, to experience the ultimate cool-down. You'll figure out one reason for the moniker the moment your body hits the icy water. Toast your polar-bear swim upon returning to the lodge, with champagne on the magnificent front porch overlooking the namesake lake at sunset. The views are nothing short of inspirational.

DETOUR ▶ The 27-mile (each way) **Bechler River Trail** is our favorite Yellowstone backcountry trip. Not only does this three-day hike give a feel for the huge park's diverse ecosystem, it also provides access to its best backcountry soak, **Mr Bubbles**. Located about halfway down the trail, the giant natural hot tub (named for the bubbling plume rising from the center) can seat 20 and is deep enough for floating – preferably under the light of a silver moon. To make night swimming a reality, reserve campsite 9D1 in advance. Less than a mile from Mr Bubbles, it's the only nearby tent spot.

The next morning, after a final horseback ride, it's time to head to Yellowstone. The drive out takes you north along the Snake River, through the rest of Grand Teton National Park, and there are a couple noteworthy pit stops, including the historic Jackson Lake Lodge. Perched on a bluff overlooking the park's biggest lake, it's worth a pause if only to ogle the views from the 60ft picture windows in the magnificent lobby. Inside the lodge, grab a milkshake and burger for lunch at the onsite **10** **Pioneer Grill**. Meals are served 1950s soda fountain–style, at countertops laid out in a serpentine shape across the room.

Protected by Ulysses S Grant in 1872, **⑪ Yellowstone National Park** was the USA's first national park and remains one of its most iconic and popular, attracting about 30,000 visitors per day in summer. Covering an astounding 3472 sq miles, it's also massive. Enter through the South Gate, remembering to show your Grand Teton admission ticket so you don't pay twice, and go west on the loop road to the **⑫ Old Faithful Visitor Center** for info. From here, it's on to **⑬ Old Faithful Inn**, your home for the next two nights. Built right next to the geyser of the same name, the national historic landmark embodies the dreamy ideal of the perfect national-park retreat. The immense timber lobby, with its huge stone fireplaces and sky-high knotted-pine ceilings, is the sort of place where you'd imagine Teddy Roosevelt lingering.

You could join the throng at the ropes in front, but our favorite way to see the park's signature geyser, **⑭ Old Faithful**, explode is from the lodge porch. After checking in, ask when the next eruption should occur – the geyser spits between 3700 and 8400 gallons of water about 150ft into the air every 1½ hours or so. Afterwards, have dinner at the lodge restaurant, which serves the best nouveau American West cuisine in Yellowstone – veggies beware, there's lots of seasoned game with eclectic sauces.

Old Faithful is just one of 250 geysers in Yellowstone, and after breakfast on day four it's time to check out some more. Today's hike is a monstrous 17-mile round trip if done in its entirety. If you aren't up for such a long haul, the trail is an in-and-out affair, meaning you can easily hike only as far as you feel comfortable, then turn around. Even just walking 2.5 miles to the first point of interest, **⑮ Lone Star Geyser**, gives a good feel for the area's trippy geothermal scenery of steaming vents, gurgling streams and oily-looking hot pools shimmering a psychedelic rainbow of red, yellow, green, grey and blue (the crazy colors are the result of sulfur and bacteria in the water). Try to synchronize your arrival at Lone Star with the solitary geyser's predicted eruption. It's quite a sight – 50ft plumes of water shooting sky high for up to 15 minutes. Lone Star goes off every two to three hours and, though there are no posted eruption times, if you ask nicely at the ranger station they'll often clue you in.

From Lone Star continue on 6 miles to **⑯ Shoshone Lake**. With no road access, it's the largest backcountry lake outside Alaska. Framed by wide grassy meadows and sitting in a geyser basin, it's far removed from the crowds and a reflective spot for lunch. You'll have to return home the way you came in, but the trail is packed with such a varied fantasy landscape you won't mind doubling back for a second look.

Go north to **⑰ Mammoth Hot Springs** on your last full day in Yellowstone. More than 115,000 years old, it is North America's oldest known, and most volatile, continuously active thermal area. After checking out the big spring, it's time for a dip in the ⑱ **Boiling River**, the park's top accessible hot-spring swimming hole, reached via an easy half-mile footpath from a parking lot on the eastern side of the road 2.3 miles north of Mammoth. The hot springs here tumble over travertine rocks into the cool Gardner River, creating a waterfall and warm swimming hole surrounded by lush vegetation below. Although it's usually crowded, soaking here is still a treat. There's also some cool trivia associated with the trail. It lies on the 45th parallel, which means the springs are on the same latitude as Minneapolis, Venice, Belgrade and northern Japan. You can snap a picture in front of an official sign marking the imaginary global line's location, just north of the trailhead parking lot, where the road crosses the Gardner River.

Spend your last night in Yellowstone at ⑲ **Roosevelt Lodge Cabins**, located slightly south and east of Mammoth Hot Springs (you'll head east on the loop road). This is the park's most remote and wild region, and it perfectly matches this hotel's rugged cowboy vibe. Make sure to partake of an "Old West dinner cookout," where horses or wagons transport guests to a big meadow for a campfire dinner. It makes a fitting farewell to this great American national-park road trip. Tomorrow you'll leave the park via the ⑳ **north entrance** at the Montana state line.

Becca Blond

SAFARI YELLOWSTONE

Shaggy grizzlies and barrel-chested black bears, solitary moose, herds of elk, mountain lions, lynxes, beavers, even the elusive gray wolf: when it comes to safari-worthy wildlife, Yellowstone has all the hot animals. **Hayden Valley**, in Yellowstone's heart, is your best all-round bet for wildlife viewing. Check along the Yellowstone River between Yellowstone Lake and Canyon Village. **Lamar Valley**, in the north of the park, is ground zero for spotting wolves. Dawn and dusk are the best wildlife-spotting times.

TRIP INFORMATION

GETTING THERE
Jackson is 563 miles northwest of Denver via I-25 north to I-80 west to Hwy 191 north.

DO

Craig Thomas Discovery & Visitor Center
Grand Teton's main visitors center, it has exhibits and info galore. ☎ 307-739-3309; www.nps.gov/grte; Grand Teton National Park; ☙ 8am-7pm Jun-Aug, 9am-5pm Sep-May

Grand Teton National Park
Grand Teton's main road closes to motorized vehicles in mid-October. ☎ 307-739-3399; www.nps.gov/grte; Teton Park Rd, Grand Teton National Park; admission $25

Old Faithful Visitor Center
The place to snag backcountry permits and reserve camping spots. ☎ 307-344-2107; www.nps.gov/yell/planyourvisit/backcountryhiking.htm; Grand Loop Rd, Yellowstone National Park; campsites $12; ☙ 8:30am-4pm Jun-Aug

Yellowstone National Park
Only the north entrance is open year-round; admission is good for a week and at Grand Teton. ☎ 307-344-2263; www.nps.gov/yell; Grand Loop Rd, Mammoth, Yellowstone National Park; admission $25; ☙ north entrance year-round, south entrance May-Oct

EAT & DRINK

Harvest Bakery & Cafe
Inside a natural-food store, the café serves wholesome breakfasts, sandwiches and smoothies. ☎ 307-733-5418; 130 W Broadway, Jackson; mains $4-10; ☙ 8am-3pm Mon-Sat

Million Dollar Cowboy Bar
This Jackson landmark, with a giant-neon-signed entrance, is kitschy West and entertaining inside. ☎ 307-733-2207; 25 N Cache Dr, Jackson; mains $8-20; ☙ 11am-late

Pioneer Grill
This 1950s-style soda fountain offers reasonably priced burgers, shakes and grilled cheese served at countertops. ☎ 307-543-1911; Jackson Lake Lodge; mains $7-15; ☙ 7am-9pm; ♿

SLEEP

Anvil Motel
Offers queen rooms with a Western motif, equipped with fridges and microwaves in a super-central location. ☎ 307-733-3668; www.anvilmotel.com; 215 N Cache Dr, Jackson; r $55-125

Jenny Lake Lodge
Digs are in 37 historic Western-styled cabins decked out with thick down comforters and handmade quilts. ☎ 307-543-3100; www.gtlc.com; cabins incl full board $585; ☙ Jun-Sep

Old Faithful Inn
Book in advance – this historic landmark is the park's most popular. The cheapest rooms share baths. The restaurant (lunch $7 to $10, dinner $17 to $30; open 11:30am to 2:30pm and 5pm to 10pm) serves nouveau American West cuisine. ☎ 307-545-4999, 307-344-7311; www.travelyellowstone.com; r $100-250

Roosevelt Lodge Cabins
A rustic and remote lodge featuring fun Wild West dinner cookouts. ☎ 307-344-7311; www.travelyellowstone.com; Roosevelt Country, Yellowstone National Park; cabins $70-120

USEFUL WEBSITES
www.jacksonholenet.com
www.wyomingtourism.org

LINK YOUR TRIP
www.lonelyplanet.com/trip-planner

Going Boho in Bozeman's Big Sky Country

WHY GO Bumped up against the beautiful Bridger Mountains in Big Sky Country's heart, Bozeman is Montana's classiest cowboy town. Whether it's boutique shopping, spa treatments and gourmet eating or a cultural and outdoor bonanza of hot-springs soaking, skiing and ice climbing, Bozeman delivers winter's perfect bohemian adventure.

TIME
4 days

DISTANCE
45 miles

BEST TIME TO GO
Dec – Mar

START
Bozeman, MT

END
Big Sky Resort, MT

Casual chic meets the great outdoors in Bozeman, a city with cowboy roots, Hollywood good looks and a modern attitude. Once the untamed domain of ranchers, cowboys, explorers and Native Americans, modern-day Bozeman is now home to a growing number of artists, real-estate developers, students and movie stars all hooked on the fabulous Montana high. Once you've had a hit of Bozeman's bountiful offerings you'll likely return to buy property – at least according to the latest census data: Bozeman's population grew 28% between 2000 and 2006. For a state where cows still outnumber people by 12 to one, that's quite an achievement.

If you can't pack up the crib and move straight to Montana, you can at least have a ball playing in ❶ Bozeman for a weekend. The location, rump up against the Bridger Mountains, means there's plenty of outdoor activities to keep you moving. But if you'd rather support the local economy with Main St shopping, eating and drinking, the historic downtown features tidy Old West brick buildings housing unique galleries, trendy boutiques and outdoor-gear shops, as well as bohemian wine bars and restaurants serving global fare under pressed-tin ceilings. In the heart of Big Sky Country, surrounded by the 1.8-million-acre Gallatin National Forest, and framed by the toothy smile of the Bridger range, Bozeman is also ideally situated for wilderness play – think Disneyland for the great outdoors. Although the town is gorgeous to visit any season, winter is particularly fun.

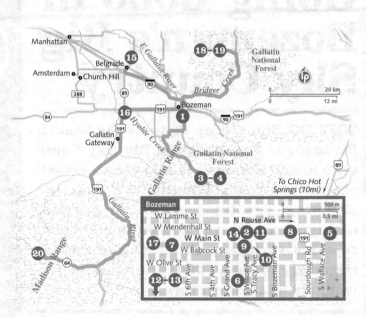

Fuel up at ❷ **Burger Bob's**, a greasy Old West spoon that's been serving cold beer and loaded burgers long enough to be considered a Bozeman institution. But don't eat too much: climbing frozen waterfalls is the next activity. When the temperature drops, ❸ **Hyalite Canyon**, just 11 miles south in the Gallatin National Forest, becomes the hottest destination for the coldest of sports. The small canyon is an ice-climber's paradise, boasting around 150 set routes. The friendly folks at ❹ **Montana Alpine Guides** will take newbies and pros. Although the steepest ascents average 600 vertical feet, the canyon has plenty of beginner climbs too, meaning you can't use the excuse that you've never ice climbed to get out of trying it.

"Bozeman is ideally situated for wilderness play – think Disneyland for the great outdoors."

Warm up after climbing with a drink at ❺ **Montana Ale Works.** In a century-old brick railroad warehouse at the historic east end of Main St, it serves upscale comfort food and 40 brews on tap. Besides the seven Northwest-style signature house drafts, Ale Works offers a sampling of Montana's best small-batch beers, with handcrafted creations from nine microbreweries across the state.

Check into the ❻ **Voss Inn**, Bozeman's most elegant sleeping option, for two nights. The charming establishment in an 1883 antique-furnished Victorian mansion is an easy stroll from downtown. It has six carefully restored rooms with terrycloth robes that are perfect for cold winter nights. Finish out the night bar hopping. Try **7** **Molly Brown**, a noisy student dive with pool tables and 20 on-tap beers. The **8** **Zebra Cocktail Lounge**, inside the Bozeman Hotel, is ground zero for the live-music scene.

After a gourmet waffle-and-whipped-cream breakfast at the Voss, search out Bozeman's bohemian underbelly. Hit the historic downtown: it's home to tidy two-story red-brick buildings, dating to the late 1880s, now housing chic boutiques and quality art galleries. Best of all, Montana has no state sales tax, which makes big-ticket purchases, like the exquisite rings or bracelets at earth-friendly **9** **Alara Jewelry**, much easier to justify. The unique jewelry is made from entirely recycled materials, and is mostly the creation of celebrated local designer Babs Noelle. The store purchases unwanted precious metal from customers and wholesalers, melts it and uses it to create new pieces of wearable art. Noelle also works directly with customers to design fantasy necklaces and engagement rings.

The **10** **Indian Uprising Gallery** is wonderful to wander, just to check out the traditional and contemporary collections by award-winning Native American artists. It features one of-a-kind artifacts and unique pieces covering centuries of Northern Plains Indian creativity. Take a lunch break at **11** **Plonk**, for an innovative and organic nouveau-American-meets-French-bistro menu in hip environs. Check out the period pressed-tin ceilings and long shotgun bar.

BOZEMAN TRIVIA

Gary Cooper fans will want to pay Bozeman Backpackers Hostel at 405 W Olive St a visit. Located in a beautiful 1890 Victorian home, the rocking independent hostel was once a boarding house where Cooper lived while attending Gallatin High School (now called the Willson School), down the corner. One of the hostel's bunk rooms is believed to have been Cooper's bedroom; today it's decorated with photos and information about the silver-screen star's early life.

With no fewer than eight museums, Bozeman claims the title of Montana's cultural. By far the cream of the crop is the award-worthy **12** **Museum of the Rockies** on the Montana State University campus. It covers an astonishing 4.6 million years' worth of Rocky Mountain history, geology, wildlife and culture. The permanent dinosaur exhibit is a must-see. The museum's curator of paleontology, Dr Jack Horner, served as a scientific consultant for *Jurassic Park*, and knows his dinosaurs. The exhibit includes a life-size cast of the world's biggest T-Rex skull and some of the only dinosaur eggs and nests known to exist. The planetarium, which features entertaining, high-tech laser shows, is also noteworthy.

Jump forward a few thousand millennia and check out a different kind of dinosaur – room-sized electronic computers, old key-punch machines and prototypes of the world's first video games – on display at the **13** **American Computer Museum**. Less than half a century ago these electronic devices were the cutting edge in technology; today they are considered museum-worthy collectables, nostalgic techie relics. Coming from the dinosaur exhibit at the Museum of the Rockies, the machines on display here seem almost comical.

All the museums and shopping and sore muscles from ice-climbing worn you out? Reboot at the totally Zen, locally owned ⑭ Loft Spa. It offers scintillating hot stone massages, rejuvenating facials and other pampering services. Remember Montana has no sales tax, so if you need upscale hair and skin products, check out the bookshelves in the comfortable, feels-like-a-living-room lobby, to stock up on both.

> **DETOUR** Soaking in the open-air mineral pools at unpretentious **Chico Hot Springs** is well worth driving 58 miles from Bozeman – follow I-90 east to Hwy 89 south. The relaxed spot has two open-air hot soaking pools. The larger one is the perfect temperature for floating (93°F); the smaller pool is hotter (103°F), but still not too hot to stay in long enough for wrinkles. The excellent restaurant serves steak and seafood, and the springs stay open until midnight.

The promised steak dinner comes courtesy of ⑮ John Bozeman's Bistro, a Montana roadhouse 8 miles northwest of town, which has made the National Register of Historic Places. It has equally impressive steak and wine menus and the big, juicy steaks, cooked as bloody as you like, are served at sleek booths. Old cowboy photos and a mounted longhorn head create the ambience. Afterwards take a romantic moonlight soak at nearby ⑯ Bozeman Hot Springs. One of 61 naturally hot mineral springs in the geothermally active region east of Yellowstone, with pools ranging from 59°F to 104°F, it's been attracting bathers since the late 1800s.

Get stoked for sick powder on day three. Grab a wake-me-up cup of fair-trade coffee from the upstairs café of the ⑰ Community Food Co-Op; then pick up picnic supplies for a slope-side lunch in its downstairs market. The nonprofit ⑱ Bridger Bowl Ski Area, owned by the community, is just 16 miles north of Bozeman. It's known for its fluffy, light powder and unbeatable lift-ticket prices. Spend night three at ⑲ Rainbow Ranch Lodge, near Bridger Bowl. It's an elegant place with a comfortable ambience that's nestled among the trees at the edge of the Gallatin River, offering guests an intimate and romantic back-to-nature experience. Don't miss the onsite Outpost Retreat Spa, which pampers with natural treatments made from indigenous ingredients.

Wrap up your Bozeman adventure by skiing the region's foremost resort, ⑳ Big Sky. With multiple mountains, 400in of annual powder and Montana's longest vertical drop (4350ft), it offers runs for all levels accessed from 21 lifts, plus three terrain parks and a super pipe. If steep and extreme are what you crave, hop off Lone Peak Tram into some of the country's best lift-accessible double black diamond runs.

Becca Blond

TRIP INFORMATION

GETTING THERE
Bozeman is 700 miles northwest of Denver via I-25 north to I-90 west.

DO
Alara Jewelry
Wearable art is the best way to describe the creative, bold and altogether unique jewelry on sale here. ☎ 406-522-8844; www.alarajewelry.com; 42 W Main St, Bozeman; ⏱ 10am-6pm Mon-Sat, 10am-4pm Sun

American Computer Museum
With each passing digital year the calculating "dinosaurs" on display at this techie museum become more comical – look for the room-sized computer. ☎ 406-582-1288; www.compustory.com; 2023 Stadium Dr, unit 1A, Bozeman; admission $5; ⏱ noon-4pm Tue-Sun Mar-May, 10am-4pm daily Jun-Aug, call for Sep-Feb hours

Big Sky Resort
With multiple mountains, 400in of annual powder, three snowboard parks and Montana's longest vertical drop, Big Sky is the region's foremost winter playground, just 18 miles north of Bozeman. ☎ 800-548-4486; www.bigskyresort.com; lift ticket $78; ⏱ 9am-3pm Nov-Mar

Bozeman Hot Springs
Newly renovated, it's the place to soak away your aches and pains, and features nine pools, plus a sauna and steam room, 8 miles west of downtown. ☎ 406-586-6492; admission $5; ⏱ 8am-1pm Sun-Thu, to midnight Fri & Sat

Bridger Bowl Ski Area
A community-owned, nonprofit ski area 16 miles north of Bozeman via Hwy 86; it's known for fluffy powder and bargain lift tickets. ☎ 406-587-2111; www.bridgerbowl.com; 15795 Bridger Canyon Rd; lift ticket day $45; ⏱ 9am-3pm Nov-Mar

Indian Uprising Gallery
From one-of-a-kind artifacts to contemporary paintings by award-winning Native American artists, this gallery covers centuries of Northern Plains Indian art. ☎ 406-586-5831; www.indianuprisinggallery.com; 25 S Tracy Ave, Bozeman; ⏱ 10am-5pm

Loft Spa
Locally owned community-oriented spa offering personalized services including hot-stone massages, facials and pedicures. ☎ 406-586-0530; www.theloftspabozeman.com; 128 W Main St, Ste B2, Bozeman; manicure from $25, 30min massage $50; ⏱ 10am-5pm Mon-Sat, 10am-3pm Sun

Montana Alpine Guides
Personalized, guided ice-climbing adventures in Hyalite Canyon; rates include gear and instruction. ☎ 406-586-8430; www.adventuremontana.com; trips around $300

Museum of the Rockies
Montana's number-one natural-history museum, showcasing the best of state culture, features an extraordinary dinosaur exhibit that includes the world's largest T-Rex skull. ☎ 406-994-2251; www.museumoftherockies.org; 600 W Kagy Blvd, Bozeman; adult/child $10/7; ⏱ 8am-8pm, with seasonal variations

EAT & DRINK
Burger Bob's
A true greasy Old West spoon, serving dozens of loaded burgers and cold beer. It caters to hungry college kids and ranchers equally; the lunch combo meal is a steal at around $6. ☎ 406-585-0800; 39 W Main St, Bozeman; mains $5-10; ⏱ 11:30am-9pm, to 10pm Fri & Sat

Community Food Co-Op
The co-op has a salad bar and full-service deli to create your own organic picnic fixings. Head to the upstairs café for decadent desserts, fair-trade coffee and great mountain views. ☎ 406-587-4037; 908 W Main St, Bozeman; mains $4-15; ⏱ 7am-7pm Mon-Sat, 7am-9pm Sun, with seasonal variations

John Bozeman's Bistro

This local landmark, 8 miles west of town, has a juicy steak-oriented menu and sophisticated wine list. ☎ 406-388-1100; 27 E Main St, Belgrade; mains $10-30; ⏰ 5-10pm

Molly Brown

A longtime favorite with the college crowd, it's a noisy dive offering 20 draft beers and a number of pool tables; perfect for cheap shots on cold winter nights. www.themolly brown.com; 703 W Babcock St, Bozeman; ⏰ 4pm-late, with variations

Montana Ale Works

This funky brewery in a huge, historic railroad warehouse serves a varied menu and features 40 beers on tap. ☎ 406-587-7700; 611 E Main St, Bozeman; mains $10-20; ⏰ 4pm-late

Plonk

Serves an innovative menu featuring organic produce and local meat. Sit on the sidewalk out front in summer. ☎ 406-587-2170; 29 E Main St, Bozeman; mains $10-30; ⏰ 11.30am-10pm

Zebra Cocktail Lounge

Inside the Bozeman Hotel, the Zebra has live bands performing most nights per week. ☎ 406-585-8851; 15 N Rouse Ave, Bozeman; cover charge varies; ⏰ 8pm-2am Wed-Sat

SLEEP

Rainbow Ranch Lodge

This luxe retreat is nestled on the Gallatin River and embraces a back-to-nature philosophy. Visiting the onsite Outpost Retreat Spa. ☎ 406-995-4132; www.rainbowranch bigsky.com; 42950 Gallatin Rd, Gallatin Gateway; r from $250

Voss Inn

This Victorian-era B&B has six charming, old-fashioned rooms featuring cozy big beds and terrycloth robes. Breakfast is a fabulous gourmet affair. ☎ 406-587-0982; www. bozeman-vossinn.com; 319 S Wilson Ave, Bozeman; s/d $120/140

USEFUL WEBSITES

www.bozemancvb.com
www.downtownbozeman.org

LINK YOUR TRIP   www.lonelyplanet.com/trip-planner

Once-in-a-Lifetime Glacier

WHY GO Glacier National Park turned a century in 2010, but the party was subdued. That's because, by 2020, Glacier's signature ice fields will reach an even bigger milestone: extinction. Steven Thompson, of the National Park Conservation Association's Glacier Field Office, explains, and helps us define the park's top five must-sees before the glaciers die.

TIME
3 days

DISTANCE
60 miles

BEST TIME TO GO
Jul – Sep

START
West Glacier

END
St Mary, MT

1 Glacier National Park sans glaciers? Sad but true, and happening faster than originally anticipated. Steven Thompson, who has been hiking, studying and living in the region for more than 20 years now, tells us: "Right now, the glaciers in the park are melting more quickly than predicted just a few years ago. The old estimate was for 2030, but according to US Geological Survey and top glacier-melting expert Dan Fagre, it now looks like the glaciers will be gone by 2020. There're about 26 now, down from 150 in the late 1800s. And there's nothing that can be done to halt the melting at this point."

But while Glacier glaciers will be nothing but a memory by the next decade, the park won't just disappear, Thompson promises: "To be clear, the predicted absence of glaciers in the park after 2020 doesn't mean everything will be dry. There will still be ice and 'permanent' snowfields. However, the size will be below the threshold of a glacier. Mountain glaciers are defined by a minimum size and physical properties, especially movement and replenishment."

That said, the disappearance of the glaciers will have a trickle-down effect on plant and animal life in the park – Glacier is known especially for its healthy grizzly population, as well as being home to some of the USA's other most endangered species, including the wolverine,

gray wolf and lynx – and a lot can still be done to reduce the global-warming problem before it's too late for the animals.

"To conserve watersheds and habitat, we need to protect and restore stream-side riparian zones, maintain free-flowing rivers, and ensure freedom to roam outside park boundaries for wildlife," Thompson says. "We need to shift to renewable energy sources and significantly reduce the burning of fossil fuels."

Start this once-in-a-lifetime adventure just inside Glacier's western entrance, with a hearty breakfast at Thompson's favorite morning spot, the ❷ **West Glacier Restaurant**. Located just inside the boundary, it looks and feels pretty much as it has for the last 50 years. Order something with huckleberry, the same Montana fruit the grizzly bears like. Afterwards, pick up Going-to-the-Sun Rd, the only paved road through the entire park. Heading north from the entrance, the road skirts shimmering Lake McDonald's eastern shore, serving up views of Stanton Mountain, before angling sharply to the Garden Wall, which forms the 9000ft spine of the Continental Divide. This part of the drive is where park promoters shoot their tourism brochures. Make sure to pull over to take your own personal postcard shot along the way.

Grab lunch at the ❸ **Lake McDonald Lodge**; the restaurant inside the old hunting lodge is known for its pizza. After dining, spend the afternoon in an ecofriendly way: rent a rowboat and paddle out onto the lake. Thompson says this is one of his favorite ways to experience the park's serenity and beauty from a different perspective – which makes going to the lodge dock and renting a rowboat from the ❹ **Glacier Park Boat Co** defining park moment No 1: oh, the views from the glassy water.

Getting off the road and up against the soaring sedimentary peaks is what Glacier's really all about, and the best way to discover just how soul soothing this ancient terra firma is, and be totally green at the same time, is to explore the backcountry on foot. The sky seems bigger and bluer amid the wilderness mountaintops than anywhere else. The air is intoxicatingly crisp, fresh and scented with pine, and you're more likely to exchange hellos on the hiking trail with a shaggy, medium-sized brown bear sipping glacier water from an ice-blue lake than with another human being. We think it's worth trekking nearly 7 miles one way to sleep at the 17-room ❺ **Sperry Chalet** on your first night in Glacier for the views alone, and Thompson agrees that this is Glacier must-do No 2. The trail starts from opposite Lake McDonald Lodge and leads to an impressive stone structure constructed by Great Northern Railway employees between 1912 and 1914. It's also ecofriendly, with outdoor modern composting toilets and cold-water-only showers, and it's set in the heart of the high country, where wildflower-strewn meadows, jagged peaks and babbling brooks make the place feel like nirvana.

GREEN GLACIER

Fewer cars on the road means less fossil-fuel emissions, so help the park combat global warming by taking the park's free shuttle bus across Going-to-the-Sun Rd rather than driving. To go totally green, use Amtrak's Empire Builder train from Minneapolis, Chicago, Seattle or Portland to get here.

Return to West Glacier in the morning for another human-powered excursion. The ❻ **Glacier Raft Co** is the oldest and arguably best of the river companies running half- and full-day guided trips down the North Fork and Middle Fork of the Flathead River, and the more interesting DIY kayak and rafting excursions from West Glacier 12 miles down the river. Prices include a bit of paddling instruction and gear including wetsuits – the water can feel, well, glacial even in August.

Back in the park, Going-to-the-Sun Rd crosses the Continental Divide atop Logan Pass, where the ❼ **Logan Pass Visitor Center** offers natural-history displays and a browse-worthy bookstore. Here you'll also come across the trailhead to Thompson's top Glacier hike (moment No 3), the rugged 18.5-mile one-way ❽ **Highline Trail** along the Continental Divide. If you can't do the whole trail, try the portion between Logan Pass and Granite Park.

"This is one of the best day or overnight hikes in America. Before you spreads the amazing panorama of glaciated valleys and jagged peaks that defines

OUTDOORS

Glacier National Park. It's relatively easy, and goes through splendid scenery and amazing rock gardens filled with wildflowers and wildlife," he says. "It's also one of the most accessible places in the world to see a wolverine. I still savor my 10-minute sighting of this elusive critter in 2002."

> **DETOUR** If the somber reality of global warming is getting you down, take a break in gorgeous, rustic, chic **Whitefish**, where gourmet restaurants, unique boutiques and the **Big Mountain Resort** await. Grab the gondola to the latter's summit and ride a mountain bike down one of the steep ski trails for white-knuckle thrills guaranteed to make you forget the planet's woes for at least a few hours. Whitefish is 30 miles west of West Glacier via Hwy 2 to Hwy 93.

Even if you aren't lucky enough to keep company with a wolverine, there are plenty of other animals to keep watch for. "For wildlife lovers it's almost always a winner. I've seen grizzly bears (at a safe distance), mountain goats, bighorn sheep and moose in addition to that wolverine," Thompson continues. "One time I passed 150 feet above a grizzly sow and cub before a hiking companion noticed. We are all cool, but constant banter or singing with your hiking partner is a good idea to let bears know you are around."

Continue on Going-to-the-Sun Rd afterwards, following it all the way to the eastern end at St Mary. From here cut north on Hwy 89 to Many Glacier Rd, backtracking west for around 20 miles to the **9 Many Glacier Hotel,** Thompson's pick for Glacier's most classic indoor sleep (memory maker No 4), where you should check in for two nights. The park is home to seven national historic landmark lodges dating from the early 1800s, of which Many Glacier is one. Modeled after a Swiss chalet (Glacier seems to love Swiss design), it sits pretty on the edge of Swiftcurrent Lake, and has a fine-dining room specializing in yummy Swiss fondue. Evening entertainment and a lounge add extra ambience.

"Before you spreads the amazing panorama of glaciated valleys and jagged peaks that defines Glacier National Park."

The area around Many Glacier also offers some of the best bear-spotting opportunities in the park, Thompson says: "Visitors have a front-row seat for viewing grizzlies in Many Glacier Valley, assuming they bring binoculars or a spotting scope, right from the road near Many Glacier Hotel. In fact, the congestion of viewers, especially in August and September, has been causing a bit of a problem with traffic congestion and bear jams."

Don't be surprised if you run into a shaggy bear yourself hiking the **10 Iceberg Lake trail** the next morning. The 9-mile hike, starting near the lodge, is this author's personal favorite defining Glacier memory (that would be No 5). The lake was named by George Grinnell in 1905, after the explorer saw icebergs calving from the glacier at the foot of the headwalls. Though the glacier is no longer active, surface ice and avalanche debris still provide sizeable flotillas of bergs as the lake melts in early summer. And while Thompson says Iceberg Lake may eventually shrink, it's not looking as though it'll be gone with the glaciers come 2020. The approach to the stunning glacial lake, enclosed by 3000ft vertical headwalls on three sides, is gentle. With most of the hiking at or above the tree line, it also affords awesome views nearly the whole way, while wildflower fiends will delight in the meadows surrounding the lake.

Saddle up after breakfast on day three. On the eastern side of Many Glacier Lodge, ⑪ **Swan Mountain Outfitters** offers guided horseback rides into the backcountry. There are routes and mounts for all skill levels. Try the half-day ride to the aquamarine wonders of ⑫ **Grinnell Lake**, which Thompson says isn't in danger of disappearing completely at this point, although its size is likely to decrease in the coming years. End your trip in style with a slice of pie – that's Thompson's recommendation, at least. At the park's eastern entrance, back in St Mary, is the family-owned ⑬ **Park Café and Grocery**, which has garnered many accolades over the years for its excellent homemade pies. Numerous selections from fruit to cream are fresh-baked each morning.

Becca Blond

DETOUR Bring your passport along, and spend the night at Glacier's sister park, Waterton Lakes National Park, in Alberta, Canada. Together the two parks compose the Waterton-Glacier International Peace Park, declared a World Heritage Site in 1995. Thompson suggests taking high tea at the venerable old **Prince of Wales Hotel** (www. princeofwaleswaterton.com), perched on a hill with stunning views. The hotel is only open June through August.

TRIP INFORMATION

GETTING THERE
West Glacier is 28 miles northwest of White-fish, the gateway town, via Hwy 93 to Hwy 2.

DO
Glacier National Park
Park headquarters are in West Glacier, between Hwy 2 and Apgar, and open year-round. Admission is valid for seven days. ☎ 406-888-7800; www.nps.gov/glac; West Glacier; admission $25; ☒ 8am-4:30pm Mon-Fri; ⚐

Glacier Park Boat Co
Runs tours, and rents rowboats and canoes from five park locations. ☎ 406-257-2426; www.glacierparkboats.com; Going-to-the-Sun Rd, Lake McDonald; rowboats per hr $18; ☒ mid-May–Sep

Glacier Raft Co
Runs guided trips down the North Fork and Middle Fork of the Flathead, and rents two-person kayaks for DIY trips from West Glacier. ☎ 800-235-6781; www.glacierraftco.com; Hwy 2, West Glacier; trips $45-120; ☒ Jun-Aug

Logan Pass Visitor Center
Atop the pass, it has info plus exhib-its. ☎ 406-888-7800; Going-to-the-Sun Rd, Logan Pass; admission free; ☒ Jun–mid-Oct

Swan Mountain Outfitters
Half-day rides depart from Many Glacier Corral, on the eastern side of Many Glacier Lodge, at 8am and 12:45pm. ☎ 877-888-5557; www.swanmountainoutfitters.com/glacier; Many Glacier Rd, Many Glacier Valley; half-day ride $105; ☒ Jun-Sep

EAT & SLEEP

Lake McDonald Lodge
The restaurant inside this 1913 hunting lodge does a delicious pizza. ☎ 406-888-5431; www.lakemcdonaldlodge.com; Going-to-the-Sun Rd, Lake McDonald Valley; mains $10-20; ☒ Jun-Sep

Many Glacier Hotel
This national historic landmark on Swiftcur-rent Lake is the park's largest hotel, with 208 rooms; decor is Swiss chalet all the way – including fondue. Yum. ☎ 406-732-4411; www.manyglacierhotel.com; Many Glacier Rd, Many Glacier Valley; r from $145; ☒ mid-Jun–mid-Sep

Park Café and Grocery
Located at the eastern end of Going-to-the-Sun Rd, it's a perennial favorite, especially if you dig pie. ☎ 406-732-4482; www.park cafe.us/aboutus.php; mains $5-10; St Mary; ☒ May-Sep

Sperry Chalet
This hike-in-only Swiss-style chalet offers phenomenal views. Mules can be hired to carry gear. ☎ 888-345-2649; www. sperrychalet.com, www.mule-shoe.com; r incl meals $170-300, mule hire $130; Lake McDonald Valley; ☒ Jul 7-Sep 8

West Glacier Restaurant
Good grub and reliable service at the park's western entrance. ☎ 406-888-5359; 200 Going-to-the-Sun Rd; mains $5-15; ☒ 7am-10pm mid-May–Oct; ⚐

USEFUL WEBSITES
www.npca.org/parks/glacier-national-park.htm

www.parkscanada.gc.ca/waterton

LINK YOUR TRIP
www.lonelyplanet.com/trip-planner

Champagne & Powder in Sun Valley

WHY GO Go glam in the Rocky Mountains' least pretentious rich and famous winter playground. From riding champagne powder at the USA's first commercial ski resort to sipping French bubbly with Ernest Hemingway's ghost afterwards, this isn't the part of Idaho they crack potato jokes about – it's the part that throws devilishly posh white-tie affairs.

Inside a volcanic crater surrounded by igneous rocks (resembling ashy versions of Idaho's famous potato doing the rippled-chip look) shooting up straight from the valley floor, Ketchum and neighboring ski area Sun Valley are the state's premier winter destinations. They're favorites with undercover high rollers and movie stars, keeping low profiles disguised in buffalo-skin jackets, turquoise-beaded cowboy hats and Chanel sunglasses. Nobel Prize–winning author (and avid sportsman) Ernest Hemingway was a frequent visitor to Sun Valley and a longtime Ketchum resident. He ended his life here with a bullet in 1961, and is buried in Ketchum. There's also a touching memorial to Hemingway in a grove of cottonwoods above Sun Valley.

Despite the swank appeal, ❶ **Ketchum**, which has 1890s blue-collar mining and smelting roots, feels more polished than pretentious. Walk Main St between First and Fifth to experience the quaint downtown's charm. Here you'll find the ❷ **Chapter One Bookstore**, which has been delighting locals and tourists for 30 years with a wide selection of literature, including out-of-print titles. Check the special fiction section dedicated to books about or by authors from Idaho and the Pacific Northwest first. After browsing, grab a revitalizing smoothie at onsite ❸ **Akasha Organics** in the shop's rear. The old-school hippie juice bar mixes fruit, root and spice concoctions that are more than delightfully refreshing – they're meant to fuel everything from mental awareness to

TIME	4 days
DISTANCE	135 miles
BEST TIME TO GO	Dec – Mar
START	Ketchum , ID
END	Hailey, ID

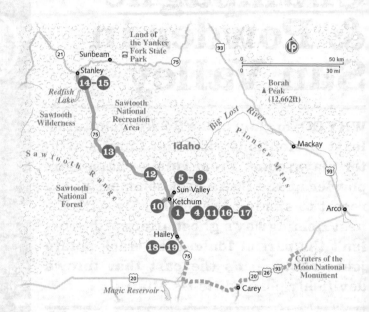

immunity. Ask the barista to mix a potion that fits your mood. The small café is also stocked with dried herbs and tinctures. In a super-cool painted shack just off Main St, have lunch at **4** **Rickshaw**. The menu is Asian fusion tapas – creative, fresh small plates inspired by the cuisine of Vietnam, Thailand, China and Indonesia, which the chef refers to as "Asian street food." Be careful how much you order: most portions are small, and it's easy to order a fortune's worth before feeling stuffed. We suggest visiting at lunch.

"fruit, root and spice concoctions are meant to fuel everything from mental awareness to immunity."

At the north end of Main St is the turn-off to **5** **Sun Valley Resort**, located another mile northeast. The name is a bit confusing, as this road doesn't lead to anything resembling ski slopes but rather to a grand old hotel, a shopping mall with several restaurants, a movie theater and a post office, plus an outdoor pedestrian boardwalk. It's also where Hemingway ended his life in 1961. That said, the doyen of Ketchum and Sun Valley does operate two excellent ski mountains (which most people confusingly refer to collectively as "Sun Valley") just west and south. Famous for light, fluffy powder, both of Sun Valley's mountains frequently take top honors as one of the USA's best snow-sport destinations.

The USA's first destination ski resort, **6** **Sun Valley** was the brainchild of Averell Harriman, chairman of the Union Pacific Railroad. The luxury resort sprang to life in 1936 and never looked back. Before long it became a favorite wealthy playground, and today trophy homes of the truly rich and famous still dot the hilltops (the town south of Ketchum is half-owned by Bruce Willis, but we'll get to that later). See the proof in photographs on the walls of the princely lobby at the **7** **Sun Valley Lodge**, your home for the next two nights. While reception is getting the details sorted, check out the impressive celluloid diary of the glitterati on skis throughout the decades – from Mary Pickford to Gary Cooper, Lucille Ball, the Kennedys and even Marilyn Monroe. Literati will especially relish slumbering at the lodge: this is where Hemingway completed *For Whom the Bell Tolls*. The resort is fading gracefully and, though it has a few cobwebs, for the most part it exudes an old-fashioned elegance that, coupled with its historic legacy, keeps it in the game. Rooms are comfortable, although some are a tad cramped, but the sauna is divine after a day on the slopes.

When you're all checked in, grab the hotel ski shuttle to the lifts at **8** **Dollar Mountain**, Sun Valley's original ski area. Its five lifts serve 13 easy runs with a maximum vertical drop of 628ft, making it a great learn-to-ride mountain (if you know how to ski, try renting a snowboard here or vice versa). Lift tickets are a steal, some of the lowest priced in the nation. If you're not up for skiing or boarding, spend the afternoon riding the lift up and sliding down the mountain's tubing hill on an inflated rubber donut. Sun Valley's top nightspot, **9** **Whiskey Jacques**, is the place to unwind with smooth cocktails, live music and dancing come dark. Purported to have been one of Ernest Hemingway's favorite watering holes, it's a rustic, Old-West-saloon-style spot.

> **DETOUR** Want to really get off the grid? Go skiing on the moon – well, not the literal moon, but Idaho's version. An hour's drive southeast of Ketchum, **Craters of the Moon National Monument** is an 83-sq-mile volcanic showcase. Lava flows and tubes and cinder cones are found along the 7-mile **Crater Loop Rd** (closed to cars in winter, when skiers and snowshoers take control). Rent gear in Ketchum.

Tackle **10** **Bald Mountain**, just west of Ketchum and Sun Valley's bigger resort, on day two. It's known for its steeps and chutes. The forested slopes of Bald Mountain (9150ft), known affectionately as "Baldy," catch tons of dry powdery snow, making this a world-class downhill destination. From the summit, 64 diverse runs served by 13 lifts plunge a maximum of 3400 vertical feet; almost two-thirds of the runs are advanced. Grab après-ski drinks at one of two day lodges and return to Ketchum for dinner at **11** **Desperado's**. Rehash the day's tumbles over margaritas and filling, tasty Mexican cuisine served in bright and busy environs.

Take a break from skiing on day three, and try a different type of adrenalin-pumping winter sport, snowmobiling. Cruise north from Sun Valley to Stanley on Hwy 75, also known as the **12** **Sawtooth Scenic Byway**. The 60-mile drive is gorgeous, winding through a misty, thick ponderosa pine forest – where the air is crisp and fresh and smells like rain and nuts – before ascending the 8701ft **13** **Galena Summit**. From the overlook at the top (make sure to pause) there are views of the 1180-sq-mile Sawtooth National Recreation Area, home to 40 glacially carved peaks over 10,000ft, more than 300 high-alpine lakes, 100 miles of streams and 750 miles of trails.

On the wide banks of the Salmon River, tiny **14** **Stanley** (population 100) is the only place in America where three national scenic byways meet. Surrounded entirely by protected wilderness and national-forest land, the remote outpost is nestled into the crook of Salmon River, miles from anywhere. It's the kind of place where peaceful high-summer twilight stretches on past 10pm.

Once in town, visit the family-run **15** **Riverside Motel** to set up tonight's lodging and the afternoon's snowmobiling trip. With more than 165 miles of groomed trails, the area around Stanley offers some of Idaho's most stupendous snow-car riding. The endless meadow stretches are a blast for lead-footed drivers, and flying at full throttle across the whitened landscape is a sensation like none other. The friendly folks at Riverside can arrange lessons and guided tours, or if you know what you're doing and just need a ride, private rentals can also be arranged.

AMERICA'S MOST SCENIC INTERSECTION?

The US Department of Transportation also thinks highly of Stanley's beauty. When deciding which of the country's two-lane highways were worthy of earning national scenic byway status, all three roads into Stanley made the cut (it's the only place in the USA where this happens). Considering there are only 125 such roads in the country, this means 2.4% of American's prettiest pavement runs through bucolic Stanley.

There's literally nothing to do in Stanley after dark besides check out the stars, which are part of its romantic appeal. The Riverside is perfectly perched above the Salmon, and eight of the well-appointed rooms have giant private porches looking right onto the wide, icy troth. At night, sleeping in the stripped-pine beds under ultra-warm duvets, the river's burps and gurgles help lull you to sleep. You'll want to pick up provisions at the grocery and liquor store at the junction of Hwys 75 and 21, as Stanley doesn't have much in the way of reliable open restaurants in winter. The Riverside's rooms come with kitchenettes, and tables to eat your creations upon, so it's a cozy way to pass an evening (plus now you'll have extra cash for tomorrow's dinner, which is deliciously pricy). On your way out for burritos and beer, make sure to look up. Stanley has zero light pollution, and the star patterns on a clear night are extraordinarily bright.

Return to Ketchum the way you came in, on Hwy 75, in the morning and go straight to Sun Valley's slopes. Today's a good day to try Bald Mountain if you haven't already. If you have, you'll more than likely be thirsting for more (of course, if you are short on time, you can also cut this day out entirely). Spend your last night in town at the ⑯ Lift Tower Lodge, a friendly small motel in downtown Ketchum. Offering free continental breakfast and a hot tub, it sits next to a landmark exhibition chairlift c 1939 and is the best budget bet in town. A local favorite, ⑰ Ketchum Grill boasts a creative menu bursting with fresh fare. The elegant offerings include lots of seafood, along with plenty of veggie options.

Tonight it's time to party ski-bum style, in ⑱ Hailey, 12 miles south of Ketchum on Hwy 75. Half owned, and partially lived in by Bruce Willis and assorted family members, Hailey has cheaper rent than Ketchum, and it's where most seasonal workers and many locals live. It has a lively bar scene, including ⑲ Sun Valley Brewing Company, the premier blue-collar after-work party spot, serving microbrews and burgers.

Becca Blond

TRIP INFORMATION

GETTING THERE
It's about 280 miles from Salt Lake City, Utah, to Ketchum via I-15 north to I-84 west. Take exit 173 and follow Sun Valley signs.

DO
Chapter One Bookstore
Check out the special fiction section dedicated to books about or by authors from Idaho and the Pacific Northwest. ☎ 208-726-5425; 160 N Main St, Ketchum; ☼ 10am-9pm

Sun Valley Resort
Advanced-terrain Bald Mountain and easier-on-the-nerves (and wallet) Dollar Mountain make up this resort. ☎ 800-786-8259; www.sunvalley.com; lift ticket Bald Mountain $55-80, Dollar Mountain $32-40, tubing $5-10

EAT & DRINK
Ashaka Organics
This organic, hippie juice bar makes a heck of a revitalizing smoothie. ☎ 208-726-5425; 160 N Main St, Ketchum; ☼ 10am-9pm

Desperado's
Specializes in reasonably priced Mexican food. Fill up on burritos, chimichangas and tacos; wash them down with a marg. ☎ 208-726-3068; 211 4th St, Ketchum; mains $7-10; ☼ 11:30am-10pm Mon-Sat

Ketchum Grill
Boasts a creative menu bursting with fresh fare including lots of seafood and veggie options. ☎ 208-726-4660; 520 East Ave, Ketchum; mains $10-20; ☼ 5:30pm-close

Rickshaw
Delicious Asian fusion tapas in a painted shack; Friday lunch is the best deal. ☎ 208-726-8481; 460 Washington Ave N, Ketchum; small plates & mains $5-12; ☼ 5:30-10pm Tue-Sat, plus 11:30am-2pm Fri

Sun Valley Brewing Company
In Hailey, locals come here for burgers and fresh-brewed beer after work. ☎ 208-788-5777; 202 N Main St, Hailey; mains $5-15; ☼ 11am-late

Whiskey Jacques
Purported to have been one of Ernest Hemingway's favorite watering holes. Come for dancing, live music or pool. ☎ 208-726-5297; 251 Main St, Sun Valley; cover up to $5; ☼ 4pm-2am

SLEEP
Lift Tower Lodge
Good affordable ski-season crash with a hot tub and free continental breakfast. ☎ 208-726-5163; 703 S Main St, Ketchum; r $65-100

Riverside Motel
Perfectly perched above the Salmon, this family-run log cabin motel features well-appointed rooms with kitchenettes; pay extra for one of the eight with a river view from its awesome private deck. ☎ 208-774-3409; www.riversidemotel.biz; Hwy 75, Stanley; r & cabins $65-150

Sun Valley Lodge
Ernest Hemingway completed *For Whom the Bell Tolls* here. It runs a ski shuttle and has a children's program. ☎ 208-622-2001; 1 Sun Valley Rd, Sun Valley; r $150-500

USEFUL WEBSITES
www.visitsunvalley.com

LINK YOUR TRIP
www.lonelyplanet.com/trip-planner

Hot Potatoes & Hot Lava: Offbeat Idaho

WHY GO Walk across a lava ocean, don your anti-radiation suit in Atomic City and see the world's largest potato chip in the planet's spud capital. When it comes to the offbeat adventure market, Idaho delivers with a hot, diversified portfolio that takes you from the moon to hell.

From Craters of the Moon to Hells Canyon (and in-between Bliss), from weapons of mass destruction to massive potato production, Idaho is dialed in with some truly weird attractions. Wedged into the space where the Pacific Northwest's lush, green curves meet the Rocky Mountain's craggy glacier-capped peaks, this state boasts more protected acreage (to the tune of 18 million acres of wilderness) than anywhere outside Alaska. And despite its laundry list of wonderful highway distractions, this northern wonderland remains a black hole on most road-trippers' navigational screens. Exploring Idaho's beguiling blue-green assets when the tourists are not is what makes this totally campy adventure so devilishly hot.

Begin with a virtual carb blast. Hard-working ❶ Blackfoot calls itself the potato capital of the world and, while any town in this spud-happy region could cash in on production fame, only Blackfoot has the ❷ Idaho Potato Museum. The mother of well-done roadside attractions, it covers all things spud. Look for the Mr Potato Head tribute, the burlap tuxedo (touching allowed!) Idaho's first Potato Commissioner first wore and, best of all, the biggest fake potato chip ever made. The 25in by 14in Pringle is the size of a large pizza, and was created in 1991 by Proctor & Gamble engineers. During summer the gift shop sells ice cream, cookies and fudge, all made from potatoes, and, as long as you pay admission to the museum, gives "free 'taters for out-of-staters." A photo-worthy massive Styrofoam potato, topped with sour cream and butter, marks the museum parking lot.

TIME
4 days

DISTANCE
450 miles

BEST TIME TO GO
May – Sep

START
Blackfoot, ID

END
Hells Canyon National Recreation Area, ID

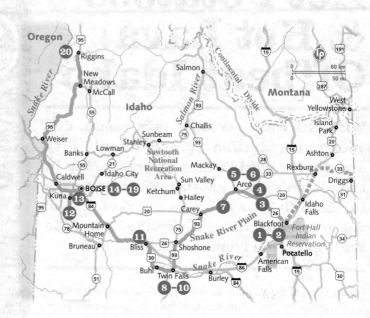

Tired of potatoes? Go nuclear. For a short time during the Cold War
3 Atomic City, 29 miles northwest on Hwy 26, served as a nuclear boom-
town thanks to its location near a secret government research facility.

Today the isolated place (population around 25) has gone just about bust. The
main road is unpaved, and the Texaco gas station serves as both the post office
and the bar. Still, Atomic City is worth a pause, if for nothing more than the
fantastic campy photo ops it provides.

The flat, empty plains stretching northeast from Atomic City have been used
for nuclear-reactor experimentation and development by the US government
since the closing days of WWII. A historical marker at a Hwy 26 pull-off
proudly proclaims: "Since 1949, more nuclear reactors – over 50 of them –
have been built on this plain than anywhere else in the world." Managed
by Lockheed Martin, the 900-sq-mile **4 Idaho National Engineering &
Environmental Laboratory** (INEEL) is still used for Pentagon-sponsored
research, and remains mostly closed to the public. You can take a self-guided
tour of the visitors center located inside the world's first nuclear power plant,
Experimental Breeder Reactor 1 (EBR-1), where the world's first peacetime
demonstration of nuclear energy's potential took place on December 20,
1951. You can see the "hot cell" where they made plutonium-239, which is
still considered radioactive. Don't worry: you'll be protected from residual
radiation by 34 layers of oil-separated glass.

Three years after the EBR-1 experiment, the government built a second reactor, BORAX II, nearby, and on July 17, 1955, plugged in its fission cord and made the small town of ❺ Arco, 16 miles north, glow. It was the world's first city lit by atomic energy (it was also the first to face the reality of a partial reactor meltdown later that same year, but no one talks that story up too much). Although its time in the atomic spotlight was ultimately short, Arco doesn't let you forget it owns the original nuclear bragging rights. Have lunch at ❻ Grandpa's Southern Bar-B-Que in town. It's a welcome surprise, serving finger-licking-good ribs and pulled-pork sandwiches, and a good place to fuel up before going lunar.

> **DETOUR**
>
> You know that novelty postcard that's been around forever? The one with "Greetings from Idaho" imposed above a picture of a potato so big it covers the entire truck bed? Well, the real deal exists in **Driggs**, 100 miles northeast of Blackfoot. Sure, the spud on the back of the flatbed is located in the middle of nowhere, but trekking here is worth more than photographs. The sculpture fronts one of only a handful of the USA's still-operating **drive-in movie theaters**, showcasing the latest blockbusters nightly in summer.

Say hello to the moon 20 miles southwest on Hwy 20/26. Established in 1924, ❼ Craters of the Moon National Monument is an 83-sq-mile volcanic showcase of uncanny lava flows, cinder cones and spatter cones. Drive the 7-mile Crater Loop Rd to scope the sci-fi landscape, but to really experience it lose the car and hike. Several short trails lead from the road to the edge of the crater and down into undeveloped lava caves (bring a flashlight to explore). The barren black basalt absorbs heat, and by midmorning on a sunny summer day temperatures quickly soar above 100°F. Try exploring in late afternoon or, better yet, pitch a tent in the surreal campground near the monument's entrance station and hike the lunar craters after dark. The road is open 24/7 between May and October (the only months the campsite has running water). Time a summer camping trip with a full moon for a doubly trippy lunar experience.

If camping is not your thing, spend the night in ❽ Twin Falls on Hwy 93 south of I-84. The sprawling agricultural center is home to the usual assortment of cheap, and slightly classier, chain motels (but not much else). The town on the Snake River was propelled to cartographic fame in 1974, when Evel Knievel promoted, then aborted, jumping the canyon here on a rocket-powered motorcycle. The walkway on the 1500ft-long and 486ft-high ❾ Perrine Bridge is the best place to view the impressive river canyon. Grab breakfast at the ❿ Buffalo Café, making sure to order fried Idaho potatoes smothered with gravy.

Cut north from Twin Falls on the Thousand Springs Scenic Byway to ⓫ Bliss. Sadly, the town doesn't quite live up to its super-cool name (and doesn't boast any weird trivia or oversized inanimate objects), but the canyon the byway meanders through to get there is geologically phenomenal. Cascades of water gush out of the canyon walls along the 48-mile stretch of Hwy 30 along the Snake River. At Bliss the road diverges, and you'll pick the interstate back up, heading west on I-84 towards Boise.

If highway driving is putting you to sleep, there is nothing like a carnivorous bird encounter to wake you up. Take exit 44 from I-84 and follow Hwy 69 south for 8 miles to Kuna and ⑫ **Morley Nelson Snake River Birds of Prey National Conservation Area** signs. The 755-sq-mile refuge encompasses North America's densest concentration of nesting birds of prey. Stretching along 80 miles of the basalt-cliff-lined Snake River, the desert refuge is home to pairs of majestic raptors, as well as red-tailed hawks, golden eagles, prairie falcons and great horned owls.

Having no success using binoculars to scan for your photographic prey? Don't get frustrated. You just need a shot of raptor rehab. Backtrack north towards I-84 to visit the ⑬ **World Center for Birds of Prey** rehabilitation center for injured or abused birds. The center runs 90-minute tours visiting the nursery where rare birds, like the peregrine falcon, are incubated, and the rehab center, where raptors are given a second chance to succeed. Some avian residents do so well they become stars in the center's outdoor flight show, showcasing choreographed raptor sky-dancing routines.

It's an easy drive west on I-84 to buzzing ⑭ **Boise**. In a dramatic location where the desert meets the mountains, tonight's sleepover spot has an outdoors slant and hippie-trendy vibe. Plus, Idaho's capital and biggest city has been named one of America's best places to live. The city boasts a unique multicultural pioneer heritage (and architectural landscape) that includes roots in the Basque homeland – strangely, Boise and southwestern Idaho have one of the biggest concentrations of Basque people outside Europe. To learn the story behind Idaho's late-19th-century Pyrenean pioneers, visit the ⑮ **Basque Museum & Cultural Center**.

"Don't get frustrated. You just need a shot of raptor rehab."

At the northeastern end of the Basque neighborhood is the ⑯ **Idaho State Capitol**, the only geothermally heated statehouse in the country. The dowdy exterior belies its handsome interior, faced with four different colors of marble and embellished with mahogany inlays. The 1st floor of the 200,000-sq-ft building contains epic sculptures and a display of rare Idaho gemstones. The rotunda dome rises nearly 200ft to end in a patch of sky blue emblazoned with 43 stars (Idaho was the union's 43rd state).

From the capitol, it's an easy eight-block walk to ⑰ **The Grove**. The brick-lined pedestrian plaza is the city's social center, packed with eating and shopping establishments. Have a wander. Summer twilight stretches nearly to 10pm in Boise, and residents who've spent a long winter cooped up in the dark flock to the Grove in droves to sip wine and catch up with friends at trendy sidewalk cafés here.

Named to honor Boise's location on the 43rd parallel and Idaho's status as the 43rd state to enter the union, ⑱ **Hotel 43** is a cozy boutique joint that's stumbling distance from the Grove. Rooms and suites are artfully decorated; ask for one with state capitol views. The swanky onsite ⑲ **Chandlers Restaurant** is one of Boise's most popular eateries. If you're still stuffed from dinner, treat yourself to one of the signature martinis.

DETOUR

A TASTE OF HEAVEN IN HELL

Like all good things, getting to heaven takes more effort than going to hell. In the Idaho portion of Hells Canyon National Recreation Area, reaching the pearly gates without a raft means driving 21 miles up a steep 4WD track to the breathtaking **Heaven's Gate Lookout** at the canyon rim. Time the trip with summer sunset – the canyon's location, on the far western edge of the MST zone, makes the evening color show start later and seemingly last forever. Reach the lookout from USFS Rd 517 (open July to September), a quarter-mile south of the Riggins Ranger Station on Hwy 95.

Now that you've set foot on the moon, stood just 34 panels away from a radioactive reactor and driven through Bliss, it's only appropriate to end this trip in Hell. Sitting in a remote area on the Idaho–Oregon border, straddling time zones, ⑳ **Hells Canyon National Recreation Area** is North America's deepest gorge. Plunging 8913ft from Mt Oore's He-Devil Peak on the east rim to the Snake River at Granite Creek, the remote, mostly roadless 652,488-acre Hells Canyon is thousands of feet deeper than the Grand Canyon.

Becca Blond

TRIP INFORMATION

GETTING THERE
Blackfoot is 260 miles east of Boise via I-15 and I-84.

DO
Basque Museum & Cultural Center
The museum tells the story of Boise's Basque people, who migrated to Idaho in the late 19th century. ☎ 208-343-2671; www.basquemuseum.com; 611 Grove St, Boise; admission $3; ⏱ 10am-4pm Tue-Fri, 11am-3pm Sat

Hells Canyon National Recreation Area Visitors Center
Good info and maps on navigating the hard-to-access wilderness area, including the scoop on campgrounds, hiking trails and river permits. ☎ 208-628-3916; Hwy 95, Riggins; ⏱ 8am-5pm Mon-Fri

Idaho National Engineering & Environmental Laboratory (INEEL)
Lockheed manages this reservation for the US Department of Energy; reach INEEL from Hwy 26 east of Arco. ☎ 208-526-2331; Hwy 26; admission free; ⏱ 8am-4pm Jun-Aug

Idaho Potato Museum
In the former railroad depot off I-15, exit 93; devoted to the state's potato story. ☎ 208-785-2517; 130 NW Main St, Blackfoot; admission $3; ⏱ 9:30am-7pm Mon-Sat, 10am-5pm Sun

Morley Nelson Snake River Birds of Prey National Conservation Area
Get a driving tour and Snake River float-trip guide info at the visitors center. ☎ 208-384-3300; www.blm.gov/id/st/en/fo/four_riv ers/01.html; Swan Falls Rd; admission free; ⏱ dawn-dusk

World Center for Birds of Prey
This raptor rehab center also features fine educational displays; take exit 50 off I-84. ☎ 208-362-8687; 5666 W Flying Hawk Lane; admission $5; ⏱ 9am-5pm Mar-Oct, 10am-4pm Nov-Feb

EAT & SLEEP
Buffalo Café
Visit this restaurant for spuds and gravy, a traditional Idaho breakfast. ☎ 208-734-0271; 218 4th Ave W, Twin Falls; mains $4-10; ⏱ 6am-2pm

Craters of the Moon National Monument & Campsite
An 83-sq-mile volcanic showcase featuring uncanny lava flows, cinder cones and spatter cones offering glimpses of past volcanic activity. All are visible from the 7-mile crater loop road. ☎ 208-527-3257; vehicle $4, hiker & cyclist $2, campsites $10; ⏱ 8am-4:30pm Sep-May, 8am-6pm Jun-Aug

Grandpa's Southern Bar-B-Que
Serving tasty ribs and pulled-pork sandwiches, it's a locals' favorite fuel-up. ☎ 208-522-1890; 434 W Grand Ave, Arco; mains $6-15; ⏱ 11am-10pm

Hotel 43 & Chandlers Restaurant
Features 112 creative rooms and suites, a swanky on-site martini bar and restaurant (mains $15 to $25), and a fitness center, all right downtown. ☎ 800-243-4622; www.hotel43.com; 981 Grove St, Boise; r $85-270

USEFUL WEBSITES
www.visitid.org

LINK YOUR TRIP
www.lonelyplanet.com/trip-planner

TRIP 72 Champagne & Powder in Sun Valley p509

SOUTHWEST TRIPS

You've stuffed the car with sunscreen, Frisbee, cooler, water sandals, hiking boots and hats. You've turned down your hot-water heater, put the lights on a timer and, yes, the neighbor will remember to water the plants. You have this book in hand, a plan and, most comforting of all, that woman's voice in your GPS.

But this is the land of cowboys and Indians, miners and mountain men, small desert towns of adobe and sprawling cities of neon, dry winds and searing skies, red rock canyons, coyotes and sagebrush. This is Thelma and Louise's road, Jack Kerouac's "mad road, lonely, leading around the bend into the openings of space towards the horizon."

PLAYLIST ♫ You drive the desert highway at twilight, cheeks still hot from the day's sun, lips chapped. It's quiet, finally cooler, and you open the window. When you've had your fill of the silence, you reach down and turn on your music.

- "New Mexico Rain," Bill and Bonnie Hearne
- "Can't Help But Wonder Where I'm Bound," Nanci Griffith
- "The Painted Desert," 10,000 Maniacs
- "Albuquerque," Neil Young
- "Atomic Power," Uncle Tupelo
- "The Gambler," Kenny Rogers
- "Wide Open Spaces," Dixie Chicks
- "New Mexico," Johnny Cash

We can tell you where to go and what to do, and, from Sin City to Santa Fe, from high country rambles to screaming rapids, there's a lot to recommend. But, in the end, the best part of the iconic American Southwest is losing yourself in its Nothing.

SOUTHWEST TRIPS

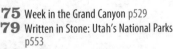

48 Hours in Las Vegas

WHY GO Las Vegas is a wild ride. It doesn't matter if you play the penny slots, lay down a bankroll on the poker tables or never gamble at all – you'll leave this town feeling like you've just had the time of your life. Guaranteed.

According to Hollywood legend, the day mobster Bugsy Siegel drove from LA into the Mojave Desert and decided to finish raising a glamorous, tropical-themed casino under the searing sun, all there was here were some ramshackle gambling houses, tumbleweeds and cacti. Nobody thought anyone would ever come here. But everybody couldn't have been more wrong, baby.

Today, Las Vegas welcomes more visitors each year than the holy city of Mecca. Admittedly, its tourist traps, especially on the infamous Strip, are nonstop party zones. But scratch beneath the surface, and you'll find Sin City has much more on tap than just gambling, booze and cheap thrills. There are as many different faces to Nevada's biggest metropolis as there are Elvis impersonators or wedding chapels here.

Sprawled immodestly along Las Vegas Blvd, the Strip is a never-ending spectacle, especially at night with all of its neon lights blazing. Ever since Bugsy's Flamingo casino hotel upped the ante back in 1946, casino hotels have competed to dream up the next big thing, no matter how gimmicky. You can be mesmerized by the dancing fountain show outside of the ❶ **Bellagio**, an exploding faux-Polynesian volcano in a lagoon fronting the ❷ **Mirage**, singing gondoliers plying the artificial canals of the ❸ **Venetian** or sexy pirates in a mock battle of the sexes with pyrotechnics galore at ❹ **TI (Treasure Island)**. Rise above the Strip's madness inside glass elevators shooting up the half-scale replica of the Eiffel Tower at ❺ **Paris Las Vegas**, or ascend the 110-story ❻ **Stratosphere Tower**, where the world's highest thrill rides await.

TIME
2 – 3 days

BEST TIME TO GO
Apr – Jun

START
Bellagio

END
The Strip

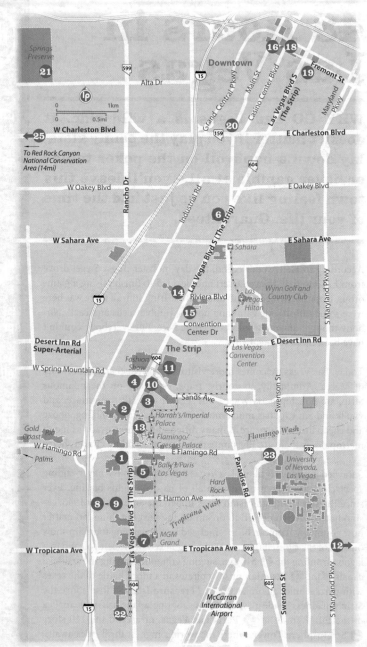

All of this showy stuff is old hat for Las Vegas. This century-old city is quickly metamorphosing into a sophisticated but still sexy and sybaritic destination. Boutique hotels within casino resorts (for example, the Signature Suites at ➐ MGM Grand), star chefs' restaurants (including a recent invasion of high-flying French folk: witness CityCenter's ➑ Twist by Pierre Gagnaire), and indulgent spas such as ➒ Spa at Aria, also at CityCenter, with Japanese-style stone sauna beds and a therapy room made of illuminated salt bricks, are what hip, younger crowds demand. Ironically, this polish and sophistication hearken back to Old Vegas' heyday in the "Fabulous '50s," when mobsters mixed with Rat Pack movie stars and even showgirls dressed in diamonds and silk to just step inside a casino. The most decadent high-roller casino resorts such as ➓ Palazzo and ⓫ Wynn Las Vegas each have their own galaxy of catwalk couture shops, epicurean restaurants and entertaining diversions, from Broadway shows to nightclubs on par with LA or NYC. To gawk at the VIPs, stroll through the front doors anytime – they're free, and they never close.

You can still find the kitschier and oh-so-cheesy side of Las Vegas. After all, this is the city that brought fame and fortune to flamboyant Liberace, and staged a 1969 comeback show for Elvis outfitted in a rhinestone-studded jumpsuit. Pay your respects at the outrageous ⓬ Liberace Museum, stuffed with hand-painted antique pianos, luxury cars including a mirror-tiled Rolls Royce, and a collection of feathered capes and million-dollar furs. Elvis has indeed left the building, but you can still play blackjack with the King at the ⓭ Imperial Palace, where "dealertainers" do double duty as casino card dealers and celebrity impersonators. Speaking of casinos, there's none tackier than the 1960s ⓮ Circus Circus, where trapeze artists, high-wire workers and contortionists steal center stage. Grab a seat at the revolving Horse-A-Round Bar, made famous by Hunter S Thompson's *Fear and Loathing in Las Vegas*. At Slots A' Fun next door, grab a coupon book, give the giant slot machine a free spin and scarf down a few $2 beers and hot dogs; then relax and enjoy the laughable lounge acts. At the retro ⓯ Fireside Lounge, a swingin' '70s hideaway, cooing couples nestle into blue-velvet couches and make out like there's no tomorrow.

When you've exhausted the hurly-burly Strip, take yourself downtown to the ⓰ Fremont Street Experience, a five-block-long pedestrian mall with a canopy steroid-enhanced by a super-big Viva Vision screen and 550,000 watts of concert-hall sound. When the 12.5-million synchronized LEDs come on, its silly sound-and-light shows hypnotize passersby (especially anyone who's already drunk on those 99¢ fluorescent-pink margaritas sold in gigantic souvenir glasses). Fremont St is the city's historic quarter, preferred by serious gamblers who find faux volcanoes beneath them; the smoky, low-ceilinged casinos have changed little over the years. Check out the nerve-wracking, no-limit Texas- hold-'em action at legendary ⓱ Binion's, where the World Series of Poker was born. Then stumble across the street to the ⑱ **Golden Nugget**, downtown's most posh address, to gawk at the Hand of Faith, the largest chunk of gold ever found, weighing 61lb 11oz. Oh, they've got an outdoor swimming pool with a three-story waterslide that shoots through a live-shark tank, too.

East Fremont St is undergoing a renaissance of cool, with indie watering holes and nightclubs popping up, like the ⑲ **Beauty Bar**. On the tattered fringes of downtown, hidden among the vintage-clothing and antiques shops, is the emerging ⑳ **18b Arts District**. On the first Friday night of each month, these streets take on a carnival atmosphere as 10,000 art lovers, hipsters and indie musicians turn it into a big block party, with gallery openings, performance art, live music, fortune tellers and tattoo artists.

Did you know that this artificial desert oasis also has a greener, more ecofriendly side? The immense ㉑ **Springs Preserve** is planted on the site of the once-bubbling springs that gave Las Vegas its Spanish name, "the meadows." The preserve weaves together cultural and natural history in the Origen Experience, then imagines a more sustainable future for Nevada at the Desert Living Center, with xeriscaped gardens and interpretive walking trails outside. Back on the Strip, Mandalay Bay's ㉒ **Shark Reef Aquarium** has some of the world's last remaining golden crocodiles. Go on a behind-the-scenes tour of this walk-through aquarium or go scuba diving in its 1.3-million-gallon shipwreck theme tank. If history rocks your world, delve into the Cold War era at the Smithsonian-affiliated ㉓ **Atomic Testing Museum**, when monthly above-ground atomic blasts shattered casino windows as mushroom clouds rose on the horizon, and the city even crowned a "Miss Atomic Bomb" beauty queen.

> **DETOUR** When the ding-ding-ding of the slot machines drives you bonkers, **Red Rock Canyon** (☎702-515-5350; www.redrockcanyonlv.org) is the antidote. The startling contrast between the Strip's artificial neon glow and the awesome natural forces at work in the canyon can't be exaggerated. A 13-mile, one-way loop drive passes striking natural features, panoramic viewpoints and hiking trailheads. To get here from Las Vegas, take I-15 south to Hwy 160 or Charleston Blvd west to Hwy 159, both about a 20-mile drive.

No matter how many of Las Vegas' multiple personalities you flirt with – kitschy, extravagant, modern, racy, retro, arty or indie – don't leave town without trying the classic stuff. Plug a few bucks into a slot machine. Catch a stage show, whether it's a chintzy showgirl revue or an all-star production in the ever-expanding ㉔ **Cirque du Soleil** galaxy. Stuff yourself at an luxury casino all-you-can-eat buffet or feast at a steakhouse with all the trimmings, of which there are dozens on the Strip (though honestly, we're just as happy with an all-natural beef burger, sweet-potato fries and a liqueur-spiked milkshake from ㉕ **LBS**). Just don't take this city too seriously – or you'll miss out on all the fun.

Sara Benson

TRIP INFORMATION

GETTING THERE

From Los Angeles, take I-210 east to I-15 north; from Flagstaff, take I-40 west, then Hwy 93 north. It's about 250 miles either way.

DO

Atomic Testing Museum

Buy your tickets for this engaging multimedia museum at the replica Nevada Test Site guard station. ☎ 702-794-5151; www.atomic testingmuseum.org; 755 E Flamingo Rd; adult/child $12/9; ⏰ 9am-5pm Mon-Sat, 1-5pm Sun; ♿

Bellagio

The Italianate resort's faux Lake Como and choreographed fountains are an absurdist take on desert life. ☎ 702-693-7111; www. bellagio.com; 3600 Las Vegas Blvd S; admission free; ⏰ casino 24hr, fountain shows 3pm-midnight Mon-Fri, noon-midnight Sat & Sun

Binion's

When the ex-Horseshoe opened in 1951, Texas gambler Benny Binion transformed Fremont St from a row of sawdust gambling halls into classy carpet joints. ☎ 800-937-6537; www.binions.com; 128 E Fremont St; admission free; ⏰ 24hr

Circus Circus

On the Midway you'll find carnival games and circus acts galore. ☎ 702-734-0410; www.circuscircus.com; 2880 Las Vegas Blvd S; admission free; ⏰ casino 24hr, shows 11am-11pm Sun-Thu, 11am-midnight Fri & Sat; ♿

Cirque du Soleil

Catch the troupe's signature aerial acrobats at various casino hotels around town. www. cirquedusoleil.com; various locations; admission $60-175; ⏰ schedules vary

Fremont Street Experience

Streaking right down the middle of downtown's historic "Glitter Gulch." ☎ 702-678-5777; www.vegasexperience.com; Fremont St, btwn Main St & Las Vegas Blvd; admission free; ⏰ shows hourly dusk-midnight

Imperial Palace

Celebrity impersonators jump up from the blackjack tables to show off their song-and-dance skills. ☎ 702-731-3311; www. imperialpalace.com; admission free; 3535 Las Vegas Blvd S; ⏰ casino 24hr, shows 11am-4am

Liberace Museum

Connoisseurs of kitschy celebrity shrines, don't miss this memorial to "Mr Showman-ship." ☎ 702-798-5595; www.liberace.org; 1775 E Tropicana Ave; adult/child $15/10; ⏰ 10am-5pm Tue-Sat, noon-4pm Sun, guided tours 11am & 2pm Tue-Sat, 1pm Sun

Mirage

When the volcano erupts, it inevitably brings traffic to a screeching halt. ☎ 702-791-7111; www.mirage.com; 3400 Las Vegas Blvd S; admission free; ⏰ casino 24hr, shows hourly dusk-11pm

Paris Las Vegas

Gustave Eiffel's original drawings were consulted before building this 460ft-high replica tower. ☎ 702-946-7000; www.parislas vegas.com; 3655 Las Vegas Blvd S; admission free, tower elevator adult/child from $10/7; ⏰ casino 24hr, tower 9:30am-12:30am, weather permitting; ♿

Shark Reef Aquarium

Over 2000 submarine beasties call M-Bay's walk-through aquarium home. ☎ 702-632-4555; www.sharkreef.com; Mandalay Bay, 3950 Las Vegas Blvd S; adult/child $16/11; ⏰ 10am-8pm Sun-Thu, 10am-10pm Fri & Sat, last entry 1hr before closing; ♿

Spa at Aria

Day-use entry fee includes the unisex outdoor therapy pool; massages, body-care treatments and salon services cost extra. ☎ 702-590-9600, 877-312-2742; www.arialasvegas. com; Aria, 3730 Las Vegas Blvd S; admission $30; ⏰ 6am-8pm

Springs Preserve

Forward-thinking ecomuseum takes visitors on an incredible trip through historical, cultural and biological time. ☎ 702-822-7700; www.springspreserve.org; 333 S Valley View Blvd; adult/child $19/11; ⏰ 10am-6pm, trails close at dusk; ♿

Stratosphere Tower
High-altitude thrill rides cost extra, but they're pretty much worth it. ☎ 702-380-7777; www.stratospherehotel.com; 2000 Las Vegas Blvd S; adult/child $16/10; ☺ 10am-1am Sun-Thu, 10am-2am Fri & Sat, weather permitting; ☝

TI (Treasure Island)
Laugh at the hilarious "Sirens of TI" show, in which feisty, bad-girl buccaneers clad in lingerie do battle. ☎ 702-894-7111; www.treasureisland.com; 3300 Las Vegas Blvd S; admission free; ☺ casino 24hr, shows 7pm, 8:30pm & 10pm, with seasonal variations

Venetian
Graceful bridges and flowing canals almost capture the romantic spirit of Venice. ☎ 702-414-1000; www.venetian.com; 3355 Las Vegas Blvd S; admission free, gondola rides $16-64; ☺ casino 24hr, gondola rides 10am-10:45pm Sun-Thu, 10am-11:45pm Fri & Sat

EAT & DRINK

Beauty Bar
Swill a cocktail and listen to live bands and DJs inside the salvaged innards of a 1950s beauty salon. ☎ 702-598-1965; www.beautybar.com; 517 E Fremont St; admission free-$10; ☺ usually 10pm-4am

Fireside Lounge
Strangely spellbinding hideaway inside a old-school round-the-clock coffee shop. ☎ 702-735-4177; www.peppermilllasvegas.com; Peppermill, 2985 Las Vegas Blvd S; mains $8-23; ☺ 24hr

LBS
Hormone-free beef, free-range turkey and homemade veggie burgers with wildly eclectic toppings. ☎ 702-835-9393; http://lbsburger.com; Red Rock Casino, 11011 W

Charleston Blvd; mains $10-15; ☺ 11:30am-10pm Sun-Thu, 11am-11pm Fri & Sat; ☝

Twist by Pierre Gagnaire
This intimate, mod French dining room is the sole US outpost of this three-star Michelin chef. ☎ 888-881-9367; www.mandarinoriental.com/lasvegas/dining/twist; Mandarin Oriental, 3752 Las Vegas Blvd S; mains $38-56, 6-course tasting menu $185; ☺ 6-10pm Tue-Sat

SLEEP

Golden Nugget
Generously cut, almost gorgeous rooms for anyone hip to the downtown scene. ☎ 702-385-7111, 800-846-5336; www.goldennugget.com; 129 E Fremont St; r & ste $39-450

MGM Grand
There are plenty of rooms and suites to choose from at what was, until recently, the world's largest hotel. ☎ 702-891-1111, 800-929-1111; www.mgmgrand.com; 3799 Las Vegas Blvd S; r & ste $70-1500; ☝

Palazzo
Luxury all-suites hotel tower, brand-name chefs' eateries, glamorous shops and A-list nightclub Lavo. ☎ 702-607-7777, 866-263-3001; www.palazzolasvegas.com; 3325 Las Vegas Blvd S; ste $189-659

Wynn Las Vegas
Five-diamond resort rooms are bigger than your apartment, and come with all the little luxuries. ☎ 702-770-7100, 888-320-7123; www.wynnlasvegas.com; 3131 Las Vegas Blvd S; r & ste $189-815

USEFUL WEBSITES
www.vegas.com
www.visitlasvegas.com

LINK YOUR TRIP   www.lonelyplanet.com/trip-planner
TRIP

OUTDOORS

Week in the Grand Canyon

WHY GO What can be said about the Grand Canyon that hasn't been said thousands of times already, in paintings and words, photographs and movies? There's nothing. And yet, when you stand on that rim for the first time or the 100th time, it's your canyon. Yours alone.

While you could zip up to the South Rim from I-40 after breakfast and be on your way to California by lunch, that won't leave you with much more than you'd get from the standard coffee-table book of glossy photographs. Beautiful views, handsome stone buildings and a quick pop into a museum along with hundreds of other visitors and you've done the canyon. The other extreme sees you packing gallons of water and salty snacks, securing a backcountry permit and tackling a challenging and treacherous multiday hike. But somewhere between the drive-by and the hard core there's a trip that offers everyone from grandparents to toddlers the chance to not only see the canyon but to feel it, so that months and years later, in the chaos of deadlines and kids' soccer meets, you can still smell the canyon dust. This is that trip.

Services at 1,218,375-acre ❶ **Grand Canyon National Park** cluster at two rim-side tourist hubs separated by overnight hikes through, or a 215-mile drive around, the 277-mile-long canyon. Each rim offers dramatically different experiences: you could head straight to the South Rim (7000ft) from Flagstaff, the closest city to the park, and be ooh-ing and ah-ing along with thousands of others in about an hour, but for maximum wow-appeal we far prefer to let the canyon speak for the first time from the cooler and quieter North Rim (8100ft), a five-hour drive from Flagstaff.

Begin and end in ❷ **Flagstaff**. Poke through historic downtown, stopping at one of the many outdoor shops for a water bottle or other supplies, and spend the night at ❸ **Little America Hotel** on the outskirts

TIME
7 days

DISTANCE
500 miles

BEST TIME TO GO
May – Oct

START
Flagstaff, AZ

END
Flagstaff, AZ

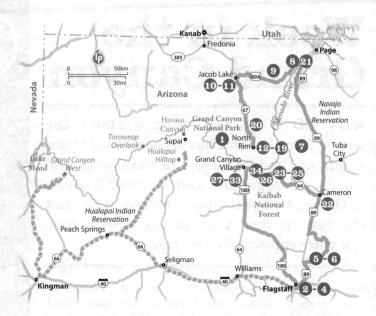

of town. Though it doesn't look like much more than a drab and sprawling 1960s highway motel with an oddly dated penguin logo, you'll find luxurious bedding, spacious rooms and an outdoor pool against 500 wooded acres with a mountain backdrop.

Grab breakfast at one of the many college hangouts in town and bone up on the natural and human history of the Grand Canyon region at the ④ **Museum of Northern Arizona**. From here, head north on Hwy 89 and follow signs onto 36-mile Park Loop Rd 545 to several sites within ⑤ **Sunset Crater Volcano and Wupatki National Monuments**. The crater, left behind by a series of eruptions between 1040 and 1100AD, spewed ash across 800 sq miles. Hopi, Zuni and Navajo were forced to flee until, when the volcano quieted, they returned to farm the fertile land. Stroll the easy 1-mile loop through the tumbling black basalt of ⑥ **Bonito Lava Flow**, stop for a picnic at the Painted Desert Overlook and explore the puebloan remains before returning to Hwy 89.

The 145-mile drive from here to the North Rim takes you through the endless expanse of the ⑦ **Painted Desert** and the Navajo Reservation, across the ⑧ **Colorado River**, past ⑨ **Vermillion Cliffs National Monument**, along which you'll find a couple of restaurants and motels, and up from 3180ft to 8000ft into the aspen and meadows of the ⑩ **Kaibab National Forest**. It's cooler up here, and you dig around for a jacket, maybe a hat, as you stretch the desert out of your bones and breathe in the butterscotch air of the ponderosa. There's a gas station and a handful of other travelers, but not much else. Pop into ⑪ Jacob Lake Inn for a milkshake and burger before tackling the final 44-mile stretch to the rim. Deer graze around here, often wandering onto the road, so drive slowly.

You wind through the woods until, finally, your drive ends at ⑫ **Grand Canyon Lodge**. Built of wood, stone and glass in 1932, this classic national park lodge perches on the canyon edge. Floor-to-ceiling windows offer 180-degree views of the canyon, and the small veranda, with a stone fireplace and rough-hewn chairs, fills with dusty, weary hikers doffing baseball caps and backpacks at the end of every day. They grab a beer from the lodge's ⑬ **Rough Rider Saloon** and mingle on the porch, comparing notes and sharing experiences. Don't even bother to check into your cabin; park the car and join them. After the

DEATH IN THE GRAND CANYON

Hundreds of tourists have died at the Grand Canyon, average Joes posing for a photograph too close to the rim or venturing into the depths without adequate water and salty food. While the ubiquitous signed warnings often end up as white noise, reading the gripping *Over the Edge: Death in the Grand Canyon,* by Michael Ghiglieri and Thomas Myers, may save your life.

sun sets, when most of the children have gone to sleep and the darkness has softened the canyon's ferocity, folks bundle in fleece and sit quietly, studying the stars, breathing in the canyon's emptiness, listening to the silence. We've hiked all the trails, seen all the viewpoints and driven all the drives on both rims, and these Adirondack chairs remain our favorite spot.

On the North Rim there are no museums, bus tours, or shuttles to overlooks. Instead, everyone here, from families to retirees to wilderness backpackers, seems to settle into an intimate, camplike routine. Miles of trails wind through meadows thick with wildflowers, aspen and ponderosa pine, and canyon views peep from behind the trees. After breakfast, head to the tiny visitors center for a schedule of ranger talks and trail guides. Our favorites include the ⑭ **Widforss Trail**, a perfect full-day hike for all ages, the hidden silence at the end of the scrambling ⑮ **Cliff Springs Trail**, and the unsurpassed view from ⑯ **Cape Final**.

"We've hiked all the trails, seen all the viewpoints…and these Adirondack chairs remain our favorite spot."

Experienced hikers can trek into the canyon on the beautiful ⑰ **North Kaibab Trail**, passing from conifer forest to scrubby desert 5 miles to Roaring Springs. The 3 miles just below the rim are steep switchback after steep switchback of grinding haul with no relief from the heat, so hit the trail by 6am to avoid hiking back up in the afternoon sun. Though the trail stretches all the way to the canyon bottom, day hikers should not venture further than Roaring Springs. Stop in the lodge or make advanced reservations to take the journey by mule. Two paved scenic drives meander through the woods to magnificent views: 15-mile **18** **Cape Royal Road** passes several overlooks on its way to a 0.6-mile paved trail to Cape Royal Point, and 3-mile **19** **Point Imperial Road** leads to the highest overlook on either of the rims.

It's hard to leave the gentle rapport of the North Rim but museums, hikes and views at the South Rim await. After four nights, retrace your drive out on Hwy 67 and follow the signs 12 dirt miles off the highway to **20** **Marble View**. Here, a 1-acre meadow, covered with Indian paintbrush and hiding Coconino sandstone fossils, feels like the edge of the earth. Views sweep over the eastern edge of the canyon to the paper-flat expanse beyond. Take time to relax in the quiet; throw the Frisbee, stretch out, read a book.

CLASSIC CANYON RIM-TO-RIM

For a spectacular but sometimes grueling 20-mile overnight journey into searing desert and across the Colorado River, pack smartly, check conditions with a ranger and hit the **North to South Kaibab Trail**. Make reservations up to 13 months in advance for dorm accommodations and dinner at lovely **Phantom Ranch** (www. grandcanyonlodges.com), set among the Cottonwoods along a creek on the canyon bottom, or secure back-country camping reservations. A five-hour rim-to-rim shuttle will run you back to your starting point mid-May to mid-October.

Dip your toes into the icy Colorado at **21** **Lees Ferry** and continue 77 miles to the **22** **Cameron Trading Post** for Navajo tacos before the final 32 miles to the South Rim's **23** **East Entrance**, the starting point for the park's scenic **24** **Desert View Drive**. Your first stop is the spectacular stone **25** **Watchtower** (open daily 8am to sunset), a 70ft Mary Colter masterpiece featuring murals depicting Indian legends and a 360-degree view from the top of its circular staircase. From here it's 26 miles past overlooks and ancient puebloan dwellings at **26** **Tusayan Ruins and Museum** (museum open 9am to 5pm, ruins dawn to dusk daily), to the historic buildings, visitors centers, shops, grocery store, museums, hotels and restaurants of **27** **Grand Canyon Village**.

This is the pulse of the South Rim, the center of the park's tourist industry, and negotiating your way through the fanny packs, cameras and panicked admonishments of parents can easily turn the canyon wow into a frustrated grunt. Embrace the mayhem and find your way to **28** **El Tovar**. Built in 1905, this grand dame of national-park lodges features elegant public spaces and a wraparound porch with views past the crowds to the canyon. Check into a room here or next door at **29** **Bright Angel Lodge** and head to the **30** **Arizona Room** for dinner. Once the day-trippers have made their way home the rim settles down a bit; relax with a prickly-pear margarita on the back porch of El Tovar and watch the day fade over the canyon.

In the morning, orient yourself at **31** **Canyon View Information Plaza**, where you'll find bulletin boards displaying concise information on ranger programs, rim and interior hikes, shuttle hours, guided tours etc. The 12-mile, mostly paved **32** **Rim Trail**, with an elevation change of a mere 200ft, stretches along the rim, connecting viewpoints and passing gift shops and museums housed in historical buildings. While the 3 miles through the village can be packed with people, the mile east of Pima Point overlook is set far back from the road and offers stunning views and relative solitude. Three shuttles, including one along the 7-mile **33** **Hermit Road** that stretches west from the village to Hermits Rest, service most of the Rim Trail's 12 vistas, so you can combine hikes and shuttles to see the entire trail.

Before driving the 80 miles southeast back to Flagstaff for the night, pick up a picnic and head east on Desert View Drive. About a mile east of Yaki Point, just past the second mapped picnic area, pull into the unmarked parking lot beside a gated dirt road. Walk the easy and often empty mile through the shade of ponderosa and past a small clearing with picnic tables and grills to magnificent and quiet **34** **Shoshone Point**. Creep out along the narrow, rocky ledge jutting over the canyon to enjoy a final panoramic view, one of the best in the park.

Jennifer Denniston

> **DETOUR**
>
> Lovely **Havasu Canyon**, with five stunning waterfalls and azure swimming holes, lies below the rim within the 185,000-acre Havasupai Reservation. Hike or ride a mule 10 miles from lonely **Hualapai Hilltop**, four hours west of Grand Canyon Village. At **Grand Canyon West**, 240 miles from Grand Canyon Village, the Hualapai tribe operates tours, including one to a glass-floored sky-walk over the canyon. Go to www.havasupai tribe.com and www.grandcanyonwest.com for details.

TRIP INFORMATION

GETTING THERE
Flagstaff lies 250 miles east of Las Vegas and 145 miles north of Phoenix.

DO
Canyon View Information Plaza
The primary visitors center and South Rim's transportation hub. ☎ bookstore 928-638-7145, visitors center 928-638-7644; Grand Canyon Village, South Rim; ☼ 8am-7pm, with seasonal variations; ♿

Grand Canyon National Park
Admission includes North and South Rims, most of the interior canyon and remote Toroweap/Tuweep Overlook. ☎ 928-638-7888; www.nps.gov/grca; 7-day pass individual/vehicle $12/25; ☼ South Rim year-round, North Rim mid-May–mid-Oct; ♿

Museum of Northern Arizona
Excellent overview of regional culture, history and geology. ☎ 928-774-5213; www.musnaz.org; 3101 N Fort Valley Rd, Flagstaff; adult/child/under 7yr $7/4/free; ☼ 9am-5pm; ♿

Sunset Crater Volcano and Wupatki National Monuments
Ancient puebloan site within miles of AD 1040 eruption. ☎ 928-526-0502, 928-679-2365; www.nps.gov/sucr, www.nps.gov/wupa; 6400 N Hwy 89; 7-day pass adult/under 16yr $5/free; ☼ 9am-5pm; ♿

EAT
Arizona Room
Antler chandeliers and picture windows. ☎ 928-638-2631; Grand Canyon Village, South Rim; mains $7-15; ☼ 11am-3pm, 4:30-10pm, with seasonal variations; ♿

Cameron Trading Post
Eating, shopping, handsome accommodations and a garden courtyard. ☎ 928-679-2231; 466 Hwy 89; mains $8-13 ☼ 6am-10pm May-Aug, 7am-9pm Sep-Apr; ♿

Jacob Lake Inn
Just about everyone stumbles out of their car to stretch their cramped bodies. ☎ 928-643-7232; Hwy 67, Jacob Lake; mains $6-15; ☼ 6:30am-9pm; ♿

SLEEP
Bright Angel Lodge & Cabins
Simple historic lodge rooms and rim-side cabins. ☎ reservations up to 13 months in advance 888-297-2757, same-day 928-638-2631; www.grandcanyonlodge.com; Grand Canyon Village, South Rim; r $79-90, cabins $111-159, ste $138-333; ♿

El Tovar
Coveted suites with spacious patios and views. ☎ reservations up to 13 months in advance 888-297-2757, same-day 928-638-2631; www.grandcanyonlodges.com; Grand Canyon Village, South Rim; r $174-268, ste $321-426; ♿

Grand Canyon Lodge
Western cabins feature gas fireplaces and porches; four rim-side jewels boast full-canyon views. ☎ reservations up to 12 months in advance 877-386-4383, same-day 928-638-2611; www.grandcanyonforever.com; North Rim; r $112, cabins $116-170; ☼ mid-May–mid-Oct; ♿

Little America Hotel
Luxury accommodation behind a roadside motel veneer. ☎ 928-779-2741; www.littleamerica.com/flagstaff; 2515 E Butler Ave, Flagstaff; r $90-180, ste $200-350; ♿

USEFUL WEBSITES
www.kaibab.org
www.flagstaffarizona.org

LINK YOUR TRIP
TRIP

www.lonelyplanet.com/trip-planner

Southwest by Train

WHY GO Stare out your window at the plaintive desert of New Mexico and Arizona, stroll downtown Santa Fe and Flagstaff, bed down in historic hotels, and choo-choo up to the canyon on a vintage train. In an age of rising fuel costs and city sprawl, riding the rails can be easy and economical.

Following the completion of the Transcontinental Railroad in 1869, travelers rode steam trains to the Wild West. Stories of Kit Carson, photographs by Edward Curtis and paintings by Thomas Moran fueled the imagination, and Americans eagerly voyaged across the country to see the mountains and the canyons. They were, after all, young America's cathedrals, billed as grander than the Swiss Alps and more stunning than the Sistine Chapel. While today the interstates, fast-food joints and ubiquitous chain motels give easy access to the West, they take something away as well. This train trip brings back a little bit of that something.

Begin with a few days exploring Santa Fe's historic landmarks, museums and galleries, most within walking distance of ❶ La Fonda. Built in 1922, the hotel was purchased by the Atchison, Topeka & Santa Fe Railroad in 1925 and leased to Fred Harvey. Nicknamed "the civilizer of the West," Harvey had exclusive rights to hotels and restaurants along the rail-line west of the Mississippi, and his elegant "Harvey Hotels" played an integral role in developing tourism in the Southwest. Today, La Fonda drips Southwestern charm, Fred Harvey–style. For a less expensive option, try the ❷ El Rey Inn, a short cab ride from downtown Santa Fe.

The westbound ❸ Amtrak departs Lamy, 20 minutes south of Santa Fe and accessible via a prearranged Amtrak shuttle from your hotel,

TIME
5 days

DISTANCE
470 miles

BEST TIME TO GO
Sep – Jun

START
Santa Fe, NM

END
Grand Canyon
South Rim, AZ

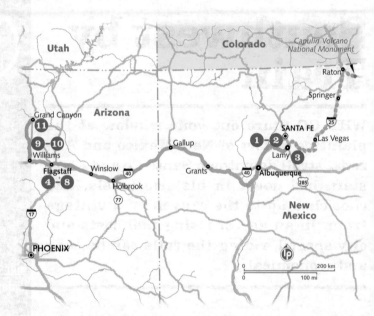

daily at 2:24pm. One-and-a-half hours later, the train arrives in Albuquerque, where vendors sell turquoise jewelry and Navajo-style blankets from the platform and new passengers board. You sit with a glass of wine as the train pulls away from the city's outskirts, and stare out at the massive red-rock mesas and plateaus of Navajo country, your book lying open and unread in your lap. The train rolls on, through the flat desert plains of western Arizona, and, in about five hours, up into the Ponderosa surrounds of ❹ Flagstaff.

NEW MEXICO R&R

Rest your rail-weary bones with a night at **Los Poblanos Historical Inn**, 6 miles and worlds away from the Amtrak station in Albuquerque. This 1934 hacienda sits on 25 acres of gardens and fields, and features lovely rooms, spectacular mountain views, trails along the acequia and breakfasts provided by its organic farm. Swim in the tiled courtyard pool or simply sit on the lawn, watching the cotton from the cottonwood trees drift into the wind.

Gather your bags and hop onto the platform. It's colder here, and even in the summer you will pull on your fleece before heading to a room for the night. The streets of this welcoming college town are busy as you walk to the ❺ **Weatherford Hotel**. Rooms here, decorated with lace curtains, period antiques and claw-foot cast-iron tubs, take you back to the 1930s. The wraparound 2nd-floor porch off the bar is a great place to kick back with a cold beer after the train ride.

Wake up for tofu scrambles and coffee at ❻ **Macy's European Coffee House**, a popular local hangout. Students tap away on computers and parents sit with the crossword puzzle while kids nurse giant mugs of hot chocolate and vegan apple turnovers. If you're feeling ambitious, rent a bike and pick up a bike-trail map at ❼ **Absolute Bikes**. Head west on Route 66 from the shop and follow it for about 3 miles to S Woody Mountain Rd; take a left and ride 4 miles through pines and meadows to the ❽ **Arboretum at Flagstaff**. Walk through and read about the landscape you've been watching from the train window. Trails wind around gardens with more than 2300 species of plants; it's a beautiful spot for a picnic.

DETOUR Riding Amtrak from Colorado, consider jumping off for a day in **Raton**. While there's not much to recommend in this tiny town, rent a car and head to **Capulin Volcano National Monument** (www.nps.gov/cavo). You can drive to the rim of this beautiful cinder cone volcano, formed 60,000 years ago, and take in the 360-degree views; there are also several short hikes.

Jump on the 8:57pm Amtrak or the 3.45pm Amtrak bus shuttle to Williams, a tiny tourist town 35 miles west of Flagstaff, and sleep at ❾ **The Lodge**, an updated Route 66 classic (or stay in Flagstaff and take a shuttle or cab in the morning). The ❿ **Grand Canyon Railway** departs from Williams. Catch the predeparture Wild West Show at 9:30am, with goofy cowboys wearing spurs, silly banter and an Old West facade, before boarding the vintage train for the 2½-hour ride to the canyon.

As the train slowly chugs north, out of town and down in elevation into the shrubbery of the desert, the mountains softly arch in the distance, nothing but shaded silhouettes, and the coolness of morning fades. The train lulls you along, passing landscape void of cars and buildings, and with few other hints of the 21st century. Cowboy singers pass through the train, plucking Johnny Cash, and someone walks down the aisle with bottles of soda and water. Folks exchange stories and talk politics until the train pulls into the station at ⓫ **Grand Canyon National Park**, a short walk from the canyon rim.

Americans resist the train, thinking that they need the flexibility of a car, and perhaps feeling anchorless without it. But this trip is easy, with no middle-of-the-night departures. No, you don't have the same freedom you have in your own car, but it offers a different kind of freedom. You don't have any choice but to slow down and enjoy the ride.

Jennifer Denniston

TRIP INFORMATION

GETTING THERE
Santa Fe lies 63 miles north of Albuquerque. There is a regular shuttle service between Albuquerque Sunport airport and Santa Fe.

DO
Absolute Bikes
A bike is perfect for exploring Flagstaff's museums and parks. ☎ 928-779-5969; www.absolutebikes.net; 200 E Route 66,Flagstaff, AZ; per day $35-70; ☾ 9am-7pm Mon-Fri, 9am-6pm Sat, 10am-4pm Sun; ☕

Amtrak
Amtrak's *Southwest Chief* stops daily in Lamy, New Mexico (with shuttle service to Santa Fe), Albuquerque, New Mexico, Flagstaff, Arizona, and Williams, Arizona, on route from Chicago to Los Angeles. It departs Albuquerque at 4:45pm and arrives at Flagstaff at 8:57pm. ☎ 800-872-7245; www.amtrak.com; one-way Santa Fe to Flagstaff $79-136; ☾ daily; ☕

Arboretum at Flagstaff
Cacti, wildflowers, a butterfly garden and more. Live birds-of-prey shows daily at noon and 2pm. ☎ 928-774-1442; www.thearb.org; 4001 S Woody Mountain Rd, Flagstaff, AZ; adult/6-17yr/ under 6yr $6/3/free; ☾ 9am-5pm Apr-Oct; ☕

Grand Canyon National Park
Make reservations for lunch at the El Tovar lodge, overnight accommodation, tours and mule rides. ☎ 928-638-2631, advanced reservations 888-297-2757, same-day reservations 928-638-2631; www.gov/grca; ☕

Grand Canyon Railway
Vintage train to the South Rim, with hotel and meal packages, and guided tours designed to fit the train schedule. ☎ 800-843-8724, 929-773-1976; www.thetrain.com; Train Depot, Williams, AZ; round-trip adult

$70-190, child $40-110; ☾ depart Williams 9:30am, Grand Canyon 3:30pm; ☕

EAT & SLEEP
El Rey Inn
Route 66 motel with gardened grounds. Some suites have a kiva fireplace. ☎ 800-521-1349; www.elreyinnsantafe.com; 1862 Cerrillos Rd, Santa Fe, NM; r & ste $99-260; ☕

La Fonda
Elegant historic hotel. Catch folk singer Bill Hearne, a Santa Fe institution, at the bar on Wednesday nights. ☎ 505-982-5511; www.lafondasantafe.com; 100 E San Francisco, Santa Fe, NM; r $230-599; ☕

The Lodge
Adobe-style roadside motel with updated rooms and friendly service. ☎ 877-563-4366; www.thelodgeonroute66.com; 200 E Route 66, Williams, AZ; r & ste $90-200; ☕ ☼

Macy's European Coffee House
Decidedly crunchy coffee shop half a block from the train depot. ☎ 928-774-2243; 14S Beaver St, Flagstaff, AZ; ☾ 6am-10pm, kitchen closes at 4pm; ☕

Weatherford Hotel
Serving travelers to the Grand Canyon since 1900. Look for the 2nd-floor porch. ☎ 928-779-1919; www.weatherfordhotel.com; 23 N Leroux St, Flagstaff, AZ; r $60-175; ☕

USEFUL WEBSITES
www.flagstaffarizona.orgwww.santafe.org

SUGGESTED READS
- *Inventing the Southwest: The Fred Harvey Company and Native American Art,* Kathleen Howard
- *Nothing Like It In the World: The Men Who Build the Transcontinental Railroad 1863–1869,* Stephen Ambrose

LINK YOUR TRIP

www.lonelyplanet.com/trip-planner

Santa Fe Arts Amble

WHY GO It's not just carved howling coyotes and neon desert landscapes at this high-country hot spot of American art. Traditional struts alongside modern, and intricate Native American pottery, jewelry and textiles share the stage with alternative performance art, world-renowned opera and a vibrant literary scene that pushes Santa Fe outside the box of regional art.

TIME
5 days

DISTANCE
20 miles

BEST TIME TO GO
May – Dec

START
**Central Santa Fe, NM
Santa Fe**

END
Shidoni Foundry

Beginning in the early 20th century, Anglo writers and visual artists found their way to the foothills of the Sangre de Cristo Mountains. Puebloan peoples had been living here for millennia, and Spanish conquistadors, pioneer settlers, mountain men and the US Army had made inroads more recently. The influx of European and American artists would be simply another layer in the City Different's constantly shifting population and emerging identity. Their influences, however, would transform the dusty trading post into an international city for art. Santa Fe today wears the confluence of its cultures on its sleeve and revels in its rich history of written and visual art. Contemporary artists continue to stir the pot of the Santa Fe arts scene, and the city's museums, galleries and art festivals hold their own on the world stage.

What better place to hunker down for a week of Santa Fe art than the former home of Witter Byner (1881–1968), a poet and pillar of the Santa Fe Writers' Colony. Now a gracious B&B, the ❶ **Inn of the Turquoise Bear** boasts courtyards and evening wine.

Begin at ❷ **Museum Hill**, a beautiful compound of four art museums, desert gardens and a recommended outdoor café with vista views of shadowed piñon-covered hills, chamisa and sagebrush. Here

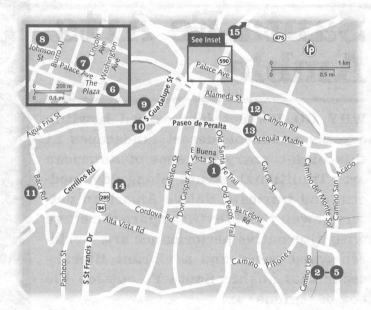

you'll find the Museum of International Folk Art (arguably our favorite of all Santa Fe museums) and the Museum of Indian Arts and Culture, two of four museums that comprise the **3 Museum of New Mexico**. Sculpture-lined trails link these to the **4 Museum of Spanish Colonial Art** and the **5 Wheelwright Museum of the American Indian**.

Another day or two of museum ambling explores a cluster of art museums within walking distance of the shops and restaurants around the Plaza. Shatter clichéd ideas of Native American art at the **6 Museum of Contemporary Native Arts**, boasting the single largest collection of paintings, beadwork, clothing and more, from more than 120 Native American nations. Images and sounds from the short films featured during our last visit linger hauntingly.

A classic 1917 adobe and the third of four museums within Museum of New Mexico, the **7 New Mexico Museum of Art** celebrates work by artists who lived in or visited the state since the arrival of the railroad in 1879, including masterpieces from the Taos Society of Artists and the Santa Fe Society of Artists. From April to November, the museum offers "art walking tours" (10am, $10). Down the street is the **8 Georgia O'Keeffe Museum**, which opened to

MARK YOUR CALENDER!

Performing arts and annual festivals require a bit of planning. Our favorites include the **Santa Fe Opera**, **Lensic Theater**, **Indian Market** and **Spanish Market**. Go to www.santafeartsandculture.org for calendar and tickets.

great fanfare in 1997. It houses more than 1000 of the iconic recluse's paintings, drawings and sculpture, and boasts an excellent restaurant.

Had enough museums? Pick up a full-color Collector's Guide (free from www.collectorsguide.com), fill your water bottle and hit the adobe-lined streets for a day of gallery crawling – the fun is in the wandering. Begin at the **9 Railyard District**, home to the decidedly urban **10 Site Santa Fe**, a hybrid gallery-museum with changing exhibits that lean towards installation pieces and cutting-edge multimedia extravaganzas, and several excellent contemporary art galleries within five minutes of one another. Dash away from tourist crowds for lunch of ahi tuna over rice noodles or an over-stuffed veggie sandwich at **11 Counter Culture** before returning to town for a stroll down historic tree-lined

> **ASK A LOCAL**
>
> "For avant-garde music, go to **High Mayhem** (www.highmayhem.org; a multimedia arts facility and record label). They can be really out there and funky but usually good quality. Young people show their art at **Meow Wolf** (1403 2nd St) – a lot of graffiti. It's probably open if there's someone there. Definitely check out the **Center for Contemporary Art** (www.ccasantafe.org) – there are two galleries and a theater screening indie and foreign films. I like **La Boca** (72 W Marcy) for flamenco dancing and tapas."
>
> *Frank Ragano, Santa Fe, NM*

12 Canyon Rd. Artists including Alice Corbin Henderson (of *Poetry Magazine*), John Sloan and Andrew Dasburg made this neighborhood, once a farming community for Spanish settlers, their home in the early 20th century. By 1925 it had become the pulse of Santa Fe's emerging arts scene.

Don't miss **13 photo-eye Bookstore and Gallery**, one block south of Canyon Rd. With contemporary exhibits and an exhaustive book collection ranging from *A Walk in Beauty: A Navajo Family's Journey Home* to Anthony Karen's chilling documentary on the Ku Klux Klan, this is one of the best of its kind anywhere. Next door is an excellent independent bookstore and a local coffee hangout with outdoor seating.

After a day of galleries, rest those aching feet over margaritas, carne adovada and housemade tortillas at **14 Maria's**. Wagon-wheel chandeliers and rough-hewn furniture, originally from La Fonda, one of the city's oldest hotels, give this under-the-radar Santa Fe institution an old-school vibe. In the morning, drive about 6 miles north on Bishops Lodge Rd to 6 grassy acres of sculptures at peaceful creek-side **15 Shidoni Foundry**. It makes a lovely spot for a picnic – pick up supplies a mile north at Tesuque Market.

DH Lawrence once wrote that in the fierce New Mexico sun, "a new part of the soul woke up suddenly." We agree. There's just something about this place that does, indeed, wake up the soul.

Jennifer Denniston

HISTORY & CULTURE

TRIP INFORMATION

GETTING THERE

Santa Fe lies 60 miles north of Albuquerque on I-25. Take the St Francis Dr exit and follow signs to the Plaza.

DO

Georgia O'Keeffe Museum

Ask about guided tours to her home and studio in Abiquiu. ☎ 505-946-1000; www.okeeffemuseum.org; 217 Johnson St; adult/under 18yr $10/free, Fri 5-8pm free; ☽ 10am-5pm Sat-Thu, 10am-8pm Fri

Museum of Contemporary Native Arts

Native art from the Southwest and beyond. ☎ 505-983-8900; www.iaiamuseum.org; 108 Cathedral Place; admission $5; ☽ 10am-5pm Mon-Sat, noon-5pm Sun

Museum of New Mexico

Encompasses four separate museums; multimuseum prices include Museum of Spanish Colonial Art. ☎ 505-946-1000; www.museumofnewmexico.org; Santa Fe Plaza & Museum Hill; 1-2 museums for 1 day New Mexico residents/nonresidents $9/12, 5 museums for 4 days $18/20, under 16yr & Fri 5-8pm free; ☽ 10am-5pm Tue-Sun, 10am-8pm Fri, with seasonal variations; ♿

Museum of Spanish Colonial Art

Traditional arts including weaving and furniture collected since 1928. ☎ 505-982-2226; www.spanishcolonial.org; Museum Hill; adult/under 16yr $6/free; ☽ 10am-5pm Tue-Sun; ♿

New Mexico Museum of Art

See Museum of New Mexico, above.

photo-eye Bookstore and Gallery

Premier resource for classic and cutting-edge photography. ☎ 505-988-5152; www.photoeye.com; 370 Garcia St; ☽ gallery 10am-5pm Tue-Sat, bookstore 10am-6pm Mon-Sat

Shidoni Foundry

Gallery and sculpture gardens. Ask about Saturday foundry pours. ☎ 505-988-8001; www.shidoni.com; 1508 Bishops Lodge Rd, Tesuque; admission free; ☽ 10am-5pm Tue-Sat, gardens dawn-dusk daily; ♿

Site Santa Fe

Cornerstone of Santa Fe's international contemporary art scene. ☎ 505-989-1199; www.sitesantafe.org; 1606 Paseo De Peralta; ☽ 10am-5pm Thu-Sat, 10am-7pm Fri, noon-5pm Sun, with seasonal variations

Wheelwright Museum of the American Indian

Native American Art with an emphasis on the Southwest. ☎ 505-982-4636; www.wheelwright.org; Museum Hill; admission by donation; ☽ 10am-5pm Mon-Sat, 1-5pm Sun; ♿

EAT & DRINK

Counter Culture

Eclectic fare and patio seating. ☎ 505-995-1105; 930 Baca St; mains $7-12; ☽ 8am-9pm Tue-Sat, 8am-2pm Sun, 8am-3pm Mon; ♿ 🐾

Maria's

New Mexico home cooking with more than 100 margaritas; the owner literally wrote the book (*The Great Margarita Book*, by Al Lucero) on the Southwest classic. ☎ 505-983-7929; 555 W Cordova; mains $8-13; ☽ 11am-10pm Mon-Fri, 11am-12pm Sat & Sun; ♿

SLEEP

Inn of the Turquoise Bear

Throngs of artists once gathered here for what Ansel Adams called "Bymer Bashes." ☎ 505-983-0798; www.turquoisebear.com; 342 E Buena Vista St; r $99-235; ♿ 🐾

USEFUL WEBSITES

www.santafe.org
www.santafegalleryassociation.org
www.lonelyplanet.com/trip-planner

LINK YOUR TRIP

Four Corners Cruise

WHY GO From the neon chaos of Las Vegas to the solitude of the Grand Canyon, the scenery on this epic 3000-mile road trip across five states is ripped straight from the silver screen. Throw in a Wild West back-story, neohippie art colonies, giant cacti and UFOs and get ready for one grand Jack Kerouac–style adventure.

Your iconic journey starts in ❶ Las Vegas, America's most scintillating adult playground. Seedy yet decadent, Sin City is a puzzling paradox where fate is decided by the spin of a roulette wheel and time seems irrelevant. Here the sight of the Great Pyramids of Egypt, the Eiffel Tower, the Italian lake country and the Brooklyn Bridge in the same mile, leave you feeling like you've stumbled into someone else's acid trip. Is that really a bible-toting Elvis kissing a giddy young couple that's just pledged eternity in the Chapel of Love? A Gucci-garbed porn star hawking her hip-hop demo amid the chaos of clanking slots and flashing neon? The answer is more than likely yes.

All that glitters is likely gold in this high-octane desert oasis, where the poor feel rich and the rich lose thousands. At the opulent ❷ Bellagio, glamour's sweet stench is thicker than the cigarette smoke of the blue-haired grandmother feeding quarters into the nickel slots. Inspired by the beauty of lakeside Italy, the casino resort is the city's original Europimp pleasure palace. Check out the ceiling in the hotel lobby. It's made from a vibrantly colored bouquet of 2000 handblown glass flowers.

Las Vegas tempts you to lose your inhibitions and indulge your naughtiest fantasies. And what better place to loosen up than Sin City's guiltiest new pleasure, the ❸ Pussycat Dolls Lounge? Lingerie-clad

TIME
2 – 3 weeks

DISTANCE
3000 miles

BEST TIME TO GO
Year-round

START
Las Vegas, NV

END
Las Vegas, NV

ladies do a little aerial swinging, play rub-a-dub-dub in a tub and flaunt their bodies during sexy song-and-dance numbers at this burlesque lounge inside Caesar's Palace. When the club opened, Busta Rhymes got so excited he jumped on stage and inadvertently started a tradition. Eva Longoria Parker, Nicole Kidman and Jessica Simpson are just a few of the celebrities who have performed impromptu with the Dolls since.

High-drama and neon drenched, the ❹ **Palms** casino hotel is just off the strip and caters to the Hollywood crowd. Paris Hilton and her pals like to play in exclusive sci-fi inspired ❺ **ghostbar** on the 55th floor. It has amazing 360-degree panoramic views of the famous Las Vegas Strip. When you can't keep your eyes open, move the party to your room. We hear the Hugh Hefner Sky Villa –with a round bed, and a glass-enclosed infinity pool on the porch – is the sexiest room in town.

After a couple days in Las Vegas, make a run for the border. The Arizona border, that is. It's about 250 miles from Sin City to Arizona's favorite crunchy college-meets-ski town, ❻ **Flagstaff**, your destination for the night. The drive itself is attractive, linking up Route 66 in Kingman and following an old stretch of the "Mother Road" east over empty umber hills and tumbleweeds before climbing into the gentle mountains outside Flagstaff. You'll be feeling road worn and weary by this point, so check into the ❼ **Hotel Monte Vista**, once the inn of choice for film stars like Humphrey Bogart, Clark Gable and

Jane Russell. As befits a place with such a pedigree, it is said to be haunted (but only by friendly ghosts, the proprietors proclaim).

It's just under 80 beautiful, winding miles from Flagstaff to America's most iconic natural attraction, the **8** **Grand Canyon**. Although many people (and tour buses) see little more of the park than the South Rim viewing center, to do so would be a shame. To make the most of this national park, you need to devote at least three days to the region. Whether you get to the bottom via mule or foot power is not important, but spending the night at **9** **Phantom Ranch** on the canyon floor is paramount. Catch a Grand Canyon sunset, an amazing play of light and shadow, from the porch of the **10** **El Tovar** on your last night. Albert Einstein and Teddy Roosevelt have both slumbered at this rambling 1905 wooden lodge, and so should you. The place hasn't lost a lick of its genteel historic patina.

"As befits a place with such a pedigree, Hotel Monte Vista is said to be haunted..."

Loop south from the Grand Canyon and drive through 110 miles of Arizona's red rock country to **11** **Sedona**. With spindly towers, grand buttes and flat-topped mesas carved in crimson sandstone the town can easily hold its own against national parks when it comes to breathtaking beauty. Memorialized in countless Western flicks, the scenery has provided a jaw-dropping backdrop for those riding tall in the saddle. Though Sedona was founded in the 19th century, the discovery of energy vortices here in the 1980s turned this once modest settlement into a bustling New Age destination – many believe this area is the center of vortices that radiate the Earth's power.

Follow Hwy 89A south from Sedona. The first part of the drive winds through the best of red rock country – when the light hits these massive rocks at the right angle they glow tomato, pumpkin and gold. It then climbs the crumbling ridge of the Mogollon Rim to **12** **Jerome**, our favorite ghost gone gallery town in the Southwest. Wedged into steep Cleopatra Hill, Jerome resembles those higgledy-piggledy Mediterranean hamlets clinging to a rocky hillside. Well, at least from afar. Close-ups reveal a history solidly rooted in the Old West. Jerome was home of the unimaginably fertile United Verde Mine, nicknamed the "Billion Dollar Copper Camp." It was also the wickedest town in the West, teeming with brothels, saloons and opium dens. When the mines petered out, the remaining residents looked to tourism as the new gold.

Spend the night at the **13** **Mile High Inn**. Once a bordello and then a hardware store, today it's a snug, but haunted, B&B. Reserve the Lariat & Lace Room for the best chance of seeing a ghost; the former madam supposedly still hangs out here. The **14** **Asylum Restaurant**, in the Jerome Grand Hotel, has the best views and food in town. The venerable dining room is decorated with deep-red walls, lazily twirling fans and gilded artwork.

A conglomeration of some 20 cities zippered together by freeways, ⑮ Phoenix, 120 miles south, resembles one giant (and not particularly pretty) strip mall upon first look. But there's much more here than seen on the initial glance. Phoenix is an excellent place to get pampered in a ritzy spa at a five-star resort, dine on juicy steaks and practice your golf game – there are more than 230 courses in the metropolis. Try staying at the ⑯ Boulders Resort, where tensions evaporate the moment you arrive. It's a desert oasis blending nearly imperceptibly into a landscape of natural rock formations that is home to the ultra-posh Golden Door Spa and an 18-hole Jay Morris–designed championship golf course.

It's just a short hop from Phoenix south to the bustling college town of ⑰ Tucson. Less intimidating than her big sister, Tucson is Arizona's second-largest city, but feels like a small town. This is a town rich in Hispanic heritage (more than 20% of the population is of Mexican or Central American descent), so Spanish slides easily off most tongues and high-quality Mexican restaurants abound. The eclectic shops toting vintage garb, scores of funky restaurants and dive bars don't let you forget Tucson is a college town at heart, home turf to the 37,000-strong University of Arizona (U of A). Right in the thick of things downtown, infamous bank robber John Dillinger and his gang were captured at the ⑱ Hotel Congress during their 1934 stay after a fire forced them out of their guest room. Today this bohemian vintage beauty remains a hot spot to slumber. Don't miss one of Tucson's best live-music venues, Club Congress, which is in the same building.

ASK A LOCAL

"What so special about Santa Fe? The light. The atmosphere. It is like not being in America, and yet I am still here. There is no place else in the country with architecture like here. One of the great things about Santa Fe is it's the classic American small town. I go to restaurants and always run into people I know. I even run into them on the sidewalk. And it's not pretentious. That's part of why I moved here."

Ted Flicker, Santa Fe sculptor

Get a good night's rest in Tucson, because your next destination is 475 miles (eight hours) away in southeastern New Mexico. It's a long haul across from Tucson to ⑲ Carlsbad Caverns National Park, but this stretch of pavement is made for road-tripping. Pump up the stereo and sing at the top of your lungs as you whiz past fields of giant cacti, huge skies and pancake-flat desert on your way to this enchanted underground wonderland. Musty-smelling limestone and fluttering free tail bats (the population is 250,000 strong) add to the creepiness as you descend 800ft into the strange underground world of one of the planet's greatest cave systems. Ranger-led tours take you into the dripping heart of the 75-sq-mile network of some 100 caves. Emerge before sunset. You don't want to miss the cartoonlike spectacle of thousands of bats flying from the mouths of the caves, cutting black lines through the crimson sky as they circle overhead, looking for a buggy dinner.

Move from bats to extraterrestrials by following Hwy 285 north to 20 Roswell, the alien capital of the world. Sure this town is about as cheesy as it gets for most of us, but conspiracy theorists and *X-Files* fanatics journey here in the utmost seriousness. Whether or not you believe a flying saucer crashed here in July 1947, Roswell merits a visit if only to experience America's alien obsession. While in town, make sure to pay a visit to the International UFO Museum & Research Center. It just might make a believer out of you...

Spunky 21 Santa Fe is the next tick on your list. The USA's oldest capital is also the country's top art destination. Home to retired cityfolk and with world-class galleries and adobe everywhere, it's the heart and soul of New Mexico. Food is just another form of art in Santa Fe, and it's always a toss-up whether the city boasts more quality restaurants or galleries. Either way, you can't go wrong at 22 Shed, a low-key restaurant right on the historic plaza. Sink your teeth into a freshly squeezed lime margarita, creamy guacamole and a spicy green chile–drenched enchilada and you'll think you've died and gone to Southwest foodie heaven. Cut northwest from Santa Fe, through the nuclear town of 23 Los Alamos, and into Indian country. The wild northern corner of the state has long been the domain of the Navajo, Pueblo, Zuni, Apache and Laguna people.

New Mexico, Arizona, Utah and Colorado meet at the 24 Four Corners Navajo Tribal Park. Plant a foot in each state – this is the only spot in America where four states touch in one corner – and take a silly picture. Then cross into southwestern Colo-

> **DETOUR** Climb aboard the steam driven **Durango & Silverton Narrow Gauge Railway** (www.durangotrain.com) for the train ride of the summer. The train, running between Durango and Silverton, has been in continuous operation for 123 years, and the scenic 45-mile journey north to Silverton – the entire town is a National Historic Landmark – takes 3½ hours each way. The voyage costs $75 for adults and $45 for children. It is most glorious in late September or early October when the trees put on a magnificent color show.

rado. With striking scenery, wild history and cool mountain towns, this part of the state looks like it belongs in a John Denver music video. There is a mystery without a conclusion in the ruins of 25 Mesa Verde National Park, your first stop in Colorado. In AD 1300 an entire civilization of Ancestral Puebloans vanished without a trace. Their disappearance has proven so intriguing that eight centuries later, historians and tourists flock to the cliffside empires in search of puzzle-solving clues. The largest, and most impressive, cliff dwellings are around Wetherhill and Chapin Mesas. Wear sturdy shoes –

hiking here involves scrambling up ancient wooden ladders and down narrow holes.

After you've gathered all your clues, head east on Hwy 160 for 65 miles to 26 **Durango**, your destination for the night. It's one of those archetypal old Colorado mining towns filled with graceful old hotels and Victorian-era saloons; a place seemingly frozen in time. The waiter slinging drinks at the scarred wooden bar is dressed straight out of the early 19th century. The antique-laden inn and the musician pounding ragtime on worn ivory keys add to the surrealism. It usually takes stepping into a classy store or modern restaurant to break the spell of yesteryear, and realize it's still the early 21st century and you haven't really traveled back to 1898. There's a dining option poised to charm the most critical of palates and a store for any desire, from outdoor apparel to fancy jewelry or funky retrogarb. Durango's lovely old-world 27 **Strater Hotel** is the best place to sleep. The museum-worthy interior features a Stradivarius violin and gold-plated commemorative Winchester in the lobby.

"you may hear spontaneous popping noises in distant rocks – the sound of arches forming."

Head west to eastern Utah when you are finished exploring Durango. Nicknamed Canyon Country, this desolate corner of Utah is home to soaring snow-blanketed peaks towering over plunging red-rock river canyons. The terrain is so inhospitable that it was the last region to be mapped on continental the USA. Utah's largest and wildest park is 28 **Canyonlands National Park**. Over 65 million years, water carved serpentine, sheer-walled gorges along the course of the Colorado and Green Rivers, which now define the park's three districts. Arches, bridges, needles, spires, craters, mesas, buttes – wherever you look there is evidence of crumbling, decaying beauty and a vision of ancient earth. Hike, raft and 4WD (Cataract Canyon offers some of the wildest white water in the West), but be sure that you have plenty of gas, food and water before leaving the hub town of Moab. Difficult terrain and lack of water render this the least developed and visited of the major Southwestern national parks. The Island in the Sky district, 32 miles south of Moab off Hwy 191 and Hwy 313, is the easiest area to visit.

It's about 50 miles from the Island in the Sky District to 29 **Arches National Park**. Northeast of Moab, the park is home to the most crimson arches in the world. Consider a moonlight exploration, when it's cooler and the rocks feel truly ghostly. Many arches are easily reached by paved roads and relatively short hiking trails. Highlights include Balanced Rock, the oft-photographed Delicate Arch (best captured in the late afternoon) and the spectacularly elongated Landscape Arch. As you casually stroll beneath these monuments to nature's power, listen carefully, especially in winter, and you may hear spontaneous popping noises in distant rocks – the sound of arches forming.

Encircled by stunning orange rocks and the snowcapped La Sal Mountains, ⓺ **Moab** lies between the two parks and is Utah's adrenaline-junkie destination. In this active and outdoorsy town with legendary slickrock mountains, it seems as though every pedestrian clutches a Nalgene water bottle and every car totes a few dusty mountain bikes. Moab bills itself as Utah's recreation capital, and it delivers. Get some rest at the ⓷⓵ **Gonzo Inn**, a fun and funky boutique with a gecko theme. Check out retro color splashes in the spacious rooms and suites, which also boast kitchenettes and cool patios.

Follow Hwy 191 south from Moab (it eventually becomes Hwy 163) for about 150 miles, dipping back into Arizona to see drop dead gorgeous Monument Valley. Home of western America's most visceral landscape, it's nearly impossible to visit this sacred place without feeling a serious sense of déjà vu. That's because the flaming-red buttes and impossibly slender spires bursting to the heavens have starred in countless Hollywood Westerns. Great views of the rock formations are found all along Hwy 163, but to get up close and personal follow the signs to ⓷⓶ **Monument Valley Navajo Tribal Park**. From the visitor center, a rough and unpaved road goes through 17 miles of stunning valley views. Continuing south on Hwy 160 from Monument Valley, you'll cross through the vast lands of the Navajo Reservation. The evidence of hard times is everywhere here, from the rusting tumbledown trailers to social services buildings in small nowhere towns. Still, gorgeous sites are peppered throughout.

> **DETOUR** An alternative way to reach Las Vegas from the Moab area takes you along Utah's most scenically orgasmic byway, Hwy 12, stopping along the way to gawk at magnificent **Bryce Canyon National Park**. The road eventually merges with Hwy 15 south to Las Vegas. Make sure to take advantage of the byway's pull-offs to watch this amazing hued landscape slide from slickrock desert to red rock canyon to wooded high plateau.

Nine miles off Hwy 160, ⓷⓷ **Navajo National Monument** is one of the lesser visited cliff dwellings in the region. Hike to the sublimely well-preserved Ancestral Puebloan cliff dwellings of Betatkin and Keet Seel. Accessible only by foot, there's something truly magical about approaching these ancient stone villages in relative solitude. You can also walk a half-mile from the visitor center to catch a glimpse of Betatkin.

The nearby Hopi Reservation is also worth exploring. Don't miss the village of ⓷⓸ **Walapi** on First Hopi Mesa –the reservation stretches across three mesa tops. The most dramatic of the Hopi enclaves, Walapi dates back to AD 1200 and clings like an aerie onto the mesa's narrow end – the mostly empty old sandstone-colored stone houses seem to organically sprout from the cliffs. The Hopi are best known for their ceremonial dances, although many, especially the super-sacred Kachina Dances, are Hopi-only affairs. These are serious, holy ceremonies not meant for photo-snapping or gawking tourists. Each village decides which dancees it allows the public to attend, but your best shot is between late August and November, when the Social and Butterfly Dances take place.

It's a grueling 370-mile drive northeast (take Hwy 264 east from the Hopi Reservation) to ㉟ **Canyon de Chelly National Monument** on the outskirts of Ganado, but the remote and beautiful park is worth the nearly eight-hour drive. A National Park Service–maintained site on private Navajo land, multipronged Canyon de Chelly (pronounced d-SHAY) is far removed from time and space and modern civilization. It shelters prehistoric rock art and 1000-year-old Ancestral Puebloan dwellings built into water-resistant alcoves.

NAVAJO CRAFTS

The Navajo rely on the tourist economy to survive; help keep their heritage alive by purchasing their renowned crafts – you'll see stalls and gift shops throughout the Navajo Nation, the reservation that is also home to Monument Valley's legendary scenery. The Navajo are best known for their intricately carved animal fetishes like turquoise bears, coyotes, bison and other animal talismans.

Follow Hwy 191 south across the psychedelic painted desert – this is another magnificent bit of pavement – until it links up with I-40 in Chambers. From here retrace your footsteps west to Las Vegas. Plan a few celebratory nights in Vegas at the end of your trip. You will have completed nearly 3000 miles around the most iconic attractions in the West, so treat yourself to some bubbly, a massage and room service at a dazzling hotel in the country and century of your choice.

Becca Blond

TRIP INFORMATION

GETTING THERE

Las Vegas is 575 miles west of Albuquerque and 300 miles northwest of Phoenix on Hwy 15.

DO

Arches National Park

Five miles north of Moab, it features the world's largest concentration of sandstone arches. ☎ 435-719-2299; www.nps.gov/arch; Hwy 191, UT; 7-day pass person/vehicle $5/10; ☉ visitors center 7:30am-6:30pm Apr-Oct, 8am-4:30pm Nov-Mar

Bellagio

The original opulent Las Vegas pleasure palazzo. Casino guests are first dazzled by the choreographed dancing fountain show every 15 to 30 minutes during the afternoon and evening. ☎ 702-693-7111; www.bellagio.com; 3600 Las Vegas Blvd S, Las Vegas, NV; ☉ 24hr

Canyonlands National Park

Covering 527 sq miles this is Utah's largest and wildest national park. The most accessible entrance is 32 miles south of Moab. ☎ 435-719-2313; www.nps.gov/cany; 7-day pass person/vehicle $5/10; Hwy 313, UT; ☉ visitors center 8am-4:30pm

Carlsbad Caverns National Park

The entrance to this giant cave system is 23 miles southwest of Carlsbad town. ☎ 575-785-2232, reservations 877-444-6777; www.nps.gov/cave; 3225 National Parks Hwy, NM; 3-day pass from $6; ☉ 8am-7pm, last entry 5pm May-Aug, 8am-5pm, last entry 3:30pm Aug-May; ♿

Mesa Verde National Park

It's about 21 miles to the visitors center from the park entrance. ☎ 800-449-2288; www.nps.gov/meve; Hwy 160, CO; 7-day pass person/vehicle $8/15, with seasonal variations; ☉ 8am-4:30pm Mon-Fri, with seasonal variations

Monument Valley Navajo Tribal Park

The visitors center has a blissfully cold water fountain and a restaurant. The road into the park is accessed from Hwy 163. ☎ 435-727-5870; www.navajonationparks.org; Monument Valley Rd, AZ; per person $5; ☉ 6am-8:30pm May-Sep, 8am-4:30pm Oct-Apr

EAT & DRINK

Asylum Restaurant

Amazing views and equally good food inside the Jerome Grand Hotel. The wine list is long. ☎ 928-639-3197; 200 Hill St, Jerome, AZ; dinner mains $18-29; ☉ 11am-3pm & 5-9pm

ghostbar

A clubby crowd, often thick with celebs, packs this sky-high ultra lounge. DJs spin pop and hip-hop mash-ups. ☎ 702-942-6832; 55th fl, Palms, 4321 W Flamingo Rd, Las Vegas, NV; cover $10-20; ☉ 8pm-4am

Pussycat Dolls Lounge

Lingerie-clad ladies do a little aerial swinging and flaunt sexy song-and-dance numbers at this SoCal import. ☎ 702-731-7873; Pure Nightclub, Caesar's Palace, 3570 Las Vegas Blvd S, Las Vegas, NV; cover $10-30; ☉ 10pm-4am Tue, Fri & Sat, performances 10:45pm & 11:45pm

Shed

This family-run, James Beard Award–winning, restaurant has been serving New Mexican fare in an atmospheric 1692 adobe since 1953. ☎ 505-982-9030; 113½ E Palace Ave, Santa Fe, NM; lunch $8-10, dinner $9-20; ☉ 11am-2:30pm & 5:30-9pm Mon-Sat; ♿

SLEEP

Boulders Resort

Relaxation is paramount at this world-class resort with a posh spa and equally fabulous golf course. ☎ 480-488-9009, 866-397-6520; www.theboulders.com; 34531 N Tom Darlington Dr, Phoenix, AZ; casitas $250-700, villas from $500

El Tovar

Standard rooms are on the small side, so those in need of elbow room should go for the deluxe rooms. Both offer casual luxury and high standards of comfort. ☎ same-day reservations 928-638-2631, up to 13 months in advance 888-297-2757; www.grandcan yonlodges.com; Grand Canyon Village, AZ; r $174-268, ste $321-426

Gonzo Inn

The ample suites can comfortably sleep four. Amenities include wi-fi and a swimming pool; rates include breakfast. ☎ 435-259-2515, 800-791-4044; www.gonzoinn.com; 100 W 200 South, Moab, UT; r $160, ste $205-340

Hotel Congress

Many rooms at this beautifully restored1919 hotel have period furnishings; ask for one at the end of the hall away from the thumping Club Congress. ☎ 520-622-8848, 800-722-8848; www.hotelcongress.com; 311 E Congress St, Tucson, AZ; r $79-119; ⚅

Hotel Monte Vista

The 50 rooms and suites have been restored to their 1920s glory, and are old-fashioned but comfortable. Wi-fi is available. ☎ 928-779-6971; www.hotelmontevista.com; 100 N San Francisco St, Flagstaff, AZ; r $70-170

Mile High Inn

Seven newly remodeled rooms have such unusual furnishings as a tandem chair and a lodge pole bed. Breakfast served until noon. ☎ 928-634-5094; www.jeromemilehighinn. com; 309 Main St, Jerome, AZ; r $85-130, ste $195

Palms

Standard rooms are generous, as are tech-savvy amenities. Request an upper floor to score a Strip view. ☎ 702-942-7777, 866-942-7770; www.palms.com; 4321 W Flamingo Rd, Las Vegas, NV; r $69-459, ste from $209

Phantom Ranch

There are six cozy cabins sleeping four to 10 and single-sex dorms outfitted for 10 people. It ain't luxury, but after a day on the trail, even a bunk is likely to feel heavenly. ☎ 888-297-2757; www.grandcanyon lodges.com; Bottom of the Grand Canyon, AZ; bunk $42

Strater Hotel

Romantic rooms feature antiques, crystal and lace. Beds are super comfortable with impeccable linens. Prices are slashed by more than 50% in winter. ☎ 800-247-4431; www. strater.com; 699 Main St, Durango, CO; r $179-289 May-Oct, $108-189 Oct-May

USEFUL WEBSITES

www.americansouthwest.net
www.notesfromtheroad.com

LINK YOUR TRIP

www.lonelyplanet.com/trip-planner

Written in Stone: Utah's National Parks

WHY GO Stare at the swirling pattern long enough and you'll swear you can see the red rock move. Hiking through Utah's five national parks, you get to test your limits and bear witness to the earth's power at its most elemental. Here the story of wind and water is written in stone.

Though the whole alphabet soup of Southern Utah's national parks – Zion to Arches, west to east – lies within the Colorado plateau, each region has its own distinctive features. Start at the lowest elevation (just 3800ft on the canyon floor) in **1** Zion National Park and you can feel the desert heat. Temperatures in July consistently top 100°F, and late October still has warm, sunny fall days. The park's red canyon cliffs are so strikingly dramatic that it's hard to imagine that the little Virgin River carved them.

The carved red rock views from the winding and main canyon drive (on a shuttle system in summer) are great. But to get a real feel for the place, hike **2** The Narrows, the slender canyons along the river's north fork. In an easy-does-it day, you can trek a few miles north from Riverside Walk to experience the sheer fluted walls closing in and then slosh back. Adrenaline junkies will shuttle out early to the Narrows trailhead near Chamberlain's Ranch so they can complete the full 16-mile, 13-hour journey in a day. Plan to get wet: at least 50% of either hike is in the river.

Prefer dry land? More than one hiker has challenged their fear of heights on **3** Angels Landing. Here the 5-mile one-way trail is so steep (1450ft ascent) and narrow (5ft at some points) that there's a wide spot known as "chicken-out point." To conquer one cleft formed by wind and water, 22 stonework switchbacks were carved into the

TIME
8 days

DISTANCE
400 miles

BEST TIME TO GO
**May – Jun,
Sep – Oct**

START
**Zion National
Park, UT**

END
**Canyonlands
National Park
– Needles
District, UT**

rock. Thankfully, an exertion-filled day doesn't necessarily need to end in a night on the hard ground. The motel rooms at the ④ **Zion Lodge** may not be much to look at, but the lodge provides a front-row seat for the kaleidoscope of colors reflected off red rock at sunset. Your best bet for dinner is in nearby Springdale, where you can savor ancho chile–seared lamb paired with one of hundreds of wines at ⑤ **Spotted Dog Café**. The town is so laid-back, you won't even have to change out of your hiking togs.

A more isolated and even-terrained hiking experience is to be had if you drive out to ⑥ **Kolob Terrace Rd**, 14 miles west of Springdale. Stunning views of carved red rock pop up at every turn as you weave in and out of park lands. Thirty-eight miles north, turn off toward ⑦ **Lava Point** for an excellent overlook, a six-site first-come, first-serve campground, and higher-elevation hikes that lead to cool, flower-filled meadows.

Stay over a second night because you also want to explore the one-10th-as visited Kolob Canyons arm of Zion NP, 40 miles (70 minutes) northwest. In some ways the 5-mile scenic route starting from ⑧ **Kolob Canyons Visitor Center** is even more stunning than the main drive. Here the cliff walls are closer and the roads are paved with red rock asphalt (yes, it's really red), making the experience all the more colorfully intense. At the end of the road, follow ⑨ **Timber Creek Overlook Trail** (half a mile) up a 100ft ascent to a small peak with expansive finger canyon views.

The next day, broad leaves and deciduous trees give way to evergreen needles and soaring pines as you make your way from Zion to ⑩ **Bryce Canyon National Park**. Though only 77 miles northeast, a 4000ft elevation change sets Bryce a world apart. Here the freeze-and-thaw of winter snows has gotten under the earth's skin. Expanding fissures created the spindly spires and sherbet-colored fins (thin walls of rock) that stand like sentinels in ⑪ **Bryce Amphitheater**. Best viewed from Sunset and Sunrise Points, you can also hike below the lookouts and experience the awe of these sand castle shapes from below. Zig-zag 521ft down from Sunset Point along Navajo Trail through Wall Street slot canyon, under arches and past hoodoos – all glowing an eerie orange.

WHAT'S A VIRGIN TO DO?

Fourteen miles west of Springdale, it's hard to miss the town of Virgin. Have your picture taken inside the "Virgin Jail" or "Wild Ass Saloon" before you feed the deer, donkey and llama in the petting zoo, or buy ice cream in the Trading Post. What pure kitschy fun! The tiny outpost town has another claim to fame – in 2000 the council passed a law requiring residents own a gun. It's a $500 fine if you don't.

Follow the Queen's Trail along the canyon floor up to Sunrise Point and back along the overlooking rim for a fairly strenuous 3-mile loop (you climbed down, you have to climb up).

Bryce does have a lodge, but you can't visit the park without noticing the sleep-shop-eat-and-outfit-for-all-adventures complex ⑫ **Ruby's Inn**, sprawling just north of the entrance. What was originally just a motel gained town status in 2007 and has been a family-owned part of the landscape since 1919. Everybody passing through to Bryce stops here at one time or another – to sleep, get gas, have a meal or book a helicopter or horseback ride; it's an experience.

Driving west from Bryce on Hwy 12, almost all you see south of the road – expansive plateaus, candy cane–striped sedimentary hills, uplifted ridges – belongs to the nation's largest park. ⑬ **Grand Staircase-Escalante**

ASK A LOCAL "For end of the day photography it's the tremendous views off Kolob Terrace Rd. Here you stand at the extreme western edge of the Colorado Plateau and can see the land fall away beneath your feet. To the north are beautiful vistas into the Kolob finger canyons and Hop Valley. If you're fortunate, you may glimpse the sizable elk herd that frequents the large meadow to the southeast of the Hop Valley trailhead."
Michael Plyler, Director, Zion Canyon Field Institute, Springdale

National Monument (GSENM) is bigger than Rhode Island (1.9 million acres) and about a zillion times more desolate. Entry is free and infrastructure is limited to the towns along the park's edge; dirt roads traverse the expanse. ⑭ **Upper Calf Creek Falls** is the GSENM's most accessible and popular day-hike trail (2 mile round-trip). Start on the spur road between mile markers 81 and 82 off Hwy 12. Cairns lead the way down a fairly steep trail with far-ranging views. When the trail splits, veer toward the lovely pools and swimming hole on the upper trail.

Your most comfortable bet is to base yourself in the microscopic town of Boulder at ⑮ **Boulder Mountain Lodge** (66 miles northeast of Bryce), a rustic ecolodge with high-thread-count sheets. Then you can dine on soulful, earthy preparations of locally raised meats and site-grown organic vegetables at the associated ⑯ **Hell's Backbone Grill**. If you can tear yourself away after waking up to birdsong on the 15-acre wildlife sanctuary you should at least go for one backroad drive through the GSENM.

> **DETOUR**
>
> A Salvador Dali–like rock fantasy, a field of giant stone mushrooms or an acid trip the creator went on? You decide what the stadiumlike valley of stunted hoodoos resembles. We think the 3654-acre **Goblin Valley State Park** (www.stateparks.utah.gov), 58 miles northeast of Capitol Reef, looks like a big playground. Follow the trail down from the overlooks, then you're allowed to climb down, around, even over, the evocative "goblins" (2ft- to 20ft-tall rock formations). Detour west off Hwy 24 along a signed, paved road 12 miles to the entrance.

Just west of town, the rough gravel-and-dirt ⑰ **Hell's Backbone Rd** climbs steadily uphill for 14 miles before reaching a one-lane bridge teetering above a plunging canyon sure to give you vertigo. Cut the engine, get out and listen to the wind funneling up the canyon while giant crows float silently on the thermals above. Look to the east, where Boulder Mountain is carpeted with deep-green forests and stands of quaking aspens that turn a gorgeous gold in September.

Do pay a visit to ⑱ **Anasazi State Park** before you continue. Thousands upon thousands of pottery shards, on display in the museum, were excavated here in the 1950s. Outside are the scant remains of the Ancestral Pueblo, an archaeological site, inhabited from AD 1130 to 1175.

Ever wondered what happens when the earth's crust buckles? See for yourself at ⑲ **Capitol Reef National Park**, 48 miles northeast of Boulder. The rocky valleys, petrified yellow sand dunes and steep switchbacks along Hwy 12 hint of the geography to come. Over the course of millions of years, a 100-mile-long monocline fractured and uplifted, creating Waterpocket Fold, the centerpiece to Capitol Reef National Park. (The formation once blocked settlers' westward migration like a "reef" blocks a ship's passage.) An interpretive drive leads south along the fold, past abandoned homesteads and orchards where the sweet smell of free-for-your-picking pears, apricots, peaches and apples hangs in the air June through October. Pitch your tent next to the fragrant fields at ⑳ **Fruita Campground** and listen as the Fremont River babbles along.

If you're camping there's little reason to go into the closest town, Torrey, 11 miles west. Well, except to eat at one of southern Utah's best restaurants, **㉑ Café Diablo.** Its stylized Southwestern cooking – including succulent vegetarian dishes – bursts with flavor. Even if you order just appetizers ($9 to $11) and dessert, you won't leave hungry.

You have to venture north into the park to get an up-close view of the monocline's Capitol Dome. Arrange a shuttle and bike rental from **㉒ Backcountry Outfitters** and you can pedal the 58-mile loop through **㉓ Cathedral Valley.** An otherworldly landscape of stark desert (bring water!) studded with rounded hills of volcanic ash and towering sandstone monoliths rewards the effort. The sedimentary layers you see – chocolate browns, ashen grays, sandy yellows and oxidized reds – together reveal 200 million years of history.

If Capitol Reef reveals the passage of time, **㉔ Arches National Park,** 142 miles northeast, captures a snapshot. Almost all of the rock you see here is entrada sandstone, a muddy-to-orangish-red stone laid down during the Jurassic period. The namesake arches formed when salt pockets raised the earth and water erosion tore it down. Freeze-and-thaw continues to slough off rock, creating arches (which will all eventually collapse). Book ahead for a **㉕ Fiery Furnace** guided hike, so you can explore the maze of spectacularly narrow fissures and giant fins that are the first step in arch formation.

RABBITS & RATTLESNAKES

No, it's not the name of a new band; rabbit and rattlesnake are the kinds of sausages you can try at **Buffalo Bistro** (www.visiteastzion.info/buffalobistro.html) in Glendale. Hang out on the rustic back porch while your buffalo ribs sizzle on the grill and the boisterous owner-chef holds court. Stop for dinner en route from Zion to Bryce (April through October, reservations advised); who knows, the Testicle Festival (serving Rocky Mountain oysters) may even be on.

The king of all named park features is **㉖ Delicate Arch.** You've seen this one: it's the unofficial state symbol and is pictured on just about every piece of Utah tourist literature ever printed. The 3-mile round-trip trail to it ascends slickrock, culminating in a wall-hugging ledge. If you've filled up on the homemade scones and jam for breakfast at the lovely **㉗ Sunflower Hill B&B** where you're staying, you

"a one-lane bridge teetering above a plunging canyon sure to give you vertigo."

may not need it. But you could bring a picnic lunch, ditch the crowds by passing beneath the arch and drop down to enjoy it on the other side several yards away.

Your sizable base town, Moab, 5 miles south of the park, is a good place for stocking up on everything. It's also ideally located to reach several other parks as day trips. In the morning you're off to see one of the Canyonlands National

Park sections, but first stop on the way in to **28 Dead Horse Point State Park**, where the views pack a wallop. Peer down 2000ft to the Colorado River and 100 miles across a mesmerizing stair-step red rock landscape. (You might remember this epic vista from the final scene in *Thelma & Louise*.) Legend has it that cowboys blockaded the mesa to corral wild horses, and that they forgot to release them upon leaving. The stranded equines died within view of the unreachable water below, hence the name.

Ten miles further (30 northwest of Moab) lies **29 Canyonlands National Park – Island in the Sky District**. Think of this as the overview section of Canyonlands, an RVer's special, with paved drives and easy-access lookouts. Here vast serpentine canyon stippled with white cliffs loom high over the Colorado and Green Rivers, their waters 1000ft below the rim at Islands in the Sky.

For the more adventurous, **30 Canyonlands National Park – Needles District**, 75 miles south of Moab, is where you can hike down in and among the skyward-jutting spindles and spires, blue-hued mesas and majestic buttes. Trek the awesome 11-mile **31 Chesler Park Loop** through desert grasslands, past towering red-and-white-striped pinnacles and between deep and narrow fractures (some only 2ft across). Elevation changes are mild, but the distance makes it a moderate-to-difficult day hike. Don't forget to stop on the way back to Moab to see the hundreds of petroglyphs at the **32 Newspaper Rock Recreation Site**. Note that the impressive panel of horse and human etchings photographs better in the late-afternoon sidelight.

JUMP OFF A CLIFF

Hiking into a slot canyon so slender you have to turn sideways, and rappelling down a cliff face (or climbing up one) are just a few of the adventures available in southern Utah. Unless you're an expert, you'll need a guide. Outfitters are found in pretty much every town adjacent to a park. In Springdale, contact **Zion Adventure Company** (www.zionadventures.com), in Escalante, **Excursions of Escalante** (www.excursions-escalante.com), and in Moab, the **Moab Adventure Center** (www.moabadventure center.com).

And leave plenty of time to get back to Moab for your reservation at casually elegant **33 Center Café**, which supports the local farmers market and youth garden. Lingering over sautéed shrimp with cheddar-and-garlic grits served in the back garden, you have ample opportunity to reflect on not only the earth's bounty but the tumultuous forces that created it. Now if your calves would just stop throbbing from so many days of hiking.

Lisa Dunford

TRIP INFORMATION

GETTING THERE

From Las Vegas, Zion National Park is a 160-mile, 70mph-plus drive northwest up I-15 and off onto smaller Hwy 9.

DO

Anasazi State Park

The ruins aren't as evocative as some in southeastern Utah, but Ancestral Puebloan museum exhibits are well worth seeing. ☎ 435-335-7308; www.stateparks.utah.gov; Main St/Hwy 12, Boulder; 7-day pass individual/family $4/10; ⏰ 9am-5pm Mon-Sat Nov-Apr, 8am-6pm daily Apr-Oct

Arches National Park

Stop at the visitors center to see a park overview video, check ranger-led activity schedules, reserve your tickets for a Fiery Furnace hike and buy maps. ☎ 435-719-2299; www.nps.gov/arch; Hwy 191; 7-day pass person/vehicle $5/10; ⏰ visitors center 8:30am-6:30pm

Backcountry Outfitters

In addition to 4WD and hiking packages, Backcountry Outfitters also rents bicycles ($38 per day) and ATVs ($150 per day) and provides shuttles. ☎ 435-425-2010; www.ridethereef.com; 677 E Hwy 24 at Hwy 12, Torrey; ⏰ 9am-6pm

Bryce Canyon National Park

The visitors center sells loads of maps and books and gives out info about weather, road conditions and campsite availability. ☎ 435-834-5322; www.nps.gov/brca; Hwy 63; 7-day pass person/vehicle $12/25; ⏰ visitors center 8am-8pm May-Sep, 8am-4:30pm Nov-Mar, 8am-6pm Apr & Oct

Canyonlands National Park – Island in the Sky District

Pick up your overlook driving tour CD for $10 (or rent it for $5) before you drive out to the fabulous vistas. ☎ 435-259-4712; www.nps.gov/cany/island; Hwy 313; 7-day pass person/vehicle $5/10, includes Needles District; ⏰ visitors center 9am-4:30pm Oct-Mar, 8am-6pm Mar-Oct

Canyonlands National Park – Needles District

Ask rangers about the 4WD roads the park is known for. Even if you're hiking, watching can be quite a show. ☎ 435-259-4711; www.nps.gov/cany/needles; Hwy 211; 7-day pass person/vehicle $5/10, includes Island District; ⏰ visitors center 9am-4:30pm Oct-Mar, 8am-6pm Mar-Oct

Capitol Reef National Park

Watch the short film, then ooh and aah over the 64-sq-ft park relief map, carved with dental instruments. Ranger-led hikes available. ☎ 435-425-3791; www.nps.gov/care; cnr Hwy 24 & Scenic Dr; 7-day pass person/vehicle $3/5; ⏰ visitors center 8am-4:30pm Sep-May, 8am-6pm Jun-Aug

Dead Horse Point State Park

To escape the small (but sometimes chatty) crowds at the main overlook points, take a walk around the mesa rim. ☎ 435-259-2614; www.stateparks.utah.gov; pass individual/family $2/5; ⏰ visitors center 8am-5pm, trails 6am-10pm

Kolob Canyons Visitor Center

Admission to Zion National Park's main section includes admission to Kolob Canyons, and vice versa. Hold onto your receipt. ☎ 435-586-9548; Kolob Canyons Rd, off I-15; 7-day pass per vehicle $25; ⏰ visitors center 8am-4:30pm Oct-Mar, 8am-5pm Mar-Oct

Newspaper Rock Recreation Area

This tiny, free turn-out showcases a single large sandstone rock panel packed with more than 300 petroglyphs attributed to Ute and Ancestral Puebloan groups. ☎ 435-587-1500; www.blm.gov; Hwy 211

Zion National Park

Rangers are on hand to answer questions and lead interpretive hikes from the main visitors center. Mandatory shuttle rides (April through October) start there. ☎ 435-772-3256; www.nps.gov/zion; Hwy 9; 7-day pass person/vehicle $12/25; ⏰ visitors center 8am-6pm, with seasonal variations

EAT

Café Diablo

Don't miss the creative Southwestern cuisine here. For something you won't find back home, try the rattlesnake cakes. ☎ 435-425-3070; 599 W Main St, Torrey; mains $20-24; ⏱ 5-10pm Apr-Oct

Center Café

Center Café's chef-owner draws from regional American and Mediterranean influences. Budgeteers: come for the small plates served from 3pm to 6pm. ☎ 435-259-4295; 60 N 100 West, Moab; small plates $6-11, mains $18-30; ⏱ 4-10pm

Hell's Backbone Grill

This is foodie destination dining. Save room for desserts such as chimayo-chile ginger cake with butterscotch sauce. ☎ 435-335-7464; Boulder Mountain Lodge, cnr Hwy 12 & Burr Trail Rd, Boulder; mains $12-22; ⏱ 7-11:30am & 5:30-9pm Mar-Nov

Spotted Dog Café

Don't be put off by the white tablecloths and black-shirted waiters; snobbery is not on the menu at this upscale hikers' fave. ☎ 435-772-3244; Flanigan's Inn, 428 Zion Park Blvd, Springdale; mains $19-28; ⏱ 7-11am & 5-10pm Mar-Oct

SLEEP

Boulder Mountain Lodge

Watch the birds flit by at the wildlife sanctuary and stroll through the organic garden. Don't forget to recycle – Boulder Mountain Lodge has a strong eco-aesthetic. ☎ 435-335-7460; www.boulder-utah.com; cnr Hwy 12 & Burr Trail Rd, Boulder; r & ste $99-190; 🚭

Fruita Campground

June through August, the 71 first-come, first-served riverside sites fill up by noon. Drinking water, pit toilets available. ☎ 435-425-3791; www.nps.gov/care; Scenic Dr, Capitol Reef National Park; campsites $10; ♿

Ruby's Inn

Motel rooms, hotel suites, post office, grocery store, ATV rental and outfitter tours are just some of the facilities at Ruby's. ☎ 435-834-5341; www.rubysinn.com; 1000 S Hwy 63, Bryce Canyon; r & ste Mar-Dec $134-190, Dec-Mar $70-119; ♿

Sunflower Hill B&B

Kick back in an Adirondack chair amid the manicured gardens of two inviting buildings – an early-20th-century home and a 100-year-old farmhouse. ☎ 435-259-2974; www.sunflowerhill.com; 185 N 300 East, Moab; r & ste Mar-Oct $165-235, Nov-Feb $125-185

Zion Lodge

Despite a late-'90s American motel style, this park lodge is admirably green: 85% of its power comes from solar and wind, and lodge vehicles are all hybrids. ☎ 435-772-7700, reservations up to 13 months in advance 888-297-2757; www.zionlodge.com; 60 N 100 West; r & ste Dec-Apr $89-120, Apr-Dec $160-185

USEFUL WEBSITES

www.nps.gov
www.utah.com

LINK YOUR TRIP   www.lonelyplanet.com/trip-planner

A Green Chile Adventure

WHY GO Nothing says New Mexico more than green chile. Come in the fall, during harvest season, when the cottonwoods along the Rio Grande are yellow, the smell of roasting chiles and piñon fires permeate the air, and hot-air balloons dot the skies around Albuquerque.

New Mexicans love their chile. Welcome signs on the interstates feature huge red and green chiles, red ristras hang from adobe homes north to south, and even McDonald's offers green chile on its burgers. Chop and scramble it in eggs, stir-fry it fresh with pork for an Asian twist, add it along with lettuce and tomato on a turkey sandwich. You can't get away from the stuff, and while some visitors never do develop a taste for its fire, others soon acquire a discerning palate that drives an obsessive search for the perfect chile. This one's too hot, that one's too gelatinous, this one has no flavor at all, and soon you're talking about chile as much as farmers around here talk about rain. To get a sampling of the state's best, from sauces loaded with chopped veggies to the perfect green-chile cheeseburger, this fiery green trail of chile hot spots takes you to local favorites.

For a tasty cup of java and the hottest green in ❶ Albuquerque, head to the decidedly crunchy ❷ Java Joe's. Hidden in a residential neighborhood off old Route 66, this tiny spot looks, at first glance, like the usual granola and herbal tea hangout. Local art hangs on the walls and half-read newspapers sit on the tables. You can grind your own coffee to take home, or grab a mug to enjoy with a homemade cranberry scone. But don't be deceived – the chile on its chicken burrito packs more punch than a triple espresso, and the black beans are as good as any you'll find in a fancy restaurant. A few miles down the road, past the 1954 Indian art stores and dance clubs along downtown Albuquerque's Central Ave and into student haunts around the University of New Mexico, is ❸ El Patio. A couple of blocks from the

TIME
3 – 4 days

DISTANCE
140 miles

BEST TIME TO GO
Aug – Oct

START
Albuquerque, NM

END
Taos, NM

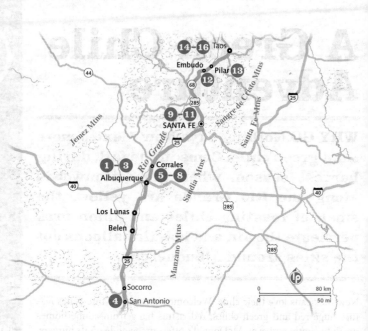

campus on Harvard St, this under-the-radar standby for simple, fresh and tasty fare is easy to miss – look for the vintage neon sign and the blue fence around the tiny patio. Sitting outside with a Dos Equis, a plate of green chile enchiladas and a basket of hot *sopapillas* just might be the closest thing to nirvana this side of the Mississippi. It doesn't take credit cards, but there's an ATM in the back.

If you still haven't found your idea of chile perfection, consider cruising about an hour south on I-25 to blink-and-you-miss-it San Antonio. Here, the dark lil' ❹ **Owl Bar** serves up no-frills chile that's the subject of statewide debate. Some folks drive miles for its green-chile cheeseburger, while others gripe that the reputation is undeserved. The best in New Mexico? You decide.

"it's the green chile that reigns supreme in the fall."

To fully appreciate New Mexican green chile, visit in the late summer or fall, when acres upon acres of chile fields throughout the state begin to ripen and farmers don straw hats to protect their faces from the still-burning desert sun and spread into the fields to hand-pick the fragile pods before they turn red. Despite the Albuquerque sprawl, it's surprisingly easy to find your way to rural pockets of orchards, chile fields and pastures. From I-40 take the Rio Grande Blvd exit (about a mile west of I-25) and head north, past fields and stables, sheep and llamas, rambling ranches and palatial estates, to the farming community of

5 **Corrales**. Here, old Hispanic farming families mingle with organic-inclined newcomers, tiny homes with thick adobe walls sit beside multimillion-dollar haciendas, and dirt roads twist and wind through the cottonwoods.

Once allowed to ripen to red, the flavor of the green chile changes distinctly, and just about every New Mexican prefers one to the other. Both green and red can be used to make sauces for the ubiquitous burrito and enchiladas, but it's the green chile that reigns supreme in the fall. Green-chile stands pop up along country and city roads all over the state, farmers bring overflowing pick-up trucks to grower markets, and New Mexicans get busy preparing the chiles for the upcoming year. In Albuquerque, folks head to **6** **Wagner Farm**, a seasonal farm stand that sells produce grown in their fields throughout Corrales. They bring their coolers or garbage bags, select a bushel for roasting at the cylinder roasters on site, and drag home bags of the blackened pods. Enjoy a fresh-made peach turnover, watch 'em roast the chiles, and pick up a gallon of apple cider.

"The smell of rain mingles with that of roasting chiles, and the Sandia Mountains glow red with the setting sun…"

Just down Dixon Rd from the farm stand is the friendly and simple **7** **Nora Dixon Place**. Take some time to sit in the courtyard, watching the hummingbirds and lizards, enjoying the roses and wisteria. If you're lucky, a passing evening monsoon will settle the dust. The smell of New Mexican rain mingles with that of roasting chiles, and the Sandia Mountains glow red with the setting sun (in fact, Sandia means "watermelon" in Spanish). During the annual balloon fiesta in early October, the skies fill with bright hot-air balloons every morning. Pull on a fleece, pour a mug of coffee and ask for your green-chile eggs outside so you can watch the balloons float in the shadow of the Sandia Mountains. They drift silently above the trees, so close that you can hear the rumble of propane burners, and it's not unusual to see them land in the fields throughout town.

The **8** **Rio Grande Bosque**, home to porcupines, muskrats, birds and more, is about a half-mile walk down

GREEN CHILE BY MAIL

Several companies cater to green-chile addicts, FedEx-ing fresh and frozen green chile anywhere in the US, from California to Maine, Texas to North Dakota.

- www.hatchnmgreenchile.com Fresh Hatch green chiles in 5lb to 25lb bushels; preorder a year in advance.

- www.hotchile.com Order 8lb to 24lb in 2lb bags of roasted, peeled, diced and frozen green chile.

- www.thechileshop.com All things chile, from salsas to jams.

Dixon Rd. Here, a wide red dirt path, popular for horseback riding, biking and walking, hugs the irrigation ditch, and several trails cut over to the Rio Grande. Standing next to the willows by the river, looking at the mountains and listening to the distinct caw of the migrating Sandhill Cranes and the wind in the wizened trees, you'd never know downtown Albuquerque is only a 20-minute drive away. Grab a burrito to go from Wagners to enjoy on your walk.

The autumn ritual of preparing green chile continues in the kitchen, as it takes hours to peel the chiles, scrape the seeds and package them into ziplocks for the freezer. Some go right into the pot, mixed up with family secrets to cook up piquant sauces of green to use year-round on heuvos rancheros, tacos and just about anything else. And some get diced up, thrown into a pot of beans with a little garlic and salt, and left to simmer all day. Unfortunately, if you're like most visitors to New Mexico, you'll hesitate to buy any chiles because, to the average cook, they're mysteriously alien. No worries. Drive up I-25 to **9** **Santa Fe**, swing by Santa Fe train depot to pick up some extra hot green at the year-round Saturday and Tuesday morning farmers market, and take an afternoon class at the **10** **Santa Fe School of Cooking**. Classes are offered just about daily, and they have an excellent collection of Southwest cookbooks and green-chile products, like green-chile pistachios, jelly and mustard. You can try out those recipes in the kitchen of a historic casita at **11** **Dunshees**. Hidden in a quiet stretch of old adobes and desert gardens, this beautifully furnished nest is within walking distance of galleries and shops along Canyon Rd. With a kiva fireplace and private patio, it makes a delightful place to hunker down with a bottle of wine, a piñon fire, and a bowl of your own green-chile stew.

FOOD FESTIVALS

Feast on green chile, piñon and tortillas at these annual celebrations of New Mexico food.

- **Hatch Chile Festival** The sleepy town of Hatch celebrates its most famous export.
- **Santa Fe Wine & Chile Fiesta** Santa Fe chefs pair Southwest dishes with wines from New Mexico and beyond.
- **Whole Enchilada Fiesta** The state's biggest enchilada and plenty of chile.
- **Lincoln County Cowboy Symposium** Cowboy food New Mexico–style.
- **New Mexico Harvest Festival** Historic adobe buildings and chile fields at Rancho de la Golondrinas.

From Santa Fe, it's an easy 1½-hour drive along the Rio Grande River to Taos. Stop at **12** **Embudo Station** for a green-chile burger with a kick – you could spend hours under the shade of a cottonwood not doing much of anything at all. Continuing north, the road passes **13** **Pilar**. Detour a mile or two west on State Rd 570, past several campgrounds, to digest your meal at the bridge over the river. This popular raft launch for white-water trips down the Rio Grande makes a pleasant spot to splash around before returning to Hwy 68 for the final 20-minute stretch to **14** **Taos**. Pedestrian-friendly downtown Taos boasts excellent art galleries, and fantastic hiking trails wind through the aspen and ponderosa of the surrounding mountains. End the day with a pint of green-chile beer and a green-chile smothered burrito at

⑮ Eske's Brew Pub & Eatery. The vegetarian chili, with huge chunks of carrots, zucchini and other goodies, is unusual even in this vegetarian-friendly town, and just the smell of the beer is ecstasy to a green-chile addict. It's an acquired taste, so ask for a sample before ordering a pint. On weekends, it features live music from country to folk to rock.

From Eske's, drive a few miles out of town to **⑯ Old Taos Guesthouse**, a historic bed and breakfast with Southwestern furnishing and viga (wood beamed) ceilings, set on 8 acres of grass and orchards. Views from the courtyard stretch across the volcano-dotted Taos Plateau into the flatness of the horizon.

ASK A LOCAL

"Once you've had green chile, you become an addict. And anytime you're anywhere away from it, you're a fiend to get it. I go to Hatch for my chile. I have my favorite vendor I go to. I bring my big ol' cooler and they roast 'em and I bring 'em home. The road that cuts southwest from Hatch to Demming goes through chile fields and ranch country. It's beautiful."
Angela Le Quieu, Rio Rancho, NM

In the morning, owner Tim will share his favorite hiking trails over a homemade breakfast of fruit, muffins and, you guessed it, green-chile casserole.
Jennifer Denniston

TRIP
80

TRIP INFORMATION

GETTING THERE
Albuquerque lies 63 miles south of Santa Fe on I-25.

DO
Santa Fe School of Cooking
Regular classes on New Mexican cuisine and an excellent selection of cookbooks and green-chile condiments. ☎ 505-983-4511; www.santafeschoolofcooking.com; 116 W San Francisco St, Santa Fe, NM; ⓧ varied

Wagner Farm
Locally grown chile in farming village outside Albuquerque. ☎ 505-898-3903; 5000 Corrales Rd, Corrales, NM; ⓧ Jul-Nov; ♿

EAT
El Patio
University of New Mexico hangout with the city's best green-chile enchiladas. ☎ 505-268-4245; 142 Harvard Dr SE, Albuquerque, NM; mains $5-10; ⓧ 11am-9:30pm Mon-Sat; ♿

Embudo Station
Old narrow-gauge railroad station along the Rio Grande River, with cottonwoods, outdoor seating and chile with a kick. ☎ 505-852-4707; Hwy 68, Embudo, NM; mains $8-15; ⓧ 11am-8pm Thu-Mon, with seasonal variations; ♿

Eske's Brew Pub & Eatery
Drink the chile with a pint of aromatic Taos Green Chile Beer. ☎ 575-758-1517; 106 Des Georges Lane, Taos, NM; mains $5-12; ⓧ 12:30-9pm Sun-Thu, to 10pm Fri & Sat, seasonal variations

Java Joe's
Comfy coffeeshop with black beans and some of the hottest chile in town. ☎ 505-765-1514;906 Park Ave SW, Albuquerque; mains $5-12; ⓧ 6:30am-3:30pm; ♿ 🐾

Owl Bar
Nothing can beat the simple green-chile cheeseburger at this hole-in-the-wall south of Albuquerque. ☎ 505-835-9946; 77 Hwy 380, San Antonio, NM; mains $4-7; ⓧ 11:30am-9pm Tue-Sun Mar-Oct

SLEEP
Dunshees
Beautifully appointed suite or casita with kiva fireplaces, private patios, and gardens. ☎ 505-982-0988; www.dunshees.com; 986 Acequia Madre, Santa Fe, NM; suites $125-162; ♿ 🐾

Nora Dixon Place
Friendly B&B in a rural village outside of Albuquerque. Ask for the Bosque Room, with a kiva fireplace and Mexican tiles. ☎ 505-898-3662; www.noradixon.com; 312 Dixon Rd, Corrales, NM; r $110-125; ♿

Old Taos Guesthouse
This 200-year-old former farm sits on 8 acres of grass and cottonwoods. ☎ 575-758-5448; www.oldtaos.com; 1028 Witt Rd, Taos, NM; r $95-185; ♿ 🐾

USEFUL WEBSITES
www.newmexico.org
www.itsatrip.org

SUGGESTED READS
- *Red or Green? New Mexican Cuisine,* Clyde Casey
- *Artisan Farming: Lessons, Lore and Recipes,* Richard Harris

LINK YOUR TRIP
www.lonelyplanet.com/trip-planner

Gunfighters & Gold Miners

WHY GO Gold, copper and silver mining was big business in the late 1800s, and it drew a motley crew to Arizona. These folks settled disputes over poker games and saloon girls with a quick-draw six-shooter. As Shipherd Reed from the Miners Story Project will show you, their legacy remains in the old mining towns that dot the state.

People who've plunged deep into the earth for copper, gold and other metals tell Tucson resident Shipherd Reed their tales. But he has to work fast – the bold breed is quickly disappearing. "The impetus for this project was the realization that there is no underground mining anymore in Arizona – it's all strip-mining now. This way of life, this culture of underground mining, was a huge part of Arizona for more than a century," he explains.

Start the journey into Arizona's rugged past in ❶ Jerome, an old mining town perched precariously on a hillside 115 miles northwest of Phoenix. Strut into the ❷ Spirit Room, an old gunslingers' saloon, and practice your 12oz quick draw. Modern outlaws, aka bikers, still hang out here. Indeed, groups of bikers rumble into Jerome almost daily, with weekends being especially crazy. And if you get a little too spirited with the Spirit Room crowd, the ultra-friendly ❸ Connor Hotel is attached for lodging.

For a more gentrified experience, drink and dine at the ❹ Asylum Restaurant in the ❺ Jerome Grand Hotel. Once a miners' hospital, it has morphed into Jerome's top address with the views to prove it.

Before leaving town, Reed recommends stopping by the ❻ Mine Museum across from the Spirit Room. The best exhibits are at the

TIME
4 days

DISTANCE
720 miles

BEST TIME TO GO
Oct – Mar

START
Jerome, AZ

END
Phoenix, AZ

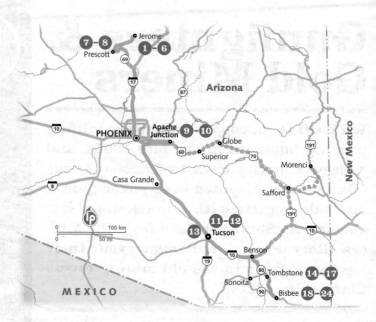

back of the gift shop, detailing early Jerome's ethnic diversity and its thriving red-light district. In ❼ **Prescott**, situated 35 miles southwest of Jerome, it's obligatory to swagger through the swinging doors of a saloon at least once. The ❽ **Palace Saloon**, on Whiskey Row, is the perfect place to give it a go. Imagine you're greeting Doc Holliday or Wyatt Earp – both former patrons – as you belly up at Arizona's oldest frontier bar.

"A disagreement over 1 cubic yard of land often put a miner 6ft under it."

After lunch at the Palace, head south and watch the scenery turn from scrubby rolling hills to towering rock formations around the ❾ **Superstition Mountain Museum** in Apache Junction, 135 miles south of Prescott. Inside you'll learn about the Lost Dutchman Gold Mine, a fabled mother lode that still draws treasure hunters. Feel the fever? You can look for fat nuggets yourself at ❿ **Lost Dutchman State Park**.

Ease 130 miles down I-10 to Tucson and watch the desert get as flat as a board. Time warp into yesteryear at the ⓫ **Hotel Congress**, with its radio-only rooms and Sam Spade movie-set decor. Speaking of drama, bank robber John Dillinger spent a night on the 3rd floor here, until a fire drove him out and, soon enough, into the cuffs of the law.

The next morning, stop by the ⓬ **University of Arizona Mineral Museum** to listen to Reed's miner interviews and ogle mondo crystals. If you're travelling with kids, you'll appreciate ⓭ Old Tucson, which provides a G-rated picture of Arizona's outlaw days. Originally built as a film set, it's now a sort of Wild West theme park set in a huge patch of gorgeous cacti. It's a few miles southeast of the Arizona-Sonora Desert Museum, off Hwy 86.

Seventy-five miles southeast of Tucson, ⓮ Tombstone is billed as "the town too tough to die." Underneath the sometimes-hokey facade lurks an intriguing Wild West history. Visitors can see a reenactment of the shoot out at the ⓯ OK Corral at 2pm daily, with an additional show at 3:30pm on busy days.

Tombstone's one-stop sin shop in the 1880s was the ⓰ Bird Cage Theater – a saloon, dance hall, gambling parlor and home for "negotiable affections." Today it's filled with dusty artifacts like Doc Holliday's old card table. Employees report ghost sightings on a regular basis.

DETOUR To see a modern mining boom town, head to **Safford**, 135 miles north of Bisbee, and the nearby **Graham County Museum** (www.visitgrahamcounty.com). An hour east of Safford, the **Morenci Mine Tour** (☎ 877-646-8687) takes visitors to an open-pit mine in a huge truck. Heading back to Phoenix, pass through **Globe**, another modern mine town, and **Superior**, where there's talk of opening the **Resolution Copper Mine** (www.resolutioncopper.com), a proposed 7000ft-deep shaft that will rely on robotic equipment.

Reed says that mining and gun fighting often came as a pair because back when the West was young, claim borders were often in dispute. A disagreement over 1 cubic yard of land – if that land happened to hold the mother lode – often put a miner 6ft under it. Lots of miners lost their lives in such fights. The ⓱ Boothill Graveyard, off Hwy 80 about a quarter-mile north of town, is where they take their final nap. The OK Corral's unlucky threesome are buried in row 2.

Twenty-five miles south of Tombstone on Hwy 80 is ⓲ Bisbee – the number-one pick for a mining tour, according to Reed, "not just because it's very picturesque, but because they've done a great job of preserving the history there." People who have visited San Francisco might have a déjà vu moment: Bisbee's Victorian buildings are set on rolling hills and the mile-high city is surprisingly cool.

"The parallels between those two cities have always fascinated me," Reed says. "It's fitting that a lot of the people who kept this place from turning into a ghost town were part of the whole Haight-Ashbury scene and came here when that broke up. Now Bisbee is a pretty, artsy place and there is no shortage of characters."

Besides hipness, Bisbee is all about copper. The ⓳ Copper Queen Hotel was built in 1902 to give visiting fat cats a place to spend the night. Cut right to the crux of the matter – literally – with **20 Queen Mine Tours** and delve a quarter-mile straight into the cold earth on a small rail car. Retired miners with firsthand stories of the place serve as guides. Dress as if you're going into a refrigerator; you'll receive a safety jacket, hat and light as accessories.

Dedicate at least two hours to the **21 Bisbee Mining & Historical Museum**, a Smithsonian affiliate. It's housed in the 1897 former headquarters of the Phelps Dodge Copper Mining Co and does an excellent job documenting the town's past and the changing face of mining. You even get to "drive" an industrial mining shovel with a dipper larger than most living rooms.

GEORGE WARREN

He may be credited with discovering Bisbee's mega-rich Queen Mine, but George Warren's tale is a hard-luck one. He was sent to investigate a promising deposit spotted by two other prospectors, and ended up filing the mining claim in his own name. So far, so good. Warren then downed a few drinks at the local pub, boasted that he could outrun a horse, bet his new mine claim on the stunt…and lost. Soon after, Queen Mine started producing a fortune. Warren's consolation prize? Artists modeled the miner on the state seal after him.

If you're lucky, the person collecting admission fees that day will be La Verne Williams, "The Hugging Mayor." The name doesn't lie – she really was Bisbee's mayor at one time, and indeed gives a serious embrace to surprised out-of-towners.

To learn more about Bisbee's unique architecture and modern-day renaissance, take the **22 Historic Walking Tour**. Led by the affable Michael London – in full gunslinger get-up – he's one of the many former San Franciscans who moved to Bisbee in the early 1970s. With historic photographs, he shows how mining irrevocably changed the city over the years.

A high-proof taste of Bisbee's yesteryear swirls in the glasses at the **23 Stock Exchange Saloon**. The original stock boards from 1919 still grace the walls, and these days it's a good place to meet locals and hear live music. For a glimpse of new, sophisticated Bisbee, peek behind the steel art-nouveau door at **24 Cafe Roka**. Modern American cuisine fills the plates here; reservations are essential.

Now that you're no longer a "dandy," or newcomer, in the slang of miners, head back to Phoenix. Take the long way (see the boxed text on p569) to see what modern mining towns look like today.
Josh Krist

TRIP INFORMATION

GETTING THERE

From Phoenix, Jerome is 110 miles northwest via I-17 and Hwy 89A. Bisbee is 210 miles southwest via I-10 and Hwy 80.

DO

Bird Cage Theater

A gaggle of ghosts haunt Tombstone's old sin pit, now transformed into a funky museum. ☎ 520-457-3421; 517 E Allen St, Tombstone, AZ; adult/child/senior $10/8/9; ⏰ 9am-6pm

Bisbee Mining & Historical Museum

Bisbee's riotous heyday comes to life through old photos and interactive exhibits. ☎ 520-432-7071; www.bisbeemuseum.org; 5 Copper Queen Plaza, Bisbee, AZ; adult/child/senior $7.50/3/6.50; ⏰ 10am-4pm

Boothill Graveyard

Gunfighters' headstones fill this old graveyard. The most poetic reads: "Here lies Lester Moore, four slugs from a 44, no less, no more." Enter via the gift shop. ☎ 520-457-9344; Hwy 80, Tombstone, AZ; admission free; ⏰ 7:30am-6pm

Historic Walking Tour

Dig deep into Bisbee's past on this one-hour walkabout. It leaves every hour on the hour. ☎ 520-432-3554; www.discoverbisbee.com; 2 Copper Queen Plaza, Bisbee, AZ; tour $10; ⏰ 10am-4pm

Lost Dutchman State Park

Search for the legendary Lost Dutchman Gold Mine. Or just hike the abundant trails; bring lots of water. ☎ 480-982-4485; www.azstateparks.com; 6109 N Apache Trail, Apache Junction, AZ; pass person/vehicle $2/5; ⏰ sunrise-10pm

Mine Museum

See the Colt pistol used by a local marshal to gun down vigilantes on Main St back in the day. ☎ 928-634-5477; 200 Main St, Jerome, AZ; admission $2; ⏰ 9am-4:30pm

OK Corral

Site of the famous gunfight (reenacted daily)and now the historic heart of Tombstone. ☎ 520-457-3456; www.ok-corral.com; Allen St btwn 3rd & 4th Sts, Tombstone, AZ; admission $10, without gunfight $6; ⏰ 9:30am-5pm

Old Tucson

Built in 1939 as the set for the film *Arizona*, these days it's a silly-fun family theme park. ☎ 520-883-0100; www.oldtucson.com; 201 S Kinney Rd, Tucson, AZ; adult/4-11yr $17/11; ⏰ 10am-4pm; ♿

Queen Mine Tours

Dress warmly and prepare to go deep into the hillside for a clamber around the hard places miners worked. ☎ 520- 432-2071; www.queenminetour.com; 119 Arizona St, Bisbee, AZ; adult/5-11yr $13/5.50; ⏰ 9am-3:30pm

Superstition Mountain Museum

Yes, it's known for its Lost Dutchman Gold Mine exhibit, but there's also the Elvis Presley Memorial Chapel. ☎ 480-983-4888; www.superstitionmountainmuseum.org; 4087N Apache Trail, Apache Junction, AZ; adult/child/senior $5/free/4; ⏰ 9am-4pm

University of Arizona Mineral Museum

Miners' oral histories and lots of rocks sit below Flandrau Science Center on the university campus. ☎ 520-621-7827; www.uamineralmuseum.org; 1601 E University Blvd, Tucson, AZ; adult/under 4yr $4/free; ⏰ 9am-5pm Fri & Sat

EAT & DRINK

Asylum Restaurant

The fantastic views and wine list make Asylum the most upscale place in town. Just ask the ghosts who haunt it. ☎ 928-639-3197; 200 Hill St, Jerome, AZ; dinner mains $18-29; ⏰ 11am-9pm

Cafe Roka

Four-course dining is the rule at this sophisticated restaurant, so prep those taste buds for dishes like the signature roast duck.

HISTORY & CULTURE

Reservations essential. ☎ 520-432-5153; 35 Main St, Bisbee, AZ; dinner mains $15-25; 🕐 5-9pm Thu-Sat, with seasonal variations

Palace Saloon

Arizona's oldest frontier bar comes complete with a swinging saloon door, framed photos and Old West memorabilia, including antique gambling machines. ☎ 928-541-1996; www.historicpalace.com; 120 S Montezuma St, Prescott, AZ; mains $8-20; 🕐 lunch & dinner

Spirit Room

A dark, old-time saloon with a pool table and bordello-scene mural. Live music every Saturday and Sunday afternoon and some weeknights. ☎ 928-634-8809; 166 Main St, Jerome, AZ; 🕐 11am-1am

Stock Exchange Saloon

Keeping the legacy of historic Bisbee alive one drink at a time, the long bar is a prime place to meet local characters. ☎ 520-432-9924; 15 Brewery Ave, Bisbee, AZ; 🕐 11am-1:30am Wed-Sun, 3pm-1:30am Mon & Tue

SLEEP

Connor Hotel

Rooms waft old-school flair while staying spiffy and comfy. Rooms 1 to 4 get most of the noise from the Spirit Room bar, below. ☎ 928-634-5006, 800-523-3554; www.connorhotel.com; 164 Main St, Jerome, AZ; r $90-165; 🔧

Copper Queen Hotel

The Copper Queen combines late-19th-century elegance with modern amenities. Its downstairs restaurant and patio bar draw locals and tourists alike. ☎ 520-432-2216; www.copperqueen.com; 11 Howell Ave, Bisbee, AZ; r $90-180

Hotel Congress

A historic property where old-fashioned radios are the in-room entertainment. Opt for a room at the hotel's far end if you're noise sensitive. ☎ 520-622-8848; www.hotelcongress.com; 311 E Congress St, Tucson, AZ; r $70-120; 🔧

Jerome Grand Hotel

Get a 3rd-floor balcony room for otherworldly views of the valley below. It's a 10-minute uphill walk from the main strip. ☎ 928-634-8200; www.jeromegrandhotel.com; 200 Hill St, Jerome, AZ; r $120-195, ste $205-460

USEFUL WEBSITES

www.azjerome.com
www.discoverbisbee.com

LINK YOUR TRIP

www.lonelyplanet.com/trip-planner

Rafting the Colorado

WHY GO There's a reason they call it the trip of a lifetime. Rafting the Colorado River is truly awesome, not only for its monster rapids, but also for the ever-changing beauty of canyon walls, and the solitude of sleeping under the stars in the inner-gorge wilderness.

So you've scored a river permit, gathered your buddies, and hired an outfitter to supply your crew with cook stoves and ammo cans. Or maybe you've booked a week on a commercial trip and can leave the planning to a pro. Either way, you're about to experience one of the most mind-blowing rivers you'll ever have the privilege of running. All told, the layers of canyon geology through which you'll travel represent at least two *billion* years, and if that doesn't get your rocks off, the white water will. With so many notable rapids, beautiful side hikes, camping beaches and put-in and take-out points, this trip's route should be viewed as a necessarily exclusive selection of highlights.

Slap on the sunscreen, keep your camera handy (but safely zipped into a plastic bag), and get ready to head down 87, 187 or maybe all 279 river miles of the mighty Colorado. You're slashing your connection to the outside world for the duration of your trip.

Take a virgin dip into the frigid river at ❶ Lees Ferry and then put in. Take a look at the low-lying cliffs of the Moenkopi Formation atop darker red Kaibab Limestone rising around you, the top layers of Grand Canyon strata. Then glide onto the Colorado and muse on the depth – literal and figurative – of this venerable canyon you're rafting. As you gently float away from Lees Ferry, you'll enter Grand Canyon National Park after several miles of smooth water and riffles. But after some fun first-day rapids like ❷ Badger Creek and Soap Creek, you'll get the hang of the Colorado River rating system, which classifies rapids from Class 1 to 10 (rather than the standard I to V).

TIME
7 – 14 days

DISTANCE
187 river miles

BEST TIME TO GO
May – Oct

START
Lees Ferry, AZ

END
Whitmore Wash, AZ

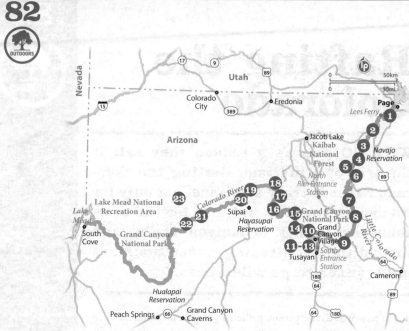

After your first day on the river, you'll also get into the groove of using those regulation ammo cans (wilderness toilets) within the privacy of tamarisk stands – giving guilty thanks for invasive flora – and sleeping on still beaches along the river. Waking on that first morning is magical, with the light slowly sliding down canyon walls and revealing the rich color of rock and river.

> "the only place you'll ever ride minirapids with a personal flotation device strapped to your bum."

On your second day, stop at **3** **North Canyon** for the hike through this side canyon leading to a small, seashell-like grotto. Depending on the weather, there may be a reflective pool here filled with tadpoles or a running tributary with little waterfalls to negotiate along the way. The curves, ridges and slabs of this side canyon give a tantalizing first taste of what you'll explore on stops along the river. Once you return to the river, you'll quickly bounce into the **4** **Roaring Twenties**, a series of smallish but not insignificant rapids along mile markers 20 through 29.

Day three you'll drift by the verdant cliffside oasis of **5** **Vasey's Paradise**, kept green by the water springing directly out of the wall, before rounding a bend and spying the wide mouth of **6** **Redwall Cavern**. As you approach, the scale of this enormous cave will surprise you. The cool sand inside may bear the tracks of ravens, frogs or kangaroo mice, but you'll want to add your own when you stop here for a snack and some Frisbee tossing. Camping isn't allowed in the cavern, but if you happen to have brought your cello, the acoustics in here are fantastic.

Though the fourth day brings hours of drifting between a few good rapids, highlights include a hike up to ancient **7** **Puebloan granaries** at Nankoweap, where ancient Native Americans stored corn for lean times. Hiking the steep trail to the granaries affords spectacular views of river and canyon from high above. Downriver, marvel at the intensely saturated purple, blue and green layers of Bright Angel Shale before stopping at the confluence of the incongruously warm, turquoise-hued **8** **Little Colorado River**. This may be the only place you'll ever ride minirapids with a personal flotation device strapped to your bum.

ASK A LOCAL

"Rafting the canyon is like a chess game, in that there are so many moves you can make – the only difference is, you never lose. As in chess, every move affects the rest of the game, but on the river you could do 20 miles every day doing short hikes, or maybe 45 miles in a day, camp there for two nights and spend all day hiking. But whatever moves you do make, you can't ever lose."

Matt Fahey, Flagstaff

Big-time white water is on tap for day five, with monster rapids like Unkar, Nevills, **9** **Hance** (rated as Class 7 or 8), Sockdolager and Grapevine Rapids socking you with some of that cold Colorado water and a fat adrenaline rush. *This* is what it's about. Between exhilarating drops, catch your breath and check out the oldest rock layer in the canyon, which now appears at river level. The smooth, black Vishnu schist shot through with pink Zoroaster granite is some of the oldest exposed rock on the planet, and it marks your arrival at **10** **Phantom Ranch**.

If you're just stopping off here, sip some cold lemonade in the canteen (keep your cup for cheap refills) and scratch out some postcards from the bottom of the canyon. This is also the only place on the river where you'll find a pay phone. If you're spending the night at Phantom, claim a comfy bunk in your air-conditioned cabin, hop in the shower, and take in a ranger talk before dinner. No one goes hungry here, and vegetarians can look forward to some killer chili.

Pre-hydrate the night before your hike out, and be sure to get started at (or before) first light to avoid hiking in the heat of midday. At the end of your six- to nine-hour haul up the **11** **Bright Angel Trail**, reward yourself with a soul-soothing chocolate ice cream at the South Rim's **12** **Bright Angel Fountain**, sitting on the low, circular stone bench on the rim as you rest your legs. After your (heavenly) shower, sup on half a citrus-glazed roast duck, sip a prickly-pear margarita on the back deck and lie down for a very sound sleep at the historic **13** **El Tovar**.

If, lucky you, your river time flows on, you'll continue floating under the suspension bridges near Phantom Ranch to hit several serious rapids, beginning with Horn Creek, with the challenge of Granite soon thereafter, and finishing with the famously burly ⑭ **Hermit Rapid**. After punching through the waves and holes of these beasts, you'll be elated, exhausted and ready to spend a calm night between the soaring schist walls of the Upper Granite Gorge.

By day six, you're well into river mode, relishing the prospect of slamming through big white water such as the 'gems' – starting with the biggest, ⑮ **Crystal Rapid**, and followed by the midsized Sapphire, Turquoise, Ruby and Serpentine Rapids. A series of smaller rapids are strung out below these, after which some floating brings you to ⑯ **Elves Chasm**. Hiking up this narrow canyon leads to a lush little grotto fed by small waterfalls, at the bottom of which lies an inviting pool amid moss and maidenhair ferns.

You may be on day seven or eight by the time you hit the churn of ⑰ **Deubendorff Rapid** and make a beeline for ⑱ **Tapeats Creek**, one of the absolute best hikes in the canyon. Even better, when made into a 10-mile loop connecting with Deer Creek, the hike takes in waterfalls, pools laced with scarlet monkey flowers and watercress, narrows carved through Tapeats sandstone and well-preserved petroglyphs. The source of Thunder River lies along this hike, an incredible waterfall shooting out of the base of a cliff into Tapeats Creek.

RIVER PERMITS

On commercial river trips, the operator takes care of your permit. If you plan a private trip, you must apply for your own through the **Grand Canyon River Permits Office** (☎ 928-638-7843, 800-959-9164; https://npspermits.us). Entering your name in the weighted lottery system requires an application fee of $25, and if you win a spot, you'll automatically be charged a non-refundable $400 deposit (which goes toward the cost of the $100-per-person permit). See www.nps.gov/grca/planyourvisit/whitewater-rafting.htm for more detailed information.

You'll bypass Granite Narrows, the narrowest point (76ft) in the canyon, if you take the Deer Creek loop, continuing down about a dozen river miles to another favorite hike at ⑲ **Matkatamiba Canyon**. Matkat's beautifully curvaceous narrows with striated, rippling walls require a little stemming and scrambling to stay above the water at the bottom of the canyon, but it's an easy hike that opens out onto a pavilion edged in green.

If you manage not to go ass over tea kettle in Upset Rapid, the river will bring you to ⑳ **Havasu Canyon** on the next day, where another hike beckons. Leading up to the famous travertine canyon and blue-green pools of the Havasupai Reservation, Havasu Creek meets the Colorado with warm, turquoise waters that beg for a swim.

Around day 13, a day of gentle drifting allows you to steel yourself for infamous Lava. As you approach, the terrifyingly thrilling maelstrom of ㉑ **Lava Falls Rapid** will reveal itself with a roar before giving you the ride of your life – this is a crucial one to scout. After Lava, you can breathe easy. Take-outs at ㉒ **Whitmore Wash** – the wash at river mile 187, where a trail leads up to the North Rim – will have you boarding a helicopter bound for the rim. Instead of jettisoning your river serenity into oblivion with an immediate return to Las Vegas, transition with a steak dinner and a down-home stay at slightly kitschy ㉓ **Bar 10 Ranch**. You can while away a few days on the ranch, skeet shootin', horseback riding and dancing before braving "civilization" again.

Wendy Yanagihara

OUTDOORS

TRIP INFORMATION

GETTING THERE
Rafting trips on the upper half of the Colorado put in at Lees Ferry, 130 miles north of Flagstaff, Arizona.

DO
River Outfitters
Grand Canyon River Outfitters Association (www.gcroa.org) is a good starting point, with listings for all 16 river concessionaires certified to run the canyon. Because prices for commercial trips vary depending on the length of the trip, we haven't listed prices; outfitters' rates tend to be competitive.

Arizona Raft Adventures
Has run paddle, oar and motorized trips since 1965; offers trips of six to 17 days. ☎ 928-526-8200, 800-786-7238; www.azraft.com; 4050 E Huntington Dr, Flagstaff, AZ 86004

Canyon Explorations & Canyon Expeditions
Family run, established in 1987, this business offers trips of six to 16 days on the river. ☎ 928-774-4559, 800-654-0723; www.canyonexplorations.com; PO Box 310, Flagstaff, AZ 86002

Canyoneers
Descended from the company originally founded by Norm Nevills, who led the first paying passengers down the Colorado. ☎ 928-526-0924, 800-525-0924; www.canyoneers.com; PO Box 2997, Flagstaff, AZ 86004

Grand Canyon Dories
One of the only companies running trips in traditional wooden dories, with trips from five to 19 days. ☎ 209-736-0805, 800-877-3679; www.oars.com/grandcanyon/dories.html; PO Box 216, Altaville, CA 95221

Hatch River Expeditions
Best known for its river-running family pedigree, Hatch is now most visible for its motorized raft trips. ☎ 928-355-2241, 800-856-8966; www.hatchriverexpeditions.com; HC 67 Box 35, Marble Canyon, AZ 86036

OARS
With trips from five to 15 days, this outfit is one of the most distinguished. ☎ 209-736-4677, 800-346-6277; www.oars.com; PO Box 67, Angels Camp, CA 95222

Outdoors Unlimited
Well respected and experienced, this company offers oar and paddle trips of five to 15 days. ☎ 928-526-2852, 800-637-7238; www.outdoorsunlimited.com; 6900 Townsend Winona Rd, Flagstaff, AZ 86004

EAT & SLEEP
Bar 10 Ranch
The place to stay when you put in or take out at Whitmore Wash. Ask about raft and ranch packages. ☎ 435-628-4010, 800-582-4139; www.bar10.com; Whitmore Wash, AZ; per person incl dinner, lodge & breakfast $100; ♿

Bright Angel Fountain
Should be your first stop after slogging up to the South Rim, for a well-earned, frosty chocolate milkshake. ☎ 928-638-2631; www.grandcanyonlodges.com; Grand Canyon Village, AZ; mains $5-10; ⏰ 8am-8:30pm; ♿

El Tovar Dining Room
A meal here or cocktail on the back porch is *de rigueur*. Rooms at the historic lodge are the best on the rim. ☎ 928-638-2631; www.grandcanyonlodges.com; Grand Canyon Village, AZ; lunch from $11, dinner $21-35; ⏰ 6:30-10:45am, 11:15am-2pm & 4:30-10pm, with seasonal variations; ♿

Phantom Ranch
The six-person dorm-cabins have air-con. Breakfast ($20), sack lunch ($13) and dinner ($26 to $42) must be reserved. ☎ 928-638-2631; www.grandcanyonlodges.com; dm $42; ♿

USEFUL WEBSITES
https://npspermits.us
www.nps.gov/grca

LINK YOUR TRIP
TRIP

www.lonelyplanet.com/trip-planner

CALIFORNIA TRIPS

Other states may lure travelers with destination dining and giant balls of twine, but only this one gives the great American road trip its Hollywood ending. From the Gold Rush to the Oscars' red carpet, the eternal quest for fortune and fame leads inevitably to California's shores – but once you take a look at the place, you may forget why you came, and where else you could possibly be headed. Gold seems overrated once you've seen the platinum glint of the Pacific, and no movie star will ever be as big as California's mighty old-growth redwoods.

PLAYLIST 🎵 Go California or bust with a full tank and these unofficial state anthems:

- "California," Joni Mitchell
- "No Rain," Blind Melon
- "Everyday People," Sly & the Family Stone
- "Better Git It in Your Soul," Charles Mingus
- "La Bamba," Richie Valens
- "I Don't Wanna Grow Up," Tom Waits
- "Welcome to Paradise," Green Day
- "Under the Bridge," Red Hot Chili Peppers

Hang tight around the curves and hug the coastline along legendary Hwy 1, eat your way around the San Francisco Bay with guidance from Alice Waters, or take the slow train through Central Valley vineyards: there's no such thing as a wrong turn in California – though you might want to bring water for detours to Death Valley salt flats. But no matter where you're headed, as shadows begin to fall, swerve to the side of the road and face the setting sun. In California, dreaming comes with the territory.

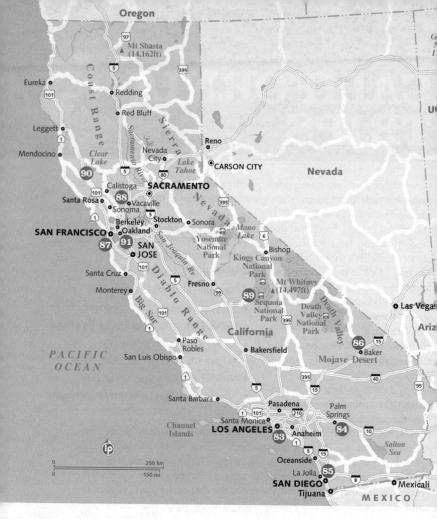

CALIFORNIA TRIPS

48 Hours in Los Angeles

WHY GO If LA's celebrities "Are just like us!" is LA just like Boise? Well, yes, if Boise bordered 75 miles of sun-dappled coast, basked in the glow of a $275-million concert hall, hosted the Oscars and lured gourmands to savory world-class restaurants. But let's just admit it, shall we? Sometimes leaving home is good.

TIME
2 days

BEST TIME TO GO
Year-round

START
Walt Disney Concert Hall, LA, CA

END
Santa Monica State Beach, LA, CA

According to LA lore, a wannabe starlet once asked Bette Davis for advice on the best way to get into Hollywood. "Take Fountain," was Davis' reply, referencing a lesser-known avenue that runs parallel to Sunset Blvd. Bitchy, perhaps. Practical, yes. But just the attitude needed for navigating this glorious mash-up of a city. In 48 hours you can stroll Hollywood Blvd, nab a studio tour, dine at world-class restaurants, savor a travertine-framed sunset, shop in celebrity style and spend a morning at the beach. Flexibility is key, and if you hear or see the word "Sig-alert," get off the freeway fast.

Downtown, long known for a bustling financial district that emptied at night, is in the midst of a massive Renaissance that's attracting party animals as well as full-time residents. The symbol of the revitalization is the ❶ Walt Disney Concert Hall, the landmark that launched a thousand metaphors. Billowing ship? Blooming rose? Silver bow? No matter which comparison you prefer, it's agreed that this iconic structure – designed by Frank Gehry and completed in 2003 – kick-started Downtown's rebirth. Cascading escalators whisk visitors from the parking garage directly into the airy lobby, where tours highlight Gehry's exquisite attention to detail – air-conditioning units are hidden inside smooth Douglas fir columns – throughout the building and gardens.

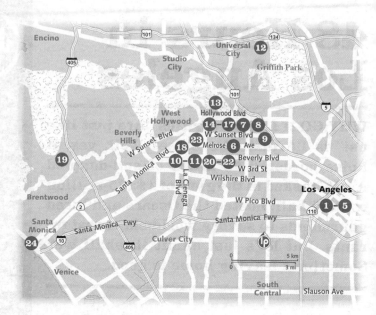

Just across Grand Ave, hard hats construct the Grand Ave Cultural Corridor, a high-end cluster of shops, hotels and restaurants scheduled for a 2011 completion. Stroll south to the postmodern charms of the ❷ **Museum of Contemporary Art**, a minimalist masterpiece housing a rotating collection of avant-garde exhibits in its underground galleries. Grand Ave then takes a watch-your-balance plunge before crossing 5th St. Peek inside the 1926 ❸ **Richard Riordan Central Library** on your right to ogle the 64ft-high rotunda with a 42ft span. Here, a 1-ton chandelier laughs in the face of fault lines, hanging with optimistic audacity above a stark marble floor.

Another two blocks – plus an escalator and elevator ride – will take you to the ❹ **Rooftop Bar at the Standard Hotel** and 360-degree views of twinkling city lights, flickering freeways and white-capped mountains. Plot your arrival for weeknights or early evening on the weekend. You'll enjoy the view and the highlights – comfy space pods, fireside lounges – without the long line, $20 cover and maddening crush of scenesters (no offense to scenesters, it's just the numbers that annoy). For downtown lodging without the scene, consider the ❺ **Figueroa Hotel**. Here, a festive Spanish-style lobby, Moroccan-themed rooms and a welcoming poolside bar infuse the hotel with a refreshing join-the-caravan conviviality.

For dinner, the evening can go one of two ways – *burrata* or burgers. For the former, you'll need to be organized (reservations accepted one month ahead) or a little bit lucky because Nancy Silverton and Mario Batali's bustling **6 Osteria Mozza** has been the hottest table in town since opening in mid-2007. The highlight at this stylish Melrose and Highland mecca is the central, first-come-first-served mozzarella bar where Silverton whips up *burrata, bufala* and other Italian cheese-based delicacies. The more casual – but almost equally crowded – Pizzeria Mozza is next door.

So…no one's moved from the mozzarella bar? Consider a deal with brightred **7 Lucky Devils** on Hollywood Blvd, just a short drive north via Highland Ave. The Kobe Diablo, a thick Kobe beef patty slathered with avocado, double-smoked bacon and Vermont cheddar, is so gob-smackingly tasty you'll be tempted to curse aloud. Or you can take another bite, sip one of 13 draft beers, and settle in for some Hollywood people-watching. Cool fact? The owner is Lucky Vanous, the hunky model from the 1990s Diet Coke ads. Just sayin'.

Clubs and condos – not to mention cranes – are transforming the once gritty **8 Hollywood & Vine** intersection into LA's next "it" neighborhood. One popular store that made its mark in the area before things got trendy is **9 Amoeba Music**. For

HAPPY BIRTHDAY, PHILLIPPE

Celebrating your 100th birthday is a big deal in LA, especially since nobody here is a day over 29. It's even more remarkable when the centennial belongs to a restaurant, in this case downtown's **Philippe the Original** (www.philippes.com), which opened in 1908. The restaurant is still hauling in hungry hordes craving juicy French-dip sandwiches, created here decades ago by the original Philippe. With 9¢ coffees, sawdust-covered floors and communal tables, Philippes remains a thriving cultural crossroads. North of Union Station, it's worth a trip.

vinyl and liner notes, follow Cahuenga Blvd south from Hollywood Blvd to Amoeba's neon-lit, warehousey digs. Here, the click, click, click of customers flipping through hundreds of thousand of CDs, DVDs and vinyl is soothing in a party-like-it's-1989 sort of way. Slip into nearby Velvet Margarita for tequila sipping and Day of the Dead decor, embrace the historic, divey charms of the Frolic Room, or simply chill out with an acoustic show at Hotel Café.

For Mid-City shut-eye, consider the retro charms of the **10 Beverly Laurel Motor Hotel**, the nondescript blue-gray building hiding in plain sight on Beverly Blvd south of Hollywood. Look for the Coffee Shop sign over Swingers, the late-night diner across from the lobby. Inside the hotel, framed photographs and diamond-patterned bedspreads add a hint of style to basic rooms which include an in-room fridge, microwave and sink.

Even the breakfast joints have valet service in LA. Just watch the perpetual flow of cars unloading by the beige umbrellas outside **11 Toast**. Here, parents with strollers, tattooed hipsters, gossiping quartets and an occasional recognizable face come for gourmet breakfasts, easygoing ambiance, and maybe, just maybe, the scene. Add your name to the list and decide on breakfast based on the heaping plates swooping past (scramblettes are always a winner).

If Hollywood is the glamorous face of the entertainment business, then Burbank, with its massive studio production lots, is the hard-working stylist hustling to prep that mug. The two major studios anchoring Burbank are Universal Studios Hollywood and ⑫ **Warner Bros**. For an engaging behind-the-scenes tour, hop the Warner Bros tram for the two-hour VIP tour. It winds past sound stages, sitcom sets and historic sites on the studio's 110-acre lot. Although no two tours are exactly the same, stops can include the Central Perk set, recognizable from the sitcom *Friends,* as well as the Transportation Garage where you'll find the Batmobile from *Batman Begins* and the Mystery Machine from *Scooby Doo.* Tell your guide at the start what you'd most like to see. The tour also includes a stop at the Warner Bros museum, a treasure trove of memorabilia with a well-stocked Harry Potter exhibit on the 2nd floor.

For a great-view detour, grab Mulholland Dr off Cahuenga Blvd, winding an eighth of a mile to the top of the hill. Turn left to enter the small ⑬ **Hollywood Bowl Overlook**. Even on hazy days, the sight of the Hollywood Bowl, Griffith Park and the city unfurling below is memorable, highlighting the rarely considered juxtaposition of raw nature and urban sprawl. Continue west a third of a mile and make a quick left at the bend onto Outpost Dr, a twisting ride past homes tucked behind hedges, trees and canyon nooks, which will take you back to Hollywood Blvd. If you're in the mood for driving, pass Outpost Dr and continue west on Mulholland Dr. As this famous roadway winds along the summit of the Santa Monica Mountains, you'll have views of the San Fernando Valley to the north and Hollywood to the south. Turn left on woodsy Laurel Canyon Dr to return to Hollywood Blvd.

> **ASK A LOCAL**
>
> "There's a store in Burbank on Magnolia called **It's a Wrap**. I bought a shirt once that I wore for a year that Tori Spelling wore on *90210*. I saw it on a repeat, so they're not lying when they say they were on the stars… On the rack it will say whatever show [it is] so you know that rack is from that show."
>
> *Allison Intrieri, Los Angeles*

So Elvis, Batman and Charlie Chaplin walk into a bar…hey, it could happen, at least at the ⑭ **Hollywood & Highland** complex where celebrity impersonators cluster for photo ops and tips. And while this block is over-the-top touristy, there's a certain undeniable energy that makes the freak-dodging, hustle-and-bustle confusion kind of fun. Be sure to wander the cement handprints and footprints left by big-screen stars from Clark Gable to Judy Garland to Johnny Depp outside ⑮ **Grauman's Chinese Theater**, a 1927 grand movie palace inspired by Chinese imperial architecture.

Crossing Hollywood Blvd here, it can be hard to envision Hollywood's A-listers walking the red carpet in front of the Kodak Theater. In contrast, inside the ⑯ **Hollywood Roosevelt Hotel**, with its dark lobby lounge, antique couches and let-you-be vibe, it's easier to imagine the Hollywood heavy-weights who've strolled through, from Marilyn Monroe to Montgomery Clift. The hotel hosted the first Academy Awards ceremony in 1929. Though recently revamped, rooms can feel small, and the elevator is unnerving if you've taken the plunge inside DCA's Tower of Terror. Overall, though, the hotel's history and Hollywood proximity make it an interesting, center-of-the-action choice.

Outside, more than 2000 pink marble stars line the sidewalks between La Brea Ave and Vine St – and a bit beyond – as part of Hollywood's Walk of Fame. Follow the stars east to ⑰ **Skooby's** red-and-white placard reading "gourmet hotdogs." Why this splash of hotdog pretension? Who knows. The chili-slathered masterpieces at this tiny walk-up don't need a fancy adjective. Maybe it's because the fries have aioli sauce.

"there's a certain undeniable energy that makes the freak-dodging, hustle-and-bustle confusion kind of fun."

To witness pretension on a grand scale, don't miss an Ivy drive-by. Tucked behind a white picket fence on uber-trendy ⑱ **N Robertson Blvd**, the Ivy still holds court as Queen Bee for see-and-be-seen weekday lunches. Scan the patio for A-listers if camera-toting paparazzi crowd the sidewalk. Neighboring boutiques Kitson, Curve and Lisa Kline sell tiny clothes from hot designers to the young, beautiful and moneyed. For designer-style duds at way cheaper prices, follow Robertson north to grittier Melrose Ave, wandering east to the trendy boutiques, denim shops and thrift stores.

If you prefer natural and cultural splendor to commercial, spend your afternoon exploring the ⑲ **Getty Center**, glowing in travertine splendor from its hill-top throne in the Santa Monica Mountains. The natural flow of walk-ways, skylights, fountains and courtyards on its 110-acre Richard Meier–designed "campus" encourages effortless wandering between Van Gogh's *Irises*, the bright Central Garden, and inspiring citywide vistas framed by Italian-cut stone. Sunsets are simply superb.

For dinner we recommend two LA restaurants that should never be mentioned in the same breath: ⑳ **AOC** and ㉑ **El Coyote**. But sometimes it's nice to have choices. To maintain the ambiance set by the Getty, make a reservation at Chef Suzanne Goin's ever-popular AOC, a smooth-as-silk wine bar that glows like the wine cellar of a very close, very rich friend. With more than 50 wines by the glass, it's easy to complement the small-plates menu that purrs with such savory morsels as truffled scallops with bacon, and grilled skirt steak with Roquefort butter.

For those who'd prefer to slurp potent margaritas, scarf messy Mexican combos and talk as loud as they want, suit up for a fun-lovin' dinner inside slightly divey El Coyote, the place with red-frocked waiters, and cars spilling out of the parking lot. Trust us, everyone in town's been here at some point. We've seen Nicole Richie chilling on the patio, and they say Sharon Tate ate her last dinner here. Down the street is ㉒ New Beverly Cinema, a 32-year-old indie movie house known for nightly double features and themed retrospectives organized by celeb hosts including Quentin Tarantino and Diablo Cody.

DETOUR For a short hike to one of LA's best sweeping views, try the 1.4-mile Charlie Walker Trail, behind Griffith Park Observatory. This switchbacking path climbs up scorched, scrubby slopes to reach the summit of Mt Hollywood (not the location of the sign). Here, a summit view captures the San Gabriel mountains, the sprawling San Fernando Valley, downtown skyscrapers, and the city grid rolling west to the Pacific Ocean. Round-trip, the hike should take about an hour.

To fuel up on your last day, head to Sunset Strip's ㉓ Griddle Cafe, a grubby but happenin' spot in the shadows of the Directors Guild. For the best view of the tousled film students and hungry screenwriters that congregate here, sit at the U-shaped bar facing the narrow interior. The pancakes are huge, and the coffee French press. Get there early.

Best way to the beach? To paraphrase Bette Davis: take Sunset. You'll pass the castlelike visage of Chateau Marmont (look up as you cross Crescent Heights), soon followed by rock icons Whiskey a Go Go, Viper Room and the Roxy. Oh-so-pink Beverly Hills Hotel lurks behind Hollywood hedges, followed by Star Maps, UCLA and posh Bel Air. Sunset then swoops over I-405, cruising west through Brentwood and Pacific Palisades before dropping at the Pacific Coast Hwy. Follow PCH south to ㉔ Santa Monica State Beach.

Once there, ride the pier's solar-powered Ferris wheel, pedal the bike path, or simply plop onto your towel on the wide beach and smile at the sun. For historic perspective, glance at the bluffs behind you. A palm-dappled greenway, Palisades Park, runs along the top, passing a marker denoting the western terminus of Route 66. Ponder for a second the appropriateness of America's famed romantic byway ending at this most gorgeous of spots. Then slather on another dollop of lotion and flip for those last few rays.

Amy C Balfour

TRIP INFORMATION

GETTING THERE
Los Angeles is located in Southern California, 381 miles south of San Francisco and 124 miles north of San Diego.

DO

Amoeba Music
Live performances, listening stations and a map are a few of the extras at this vinyl and CD emporium. ☎ 323-245-6400; www.amoeba.com; 6400 W Sunset Blvd; ⏰ 10:30am-11pm Mon-Sat, 11am-9pm Sun

Getty Center
A driverless tram whisks visitors to art, architecture, gardens and stellar views. ☎ 310-440-7300; www.getty.edu; 1200 Getty Center Dr; admission free, parking $10; ⏰ 10am-5:30pm Tue-Fri & Sun, 10am-9pm Sat; ♿

Grauman's Chinese Theater
Stand in the footprints of Gable, Clooney and Schwarzenegger just west of Hollywood & Highland while 200 people jostle you. ☎ 323-464-8111; www.manntheatres.com; 6925 Hollywood Blvd; admission free; ♿

Hollywood & Highland
Shops, restaurants and movie screens are just part of the spectacle at this towering Hollywood complex. ☎ 323-467-6412; www.hollywoodandhighland.com; 6801 Hollywood Blvd; admission free; ⏰ 10am-10pm Mon-Sat, to 7pm Sun; ♿

Museum of Contemporary Art (MOCA)
Collection spans 1940s to present. ☎ 213-626-6222; www.moca.org; 250 S Grand Ave; adult/under 12yr/student & senior $10/free/5; ⏰ 11am-5pm Mon & Fri, to 8pm Thu, to 6pm Sat & Sun

New Beverly Cinema
Indie cinema screens double features and eclectically themed retrospectives. ☎ 323-938-4038; www.newbevcinema.com; 7165 W Beverly Blvd; general/senior & child/student $7/4/6

Richard Riordan Central Library
This 1926 building boasts a grand rotunda, stunning murals, whimsical cascading elevators and 2.1 million books. ☎ 213-228-7000; www.lapl.org; 630 W 5th St; admission free; ⏰ 10am-8pm Mon-Thu, 10am-6pm Fri & Sat, 1-5pm Sun; ♿

Walt Disney Concert Hall
Tours highlight architect Frank Gehry's attention to detail, but concert tickets are needed to see the acoustically precise auditorium. ☎ 323-850-2000 concert tickets, 213-972-4399 tours; www.laphil.com; 111 S Grand Ave; tours free; ⏰ 10am-2pm most days

Warner Bros
Hop a tram for a two-hour tour in which the secrets of Hollywood are revealed – forced perspective, fancy facades and fake bricks. ☎ 818-972-8687; www.wbstudiotour.com; 3400 Riverside Dr, Burbank; tours $45, min age 8; ⏰ 7:30am-7pm Mon-Fri, tours 8:20am-4pm

EAT & DRINK

AOC
From goat cheese to blue cheese, fancy fromages fill one full page on the menu and add to the epicurean fun. ☎ 323-653-6359; www.aocwinebar.com; 8022 W 3rd St; small plates $14-18; ⏰ 6-11pm Mon-Fri, 5:30-11pm Sat, 5:30-10pm Sun

El Coyote
Combos are messy and margaritas are strong at this lively Mexican cantina that's been pulling in locals for years. ☎ 323-939-2255; www.elcoyotecafe.com; 7312 Beverly Blvd; mains $5-12; ⏰ 11am-10pm; ♿

Griddle Cafe
Items named Banana Nana Pancakes and Peanut Bubba Crunchy French Toast make reading the menu fun. ☎ 323-874-0377; 7916 W Sunset Blvd; mains $9-12; ⏰ 7am-4pm Mon-Fri, 8am-4pm Sat & Sun

Lucky Devils

From Kobe burgers and veggie burgers to fries and shakes, it's all good. ☎ 323-465-8259; www.luckydevils-la.com; 6613 Hollywood Blvd; mains $8-16; ☽ lunch & dinner; ♿

Osteria Mozza

Watch chef Nancy Silverton craft mouth-watering morsels from Italian cheese; reserve a month ahead. ☎ 323-297-0100; www.mozza-la.com; 6602 Melrose Ave; mains $11-30, Sun-Thu 3-course bar special $35; ☽ 5:30pm-midnight

Rooftop Bar at the Standard Hotel

Citywide views from the roof are worth hipper-than-thou hassles to get there. ☎ 213-892-8080; www.standardhotel.com; 550 S Flower St; cover after 7pm Fri & Sat $20; ☽ noon-1:30am

Skooby's

Be sure to order fries with that chili-smothered dog. ☎ 323-468-3647; www.skoobys.com; 6654 Hollywood Blvd; mains $2.50-4; ☽ 11am-midnight; ♿

Toast

Frothy lattes, hearty scrambles and valet parking at the corner of 3rd St and N Harper Ave. ☎ 323-655-5018; www.toastbakerycafe.net; 8221 W 3rd St; mains $8-17; ☽ 7:30am-10pm; ♿

SLEEP

Beverly Laurel Motor Hotel

Let the retro times roll at this spare but stylin' budget option close to Mid-City and Hollywood. ☎ 323-651-2441; 8018 Beverly Blvd; r $115, pet fee $25; ♿

Figueroa Hotel

Spanish touches and Moroccan-style rooms liven up this property, conveniently located next to the Staples Center. ☎ 213-627-8971; www.figueroahotel.com; 939 S Figueroa St; r $148-184, ste $225-265

Hollywood Roosevelt

Who said historic can't be hip? Open since 1927; reborn in 2005. ☎ 323-466-7000; www.hollywoodroosevelt.com; 7000 Hollywood Blvd; r $250-400, ste $340-1200

USEFUL WEBSITES

www.laweekly.com
http://theguide.latimes.com

LINK YOUR TRIP

www.lonelyplanet.com/trip-planner

Retro-Modern Palm Springs

WHY GO For this fab midcentury modern architectural tour of Palm Springs, where you can drive by masterpieces from the Rat Pack era, tour Elvis' honeymoon hideaway and stay overnight inside Frank Sinatra's vacation home, we've teamed up with local expert Tony Merchell, a well-known architectural historian.

After WWII, Hollywood celebrities flocked to Palm Springs, where their newfound wealth built desert palaces, many in the midcentury modern architectural style. Today, this retro-flavored resort town shows off some of the best-preserved modern buildings in Southern California.

Your first stop is at the ❶ **Palm Springs Visitor Center**. "This building, with its hyperbolic paraboloid roof structure," Merchell points out, "is an icon of Palm Springs. It's an adaptive reuse of the Tramway Gas Station designed by Albert Frey and Robson C Chambers in 1965." The distinctive space-age structure, with its stark metal roof cutting diagonally across an organic background of toothily peaked San Jacinto Mountains, is a standout example of modern design, rescued from demolition by the city in 2002. You can pick up a copy of the Palm Springs Modern Committee's full-color tour map here; the self-driving tour takes you past many of the important architectural buildings still standing in Palm Springs.

Everyone interested in modern architecture visits the ❷ **Kaufmann Desert House** designed by Richard Neutra, an Austrian-born architect who worked with Frank Lloyd Wright and later Rudolph Schindler. We admit it's partly concealed by mature landscape, but don't worry: parts of this masterpiece are still visible from the road. Its exterior is

TIME
2 days

DISTANCE
16 miles

BEST TIME TO GO
Oct – Mar

START
Palm Springs Visitor Center, FL

END
Central Palm Springs, FL

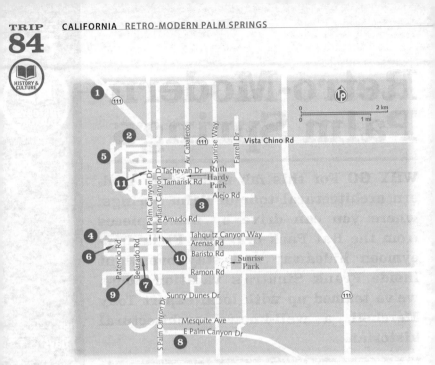

dominated by square lines and flat-topped metal roofs. But some building materials, including sandstone and sliding glass walls, soften the look, making the house fit more harmoniously with the desert landscape.

Next up is the ❸ **Frank Sinatra House**, designed by modern architect E Stewart Williams. Ol' Blue Eyes wanted a Georgian-style mansion, but Williams, a contemporary of Frey and Neutra, proposed a low-lying modern design. You can only get a good view of the Sinatra House if either the front or rear gate is open – but it's also available to rent. Famous for its grand piano–shaped pool, the house is stylishly outfitted with authentic period pieces.

Very few modern houses are open to the public in any regular manner. However, as Merchell points out, "Architect Albert Frey's own house, ❹ **Frey House II**, now owned by the Palm Springs Art Museum, is open on rare occasions." It's an incredible piece of art, with sheer glass walls and corrugated roofs built dramatically into a rocky canyon. The Swiss-born architect apprenticed with Le Corbusier, master of the International Style, before moving to Palm Springs in 1939. Other modernist designs by the prolific Frey include the 1952 City Hall.

One house that is regularly open to the public is the ❺ **Alexander Estate**, also known as "The House of Tomorrow" and the "Elvis Honeymoon Hideaway." This spectacular midcentury modern party house was built for Robert Alexander, who, along with his father George, was the largest builder of modern homes in Palm Springs. Elvis leased it for a year and, after marrying Priscilla Beaulieu at the Aladdin casino hotel in Las Vegas, he escaped to Palm Springs, as many celebs did both then and now, to get away from Hollywood paparazzi.

"There are many hotels to choose from in Palm Springs," Merchell points out, "but if you want something of the retro Rat Pack experience, you've got a few good choices." Just off the main drag in downtown Palm Springs, Merchell highlights the **6 Orbit In.** "It was the first modern hotel to be refurbished in Palm Springs. It's all first-class, with serious furniture and a great outdoor bar by the pool." Throwback touches include LP record players (juxtaposed with plasma-screen TVs), a fire pit by the Jacuzzi and 1950s-style beach cruiser bikes for guests to borrow.

STAR HOMES

Another way to get the "Rat Pack" experience is to rent a Palm Springs vacation home. "There are hundreds of vacation rentals available in the desert, many of which are perfectly furnished in the modern style," says our expert Tony Merchell. Many can be found through **Vacation Rentals by Owner** (www.vrbo.com). Listings include the immaculately furnished "Alexander," which was restored "with the assistance of the original architect William Krisel, who also designed the new front landscape," says Merchell.

Also conveniently downtown, the **7 Del Marcos Hotel** dates from 1947. This was the first building in the desert designed by architect William F Cody, who worked on many other private homes, hotels and country clubs around Palm Springs. "It has a great pool with a wonderful view of the mountains. Two of the upper-level rooms have private balconies that offer a view of Frey House II," Merchell comments. Groovy tunes in the lobby usher you to a saltwater pool and ineffably chic rooms named for local architectural luminaries. On the south side of Palm Springs, you'll find the **8 Horizon Hotel**, which was also designed by Bill Cody and has been meticulously restored to its former glory. Notice there are no 90-degree angles visible anywhere on the property.

"There aren't that many Rat Pack–era restaurants left in Palm Springs," Merchell remarks. "One of the best is **9 Melvyn's** at the Ingleside Inn. The restaurant is good, but the bar is fantastic: a small dance floor, and old-timers partying down to the wee hours." Come for the Sunday-afternoon jazz jams. Casual **10 Sherman's Deli & Bakery** is "where old Palm Springs and tourists hang out," Merchell reveals. "Sandwiches are enormous!" Grab a sidewalk table and watch PS society pass by, often dressed in outrageously colorful California-chic resortwear by **11 Trina Turk**, whose original storefront boutique looks right at home inside a 1960s Albert Frey design.

Sara Benson

HISTORY & CULTURE

TRIP INFORMATION

GETTING THERE

From Los Angeles, take I-10 east, then follow Hwy 111 south into downtown Palm Springs.

DO

Alexander Estate

Tour the midcentury modern home that's nicknamed the "Elvis Honeymoon Hideaway." ☎ 760-322-1192; www.elvishoneymoon. com; 1350 Ladera Circle, Palm Springs; admission $25-35; 🕙 tours 1pm Mon-Fri, by reservation only Sat & Sun

Frey House II

Owned by the Palm Springs Museum, which has an impressive collection of Julius Shulman's midcentury modern architectural photographs. ☎ 760-322-4800; www.ps museum.org; 686 Palisades Dr, Palm Springs; tour $50-100; 🕙 tours mid-Feb (Modernism week)

Kaufmann Desert House

Painstakingly restored, this home's pavilions are the final evolution of Neutra's domestic style. There's no public entry. **470 W Vista Chino Rd, Palm Springs**

Palm Springs Visitor Center

Look for the converted gas station at the start of the Tramway Rd. ☎ 760-778-8418; www.visitpalmsprings.com; 2901 N Palm Canyon Dr, Palm Springs; admission free; 🕙 9am-5pm

Trina Turk

Find shagadelic retro-print fashions at PS' signature clothing boutique. ☎ 760-416-2856; www.trinaturk.com; 891 N Palm Canyon Dr, Palm Springs; 🕙 10am-5pm Mon-Fri, 10am-6pm Sat, noon-5pm Sun

EAT

Melvyn's

Frank Sinatra was an early customer at this swanky resto lounge. ☎ 760-325-2323; www. inglesideinn.com; Ingleside Inn, 200 W Ramon Rd, Palm Springs; mains $9-38; 🕙 restaurant 11:30am-3pm Mon-Fri, 9am-3pm Sat & Sun, 6-11pm daily, lounge 10am-2am daily

Sherman's Deli & Bakery

This deli serves early-bird dinners and is festooned with headshots of aficionados like Don Rickles. ☎ 760-325-1199; www.shermansdeli. com; 401 E Tahquitz Canyon Way, Palm Springs; mains $8-16; 🕙 7am-9pm; 🚼 🐾

SLEEP

Del Marcos Hotel

After suffering years of bad remodels, this 16-room oasis shines at last. ☎ 760-325-6902, 800-676-1214; www.delmarcoshotel.com; 225 W Baristo Rd, Palm Springs; r $89-174

Frank Sinatra House

A three-night minimum rental is required at Blue Eyes' "Twin Palms" estate. ☎ 877-318-2090; www.sinatrahouse.com; 1148 E Alejo Rd, Palm Springs; house rental per night $2600

Horizon Hotel

Marilyn Monroe and Betty Grable once lounged by the poolside bar at this modern gem. ☎ 760-323-1858, 800-377-7855; www.thehorizonhotel.com; 1050 E Palm Canyon Dr, Palm Springs; r $99-700

Orbit In

Swing back into the 1950s during the complimentary "Orbitini" happy hour. ☎ 760-323-3585, 877-996-7248; www.orbitin.com; 562 W Arenas Rd, Palm Springs; r $99-259

USEFUL WEBSITES

www.psmodcom.com
www.pspf.net

LINK YOUR TRIP

www.lonelyplanet.com/trip-planner

A Wild Ride in the Parks

WHY GO The world's first theme park opened in 1940 when Walter Knott threw open the gates to an Old West attraction beside his fried chicken restaurant in Buena Park. More than 70 years later, parks circle the globe, but for sheer density, variety and scream-your-head-off craziness, SoCal remains King of the Thrill.

When it comes to 8000lb killer whales, Shamu at San Diego's ① SeaWorld is pretty darn cute. In fact, if you're not yelling "Shamu, Shamu!" with the rest of the crowd during the 25-minute show "Believe," your heart is surely made of plankton. For ooohs and ahhhs beyond the Shamu zone, wander habitats housing frolicking polar bears, menacing reef sharks and honking seals (you can feed 'em sardines for $6). The handful of rides are low-key, but coaster junkies can get a tiny fix on the plummeting coaster-flume Journey to Atlantis. Avoid the front seat if you're wearing white.

For nearby shut-eye, unpack your bags inside an oceanfront cottage at ② Beach Cottages in Pacific Beach. Shuffleboard and ping-pong – not to mention the beach – keep the under-12 set occupied. For breakfast, dodge joggers and dog walkers on an oceanside stroll north to scruffy ③ Kono's across from Crystal Pier. The line moves fast and, for a hearty breakfast burrito under $5, what's a short wait?

If you're traveling with kids under 13, take a coastal drive north on Hwy 101 to Carlsbad's ④ Legoland. The rides aren't constructed of Lego, but almost everything else is. Just ask that nice-looking family in the parking lot...oh, wait, they're made out of plastic blocks. Inside the park, people can't stop staring at the tiny Lego newlyweds gliding blissfully from the quickie wedding chapel in Miniland Las Vegas.

TIME
5 – 6 days

DISTANCE
160 miles

BEST TIME TO GO
Apr – Sep

START
San Diego, CA

END
Valencia, CA

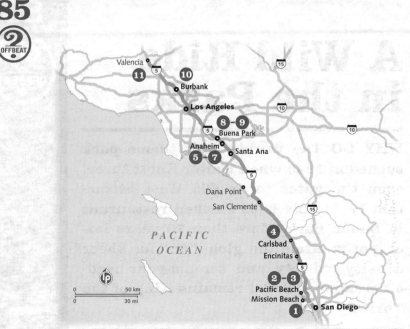

Will they be getting a quickie Lego divorce or is life somehow better when you're made of connectible blocks? Young sharpshooters will enjoy 2008's Lost Kingdom Adventure with its point-and-blast laser guns (the 16ft Pharaoh is made from 300,000-plus blocks). For small-sized shrieks, climb aboard the twisting Technic minicoaster.

For sheer attention to detail, no park does it better than Anaheim's **5** **Disneyland**, 60 miles north, which welcomed 14.3 million guests in 2008. From the bright floral Mickey at the entrance to the buffeting Star Speeder in Star Tours to the screeching monkeys inside the Indiana Jones Adventure, there's a magical detail ready to tease one of your senses. The latest high-dollar attraction is 2007's $100-million Finding Nemo Submarine Voyage. Look for Nemo from inside a sub and rumble though an underwater volcanic eruption. Coasterwise, use the Fastpass system and you'll be hurtling through Space Mountain – still the park's best adrenaline pumper – in no time.

Elevator issues? Avoid the Tower of Terror at **6** **Disney's California Adventure** (DCA), across from Disneyland. The heart-stopping plunge down a 183ft elevator shaft is an experience you won't forget. Themed areas in DCA highlight the best of California, including numerous adventures that don't involve losing your lunch – except Rockin' California Screamin' at Paradise Pier. This whip-fast coaster looks like an old-school carnival ride, but from the moment it blasts forward with a cannon-shot whoosh, this 10-acre monster never lets go.

DCA began a $1.1-billion makeover in 2008, with the new *Toy Story*–themed 3D carnival, Little Mermaid "dark ride," and high-speed auto ride inspired by Pixar's *Cars* in the works. Of the resort's three Disney lodgings, the one most enjoying its theme is 481-room **7** **Paradise Pier Hotel**. Swaying palms frame the rooftop pool, mini surfboards display your room number, and interiors celebrate coastal living with palm-pattern bedspreads, lighthouse lamps and sunburst mirrors.

For 11th-century joie de vivre, get your steed to rowdy **8** **Medieval Times**, 7 miles northwest of Disneyland. Here, crown-wearing guests tear at roast chicken with their hands while knights joust, fence and display their horse-back-riding skills in a central arena. The next morning, slow down at the corner of Beach and La Palma Aves. Hear the screams? Got your teens?

Pompadoured waiters, "Splish Splash" on the stereo, cherry-topped milkshakes. What is this? *Happy Days?* Nope, it's the next best thing: **Corvette Diner** (www.cohnrestaurants.com/restaurants/corvettediner) in downtown San Diego, about 3 miles from Sea World. At this doo-wop diner the singing waitstaff has happily forgotten it's a new millennium, but nobody seems to mind. We dare you not to finish the all-shook-up banana, peanut butter and marshmallow Elvis Shake.

Hello, **9** **Knott's Berry Farm**, America's first theme park, where nine high-scream coasters lure middle-schoolers and fast-track fanatics. Look up as you enter. The suspended coaster careening past is the Silver Bullet, popular for its corkscrew, double spiral and outside loop. Barefoot riders removed their flip-flops for a reason. The *Peanuts* gang keeps moppets happy in Camp Snoopy.

Thirty miles north, it's bye-bye to the future, hello to *The Simpsons* at **10** **Universal Studios Hollywood**, where a $40-million simulator ride featuring Homer and the gang has replaced the lurching *Back to the Future*. An 80ft screen is the backdrop for a whirlwind journey through Krustyland. The short-but-screamworthy *Revenge of the Mummy* hurtles through Imhotep's Tomb (ride solo to avoid long lines) and *Jurassic Park* ends with a splashy plunge. Hop a tram for the Studio Tour, the park's best "ride." The guided tram winds past the Bates Motel from *Psycho,* a lunging Jaws, and Wisteria Lane from *Desperate Housewives* (when the show's not shooting). After a devastating 2008 fire, the studio relaunched the beloved *King Kong* attraction as a hair-raisingly close 3-D encounter with the giant ape.

Ready to ratchet and roll? Look north to the steel-framed harbingers of doom rising from the grounds of Valencia's **11** **Six Flags Magic Mountain** off the I-5 northwest of Burbank. With 15 daredevilicious coasters ranging from Scream (which rips through seven loops) to revamped X2 (with a hurtling car spinning 360 degrees), Magic Mountain caters to its base. Bumper cars, kiddie plunges and Thomas the Tank Engine are tyke-friendly alternatives.

Amy C Balfour

TRIP INFORMATION

GETTING THERE
SeaWorld is 5 miles northwest of San Diego International Airport via I-5 and SeaWorld Dr.

DO
Disneyland & Disney's California Adventure
Happiest Place on Earth still lures 'em by the tram load. ☎ 714-781-4000; www.disneyland.com; 1313 S Harbor Blvd, Anaheim; 1-day Disneyland or DCA adult/3-9yr $72/62; ♿

Knott's Berry Farm
A shriek-fest of horrorific mazes and spine-tingling shows complement the coasters during Halloween season. ☎ 714-220-5200; www.knotts.com; 8039 Beach Blvd, Buena Park; adult/3-11yr & senior $54/24, online printout adult $46; ♿

Legoland
A Lego-made family greets DNA-made families in the parking lot at this mazelike ode to plastic connectable blocks. ☎ 760-918-5346; www.legoland.com; 1 Legoland Dr, Carlsbad; adult/3-12yr & senior $67/57; ☼ 10am-6pm, with seasonal variations; ♿

SeaWorld
Creatures of the deep are the reason to come. ☎ 619-226-3901; www.seaworld.com; 500 SeaWorld Dr, San Diego; adult/3-9yr $69/59; ☼ 9am-11pm Jul–mid-Aug, shorter hours rest of year; ♿

Six Flags Magic Mountain
Scream. Ninja. Viper. Goliath… 16 roller coasters, 16 ways to lose it. ☎ 661-255-4100; www.sixflags.com/parks/magicmountain; 26101 Magic Mountain Pkwy, Valencia; adult/child under 4ft $55/28, Mar-May adult $30; ☼ varies by season; ♿

Universal Studios Hollywood
Rides are tied to movies at this Burbank theme park, and the highlight is the Studio Tour. ☎ 818-622-3801; www.universalstudioshollywood.com; 100 Universal City Plaza, Universal City; admission over/under 48in $69/59 (see online specials); ☼ varies by season; ♿

EAT
Kono's
Join the quick-moving line for plates piled high with eggs, bacon, pancakes and hearty burritos. ☎ 858-483-1669; 704 Garnet Ave, Pacific Beach; dishes from $5; ☼ 7am-3pm Mon-Fri, 7am-4pm Sat & Sun; ♿

Medieval Times
Feast on roast chicken while knights on horseback joust before you. ☎ 866-935-6878; www.medievaltimes.com; 7662 Beach Blvd, Buena Park; adult/12yr & under $56/35; ☼ daily, show times vary; ♿

SLEEP
Beach Cottages
Smack on the beach, this mom-and-pop motel with vintage whitewashed cottages is south of Crystal Pier. ☎ 858-483-7440; www.beachcottages.com; 4255 Ocean Blvd, Pacific Beach; r $90-160, apt $205-345, cottage $210-335; ♿

Paradise Pier Hotel
Ask for a room overlooking DCA at this beach-inspired retreat, the newest and best value of the three Disney hotels. ☎ 714-999-0990; www.disneyland.com; 1717 S Disneyland Dr, Anaheim; r $210-320; ♿

USEFUL WEBSITES
www.latimes.com/funland
www.westcoaster.net

LINK YOUR TRIP
TRIP
www.lonelyplanet.com/trip-planner

7 Wet & Wild West Coast p105
83 48 Hours in Los Angeles p581

Life in Death Valley

WHY GO Dive deep into the Mojave Desert on our grand tour of Death Valley National Park, a forbidding-sounding place where the incredible forces of natural and human history collide. Time your trip for early spring to catch blossoming wildflowers and blessedly lower temperatures.

Death Valley is a land of extremes – you'll find the lowest elevation in the USA here, not far from Mt Whitney, the highest peak in the lower 48 states. Death Valley is also the hottest place in the nation. If you don't believe us, just take a look at the ❶ World's Largest Thermometer, off I-15 in Baker. It stands 134ft tall to commemorate the record-breaking temperature of 134°F measured in nearby Death Valley on July 10, 1913. Try to visit the desert in the cooler spring months, when wildflowers are in full bloom – that is, if enough rain has fallen over the winter.

Even when the desert is bone dry, you can still find an oasis at ❷ Tecopa Hot Springs Resort. Soak in the natural mineral springs used by Native Americans for centuries, then try the fresh, organic cooking at ❸ Pastels, a laid-back desert bistro. On new-moon nights, when the desert sky twinkles with celestial diamonds, you can roll out your sleeping bag for star-viewing parties. Further north in Shoshone, look for ❹ Cafe C'est Si Bon, a solar-powered internet café decorated with vibrant local art and UFOs ("Unusual and Found Objects").

Harley riders speed along Hwy 178 on the winding, southern approach to ❺ Death Valley National Park. Cresting Jubilee Pass, the highway at last dips down into the valley itself, enfolded by steep, rugged mountains. The peaks are the ages-old product of geological uplift and erosion along thrust faults. Despite its name, this harsh-looking valley

TIME
2 – 3 days

DISTANCE
350 miles

BEST TIME TO GO
Feb – Apr

START
Baker, CA

END
Death Valley National Park, CA

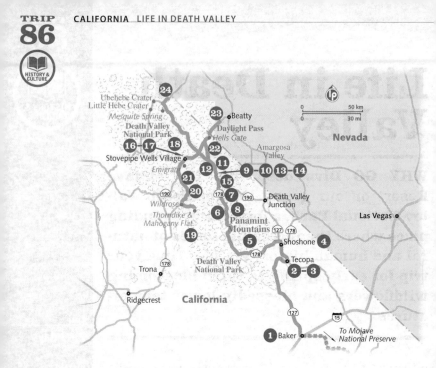

is a diverse habitat for wildlife and has supported human life for millennia, starting with the Timbisha Shoshone people, followed much later by Old West pioneers, gold seekers and borax miners. It's the silence and solemnity of the vast expanse that inspires travelers today.

That cracked, parched-looking salt pan extending across the valley floor is **6 Badwater**. At 282ft below sea level, Badwater is the lowest point in North America. Here a boardwalk hovers over the constantly evaporating bed of salty, mineralized water, otherworldly in its beauty. Prehistoric Lake Manly, which covered the entire valley during the ice age, reappeared here in 2005 for the first time in recorded human history. Although the lake evaporated again within weeks, its surprising reemergence just goes to show the tenacity of life in this barren-looking valley. And that means human endurance, too: in July, the Badwater Ultramarathon race travels 135 miles from Badwater to Mt Whitney Portal (elevation 8300ft) in 120°F-plus heat.

Many of Death Valley's most outstanding natural features also reflect the human history of the place. Take **7 Zabriskie Point**, for example. Rising over 5000ft above the valley floor, this panoramic stretch of badlands gets its name from an early-20th-century manager of the Pacific Borax Company. **8 Twenty Mule Team Canyon** is where the mule "skinners" (drivers) once guided wagon trains hauling borax out of Death Valley to a railway stop nearby in the Mojave Desert. As your car rattles along an unpaved road through the canyon, pause to ponder the arduous 165-mile, 10-day trip made by borax miners in the late 19th century.

The mule teams' journey actually began far below at **9 Furnace Creek**. Find out exactly why borax, a multipurpose mineral used in hundreds of household products, was so valuable, at the **10 Borax Museum**. Out back is a pioneer-era collection of old wagons and stagecoaches. A short drive north, passing the interesting **11 Furnace Creek Visitor Center**, you can walk in the footsteps of the Chinese laborers who dug borax out of the earth and examine the adobe ruins of the **12 Harmony Borax Works**, which operated for just five years during the 1880s.

When sunset seems to set the desert rocks aflame, check into the rustic, family-style motel rooms or Western cabins at **13 Furnace Creek Ranch**, which can arrange horseback rides.

> **DETOUR** For even more Wild West history, visit the **Mojave National Preserve** (www.nps.gov/moja), south of Baker. Tour the gloriously restored Kelso Depot, with its fascinating historical museum. At Hole-in-the-Wall, scale the cliffs Native Americans used to escape Western ranchers, then drive through Wild Horse Canyon or follow the old Mojave Rd blazed by Spanish missionaries, fur trappers and traders, and oddly enough, camels on an 1867 military expedition. Bunk in **Nipton** (www.nipton.com), a turn-of-the-20th-century town with a renovated adobe hotel and "ecolodge" cabins.

Beside the general store, chow down at the **14 Forty-Nine Cafe & Wrangler Steak House**. Over at the elegant oasis of the **15 Furnace Creek Inn**, guests soak up elevated views across the desert salt pans as they swim laps in a warm, natural spring–fed pool. On the site of the valley's original tourist camp, **16 Stovepipe Wells Village** is a quieter, more down-to-earth place to rest your head, with renovated motel rooms. At its cowboy-style **17 Toll Road Restaurant** the flapjacks and biscuits-and-gravy breakfasts go like gangbusters.

The next day, take up another strand of history in Death Valley: the story of the lost '49ers. When the California gold rush began in 1849, a small group of pioneers took what they hoped would be a shortcut to the California goldfields, leaving behind the Old Spanish Trail. Exhausted, dangerously running out of food and water, and struggling with broken wagons and worn-out pack animals, the woeful group arrived near Furnace Creek on Christmas Eve. An Old West festival featuring a historical reenactment of the ill-fated '49ers takes place here every November.

Failing to get their wagons across the Panamint Mountains, the survivors slaughtered their oxen and burned their wagons near **18 Mesquite Flat sand dunes**, outside of what was later named Stovepipe Wells Village. The pioneers proceeded to walk out of the torturous valley over Emigrant Pass. As they left, one woman reportedly looked back and uttered the words "Good-bye, death valley." Follow the '49ers' escape route by driving up Emigrant Canyon Rd, which winds through Wildrose Canyon up to the ⑲ **Charcoal Kilns**. Built in the 1876, these beehive-shaped kilns produced the fuel needed to process silver and lead ore. Historically, it wasn't just borax that miners unearthed in Death Valley.

During the 19th and 20th centuries, gold was discovered around Death Valley, including at ⑳ **Eureka Mine**, a short detour off the main road out toward vertigo-inducing Aguereberry Point, and at the ghost-town site of ㉑ **Skidoo**, a boomtown that went bust in the early 20th century, and where the influential silent movie *Greed* was filmed in 1923. The ㉒ **Keane Wonder Mine** also sparked a mini–gold rush in Death Valley. It's still standing but closed to visitors, due to mine shafts that have been known to collapse without warning. Finally, just over the Nevada state line is ㉓ **Rhyolite**, the queen of Death Valley's mines during its heyday (1905–11). Today it's the best-preserved ghost town around, featuring the photogenic ruins of a three-story bank, ghostly statues by Belgian sculptor Albert Szukalski, and a miner's house built with 50,000 glass beer, whiskey and medicine bottles.

> *"As they left, one woman reportedly looked back and uttered the words 'Good-bye, death valley.'"*

No historical tour of Death Valley would be complete without a tour of ㉔ **Scotty's Castle**, where guides in authentic period dress lead you around a grandiose Spanish villa built by a wealthy Chicago businessperson, Albert Johnson, and his wife in the 1920s. The castle's most famous resident was a bogus prospector named "Death Valley Scotty." This ex-Buffalo Bill sideshow performer, hustler and raconteur claimed that this ranch in Grapevine Canyon actually was his, and that he had built it from gold he mined in Death Valley. That was a big, fat lie, but Albert Johnson played along, even after he had lost a ton of money investing in Scotty's legendary mine. Scotty himself lived at the ranch off and on until his death in 1954; his passing signaled the end of the Old West era in Death Valley.

Sara Benson & Alison Bing

TRIP INFORMATION

GETTING THERE
From Los Angeles, take I-10 east toward San Bernardino, then I-15 north past Barstow to Baker.

DO

Borax Museum
Poke around historical exhibits covering mining and the famous 20-mule teams that hauled mineral ore out of Death Valley. ☎ 760-786-2345, ext 215; Hwy 190, Furnace Creek; admission free; ⏱ 9am-9pm

Death Valley National Park
Pay your entrance fee at the Furnace Creek visitor center. If you didn't fill up outside the park, there are gas stations with 24-hour credit-card pumps at Furnace Creek and Stovepipe Wells. ☎ 760-786-3200; www.nps.gov/deva; PO Box 579, Death Valley; 7-day entry pass per vehicle/bicycle or motorbike $20/10; ⏱ 24hr; ♿

Furnace Creek Visitor Center
Free information and brochures, including schedules of free ranger-guided hikes and kid-friendly programs, plus educational slide shows and a well-stocked bookstore. ☎ 760-786-3200; www.nps.gov/deva; Hwy 190, Furnace Creek; ⏱ 8am-5pm; ♿

Rhyolite
A worthy detour east of Death Valley, this mining ghost town is made for just wandering around, from the 1906 bottle house to the bike-riding ghost sculpture. ☎ 775-553-2967; www.rhyolitesite.com; Hwy 374, 4 miles west of Beatty, NV; admission free; ⏱ 24hr; ♿ ☀

Scotty's Castle
Show up early, because 50-minute living-history and underground house tours accommodate 19 people maximum. Lower Vine Ranch tours of Death Valley Scotty's cabin are available seasonally on Wednesdays and Saturdays. ☎ 760-786-2325; www.nps.gov/deva; Hwy 267, Death Valley National Park; house tours adult/senior/6-15 yr/under 5yr $11/9/6/free, Lower Vine Ranch tour

$15; ⏱ 9am-4:30pm Apr-Oct, 8:30am-5pm Nov-Mar

Tecopa Hot Springs Resort
Sex-segregated bathhouses shelter therapeutic mineral springs plus sauna ($30 per half-hour); try the $5 local mud mask. ☎ 760-852-4420; www.tecopahotsprings.org; 860 Tecopa Hot Springs Rd, Tecopa; day use $8; ⏱ 6am-10pm daily Oct-May

EAT

Cafe C'est Si Bon
Savor fresh-cooked, chef-made crepes, and quiche packed with goat cheese and organic veggies, while world music plays in the background. Cash only. ☎ 760-852-4307; www.tecopaca.com; Hwy 127, Shoshone; mains $6-8; ⏱ 8am-4pm Wed-Sun; ♿

Forty-Niner Cafe & Wrangler Steak House
Expect long waits and only average American food at this family-style restaurant and steakhouse. ☎ 760-786-2345; www.furnacecreekresort.com; Hwy 190, Furnace Creek; mains $12-38; ⏱ café 7am-9pm mid-Oct–mid-May, 11:30am-9pm mid-May–mid-Oct, steakhouse 5:30-9:30pm mid-Oct–mid-May, 6:30-9:30pm mid-May–mid-Oct; ♿

Furnace Creek Inn Dining Room
Reserve a table in the formal dining room (no tanks, tees or shorts) or stay casual at the sociable bar, where you can order sizable Southwestern snacks. Afternoon tea ($18) from 3:30pm to 5pm daily, except in summer. ☎ 760-786-3385; www.furnacecreekresort.com; Hwy 190, Furnace Creek; mains $13-38; ⏱ 7-10am & 11:30am-9pm mid-Oct–mid-May

Pastels
Chef John Muccio runs the friendly "flexitarian" kitchen here, where the California fusion menu changes weekly. Powerful espresso; $5 corkage for BYO. ☎ 760-852-4420; http://pastels1.tripod.com; Tecopa Hot Springs Resort, Tecopa Hot Springs Rd, Tecopa; mains $10-18; ⏱ 10am-4pm Thu-Mon, 6-10pm Thu-Sun

HISTORY & CULTURE

Toll Road Restaurant

Above-par cowboy cooking and generic salad bar inside a ranch house with a toasty fireplace, Native American blankets on the walls, and wooden chairs and tables that really feel like the Old West. ☎ 760-786-2387; www.stovepipewells.com; Stovepipe Wells Village, Hwy 190, Stovepipe Wells; mains $10-25; ⏱ 7am-10am, 11:30am-2pm & 5:30-9pm; ♿

SLEEP

Death Valley National Park Campgrounds

Furnace Creek Campground accepts reservations from mid-October through mid-April. All other campgrounds are first-come, first-served; some have potable water. Emigrant is tents-only; more remote Wildrose, Thorndike and Mahogany Flat are free with park admission. Mesquite Springs has spacious sites that are much less congested than Furnace Creek. ☎ reservations 877-444-6777; www.recreation.gov; campsites 1-8 people free-$18, 9-40 people $52; ⏱ some campgrounds year-round; ♿ 🐾

Furnace Creek Inn

At this hilltop adobe hotel, elegant Mission-style buildings dating from 1927 lie among palm-shaded garden terraces. Stripped-down rooms with cable TV are overpriced, yet the Zenlike atmosphere is priceless. Perks include a swimming pool and tennis courts. ☎ 760-786-2345, reservations 303-297-2757, 800-236-7916; www.furnacecreekresort.com; Hwy 190, Furnace Creek; r $227-440; ⏱ mid-Oct–mid-May; ♿

Furnace Creek Ranch

Popular with families, this dusty ranch just south of the Furnace Creek Visitor Center has ordinary cabins and motel rooms, but also a swimming pool, tennis, horseback-riding stables (winter only) and a desert golf course. ☎ 760-786-2345, reservations 303-297-2757, 800-236-7916; www.furnacecreekresort.com; Hwy 190, Furnace Creek; r $102-286; ⏱ year-round; ♿

Stovepipe Wells Village

Basically, it's just a roadside motel with a small swimming pool, but it's the best bargain in the valley itself. Standard rooms have air-con but no phone; deluxe rooms have TVs and fridges. ☎ 760-786-2387; www.stovepipewells.com; Hwy 190, Stovepipe Wells; r $75-115; 🐾 ♿

USEFUL WEBSITES

www.deathvalleychamber.org
www.nps.gov

LINK YOUR TRIP

www.lonelyplanet.com/trip-planner

TRIP
74 48 Hours in Las Vegas p523
78 Four Corners Cruise p543

48 Hours in San Francisco

Why Go Flower power, Beatniks, blue jeans, biotech...what will SF dream up next? Get to know the world capital of weird inside out, from mural-lined alley-ways named for poets to hilltop parks where wild parrots curse their hellos. Ditch your car, come as you are, and find your niche in San Francisco.

TIME
2 days

BEST TIME TO GO
Sep – Nov

START
Ferry Building

END
Castro

Snow globe of a city that it is, San Francisco is small, easy to grasp and likes nothing better than shaking things up and getting coated with glitter. In two days you can do up this 7 x 7–mile city, mingle with pirates and graffiti artists, shop with drag queens and brunch amid top chefs in a working kitchen.

San Francisco slackers have the right idea at the Ferry Building, the transport hub turned gourmet emporium where no one's in a hurry to get anywhere. Why rush when you can linger over poached eggs with truffled sheep's cheese and polenta, watching chefs prep the evening meal at ❶ Boulette's Larder? Once you're good and ready you can roll up the waterfront Embarcadero to Union St, where you'll cross the plaza named for the local entrepreneur without whom the city would be permanently half-naked: Levi Strauss.

Passing pet rocks and Zen gardens, head up Filbert St Steps. You'll know you're getting close to the top of Telegraph Hill (named for San Francisco's proto-internet invention) when you start getting heckled by the flock of trash-talking wild parrots who have taken over the tree-tops. Finally you'll reach ❷ Coit Tower, with wall-to-wall 1930s murals honoring San Francisco workers, which were almost painted over during the communist-baiting McCarthy era. The tower is capped by 360-degree top-floor panoramas revealing the Golden Gate Bridge in all its glory.

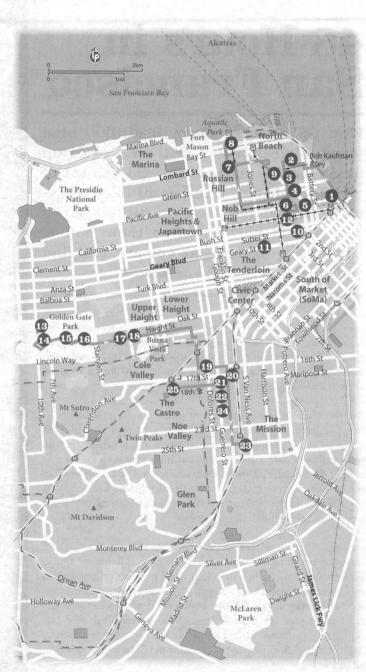

Downhill from Telegraph along Greenwich and Grant is North Beach, the Italian neighborhood where the US Navy dumped insubordinate sailors during WWII. It became a magnet for 1950s rebels: jazz musicians, civil rights agitators, topless dancers, Beat poets and dharma bums. One individual who defied all categories and conventions now has a street named after him: Bob Kaufman, the bebop-jazz-poet-voodoo-anarchist-Jewish-biracial-African-all-American-street-corner-prophet.

On Grant St you'll pass boho boutiques and bars on your way to ❸ **Caffe Trieste**, the legendary Beat poet hangout with opera on the jukebox and accordion jam sessions on weekends. Throw back an espresso to power you two blocks to Columbus and the landmark ❹ **City Lights** bookstore, which fought charges of "willfully and lewdly" publishing Allen Ginsberg's epic *Howl and Other Poems* in 1957 and won a groundbreaking court ruling against book banning. Celebrate your freedom to read willfully and lewdly in the upstairs poetry section or downstairs in free-form nonfiction sections dedicated to Muckracking and Stolen Continents.

Turn right out the door to Jack Kerouac Alley, the mural-covered byway named for the *On the Road* author, with his thoughts on San Francisco embedded in the sidewalk: "The air was soft, the stars so fine, and the promise of every cobbled alley so great..." Walk across the pavement poetry to Chinatown's Grant St, where phone booths are topped with tiled pagodas and the smoky-rich aroma of roast duck wafts out deli doors. Hungry yet? Follow Grant past souvenir shops packed with butterfly kites and chirping toy crickets, turn left onto Clay St, with its fierce chess games in progress in Portsmouth Sq, and turn right one block south to Commercial St. In the 19th century, this was one of the most notorious brothel byways in the Wild West, conveniently located close to waterfront saloons and bawdy Jenny Lind Theater, which with a few modifications became San Francisco's first City Hall. Today the greatest temptations on this block are the dim sum (dumplings) at ❺ **City View**, where servers narrowly avoid collisions between trolleys loaded with fragrant bamboo steamers during the lunch rush.

Indulge at your leisure, then walk one flat block down Kearny and one very steep block up Sacramento St to Waverly Pl, where prayer flags flap and incense wafts from 4th-floor temple balconies. When Chinatown crumbled and burned in the 1906 earthquake and fire, residents fled for their lives, and opportunistic real estate speculators urged City Hall to relocate Chinatown south of the city. But even before the smoke had cleared, Chinatown residents returned to pray in these temples, and if you visit ❻ **Tien Hou Temple** you can see the charred altar that has become a symbol of community endurance against the odds. Revolution is only a block away, left on Clay St and right on Spofford Alley, where Sun Yat-sen plotted the overthrow of China's last emperor. The

1920s brought bootleggers and gun battles, but Spofford has mellowed with age, and in the evenings you'll hear the shuffling of tiles as octogenarians plot winning mah-jongg moves and an *erhu* (two-stringed Chinese fiddle) warms up with a plaintive note. Head right on Jackson half a block and left onto Ross, where colorful murals mark the entry to a street with a colorful history. SF's oldest alley was formerly known as Manila, Spanish and Mexico St after the origins of the women who once worked this block – until the 1906 fire tore through the alley, trapping the women and their clients behind locked bordello doors.

DETOUR Duck into the Bob Kaufman Alley in North Beach and enjoy a moment of profound silence in tribute to the poet who refused to speak for 12 years, beginning at the assassination of John F Kennedy. On the day the Vietnam War ended, he walked into a café and recited "All Those Ships That Never Sailed": "Today I bring them back/Huge and transitory/And let them sail/Forever."

On Jackson and Powell you can catch the Powell–Hyde cable car, which is not equipped with seat belts or air bags – for safety you just grab a leather strap and pray. You'll notice these vintage trolleys emit mechanical grunts on uphill climbs, and require burly brakemen and bionic brakewomen to keep from careening down Russian Hill – for a city of risk takers, this is the perfect joyride. Leap on for a rickety ride uphill to ❼ **Sterling Park**, named for San Francisco's "King of Bohemia," poet and 1920s free-love advocate George Sterling, who loved verse, women, men, nature, opium and San Francisco, though not necessarily in that order. The Golden Gate Bridge and Pacific stretch past the wind-sculpted pines in this hilltop park and anyone not moved to poetry by sunsets here must've already left a heart elsewhere in San Francisco.

PLAYLIST Eclectic doesn't begin to describe San Francisco's music scene, or the unlikely hits local bands have produced. Listen for yourself and, for the ultimate SF DJ challenge, try mashing them up into one freakified song…

- "Take Five," Dave Brubeck
- "Sugar Magnolia," Grateful Dead
- "California Uber Alles," Dead Kennedys
- "San Francisco Anthem," San Quinn
- "Enter Sandman," Metallica
- "Lights," Journey
- "Me and Bobby McGee," Janis Joplin
- "Thank You (Falettinme Be Mice Elf Agin)," Sly and the Family Stone

To keep the romance going, head downhill and splash out for dinner with a view at ❽ **Gary Danko**, winner of multiple James Beard awards and inventor of tasting menus San Francisco foodies swear are the culinary equivalent of Viagra. For crowd-pleasing, family-friendly fare, head down zigzagging Lombard to Columbus and walk four blocks to ❾ **Cinecittá Pizzeria** for the capricciosa, loaded with artichoke hearts, prosciutto, olives, fresh mozzarella and an egg.

The next morning while the fog's still clearing, take public transit from your downtown digs at funky artist-decorated ⑩ **Hotel des Arts**, designer-fabulous ⑪ **Hotel Adagio** or certified green ⑫ **Orchard Garden Hotel** to the ⑬ **MH de Young Memorial Museum** in Golden Gate Park (best options: N Judah streetcar or bus 71 from Powell and Market). Follow Andy Goldsworthy's simulated sidewalk earthquake cracks into the museum, which celebrates artists from Oceania to California. Blockbuster temporary shows range from Hiroshi Sugimoto's haunting time-lapse photographs of drive-ins to Dale Chihuly's bombastic glass sculpture. Access to the tower is free; catch the elevator by Ruth Asawa's mesmerizing meshwork sculptures, which dangle from the ceiling and cast psychedelic shadows around the gallery.

The copper-clad de Young is a shy landmark that's just trying to blend in – architects Herzog & de Meuron (of Tate Modern fame) treated the copper exterior to oxidized green to match the park. Across the plaza, Pritzker

"Movies in San Francisco are a spectator sport. San Francisco crowds don't realize the movie is not about them – audiences will hiss, yell and backtalk at the screen like it's going to change the ending. We have the best audiences in the world, period."

Peaches Christ, drag diva and San Francisco movie maven

Prize–winning architect Renzo Piano has taken camouflage to the next level, capping the ⑭ **California Academy of Sciences** with a "living roof" of California wildflowers. The academy houses 38,000 weird and wonderful animals in custom habitats: a white alligator stalks the swamp, butterflies flutter through the four-story rainforest dome, and Pierre the Penguin and friends paddle their tank by day, and nuzzle and doze off to artificial sunsets during NightLife Thursdays.

Stroll through the redwoods of the ⑮ **National AIDS Memorial Grove**, where volunteers have brought life back to a forgotten corner of the Golden Gate Park and created a haven of peace. Emerge in ⑯ **Sharon Meadow**, better known as the site of the Summer of Love. Spelunk through the faux-cavern tunnel to Haight St, where the parade of nonconformists has continued for 40 years.

Browse your way along five blocks of skate shops and tattoo parlors to the Victorian storefront with fishnet-clad legs kicking out the window. This is ⑰ **Piedmont**, the legendary drag supply store where counter staff call everyone "baby doll" and no one obeys the sign that reads: "No Playing in the Boas."

All that glamour is bound to make you hungry and possibly in need of a drink and, right across the street, ⑱ **Magnolia Brewpub** obliges. Make yourself at home at the communal table, consult your neighbors on the all-local, organic menu (bet they'll recommend the Prather Ranch burger) and work your way through the beer sampler. You may have to peel yourself off your chair to continue your long, strange trip down Haight St, past flamboyant gilded Victorians, windswept Buena Vista Park and painfully punning storefronts: Haight Mail, Love & Haight, Lower Haighter.

Pass the medicinal marijuana club (sorry dude, prescription required), hang a right on Steiner and an immediate left onto Victorian-lined Laussat, which includes a Rasta house painted red, gold and green. Turn right on Fillmore, walk 2½ blocks to Hermann, go left and walk two blocks to Church. Follow Church four blocks south across Market to 16th St and turn right – you'll see the spectacular cake-frosting *churrigueresque* towers of ⑲ **Mission Dolores**. Duck inside to peek at spectacular stained-glass windows depicting California's 21 missions and San Francisco's gentle namesake saint, and pay respects to the native Miwok and Ohlone who built this mission at the memorial hut.

The Mission District has more than 250 murals hidden on side streets, and two blocks up on Valencia between 17th and 18th St is San Francisco's best open-air graffiti art gallery, ⑳ **Clarion Alley**. Only the strong murals survive here: anything that fails to inspire gets peed on or painted over. Half a block further down Valencia, you'll spot San Francisco's biggest mural, ㉑ **Maestrapiece**, a show of female strength that wraps around the trailblazing Women's Building.

Comic-artist Chris Ware's mural marks ㉒ **826 Valencia**, the nonprofit youth writing program and purveyor of pirate supplies. Pick up eye patches, tubs of lard and tall tales for long nights at sea, published by McSweeney's. Stop by the Fish Theater to see Vaclav the pufferfish immersed in Method acting. He's no Sean Penn but as the sign says: "Please don't judge the fish."

Everyone in the Mission has strong opinions about burritos, Cal-Mex feasts wrapped in tortillas and tinfoil. At ㉓ **La Taqueria** they don't mess around with debatable rice or tofu but stick to mesquite-grilled meats, plump beans, fresh salsa, and optional cheese and housemade spicy pickles. If you prefer to remain neutral on the great burrito debate, head to ㉔ **Range**, where the menu is seasonal Californian, prices are reasonable, and style is repurposed industrial chic – think fan-belt lamps and blood-bank refrigerators for beer.

End your 48 hours in San Francisco with a roar at the historic ㉕ **Castro Theatre**, where the crowd goes wild when the giant organ rises from the floor (no, really) and pumps out show tunes until the movie starts. Fingers crossed you'll get a Bette Davis double feature, where the crowd shouts lines like: "Fasten your seat belts, it's going to be a bumpy night!" Now that you know San Francisco, you should expect nothing less.

Alison Bing

TRIP INFORMATION

GETTING THERE
San Francisco is the capital of the breakaway republic of Northern California, a convenient 70 miles from Santa Cruz and a safe 381 miles north of Los Angeles.

DO
826 Valencia
Pirate supply sales fund 826's after-school programs, and a heartfelt, pirate-to-pirate "Arrrr!" is free with any booty purchased here. ☎ 415-642-5905; www.826valencia.org; 826 Valencia St; ☾ noon-6pm

California Academy of Sciences
Creature features and wild scenes unfold under the flower-topped roof, plus rainforest-themed cocktails on NightLife Thursdays (21-years plus, with ID; $12). ☎ 415-321-8000; www.calacademy.org; Concourse Dr; adult/senior & student/4-11yr/under 4yr $24.95/19.95/14.95/free, 3rd Wed of month free; ☾ 9:30am-5pm Mon-Sat, 11am-5pm Sun, NightLife 6-10pm Thu

Castro Theatre
Independent cinema, silver-screen classics and cult-hit double features, plus the Lesbian/Gay/Bi/Trans Film Festival in June. ☎ 415-621-6120; www.castrotheatre. com; 429 Castro St; adult/child & matinee $10/7.50

City Lights
Purveyor of poetry and inspiration since 1953. The sign by the door paraphrases Dante: "Abandon All Despair, Ye Who Enter Here" – without that bummer baggage, there's more room for books. ☎ 415-362-8193; www.citylights.com; 261 Columbus Ave; ☾ 10am-midnight

Coit Tower
This monument to San Francisco's firefighters was named after eccentric millionaire Lillie Hancock Coit; Saturday 11am tours cover hidden murals. ☎ 415-362-0808; 1 Telegraph Hill Blvd; adult/senior & 12-15yr/5-11yr/under 5yr $5/3/2/free; ☾ 10am-6pm

MH de Young Memorial Museum
Travel around the world and back through the international collection of arts in this landmark copper-clad building. ☎ 415-750-3600; www.famsf.org/deyoung; 50 Hagiwara Tea Garden Dr; adult/senior/student/under 12yr $10/7/6/free, 1st Tue of month free; ☾ 9:30am-5:15pm Tue-Sun, 9:30am-8:45pm Fri

Mission Dolores
Our Lady of the Sorrows doesn't look a day over 225 years, with original Ohlone ceilings and an adjoining basilica aglow with stained-glass scenes of California missions. ☎ 415-621-8203; www.missiondolores. org; 3321 16th St; adult/student & senior $5/3; ☾ 9am-4pm Nov-Apr, 9am-4:30pm May-Oct

Piedmont
Glam up or get out at this emporium of inch-long eyelashes, feather boas and Day-Glo pleather hot pants designed on the premises. ☎ 415-864-8075; 1452 Haight St; ☾ 11am-7pm

Tien Hou Temple
Dedicated in 1852 to the Buddhist Goddess of Heaven, this survivor of the 1906 earthquake and fire is a Chinatown icon. **125 Waverly Place; admission free but offerings appreciated;** ☾ 10am-5pm

EAT & DRINK
Boulette's Larder
Local and organic products become sumptuous breakfasts before your eyes at communal chefs' tables. ☎ 415-399-1155; www. bouletteslarder.com; 1 Ferry Bldg Marketplace; breakfast/brunch mains $9-25; ☾ 8-10:30am & 11:30am-2:30pm Mon-Fri, 10am-2:30pm Sun

Caffe Trieste
Powerful espresso, bathroom-stall poetry, free wi-fi and jukebox opera at the Beats' favorite hangout; cash only. ☎ 415-392-6739; 601 Vallejo St; ☾ 6:30am-11pm Sun-Thu, 6:30am-midnight Fri & Sat

Cinecittà Pizzeria

Local Italians throng this hole-in-the-wall pizzeria for thin-crust pies, draft beer and sass from Roman owner Romina. ☎ 415-291-8830; 663 Union St; pizzas $8-13; ⏱ noon-10pm Sun-Thu, noon-11pm Fri-Sat

City View

Flag down rolling dim sum carts for plump shrimp and leek dumplings, savory spare ribs and garlicky Chinese broccoli. ☎ 415-398-2838; 662 Commercial St; small plates $2-8; ⏱ 11am-2:30pm Mon-Fri & 10am-2:30pm Sat & Sun

Gary Danko

All the right moves: James Beard Award–winning California cuisine, waterfront location, smart yet easy-going service and tiny cakes as parting gifts. ☎ 415-749-2060; www.garydanko.com; 800 North Point St; 3-/4-/5-course tasting menu $66/83/98; ⏱ 5:30-10pm, book ahead

La Taqueria

Pure burrito bliss: classic tomatillo or mesquite salsa, smoky meats and beans inside a flour tortilla, with housemade spicy pickles. ☎ 415-285-7117; 2889 Mission St; burritos $6-7 ⏱ 11am-9pm

Magnolia Brewpub

Organic pub grub and homebrews with laid-back, Deadhead service in the hippie heart of the Haight. ☎ 415-864-7468; www.magnoliapub.com; 1398 Haight St; mains $10-21; ⏱ noon-midnight Mon-Thu, 10am-1am Fri & Sat, 10am-midnight Sun

Range

Clean flavors, inventive veggie offerings, euphoric desserts and clever appliance-store decor at surprisingly fair prices. ☎ 415-282-8283; www.rangesf.com; 842 Valencia St; mains $19-25; ⏱ 6-10pm Mon-Thu, 5:30-11pm Fri-Sun

SLEEP

Hotel Adagio

Downtown designer chic, with chipper staff, killer bar, deco building and shopping-central location. ☎ 415-775-5000, 800-228-8830; www.thehoteladagio.com; 550 Geary St; r $129-239

Hotel des Arts

Shack up in an art installation piece by an emerging local artist. ☎ 415-956-3232, 800-956-4322; www.sfhoteldesarts.com; 447 Bush St; r $59-89, ste $119-139

Orchard Garden Hotel

High style gets down to earth with this LEED-certified green hotel's roof gardens, nonchemical cleaners, fresh air indoors, and nature-friendly policies. ☎ 415-399-9807, 888-717-2881; www.theorchardgardenhotel.com; 466 Bush St; r $279-339

USEFUL WEBSITES

www.sfgate.com
www.sfbg.com
www.craigslist.org
www.7x7.com

LINK YOUR TRIP
www.lonelyplanet.com/trip-planner

Alice Waters' Culinary Tour

WHY GO Alice Waters' vision for local, organic, sustainable food continues to change and challenge the way we think about what we put in our bodies. True to this vision, her tour of California eating focuses on foods that stay close to the source, ending with dinner at her own Chez Panisse.

TIME
2 days

DISTANCE
146 miles

BEST TIME TO GO
Aug – Oct

START
Vacaville, CA

END
Berkeley, CA

Other revolutions start with a manifesto, but Alice Waters began changing how Americans eat by using a menu. The year was 1971, and diners at Chez Panisse lacked the terminology to describe the food they were tasting – it would be years until terms like "California cuisine," "certified organic" and "locavore" were coined. But who needs words when you have such a meal? Alice Waters made US food a pure pleasure.

Your own journey of culinary discovery begins down on the farm – the inspiration for Chez Panisse's pioneering menu, and most California culinary triumphs since. From San Francisco or Berkeley, go north on I-80 and exit near Vacaville at Pena Adobe Rd. The winding Cherry Glen Rd crosses under the highway to come to Pleasant Valley Rd, home of ❶ **Soul Food Farm**. Run by Alexis Koefoed, it earns Waters' raves and supplies chickens and eggs to a select handful of other restaurateurs throughout the Bay Area.

Waters reminisces about Soul Food's humanely raised "Freedom Rangers" breed, which peck around the 45 acres. "I had one of those the other week. I made it at home, this simple chicken, and you know what, I'm pretty used to good chicken. It tasted like no other chicken I've had in the United States. The dark meat was richer, more flavorful, and it was a revelation. It reminded me of the chicken I had 35 years ago in France."

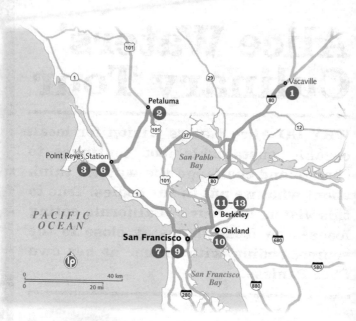

Pick up some of the eggs from the cooler at the end of the drive and leave your money in the jar. "Her eggs are fantastic," Waters says. "I just feel like I'm making a donation to the cause."

From Vacaville, go south on I-80 for 20 minutes and follow the exit for Hwy 37, which skirts the marshes of the San Pablo Bay and leads into Novato. Head north on 101 20 miles to Petaluma, home of another Alice Waters standby, **②** **Green String Farm**. Bob Cannard has pioneered sustainable farming in the North Bay for 30 years, and you can taste the chemical-free fruits of his labors at Green String's farm store.

The only weed-eaters around this farm are the fluffy sheep you can pet near the store. Instead of battling weeds with herbicides, Green String's philosophy is to let them coexist with cover vegetation and planted crops, creating a symbiotic ecosystem that yields a smaller crop but richer soil. While on the farm you may meet strutting chickens, members of the Green String Farm Band (theme song: "Favorite Chicken"), and Farmer Bob himself. "Bob is doing amazing things with that land," Waters says with admiration.

With ingredients from Green String you've got the beginnings of an exemplary picnic. To complete the feast, take the Point Reyes–Petaluma Rd 19 miles west of town to Point Reyes Station, home to a pair of North Bay food artisans that earn raves from Waters.

Point Reyes Station may look like a sleepy cow-town but at 3am baker Celine Underwood is stoking her wood-fired brick oven. Her dedication yields Brickmaiden bread, a Waters favorite sold at nearby ❸ **Bovine Bakery**. "That crust…" Waters trails off into reverential silence.

With loaf under arm, step down the block to the restored barn that houses ❹ **Cowgirl Creamery**, another Waters staple. In springtime the must-buy cheese is the St Pat's, a smooth, mellow round that comes wrapped in nettle leaves. There is also a gourmet deli and tour available on Friday mornings.

For the perfect picnic spot, Waters says to look on the surrounding coast. "Go up there in the headlands and find a little spot by Bolinas and Inverness and along the ❺ **Point Reyes National Seashore**," she says. "I think that is one of the greatest park areas I've ever been in."

Another idyllic picnic spot awaits 10 minutes north of Point Reyes Station, at the salty turnout for the ❻ **Hog Island Oyster Company**. It has a handful of silky oysters available to go (by the pound) but, to Waters, "there's nothing better than eating them right there on the beach." For a fee you can arrange for a table and borrow some shucking tools. The company even offers lessons on how to crack open and grill the oysters for those who like them barbecued.

After lunch, explore the misty coastal forests before winding down Hwy 1 back into San Francisco. From the center of the Golden Gate Bridge it's possible to view the clock tower of the city's ❼ **Ferry Building Marketplace**, which hosts not only a broad selection of gourmet organic produce but is also a one-stop destination for many of Waters' recommendations. Tuesday, Thursday and Saturday year-round, the Ferry Building is encircled by up to 82 family farmers and 42 food artisans, selling sustainably produced wares to top chefs and picky eaters. From dry-farmed tomatoes to organic kimchi fried rice, this bounty may seem like an embarrassment of riches – but not to Waters. "We have to start looking at food as a right and not a privilege," she says flatly. "That is important."

THE ENDANGERED ELBERT PEACH

At **Masumoto Family Farm**, near Fresno, you can sink your teeth into the endangered Elbert peach, a variety deemed "too fragile" for the modern supermarket. Waters calls the farm "one of the most gratifying places on earth," but the public can only visit if they adopt a tree through www.masumoto.com. The adoptive parents harvest the buttery peaches themselves – all 400lbs to 500lbs of them. "It's no vacation," Masumoto says. "But it's the kind of thing that really helps people understand the rhythms of nature."

Even if your SF arrival doesn't coincide with a Ferry Building market day, never fear: 35 local food purveyors have set up shop indoors. "Inside there are really quite exceptional vendors," Waters says. "It's one of the only places where you can get real food all in one place. There's obviously Cowgirl Creamery and Acme Bread, and McAvoy Olive Oil. And we have a reliable source of humanely raised, clean meat at Prather Ranch."

To stay within skipping distance of the Ferry Building, check into the bay-front luxury ⑧ **Hotel Vitale**. Those worn out from all the organic veggie hunting can blow off some steam in the rooftop soaking tubs surrounded by a bamboo forest – with local, seasonal bath products, of course.

SEASON'S EATINGS

California is the most agriculturally diverse region in the United States and many of its farmers markets stay open year-round. Look for these seasonal delights during your romp through the state: spring's artichokes, asparagus, snow peas, lettuce greens and avocados; summer's berries, watermelon, peppers, zucchini, corn and stone fruit; fall's squash, tomatoes, apples, pumpkins and cucumbers; and winter's Swiss chard, Meyer lemons, fennel and kiwi.

For dinner, a San Francisco institution is just up Market St at ⑨ **Zuni Café**, a place Waters merrily refers to as her "home away from home." She'll quickly admit that it's a distinctively different atmosphere than the one at Chez Panisse, but adds, "Zuni is run in the right spirit. It's real food." By the way she offers these straightforward compliments – her voice going from a kind of gregarious, playful lilt to dead-serious in a second – it's clear that a declaration of "real food" is her highest praise. It's not doled out all that often but reserved for a select handful of students who have passed through the kitchen of her restaurant and other like-minded chefs in what she calls "the cause."

Asked about menus she admires, her response is uncomplicated: "It's about seasonality, no question," she says. "And obviously locality. I'm looking for people who are using organic produce and meat. So I want grass-fed beef. I want organic vegetables. I want organic breads. I want people who care about farmers and ranchers. I'm looking," and she pauses just a beat, "for the *purists*."

To get a tantalizing taste of what US food could taste like after Waters' food revolution is won, head across the Bay Bridge to downtown Oakland, and claim your rightful place at the 30ft communal table at ⑩ **Camino**. A 20-year veteran at Chez Panisse, chef Russell Moore brings farm-fresh food to gritty Grand Ave in a converted furniture showroom. The massive central fireplace isn't just there for looks: wood-fired meats and pizzas are pulled sizzling from the flames. The daily menu is abbreviated, but nothing short of heartwarming. As Waters says with relish, "Russell is a purist."

Another celebrated Chez Panisse alum is Steve Sullivan, the master baker behind ⑪ **Acme Bread Company.** Sullivan started bussing tables at Chez Panisse while he was a student at UC Berkeley and began what local foodies refer to as the "San Francisco bread revolution." On the western end of the so-called "Gourmet Ghetto" – a neighborhood that married the revolutionary ideals of Berkley in the late '60s with a haute dining sensibility – you can smell the cinnamon bread floating across Shattuck St, intoxicating passersby every morning.

To taste the sunny, California-grown flavors that redefine "good food," head to ⑫ **Chez Panisse,** just up the street. It's casual and unpretentious, and every mind-altering bite of the food served in the dining room downstairs and the slightly less formal café upstairs is emblematic of Waters' principles. The service is impeccable, the atmosphere is comfortably elegant and the kitchen is open for a peek behind the scenes.

The full effect of Chez Panisse may hit the next day when, in the thrall of culinary inspiration, you mysteriously find yourself at the ⑬ **Berkeley farmers' market,** run by the Ecology Center since 1987. Don't be surprised to find Alice Waters here, in her element and in raptures. "You have to

PANISSE PROTÉGÉS

"When you operate a restaurant for 37 years, a whole lot of people come through the kitchen," Waters says. Of her alumni in San Francisco, try Michael Tusk, who offers shrewd Italian-French fusions at Quince (www.quincerestaurant.com), or Gayle Pirie, who operates Foreign Cinema (www.foreigncinema.com), a gourmet movie house in the Mission District. More casual eats are across the bay, where Charlie Hallowell offers immaculate wood-fired pizzas at Pizzaiolo (www.pizzaiolooakland.com), and Alison Barakat marries classic comfort food with '50s kitsch at Bakesale Betty (www.bakesalebetty.com).

try Prima Vera's organic tortillas," she urges, "and Annabelle's stand [La Tercera] has wonderful Italian greens. Oh, that *puntarella*…" Enough said: by now your tastebuds are standing at attention, ready to join the revolution.

Alison Bing & Nate Cavalieri

FOOD &
DRINK

TRIP INFORMATION

GETTING THERE
Eat your way around the bay. To begin, head north to Vacaville.

DO

Berkeley Farmers Markets
Markets are held Tuesday on Derby St and Thursday on Shattuck, but Saturday's Center St one doubles as a block party. ☎ 510-548-3333; www.ecologycenter.org/bfm; ☿ 2-6pm Tue, 3-7pm Thu, 10am-3pm Sat; ♿

Ferry Building Marketplace
A one-stop shop of Waters' favorites. ☎ 415-983-8000; www.ferrybuildingmarketplace. com; One Ferry Building, San Francisco; ☿ stores 10am-6pm Mon-Fri, 9am-6pm Sat, 11am-5pm Sun, market 10am-2pm Tue & Thu, 8am-2pm Sat; ♿

Green String Farm
Bucolic splendor at its best. ☎ 707-778-7500; www.greenstringfarm.com; 3571 Old Adobe Rd, Petaluma; admission free; ☿ 10am-5pm winter, 10am-6pm summer; ♿

Soul Food Farm
Its chickens are also available at Bay Area farmers markets. ☎ 707-469-0499; www. soulfoodfarm.com; 6046 Pleasants Valley Rd, Vacaville; ♿

EAT

Acme Bread Company
Waters' protégé Steve Sullivan ignited the "San Francisco bread revolution." ☎ 510-524-1327; 1601 San Pablo, Berkeley; ☿ 8am-6pm Mon-Sat, 8:30am-3pm Sun

Bovine Bakery
Just-baked goods and organic coffee. ☎ 415-663-9420; 11315 Shoreline Hwy, Pt Reyes Station; pastries $1-8; ☿ 6:30am-5pm; ♿

Camino
Gather round the roaring fire at reclaimed-wood communal tables for sophisticated rustic fare and seasonal cocktails. ☎ 510-547-5035; www.caminorestaurant.com; 3917 Grand Ave, Oakland; mains $13-26; ☿ 10am-2pm Sat & Sun, 5:30-10pm Mon & Wed-Sat, 5-10pm Sun

Chez Panisse
Changing palates and preserving ecosystems, one dish at a time. ☎ 510-548-5525 restaurant, 510-548-5049 café; www.chezpanisse. com; 1517 Shattuck Ave, Berkeley; prix fixe café $26, restaurant $60-95; ☿ café 11:30am-3pm & 5-10:30pm Mon-Thu, 11:30am-3:30pm & 5-11:30pm Fri & Sat, restaurant seatings 6pm & 8:30pm Mon-Sat

Cowgirl Creamery
The triple-cream soft cheese has a nationwide rep. ☎ 415-663-9335; www. cowgirlcreamery.com; 80 Fourth St, Pt Reyes Station; artisan cheese from $8; ☿ 10am-6pm Wed-Sun; ♿

Hog Island Oyster Company
The sustainably farmed oysters can be grilled on the beach. ☎ 415-663-9218; www. hogislandoysters.com; 20215 Hwy 1, Marshall; 12 oysters $13-$16, picnic area $5-10; ☿ 9am-5pm

Zuni Café
This hip spot is great for sustainably sourced, mesquite-grilled meats, brick-oven pizzas and people-watching. ☎ 415-552-2522; www. zunicafe.com; 1658 Market St, San Francisco; mains $15-30; ☿ 11:30am-11pm Tue-Thu, 11:30am-midnight Fri & Sat, 11am-11pm Sun

SLEEP

Hotel Vitale
Deep soaking tubs and huge views of the Bay Bridge are an easy stroll from the Ferry Building Marketplace. ☎ 415-278-3700; www. hotelvitale.com; 8 Mission St, San Francisco; r $279-319

USEFUL WEBSITES
www.ccfm.com
www.farmtrails.org

www.lonelyplanet.com/trip-planner

LINK YOUR TRIP

Tree Time in Sequoia & Kings Canyon

WHY GO If you want to feel small, crane your neck to the heavens and marvel at the heft of these giant sequoias. Home of one of the deepest canyons in the US and some of the biggest trees on earth, these Sierra-straddling parks collect superlatives but not the Yosemite crowds.

The roads in ❶ **Sequoia & Kings Canyon National Parks**, two parks managed together like fraternal twins, seem to barely scratch the surface of the parks' beauty. To see their treasures, you'll need to get out and stretch your legs.

On Hwy 180, trace the path of Kings River and drop down into Kings Canyon on the 30-mile Kings Canyon Scenic Byway. With a steep drop of 8200ft, this glacier-sculpted canyon is deeper than the Grand Canyon. Pull over at the sweeping ❷ **Junction View** overlook to get an eyeful of the river's Middle and South Fork and the steely peaks clustered nearby.

If the day's hot and your suit's handy when you reach Road's End, stroll from the wilderness permit office to ❸ **Muir Rock**. A large flat-top river boulder where John Muir gave talks during early Sierra Club field trips, it's a popular spot for shrieking cannonball dives and wet summer fun. Spend the night creekside at ❹ **Sheep Creek Campground**. Located a bit further from the Cedar Grove Village area than the three other area campgrounds, it's often less used.

For a sobering reminder of what the parks protect, reverse course and head back west 26 miles from Cedar Grove, making an easy detour to the ❺ **Converse Basin Grove**. Now a sequoia cemetery, it once held the world's largest grove of mature sequoias. The one colossus left to live was the Boole Tree, the seventh-largest giant sequoia. On the

TIME	
3 – 4 days	
DISTANCE	
195 miles	
BEST TIME TO GO	
Jun – Sep	
START	
Big Stump Entrance, Kings Canyon, CA	
END	
Mineral King, CA	

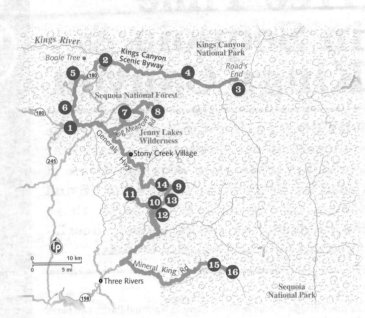

road in, stop at Stump Meadow to see the oversized vestiges of 19th-century logging. Check your park map to locate the unpaved Forest Service roads to the grove.

Continue about 6 miles south to the ⑥ **General Grant Grove**, where you'll see some of the big ones of yore. Saunter along the paved third-of-a-mile General Grant Tree Trail, an interpretive walk that visits a number of skyscraper-sized sequoias, including the 27-story General Grant Tree, the world's third-largest living tree. Kids will adore the Fallen Monarch, a massive, fire-hollowed walk-through trunk that's done duty as a cabin, hotel, saloon and horse stable.

To see one of the most evocative fire lookouts in the country, go south on the Generals Hwy, east on Big Meadows Rd and follow signs to the staffed ⑦ **Buck Rock Fire Lookout**. Built in 1923, a wooden panoramic-view cabin lords over the horizon from 8500ft atop a granite rise, reached by 172 stairs.

A bit further east, hike a mile into the forest for ice water and gourmet meals at the ⑧ **Sequoia High Sierra Camp**. A luxurious off-the-grid tent-cabin resort perched at 8282ft, it's nirvana for active, sociable people who don't think "luxury camping" is an oxymoron.

The next day, rejoin Generals Hwy and motor south to Lodgepole Village. Duck into the visitor center to buy afternoon tickets for Crystal Cave and pick up a salad or wrap at the ❾ **Watchtower Deli** for a picnic lunch outside. If you have curious little ones, head south to the Giant Forest Area and spend an hour or two at the indoor/outdoor ❿ **Beetle Rock Education Center**, where activity stations let kids ogle and interact with bones, bugs and (fake) animal poop. Afterwards, continue 2 miles south and then about 7 miles northwest to take your tour of ⓫ **Crystal Cave**, a chilly otherworld carved by an underground river. Stalactites hang like daggers from the ceiling, and milky white marble formations 10,000 years old take the shape of ethereal curtains, domes, columns and shields.

Back in the daylight, backtrack 2 miles north on Generals Hwy to get schooled on sequoia ecology and fire cycles at the ⓬ **Giant Forest Museum**, and then have a gander at

DREAMS TO SAWDUST

Before Sequoia National Park existed, an idealistic organization of workers called the **Kaweah Colony** began a utopian community in the pristine foothills below Giant Forest. It developed a labor-based currency, organized a school and farmed the land. But the 1890 victory of park designation wiped out its land claims and quashed its socialist dreams. Remaining Kaweah relics include the simple **Squatters Cabin** near Crescent Meadow and the one-room **Kaweah Post Office**, just north of Three Rivers.

⓭ **Giant Forest**, a mind-blowing throng of ancient giant sequoias. By volume the largest living tree on earth, the massive General Sherman Tree rockets 275ft to the sky. Then return a few miles north to the ⓮ **Wuksachi Lodge**, the parks' most upscale lodging and dining. Spacious rooms have a Southwestern feel, and the wood-paneled dining room enchants with a stone fireplace and forest views. Hearty dinners and decadent desserts such as chocolate mousse and ice-cream sundaes top off your day.

Continue south on Hwy 198 and, as you exit east before Three Rivers, clench the steering wheel for the hairraising and winding 1½-hour ride to Mineral King, a remote and marmotoverrun section of the park and his-

ASK A LOCAL "I first went there in the summer of 1943 and I've gone most summers since. There are 67 cabins in all; mostly built by people's grandfathers or great-grandfathers. It's a historic and continuing community – the majority of us are descendants of those first miners. My family's cabin is one of the oldest, and we cook on an old wood stove that probably dates from the 1880s. Nobody has electricity."

Jane Coughran, Mineral King cabin owner

toric mining hamlet. *Almost* at the end, mop your brow and stop for pie and burgers at the ⓯ **Silver City Mountain Resort**, the only restaurant on the road. Situate your tent at ⓰ **Cold Springs Campground**, set along a peaceful creek with gorgeous ridge views. Trailheads to the high country begin at the end of the road, where historic private cabins dot the valley floor flanked by massive mountains and jagged peaks.

Beth Kohn

TRIP INFORMATION

GETTING THERE
From Fresno, take Hwy 180 to the Big Stump Entrance. Return from Mineral King via Hwy 198 and Hwy 99.

DO
Beetle Rock Education Center
A bright and cheerful activity cabin run by the Sequoia Natural History Association, it's appropriate for kids aged three to 15. ☎ 559-565-4251; admission free; 🕙 10am-4pm summer; 👤

Buck Rock Fire Lookout
An active 1920s fire lookout, its long staircase leads to a dollhouse-sized wooden cabin on a dramatic 8500ft granite rise. www.buckrock.org; admission free; 🕙 9:30am-6pm Jul-Oct

Crystal Cave
Buy tickets in advance and bring a sweater for fantastical river-cave experiences. ☎ 559-565-3759; www.sequoiahistory.org; Crystal Cave Rd; 45min tour adult/senior/child $11/10/6, 1½hr tour $19, 4-6hr tour $129; 🕙 tours 11am-4pm mid-May–Oct, with variations

Giant Forest Museum
A fun primer in sequoia ecology, this pint-sized museum has hands-on exhibits about some very big trees. ☎ 559-565-4480; admission free; 🕙 9am-7pm Jul-Aug, 9am-5pm Apr-Jun & Sep-Oct, 9am-4:30pm Nov-Mar; 👤

Sequoia & Kings Canyon National Parks
Towering trees and a deep, deep canyon are but two reasons to visit the parks. ☎ 559-565-3341; www.nps.gov/seki; per car $20, per motorcycle, bicycle or pedestrian $10; 👤 🐾

EAT
Silver City Mountain Resort
Mineral King's only restaurant serves homemade pie and simple meals under a pleasant tree canopy. ☎ 559-561-3223; www.silvercityresort.com; Mineral King Rd; 🕙 8am-7pm Thu-Mon, 8am-2pm Tue & Wed late May-Oct; 👤

Watchtower Deli
Conveniently located gourmet deli that sells healthy to-go fare like foccaccia sandwiches and prepared salads. Lodgepole Village; mains $6-8; 🕙 11am-6pm May-Aug

Wuksachi Lodge
The most upscale option in the parks, Wuksachi's dining room serves a breakfast buffet, soup-and-salad lunches, and extravagant dinners (reservations recommended). ☎ 559-565-4070; dinner mains $15-35; 🕙 7:30-9:30am, 11:30am-2:30pm & 5-9:30pm; 👤

SLEEP
Cold Springs Campground
Towards the end of a tortuous 23-mile road, these nonreservable tent sites sit by a creek near the ranger station. Mineral King Rd; campsites $12; 🕙 late May-Oct; 👤 🐾

Sequoia High Sierra Camp
Settle in for gourmet meals and comfy beds at this luxury tent-cabin oasis. ☎ 866-654-2877; www.sequoiahighsierracamp.com; r incl meals per adult/child over 3yr $250/100; 🕙 mid-Jun–early Oct; 👤

Sheep Creek Campground
In the Cedar Grove region at the bottom of Kings Canyon, choose from 111 well-spaced sites situated along pretty creekside loops. campsites $18; 🕙 May–mid-Nov; 👤 🐾

USEFUL WEBSITES
www.sequoiahistory.org
www.sequoiaparksfoundation.org

LINK YOUR TRIP
www.lonelyplanet.com/trip-planner

TRIP
78 Four Corners Cruise p543
86 Life in Death Valley p597

California's Other Wine Countries

WHY GO Everybody knows the Napa and Sonoma Valleys. So now it's time to venture into California's less famous wine regions, where family-owned wineries welcome novices and experts alike, and tasting fees are low. Most of these well-hidden wine countries are near the San Francisco Bay area, perfect for weekend escapes.

TIME
4 days

DISTANCE
650 miles

BEST TIME TO GO
Apr – Oct

START
Hopland, CA

END
Paso Robles, CA

Beyond Napa and Sonoma, and past the Russian River Valley, lie the wineries of Mendocino County. No more than 150 miles north of San Francisco, this unsung winemaking region is hospitable to elegant pinot noirs, crisp Alsatian whites and saucy, food-loving zinfandels. Family farms line Hwy 101 just south and north of Hopland, a tiny farm town. The downtown wine shop ❶ Sip! Mendocino should be your first stop. There the expert proprietor pours handpicked flights of wines ranging from across the county, including rare vintages you might not even get to taste at the wineries themselves. Down the street next to a bakery, sunlight-filled ❷ Graziano Family of Wines brings together four different labels and continues to farm vineyards first planted by the owner's grandparents, Italian immigrants who kept right on making wines in Mendocino County through the Prohibition era. For earthy, flavor-packed wine-country cooking, dash north to ❸ Patrona in Ukiah. Locally grown ingredients glow in garden salads, flatbread pizzas and sublime sustainable fish tacos.

The biggest appellation within Mendo is the Anderson Valley, known for its delicate Alsatian whites and sparkling wines as much as for its specialty pinot noirs, all thanks to sun-drenched days and coastal fog drifting over the vineyards at night. Follow winding Hwy 153 west to the podunk town of Boonville. Rest up for more tastings at the ❹ Boonville Hotel, with its chicly rehabbed, yet still rustic rooms

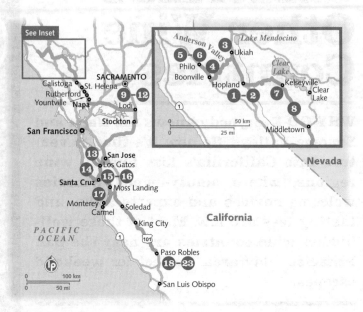

off the highway. From Boonville past Philo, Hwy 128 is lined with family-run wineries. With its sustainably produced wines and sunny picnic deck, **5 Navarro Vineyards** is the most popular stop. Starring on a free tasting menu are Navarro's dry, estate-bottled gewürtztraminer and nonalcoholic pinot noir grape juice. The sparkling wines of **6 Roederer Estate** are hand-crafted by the same French family that makes Cristal champagne. At this upscale countryside winery, only delicate first pressings of estate-grown char-donnay and pinot noir grapes are used for the cuvée (signature blend) – the winemakers are picky, and it pays.

In the northern San Joaquin Valley of central California, breezes from the Sacramento River delta soothe the hot vineyards of Lodi, yielding 40% of California's zinfandel grapes. Century-old oaks thrive alongside vineyards adhering to groundbreaking Lodi Rules, third-party-certified sustainable growing methods. Lodi's diverse soil is sometimes rocky, sometimes a fine sandy loam, giving its zins distinctive character. To get here from Hopland, the scenic route takes you east into Lake County around Clear Lake, which boasts its own noteworthy winemakers like deeply rooted **7 Steele Wines**, where an adventurous lineup of whites and reds includes Writer's Block Cunoise, bottled with a portrait of the Bard; and high-society **8 Langtry Estate & Vineyards**, a Napa-style winery that makes a bright, soft petite sirah from vineyards first planted in the late 19th century by actor Lillie Langtry.

Hwy 29 flows slowly south through Calistoga, St Helena, Yountville and finally Napa, after which Hwy 12 slingshots east across the delta toward Lodi. Get your first taste of Lodi's powerful, sun-soaked zins at the **9 Lodi Wine & Visitor Center**, where 200 local vintages are sold by the solid-wood tasting bar. Then drive out into the vineyards to sample straight from the source. **10 Michael-David Winery** is shockingly touristy, with its farm stand, café and tasting-room complex, but its flagship 7 Deadly Zins, a jammy blend of seven different old-vine zinfandels, merits a stop.

The Lange family has been tilling Lodi fields for five generations, and their savvy shows in LangeTwins' small-batch zin, viognier and petit verdot made with Lodi Rules–certified grapes. Swing by **11 LangeTwins'** solar-powered winery a few miles north of Lodi for complimentary tastings of their silky Midnight Reserve Cab blend and spiced-cherry reds – at $12 to $15 a bottle you might even ship some to the folks back home in the winery's biodegradable packaging. With historical atmosphere and ultramodern amenities, the **12 Wine & Roses** inn back in Lodi distinguishes itself with a swanky spa and Cal-Ital restaurant, where Dungeness crab cakes and rose-petal salads are served on a leafy patio.

GREENING THE VINEYARDS

Some of California's smallest wineries and wine regions are among the "greenest," environmentally speaking. A buzz word you'll hear as you travel about is "biodynamic," referring to vineyards that create self-sustaining farm eco-systems and aim to keep crop quality high. Organic, pesticide-free vineyards at wineries using solar-energy panels and biodiesel-fueled vehicles abound, especially in Mendocino County, where you can tour the educational **Solar Living Institute** (☎707-744-2017; www.solarliving. org). It's located at 13771 S Hwy 101, Hopland, and is open from 10am to 6pm daily.

Backtracking to the Bay area, you'll pass the emerging Livermore wine country, then coast down the peninsula into the Santa Cruz Mountains. Vines were first planted among these coastal redwood forests in the mid–19th century. One of the first US regions to be awarded its own appellation, these rugged, little-known mountains produced a cabernet sauvignon that bested mighty French Bordeaux in the Judgment of Paris in 1976. Taste the championship winemakers' most recent harvests at legendary **13 Ridge Vineyards**. Heading over the mountains on twisted Hwy 9 or Skyline Dr to Santa Cruz, you'll pass dozens more wineries, most open for tastings only on Saturday afternoons or during the quarterly "Passport Weekend" festivals. In case you're wondering, estate-bottled pinot noirs are the specialty around here.

Off Hwy 1 heading into downtown Santa Cruz, **14 Bonny Doon Vineyard** has a cult following for its unusual varietals and original Rhône blends like Le Cigare Volant ("The Flying Cigar" – ask about the actual French law that prohibits UFOs from landing in vineyards). In downtown Santa Cruz, **15 Vinocruz** is an airy wine shop with a modern stainless-steel tasting bar, where an ever-changing lineup of wines by famous Santa Cruz Mountain winemakers like Kathryn Kennedy, Thomas Fogarty and David Bruce, to name just a few, are poured. Also downtown, **16** **Soif** (French for "thirst," get it?) is where bon vivant foodies flock for a heady selection of 50 international wines by the glass and organic small-plate pairings.

Further south, Monterey County is a much younger wine region, and you can taste vintages from 70 different Monterey County wineries in a converted sardine cannery right on Cannery Row at **17** **A Taste of Monterey**. This wine shop and tasting room has panoramic sea views and thoughtful exhibits on barrel-making and cork production. East of Carmel-by-the-Sea, Carmel Valley Rd takes you past organic farms, vineyards and equestrian ranches and into the tiny village of Carmel Valley, where a half-dozen established Monterey County wineries have tasting rooms, and country bistros have invitingly shady garden patios.

Further south is **18** **Paso Robles**, a hot spot for San Luis Obispo County wines. Travel west along Hwy 46 to discover scores of small family-run wineries, including many zinfandel specialists, like **19** **Dark Star Cellars**, which also crafts a plummy merlot and signature Bordeaux-style ricordati blends. Nearby **20** **Linne Calodo** specializes in red blends that are unfined, unfiltered, and ripe with intrigue: Stick & Stones is a grenache/syrah/mourvedre blend with serious attitude, while the syrah/zin/mourvedre Problem Child blend is a big, fruity kick in the pants.

ASK A LOCAL

"Paso Robles is a charming town that has been making a transition from cowboy town to a wine- and food-oriented urban center, but it's still unpretentious, friendly and outdoorsy. The area is known for full-bodied red varietals, and they're taking the lead on nontraditional blends that might combine tempranillo and petite sirah, or syrah and sangiovese."

Steve Heimoff, Wine Enthusiast West Coast editor and blogger (http://steveheimoff.com)

Closer to Hwy 101, **21** **Zenaida Cellars** is a Zen master of zin, along with lush estate-bottled red blends like Fire Sign and Zephyr. Rent its Winemaker's Loft and watch the sunset over the vineyards from your own private porch. For some dinner with your drinks, Paso Robles' downtown square is bordered by even more boutique tasting rooms and outstanding California and European-style wine-country restaurants. Just off the square, you can raise a toast to clean drinking water around the world at **22** **Paso Wine Center**, where proceeds from your choice of 42 wines by the glass, bottle or taste help build wells in developing nations. Settle in at **23** **Vinoteca** for wine flights, artisan cheese plates and live music on weekends – Napa and Sonoma pour on the charm, but California's indie wine regions rock.

Alison Bing

TRIP INFORMATION

GETTING THERE
From San Francisco, take Hwy 101 across the Golden Gate Bridge and north to Hopland.

DO & DRINK

Bonny Doon Vineyard
Eccentric wines from the original "Rhône Deranger" Randall Grahm. ☎ 831-425-4518; www.bonnydoonvineyard.com; 328 Ingalls St, Santa Cruz; tasting fee $5 (refundable with purchase); ☉ noon-9pm Wed-Sun

Dark Star Cellars
For intense, brooding reds – zinfandel, cabernet sauvignon and, yes, even merlot. ☎ 805-237-2389; www.darkstarcellars.com; 2985 Anderson Rd, Paso Robles; tasting fee $3; ☉ 10:30am-5pm Fri-Sun

Graziano Family of Wines
Reasonably priced Burgundy, Tuscan and Piedmont varietals, plus Mendo-style organically grown zinfandels. ☎ 707-744-8466; www.grazianofamilyofwines.com; 13251 S Hwy 101, Hopland; tasting fee $5; ☉ 10am-5pm

LangeTwins Winery
Great values on small-lot, sustainable wines to please every palate. ☎ 209-334-9780; www.langetwins.com; 1525 E Jahant Rd, Acampo; tasting free; ☉ by appointment 8am-5pm Mon-Fri

Langtry Estate & Vineyards
With a unique *terroir*, this elegant winery owns the Guenoc Valley appellation. ☎ 707-987-9127; www.langtryestate.com; 21000 Butts Canyon Rd, Middletown; tasting fee $5; ☉ 11am-5pm

Linne Calodo
Get bragging rights among wine collectors with tastings of limited-production cult classics such as syrah/mourvedre/grenache Slacker. ☎ 805-227-0797; www.linnecalodo.com; 3030 Vineyard Dr, Paso Robles; tasting fee $10; ☉ 11am-5pm

Lodi Wine & Visitor Center
Pick up wine-tasting maps here and ask about the ZinFest in May. ☎ 209-365-0621; www.lodiwine.com; 2545 W Turner Rd, Lodi; tasting fee $5; ☉ 10am-5pm

Martin & Weyrich
Italianate winery with a westside York Mountain vineyard producing pinot noirs and citrusy Albariño. ☎ 805-238-2520; www.martinweyrich.com; 2610 Buena Vista Dr, Paso Robles; tasting fee $5; ☉ 10am-6pm daily summer, 10am-5pm Sun-Thu & 10am-6pm Fri & Sat winter

Michael-David Winery
Famous for its zinfandels, all fruit-forward and most under $20. ☎ 209-368-7384; www.lodivineyards.com; 4580 W Hwy 12, Lodi; tasting fee $5; ☉ 10am-5pm

Navarro Vineyards
The busiest and friendliest tasting room in the Anderson Valley, with well-priced, sustainable wines. ☎ 707-895-3686; www.navarrowine.com; 5601 Hwy 128, Philo; tasting free; ☉ 10am-5pm; ✿

Paso Wine Center
Sip local sensations, from Alban's honeysuckle-scented viognier to Saxum's sexed-up spicy red blends; proceeds support Wine for Wells (www.wineforwells.org). ☎ 805-239-9156; www.pasowines.com; 1240 Park St, Paso Robles; per oz $1.50-3; ☉ 11am-8pm Tue-Thu, 11am-9pm Fri & Sat, noon-7pm Sun

Ridge Vineyards
This top-tier producer astride Monte Bello Ridge is known for complex estate cabs and old-vine carignane. ☎ 408-867-3233; www.ridgewine.com; 17100 Monte Bello Rd, Cupertino; tasting free-$20; ☉ 11am-5pm Sat & Sun Apr-Oct, 11am-4pm Sat & Sun Nov-Mar

Roederer Estate
French sparkling-wine specialists conduct winery tours and tastings of vintage-reserve and rosé bubbly. ☎ 707-895-2288; www.roedererestate.com; 4501 Hwy 128, Philo; tasting fee $6; ☉ 11am-5pm

Sip! Mendocino

Expertly selected wines of all types, often served with chef-made appetizer plates on Thursday and Saturday nights. ☎ 707-744-8375; www.sipmendocino.com; 13420 S Hwy 101, Hopland; tasting fee $5; ⏱ 11am-5pm Sun-Thu, 11am-6pm Fri & Sat

Steele Wines

No varietal goes unfermented here! Dare to sip its caramel-tinged Roussanne or Black Bubbles, an Aussie-inspired sparkling syrah. ☎ 707-279-9475; www.steelewines.com; 4350 Thomas Dr at Hwy 29, Kelseyville; tasting fee $5; ⏱ 11am-5pm Mon-Sat

A Taste of Monterey

This outfit also has a cheaper, less picturesque, tasting room in Salinas, off Hwy 101. ☎ 831-646-5446; www.tastemonterey.com; 700 Cannery Row, Monterey; tasting fee $10-15; ⏱ 11am-6pm

Vinocruz

Unlock the secrets of the Santa Cruz Mountains at this chilled-out wine shop. It's off Cooper St, between Front St and Pacific Ave. ☎ 831-426-8466; www.vinocruz.com; Abbott Sq, Santa Cruz; tasting fee $9; ⏱ 11am-7pm Mon-Thu, 11am-8pm Fri & Sat, noon-6pm Sun

EAT

Patrona

A "simply seasonal" bistro and wine bar adheres to a sustainable-food mission. ☎ 707-462-9181; www.patronarestaurant.com; 130 W Standley St, Ukiah; mains $12-21; ⏱ 11am-9pm Tue-Sat

Soif

Extensive wine bar and seasonal, organic California cuisine make for a swanky local hangout. ☎ 831-423-2020; www.soifwine.com; 105 Walnut Ave, Santa Cruz; small plates $4-14; ⏱ kitchen 5-10pm Mon-Thu, 5-11pm Fri & Sat, 4-10pm Sun, store noon-close Tue-Sat & 5-10pm Sun & Mon

Vinoteca

Friendly wine bar with cushy sofas and satisfying small plates; score winemaker flights on Wednesday and half-off on Tuesday. ☎ 805-227-7154; www.vinotecawinebar.com; 835 12th St, Paso Robles; share plates $5-20; ⏱ 4-11pm Mon-Sat

Wine & Roses

Seasonal California wine-country cuisine highlighting garden-fresh flavors. ☎ 209-334-6988; www.winerose.com; 2505 W Turner Rd, Lodi; mains $12-35; ⏱ 6:30am-2pm daily & 5-9pm Mon-Thu, 5-10pm Fri & Sat

SLEEP

Boonville Hotel

For laid-back style in the country. Locavore feasts and parking-lot farmers market on weekends. ☎ 707-895-2210; www.boonvillehotel.com; 14050 Hwy 128, Boonville; r $125-275; 🌐

Zenaida Cellars

Bring friends to the apartment-style loft, taste wine ($3) or get romantic in an ecofriendly suite with bamboo furnishings, organic cotton sheets and an outdoor hammock. ☎ 866-936-5638; www.zenaidacellars.com; 1550 W Hwy 46, Paso Robles; r $250-375

USEFUL WEBSITES

www.gomendo.com
www.lakecountywinegrape.org
www.montereywines.org
www.pasowine.com
www.scmwa.com

LINK YOUR TRIP

www.lonelyplanet.com/trip-planner

All Aboard Amtrak

WHY GO Beaches, beaches, beaches. That's the theme for this trip down California's coast. Leave the driving to Amtrak while you enjoy sandy vistas and chances to pause at numerous stops for everything from wine tasting to iconic meals to a baseball game.

TIME
2 – 4 days

DISTANCE
600 miles

BEST TIME TO GO
Mar – Oct

START
Oakland, CA

END
San Diego, CA

Amtrak's *Coast Starlight* begins its 1377-mile run far north in Seattle but to start this trip you'll hop aboard in ① **Oakland** for a 464-mile daylight run through the heart of California to San Diego. The train skirts the San Francisco Bay and runs through the middle of sprawling Silicon Valley. You can extend this trip over many days by getting on and off the train at various stops, the most interesting of which are detailed below.

As you near ② **Salinas**, the tracks enter the Salinas Valley, which fully lives up to its hackneyed moniker "America's Salad Bowl." Lettuce, broccoli, celery, strawberries and much more grow here in profusion. Try not to feel too guilty as you recline in your seat and watch squads of people laboring amid the orderly rows of produce.

After 100 miles of agricultural splendor, the terrain gets brown and hilly as you reach ③ **Paso Robles**. You'll notice striations across the landscape, which are the twisted vines of the region's vast vineyards. More than 180 wineries produce some excellent zinfandels and syrahs. If you exit the *Coast Starlight* here you can spend the night at the historic ④ **Paso Robles Inn**, and the next morning tour wineries with the ⑤ **Wine Wrangler** before reboarding the train.

The line then makes a dramatic looping descent to ⑥ **San Luis Obispo**. The next 120 miles or so are among the most spectacular of any railroad in the world. Trains hug the Pacific Ocean, passing countless isolated beaches – some deserted except for the odd puffin and seal, others

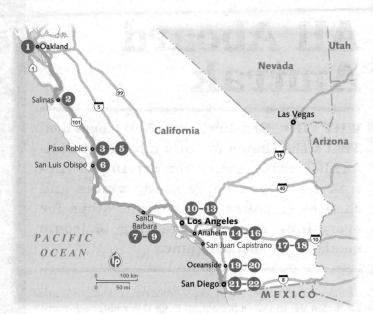

dotted with frolicking naked sunbathers (sit on the right side for views of the wildlife, fur-clad and otherwise). A good portion of this segment lies within the off-limits expanse of Vandenberg Air Force Base. Look for the gantries used for launching spy satellites poking up amid the rugged terrain.

A perfect place to break your journey, **7** **Santa Barbara** combines beautiful buildings, a top-notch beach and orange blossom–scented air in one beguiling package. Only three blocks from the train station and near the beach, the **8** **Villa Rosa Inn** has the city's signature Spanish adobe architecture. Nearby State St is one of the most beautiful main streets in the USA; perfect for walking, it is lined with shops, cafés and fine restaurants such as locally beloved **9** **Tupelo Junction**.

There are frequent trains south from Santa Barbara all the way to San Diego. The next important stop is 100 miles south in **10** **Los Angeles**, and it's a big one: **11** **Los Angeles Union Station**. This 1939 Mission-style gem has commodious leather chairs in its waiting area and is a popular location for films. Nearby **12** **Olvera St** is a Mexican marketplace in the middle of LA's oldest neighborhood. Amid plenty of tourist tchotchkes are stalls selling quality arts and crafts and numerous restaurants as authentic as any in Mexico City. Or head just north to **13** **Philippe the Original**, where the French-dipped sandwich debuted a century ago. Photos show trains at Union Station through the decades.

The tracks to San Diego first head east through an endless sprawl of factories and warehouses. After about 30 minutes the route turns south through thickets of suburbs. Views open up at ⑭ **Anaheim**, where the station sits right across the parking lot from ⑮ **Angel Stadium of Anaheim**, home of the alliterative Los Angeles Angels at Anaheim. Fortunately the team is more deft on the field, and frequently sparks flamboyant displays of fountains and fireworks with their home runs and victories.

Fewer than 3 miles from Anaheim (and linked to the station by shuttle bus), ⑯ **Disneyland** is *the* stop on many a SoCal itinerary.

 One block from the station, Salinas' **National Steinbeck Center** (www.steinbeck.org) gives context to both the Salinas Valley and the John Steinbeck works set here, such as *East of Eden*. Spend the night in Salinas or nearby Monterey before continuing on the train the next day.

About the time you may be reaching subdivision fatigue, the train pulls into ⑰ **San Juan Capistrano**, some 27 miles south of Anaheim. This cute-as-a-button village exudes old California for several blocks in all directions from the station. Amid the quaint shops, cafés and attractions is the local star: ⑱ **Mission San Juan Capistrano**, which dates from 1776. As you wander the flower-bedecked grounds and breezeway-surrounded old buildings, you'll see why not only swallows flock here.

As it did up north, the rail line now heads straight for the coast and follows the beaches most of the way to San Diego. Unlike the stretch north of Santa Barbara, these beaches are lined with people sunning themselves between bouts of volleyball and surfing. At the classic beach town of ⑲ **Ocean-side** you can revel in surf culture at the 2009-relaunched ⑳ **California Surf Museum**, just four blocks from the station.

Your Amtrak adventure hits the end of the line 130 miles south of LA, in downtown ㉑ **San Diego**. The best way to start your exploration of this town, which mixes sunshine, beaches,

RIDING AMTRAK

North of San Luis Obispo, Amtrak's **Coast Starlight** service runs only once a day. It has comfy coaches and a diner, and you can splurge and enjoy wine tastings in the private Pacific Parlor Car. South of SLO, most services are on frequent **Pacific Surfliner** trains featuring double-deck coaches, big windows and snack bars.

Full fare from Oakland to San Diego is $59-72; 21-day California rail passes are adult/child $159/80. Reserve the *Coast Starlight* well ahead (www.amtrakcalifornia.com).

loads of attractions and the navy, is on a tour of the vast bay. ㉒ **Hornblower Cruises** depart the waterfront north of the historic old train station. Bon Voyage!

Ryan Ver Berkmoes

TRIP INFORMATION

GETTING THERE
Oakland is just across the Bay Bridge from San Francisco. Amtrak buses link the train station with stops in San Francisco.

DO
Angel Stadium of Anaheim
The fun-filled home of Major League Baseball's Los Angeles Angels at Anaheim. ☎ 888-796-4256; http://losangeles.angels. mlb.com; 2000 Gene Autry Way, Anaheim; tickets adult $12-200, child from $5, under 2yr free; ☾ Apr-Sep; ♿

California Surf Museum
Boards galore and tributes to surf culture dating back almost 100 years. ☎ 760-721-6876; www.surfmuseum.org; 312 Pier View Way, Oceanside; admission adult/student & senior/under 12yr $3/1/free; ☾ 10am-4pm Fri-Wed, 10am-8pm Thu; ♿

Disneyland
Adults are often as entranced as the kids at the Magic Kingdom. ☎ 714-781-4565; www.disneyland.com; Anaheim; adult/child from $72/62; ☾ hours vary; ♿

Hornblower Cruises
One- and two-hour tours of the famous San Diego harbor often include Coronado Island; whale- and dolphin-watching cruises run December to April. ☎ 888-467-6256; www. hornblower.com; 1066 N Harbor Dr, San Diego; harbor cruise adult/senior/child 1hr $20/18/10, 2hr $25/23/12.50, whale-/dolphin-watching cruises from $32; ☾ hours vary; ♿

Mission San Juan Capistrano
This vast old Spanish Mission is famous for both the annual migration of swallows (mid-March) and its evocative buildings and ruins. ☎ 949-234-1300; www.missionsjc.com; 26801 Ortega Hwy, San Juan Capistrano; adult/senior/child $9/8/5; ☾ 8:30am-5pm; ♿

Olvera St
Unearth Mexican treasures at this chaotic market in the midst of buildings that are ancient by LA standards (1870s!). www.olvera -street.com; Los Angeles; ☾ 10am-7pm; ♿

EAT & DRINK
Philippe the Original
Everyone loves Philippe's. Order a crusty roll filled with meat and hunker down at communal tables on the sawdust-covered floor. ☎ 213-628-3781; www.philippes.com; 1001 N Alameda St, Los Angeles; sandwiches $3-7; ☾ 6am-10pm; ♿

Tupelo Junction
Local ingredients star in dishes with a Southern flair; enjoy 'em at the sidewalk tables. ☎ 805-899-3100; www.tupelojunction.com; 1218 State St, Santa Barbara; mains $13-33; ☾ 8am-2pm daily & 5-9pm Tue-Sat

Wine Wrangler
Let this enterprising tour company haul your besotted butt between some of the area's best wineries. ☎ 805-238-5700; www. thewinewrangler.com; Paso Robles; tours from $52; ☾ hours vary

SLEEP
Paso Robles Inn
Some of the 108 rooms have mineral hot-springs tubs or fireplaces; most have garden views. ☎ 805-238-2660, 800-676-1713; www.pasoroblesinn.com; 1103 Spring St, Paso Robles; r $99-179

Villa Rosa Inn
An 18-room Spanish colonial inn wrapped around a courtyard swimming pool and whirl-pool. ☎ 805-966-0851; www.villarosainnsb. com; 15 Chapala St, Santa Barbara; r $129-210

USEFUL WEBSITES
www.amtrakcalifornia.com
www.visitcalifornia.com

www.lonelyplanet.com/trip-planner

LINK YOUR TRIP

PACIFIC NORTHWEST TRIPS

If the United States has a proverbial end of the line, it's the Pacific Northwest. This is where, amid the volcanoes and rain, people just seem to end up. Like the fur traders and trappers who braved the Oregon Trail in the 1800s, people ple leave their homes back east and down south to start anew up here. Artists and chefs leave New York and make Portland their home. Vintners head north from California and plant pinot noir, and techies abandon their jobs in Silicon Valley and become cheese makers in the Cascades. As much as the region's old-timers resent it (or talk like they do), people just keep coming and coming. Why? Travel the trips in this chapter and you'll know. En route, you'll discover hot springs steaming beneath dark forests of Douglas Fir, Portland's vibrant food scene, Seattle's waterbound beauty, gorgeous national parks, Oregon's epic coastline and some of the country's finest wine (and beer!). You may, heaven forbid, be tempted to stay.

PLAYLIST ♫♪ Whenever you're in radio-wave distance of Seattle, tune into KEXP (90.3 FM), which cranks out some of the best indie, old-school country and modern world music in the Pacific Northwest. The rest of the time, just play the following songs over and over again:

- "Chinese Translation," M Ward
- "Gone for Good," The Shins
- "Taking Too Long," The Wipers
- "Rose Parade," Elliott Smith
- "The Soldiering Life," The Decemberists
- "Druganaut," Black Mountain
- "Keep Your Eyes Ahead," The Helio Sequence
- "Northwestern Girls," Say Hi
- "Find Me in the Air," The Builders and the Butchers
- "Come as You Are," Nirvana

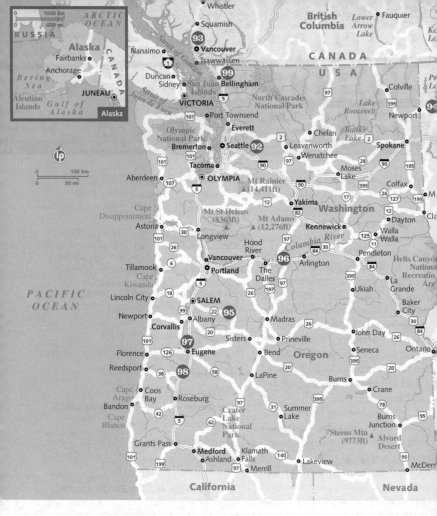

PACIFIC NORTHWEST TRIPS

48 Hours in Seattle

WHY GO A little rain never hurt anybody. All the more reason to stroll through a museum or linger over coffee. The second the sun comes out, you'll relish your time outdoors all the more, and the nonstop spectacle of rhododendron and evergreens will make the rain all seem worthwhile.

TIME
2 days

BEST TIME TO GO
Apr – Aug

START
Downtown Seattle

END
Downtown Seattle

The heavily caffeinated Seattle coffee drinker isn't just a stereotype: Seattleites drink it all day long and lots of it so they can power through weather-induced energy lags. So start this trip the way locals start their every day: with a latte. You'll find chain coffee shops on every corner, but ❶ Zeitgeist Coffee, located in a converted warehouse space in downtown, is a great place to hang out and get caffeinated.

If you need something a little more solid to sustain you, head straight to ❷ Salumi. Known for their cured meats and cheeses, this deli owned by Mario Batali's dad serves downright addictive sandwiches that have people lining up out the door. They close at four and are only open Tuesday through Friday, so depending on your timing, this might be your only chance to indulge.

Ready for a little culture? The ❸ Seattle Art Museum is the place to get it. The collections span multiple genres, from modern to tribal to classic. Whether it's Warhol's version of a gun-slinging Elvis, Northwestern totem poles, or flowery stained glass, everyone will find something they wish they owned.

When you're done, pop around the corner and check out the ❹ Seattle Public Library, one of the most dazzling modern structures in the city. The building is made almost entirely of diamond-shaped panes of glass, and, on certain days, it manages to feel sunnier indoors than out. Be sure to check out the wow-inducing, 12,000-sq-ft reading room with 40ft glass ceilings.

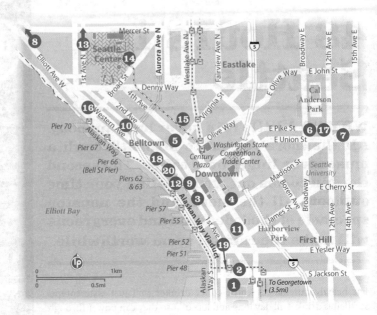

For dinner, make reservations for ⑤ **Dahlia Lounge**. It's an institution, and one of those rare places that locals and tourists seem to agree on. With crimson walls, fabulous desserts, and celebrity chef Tom Douglas, it's an easy choice for dinner, but, if nothing else, stop by and get something sweet to go from the Dahlia Bakery next door.

FUNKY FREMONT

If you have a few extra hours, head north to the neighborhood of Fremont – although let's be clear: it seceded in 1994 and now the preferred title is "Republic of Fremont, Center of the Known Universe." Its most famous denizen is the **Fremont Troll**, a concrete sculpture that lurks under the Aurora Bridge, but it's also known for an art-filled Saturday Market and the Fremont Fair, a colorful street party held each year during the summer solstice.

If there's anything else besides coffee that Seattle is known for, it's – well, you already know, it's live music. Check out the local listings to see what's playing. If you're not sure where to start, try ⑥ **Neumo's** for indie rock, ⑦ **Tractor Tavern** for rockabilly, alt country and acoustic, or ⑧ **Chop Suey** for an eclectic lineup that includes both live music and local DJs.

By now, you're surely ready for bed. Many travelers on a budget have found the ⑨ **Green Tortoise Hostel** – located mere steps from Pike's Market – to be a cheap, pleasant and convenient place to bunk down for the night. Belltown's ⑩ **Ace Hotel** is artsy in a hip, minimalist kind of way, although it's more fit for heavy drinkers than light sleepers, since the downstairs bar is always hopping.

A fairly recent addition to your sleeping options is the elegant ⓫ **Arctic Club**, opened in 2008. This historic building – known for decades as the "walrus building" for the plaster walrus medallions adorning the exterior – was established in 1908 as a men's club for Klondike explorers. Now it's a lavish hotel, where you can slumber in rooms that look like they could have been teleported from the 1920s.

The next morning, hit ⓬ **Pike Place Market** early so you can spend more time dodging flying fish and less time dodging hordes of people. Locals love it because you can buy fresh flowers, produce, and seafood. Out-of-towners love it because of its buzzing energy, and its big neon sign is a quintessential Seattle photo op.

> **ASK A LOCAL**
>
> "One of my favorite things to do in Seattle is rent a kayak and go out on **Lake Union**, especially when the weather's nice. You get great views of Downtown and the Space Needle, and you can row right by Gas Works Park, which has the neat old towers and generators from when it was a power plant."
>
> *Tameika Taylor, Seattle, WA*

Afterwards fuel up for a full day with breakfast at ⓭ **5 Spot** in Queen Anne. The five spots in question refer to the five US regions from which the eatery takes inspiration, with a changing decor to match the mood. For a gastronomic homage to Seattle grunge scene, try the Red Flannel Hash.

You may have noticed that huge, crazily colorful building at the foot of the Space Needle that looks like a huge blob of children's toys melted under a heat lamp. That would be the ⓮ **Experience Music Project & Science Fiction Museum**. Say what you will about Frank Gehry's design (many already have), this pair of genre museums is a fun place to immerse yourself in rock and roll and/or sci-fi for one admission price.

The music side, while a little Seattle-centric, does have some significant memorabilia, as well as crazy stage costumes that include touches such as fur leg warmers or spiked codpieces. The sci-fi side has beamed up a multidimensional collection ranging from Klingons to *The War of the Worlds* to *The Jetsons*. (Geek out if you must.)

More caffeine? Coming right up. Head downtown to ⓯ **Top Pot Doughnuts** for some brew and something to dunk in it. Floor-to-ceiling windows and a mezzanine level make it an ideal place to people watch while you refuel.

If the weather is cooperating, head toward the water and check out the new ⓰ **Olympic Sculpture Park**, where the artwork and the view compete for your attention. This 9-acre strip of park gives you the chance to wander among major works of art in front of a backdrop of Puget Sound and the Olympic Mountains.

> *"At the Olympic Sculpture Park, the artwork and the view compete for your attention."*

You've had your nice dinner out; now it's time for some casual dining that's uniquely Seattle: **⑰ Bimbo's Cantina.** They serve killer quesadillas and fab burritos in a funky, colorful room decorated in the wrestling theme of *lucha libre.* The music is always way too loud SO YOU'LL HAVE TO TALK LIKE THIS, but there will be plenty of time to chat later and the carbs will come in handy as you end your evening with a good, old-fashioned pub crawl.

A delicious, next-morning follow-up to what we hope was a satisfying evening is brunch at **⑱ Etta's Seafood.** Their Bloody Mary's have a huge following among the late-night crowd, and their eggs benedict with fresh Dungeness crab make everything all feel better.

DETOUR

Ballard is known for its nightlife, but if you've been there, done that, head south to **George-town** and a row of worthwhile watering holes that are ideal for pub-hopping. **Georgetown Liquor Company** (www.georgetownliquorcompany.com) offers industrial-chic design, retro video games and a hipster scene. **Jules Maes Saloon** is an old-fashioned saloon stocked with punk rockers and tattoos. And **Smartypants** (www.smartypantsseattle.com) has a thriving sports-bike scene. Mix them together and you've got **Nine Pound Hammer** (www.ninepoundhammer.com), a reassuring blend of hipster, punk, biker and you.

Book lovers shouldn't miss **⑲ Elliott Bay Bookstore.** Taking up an entire block near Pioneer Square, it's one of those great independent bookstores with warmth, character, author events, and displays that help you find something even if you don't know what you're looking for. (There's also a café in the basement, so you really can kill a whole afternoon if you want.)

Finally, we end our trip where it began: with coffee. And, believe it or not, we're actually going to suggest a **⑳ Starbucks.** The first-ever store is located downtown right near Pike's Market. It's small, and it's usually packed, but remember: before it became the megachain that it is, it was once part of what was unique about Seattle.

Mariella Krause

CITY

TRIP INFORMATION

GETTING THERE
To get to Seattle from Portland, drive 175 miles north on I-5. From Vancouver, drive 140 miles south on Hwy 99 and I-5.

DO
Chop Suey
The intimate setting with kitschy Asian touches makes this a great place for catching up-and-coming indie artists. ☎ 206-324-8005; www.chopsuey.com; 1325 E Madison St; admission $5-15; ⊙ 7pm-2am, door times vary

Elliott Bay Bookstore
This huge independent bookstore is ideal for browsing on a rainy afternoon. ☎ 206-624-6600; www.elliottbaybook.com; 101 S Main St; ⊙ 9:30am-9pm Mon-Sat, 11am-7pm Sun

Experience Music Project & Science Fiction Museum
One admission gets you into both, and there's plenty of memorabilia to keep you amused. ☎ 877-367-7361; www.empsfm.org; 325 5th Ave N; adult/youth, student & senior/under 5yr $15/12/free; ⊙ 10am-7pm

Neumo's
It gets hot and crowded, sure, but their lineup keeps people coming back. ☎ 206-709-9467; www.neumos.com; 925 E Pike St; admission $7-21; ⊙ schedule varies

Olympic Sculpture Park
When the sun comes out, you don't want to be inside an art museum. ☎ 206-654-3100; 2901 Western Ave; admission free; ⊙ sunrise-sunset

Pike Place Market
Come watch the fishmongers tossing huge king salmon, and soak in the Seattle atmosphere. ☎ 206-682-7453; www.pikeplacemarket.org; 1501 Pike Pl; admission free; ⊙ stores 10am-6pm Mon-Sat, 11am-5pm Sun

Seattle Art Museum
This excellent museum, which doubled in size in 2007, packs in everything from tribal masks to tea cups. ☎ 206-654-3100; www.seattleartmuseum.org; 1300 1st Ave; adult/senior/student/under 12yr $15/12/9/free; ⊙ 10am-5pm Tue-Sun, 10am-9pm Thu & Fri, closed Tue in winter

Seattle Public Library
When everyone says you have to go to the library, you know it must be good. ☎ 206-386-4636; www.spl.org; 1000 4th Ave; ⊙ 10am-8pm Mon-Wed, 10am-6pm Thu-Sat, 1-5pm Sun

Tractor Tavern
Check out live rockabilly, alt country and acoustic sets (but be prepared to stand). ☎ 206-789-3599; www.tractortavern.com; 5213 Ballard Ave NW; admission $6-20; ⊙ door times vary

EAT
5 Spot
Huge portions and a cute neon sign make this local spot a favorite. ☎ 206-285-7768; www.chowfoods.com/five/; 1502 Queen Anne Ave N; mains $8-14; ⊙ breakfast, lunch & dinner

Bimbo's Cantina
Killer burritos in a fun, loud atmosphere that's decorated in a *lucha libre* style. ☎ 206-322-9950; 1013 E Pike St; mains $6-10; ⊙ kitchen noon-midnight, cantina to 2am

Dahlia Lounge
Chef Tom Douglas is Seattle's favorite foodie; at least come for dessert. ☎ 206-682-4142; www.tomdouglas.com; 2001 4th Ave; mains $24-38; ⊙ brunch Sat & Sun, lunch Mon-Fri, dinner Mon-Sat

Etta's Seafood
Make reservations for this popular seafood spot near Pike's Place Market. ☎ 206-443-6000; www.tomdouglas.com; 2020 Western Ave; mains $12-25; ⊙ lunch & dinner Mon-Sat, brunch 9am-3pm Sat & Sun

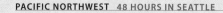
CITY

Salumi
Hope for a table in this tiny deli, but be prepared to take your sandwiches to go. ☎ 206-621-8772; www.salumicuredmeats.com; 309 3rd Ave S; mains $7-14; ⏲ 11am-4pm Tue-Fri

Top Pot Doughnuts
Whether or not this place serves the finest coffee in town, it's definitely got the best doughnuts. ☎ 206-728-1966; 2124 5th Ave; ⏲ 6am-7pm Mon-Fri, 7am-7pm Sat & Sun

DRINK
Starbucks
Once it was a little independent coffee shop. ☎ 206-448-8762; 1912 Pike Pl; ⏲ 6am-9pm Mon-Fri, 6:30am-9pm Sat & Sun (reduced hrs in winter)

Zeitgeist Coffee
Zeitgeist will keep you from going to a chain you have at home. ☎ 206-583-0497; www.zeitgeistcoffee.com; 171 S Jackson St; ⏲ 6am-7pm Mon-Fri, 8am-7pm Sat & Sun

SLEEP
Ace Hotel
Stylish and modern, this place has the feel of a converted loft that your artist friend owns. ☎ 206-448-4721; www.acehotel.com; 2423 1st Ave; r $75-199

Arctic Club
Nostalgia is just one of the amenities of this plush, retro hotel; don't miss the Dome Room's leaded-glass ceiling. ☎ 206-340-0340; www.arcticclubhotel.com; 700 3rd Ave; r $90-250

Green Tortoise Hostel
Located just steps from Pike's Place Market, this place has got the best location and the lowest prices in town. ☎ 206-340-1222; www.greentortoise.net; 105 Pike St; d $28-32

USEFUL WEBSITES
www.thestranger.com
www.visitseattle.org

LINK YOUR TRIP
www.lonelyplanet.com/trip-planner

TRIP

Pacific Northwest Grand Tour

WHY GO This meandering journey through the Pacific Northwest takes you from western Canada's largest city to the California border. En route, you'll cruise the San Juan Islands, traverse the mighty Cascades and explore the grooviest neighborhoods of the region's most exciting cities.

There's simply no better place to kick off a trip down the northwestern seaboard than ❶ Vancouver. From the spectacular Stanley Park Seawall to the galleries and coffee shops of bohemian South Main, Vancouver offers fun aplenty – outside *and* in. Best of all, the city's top attractions are all accessible on foot. Historic Gastown is where the city started, so it makes perfect sense to begin here. Hit Chinatown (it's one of North America's largest) and wander west to Yaletown, the center of the city's gay community, chockablock with heritage homes, old-school apartment buildings, restaurants and shops. It's bordered by English Bay, whose narrow stretch of sandy beach and adjacent grass offers superb people-watching opportunities and panoramic views.

Needless to say, Vancouver has outstanding restaurants, but our favorite place to fill up is ❷ Go Fish, between Granville Island and Vanier Park. Little more than a waterfront shack, it serves up the city's best fish-and-chips, along with wild-salmon tacos and scallop burgers. And when sleep finally calls, slumber in style at the ❸ Opus Hotel, Vancouver's definitive boutique hotel.

After a stint in Vancouver, head 18.5 miles (30km) south to Tsawwassen, purchase a BC Ferries SailPass, ride the ferry across the Strait of Georgia and tool around the ❹ Southern Gulf Islands for a few days. This is where stressed-out Vancouverites go to chill out and – even though we know you're *already* chilled out – so should you. Trust us,

TIME
3 weeks

DISTANCE
1675 miles

BEST TIME TO GO
Jun – Sep

START
Vancouver, BC

END
Ashland, OR

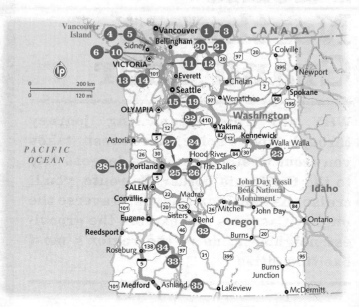

you'll love them. On Salt Spring Island, the so-called "island of the arts," don't miss the Saturday Market, where you can stock your cooler with ambrosial island-grown fruit and locally produced cheeses and fill your trunk with locally made arts and crafts. Salt Spring Island also happens to be home to the **5** Oceanside Cottages, one of our favorite places to stay, if only because one of the three rustic cabins here is the shagadelic Love Shack! As for the other islands, they're all worth visiting, but Saturna Island, the closest of the islands to the US, is remote enough to discourage most casual visitors. Hence, it's a stunning nature-locked retreat offering the quintessential island escape from the busy mainland life.

From Salt Spring or North Pender Island, ferry to Swartz Bay, zip down to nearby Sydney and take a Washington State Ferries boat to the **6** San Juan Islands, your red-carpet entry into the US. Blanketed in trees, this astoundingly scenic archipelago – where the Georgia Strait, Puget Sound and Strait of Juan de Fuca meet – is a definitive Pacific Northwest highlight. After landing at Friday Harbor's ferry terminal, on San Juan Island, and exploring Friday Harbor itself, travel up to **7** Lime Kiln Point State Park. Clinging to the island's rocky west coast, this park overlooks the deep Haro Strait and is, reputedly, one of the best places in the world to view whales from the shoreline. Of San Juan Island's handful of accommodations, **8** Roche Harbor Resort makes a superb getaway. More than 100 years after its initiation as the company hotel of limestone king John McMillin,

the place is *still* taking guests. If you'd rather pitch a tent, head directly to
9 **San Juans County Park Campground**, beautifully situated on the island's scenic western shoreline.

During your San Juans adventure, see tranquil, quirky Shaw Island, then Lopez Island (aka *Slow-pez*) and finally Orcas Island. Precipitous, unspoiled and ruggedly beautiful, Orcas is the San Juans' emerald jewel. This steeply, densely wooded and sparsely populated outpost is home to a motley mix of folk, from wealthy retirees and second-homers to traditional farmers, eccentrics, innkeepers, back-to-the-landers, and plenty of other assorted dropouts from the big-city rat race. Be sure to hit **10** **Moran State Park**, which is dominated by 2409ft Mt Constitution, the archipelago's highest peak. Hiking to the top affords one of the Pacific Northwest's most awe-inspiring views.

From Orcas Island, ferry over to Anacortes and drive down scenic Hwy 20 to **11** **Whidbey Island**. This fiercely independent 41-mile-long island is endowed with six state parks, a unique National Historical Reserve, a community of budding artists and writers, and a free – yes, free – island-wide

ASK A LOCAL

"**Deadman's Bay**, at low tide, has great tide pools and you can often see orcas going by. It's next to Lime Kiln Point. Go to South Beach, on the southern end of the island. You can see the Cascades to your left, Vancouver Island to the right and the Olympic Peninsula in front of you. It's a big wide beach with tons and tons of driftwood. And at **America's Camp**, there are trails down to the beach that no one ever goes on. "

Captain Jim Maya, Maya's Westside Charters, Friday Harbor, WA

public bus service. It's also home to approximately 140 B&Bs! Our pick of the lot is **12** **Captain Whidbey Inn** because, well, they just don't come any more outlandish than this quaint and cozy 1907 inn built of rust-colored madrone wood. So park your car, check in, jump on the bus and start exploring.

From Whidbey, continue south and swing west on mainland Highway 101 for a visit to Washington's **13** **Olympic National Park**. Spanning 1406 sq miles, this astounding national park protects wildly diverse landscapes, from glaciated mountain peaks to a 57-mile strip of coastal wilderness, to the lush old-growth Hoh Rain Forest. To figure out exactly what you want to see, stop into the **14** **Olympic National Park Visitor Center**, about 1 mile south of Port Angeles. Be sure to drive to the top of 5200ft Hurricane Ridge, which often puts you above the notorious cloud cover. To the west, take a hike (whether it's raining or not) in the Hoh Rain Forest.

After exploring the park, haul your wet, mud-covered, travel-weary body 58 miles east to **15** **Seattle**, and check into the masterfully designed **16** **Ace Hotel**. Inside, street style meets chic minimalism and decor can mean anything from stark white walls to murals of Andre the Giant to refurbished, retro furniture. After freshening up, head over to ⑰ **Brouwer's**, where you can nurse yourself back to life quaffing any of 64 beers on tap (not to mention 300 types in bottles) at this cathedral-sized beer emporium. Then take to the streets of the Emerald City. Hit the hip restaurants, boutique shops and cafés of the Ballard neighborhood by day and, come sundown, head to industrial Georgetown for bars and brews aplenty. ⑱ **Pike Place Market**? Yep, it's tourist flypaper, but don't miss it: The buzzing warren of fruits stands, cafés and wee shops makes for superb street theater. Just get there early and avoid weekends. When the midday hordes descend upon Pike Place, head instead to ⑲ **Gas Works Park**, Seattle's monument of urban reclamation, and take in the panoramic views of downtown. The park was converted from gas plant to public park in 1976 (20 years after the plant closed) and looks like the rusty remnant of a science-fiction novel. Of course, you can't miss stylish Capitol Hill, Seattle's primary gay and lesbian neighborhood either.

DETOUR Instead of heading south from Anacortes, detour west on Hwy 20 to the mainland and drive up **Chuckanut Drive** (Rte 11). It's one of the West Coast's most spectacular coastal back roads and ends in the fabulous city of Bellingham. The 35-mile (one way) trip takes just over an hour, provided you don't stop for the views. And you could spend a full day exploring the second-hand bookstores, coffee bars and myriad restaurants of **Bellingham**.

With Seattle in your pocket (and a bag of fresh roasted coffee in your kit) head to ⑳ **North Cascades National Park**, where you'll plunge into the glacier-riddled wilderness of the northern Cascades. Stop at the visitors center for information and continue up Hwy 20 to ㉑ **Colonial Creek Campground** on Diablo Lake. Then hike the 3.5-mile trail to Cascade Pass. After ascending into this flower-carpeted glacier-flanked paradise, you can either turn back or stand around struggling for superlatives that will simply never measure up to the scenery.

Spend a few days hiking and relaxing before heading south to ㉒ **Mt Rainier National Park** where, if the clouds aren't covering it, you can marvel at the Cascades' highest peak, 14,411ft Mt Rainier. Set up camp at one of several campgrounds and take to the trails that wind through swathes of flower-blanketed meadows beneath the conical peak.

When you're peaked out, head southeast along Hwy 12, through the vine-yards and apple orchards of the Yakima River Valley, to ㉓ **Walla Walla**, where you can shack up in a small inn and immediately start wine tasting. That's right – the old sweet-onion town is now the epicenter of a flourishing wine-growing region, arguably the most important in the Pacific Northwest. It's also home to a staggering number of historic houses which are mapped on free walking tour maps, available from a dispenser in Heritage Park on Main St.

From Walla Walla, follow the mighty Columbia River into Oregon and travel west along Hwy 84, into the Columbia River Gorge. Mt Hood, Oregon's highest peak, soon pops into view, and the landscape changes from dry to lushly forested. Stop in the town of **㉔ Hood River** where you'll find loads of great restaurants, two breweries and some of the best windsurfing and kiteboarding conditions in the world. It's a great place to spend a few days taking windsurfing lessons, hiking and exploring Mt Hood, only 45 minutes away via Hwy 35. Be sure to eat at, sleep at or just plain walk around the historic **㉕ Timberline Lodge** on the south side of the mountain. Built by Oregon's Works Progress Administration in 1936 and 1937, the 73,700-sq-ft log-and-stone lodge is a masterpiece of national-park architecture. Inside, the **㉖ Cascade Dining Room** serves expertly prepared, gourmet meals with an emphasis on local cuisine. The all-you-can-eat buffet breakfasts are a great way to enjoy the dining room if you'd rather not shell out for dinner. Continue west from Hood River along Hwy 84 and be absolutely certain to stop at **㉗ Multnomah Falls**. At 620ft, it's the second highest year-round waterfall in the country.

From Multnomah Falls, it's less than 40 minutes to **㉘ Portland**, where, once again, you can fill yourself up on the very best food, beer, wine, art and music that the Pacific Northwest has to offer. If you didn't book a room at the **㉙ Kennedy School**, you should at least pop into this elementary school turned brewpub, hotel and all around fun zone (have a drink in the detention room – it's now a bar!). Be sure to poke around the hip boutiques, cafés, bars, bike shops and bookstores along three eastside streets: N Mississippi Ave, NE Alberta St and SE Hawthorne Blvd. Then walk across the Willamette River on the Burnside Bridge (or, for that matter, one of five other pedestrian-friendly bridges that link the east side with downtown) and explore the art galleries and museums of downtown Portland and the Pearl District. Of course, no visit to Portland is complete without getting lost in **㉚ Powell's City of Books**, likely the largest independent new-and-used bookstore on the planet. And if you're lucky enough to be in town on a weekend don't miss the craft and food frenzy of the **㉛ Saturday Market** (held Sundays, too) beneath the west end of the Burnside Bridge.

SLEEPING GIANT

Mt Rainier is a marvel to look at and more fun to explore, but beneath its placid exterior, ominous forces brew. As an active stratovolcano, Rainier harnesses untold destructive powers which, if unleashed, could threaten Seattle with mudslides and cause tsunamis in Puget Sound. Not surprisingly, the mountain has long been mythical. Native Americans called it Tahoma or Tacoma, meaning the "mother of waters," George Vancouver named it Rainier after his colleague Rear Admiral Peter Rainier, while most Seattleites simply call it "the Mountain."

Whew. From Portland, journey south to Salem and head west along Hwy 22 to Hwy 126. Follow this up and over gorgeous Santiam Pass (4817ft) to the outdoorsy, high-desert town of Sisters and on to the adventure mecca of **32** Bend. Make your way through all the ugly housing developments (the result of an unfortunate media-driven population boom) and treat yourself to a cold pint at either of Bend's two microbreweries. With all its restaurants and lodging options, not to mention everything there is to do within an hour's drive of town, you could easily spend three days shacked up in Bend before returning to the road.

From Bend, wind your way south along the wildly scenic Cascade Lakes Hwy (Hwy 46), past Mt Bachelor, and camp beside whichever lake looks best. It's hard to go wrong, regardless of the lake you choose. Most of the campgrounds are first-come, first-served and if you roll in midweek or early on a weekend morning, you should have no problem landing a campsite. From this lake-riddled national scenic byway, make your way south to the Cascade Range's crown jewel, **33** Crater Lake National Park. You could spend days hiking the trails, motoring around the 33-mile Rim Drive and exploring The Pinnacles. Once you're acclimated to the thin air, hike the strenuous 2.5 miles (one way) to the top of 8929ft Mt Scott for the most epic views of all.

> **DETOUR** With an extra two days it's an easy detour northwest of Bend to the wildly eroded badlands of **John Day Fossil Beds National Monument** in eastern Oregon. Head west via Hwy 26 to the town of Mitchell, where you can bed down for the night at the old-fashioned, two story Oregon Hotel. See the multicolored hills of the Painted Hills Unit and, if there's time, drive to the Sheep Rock Unit, where you'll find the park's only visitor center.

Descend from on high via Hwy 138 west (toward Roseburg) and stop for a soak at the spectacular hike-in **34** Umpqua Hot Springs. Trust us, this will be one of your most memorable stops on the trip. From there, continue west along the "Wild and Scenic" section of the North Umpqua River and make your way down I-5 to **35** Ashland, home of the world famous Oregon Shakespeare Festival. Even if you don't time it right for the Bill-fest, this well-heeled mountain town just over the border from California is home to so many B&Bs and groovy little restaurants that its worth a stop any time – especially at the end of a very long drive.

Danny Palmerlee

TRIP INFORMATION

GETTING THERE
Vancouver lies 140 miles north of Seattle and 315 miles north of Portland; to get there, take I-5 and then Hwy 99.

DO

Crater Lake National Park
Information centers in Rim Village and Steel Visitors Center, both on south side of lake. Roads closed in winter. ☎ 541-594-2211; www.nps.gov/crla; per vehicle $10, free in winter; ☾ year-round; ♿ ⊛

Lime Kiln Point State Park
This 36-acre day-use park lies 10 miles from Friday Harbor, San Juan Island. Shuttles available in summer. **Admission free;** ☾ **8am-dusk;** ♿ ⊛

Moran State Park
Washington's fourth-largest state park, on Orcas Island, has enough attractions to consume a day, easily. ☎ 360-376-2326; www.parks.wa.gov; San Juan Islands, WA; admission free; ☾ 6:30am-dusk Apr-Sep, 8am-dusk Oct-Mar; ♿ ⊛

Mt Rainier National Park
Of four entrances, the most popular (and only year-round) is Nisqually entrance, Hwy 706, about 1½ hours southeast of Seattle. www.nps.gov/mora; per vehicle $15; ☾ year-round; ♿ ⊛

Olympic National Park
Fees collected year-round at Hoh and Heart o' the Hills entrances, and May to October at Elwha, Sol Duc and Staircase entrances. www.nps.gov/olym; per vehicle $15; ☾ year-round; ♿ ⊛

Olympic National Park Visitor Center
The park's most comprehensive information center offers excellent free maps and leaflets, and has exhibits for children and a bookstore. ☎ 360-565-3130; www.nps.gov/olym; 3002 Mt Angeles Rd, Port Angeles, WA; ☾ 8am-6pm summer, 9am-4pm winter; ♿

Pike Place Market
Baked goods, fruits, veggies, meat and more. Don't miss the oddball shops on lower levels. ☎ 206-682-7453; www.pikeplacemarket.org; 1501 Pike Pl, Seattle, WA; ☾ stores 10am-6pm Mon-Sat, 11am-5pm Sun

Powell's City of Books
Portland's giant independent bookstore occupies an entire city block and deals in new and used titles. ☎ 503-228-4651; www.powells.com; 1005 W Burnside St, Portland, OR; ☾ 9am-11pm; ♿

Saturday Market
Fun outdoor crafts fair with street entertainers and food carts. ☎ 503-222-6072; www.portlandsaturdaymarket.com; 108 W Burnside St, Portland, OR; ☾ 10am-5pm Sat, 11am-4:30pm Sun Mar-Dec; ♿

Umpqua Hot Springs
From Hwy 138, turn onto Rd 34 at Toketee Lake. Drive 1 mile past the campground; turn right on gravel road; continue 2 miles to parking area. **Oregon; Northwest Forest Pass $5;** ☾ **24hr**

EAT & DRINK

Brouwer's
Outstanding international selection of craft brews, including many Belgian selections. ☎ 206-267-2437; www.brouwerscafe.com; 400 N 35th St, Seattle, WA; ☾ 11am-2am

Cascade Dining Room
Serves gourmet meals with an emphasis on Pacific Norwest cuisine; breakfast buffets also available. ☎ 503-272-3104; www.timberlinelodge.com; Timberline Lodge, OR; breakfast $13, mains $24-40; ☾ breakfast, lunch & dinner

Go Fish
Best fish-and-chips around. Not much seating, but take it to go to nearby Vanier Park. ☎ 604-730-5040; 1505 W 1st Ave, Vancouver, BC; mains $8-14; ☾ 11:30am-6pm Tue-Fri, noon-6pm Sat & Sun

SLEEP

Ace Hotel
The 28 unique rooms are so stylish you finally get something worthy of the rock star you are. ☎ 206-448-4721; www.acehotel.com; 2423 1st Ave, Seattle, WA; r $75-199

Captain Whidbey Inn
Captivating, surreal inn built in 1907, constructed entirely from rust-colored madrone. Rates include full breakfast. ☎ 360-678-4097; www.captainwhidbey.com; 2072 W Captain Whidbey Inn Rd, Whidbey Island, WA; r $95-190, cabins $195-230

Colonial Creek Campground
Nearly 170 campsites skirt the Thunder Arm of Diablo Lake on either side of Hwy 20. Several walk-in campsites are also available. ☎ 206-386-4495; Hwy 20, mile post 130, WA; campsites $12; ☽ Jun–mid-Oct, walk-in only in winter

Kennedy School
Portland's most unusual hotel has several bars, a theater, restaurant, microbrewery and a soaking pool. ☎ 503-249-3983, 888-249-3983; www.mcmenamins.com; 5736 NE 33rd Ave, Portland, OR; r $109-130; ♿

Oceanside Cottages
Three stunningly situated, fully equipped seafront cottages with ocean views, surrounded by greenery. ☎ 250-653-0007, 866-341-0007; www.oceansidecottages.com; 521 Isabella Rd, Salt Spring Island, BC; cottages $135

Opus Hotel
Vancouver's best boutique hotel combines designer aesthetics with loungey West Coast comforts. ☎ 604-642-6787, 866-642-6787; www.opushotel.com; 322 Davie St, Vancouver, BC; r from $240

Roche Harbor Resort
Self-contained resort on historic country estate with waterfront restaurants and a delightfully old-fashioned hotel. Hotel bathrooms are shared. ☎ 800-451-8910, 360-378-2155; www.rocheharbor.com; Roche Harbor, San Juan Island; r $140-450

San Juan County Park Campground
Includes a beach, boat launch, 20 campsites and flush toilets. Summer reservations mandatory. ☎ 360-378-1842; 380 West Side Rd, San Juan Island, WA; campsites $28-40; ☽ year-round; ♿ ❄

Timberline Lodge
Landmark hotel, which is worth a visit even if you're not staying; options range from rustic bunks to luxury suites. ☎ 503-622-0717; www.timberlinelodge.com; Mt Hood, OR; r $110-290

USEFUL WEBSITES
www.bcferries.com
www.wsdot.wa.gov/ferries

LINK YOUR TRIP

www.lonelyplanet.com/trip-planner

International Selkirk Loop

WHY GO It's an understatement to say this Selkirk scenic drive is somewhat off the beaten track; "crowded" here means the occasional moose blocking your views of stunning Kootenay Lake. Pack your passport and shake the crowds on this uncommonly scenic binational loop through the forgotten corners of Washington, Idaho and British Columbia.

Following lakes and rivers for most of this journey, you'll quickly realize that water is a major component of this trip. So bring a swimsuit and preferably some kind of boat. Within 45 minutes of leaving Washington at Newport you hit one of the Northwest's undiscovered gems at ❶ **Sandpoint**, Idaho. Squeezed between the downhill runs of Schweitzer Mountain and the glittering waters of Lake Pend Oreille, Sandpoint is the kind of town that you want to tell your friends about, but only once you're sure no-one else is listening (*Outside* magazine voted it one of America's "Top Ten Towns"). Budget a couple of hours to stroll the bars, restaurants and shops of First Ave, including the flagship store of local hero Coldwater Creek. The nearby ❷ **Pend D'Oreille Winery** offers tastings and a tour of the French-influenced production process. Try the Huckleberry Blush, a tasty combo of riesling and huckleberry wine.

As the summer temperatures rise, Sandpoint residents shift their focus two minutes' walk east to the City Beach, where the white sand and jet skis provide the closest the Idaho Panhandle ever gets to a Caribbean vibe. ❸ **Lake Pend Oreille** screams out summer fun and gets its unusual French name from the earrings of the local Kalispel tribe and is one of the deepest lakes in the nation, still used by the US Navy for sonar research.

TIME
3 days

DISTANCE
280 miles

BEST TIME TO GO
May – Oct

START
Newport, WA

END
Newport, WA

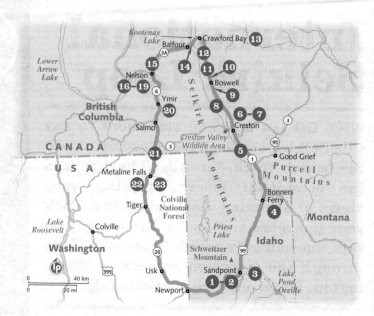

Hwy 95 heads to ④ **Bonners Ferry**, originally built on stilts at the site of a gold-rush river crossing, and continues north past ranches, Christmas tree farms and the world's largest hops farm at Elk Mountain (supplier to brewing giants Anheuser-Busch). It's tempting to continue to Good Grief, if only to take your photo next to the road sign, but turn instead onto Hwy 1 for the ⑤ **Porthill–Rykerts border crossing**. Apart from the change to Canadian dollars, kilometers and noticeably slower driving speeds, you shouldn't notice too many cultural differences, eh? Remember that border regulations implemented in 2009 require you to have a passport or enhanced drivers license (EDL) when crossing between Canada and the United States.

As you pull into Creston, don't freak out if you spot a 7ft Sasquatch carrying a six-pack. The mascot marks the entrance to ⑥ **Columbia Brewery**, home to the Kokanee and Kootenay brands, where you can take a tour and visit the sample room. They may not be the most interesting brews in the region but, hey, free beer, dude!

For a different taste of Creston head east out of town to the fruit stands that line Hwy 3 and pop into the ⑦ **Chocolate Orchard**, where a European chocolatier concocts chocolate-covered cherries, pinot noir truffles and caramel dips with the attention of a Canadian Willy Wonka. This is one shop that may just leave you drooling in the aisles. Load up on red and juicy Lapin cherries and strawberries for the drive ahead, but remember you can't take fruit back with you into the US.

The jewel-like fjord of **8** **Kootenay Lake**, which bursts into view a few miles outside Creston, is a 145km-long (90 mile) slice of turquoise framed by the peaks of the Selkirk and Purcell ranges. This section is the most scenic of the entire drive and is a favorite among adrenaline-charged motorcyclists.

The wackiest sight on the eastern shore is without doubt **9** **The Glass House**. With a mortuarist's sense of humor, funeral director David H Brown decided to build his dream retirement home out of used embalming fluid bottles, half a million of them in total (and more incredibly then persuaded his wife this was a good idea). The result is a whimsy of turrets, towers, bridges and even a garden shed, all made from recycled bottles. Brown then topped his creation off with an interior decorated with fearless 1970s panache (imagine your color-blind grandma choosing fabric on LSD) and a small army of garden gnomes. No, it ain't pretty, but it is enticingly weird.

> **DETOUR** ➤ Nature lovers and birders should detour 6 miles west of Creston to the **Creston Valley Wildlife Area** (www.crestonwildlife.ca), part of the region's most important wildlife corridor. Walk the boardwalks and spot osprey, tundra swans, pelicans or great blue herons from the two birding towers, or sign up for an hour-long guided canoe paddle through the wetlands. Dawn and dusk are the best times to spot wildlife, including the occasional moose chomping in the shadows. Don't miss the very sweet "turtle crossing" road sign.

With so much lakeshore property available, it's tempting to put down roots on Kootenay Lake, but if you're just here for the night it's hard to beat the waterfront cottages of **10** **Destiny Bay Resort** in Boswell. The giant garden chess set and the goats grazing on the sod roofs of the half-dozen cottages add an Alice-in-Wonderland feel but it's the fairy-tale private beach, with lakeside sauna, fire pit and kayak that provide the real magic.

Several spots north of Destiny Bay offer the best public access to the lake. **11** **Lockhart Beach** offers picnic tables on the fine pebble beach but the more clandestine option is the lovely, secluded cove 5 miles further at **12** **Burden's Cut**. Should you choose to find the spot, park opposite the interpretive sign and follow the trail down to what will probably be your own private shoreline.

"don't freak out if you spot a 7ft Sasquatch carrying a six-pack."

Fans of Harry Potter and the Amish will want to stop at nearby Crawford Bay to visit **13** **North Woven Broom**, maker of traditional brooms since 1975. The workshop's feathery golden hues and musky broomcorn fragrance are surprisingly beguiling, almost sensual, and there's something comforting about the workshop's almost total lack of modernity. Anyone who understands the word "Quidditch" will want to check out the replica Nimbus 2000 (Harry Potter's broomstick), 50 copies of which the owners created for a Vancouver book launch (the broom makers also supplied the props for the film *Bewitched*). While you're here, check out the glass blowers, blacksmith's forge and weavers' studio across the road.

Just 3 miles north of Crawford Bay, it's time for another freebie, the world's longest free ferry ride, courtesy of the Canadian government and the ⑭ **Kootenay Lake Ferry**. The scenic crossing departs every hour or so and offers 40 minutes of superb lake views before docking at Balfour, some 20 miles northeast of Nelson. Nelson's quirkiness precedes it and even before you reach town you'll get a hint of the residents' lateral thinking as you pass the antique paddle steamer ⑮ **SS Nasookin**, moored in someone's garden and converted into a wacky private residence.

You could easily spend a full day soaking up the Victorian charms of ⑯ **Nelson**. Outdoorsy, alternative and organic, the historic former mining town has a Victorian charm that makes it one of the most interesting towns east of Vancouver. Pick up a free architectural walking-tour pamphlet to track down the most interesting of the town's 360 heritage buildings, or stroll the waterfront pathway 1.2 miles to the beaches of Lakeside Park, returning on the restored century-old "Streetcar No 23." If you find yourself on Vernon St, head to the school of Chinese medicine and look for the mural of Steve Martin dressed as a Nelson volunteer firefighter in a scene from *Roxanne* (filmed in town).

> **ASK A LOCAL**
>
> "There's no better place to understand the local community than the **Kootenay Co-op** on Baker St, where you can find out about upcoming Tibetan Buddhist lectures while shopping for organic, locally sourced cheeses. For a caffeine fix try the excellent **Oso Negro**, on the corner of Victoria and Ward Sts, which in true Nelson style roasts its own organic fair-trade coffee. "
>
> *Chris Drysdale, Nelson, BC*

Fight your way past Baker St's sitar music and "positive energy generators" and you'll find the town's most interesting shopping, with local fashions running the gamut from hemp to Gore-Tex. For liquid refreshment head for the historic 1898 Hume Hotel, pull up a pew at the ⑰ **Library Lounge** and order a pint of organic Liplock or Wild Honey ale, brewed right in town at the Nelson Brewery. If you discover your new favorite brew, pick up a six-pack in the attached liquor store.

The most widely lauded of Nelson's fine restaurants is ⑱ **All Seasons Café**, whose romantic patio also offers one of the town's nicest hideaways. The seasonally changing menu pairs locally sourced produce and global influences to create "Left Coast Inland Cuisine" – think artisanal British Columbian cheeses with Armenian flatbread and fig chutney. Just a stumble away is the contemporary ⓳ **Cloudside Inn,** a good choice if you prefer your Victorian-era B&Bs fresh rather than frilly. Global travelers will find a kindred spirit in the peripatetic British owners, whose continent-spanning travel photos line the hallways.

Leaving Nelson, the final day's drive takes you south along the Pend Oreille Scenic Byway, past remote, forested (and slightly odd) communities like

historic ⓴ **Ymir** (pronounced why-mur, though grinning locals may well try to persuade you the name stands for "Why Am I Here?"). Connoisseurs of the unusual should pop in to the Ymir Hotel, a 1916 flophouse that stands frozen in time. Try to imagine a Western saloon-style boarding house run by Bela Lugosi and you'll get an idea of the vibe here (and one reason why the rooms cost under $30).

> **DETOUR**
>
> If you have some time to kill before the next ferry departure, drive south from the ferry terminal for 3 miles (partially on a gravel road) to a turn-out that marks a section of Pilot Bay Provincial Park. A short trail leads through forest to the charming white clapboard 1907 **Pilot Bay lighthouse,** where you can clamber to the upper story for fine views over Pilot Bay and Kootenay Lake. An overlook and bench offer a stellar spot for a picnic.

After completing your US border formalities at the sleepy ㉑ **Nelway–Metaline border crossing,** continue straight down Washington Hwy 31 to the town of ㉒ **Metaline Falls,** back-drop to the dreadful Kevin Costner film *The Postman* (the residents ask you not to hold it against them). Campers should detour to picturesque ㉓ **Sullivan Lake,** where three national forest campgrounds offer lakeshore sites, a swimming beach and the occasional bear visitor. Back on the highway it's a straight shot along the languid banks of the dammed Pend Oreille River, through the tiny settlements of Tiger (with its restored 1914 general store) and Usk and past the bison herds and log mills of the Kalispell Indian Reservation back to Newport.

Bradley Mayhew & Danny Palmerlee

TRIP INFORMATION

GETTING THERE
From Seattle, drive 280 miles east on I-90 to Spokane, then north on Hwy 2 for 47 miles to Newport.

DO
Columbia Brewery
Tour the brewing process before sampling the finished product. ☎ 250-428-9344; 1220 Erikson St, Creston, BC; ☾ tours every 30min Mon-Fri, 9:30am, 11am, 1pm & 2:30pm Sat & Sun Jul & Aug, reduced hrs May, Jun, Sep & Oct

Glass House
Admission to British Columbia's ground zero of kitsch includes a tour of the residence and gardens. ☎ 250-223-8372; Hwy 3A, Boswell, BC; admission C$8; ☾ 9am-5pm Apr–mid-Oct

North Woven Broom
One of half a dozen studios and artist work-shops that line crafty Crawford Bay. ☎ 250-227-9245; www.northwovenbroom.com; Hwy 3A, Crawford Bay, BC; ☾ 9am-5pm Mar–mid-Oct

Pend D'Oreille Winery
Award-winning wine bar and retail store, with live music Friday and Saturday evenings. ☎ 208-265-8545; www.powine.com; 220 Cedar St, Sandpoint; ☾ 10am-6pm Mon-Thu, 10am-7pm Fri & Sat, noon-5pm Sun

EAT & DRINK
All Seasons Café
Elegant and eclectic bistro hidden down a side alley. ☎ 250-352-0101; www.allseasonscafe

.com; 620 Herridge Lane, Nelson, BC; mains C$17-30; ☾ 5-10pm

Chocolate Orchard
Gourmet housemade toffees, caramels, truffles and dried fruit at this sweet treat. ☎ 250-428-7067; 2931 Hwy 3, Creston, BC; ☾ 8am-8pm, reduced hrs in winter; ♿

Library Lounge
Wood paneling, period detail and prime outdoor seating make this the most charming of the Hume Hotel's three bars. ☎ 250-352-5331; www.humehotel.com; 422 Vernon St, Nelson, BC; ☾ 11am-midnight

SLEEP
Cloudside Inn
Formerly Inn the Garden, this contemporary-styled B&B boasts bright rooms, a sun deck and a top-floor family suite. ☎ 250-352-3226; www.cloudside.ca; 408 Victoria St, Nelson, BC; r C$95-145, ste C$199

Destiny Bay Resort
Rates at this superbly romantic lakeshore hideaway include a four-course dinner and breakfast. ☎ 250-223-8234; www.destiny bay.com; 11935 Hwy 3A, Boswell, BC; r C$235-255; ☾ May-Oct

Sullivan Lake
The two national forest campgrounds here offer 67 reservable campsites, plus great boating and swimming. ☎ reservations 877-444-6777; www.reserveusa.com, www.fs.fed.us/r6/colville; Colville National Forest, WA; campsites $14

USEFUL WEBSITES
www.discovernelson.com
www.selkirkloop.org

LINK YOUR TRIP
www.lonelyplanet.com/trip-planner

TRIP
93 Pacific Northwest Grand Tour p639

OUTDOORS

Dippin' Down the Cascades

WHY GO Because nothing beats a good soak. And when the tub in question sits beside a cold river, deep in the old-growth forests of the Cascade Range, and the water, rich in minerals, burbles from a hole in the forest floor, you're guaranteed one thing: bliss.

The Cascade Range lies on the Pacific Ring of Fire, that horseshoe-shaped chain of volcanic peaks that wraps the Pacific Ocean and coughs up most of the world's volcanic eruptions. For Oregon, that means there's a lot of geothermal activity beneath its tree-covered surface. The perk? Hot springs – *lots* of them.

Hidden within the Cascades' thick expanses of western hemlock and Douglas fir, edged with maidenhair ferns and often set beside a river, are some of the most paradisiacal hot springs imaginable. But they're no secret. Like it or not, most of the Cascades' hot springs are as much a social (if not cultural) phenomena as they are an excuse to spend some time in nature. At some, folks turn up with guitars and wads of burning sage, and joints get fired up when the atmosphere is right. At others, cans of beer outnumber Nalgene bottles, and bathing suits can outnumber bare buns. Often, it all depends on the day.

Of the dozens of hot springs spread around the state, we've chosen six that are accessible enough to make for a relaxing four-day trip, allowing you to soak yourself silly *at least* once a day. At all but one (Belknap), nudity is generally the norm, but no one should feel uncomfortable donning a bathing suit either. If anything, the vibe at all these places is *relaxed*. For exact directions to the hot springs, refer to Trip Information.

There's no better place to start a trip down the thermal trail than at ❶ **Breitenbush Hot Springs**. Set above the Breitenbush River on a

---

TIME
4 days

DISTANCE
240 miles

BEST TIME TO GO
Jun – Sep

START
Breitenbush Hot Springs, OR

END
Umpqua Hot Springs, OR

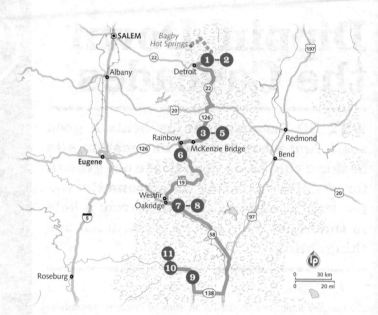

154-acre reserve inside Willamette National Forest, this place is as Oregon as it gets and, along with a fantastically relaxing soak, you'll get a solid dose of earthy Oregonian mellowness. Hot mineral water burbles out of several springs at a scorching 180°F to 200°F and is cooled to prime soaking temperatures with water from the river. There are seven pools in all. Three overlook a pretty meadow and one of these is a silent pool. Another four pools (the Spiral Tubs) are arranged in order of temperature, from 100°F to 107°F. Elsewhere, a sauna sits over an open spring and is entirely heated by steam from hot water below. You can stay in a cabin, a lodge room, a dorm room or in a tent (yours or one provided by Breitenbush). The rooms are geothermally heated, and all electricity is generated by turbines on the river (once you're here, you're off the grid). Three organic vegetarian meals are included and served in a historic lodge. In all, it's one heck of a treat. You can also visit as a day guest and camp at nearby ② **Humbug Campground**, only 3 miles below Breitenbush.

> "sitting in the deep pools and staring up at the trees remains an utterly sublime experience."

The following day (after an early morning soak, of course), make your way south along Hwy 22 to Hwy 126 East (south). About 9 miles south of Clear Lake, pull into ③ **Olallie Campground** and set up camp. There's heaps to do around here, including fishing on the McKenzie River, hiking on the nearby McKenzie River National Recreation Trail, and waterfall watching at Sahalie and Koosah Falls, only a stone's throw from the campground. By the end of the day you'll be well ready for a soak. Worry not, ❹ **Bigelow Hot Springs** is only a short distance away. This well-hidden, little-known hot spring sits on the banks of the McKenzie River, tucked into a sort of miniature grotto that drips into a perfectly heated pool (100°F to 104°F). It's shallow but a real treat, especially in the early morning, when you're likely to have it all to yourself. From the parking lot, cross to the downstream side of the bridge and take the first path down to the water. Follow the trail downstream 150 yards to the pool.

If you'd prefer to do your soaking in a bigger, clearer, sometimes hotter but always more crowded pool, stop at

> **DETOUR** For more great soaking, detour one hour (40 miles) northwest of Breitenbush Hot Springs to the eternal soakers' favorite, **Bagby Hot Springs**. From the former, continue on Forest Rd 46 (Breitenbush Rd) to Forest Rd 63. Turn left, then veer right on Forest Rd 70 and follow it 7 miles to the parking lot. Hike 1.5 miles on the well-marked trail to the free bathhouses with hollowed-log tubs. A $5 Northwest Forest Pass is required at the parking lot.

❺ **Belknap Hot Springs Resort**, only 4 miles south. Belknap is the sort of hot spring you can take your grandmother to and she won't feel out of place. But neither will you – and you'll both love the water. Two giant swimming pools filled with 103°F mineral water provide optimum soaking conditions in a family environment. The McKenzie River rushes by below, trees tower over everything and, as far as we could tell, everyone has a darn good time. The resort boasts an 18-room lodge, 14 private cabins and 15 tent sites, so it's affordable for nearly all budgets. It's also an excellent alternative to camping and, if you are camping elsewhere, it's the perfect place to pop into on a day-use basis.

On day three, journey west of McKenzie Bridge and turn left on Hwy 19, better known as Aufderheide Memorial Drive (the turnoff is just past Rainbow). After almost 8 miles, you'll come to the well-signed ❻ **Terwilliger Hot Springs**. From the parking lot, a 0.25-mile trail leads through old-growth forest to one of the state's most stunning hot springs. From a fern-shrouded hole below the trees, thermal water spills out at a scorching 116°F and into a pool that maintains a steady minimum temperature of 108°F. Only hard-core soakers can handle it. From the upper pool, the water then cascades into three successive pools, each one cooler than the one above it. Over the years, Terwilliger became so popular and so party-prone that local caretakers and the US Forest Service were forced to institute a no-alcohol policy. Despite its continuing popularity, sitting in the deep pools and staring up at the trees remains an utterly sublime experience. After hiking back to the car, you can even jump into Cougar Reservoir from the rocky shore below the parking lot.

You could stretch this trip out by camping in one of several nearby campgrounds, but to stick with the four-day program continue south along glorious Hwy 19 to the sister towns of Westfir and Oakridge. From Oakridge, drive 8.7 miles east along Hwy 58 to **7 Blue Pool Campground**, the only campground in the immediate area. It's on the banks of Salt Creek with several tent-only sites and enough trees to make most of the campsites feel secluded.

After pitching your tent and blowing up your sleeping pad, drive 0.5 miles east along Hwy 58 to **8 McCredie Hot Springs**. Because McCredie lies just off the highway it's a very popular spot, for everyone from mountain bikers fresh off the trails near Oakridge to truckers plying Hwy 58. Despite this, it's worth a stop if only because it's the site of one of the largest – and hottest – thermal pools in Oregon. If you can hit it early in the morning – and we highly recommend you do – or late in the evening midweek, you could very well have the place to yourself. There are five pools in all: two upper pools that are often dangerously hot (as in don't-even-dip-your-foot-in hot), two warm riverside pools and one smaller, murkier but usually perfectly heated pool tucked back into the trees. Salt Creek, which rushes past only steps from the springs, is perfect for splashing down with icy water. Since you'll be camped only half a mile away, it's easy to visit before or after prime time.

From Blue Pool Campground, continue east on Hwy 58, to Hwy 97 S and swing west on Hwy 138 toward Crater Lake. About 22 miles from Hwy 97, you'll pass stunning Diamond Lake and **9 Diamond Lake Resort**, the only hotel around. Shack up here if you don't plan to camp the final night. After passing several other lakes, a handful of campgrounds and some extremely high waterfalls that lie hidden in the forest, you'll come to **10 Toketee Lake Campground**, just off Hwy 138 on the North Umpqua River. Although some of the other nearby campgrounds are arguably more scenic (though not by much),

ADD A HIKE TO HOT WATER

Hiking and hot springs make a fabulous combination. Fortunately, outstanding trails can be found near almost every hot spring on this trip. Two major trails from Breitenbush lead eventually to the Pacific Crest Trail. The McKenzie River National Recreation Trail leads from Bigelow Hot Springs south to three major waterfalls. Before (and after) soaking in Umpqua Hot Springs, hike as much of the North Umpqua Trail as you can – it passes the trail to the springs.

Toketee Lake Campground is all about location. It offers excellent access to the spectacular 79-mile North Umpqua Trail, which you can hike in either direction along the federally designated "Wild and Scenic" section of the North Umpqua River. Best of all, it's the closest established campground to this trip's grand finale: **11 Umpqua Hot Springs**.

Umpqua Hot Springs is the sort of place that sets you thinking, "Is this place real *and* free?" It's both. And although you have to work a little to get here, it is the remote setting that makes these springs so magical. Cascading down a precipitous ridge overlooking the North Umpqua River, seven warm pools range in temperatures from 110°F in the upper pools to about 99°F in the lower pool. Each is formed by colorful mineral deposits, and the lower pools are just big enough to accommodate two happy soakers. Sitting in the pools on a cold, misty morning, looking out over the river and the trees towering above the opposite side of the gorge must be one of Oregon's most memorable experiences.

To reach the springs from the parking lot, you need to cross the North Umpqua River. Winter storms destroyed the old footbridge, and it may be out for years. Until it's replaced, head downstream 100yd or so from the old bridge and walk across the wide log over the river. Once you're across, walk back upstream to the site of the old bridge and then hike uphill, away from the river, until you reach the main trail. Turn right and follow the trail about 0.25 miles up and over a ridge to the pools. Once you're there, slide into one of the natural tubs and enjoy the view – after all the hot tubbing you've done this week, you deserve every minute of it.

Danny Palmerlee

TRIP INFORMATION

GETTING THERE
To get to Breitenbush Hot Springs from Port-land, drive 50 miles south on I-5 to Salem; head east for 49 miles on Hwy 22, then go 10 miles northeast on Breitenbush Rd.

DO
Bigelow Hot Springs
Traveling south on Hwy 126 from Clear Lake, turn right on the unsigned road between mileposts 14 and 15. Cross the McKenzie River and park on the right. **Admission free; 24hr**

Breitenbush Hot Springs
Fees at this rustic resort include three meals, meditation rooms, soaking pools and saunas. **503-854-3320; www.breitenbush.com; Breitenbush Rd, Detroit, OR; dm $50-72, tents $54-72, cabins $84-115**

McCredie Hot Springs
Extremely popular soaking pool 9.2 miles east of Oakridge on Hwy 58. Pools are directly below the parking lot. **Admission free; dawn-dusk**

Terwilliger Hot Springs
Closes for cleaning after around 10am on Thursdays in summer. (If you accidentally show up, you can help clean.) No alcohol, pets or glass bottles allowed. **Aufderheide Memo-rial Dr, OR; admission $5; dawn-dusk**

Umpqua Hot Springs
From Hwy 138, turn onto Road 34 at Toketee Lake. If the road to the springs is closed, hike 3 miles to the springs from Toketee Lake Camp-ground via the North Umpqua River Trail. When the road opens, drive 1 mile past Toketee Lake Campground; turn right on the unsigned gravel road and continue 2 miles to the parking area on the left. **Admission free; 24hr**

EAT & SLEEP
Belknap Hot Springs Resort
Family-oriented resort with two huge pools. Grill open in summer. **541-822-3512; www.belknaphotsprings.com; Hwy 126 near Hwy 242, OR; campsites $35, r $100-185, cabins $65-400, hourly/day use $7/12**

Blue Pool Campground
Wooded, 24-site campground near McCredie Springs. Water and pit toilets available. First-come, first-served. **Hwy 58, OR; campsites $14; May-Sep**

Diamond Lake Resort
This widely loved family resort offers hotel rooms and cabins on the lakeshore. **541-793-3333, 800-733-7593; www.diamond lake.net; 350 Resort Dr, Diamond Lake, OR; r $89-199, cabins $189-559;**

Humbug Campground
Lovely, 22-site campground on Breiten-bush River with some very secluded sites. Water and pit toilets available. First-come, first-served. **Breitenbush Rd, Detroit, OR; campsites without/with hookups $10/20; May-Sep;**

Olallie Campground
The closest campground to Bigelow Springs has a prime location on the McKenzie River. **877-444-6777; www.recreation.gov; Hwy 126, OR; campsites $14; Apr-Sep**

Toketee Lake Campground
First-come, first-served campground with shady sites on the North Umpqua River; near Toketee Falls and Umpqua Hot Springs, 56 miles east of Roseburg. **Rd 34 at Hwy 138, OR; campsites $7;**

USEFUL WEBSITES
www.fs.fed.us/r6/willamette
www.oregonhotsprings.immunenet.com

LINK YOUR TRIP

www.lonelyplanet.com/trip-planner

TRIP
93 Pacific Northwest Grand Tour p639

Journey Through Time Scenic Byway

WHY GO During this epic drive across windswept plains, desolate badlands and forested mountain passes, you'll dig deep into Oregon's history. Along the way you'll visit everything from ghost towns to fossil beds, from gold-mining sites to small-town museums. The one thing you won't see much of? Crowds.

Unless you count the futuristic-looking windmills around the town of Wasco, a more precise name for this state scenic byway would be Journey *Back* in Time Scenic Byway. From the moment you leave Hwy 84 it's truly a time warp: ghost towns lie off the roadside, fossils expose millions of years of history, and even the restaurants and hotels make you feel you've driven into decades past.

Although it's not part of the official byway, the perfect place to kick off your time travel is at the full-scale replica of ❶ **Stonehenge**, on the Washington side of the Columbia River, just east of Hwy 97. Built by eccentric businessperson Sam Hill, the site is a complete version of the Salisbury Plain monument, although its detractors argue that the keystone is incorrectly aligned with the stars.

After Stonehenge, stop at nearby ❷ **Maryhill Museum of Art**, just west of the Hwy 97 junction on Hwy 14. This spectacular mansion, set on a bluff above the Columbia River, was another Sam Hill project. Among its eclectic exhibits is a noteworthy collection of Native American baskets and other artifacts, including a seal-intestine parka and carved walrus tusks.

Traveling south on Hwy 97, you begin the *official* scenic byway as soon as you cross the Columbia River. South of the river, the two-lane road winds over rolling, grain-covered hills, past the town of Wasco

TIME
4 days

DISTANCE
301 miles

BEST TIME TO GO
Jun – Sep

START
Maryhill, WA

END
Baker City, OR

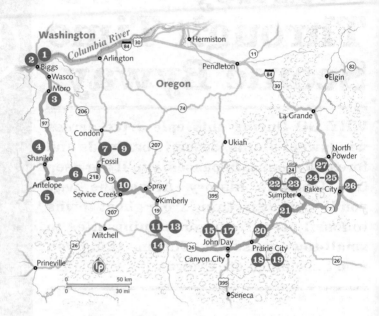

to Moro, where you'll find **3** **Sherman County Historical Museum**. For a small-town museum it has some surprisingly interesting exhibits, including those on the history of wheat production, Native Americans and rural living in the days of old. Back on Hwy 97, you'll be treated to views of several volcanoes in the distance as you head south, including Oregon's Mt Hood and Mt Jefferson and Washington's Mt Adams.

> *"After the road behind, entering the one-stoplight town of John Day is like rolling into the big city."*

Then you hit **4** **Shaniko** (population 26). This wee ghost town, contrary to everything it now seems, was once the wool shipping center of the US. Its decrepit old buildings make for exceptional photo ops, and its architectural *grand dame,* the Shaniko Hotel, is one of the finer historic buildings in eastern Oregon. (It was closed and up for sale at the time of publication.)

From Shaniko, continue south on Hwy 218 and you'll soon hit the town of **5** **Antelope** (population 59), founded in the 1870s and named for the pronghorn antelope that roamed the surrounding hills. After the boom days of the wool trade were over, Antelope floundered. It then (miraculously?) sprang back to life in the mid-1980s when "Rajneeshees," followers of Indian guru Bhagwan Shree Rajneesh, settled here after the mystic founded the nearby religious community of Rajneeshpuram.

About 16 miles west of Antelope, the dramatically eroded Palisade Cliffs come into view and mark your arrival at the ⑥ **John Day Fossil Beds Clarno Unit**. The short trails and fossil remains here plunge you into a far more distant past, to a time more than 40 million years ago, when the region was subtropical forest. The astounding collection of fossils found in the area are exactly what gave the town of ⑦ **Fossil** (population 370), 18 miles northeast, its name.

In Fossil, check into the homey ⑧ **Bridge Creek Flora Inn**, which – we coincidentally discovered – is owned by Lyn Craig, the creator of the official Journey Through Time Scenic Byway. Needless to say, Craig is a wealth of information. She's also an inspired cook and serves a whopping all-natural breakfast to her overnight guests. Tonight though, grab dinner at ⑨ **Big Timber Family Restaurant**, where good grub and small-town hospitality both come in big doses.

On day two, take Hwy 19 south to ⑩ **Service Creek** (population 2), another old stagecoach stop which today consists of an inn (where you'll find the town's two residents) and a rafting-put-in-cum-campground on the John Day River (just south of the junction). Follow Hwy 19 east from Service Creek through the town of Spray (which, with a population of 140, actually *is* a town) and on to Kimberly, where you'll find a store with snacks and cold drinks. From Kimberly south, the road follows the swift and increasingly scenic John Day River. The rust-colored walls of the river canyon narrow and then open up again before reaching the spectacular ⑪ **John Day Fossil Beds Sheep Rock Unit**. For a fascinating paleontology lesson stop at the ⑫ **Thomas Condon Paleontology Center**, which doubles as the visitors center for the surrounding John Day Fossil Beds National Monument. The museum, packed with fossilized skulls, leaves, skeletons and superb murals, will help you understand exactly what you're seeing in the mountains around you.

> **ASK A LOCAL**
>
> "If you're heading east through Picture Gorge [on Hwy 26], at the far end you'll see a sign on the left and a gravel parking area big enough for about two cars. There's a little footpath from the pullout. Walk down the footpath and then hang onto the rock wall on your left and lean around and you'll see some red pictographs. It's really cool. And you can't hurt them because you can't reach them."
>
> *Lyn Craig, Fossil, OR*

Just south of the paleontology center, Hwy 19 becomes Hwy 26, and you follow the John Day River east through a narrow basalt-walled canyon known as ⑬ **Picture Gorge**. Upon leaving here, watch for the turnoff about 2 miles east of the gorge on your right that leads up to the ⑭ **Mascall Formation Overlook**, where you can take in astounding 360-degree views of the surrounding mountains.

Back on Hwy 26, about 38 miles from the paleontology center, is ⓭ **John Day** (population 1821). After the road behind, entering the one-stoplight town of John Day is like rolling into the big city. Watch out for all those cars and make your way to the outstanding ⓰ **Kam Wah Chung State Heritage Site**, which served as an apothecary, community center, temple and general store for Chinese gold miners and settlers from the late 19th century until the 1940s. Today it's a widely acclaimed museum featuring the history of the building and the region's Chinese past. John Day is the logical place to spend the night and, although the town is hardly acclaimed for its sleeping options, the kitschy ⓱ **Dreamers Lodge** (actually a motel) does the trick.

Get an early start to day three and eat breakfast 12 miles east in ⓲ **Prairie City**, at ⓳ **Chuck's Little Diner**. This snug family diner serves nothing but the classics: bacon-and-egg breakfasts with butter-laden toast, hot pancakes and – in true diner fashion – mediocre coffee. With Strawberry Mountain towering over the town, Prairie City has a stunning setting. The town is also home to the DeWitt Depot Museum (currently closed), which is worth a quick peek just to see the depot building itself. Prairie City was the terminus of the narrow-gauge Sumpter Valley Railroad that ran between here and Baker City.

From Prairie City, leave the barren scenery of the John Day River Valley behind and make your way east into the lush, conifer-clad Blue Mountains. As you head up the first grade, pull off at the ⓴ **Strawberry Mountain Overlook** (on the left), which affords stunning views of the John Day River Valley below and the Strawberry Mountains in the distance. Continue northeast over Dixie Pass (elevation 5280ft), swing left onto Hwy 7, cross Tipton Summit (elevation 5124ft) and you'll eventually drop into a lovely valley hemmed in by trees before hitting ㉑ **Whitney**. This isolated prairie settlement, a ghost town in the best sense of the word, was once a busy logging town and the primary stop on the Sumpter Valley Railroad. Its sagging wooden buildings, which lie on either side of a dirt road that branches south (right) from Hwy 26, are certainly worth a stop.

DETOUR ▶ Two miles south of John Day lies the tiny town of Canyon City, home of the **Grant County Historical Museum** (open May to September only). Depending on your perspective, it's either (a) just another Podunk museum or (b) a fascinating glimpse into the region's human history. Just don't lose yourself among the relics: wood clamps, antique clothing, house wares, pianos and other musical instruments, a Native American exhibit and loads of interesting old photographs. You can easily see the museum in an hour.

About 9 miles east of Whitney, turn left on Sumpter Valley Hwy to visit the former gold-mining camp of ㉒ **Sumpter**. Once home to 3500 people, the town today is a sleepy cluster of Old West buildings huddled along a dusty main drag – reason alone to visit. The official attraction, however, is the **㉓ Sumpter Valley Dredge**, a massive relic of gold-mining engineering sitting beside the river. The dredge's 72-bucket "digging ladder" cost $300,000 to build and, during its operational lifespan, extracted some 9 tons of gold.

Return to Hwy 7 and make your way 26 miles east to the bustling eastern Oregon hub of **㉔ Baker City**. In the gold-rush days, Baker City was the largest metropolis between Salt Lake City and Portland, and a heady mix of miners, cowboys, shopkeepers and loggers kept the city's many saloons, brothels and gaming halls boisterously alive. Today, the city's wide downtown streets and historical architecture recall its rich bygone days. Before you live it up (now that you're in civilization once again), check into the landmark **㉕ Geiser Grand Hotel**. This masterpiece of Italian Renaissance revival architecture will keep you firmly planted in the past, *and* you'll sleep in style.

"miners, cowboys, shopkeepers and loggers kept the city's many saloons, brothels and gaming halls boisterously alive."

If you're not too beat from the drive, head to the evocative **㉖ National Historic Oregon Trail Interpretive Center**, the nation's foremost memorial to the pioneers who migrated west along the Oregon Trail. Lying atop a hill 7 miles east of town, the center contains interactive displays, artifacts and films that brilliantly illustrate the day-to-day realities of the pioneers. Outside you can stroll on the 4-mile interpretive path and spot the actual Oregon Trail.

Return to Baker City and make your way to **㉗ Barley Brown's Brewpub**, with pressed-tin ceilings, big wooden booths and a good-old pub-style menu. Most importantly, it serves some seriously good award-winning beer, which is brewed in small batches just like it was in the days back when…

Danny Palmerlee

TRIP INFORMATION

GETTING THERE
From Portland, follow Hwy 84 east to Hwy 97, go north to Hwy 14 and then follow the signs east to Stonehenge (100 miles in total).

DO

Kam Wah Chung State Heritage Site
This must-see museum shows the history of Chinese settlement and culture in eastern Oregon. ☎ 541-575-2800; 250 NW Canton St, John Day, OR; admission free; ⏰ 9am-5pm May-Oct 31; ♿

Maryhill Museum of Art
Eclectic museum in a stunning location and building to match. ☎ 509-773-3733; www.maryhillmuseum.org; 35 Maryhill Museum Dr, Goldendale, WA; adult/child/senior $7/2/6; ⏰ 9am-5pm Mar 15-Nov 15; ♿

National Historic Oregon Trail Interpretive Center
Don't miss this brilliant memorial to Oregon Trail pioneers. ☎ 541-523-1843; www.oregontrail.blm.gov; 22267 Hwy 86, Baker City, OR; adult/senior/15yr & under $8/4.50/free; ⏰ 9am-6pm Apr-Oct, 9am-4pm Nov-Mar; ♿

Sherman County Historical Museum
Thousands of artifacts bring Oregon's Native American and early US history to life. ☎ 541-565-3232; www.shermanmuseum.org; 200 Dewey St, Moro, OR; adult/student $3/1; ⏰ 10am-5pm May 1-Oct 31; ♿

Stonehenge
America's first Stonehenge replica dates back to 1918. Just south of OR-14 on Stonehenge Dr, Maryhill, WA; admission free; ⏰ dawn-dusk

Thomas Condon Paleontology Center
Visit John Day Fossil Beds National Monument's visitors center for its extraordinary fossils and knowledgeable staff. ☎ 541-987-2333; 32651 Hwy 19, Sheep Rock Unit, OR; admission free; ⏰ 9am-5:30pm, reduced hrs in winter; ♿

EAT

Barley Brown's Brewpub
Baker City's brewpub serves everything from clam linguini to teriyaki salmon and barbecue ribs – and eight delicious microbrews. ☎ 541-523-4266; www.barleybrowns.com; 2190 Main St, Baker City, OR; mains $12-18; ⏰ 4-10pm Mon-Thu, to 11pm Fri & Sat

Big Timber Family Restaurant
Big breakfasts, burgers and country-style dinners. ☎ 541-763-4328; 540 1st St, Fossil, OR; mains $5-19; ⏰ 7am-8pm; ♿

Chuck's Little Diner
With its Formica-top bar, tarnished chrome bar stools, friendly staff and greasy classics, this is a diner par excellence. ☎ 541-820-4353; 142 Front St, Prairie City, OR; mains $6-9; ⏰ 6am-2pm Wed-Sun

SLEEP

Bridge Creek Flora Inn
Occupying two adjacent, historic homes, this country-style B&B minimizes frilliness and maximizes friendliness; superb breakfasts. ☎ 541-763-2355; www.fossilinn.com; 828 Main St, Fossil, OR; r $75-95; ♿

Dreamers Lodge
Friendly, immaculately kept 1960s-era motel with spacious rooms, coffee makers, mini-fridges and a decor that's brilliantly outdated. ☎ 541-575-0526, 800-654-2849; www.dreamerslodge.com; 144 N Canyon Blvd, John Day, OR; r $54

Geiser Grand Hotel
Baker City's downtown landmark and fanciest lodgings. Elegant rooms are spacious and decorated with old-style furniture. Don't miss the saloon. ☎ 541-523-1889, 888-434-7374; www.geisergrand.com; 1996 Main St, Baker City, OR; r $109-219

USEFUL WEBSITES
www.eova.com

LINK YOUR TRIP

TRIP 93 Pacific Northwest Grand Tour p639

www.lonelyplanet.com/trip-planner

TRIP
97

FOOD &
DRINK

Whistle-Stop Brewery Tour

WHY GO Despite the coffee explosion and inroads made by the wine industry, beer – microbrewed beer – is still the Pacific Northwest's definitive beverage. It therefore follows that a brewery tour is the region's definitive trip. But rather than tearing across the region by car, travel by train. Best of all: no designated driver necessary.

TIME
10 days

DISTANCE
466 miles

BEST TIME TO GO
Apr – Oct

START
Eugene, OR

END
Vancouver, BC

With more microbreweries than any region in the US, the Pacific Northwest is heaven on earth for beer drinkers. Name a town that's halfway worth visiting, and odds are it has a brewery. But that makes crafting a brewery tour an impossible task. So we wondered, what would really make a brewery tour great? Answering took all of 30 seconds: not having to drive. Of course, riding the bus in the USA is the traveler's equivalent of quaffing flat beer, which left one option: the train. So here you have it, the no-car-is-necessary, environmentally friendly, Pacific Northwest whistle-stop brewery tour.

Thanks to Amtrak's *Cascades* and *Coast Starlight* train routes, you can ride the rails all the way up the western flanks of the Pacific Northwest. For the sake of sampling beer, this tour begins in Eugene, Oregon (the southern terminus of the *Cascades* route), and ends in Vancouver, British Columbia, the northern terminus of both routes. But first, a few logistics: purchase your tickets by leg (ie Eugene to Portland, Portland to Centralia) ahead of time to save yourself money and guarantee you get a seat. You can change your ticket anytime (simply call up Amtrak), but you'll be charged additionally if the fare has gone up (fares get higher the closer you get to the day of travel).

Enough train talk. How about ❶ **Eugene**? With its vibrant mix of university students, track stars in training, and good ol', thirsty

665

working-class folks, it's no wonder the town is home to several brewpubs. Make your way first to the **2 Eugene City Brewery**. Although it's owned by Rogue Ales (one of Oregon's largest breweries), Eugene City brews its own beers, too, and always has at least four of them available on tap. The other 31 taps (count 'em) are mostly Rogue Ales flavors with a few guest taps thrown in for fun. For happy hour, head to the **3 Starlight Lounge**, where you can quaff Ninkasi Brewing's Total Domination IPA and five other Ninkasi beers for a measly $2 a pint. (Ninkasi Brewing is production-only, and the Starlight pours the best selection of its beer). Save room for a pint at **4 Steelhead Brewing Co**, which brews much better beer than its run-of-the-mill dining room and bar area might suggest. At the end of the night, taxi on over to **5 C'est La Vie Inn**, a gorgeous B&B in a converted Victorian home.

From Eugene, ride up to the handsome Union Station in **6 Portland** and take a bus or taxi across the Willamette River to the **7 Bluebird Guesthouse**, in Southeast Portland. Situated on a happening stretch of SE Division St, the guesthouse offers modest but immaculate rooms (most with shared bathrooms) in a converted Arts and Crafts home. Visitors tend to gravitate toward downtown, but hunkering down in the southeast will allow you to hit some of Portland's best breweries without having to taxi all over the city. Plus, SE Hawthorne Blvd and SE Division St are packed with shops, cafés, restaurants and pubs.

First hit ⑧ **Hopworks Urban Brewery**, a new one on the Portland scene. Likely Bridgetown's most sustainable brewery, Hopworks composts all of its brewing waste, serves food made from organic, locally sourced products and, not surprisingly, pours organic beer. Long before Hopworks was even a notion, however, there was ⑨ **Roots Organic Brewery**. Opened in 2005, this was Oregon's first certified-organic brewery, and you should probably sidle in to pay your respects (sipping a pint of eXXXcalibur Imperial Stout is probably the best way to do so). Plus, its wooden surfboard tap handles are undoubtedly the coolest around.

Only four blocks away, in a refurbished warehouse, lies ⑩ **Lucky Labrador Brew Pub**. Around since 1994, Lucky Lab pours three to five of its own brews, plus a guest beer, and serves sandwiches, salads and bento boxes. And if you want to taste a wide variety of beers in one great spot, head six blocks up to ⑪ **Green Dragon Bistro & Brewpub**. It's inside a converted warehouse, now filled with picnic tables and an expansive wooden bar. During summer, the big roll-down doors get rolled up, making sunny afternoons prime times to drop in for a pint.

SPIN CYCLE

Traveling by train means you're car-less once you get wherever you're going. Portland, Seattle and Vancouver all have great public bus systems, but why not rent a bike? In Southeast Portland, head to the cooperative **Citybikes Annex** (www.citybikes.coop) or, for something closer to Bluebird Guesthouse, **Veloce Bicycles** (www.velocebicycles.com). For something weirder try **Clevercycles** (http://clevercycles .com). In Seattle, try **Montlake Bicycle Shop** (www.montlakebike.com), about 2 miles north of the Gaslight Inn. In Vancouver, head to **Reckless** (www.rektek.com), which has shops on either side of Granville Island.

From Portland, it's two hours by train to Centralia, home of the McMenamin Brothers' ⑫ **Olympic Club Hotel**. One of Washington's funkiest and most innovative gathering spots, the legendary Olympic Club dates from 1908 when it was billed as a "gentlemen's resort" designed to satisfy the various needs of local miners and loggers. Now it's a boisterous brewpub, billiard hall, restaurant, hotel and movie theater all rolled into one. And it's a great reason to spend the night in little old Centralia.

The following day (or the same day, if you plan it right), make the 21-minute hop north to Olympia and hit the cozy ⑬ **Fish Tale BrewPub**, where you can drink the beers and ciders brewed by Washington's second-largest brewery, Fish Brewing Company. The brewpub pours the company's Fish Tale Ales, Leavenworth Beers and Spire Mountain Ciders. They're all organic. If you need to hole up in Olympia for the night, do so at the ⑭ **Olympia Inn**. The no-frills rooms have the usual mod cons, but the real advantage is you're situated just blocks from both the State Capitol complex and the downtown coffee bars, and only eight blocks from the brewpub.

From Olympia, it's a short train ride north to King Street Station, on the southern edge of downtown ⓵⓹ Seattle. Head first to the ⓵⓺ Gaslight Inn, about 2 miles away on Capitol Hill, and drop your bags. The Gaslight is a magnificently restored turn-of-the-20th-century home with touches including sleigh and four-poster beds, plush chairs and antique furniture. From there it's only five blocks to ⓵⓻ Elysian Brewing Co, to which you should walk immediately. Knock back a pint of crisp, cold Zephyrus Pilsner while feasting on a juicy hamburger, and then wander over toward the corner of Broadway and E John St for some of Seattle's funkiest shopping and best people-watching. Then tromp down to Pike Place Market and brave the tourists (it's worth it if you've never been there) before heading into ⓵⓼ Pike Pub & Brewing, where you can order a six-beer tasting flight, thus saving yourself the need to drink 96oz of beer.

> **DETOUR**
>
> Detour back in time by getting off the train at Skagit Station in Mt Vernon (about 1½ hours north of Seattle), and taking bus No 615 west to the historic town of La Conner, on Skagit Bay. Undisturbed by modern development, La Conner itself is one of the Lower Skagit River Valley's oldest trading posts and still retains much of its 19th-century charm. When you arrive, head to **La Conner Brewing Co** (www.laconnerbrew .com), where you can enjoy your IPA with wood-fired pizza. Spend the night at the beautiful **Queen of the Valley Inn** (www.queenofthe valleyinn.com).

Minimizing your beer consumption at Pike Pub is key, considering the only train to ⓵⓽ Vancouver departs at 7:40am. The good news is, four hours later you end up in a beautiful city with plenty to explore, including a half-dozen breweries. Of these, put ⓶⓪ Granville Island Brewing first on your list, if only to allow yourself one brewery tour on the trip. Three times a day, guides walk visitors through the brewery before depositing them in the taproom for samples of the beer, all of which are named after Vancouver neighborhoods. Since you're on the island, wander over to the Granville Island Hotel, which just happens to be home to the ⓶⓵ Dockside Restaurant & Brewing Co. The beer is undoubtedly delicious, but this place is really about the patio, which has stunning views of False Creek and downtown Vancouver.

Another Vancouver institution is ⓶⓶ Steamworks Brewing Co, in Gastown. In the cavernous downstairs section of this big converted brick warehouse, folks get noisy over pints of Lions Gate Lager, while, upstairs, they lounge in cushy leather seats and take in the views across to the North Shore. It's a spectacular spot, and well worth the train ride north.

Danny Palmerlee

TRIP INFORMATION

GETTING THERE

When traveling nonstop between Eugene and Vancouver, you must do the Seattle–Vancouver leg by bus, unless you spend a night in Seattle.

EATING & DRINKING

Dockside Restaurant & Brewing Co
Brewery restaurant with a fabulous patio; inside the outstanding Granville Island Hotel. ☎ 604-685-7070; www.docksidebrewing.com; 1253 Johnston St, Vancouver, BC; mains C$14-30; ☷ restaurant 7am-10pm daily, lounge 5pm-midnight Tue-Sat; ☷

Elysian Brewing Co
Offers 15 beers on tap, usually including a barley wine and a Hefeweizen. ☎ 206-860-1920; www.elysianbrewing.com; 1221 E Pike St, Seattle, WA; mains $9-12; ☷ 11:30am-2am Mon-Fri, noon-2am Sat & Sun

Eugene City Brewery
Inside a historic brewery building owned by Oregon's Rogue Ales; expansive menu. ☎ 541-345-4155; www.rogue.com; 844 Olive Street, Eugene, OR; mains $8-15; ☷ noon-10pm Mon-Thu, noon-midnight Fri & Sat, noon-9pm Sun; ☷

Fish Tale BrewPub
Fourteen taps, plus a huge menu, including emu burgers, oyster burgers, beef burgers, salads and sandwiches. ☎ 360-943-3650; www.fishbrewing.com; 515 Jefferson St, Olympia, WA; mains $7-13; ☷ 11am-midnight Mon-Sat, noon-10pm Sun

Granville Island Brewing
Tours of this classic Vancouver brewery include four samples. Or just hit the taproom. ☎ 604-687-2739; www.gib.ca; 1441 Cartwright St, Vancouver, BC; tours C$9.75; ☷ tours noon, 2pm & 4pm, taproom noon-8pm

Green Dragon Bistro & Brewpub
Excellent taproom and restaurant in a spacious converted warehouse. ☎ 503-517-0660; www.pdxgreendragon.com; 928 SE 9th St, Portland, OR; mains $6-10; ☷ 11am-11pm Sun-Wed, 11am-1am Thu-Sat; ☷

Hopworks Urban Brewery
Slick brewery with penchant for sustainability and great pizza. ☎ 503-232-4677; www.hopworksbeer.com; 2944 SE Powell Blvd, Portland, OR; pizzas $16-25; ☷ 11am-11pm Sun-Thu, 11am-midnight Fri & Sat; ☷

Lucky Labrador Brew Pub
Converted warehouse with brewery and a big dog-friendly back patio. Kids permitted till 9pm. ☎ 503-236-3555; www.luckylab.com; 915 SE Hawthorne, Portland, OR; ☷ 11am-midnight Mon-Sat, noon-10pm Sun; ☷ ☷

Pike Pub & Brewing
Serves great burgers, pizzas and brews in a funky neo-industrial space. ☎ 206-622-6044; www.pikebrewing.com; 1415 1st Ave, Seattle, WA; sandwiches $10-13, mains $13-24; ☷ 11am-11pm, 11am-midnight Fri & Sat; ☷

Roots Organic Brewery
Aim for $2.50 Tuesdays (when pints cost that all day): definitely *the* day to go. ☎ 503-235-7668; www.rootsorganicbrewing.com; 1520 7th Ave, Portland, OR; ☷ 11am-11pm Mon-Thu, 11am-midnight Fri, 11:30am-midnight Sat, 11:30am-10pm Sun

Starlight Lounge
Eugene's Ninkasi Brewing is production only, but you'll find six of its beers on tap here. Happy hour runs from 4pm to 7pm. ☎ 541-343-3204; 830 Olive St, Eugene, OR; ☷ 4pm-2:30am

Steamworks Brewing Co
A giant Gastown microbrewery and a favorite place for the city's after-office crowd. Outstanding food. ☎ 604-689-2739; www.steamworks.com; 375 Water St, Vancouver, BC; mains C$14-22; ☷ 11:30am-midnight Sun-Wed, 11:30am-1am Thu-Sat

Steelhead Brewing Co
Local fave with standard pub fare, plus a dozen homemade brews. ☎ 541-686-2739; www.steelheadbrewery.com; 199 E 5th Ave, Eugene, OR; ☷ 11:30am-11:30pm Sun-Thu, 11:30am-12:30am Fri & Sat

SLEEPING

Bluebird Guesthouse
Seven comfy rooms, two with private bath; superb common areas, one fireplace. ☎ 503-

238-4333, 866-717-4333; www
.bluebirdguesthouse.com; 3517 SE Division,
Portland, OR; r $55-95

C'est La Vie Inn

Neighborhood show-stopper with antique
furniture, living room, dining room and four
tastefully appointed guest rooms. ☎ 541-
302-3014; www.cestlavieinn.com; 1006
Taylor St, Eugene, OR; r $125-250

Gaslight Inn

Offers 15 rooms in two neighboring homes.
In summer, it's refreshing to dive into the
outdoor pool or just hang out on the sun
deck. ☎ 206-325-3654; www.gaslight-inn
.com; 1727 15th Ave, Seattle, WA; r $98-158

Olympia Inn

This unpretentious downtown hotel is all
about location. Rooms are clean and have
fridge, microwave and cable TV. ☎ 360-352-
8533; 909 Capitol Way S, Olympia, WA; r $57

Olympic Club Hotel

McMenamin Brothers masterpiece offering
groovy old rooms with shared bathrooms.
It's walking distance from the train station.
☎ 360-736-5164; www.mcmenamins.com;
112 N Tower Ave, Centralia, WA; d $40, r
$60-80

USEFUL WEBSITES

www.amtrakcascades.com
www.amtrak.com

LINK YOUR TRIP

www.lonelyplanet.com/trip-planner

The Simpsons to The Shining

WHY GO When Hollywood needs a remote film location, it heads up the coast to the Pacific Northwest. It's got waterfalls, army bases, creepy mountain lodges, and towns that are willing to dress up like Alaska. So turn off your TV and discover some of the famous sites you've already seen.

Cottage Grove, Oregon, is known for its covered bridges, but the most famous bridge here is an open-top railroad trestle that had a cameo in the movie *Stand By Me*. It's on screen for less than a minute, but the four pre-teen boys crossing over it as they set off on their journey into the woods has become one of the film's most iconic images. The rails have been paved over, and the ❶ **Mosby Creek Trestle Bridge** is now part of the Row River Trail, easily accessible for hikers, bikers and film buffs.

Just north in Eugene, you'll find the ultimate party school: Faber College. It wasn't easy finding a campus that would agree to be in the movie *Animal House* but the University of Oregon at Eugene had the good sense (of humor) to say yes. The president of the University, who was no Dean Wormer, even let scenes be filmed in his office in ❷ **Johnson Hall**. You can't visit the Delta house anymore – it's been torn down – but you can still eat in the ❸ **Erb Memorial Union Fishbowl**, famous for the food fight John Belushi's character started by spewing mashed potatoes at Kevin Bacon.

Just north in Salem, you'll find the hospital where they shot what many people consider to be one of the greatest American movies of all time: *One Flew Over the Cuckoo's Nest*, which swept the Oscars, taking Best Picture, Best Director, Best Actor, Best Actress and Best Screenplay. The ❹ **Oregon State Hospital** is still an operating facility, so don't expect a tour, but the beautiful old building surrounded by rhododendrons is still worth driving by for any Jack Nicholson fan.

TIME
5 – 6 days

DISTANCE
700 miles

BEST TIME TO GO
May – Sep

START
Cottage Grove, OR

END
Roslyn, WA

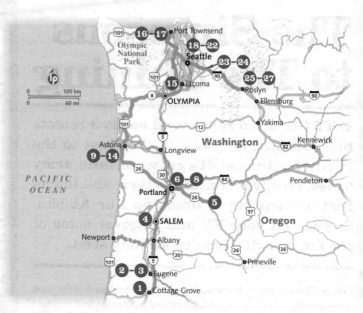

Continuing your Nicholson-goes-nuts tour, head north on I-5 and then east on Hwy 26 to **⑤ Timberline Lodge**, which, if you've ever seen *The Shining*, will give you the creeps before you even get out of the car. It was used for exterior shots of the haunted Overlook Hotel, and, while you can't wander the hedge maze (that was just Hollywood magic) you can enjoy cocoa in front of the massive stone fireplace and be glad you're not trapped in for the winter with a crazed Jack Torrance.

"be glad you're not trapped in for the winter with a crazed Jack Torrance."

In **⑥ Portland**, it seems **⑦ Jake's Famous Crawfish** is famous for more than just its crawfish. It's frequently used as a film location, including a scene in Gus Van Sant's *My Own Private Idaho*. Much of downtown was used in the dark indie flick, including the **⑧ Thompson Elk Fountain** near City Hall, where the narcoleptic hustler played by River Phoenix lies passed out in Keanu Reeves' arms.

On a cheerier note, Portland is also the hometown of Matt Groening, and there are signs of *The Simpsons* all around town – literally. Several of the surnames used on the show are also downtown street names, including NW Quimby St, Lovejoy St, and NE Flanders St, which frequently gets the letter D spray painted in after the abbreviation for northeast.

Ready to roll credits on Portland? Head west to the coastal village of **⑨ Astoria** , a virtual Hollywood by the Sea. Several movies have been filmed here, including *Short Circuit*, *Free Willy*, and *Kindergarten Cop*, but it's best known as the setting for the cult hit *The Goonies*. The opening scene with the Fratellis was shot in front of the ⑩ Clatsop County Jail, and the most popular location in town is the ⑪ Goonies House. You can't actually go inside the house where Mikey and Brandon Walsh lived, but you can walk up the gravel driveway and do your own version of the Truffle Shuffle in front of the famous Victorian.

Just over the bridge, fans of the movie *Free Willy* can visit ⑫ Hammond Mooring Basin, site of the thrilling climax where Willy leaps through the air as he heads toward open waters. There are tons of other movie locations in Astoria, warranting at least an overnight stay to see them all. So

DETOUR If **Yaquina Head Lighthouse** in Newport, Oregon, seems a little creepier than a lighthouse ought, that's because it was featured in the US version of the movie *The Ring*. Built in 1873, it was originally called Cape Foulweather Lighthouse, but in the movie it was known as the Moesko Island Lighthouse. (It was also in the 1977 TV masterpiece *Nancy Drew: The Mystery of Pirate's Cove*.) To get to Newport, turn off the I-5 between Eugene and Salem and drive 60 miles on Hwy 20.

where do filmmakers go when they're in town? ⑬ Hotel Elliott is a stylish boutique hotel that offers star-worthy accommodations in its deco-light rooms. And ⑭ Baked Alaska is a seafood-on-white-tablecloths kind of place, where cast and crew alike often dine after a day of shooting.

After you've had your fill of Astoria film locations, head north to Tacoma, a four-hour drive through farmlands and general greenery. Whether or not you're a fan of the movie *10 Things I Hate About You*, the school where it was shot is worth a stop. ⑮ Stadium High School was built in the late 1800s as a luxury hotel. Drive around back, where the castlelike structure – modeled after an actual château in France – looms over the sunken football field, where Heath Ledger's character pays the marching band to help him serenade Julia Stiles.

From Tacoma, head north for a meandering two-hour drive along two-lane highways to Port Townsend. This seaside town with a military base doubled as Pensacola in the filming of *An Officer and a Gentleman*. You might recognize some of the areas around ⑯ Fort Worden State Park, and you can reenact the love scenes in the exact same room at ⑰ The Tides Inn where Richard Gere and Debra Winger stayed the night. Although it doesn't have its original furnishings from the movie, the room is stuck somewhere back in the 1980s, and there's a plaque outside the door and a movie poster over the bed, just to make sure you don't miss the point.

Head back down into ⑱ Seattle, which has had many a star turn since its film debut in 1933's *Tugboat Annie*. The trip from Port Townsend is only about 50 miles but the ferry ride in the middle makes it a two-hour trip. Once you're back in the big city, stay at the centrally located ⑲ **Inn at the Market**, a small, elegant boutique hotel perfectly located for exploring the city. It's right across the street from ⑳ **Pike Place Market**, a perennial tourist attraction that is almost a mandatory location for any film set in Seattle. Rob Reiner and Tom Hanks wandered through this Seattle icon in *Sleepless in Seattle*, and Jeff Bridges filmed here for *The Fabulous Baker Boys*, among others.

> **ASK A LOCAL**
>
> "Almost everyone who comes to visit wants to see the **Sleepless in Seattle houseboat**. You can't see it from the street, but there are a couple of boat tours that take you by – the Duck Ride and the Argosy tour. You could also try renting a kayak and paddling out to it. It's on the northwest side of Lake Union up by Gas Works Park, and Tom Hanks' houseboat is right at the end of the dock."
>
> *Rick Bartley, Seattle, WA*

Seattle's ㉑ **Gas Works Park** is a popular spot among both locals and filmmakers for its views of Lake Union and freaky industrial structures. It was the setting for a paintball fight in *10 Things I Hate About You*, as well as a heart-to-heart between Kyra Sedgwick and Campbell Scott in *Singles*.

In fact, the whole city features prominently in *Singles*, which was seen as practically a documentary of life and love in early 1990s Seattle. The unifying element was the ㉒ **Coryell Court Apartments**, where the 20-something main characters lived. You won't find Matt Dillon hanging out in a flannel shirt in the courtyard, but driving by will bring back memories of the grunge-era film.

If you watched David Lynch's *Twin Peaks*, you'll instantly recognize the ㉓ **Salish Lodge** from the opening credits. Half an hour east of Seattle, the lodge was used as the exterior for the Great Northern Hotel, and it sits right above Snoqualmie Falls, which was also featured on the show. Stop for Northwestern cuisine in one of their two restaurants, or just hike down to the falls for a fabulous photo op. And speaking of *Twin Peaks*, you can still get cherry pie at ㉔ **Twede's Cafe** – also known as the "Double R" – where Kyle MacLachlan enjoyed a "Damn fine cup o' coffee."

Finally, head east for about 45 minutes to the little town of ㉕ **Roslyn**, which doubled for Cicely, Alaska, in the show *Northern Exposure*. The main street looks just like it did in the show, and you can grab a beer at the ㉖ **Brick Tavern** or have dinner at ㉗ **Roslyn Cafe**, which still has the famous mural painted on its side, although the moose has since moved on.

Mariella Krause

TRIP INFORMATION

GETTING THERE
From Portland, Cottage Grove is 130 miles south on I-5.

DO

Clatsop County Jail
This tiny building was the pokey from 1914 to 1976; now it's just a great photo op for *Goonies* fans. **732 Duane Street, Astoria, OR**

Coryell Court Apartments
The reddish-brown brick apartment building built around a courtyard will be recognizable to *Singles* fans. **1820 E Thomas St, Seattle, WA**

Fort Worden State Park
Do some push-ups or run some laps at this film double for Pensacola's Naval Aviation Officer Candidate School. ☎ **360-344-4400; www.parks.wa.gov/fortworden; 200 Battery Way, Port Townsend, WA**

Gas Works Park
Even if you're unfamiliar with its film work, this cool park on Lake Union has great views of downtown. **Meridian Ave & N Northlake Way, Seattle, WA;** ☽ **dawn-dusk**

Goonies House
Park at the bottom of the gravel driveway and walk up; feel free to snap a picture, but, remember, it's a private residence. **368 38th St, Astoria, OR**

Hammond Mooring Basin
If you're a fan of *Free Willy*, it's a must-see; if not, there's not much to look at. **1099 Iredale St, Hammond, OR**

Johnson Hall
This stately administration building is where Dean Wormer tried to shut down the Deltas, back in the day. **E 13 St btwn University & Kincaid Sts, Eugene, OR**

Mosby Creek Trestle Bridge
Part of the Row River Trail, this bridge is 3 miles southeast of town near the Mosby Creek Trailhead. **Cnr Mosby Creek & Mosby Ranch Rds, Cottage Grove, OR;** ♿

Oregon State Hospital
Used as both exterior and interior for *One Flew Over the Cuckoo's Nest*, this facility is still operating as a state hospital. **2600 Center St NE, Salem, OR**

Pike Place Market
This crazily popular Seattle landmark has seen its share of celluloid. ☎ **206-682-7453; www.pikeplacemarket.org; 1501 Pike Pl;** ☽ **stores 10am-6pm Mon-Sat, 11am-5pm Sun**

Stadium High School
Built as a luxury hotel, it was gutted by fire in 1898 and rebuilt to be an incredibly impressive high school. **111 N E St, Tacoma, WA**

Thompson Elk Fountain
This downtown elk statue is considered a traffic hazard — especially when it's got stars sleeping on it. **SW Main St btwn 3rd & 4th Aves, Portland, OR**

EAT

Baked Alaska
A favorite of film folk on a shoot, this seafood place overlooks the Columbia Gorge. ☎ **503-325-7414; www.bakedak.com; 1 12th St, Astoria, OR; mains $8-26;** ☽ **11am-10pm**

Brick Tavern
Where the locals go to get a beer, whether they live in Roslyn, Washington, or Cicely, Alaska. ☎ **509-649-2643; 1 Pennsylvania Ave, Roslyn, WA; mains $8-13;** ☽ **11:30am-11pm Sun-Thu, 11:30am-2am Fri & Sat**

Erb Memorial Union Fishbowl
The cafeteria has been replaced with fast-food chains, but you'll still recognize the dining area from *Animal House*. ☎ **541-346-3705; www.emu.uoregon.edu; 1222 E13 Ave, Eugene, OR;** ☽ **7am-7pm Mon-Thu, 7am-5pm Fri, reduced hrs in summer**

Jake's Famous Crawfish
Killer crawfish, elegant digs and over 100 years of history — no wonder it's famous. ☎ **503-226-1419; 401 SW 12th Ave, Portland, OR; mains $7-18;** ☽ **11:30am-10pm Mon-Thu, 11:30am-midnight Fri & Sat, 3-10pm Sun**

Roslyn Cafe

Surprisingly cute for a small-town café; be sure to get a picture of the mural. ☎ 509-649-2763; 201 W Pennsylvania Ave, Roslyn, WA; mains $9-25; ⏱ 11am-3pm & 5-8pm Wed-Sat, 11am-3pm Sun, closed Mon-Thu in winter

Salish Lodge

This hotel lacks the quirkiness of the Great Northern but, then, no dead bodies either. ☎ 425-888-2556; www.salishlodge.com; 6501 Railroad Ave SE, Snoqualmie, WA; mains $12-28; ⏱ 7am-10pm Mon-Fri, breakfast & dinner Sat & Sun

Twede's Cafe

Cherry pie and coffee are still on the menu at the former Double R. ☎ 425-831-5511; www.twedescafe.com; 137 W North Bend Way, North Bend, WA; mains $5-15; ⏱ 6:30am-8pm Mon-Thu, 6:30am-9pm Fri & Sat, 6:30am-7pm Sun

SLEEP

Hotel Elliott

Plush, deco-style rooms make this boutique hotel Astoria's leading lady. ☎ 877-378-1924; www.hotelelliott.com; 357 12th St, Astoria, OR; r $109-229, ste $179-650

Inn at the Market

Elegant, modern, and located right above Pike's Place Market. ☎ 206-443-3600; www.innatthemarket.com; 86 Pine St, Seattle, WA; r $195-399

The Tides Inn

The furniture is so dated, you might think it was left over from the film. But this age-ing movie star is still a fun star sighting. ☎ 360-385-0595; www.tides-inn.com; 1807 Water St, Port Townsend, WA; r $60-269

Timberline Lodge

Built as a Works Project Administration project, this National Historic Landmark made of timber and stone has rustic, woodsy rooms. ☎ 503-231-5400; www.timberlinelodge.com; Timberline Lodge, OR; r $125-310

USEFUL WEBSITES

www.ci.seattle.wa.us/filmoffice/filmmap.htm

LINK YOUR TRIP

www.lonelyplanet.com/trip-planner

Up the Inside Passage

WHY GO Alaska is thousands of rugged miles from the Lower 48 – so remote and wild that it's almost a mythical land. But there's a link between dream and reality: every Friday the Alaska Ferry sets sail from Bellingham, Washington, tracing the Canadian coastline before slipping into the foggy emerald maze of Alaska's Inside Passage.

TIME
4 days

DISTANCE
1119 miles

BEST TIME TO GO
Jun – Sep

START
Bellingham, WA

END
Skagway, AK

Of the 27 All-American Roads, the Alaska Marine Highway is the only one that floats. Churning 3500 nautical miles from Bellingham and out to the far tendril of the Aleutian Chain, some of the highway's most dramatic scenes are pressed into the steep fjords and waterlogged fishing towns of the Inside Passage. A three-day trip on the ❶ Alaska State Ferry ends in Skagway, traveling through the US's largest national forest, the Tongass, and stopping in several ports along the way. If you have more time, your options for detours are unlimited. A through-ticket will give you a small sample of time in each port, while point-to-point tickets let you decide how long to stay in each town.

In ❷ Bellingham, you can walk, bike or drive onto the vessel, which departs from brick-paved, historic ❸ Fairhaven District. Make sure to give yourself at least an afternoon to explore this city neighborhood, stamped onto several blocks and crammed charmingly with flower shops, cafés and bookstores. Arrive the night before and sack out at the vintage-style ❹ Fairhaven Village Inn. An excellent district-center option, the Inn is across the way from the Village Green Park's farmers market and outdoor evening movies. Be sure to fill up with housemade desserts at the nearby ❺ Colophon Café & Deli, and choose your reading material for your trip at the stacked Village Books, which mingles with the café.

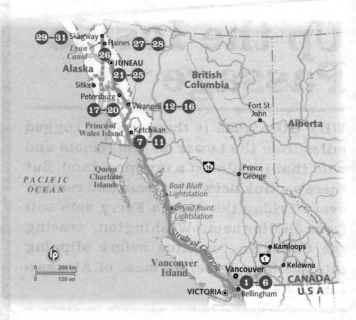

As the ferry slides out in to ⑥ **Bellingham Bay**, you'll be treated to views of Mt Baker, sienna-colored brick buildings, and Victorian homes peering from the town's hillside. Not long after leaving port, the ferry squeezes between Canada's Vancouver Island and the mainland through the Strait of Georgia. This is the time to mix with the locals and travelers who share the ferry with you. This isn't a cruise ship, but that makes the experience all the more authentic. The solarium will be filled with the sleeping bags of adventurers hunkered down under heat lamps, while brightly colored tents flap in the wind on deck. The snack-bar fare is what you'd expect of public transportation, but warming up with a cup of coffee in a booth is a comfortable way to watch the coast pass by.

Thirty-six hours after departing Bellingham, the ferry makes its first stop in ⑦ **Ketchikan**. Here you'll skim along the town's thin band of colorful buildings – with equally colorful histories – before docking north of the town center. The ferry stays in port long enough for you to explore the historic, albeit touristy, ⑧ **Creek Street**. Though this boardwalk is now safe for families, in Ketchikan's early boom-town years the street was a clatter of brothels and bars. Pop into ⑨ **Dolly's House Museum**, where you can get an insider's view of what was a working parlor. Namesake Dolly Arthur operated the brothel until prostitution was outlawed in the 1950s, and lived here until her death in the '70s.

A quality introduction to the Southeast region (simply called "Southeast" by locals) is at the ⑩ **Southeast Alaska Discovery Center**. Exhibits on Southeast's ecosystems and Native Alaskan traditions are showcased upstairs, while a re-created rain forest looms downstairs. It's a good place to help you identify what you're seeing from the windows of the ferry.

For some spiced-up local flavor head to ⓫ **That One Place**, on the ground floor of the New York Hotel. This seafood-stuffed tapas restaurant is an inexpensive place to fill up on local fare before heading back to the boat.

After departing Ketchikan, the ferry hums through Clarence Strait before arriving at tiny, false-fronted ⓬ **Wrangell** several hours later. You'll be greeted by the town's children, who set up folding tables (often in the rain) to sell their wares – deep-purple garnets that they've mined from the nearby Stikine River.

Wrangell practically spills over with historic, cultural and natural sights, including compelling ⓭ **Petroglyph Beach**. Less than a mile from the ferry terminal, the beach is dotted with boulders depicting faces and figures that were carved thousands of years ago. Lifelike whales and owls peer up at you, while some spirals eerily resemble crop circles. If you're just popping off the ferry during its quick stop, you can lace up your running shoes and jog there and back for a speedy examination of the stones. More recent Tlingit culture is showcased on the other side of town at ⓮ **Chief Shakes Island & Tribal House**, an oddly peaceful site in the middle of the humming boat harbor. Here, six totem poles tower among pines, and eagles often congregate in the trees' branches. The island is always open to walking, though the tribal house usually only opens for cruise-ship groups.

BC'S STAFFED LIGHTHOUSES

The misty stretch of Canada between Washington and Alaska is home to 40 lighthouses, more than half of which require keepers. The ferry glides by picturesque **Dryad Point Lightstation**, which features an old-school style lighthouse perched on the northeastern tip of Campbell Island. Further north, **Boat Bluff Lightstation** is a simple aluminum skeleton, but the red-roofed outbuildings cling pleasantly to a small hillside and the keepers often emerge to wave to ferry passengers.

For an overnight stay – and Wrangell is certainly worth it – check out the ⓯ **Alaskan Sourdough Lodge**. This family-owned lodge features a sauna, steam room and 16 spotless rooms, and it's a nice place to thaw out if you've been exploring in the rain.

Just after leaving Wrangell, the ferry enters the 22-mile long ⓰ **Wrangell Narrows**. Too skinny and shallow for most large vessels, the Narrows (dubbed "Pinball Alley") requires nearly 50 course corrections as boats thread between more than 70 green and red channel markers. The ferry M/V *Columbia* is the largest boat to navigate the Narrows, as water depth can get as shallow as 24ft at low tide.

At the end of the Narrows sits ⑰ **Petersburg**, a fishing village with blond roots. Petersburg's rich Norwegian history is evident not just in the phonebook full of Scandinavian names, but also in the flowery rosemaling, a decorative Norwegian art form found on buildings throughout town. But to really get into the heart of Petersburg, walk the docks of its ⑱ **North Boat Harbor**. Here fisherfolk unload the day's catch from small purse seiners, distinguishable by the large nets piled in the stern. To sample locally caught seafood, plant yourself at a window seat at ⑲ **Rooney's Northern Lights Restaurant**, where you can watch fisherman in the harbor unload your potential dinner.

MOUNTAIN BIKING POW ISLAND

The third-largest island in the USA, mountainous Prince of Wales Island isn't a well-known mountain-biking destination, but that's due more to its remote location than its lack of spectacular terrain. Veined with over 1300 miles of mostly unpaved road and spotted with tiny villages, POW also has 21 public-use cabins scattered along its inlets and alpine lakes. There are dispiriting clear-cuts, but they're the reason for all those roads.

The Inter-Island Ferry (www.interislandferry .com) has service from Ketchikan, Wrangell and Petersburg.

Complement a layover in Petersburg with a kayak tour to ⑳ **LeConte Glacier**, at the head of serpentine LeConte Bay. Constantly calving, the glacier is somewhat infamous for icebergs that release under water and then shoot to the surface like icy torpedoes. If you're lucky you'll see one – from afar.

After brushing through quiet fishing towns, arriving to hustle of ㉑ **Juneau** can be somewhat surprising. This is the only US capital with no road access, yet it still bustles with the importance of a government center. It's also postcard perfect, with massive green cliffs rising importantly above the city center. Be sure to stroll past the ㉒ **Governor's Mansion**, its assertive columns and articulately landscaped shrubs a sharp contrast to the usual rain forest–rotted cabins of Southeast. If the political climate gets to be too much, head back toward the ferry terminal to the laid-back ㉓ **Alaskan Brewing Company** for a tour and samples of beers that rival the Pacific Northwest's. The brewery is in the same neighborhood as the massive ㉔ **Mendenhall Glacier**, which tumbles down from the Juneau Icefield and is one of the few glaciers in Southeast you can drive up to. The sleek visitors center offers a movie with the glacier as its star, as well as hiking trails and a salmon-viewing platform.

If your trip calls for a night in town, cozy up at the ㉕ **Silverbow Inn**, where the smell of baking bread from the bakery downstairs wakes you in the morning. One of the amenities of this historic hotel is a bottomless cookie jar – at least it's easy to work them off on one of Juneau's many downtown hiking trails.

From Juneau, the ferry travels up the ㉖ **Lynn Canal**, which is North America's longest (90 miles) and deepest (2000ft) fjord. The Canal is equally endowed with glaciers and waterfalls, and it's hard not to stare at the scenery. Seventy-five miles from Juneau lies **27** **Haines**, where most passengers with cars disembark as the town is the main link to the Alaska Hwy. Free from cruise-ship crowds, Haines has a laid-back vibe with almost extravagant scenery. Don't miss the **28** **Hammer Museum**, which displays 1500 hammers and chronicles the history of man through them.

The ferry continues to **29** **Skagway**, a gold-rush era town that revels in all its gaudy glory. The ferry deposits you about 100yd from the action of **30** **Broadway Street**, where you'll find women dressed in feathered hats and bright satiny dresses vying for the attention of the many tourists wandering off cruise ships. Since Skagway is likely your last ferry stop, you'll have time to take the **31** **White Pass & Yukon Railroad**, a narrated sightseeing tour aboard vintage parlor cars. This dramatic ride rumbles along a narrow-gauge line, through

> **DETOUR** **Sitka** is off the main route, but if you have some extra days or want to end your journey there, this town of 8800 people is well worth the extra time. The only city in Southeast that fronts the Pacific Ocean, Sitka looks out to the cone of Mt Edgecumbe as well as a clutter of small, treed islands. A hikers' and kayakers' delight, Sitka is a full day's journey from Juneau or Petersburg.

Glacier Gorge and over White Pass (a 2885ft climb), and also connects to the Yukon Territory. It's a refreshing change from the ferry, and, if you fly home, you'll be able to say you traveled by boat, rail and air.

Whether you end your trip in Skagway or another port, you'll need to backtrack on the ferry, or fly south, to get home. There are few commercial flights from smaller towns, and to catch a major airline flight to Seattle you'll first need to fly to Juneau, Ketchikan or Sitka on a smaller carrier.

Catherine Bodry

TRIP INFORMATION

GETTING THERE

From Vancouver, drive south on Hwy 99 and I-5 53 miles to Exit 250 in Bellingham. From Seattle, take I-5 north 89 miles to Exit 250. Follow the signs to the Alaska Ferry Terminal.

DO

Alaska State Ferry

Ride from point to point, or directly from Bellingham to Skagway ($363). Accommodation includes camping on deck (no charge) or basic cabins (r from $337). ☎ 907-465-3941, 800-642-0066; www.alaska.gov/ferry; terminal at end of Harris Ave, Bellingham, WA; ♿

Alaskan Brewing Company

The largest brewery in Alaska offers complimentary tours (and beer samples!). ☎ 907-780-5866; www.alaskanbeer.com; 5429 Shuane Dr, Juneau, AK; ⏱ 11am-6pm, closed Mon-Wed Oct-Apr

Dolly's House Museum

This was the home of Ketchikan's most famous madam. ☎ 907-225-6329; 24 Creek St, Ketchikan, AK; adult/child $5/free; ⏱ 8am-5pm

Hammer Museum

See 1500 hammers on display, from Roman relics to Tlingit artifacts. ☎ 907-766-2374; www.hammermuseum.org; 108 Main St, Haines, AK; adult/child $3/free; ⏱ 8am-5pm Mon-Fri May-Sep

Southeast Alaska Discovery Center

A great introduction to the great outdoors, with cultural and natural exhibits and wildlife viewing. ☎ 907-228-6220; 50 Main St, Ketchikan, AK; adult/child $5/free; ⏱ 8am-5pm Mon-Fri, 8am-4pm Sat & Sun; ♿

White Pass & Yukon Railroad

Several tours available; note that some cross into Canada so you'll need your passport. ☎ 907-983-2217, 800-343-7373; www .whitepassrailroad.com; depot on 2nd Ave, Skagway, AK; Yukon Adventure one-way adult/child $170/85, White Pass Summit Excursion round-trip $103/51.50

EAT

Colophon Café & Deli

Renowned for its African peanut soup and chocolate brandy cream pies, the café has an outside wine garden and is popular with local literati. ☎ 360-647-0092; www.colophon cafe.com; 1208 11th St, Bellingham, WA; mains $7-13; ⏱ 9am-8pm Mon-Thu, 9am-10pm Fri & Sat, 10am-8pm Sun

Rooney's Northern Lights Restaurant

Overlooks the bustling harbor; the crab, halibut and shrimp on its seafood platter is locally caught. ☎ 907-772-2900; 203 Sing Lee Alley, Petersburg, AK; breakfast $5-10, dinner $16-30; ⏱ 6am-9pm

SLEEP

Alaskan Sourdough Lodge

Offers free shuttle from the ferry, and home-cooked meals are served family-style. ☎ 907-874-3613, 800-874-3613; www.ak gateway.com; 1104 Peninsula St, Wrangell, AK; s/d $105-199

Fairhaven Village Inn

A vintage hotel that is a class above standard motel fare. ☎ 360-733-1311, 877-733-1100; www.fairhavenvillageinn.com; 1200 10th St, Bellingham, WA; r $149-289

Silverbow Inn

This artsy, six-room hotel has a rooftop hot tub and serves a full breakfast. ☎ 907-586-4146, 800-586-4146; www.silverbowinn .com; 120 2nd St, Juneau, AK; r $99-220

USEFUL WEBSITES

www.fs.fed.us/r10/tongass
www.wingsofalaska.com

www.lonelyplanet.com/trip-planner

LINK YOUR TRIP

TRIP
7 Wet & Wild West Coast p105
93 Pacific Northwest Grand Tour p639

Behind the Scenes

THIS BOOK

This book features trips from the original six titles in this series. Those trips were written by Ginger Adams Otis, Catherine Bodry, Jeff Campbell, Nate Cavalieri, Gregor Clark, Adam Karlin, Beth Kohn, Mariella Krause, Josh Krist, Emily Matchar, Bradley Mayhew, Kevin Raub, Adam Skolnick, Ryan Ver Berkmoes and Wendy Yanagihara. This guidebook was commissioned in Lonely Planet's Oakland office and produced by the following:

Commissioning Editor Jennye Garibaldi
Coordinating Editor Kirsten Rawlings
Coordinating Cartographer Corey Hutchison
Coordinating Layout Designer Nicholas Colicchia
Managing Editor Bruce Evans
Managing Cartographers David Connolly, Alison Lyall
Managing Layout Designer Celia Wood
Assisting Editors Sarah Bailey, Kate James, Helen Koehne, Nigel Chin, Jeanette Wall
Assisting Layout Designer Jim Hsu
Cover Naomi Parker, lonelyplanetimages.com
Internal image research Sabrina Dalbesio, lonelyplanetimages.com
Project Manager Glenn van der Knijff

Thanks to David Burnett, Jay Cooke, Catherine Craddock, Heather Dickson, Owen Eszeki, Suki Gear, Mark Germanchis, Chris Girdler, Michelle Glynn, Brice Gosnell, James Hardy, Liz Heynes, Lauren Hunt, Laura Jane, John Mazzocchi, Wayne Murphy, Darren O'Connell, Julie Sheridan

THANKS

Sara Benson Biggest thanks to my dad and Mike for driving thousands of miles with me around Florida, and to Lee Britos for revealing Miami's foodie secrets. I'm grateful to Jennye Garibaldi for expertly guiding this project, and to my co-authors for sharing their expertise – and lotsa laughs, too.

Amy Balfour Hearty thanks to those who shared their Great Plains expertise: Anne & Keene Pollard, Cindy Lovell, Hillary Wiessinger, Ron and Judy Elliott, Judy Dollard, Kelly Seed Bucceri, Molly Murphy, Marilyn Weiser, Bob Stein, and Molly and Geoffrey Baker. Thanks Jennye for a great assignment and Sam for answering all of my crazy questions.

Alison Bing Many thanks and California bear hugs to: road-tripper extraordinaire Jennye Garibaldi; coordinating author Sam Benson; fearless leaders Brice Gosnell and Heather Dickson; the Sanchez Writers' Grotto for steady inspiration; and Marco Flavio Marinucci, for the best-ever bus ride.

Becca Blond Big thanks to my parents, David and Patricia Blond, without whose support I would never have made it through the last year. Also to my husband, Aaron, and our bulldog, Duke. I'd also like to thank Jason Spallek for his amazing generosity. At Lonely Planet, big thanks to Jennye Garibaldi for commissioning me on this important project, Sam Benson for being such a great coordinating author,

SEND US YOUR FEEDBACK

Got feedback? We'd love to hear your corrections, suggestions, compliments or complaints, so feel free to use our feedback form: **lonelyplanet.com/contact**.

Note: We may edit, reproduce and incorporate your feedback comments in Lonely Planet products such as guidebooks, websites and digital products. If you send it in, then that counts as permission for us to use it. If you don't want your name acknowledged, please let us know.

To read our privacy policy, visit **lonelyplanet.com/privacy**.

my team of co-authors, and thanks so much to Kirsten Rawlings, Sarah Bailey and Corey Hutchison for their careful, extensive and awesome editing and cartography!

Jennifer Denniston Huge thanks to Lonely Planet colleagues – Jennye Garibaldi, Suki Gear, Alison Lyall, and fellow authors, especially Karla Zimmerman, David Ozanich, Amy C Balfour, Sam Benson, Alison Bing and Becca Blond. To Heather, endless thanks. Finally, thank you Rhawn, Anna and Harper, always willing to road trip and loving it almost as much as I do.

Lisa Dunford Thanks much to all my friends and family across Texas, especially to my beloved mother-in-law, Helen Dickman.

Alex Leviton A huge thanks goes to *Carolinas, Georgia & the South Trips* co-authors Emily Matchar, Adam Karlin and Kevin Raub. This time around, the thanks go to Sam Benson, Brandon Presser, Karla Zimmerman and the rest of the Tripper author crew, along with editor/author wrangler Jennye Garibaldi.

David Ozanich David thanks God. Also: Chris Tuttle, Nate Harris, Buck Drummond, Tim Federle, Jennye Garibaldi, his hilarious co-authors, Lonely Planet's crack staff, and finally, most of all, Liza Minnelli.

Danny Palmerlee Big thanks to my editor Jennye Garibaldi for bringing me onboard and sending me into the remote corners of the Pacific Northwest once again. Pat, Leslie, thanks for your hot-spring trail tips! Sandra, Ben, thanks for the sound advice on coastal hideaways. And thank you to all the park rangers who fielded my endless barrage of questions.

Brandon Presser A big shout-out to my fab(lantic) co-authors and everyone at the Lonely Planet mothership! To Jennye: marry me.

Karla Zimmerman Many thanks to experts Josh Chicoine, J O'Leary and Miki Greenberg, plus Marie Bradshaw, Jim and Susan Stephan, and Don and Karen Zimmerman. Bucketloads of appreciation to Lonely Planeteers Sam Benson, Jennye Garibaldi, Amy Balfour and Alex Leviton for all the help. Thanks most to Eric Markowitz, the world's best partner-for-life.

ACKNOWLEDGMENTS

Many thanks to the following for the use of their content:

Internal photographs: p10 (bottom) Andre Jenny/Alamy; p8 (middle) Ellen McKnight/Alamy; p15 (top) Paul Giamou/Aurora Photos/Corbis; p17 (top) fromagination.com; p13 (middle), p19 Danny Palmerlee.

All other photographs by Lonely Planet Images: Eddie Brady p24 (bottom); Charles Cook p8 (top); Richard Cummins p5, p7 (top), p7 (bottom), p11 (top), p11 (bottom), p23 (bottom); Jon Davison p24 (top); John Elk III p13 (top), p18 (top); Lee Foster p15 (middle); Rick Gerharter p17 (bottom); Kim Grant p23 (top); Jeff Greenberg p17 (middle), p21 (bottom); Johnny Haglund p6; John Hay p14, p16; Richard l'Anson p10 (top); Greg Johnston p18 (bottom); Lou Jones p9 (bottom); Holger Leue p12 (bottom), p20, p21 (top); Carol Polich p12 (top); Emily Riddell p15 (bottom); Cheyenne Rouse p9 (top); Stephen Saks p8 (bottom); Witold Skrypczak p7 (middle), p10 (middle); Oliver Strewe p22; Jan Stromme p13 (bottom).

All images are the copyright of the photographers unless otherwise indicated. Many of the images in this guide are available for licensing from Lonely Planet Images: www.lonelyplanetimages.com.

Index

B

000 map pages
000 photograph pages

000 map pages
000 photograph pages

000 map pages
000 photograph pages

000 map pages
000 photograph pages

000 map pages
000 photograph pages

N

000 map pages
000 photograph pages

000 map pages
000 photograph pages

000 map pages
000 photograph pages

U

V

W

GreenDex

It seems as though everyone's going "green" these days, but how can you know which businesses are actually ecofriendly and which are simply jumping on the bandwagon?

The following have been selected by our authors because they demonstrate an active sustainable-tourism policy. Some are involved in conservation or environmental education, others engage with biodynamic agriculture, and many are locally owned and operated, thereby maintaining and preserving local identity, arts and culture.

For more information about sustainable tourism and Lonely Planet, see www.lonely planet.com/responsibletravel.

LONELY PLANET OFFICES

USA
150 Linden St, Oakland, CA 94607
☎ 510 250 6400, toll free 800 275 8555
fax 510 893 8572
info@lonelyplanet.com

Australia
Head Office
Locked Bag 1, Footscray, Victoria 3011
☎ 03 8379 8000, fax 03 8379 8111
talk2us@lonelyplanet.com.au

UK
2nd fl, 186 City Rd,
London EC1V 2NT
☎ 020 7106 2100, fax 020 7106 2101
go@lonelyplanet.co.uk

Published by Lonely Planet
ABN 36 005 607 983

Mixed Sources
Product group from well-managed
forests and other controlled sources
www.fsc.org Cert no. SGS-COC-005002
© 1996 Forest Stewardship Council

Although the authors and Lonely Planet have taken all reasonable care in preparing this book, we make no warranty about the accuracy or completeness of its content and, to the maximum extent permitted, disclaim all liability arising from its use.